The Sèvres Porcelain Manufactory

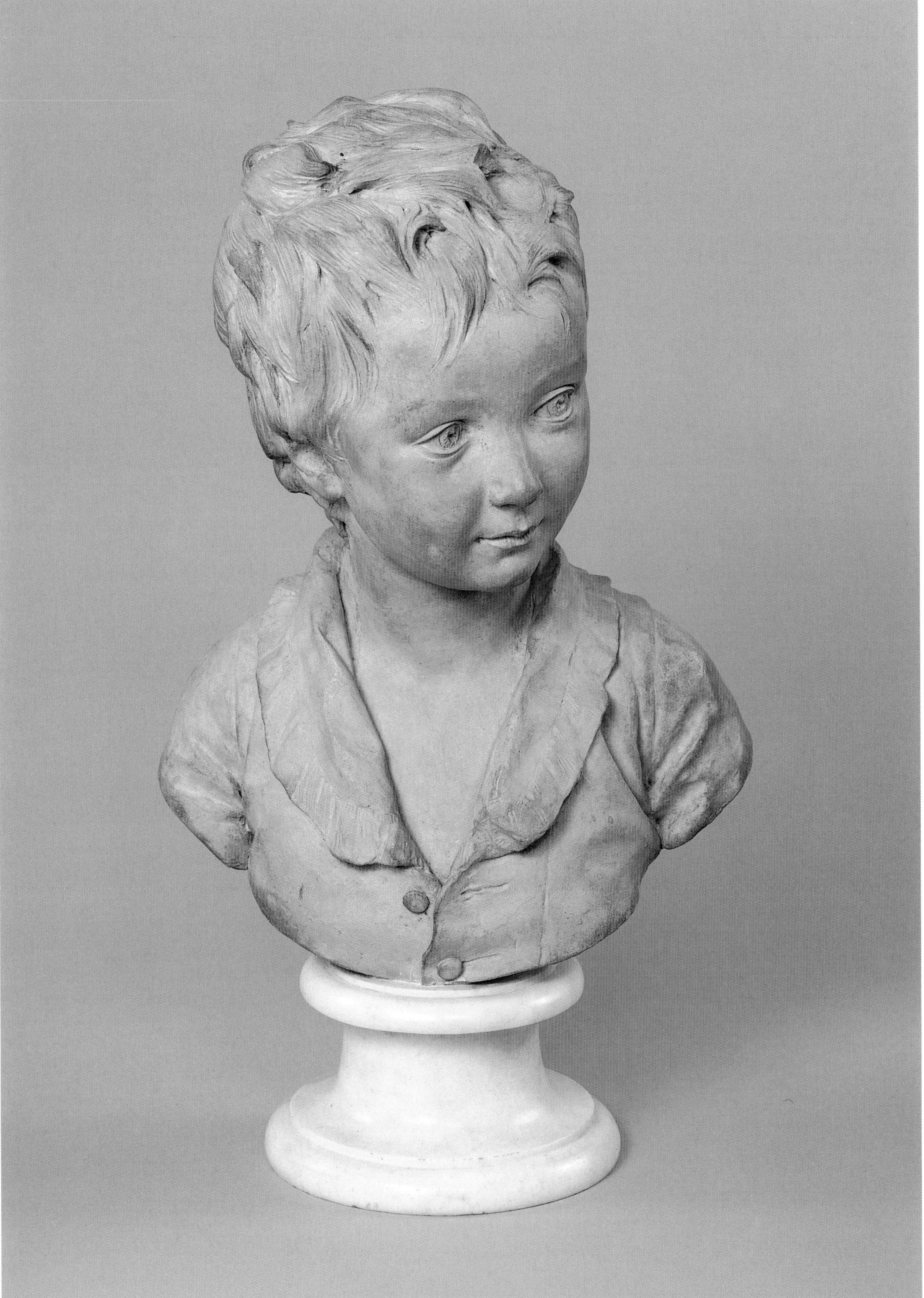

The Sèvres Porcelain Manufactory

Alexandre Brongniart and the Triumph of Art and Industry, 1800–1847

Tamara Préaud

Karole Bezut
Antoine d'Albis
Laurie Dahlberg
Anne Lajoix
Sylvie Millasseau
Béatrice Pannequin

Derek E. Ostergard, Editor

Published for The Bard Graduate Center for Studies in the Decorative Arts, New York, by Yale University Press, New Haven and London

This catalogue is published in conjunction with the exhibition "The Sèvres Porcelain Manufactory: Alexandre Brongniart and the Triumph of Art and Industry, 1800–1847" held at The Bard Graduate Center for Studies in the Decorative Arts from October 17, 1997 to February 1, 1998.

Exhibition curator: Tamara Préaud
Project director: Derek E. Ostergard
Project assistant: Vincent Plescia
Catalogue production: Martina D'Alton, Roberta Fineman, Alice Hopkins, Michael Shroyer and Kelly Spencer, New York; Sally Salvesen, London

Director of exhibitions: Nina Stritzler-Levine
Exhibition coordinator: Lisa Arcomano

Translations: John Goodman, Caroline Beamish, Richard Wittman

Composition by U.S. Lithograph typographers, New York
Printed in Singapore

Library of Congress Catalog number: 97-61445
ISBN: 0 300 07338 0 (cloth); 0 300 07425 5 (paper)

On the cover: Design for a Teapot, called *Théière 'Etrusque B'*, 1804; watercolor, gouache, pencil and ink on paper (cat. no. 11a). (Manufacture nationale de Sèvres, Archives)

Frontispiece: *Bust of Alexandre Brongniart*, by Jean-Antoine Houdon, ca. 1777; terracotta. (Paris, Musée du Louvre).

Front endpaper: *View of the Sèvres Manufactory,* by [?] Le Guay: watercolor on paper glued to cardboard (cat. no. 36). (Manufacture Nationale de Sèvres, Archives)

Back endpaper: *The Visit of King Louis XVIII to the Sèvres Salesroom, June 25, 1816*, by Jean-Charles Develly, 1816; decoration for the *Déjeuner 'L'Art de la Porcelaine'*; gouache on paper (cat. no. 39). (Manufacture Nationale de Sèvres, Archives)

Partial funding for "The Sèvres Porcelain Manufactory: Alexandre Brongniart and the Triumph of Art and Industry, 1800–1847" has been generously provided by the following:

The Florence Gould Foundation

Dresdner Kleinwort Benson

Samuel H. Kress Foundation

The Y. A. Istel Foundation

This exhibition has been organized in collaboration with the Manufacture Nationale de Sèvres.

Contents

Foreword

The tumultuous years of the French Revolution left the prestigious decorative arts industries of France poised on the brink of ruin. It was not until after the fall of the monarchy and the ascendancy of the Consulat and Empire under Napoleon that they would begin to recover. *The Sèvres Porcelain Manufactory: Alexandre Brongniart and the Triumph of Art and Industry, 1800-1847* is the first in- depth examination of the renowned French porcelain works during its virtual rebirth under the direction of Alexandre Brongniart.

Appointed director of the Sèvres manufactory in 1800, Brongniart was a gifted scientist, teacher, and enlightened administrator. He encouraged the development of technical innovations in many areas, from the formulation of clays and glazes to the design and construction of kilns at Sèvres. He established a workshop for glass painting and the making of stained glass, and he reorganized the factory's marketing practices. Recognizing the great debt owed by the decorative arts to past artists, he also founded a museum at the manufactory whose collection would serve both as inspiration for the Sèvres artists and as a record of their achievements. His books and other publications established new standards for the study and analysis of the ceramic arts. To all these ends, Brongniart traveled widely, meeting with scientists, craftsmen, and connoisseurs and promoting the Sèvres accomplishments.

As part of the Bard Graduate Center's ongoing program of exhibitions and publications, *The Sèvres Porcelain Manufactory* occasions the rediscovery and evaluation of a seminal figure in the decorative arts. The study of French porcelain has largely focused on work produced at Sèvres during the eighteenth century, while the history of the factory in the first half of the nineteenth century has for the most part been ignored by scholars, curators and collectors. It is our goal to draw attention to Alexandre Brongniart and his accomplishments, bringing him out of obscurity and shedding new light on a period of French porcelain production that truly deserves greater recognition. This re-evaluation of Brongniart's directorship at Sèvres represents another step in our effort to redress critical attitudes toward nineteenth-century decorative arts, a period which has often been judged devoid of innovation and unworthy of scholarly attention.

* * *

Without the assistance of a generous and enlightened group of supporters, the production of this catalogue and presentation of the exhibition at the Bard Graduate Center would not have been possible. I am especially grateful for the support of the Florence Gould Foundation; Dresdner Kleinwort Benson; and The Y. A. Istel Foundation. I am also most appreciative of a grant provided by the Decorative Arts Society for the symposium that has been organized in conjunction with the exhibition.

I want to express my deepest gratitude to George Touzenis, director, and Tamara Préaud, archivist, of the Manufacture Nationale de Sèvres for enabling this exhibition to take place at the Bard Graduate Center and for allowing the magnificent drawings from Sèvres to be shown in our gallery. Mr. Touzenis and Ms. Préaud also attended to innumerable organizational and logistical details. Ms. Préaud contributed rigorous scholarship, a fine curatorial eye, relentless hard work in preparing the manuscripts for publication, and incomparable devotion to this project.

No exhibition would be possible without the support of lenders. I want to thank the institutions and individuals who loaned objects from their collections: Lee Anderson; Comte and Comtess Alexandre and Elaine de Bothuri Báthory; the Cooper-Hewitt Museum, National Museum of Design; the Detroit Institute of Arts; Fred A. Krehbiel; the Hillwood Museum, Washington D.C.; the Manufacture Nationale de Sèvres; the Museum of Fine Arts, Boston; the Sterling and Francine Clark Art Institute; the Wadsworth Atheneum; The Walters Art Gallery, Baltimore; The Metropolitan Museum of Art; The Minneapolis Institute of Art; the Museum of Art, Rhode Island School of Design; The Nelson-Atkins Museum of Art, Kansas City; the National Gallery of Art; and two anonymous lenders.

The concept for this exhibition and publication on Alexandre Brongniart was first brought to my attention by Derek E. Ostergard, associate director of the Bard Graduate Center. His passion for the early nineteenth century and great interest in enhancing the history of Sèvres led to the realization of the project at the Bard Graduate Center. This catalogue should stand as an invaluable resource on French porcelain for many years to come. The authors — Karole Bézut, Laurie Dahlberg, Antoine d'Albis, Anne Lajoix, Sylvie Millasseau, Béatrice Pannequin, and Tamara Préaud — have all made a major contribution to the history of the decorative arts.

By co-publishing this book with the Bard Graduate Center, Yale University Press demonstrated their vision and dedication to scholarship in the decorative arts. We are fortunate to have worked with John Nicoll and Sally Salvesen at Yale University Press in London on the production of the catalogue. The line editing and assembly and production of the book in New York was beautifully orchestrated by Martina D'Alton and Michael Shroyer.

The commitment and hard work of many individuals on the staff of the Bard Graduate Center contributed to the realization of the catalogue and exhibition. Vincent Plescia attended to endless details and was an invaluable assistant to Derek Ostergard. In the exhibition department I want to acknowledge the assistance of Nina Stritzler-Levine, Lisa Arcomano, Osanna Urbay, and Steven Waterman. The staff of the library and slide library of the Bard Graduate Center including Bobbie Xuereb, Peter Gammie, Stephanie Sueppel, Marcial Lavina, and Danika Volkert provided great support for research and photography. Lisa Podos assisted by Jiff Gustafson and Rosalyn Weinstein created a marvelous series of public programs in conjunction with this project. I also wish to thank my assistant, Stacia Jung.

Each of the administrative departments of the Bard Graduate Center gave their time and professionalism to this project. Linda Hartley and Susan Wall assisted by Tara D'andrea devoted themselves to the fundraising effort. Tim Mulligan directed the press campaign. I am grateful for the assistance and leadership of Lorraine Bacalles in the finance office, and I also want to thank John Donovan, facilities manager, and the reception, security, and maintenance staffs for willingly responding to requests for assistance and attending to many details in the day-to-day operation of the Center.

Susan Weber Soros
Director

Preface

Since the middle of the eighteenth century, excellence and innovation have been the hallmarks of the Manufacture de Sèvres. Through the efforts of a skilled and dedicated staff, an array of remarkable masterpieces of consistently high quality was produced. Sèvres porcelain has been coveted by kings and emperors, by privileged collectors and ordinary art lovers, and by museums and other institutions. Throughout its 250-year history, however, no one has made a greater contribution to Sèvres than Alexandre Brongniart, who served as its director for nearly half a century. Both artist and scientist, Brongniart brought his considerable talents to the manufactory. His entrepreneurial spirit enabled it to thrive despite the many economic, political, and social upheavals that beset France in the early nineteenth century.

Brongniart's devotion to ceramics went beyond the confines of Sèvres. Not only did he run the manufactory, but he also helped to create a highly respected museum of ceramics, he published widely on many subjects, including two seminal books on ceramics, and he shared his knowledge of ceramics with friends and competitors, fellow countrymen and foreigners alike. Even today his name is accorded an almost religious veneration and respect within the international community of ceramists.

The Sèvres Porcelain Manufactory: Alexandre Brongniart and the Triumph of Art and Industry, 1800 – 1847 is a truly fitting tribute to this remarkable man on the 150th anniversary of his death. I have the inestimable privilege to be one of Brongniart's successors, and as the director of Sèvres, I can readily grasp the many challenges Brongniart faced. I would like to thank the eminent scholars, collectors, museum curators, and others at both private and public institutions who have made this catalogue and the exhibition it accompanies possible. Most particularly, I wish to express my gratitude to Tamara Préaud and Derek Ostergard, the two dedicated architects of this project. Theirs is a landmark achievement in the studies of the nineteenth-century decorative arts, an area so often neglected. They have been admirably supported in their efforts by Susan Weber Soros and the staff at The Bard Graduate Center in New York City, as well as many others involved with this important venture. Madame Georges Pompidou most kindly accepted the chair of the honorary committee. Her commitment to French artistic patrimony is long standing and well known. I hope that the high standards we have set will honor her confidence in this project, and I wish to thank her for her ongoing support.

This exhibition represents a milestone in the exploration of French decorative arts. Once again The Bard Graduate Center, with generosity and scholarly commitment, has broadened our understanding of the way in which history was made. For all of this and for the opportunity they have given us, I extend my warmest thanks.

George Touzenis
Director, Manufacture Nationale de Sèvres

Introduction

The Sèvres Porcelain Manufactory: Alexandre Brongniart and the Triumph of Art and Industry, 1800–1847 examines the distinguished career of Alexandre Brongniart, director of the manufactory, and the remarkable ceramics produced during his tenure. In 1791, the year Brongniart reached his majority, he personified modern Europe in many respects, poised between a reassuring past and an uncertain future. The world of his youth was in the throes of the French Revolution, and the events of the next few years would irrevocably alter not only his life but the history of France as well, issues explored in chapter 1 ("France Between the Revolutions, 1789–1848"). By Brongniart's death in 1847, the course of the nation had been set; it would not be so violently altered again until the First World War.

A product of the ancien régime, Brongniart was raised in a world of heightened expectations, where there was a belief in the power of logic, science, and the human will. Much of Brongniart's family background and education, as well as its impact on his later career, are examined in chapter 2 ("Alexandre Brongniart: Scholar and Member of the Institut de France").

In 1800, at the age of thirty, he was appointed director of the Manufacture de Sèvres. The institution that had been entrusted to him was but a shadow of its glorious past. As a symbol of the despised monarchy, it had suffered greatly during the Revolution. Chapter 3 ("Brongniart as Administrator") focuses on his new role at the manufactory, confronting problems and devising solutions. Despite his lack of experience as an administrator, Brongniart set out to stabilize the manufactory. To do this, he was given a certain latitude by the government and allowed to implement fundamental changes. He became an advocate for the employees, many of whom had not been paid for sometime, a situation he partially remedied early in his tenure.

Bridging the philosophies of the Age of Enlightenment and the emerging Industrial Revolution, Brongniart was a pragmatist with a superbly trained scientific mind, who understood the new world of the early nineteenth century in all its uncertainties. He brought his scienctific side to bear on improving the way in which ceramics were made at the manufactory. His contributions to the technical production of ceramics, porcelain in particular, are discussed in chapter 4 ("Brongniart as Technician").

As director of a company with a reputation that far exceeded the reality of its condition in 1800, Brongniart also used his early training to forge alliances with other ceramists, including rival porcelain makers, and to work within the international marketplace to assure not only the survival of Sèvres and the livelihood of its employees, but its supremacy as well. The manufactory was heavily subsidized by the government, and this circumstance — the stipend — has sometimes obscured Brongniart's importance. Many of the rival Parisian porcelain manufactories often charged that Sèvres enjoyed an unfair advantage in the marketplace thanks to government backing. Brongniart's first loyalties were to France, however; he deeply believed that if Sèvres succeeded, the nation and its artistic reputation would gain luster. The benefit of this to other French porcelain makers was obvious. Brongniart's role within the wider field of ceramics is the subject of chapter 5 ("Brongniart and the Art of Ceramics").

Part of Brongniart's success as director during this tumultuous period of French history was due to his own adroit understanding of politics and political behavior. In his forty-seven-years career at Sèvres, he witnessed six changes in government: the Consulate (1799-1802), Napoleon's term as first consul for life (1802-4), the Empire (1804-14/15), and the reigns of Louis XVIII (1814/15-24), Charles X (1824-30) and Louis-Philippe (1830-48). Brongniart was forced to contend with different political attitudes and intermittent changes in personnel. The mercurial attitudes and diversity of taste displayed by the various heads of state often played a considerable role in the state of the manufactory, and the evolution of the production during the first half of the nineteenth century is traced in chapter 6 ("The Nature and Goals of Production at the Sèvres Manufactory").

Brongniart did not work solely as an administrator, but as someone deeply invested in the artistic development of the manufactory itself. He also sought to widen the repertoire of the manufactory, exploring new aesthetics and techniques, and thus develop new markets. One of his initiatives was the opening of a workshop devoted to stained glass and related works. This is the subject of chapter 7 ("The Stained Glass and Painting-on-Glass Workshop at Sèvres"). He also revitalized the sculpture workshop at the manufactory, a development explored in chapter 8 ("Sculpture at Sèvres during the Brongniart Administration").

Within the tiny community of the manufactory, Brongniart helped to build a museum that would form the basis for a modern museological and historical view of ceramics. Its holdings were not only for use by the staff at Sèvres, but through Brongniart's generosity of spirit, they were made available to all makers of ceramics, many of whom were active rivals of Sèvres. Brongniart readily encouraged other makers to examine the collection in their efforts to improve of their own production. For Brongniart, the collection played a significant part in establishing his later reputation. From studies of the holdings, he produced a multivolume treatise on ceramics, the *Traité des Arts céramiques*. Throughout the first half of the nineteenth century, the museum served as a repository of objects and data collected and donated by government officials, citizens involved in global travel, and even friends, whom Brongniart importuned to retrieve objects and clay and soil samples during their travels. This fascinating history has been addressed in chapter 9 ("Brongniart as Taxonomist and Museologist: The Significance of the Musée Céramique at Sèvres").

During the first years of his tenure, Brongniart had taken the difficult step of eliminating the production of soft-paste porcelain, the material that had formed the basis of Sèvres high reputation in the previous century. Almost simultaneously he sold off most of the manufactory's old stock of undecorated, old-fashioned, or flawed objects. Both of these decisions and their long-term repercussions are considered in chapter 10 ("Two Controversial Decisions by Alexandre Brongniart").

One of Brongniart's most important initiatives was a broad inquiry into ceramics production that was conducted with government support. This survey, discussed in chapter 11 ("Clay, Pedagogy, and Progress: The Enquête des Préfets, 1805–1810") allowed Brongniart to collect a crucial body of information on the clays, glazes, and technical innovations by other ceramists throughout France. The results were made available to other ceramists, and the objects collected were deposited into the Musée Céramique.

The drawings and objects in the catalogue section reveal the surprising intellectual and aesthetic eclecticism that existed in Europe from the early to the mid nineteenth century. This was a time of intense scientific investigation and analysis, during which there was a re-examination of Western European history and many of its associated myths. As the Industrial Revolution which overran the social and economic systems that had supported the agrarian-based European society for centuries, there was a sentimental looking back. At Sèvres Brongniart encouraged the study of history, especially ceramics history, as a source of inspiration for new models and decorations. These appealed to a market seeking comfort and reassurance in a vanished past or broadening their interests beyond the Greco-Roman tradition to encompass other cultures. Eventually, there was even a revival of enthusiasm for the rococo aesthetics of the previous century, which had been denigrated in Brongniart's youth.

The globe also appeared to shrink as travel and new publications brought Western Europe closer than ever to non-Western cultures, from the Near and Far East to Africa, Asia, and the Americas. Aspects of each of these reverberated in art, albeit in an often highly interpretive manner. In the decorative arts and design this exoticism acquired a richness and complexity that had been unknown in the seventeenth or eighteenth centuries. The possession of such works of art often conveyed the impression of an individual's sophistication and education. In an increasingly competitive society, objects acquired a greater intensity of meaning. Brongniart's own interest extended far beyond the geographical boundaries of France. He was a scientist and writer, a student of history and a keen observor of other cultures, all of which contributed to his great achievements at Sèvres. His passions are evident in his many skills as professor, author, curator, and director of the porcelain manufactory at Sèvres for nearly half a century.

* * *

A catalogue of this size and complexity could only be brought to completion through the considerable efforts of many individuals. The most important of these has been Tamara Préaud, who as archivist at Sèvres for almost twenty-eight years, has acquired an unparalleled expertise. She has contributed her knowledge generously, just as Brongniart shared his considerable experience with his colleagues and competitors so many years ago.

Over a decade ago, I had the opportunity to listen to Tamara trace the history of the manufactory from the late eighteenth to the middle of the nineteenth century through the use of works on paper. Her eloquence and command of her subject was remarkable and her interpretation has partly formed the basis for this catalogue. As curator of the exhibition, Tamara wrote all of the entries except one and contributed five major essays. She selected authors to research and write essays, and she led them into the vast archives of the manufactory to examine this neglected period. At Sèvres, considerable support also came from George Touzenis, the director, who assisted in fundraising and staffing and gave considerable encouragement to the project.

At The Bard Graduate Center, first and foremost, Vincent Plescia has participated in this project from the start with enormous care, enthusiasm, and commitment to making certain that this catalogue lived up the expectations that were so enthusiastically applied to it when it was first envisioned. His role in this project has been decisive. Nina Stritzler-Levine, director of exhibitions, has attentively seen to the many details involved in bringing this book to completion. Lisa Arcomano, exhibitions coordinator, worked closely with lenders, shippers, and art handlers. Osanna Urbay helped with manuscripts. Several Bard Graduate Center students were very helpful, especially the project's curatorial assistants Judith Gura, Elizabeth Caffrey, and Ron Labaco. They devoted a great deal of time and attention to the details of manuscript preparation. They were assisted by Amy Miller and Kersti Kuldna. For the superb photography of the works on paper and objects in this exhibition, my thanks to Bruce White, Jean-Loup Charmet, and Cathy Carver.

The other authors have contributed significant essays to the catalogue; Laurie Dahlberg, Antoine d'Albis, Sylvie Millasseau, Karole Bezut, Béatrice Pannequin, and Anne Lajoix. Together they have produced a three-dimensional portrait of one of the great figures of the nineteenth century. Florence Slitine assembled an extensive bibliography for this publication.

In the United States, colleagues at various institutions were generous with research information, time, and loans: Anne Poulet and Jeffrey Munger at The Museum of Fine Arts, Boston; Alan P. Darr, Jr. and Tracey Albainy at The Detroit Institute of Arts; Beth Carver Wees at The Francine and Sterling Clark Institute in Williamstown, Vermont; Dianne Pilgrim, Deborah Shinn, and Cordelia Rose at the The Cooper-Hewitt Museum, New York; Clare Le Corbeiller at The Metropolitan Museum of Art, New York; Christina Nelson at The Nelson Atkins Museum of Art, Kansas City; Thomas Michie and Jayne Stokes, The Museum of

Art, Rhode Island School of Design, Providence; Linda Roth and Cindy Roman at the Wadsworth Atheneum; Christopher Monkhouse and Caroline Wanstall at The Minneapolis Institute of Art; and Anne Odom and Liana Paredes Arendt at the Hillwood Museum. My sincere thanks also to the private lenders to this exhibition, Mr. and Mrs. Alexandre de Bothuri Báthory, Roger Prigent, Richard Cohen, Mr. and Mrs. Fred A. Krehbiel, and Lee Anderson, as well as two private lenders. Letitia Roberts of Sothebys' was a great help, as were her assistants Lauren Tarshis and Eliza Osborne; at Christie's, Jody Wilkie was very helpful.

Other individuals at The Bard Graduate Center worked hard to complete this project: Lisa Podos, Director of Public Programs; Linda Hartley, Director of Development; Susan Wall, Associate Director of Development; Tim Mulligan, Director of Communications; Bobbie Xuereb, Chief Librarian; Lorraine Bacalles, Director of Finance; Carolee Goldstein; Steve Waterman and the entire installation crew who assisted with the exhibition; Stacia Jung who gave considerable support; Peter Gammie and Stephanie Sueppel who helped with research; John Donovan; Jill Gustafson and Rosalyn Weinstein in Public Programs; Tara D'andrea; Marcial Lavina and Danika Volkert who helped with photography; Greg Negron; Kelly Moody; Miao Chen; Orlando Diaz; Roy Martinez; Jose Olivera; Jorge San Pablo; Terence Lyons; Chandler Small; Dave Rio; Kenneth Talley; and Helen Aravantinos at the Leeman Agency who made travel arrangements. In addition, for their support of the exhibition, I wish to thank Mme Claude Pompidou, Hubert de Givenchy and Elieth Roux, and Bernard Dragesco. Genevieve Gallot was exceptionally kind.

The editorial work and production of the catalogue was accomplished by Martina D'Alton, Michael Shroyer and Kelly Spencer. Sarah Lowengard assisted with researching dates for the catalogue. Glorieux Dougherty prepared the index. For their sensitive translations, my thanks to John Goodman, Richard Wittman, and Caroline Beamish, each of whom brought their own distinctive approach to the difficult task of turning nineteenth- and twentieth-century French into English.

Finally and most importantly, I am most grateful to Susan Weber Soros, director of The Bard Graduate Center, who has enthusiastically supported this challenging project, another in the ongoing series of scholarly investigations, shedding light on an under-appreciated but significant area of nineteenth-century decorative arts.

Derek E. Ostergard

Editor's note: In the texts that follow, there are many quotations taken directly from the writings of Alexandre Brongniart, primarily drawn from papers in the archives of the Manufacture Nationale de Sèvres. The challenges of translating an early nineteenth-century text into modern English are manifold, and the translations that follow largely preserve the often eccentric style with which Brongniart wrote, especially his use of punctuation. Any emphasis, where given, was found in the original text.

In most cases, the original French will be found in the appropriate footnote. In addition, the early nineteenth century witnessed a proliferation of bureaucratic offices and titles in France, and these are given in French. The names of the various porcelain objects and services are also given in French, according to the designations found in the manufactory archives. Bibliographical references in the notes are cited in a shortened form consisting of author's last name, an abbreviated title, and the year of publication. Full references will be found in the bibliography.

Fig. 1-1. *Napoleon Bonaparte with the Château de Chambord in the Background*, by Antoine-Jean Gros, 1802; oil on canvas. Even relatively early in his political career, Napoleon chose to be represented with images of a royal France. (Private collection)

Chapter 1

France Between the Revolutions, 1789 – 1848

Laurie Dahlberg

In 1800, when Alexandre Brongniart received his appointment to direct the Manufacture de Porcelaine de Sèvres, France was emerging from one of the most chaotic, terrifying, and influential periods in its history. Napoleon had recently effected his *coup d'état* of 1799, ending a full decade of unrelenting confusion and bloodshed, and optimists both within France and without hoped his strong leadership would finally bring the nation a much-needed respite of stability and prosperity (fig. 1-1). This was not to be the case, however, for the next fifty years of French life would be repeatedly marked by major political, social, and economic upheavals.[1]

It was this instability — combined with highly conservative attitudes toward banking and investment and the ingrained resistance of small producers to changing their traditional production methods — that worked to delay industrial modernization in France. Although Napoleon would act quickly and decisively to build the national economy through subsidies and incentives to industry and manufacturing, neither France nor any other country could compete in this respect with Great Britain, which reigned supreme over industry and international commerce during the first half of the nineteenth century. An implicit part of Brongniart's mandate was to enlist his commanding knowledge of science and technology in an uphill battle with Great Britain over supremacy in the industrial arts, especially in the production of ceramics. At this early date, it was clear that Great Britain already had undisputed control over the market in mass-produced goods, while France occupied a small but highly respectable niche as a leader in the luxury trade. In the climate of accelerating industrial capitalism, however, neither country could afford to remain content with its existing status.

The relationship between France and Britain was a complex one. Notwithstanding their mutual distrust and recurring rivalries as declared enemies, each nation admired the other's culture and traditions, if at times begrudgingly. Even through the tensions of intermittent war, "Anglomania" made a cyclical appearance in France, manifesting itself in such trends as the fashionable rages for afternoon tea, English-style gardens, and British landscape painting, just as the English gentry continued to consider the close study of French language, art, and architecture as essential to a proper education. As the eighteenth century drew to a close, the two countries were further separated, temporarily, by two distinct but equally inexorable forces: the Industrial Revolution and the French Revolution, each of which would soon have reciprocal effects and worldwide consequences. Compared to the circumstances of other French ceramic producers, the Manufacture de Sèvres was singularly insulated from the early pressures of the Industrial Revolution due to the outright subsidies it received from the government. It had, however, an uncommonly, even uncomfortably, close view of the outbreak of the French Revolution.

Sèvres During the Revolution

On October 5, 1789, the townspeople of Sèvres watched as a swelling crowd of several thousand angry people — reputedly led by market women — passed through their streets en route to Versailles, shouting revolutionary slogans.[2] Demonstrators urged spectators to join them as they marched the last five miles to the royal palace, where they intended to confront Louis XVI, who was ensconced there under protective guard with his family. The following day, the crowd, this time numbering some 60,000, passed through Sèvres again on the way back to Paris, triumphantly escorting the reluctant king, queen, and young dauphin.

This scene presented an absurd contrast to the royal family's many previous trips through Sèvres, leading an elegant entourage between Paris and Versailles, or stopping at the Royal Manufacture of Sèvres to inspect the establishment and its latest accomplishments. Those visits would surely have been occasions of great pomp and majesty, with the Sèvres staff paying respectful attendance as the monarch entered the premises by way of the ceremonial *cour royale*, which was probably decorated with festoons and Bourbon flags. At the rear of this courtyard, the private royal entrance and staircase led to a private ceremonial chamber. In October 1789, although they were still conveyed in their royal carriage and attended by General Lafayette and an honor guard, the king and his family were effectively prisoners of the people.[3] As unprecedented as this forced journey may have been, few at that moment could have guessed that this would be the last time the king and queen would travel the *route de Versailles*.

Whatever their political beliefs, many workers of the Manufacture Royale de Sèvres must have watched the spectacle with anxiety, for their livelihoods were also held in the balance. It is true that they suffered from the same bread shortages that had touched off this latest event in the spontaneous progression of the Revolution. Moreover, they had been placed in desperate circumstances by the king, who owed them back wages. To see their patron taken by force by the unpredictable mob, however, was to

Fig. 1-2. *The Burning of the Manor House*, by Hubert Robert, ca. 1789–94; oil on canvas. While the artist's prerevolutionary canvases depicted a bucolic way of life, here he adeptly portrayed a scene of the Revolution with its violence against the ancien régime. (Wildenstein, New York)

entertain the possibility that their way of life at the manufactory might be at an end. If any of them had considered the most radical possible outcome of the popular will, they might have wondered what use a classless society could possibly have for the kind of luxury goods produced by the Manufacture Royale de Sèvres.

Looking back on the extremes of the Revolution and its immediate aftermath, it now seems astonishing that the manufactory never closed its doors, even temporarily, during the more than ten years of extreme political, social, and economic turmoil that followed the events of that October (fig. 1-2). Through all the changes in power among the governing factions, from the founding of the Constitutional Monarchy (1789) to that of the First Empire (1804), none of the successive ruling bodies of the Revolution was entirely willing to sacrifice the manufactory. By the king's own request, it officially remained his property until the founding of the Republic in 1792 when, along with other royal buildings and domains, Sèvres was placed under the control of the Minister of Public Contributions.

Although there were those who advocated the manufactory's closure, it was difficult to justify the dismantling of a celebrated establishment that was capable of earning limited capital and considerable honor for France, at least through its reputation abroad. Of great concern to the new government was the fact that the manufactory was so deeply associated with the old regime; a sustained and concerted effort was needed to extinguish this image in the public imagination. To that end, "liberty trees" were planted on the grounds, public celebrations were held to demonstrate Sèvres's commitment to the Republic's aims, and even the manufactory's old *cour royale* was rechristened the *cour de l'Egalité*, in keeping with a symbolic reordering of public spaces that was occurring across the country.[4] The manufactory's director, Antoine Régnier (1773 – 93), did his best to weather the political winds and adjust to changing demands, which included supplying wares to the army, designing new pieces that reflected the ideology of the Revolution, and destroying the molds and other items related to the Bourbon dynasty.[5] Régnier made a serious mistake, however, in briefly hesitating to follow the initial order to destroy the old molds and models, which brought him a severely worded reprimand.[6] Although he acted quickly on this second order, dispatching seven workers who spent one day smashing the stock it had taken scores of employees months or even years to build, Régnier's reputation with the new regime was irreparably damaged.[7] It was a confused, halting period for the factory, and with Régnier arrested, reinstated, and finally definitively ousted from the establishment in 1793, Sèvres hobbled through the closing years of the eighteenth century, ending its first half-century in much the same uncertain and fitful way that it began.

The gradual recovery of the Manufacture de Sèvres — renamed the Manufacture Impériale de Sèvres after the founding of the Empire in 1804 — began with the appointment of Alexandre Brongniart to the directorship. The regeneration of the manufactory, which survived and ultimately thrived despite the vicissitudes of the early nineteenth century, owed much to Brongniart's acumen, vision, and energy. Fortunately, there were also external forces and conditions that aided Brongniart in his efforts to restore the Sèvres manufactory to its former importance.

The Manufacture de Sèvres as a Workplace

During the *ancien régime*, in an effort to prevent competitors from luring away Sèvres's master craftsmen and other personnel who knew the factory's secrets, workers were prevented by law from leaving the manufactory's employ without the king's consent. Special benefits, such as exemption from certain taxes and the military draft, made up for the limitations placed on the workers' personal freedoms. The special privileges enjoyed by both the manufactory and its employees, however, were swept away by revolutionary reforms.[8] With the future of the establishment uncertain, their former civil protections eliminated, and their payroll cut to the bone, why did the *chefs*, artists, and workers stay on? The simplest answer to this question is that in the wake of the Revolution, with the country's economy in ruins, most had nowhere else to go. It is true enough that some of the able-bodied men, especially the unmarried ones, could have joined the army, for which Napoleon found no shortage of engagements. It is also the case, however, that many Sèvres employees had established deep roots in the community, and during more than a decade of privation and uncertainty that followed the Revolution, most workers at Sèvres held out the hope that the manufactory would eventually return to some semblance of normal operation.

The Manufacture de Sèvres was more than a workplace; it was a complete society, held together by bonds of real and figurative kinship. At the head of the "family" was the director, whose efficacy as a leader depended upon the mutual respect and loyalty exchanged between him and his employees. The familial structure of the factory's population was literally reinscribed each time workers intermarried, which was often, and each time a child entered the factory rolls as an apprentice in the workshop of its father or mother. Many workers and their families lived rent free within the walls of the manufactory itself, or in dwellings on or adjacent to its grounds. They could worship in the factory's chapel, and in sickness they were attended by the factory's own physician.[9] Although these privileges were eliminated by the revolutionary government, Brongniart reinstated many, including free medical assistance and a retirement plan. It is therefore not surprising to find many families represented by six or more generations in the historical lineage of Sèvres's employees.

Beyond the comfort it offered as a home, the manufactory was also a truly desirable place to work. Living and working at Sèvres must have seemed infinitely more salubrious than the alternative of working in a Parisian porcelain factory, where the quality of life for most workers was dismal to say the least. Cholera and typhoid, frequent in Paris, still surfaced occasionally at Sèvres, but with far less overcrowding and greater availability of potable water from local springs and fountains, full-blown epidemics were less of a threat. Milk from Sèvres farms was even in demand by Parisians for its perceived superior wholesomeness.[10]

The manufactory was virtually surrounded by pastoral countryside and woods (albeit somewhat deforested for the factory's use during the lean years of the Revolution)[11]; the Parc de Saint Cloud and the Bois de Meudon were just a short walk away, as was the Seine. At a time when Paris was a place of inadequate sewers, narrow, ill-paved streets, and dense clusters of ancient, dilapidated buildings, Sèvres was acclaimed as a peaceful, picturesque retreat from the city and was frequented by such luminaries as Diderot and Balzac.[12] Employees at Sèvres, though typically working eleven hours a day in summer and nine in winter, had more leisure time and more healthy ways to enjoy it than most factory workers, who commonly worked thirteen or more hours a day.[13] In contrast to their Parisian counterparts, most of whom were crowded together in the medieval working-class quarter of the Faubourg St. Antoine, meritorious workers at the manufactory were even awarded garden plots on the grounds, by which they might industriously supplement their family tables.[14]

Finally, although the private porcelain factories that reemerged in Paris after the Revolution may have offered better wages, Sèvres was subsidized by the state and therefore its workers did not face the risk that their jobs might be eliminated overnight as a result of bankruptcy.[15] In addition a certain pride and status came with contributing one's talents to the establishment that was widely acclaimed to be the premier maker of fine porcelain in Europe. "Perhaps nothing in French art or industry will be found to equal the influence gained for us in Europe by the manufactory of Sèvres," wrote the Second Empire critic Philippe Burty. "Saxony had spread the fashion [for porcelain], but the French taste and charm was now seen to triumph, while during and since the middle of the eighteenth century, nothing has surpassed it."[16]

Reemergence of a Clientele

The start of the Revolution and its savage aftermath caused the majority of the wealthy nobility — a crucial component of the manufacture's clientele — to withdraw into hiding in the provinces, or to emigrate. Describing the wealthiest quarter of Paris in 1796, an English diplomat wrote in dismay, "The Fauxbourg [sic] St. Germaine can never recover . . . its hotels are almost all seized by Government, and the streets near the Boulevard are choked with weeds."[17] With mottos such as "War on the castles, peace to the cottages!" circulating, these were dangerous years to display one's personal wealth, regardless of its source.[18] The suppression of the Church also eliminated a small, yet traditionally dependable customer from Sèvres's trade.

Upon Napoleon's overthrow of the Directory and the establishment of the Consulate (1799), the precarious situation facing the nobility eased considerably. Some more confident emigrés had begun to quietly return home even earlier (fig. 1-3).[19] Although believing in equality enough to practice the revolutionary dictum of opening careers to talent, Napoleon did not make himself an

Fig. 1-3. *Le Petit Coblenz*, by Jean-Baptiste Isabey, ca. 1797. Soon after the Revolution, aristocrats began to return to Paris. Some, known as the *incroyables*, flaunted their fashionable tastes with seeming indifference to the recent troubles. (Collection Ostergard)

enemy of the old nobility. On the contrary, he was favorably disposed toward its members if they were similarly inclined. He was busy building a new nobility and was eager to enhance its cultural and economic power by liberally seasoning its ranks with established aristocrats.[20] By 1802, the year Napoleon had himself proclaimed first consul for life, visitors to France reported that crowds of the rich and fashionable were again on display in the capital, even if many of the old private mansions and villas were still boarded up.[21]

In theory, the former royal manufactories of Sèvres, Gobelins, and Beauvais were able to survive because those policies of the Revolution that were allowed to stand did not ultimately effect great change on French social strata and economic distribution. Several initial years of conspicuous austerity notwithstanding, very few members of the wealthiest classes, and even fewer of the poorest, found their economic condition permanently changed.[22]

Several policies of the Empire, however, had far-reaching effects on French industry. In the first instance, Napoleon was dedicated to the economic growth of the country, primarily as a means to support his ambitious military campaigns. The encouragements he gave private industry, however, such as subsidizing cooperative efforts between factory owners and scientists or engineers on matters of new technology, had real impact, especially in the textile industry.[23] Considering the former protections from private industry that Sèvres enjoyed during the *ancien régime*, Napoleon's policies seemed to turn the tables on the manufactory. The appointment of the scientist Brongniart, however, was purposely made to guarantee Sèvres an important part in the greater economic plan. Moreover, the increasing use of industrial technology in the private French ceramic industry, including such innovative procedures as jiggering and transfer printing, did not significantly affect Sèvres, whose clientele expected only the finest handcrafted pieces.

If the liberality of the Empire period encouraged the return and growth of the monied classes and led to a renewal of domestic commissions for the manufactory, not to mention Napoleon's own extensive commissions to refurbish many of the former royal residences, the Napoleonic Wars (1796 – 1815) had the reverse effect on Sèvres's foreign market. The formidable reputation that Sèvres porcelain enjoyed abroad assured it of a brisk business with foreigners — when the product could reach its customers. With France variously at war with England, Russia, the Ottoman Empire, Austria-Hungary, Prussia, Holland, and Spain, however, trade routes were seriously impeded, and exports and shipping of materials intermittently came to a halt.

Napoleon's support of commerce and mercantilism also nourished the slow but steady growth of the bourgeoisie, a diverse socioeconomic class that encompassed a wide range of professions, incomes, and social aspirations. The haute bourgeoisie consisted of wealthy non-noble financiers, officials, professionals, and landowners who actually had more in common politically and economically with the nobility than with the petite bourgeoisie, which represented a much wider range of professions among its constituents, such as manufacturers, small landowners, self-employed artisans, and shopkeepers.[24] As it gradually grew larger and wealthier during the first half of the nineteenth century, the bourgeoisie and its ascension played an important part in expanding the clientele for the products of the Manufacture de Sèvres.[25]

To conduct one's life with taste and elegance, whatever the limits of one's means, was a desire shared by all but the poorest classes, from the petite bourgeoisie to the rarefied strata of the pedigreed nobility. Material displays of taste and refinement among the bourgeoisie — through the disposition of one's home furnishings, the cut of one's costume, or the style of one's carriage — were inevitably perceived by their critics as the aspiring classes' pathetic attempts to mimic their social betters.

The possession of fine objects of true usefulness that were simple and beautifully made was also an end in itself; it was a pleasure that could always stand independent of any further exigencies. Many nineteenth-century writers asserted that the effortless command of taste and style was a uniquely French characteristic. Writing home to America in 1827, James Fenimore Cooper observed of the French, "The only difference between them and the English, or them and ourselves, is in the better taste and ease with which they regulate their [social entertainments]. While there is a great deal of true elegance, there is no fuss at a French entertainment . . . ."[26] Such writers, however, unfailingly spoke of Parisian society as though it represented the whole of France, when in fact it was the stunning exception. In truth, apart from a handful of small industrial, provincial cities like Lyon and Lille, the rest of the country was dominated by an ancient rural economy, culture, and customs.

French manufacturing had therefore always devoted its greatest energies to serving the only population with disposable income and the willingness to spend it: wealthy urban elites, who above all were consumers — and often connoisseurs — of objects of refinement and luxury. It is telling that on his visit to a French industrial exhibition Cooper was astounded by the contrast between ordinary objects and luxury goods. Comparing displays of decorative furnishings with those of everyday utensils and hardware, Cooper reported that "the former abounded, were very generally elegant and well imagined, while the latter betrayed the condition of a nation whose civilization has commenced with the summit, instead of the base of society,"[27] but, he continued, "when it came to the articles of elegance and luxury, as connected with forms, taste, and execution, though not always in ingenuity and extent of comfort, I should think that no Englishman . . . could pass through this wilderness of elegancies without wonder."

Foreign writers like Cooper were surprisingly willing to concede to the French in all matters of art and taste, and this rather automatic deference held sway throughout the century. French manufacturing's commitment to an artisanal production of fine articles of style and elegance was thus reinforced by this widespread presumption of the superiority of French design, in distinct contrast to English manufacturing's vigorous development of cheaper goods for mass markets.[28]

The Social Relevance of the Dinner Party

In a feverish moment of commitment to the doctrine of equality for all members of society, the Revolution had briefly given women unprecedented freedom, such as the right to divorce. Women's gains as autonomous individuals in French society during the Revolution, however, were immediately rescinded by legislations like the Napoleonic Code, and soon the social role of the French woman seemed more circumscribed than ever. In a culture where "good" women were rather strictly confined to their homes, one of the few arenas women had for earning public recognition was the hosting of entertainments. Napoleon, in fact, was particularly eager to reestablish the social circulation between members of high society and the government that had once been nourished by elegant entertainments in both the private *hôtels* and at court; the woman who could contribute to this cause was acting as a good citizen.

It was thus that Napoleon encouraged the young Mme Junot (later, the duchesse d'Abrantès) to enlist her talents as a society hostess, remarking that she had the natural ability "to hold a drawing-room." "Accomplish that and you will be a charming little woman," the first consul told her, adding his hope that her example would show others that "for this purpose, it is not sufficient merely to give a dinner."[29] Magnificent state parties, dinners, and balls were a regular feature of Napoleon's government after the peace with Austria and Britain in 1801 – 02. As the duchesse d'Abrantès recorded in her memoirs, these glorious state entertainments were "a signal not only to Paris, but to the whole of France" to follow suit in demonstrably, joyfully declaring an end to the Spartanism demanded by the Revolution and the shortages of war.[30] Not only did such festivities animate the spirits of the nation, but for a decade they poured money into the hands of artisans and tradesmen of all kinds, from haberdashers to cabinetmakers.

Those who could afford to treat guests to less than pure luxury at their entertainments had to proclaim the appeal of more abstract kinds of wealth. "[T]he tolerance of my salon procures me friends," lamented Mme de Rémusat to her husband. "But all this would be much better if I had more money; for, begging the pardon of the idealists, the metal that is so greatly despised, and yet so sought after, forms more than half the attractions of a hostess, and if to all my own I could add the very superior [silver] of a good table, I should really be celebrated."[31]

The brilliance of the Empire was never matched by the succeeding government of the Bourbon Restauration (1814/15 – 30). Unable to compete with the spectacular image that Napoleon and his court had set before the public, Louis XVIII (1814 – 24; fig. 1-4) neither entertained lavishly nor appeared in public freely. Charles X (1824 – 30) was more sociable than his brother, but he, too, lacked real interest in nourishing his public image. Foreigners reported that in public the royal family was treated with plain indifference

Fig. 1-4. *Louis XVIII Surrounded by Members of the Royal Family at the Palais des Tuileries, Receiving the Duc d'Angoulême on his Return from Spain, December 2, 1823*, by Antoine-Jean-Baptiste Thomas, 1823; oil on canvas. (Versailles, musée national des chateaux de Versailles et de Trianon)

by all but the most devoted ultraroyalists. Those who were not attached to life at the Bourbon court conducted their socializing in private, as if by stealth, according to the Irish novelist Lady Morgan.[32] Despite its underground status, Lady Morgan averred that intellectual Parisian society flourished in small, brilliant pockets that centered around intimate gatherings. "Dinners, in France, have two objects," she wrote, "sociality and gastronomy; the most perfect intellectual enjoyment, or a refined and elaborated sensuality."[33] An ideal dinner hostess would balance these objectives with creative elegance, by inviting the most fascinating guests, having the most delectable menu prepared, and placing the two together in an environment that brought out the utmost charm in each.

In the waning years of the Restauration, James Fenimore Cooper noted the surprising failure of the ostensible tastemakers of the nation — the royal family of Charles X (fig. 1-5) — to make even the slightest effort to live up to these expectations for distinctive entertaining. Having procured a ticket to a semiannual ceremonial public dinner with the king, Cooper observed a peculiar contrast between the unrelenting dreariness of the court of Charles X and its sparkling surroundings. The mediocrity that Cooper observed in the food itself seemed to him to infuse the entire entourage of the king and his courtiers. He noted with wry amusement that "The whole party appeared greatly relieved by having something to do during the dessert, in admiring the service, which was of the beautiful Sèvres china. They all took up the plates, and examined them attentively, and really I was glad they had so rational an amusement, to relieve their *ennui*."[34] In its twilight, the Bourbon family was upstaged by its own dinnerware. One suspects this was a fairly frequent occurrence among Sèvres's customers, as much thought and effort went into the making of the porcelain, but nothing more than capital was required to purchase it.

Although well established earlier, materialism as a cultural value in France reached a high mark during the July Monarchy (1830 – 48), the first major period of bourgeois ascension, when untitled individuals began to have an impact on the art, economy, and society of France (fig. 1-6).[35] In July 1830 the highly conservative Restauration government was finally overthrown in a brief "revolution" fought mostly by workers and liberal students who held similar republican sentiments. It was the haute bourgeoisie, however, that seized governmental power in the midst of the con-

Fig. 1-5. *Charles X in his Coronation Robes*, by François Gerard, 1824; oil on canvas. The government of Charles X was characterized by its increasingly reactionary position. (Versailles, musée national des chateaux de Versailles et de Trianon)

Fig. 1-6. *The Industrialist*, by Charles Joseph Travies, after 1828; lithograph. Industrialization in France created many new fortunes, and newly wealthy individuals were often ridiculed for their habits and behavior. (Bibliothèque nationale de France, Paris)

fusion. Fearing the radical possibilities of another republic, these wealthy liberals effected the establishment of another constitutional monarchy. Soon after that time, appointments to the Chamber of Peers were no longer hereditary. Simultaneously, the new power brokers gave the crown to Louis-Philippe, the former duc d'Orleans, who was a distant cousin of Charles X and head of the rival branch of the royal family (fig. 1-7). Known as the "Citizen King," Louis-Philippe was unlike all previous French monarchs in that he accepted the provision that he was elected by parliament and therefore essentially by the will of the people. Increasingly, those of wealth began to enter the life of the nation as never before.

This meant little to the proletariat, since the vote was still reserved for owners of substantial properties. It meant a great deal, however, to members of the bourgeoisie, who were now guaranteed as much social mobility as they had wealth. Moreover, Louis-Philippe was especially solicitous of his bourgeois supporters, and his laissez-faire economic policies greatly helped bankers, manufacturers, and industrialists to expand their interests. The July Monarchy was immediately characterized by the disenchanted as a regime that lacked imagination and soul and that was driven solely

Fig. 1-7. *Louis-Philippe and his Sons Outside the Gates of the Palais de Versailles*, by Horace Vernet, 1846; oil on canvas. Louis-Philippe promoted his family through their depiction in works of art.(Versailles, musée national des chateaux de Versailles et de Trianon)

Fig. 1-8. *The Baroness (Betty) de Rothschild,* by Jean-Dominique Ingres, 1848; oil on canvas. The baroness de Rothschild, depicted here nearly twenty years after the dinner witnessed by Lady Morgan, presided over many lavish entertainments. (Private collection)

by the base pursuit of material wealth — the image of the bourgeoisie immortalized by Balzac in his novels of the period. Ultimately, as the levels of wealth proliferated, so did the subtle means of distinguishing oneself from the ranks beneath, allowing more people to join the complex game of connoisseurship and collecting. By the 1840s, "Old Sèvres" thus ranked among the most sought-after of porcelain, conferring upon its owners respectability and taste beyond that of those who acquired the new production of the manufactory.

In the hothouse environment of social distinction, the ideal host or hostess was one who could bring inspiration to the art of dinner-giving and creativity to the art of dressing a table; one who could plan a dining experience that would satisfy the palate, the mind, and the eye. In her memoirs of her travels in France, Lady Morgan wrote admiringly of one such dinner, held in 1829 at the Baron James de Rothschild's lavish residence in the Bois de Boulogne (fig. 1-8).[36] For her, the porcelain served as nothing less than a symbol of the transforming power of human creativity in taking a humble ingredient like clay and fashioning it by hand and mind into something rare and lovely. Lady Morgan did not mention Sèvres porcelain by name, but it may well have dressed the table on this occasion:

> The dining-room stood apart from the house, in the midst of orange trees. It was an elegant oblong pavilion, of Grecian marble, refreshed by fountains that 'shot in the air in scintillating streams;' and the table, covered with the beautiful and picturesque dessert, emitted no odor that was not in perfect conformity with the freshness of the scene and the fervor of the season. No burnished gold reflected the glaring sunset; no brilliant silver dazzled the eyes. Porcelain, beyond the price of all precious metals, by its beauty and fragility — every plate a picture — consorted with the general character of the sumptuous simplicity which reigned over the whole, and showed how well the masters of the feast had 'consulted the genius of the place in all.'[37]

1. From 1799 to 1848, there were seven changes of political regime and two revolutions in France, in addition to nearly fifteen successive years of war under Napoleon, and severe economic crises in 1817 – 18, 1825, 1837, and 1846. There were a few periods of relative economic health during this half-century — for example, the first decade of the July Monarchy (1830 – 48) — but the country did not experience sustained and widespread stability and economic growth until the Second Empire (1852 – 70).

2. Portet, *Sèvres en Île-de-France* (1975), p. 154.

3. Doyle, *The Oxford History of the French Revolution* (1990), p. 122.

4. Portet, *Sèvres en Île-de-France* (1975), p. 159.

5. Indeed, all displays of insignia or coats of arms were outlawed, abruptly terminating one of the more traditional decorative elements in porcelain services.

6. Portet, *Sèvres en Île-de-France* (1975), pp. 156 – 7.

7. Ibid.

8. Plinval de Guillebon, *Porcelain of Paris* (1972), p. 85.

9. During the Revolution the chapel was presumably converted to another use, perhaps as a club space for worker-patriots.

10. Portet, *Sèvres en Île-de-France* (1975), p. 192.

11. Ibid., p. 159.

12. Ibid., pp. 149, 195.

13. Archives Nationale, F21-682. Overtime hours at the Manufacture de Sèvres were frequent but voluntary. This information is in an 1853 document, but since most skilled workers at Sèvres were paid by the piece and not by the hour, it is unlikely the working schedule was any more demanding during Brongniart's tenure. As regards the average working day elsewhere, see Frederick Artz, *France Under the Bourbon Restauration* (Cambridge: Harvard University Press, 1931), p. 271. Artz reports that skilled and unskilled factory workers under the Restauration normally worked at least thirteen-hour days, with the rate sometimes rising to seventeen hours daily.

14. Archives Nationales, f21-682.

15. Plinval de Guillebon, *Porcelain of Paris* (1972), p. 41.

16. The Meissen manufactory was located in Saxony. Burty, *Chefs d'oeuvre of the Industrial Arts* (1869), p. 159.

17. Doyle, *The Oxford History of the French Revolution* (1990), p. 402.

18. Ibid., p. 199.

19. Ibid., p. 395.

20. Ibid.

21. Ibid., p. 392.

22. Price, *A Social History of Nineteenth-Century France* (1987), p. 96.

23. Breunig, *The Age of Revolution and Reaction* (1977), p. 72.

24. Price, *A Social History of Nineteenth-Century France* (1987), p. 121.

25. The most vigorous growth of the bourgeoisie occurred during the economic boom of the Second Empire (1852 – 70), when opportunities in finance, banking, and industrial production proliferated.

26. Cooper, *Gleanings in Europe*, vol. 1 (1928), p. 105.

27. Ibid., p. 221.

28. For an excellent socioeconomic study, see Walton, *France at the Crystal Palace* (1992).

29. Duchess d'Abrantès, *Memoirs of Napoleon* (1873), vol. 1, p. 387. Napoleon's criticism of lackluster entertaining was aimed at his third consul, Cambacérès (Jean Jacques Régis de Cambacérès, 1753 – 1824), a well-known host of the period. Despite Cambacérès's elegance and the budget he had for his dinners, the duchesse d'Abrantès recorded these affairs in her memoirs as being mortally dull.

30. Ibid., pp. 472 – 73.

31. Rémusat, *A Selection from the Letters of Madame de Rémusat* (1881), p. 165.

32. Morgan, *Lady Morgan in France* (1971), p. 71.

33. Ibid, p. 228.

34. Cooper, *Gleanings in Europe* (1928), pp. 172, 226. Cooper himself pronounced each article of Sèvres "fit to be framed and suspended in a gallery."

35. I am grateful to Derek Ostergard for his insightful comments and ideas regarding the July Monarchy, relative to this discussion.

36. Baron James de Rothschild exemplified the social gains made possible in France after the Revolution. In the nineteenth century James and his brothers parlayed their German father's banking house into the world's wealthiest financial institution. As the head of the family operations in France, James financed virtually every loan sought by the Restauration, July Monarchy, and Second Empire governments. Although of bourgeois Jewish origins (the family's ennoblement was granted by the Austrian emperor in 1815), under the new social order, Baron James de Rothschild ascended to the highest social circles in France.

37. Morgan, *Lady Morgan in France* (1971), p. 237.

Fig. 2-1. *Portrait of Alexandre Brongniart*, by Henriquel Dupont, 1840; pencil on paper. (Manufacture nationale de Sèvres, Archives)

Chapter 2

Alexandre Brongniart: Scholar and Member of the Institut de France

Anne Lajoix

The life of Alexandre Brongniart encompassed a wide range of interests and numerous professions and avocations. In an age of specialization, it is difficult to believe that one person could simultaneously serve as physician, chemist, zoologist, geologist, mineralogist, and paleontologist, yet Brongniart studied and mastered all these professions. Throughout his life, he remained a student of the world, pursuing his ongoing education with a passion and zeal that was rarely matched by his contemporaries.

Brongniart the Scientist

Thanks to the circumstances of his birth, Alexandre Brongniart (fig. 2-1) had the good fortune to grow up in intimate contact with both science and the arts. From this exposure, he developed scientific integrity and character, and the optimism that is characteristic of those who believe in progress. He enjoyed personal relationships with the most eminent artists and scientists of his time, he watched the public and private collections of Europe open before his eyes, and he synthesized his immense knowledge in numerous publications of great significance.

At the end of the eighteenth century, the natural sciences were being systematically organized.[1] What was considered improvization one day became precedent the next. As a true son of the Age of Enlightenment, Brongniart took advantage of this situation. At the time, France stood at the pinnacle of scientific achievement. As the largest and one of the wealthiest nations in Europe, France was viewed as the intellectual epicenter of Europe and the Americas. The French language, along with Latin, was the principal means of communication between educated Europeans; it provided a matrix for the study of science. Finally, the powerful independent French academies assembled, stored, and disseminated information throughout the international scientific community.

The scientific revolution gathered considerable momentum throughout the eighteenth century. While it took great minds to bring it about, there also had to be a community to accept and receive it. The revolution in geology was launched by Jean-Andre Deluc and James Hutton, but the task of founding paleontological stratigraphy fell to Georges Cuvier and Alexandre Brongniart. Interested in geognosy,[2] Brongniart eventually published several treatises that showed how its principles could be extended to other fields. As a geologist and zoologist, he also discovered and demonstrated the importance of fossils to the dating of rock strata.

Knowledge is created through a combination of three factors: instrumental practices, trades, and institutions. Only twenty years old in 1790, a year after the start of the French Revolution, the precocious Brongniart applied all his political weight and institutional background and connections to his emerging career. Two principal figures of the arts and sciences presided over young Brongniart's future: his father, an architect, and his uncle, a chemist.

Brongniart's father, Alexandre-Théodore Brongniart, a distinguished and successful architect,[3] came from a family with two other architects in its ranks — the highly influential Charles de Wailly and Michel-Barthélemy Hazon (Brongniart's maternal great-grandfather). The role and mentality of the chemist were most immediately imparted to Brongniart by his uncle, Antoine-Louis Brongniart, as well as by his grandfather, through whom Brongniart was also related to another well-known chemist and political activist, Antoine-François Fourcroy, a member of a family that was deeply involved with the sciences.

Brongniart the Architect

In 1767 Alexandre-Théodore Brongniart married Anne Louise d'Egremont, who had a linen business in the Temple quarter of Paris. She was the granddaughter of Michel-Barthélemy Hazon,[4] who had studied with Blondel. It may be through this connection that her husband succeeded Etienne Boullée in 1782 as architect of the École Militaire.[5]

The apex of A.T. Brongniart's career was from the late 1760s until the Revolution, when his friendship with Mme de Montesson, the morganatic wife of the duc d'Orléans, assured him of the patronage of the best-known members of eighteenth-century French royal and aristocratic society. Once admitted to her salon, he became well-liked by several individuals, including Talleyrand and the artists Isabey, Garat, and Clodion, who would later play roles in the life of his son. Brongniart was also admired by Jacques-Louis David, who gave drawing lessons to his daughter Louise Brongniart, and by Houdon, who executed busts of his children, Louise and her brother Alexandre. In addition, the elder Brongniart maintained close relationships with the painters Hubert Robert and Élisabeth Vigée-Lebrun.

As a result of his father's position, the young Brongniart met all these artists, as well as other important figures such as Benjamin Franklin and A. L. Lavoisier, who were guests in his parents' home in Paris (fig. 2-2). It was from these associations that he acquired the clarity of elocution that was one of his assets as a professor.

Fig. 2-2. Childhood home of Alexandre Brongniart at 49, boulevard des Invalides, Paris.

Brongniart's parents were also close friends with Pierre-Joseph Macquer, an eminent chemist. Their visits to his estate of Gressy-en-France, in the Brie region, were so frequent that one of Houdon's busts of the young Brongniart was installed there.[6]

Despite the privileged world the family inhabited, the elder Brongniart found opportunities in the impending changes that also threatened this world. "Liberal and Orléanist, and a Freemason,"[7] he welcomed the coming of the Revolution with optimism. In 1791 he achieved a great success when he designed the Théâtre des Amis des Arts. He used his talents during the period to plan civic festivals designed to turn political events into spectacle. Nevertheless, he was judged to be too moderate by the governing Convention, which on October 1, 1792, removed him from his official posts as architect of the Hôtel des Invalides and Ecole Militaire.[8] This removal from office may explain, in part, why he tried his luck in Bordeaux in 1793, opening the Théâtre de la Montagne (Theater of the Mountain) in somewhat obscure circumstances.[9] It appears that Brongniart was invited to Bordeaux by one of his numerous friends, perhaps Maudit de Larive, the famous actor from the Comédie-Française, in order to construct an important new theater there. He did not return to Paris and his family until some twenty-one months later.

In 1795, after the end of the Revolution, he was named a member of the Conseil des Bâtiments Civils (Civil Buildings Council). This appointment probably had something to do with J.-L. David's respect for him and with the position of his wife's powerful cousin, Antoine François Fourcroy.[10] A.-T. Brongniart was soon reunited with his old friends such as Mme de Montesson, who returned to Paris soon after the Revolution and became increasingly close to Josephine de Beauharnais, soon to marry Napoleon Bonaparte. In the coming years, the elder Brongniart accrued honors such as that of knight of the Légion d'Honneur, which he was awarded in 1808,[11] and was named to several official posts — Inspecteur du Mobilier Impérial (after 1804), Conseiller d'Art à la Manufacture Imperiale de Sèvres, Inspecteur Géneral des Bâtiments, and Architecte des Eglises de Paris.

The Chemist and His Connections

From a very early age Alexandre Brongniart showed an interest in the sciences. This interest was nurtured by his uncle, Antoine-Louis Brongniart (fig. 2-3), who in 1765 succeeded his own father as master apothecary and lecturer in chemistry at the Collège de Pharmacie. The familial relationships and professional connections passed on to Brongniart through his uncle were critical to his career. In 1780 Antoine-Louis also became professor of chemistry and physics, giving extremely well-attended private classes "at Versailles . . . , in his office and laboratory, in the boulevard du Roi." At that time, chemistry was a fashionable pursuit in France: like the concurrent experiments in electricity, it attracted those who enjoyed demonstrations, and knowledge of it was disseminated via the salons and in public and private courses (though, curiously, not at the university, as in Germany and Sweden).[12]

In 1771, soon after Antoine-Louis had been named lecturer in chemistry at the Ecoles du Jardin-Royal des Plantes,[13] he purchased one of the four posts of first apothecary to the king. In 1787 he gave chemistry lessons to the dauphin, the son and heir of King Louis XVI. The materials used in these lessons were extremely luxurious:

Fig. 2-3. *Portrait of Antoine-Louis Brongniart.* A chemist, A.-L. Brongniart, Alexandre's uncle, was a mentor to the young scientist. (Paris, Muséum d'Histoire naturelle, Bibliothèque Centrale)

"large and small silver basin, a large skimming ladle and spatula, the same."[14] Some extremely interesting names appear in his accounting notes from his private classes, including Antoine-François Fourcroy, the Abbé Siéyès, Molly from the Academy of Sciences, Lacépède, Corvisart, and again, Benjamin Franklin.[15]

At the Jardin du Roi (fig. 2-4) at that time, there were five courses taught by three professors and three professors' assistants. Some classes were in chemistry and anatomy and the others in botany. The animal and plant kingdoms were studied only to the extent that any one of the very mixed crowd of visitors — for the natural sciences were then equally fashionable — happened to pose questions about them to the professors.[16] The death of Georges-Louis Leclerc, comte de Buffon, on April 16, 1788, caused difficulties at the Jardin. Only the chemists kept to the old way of doing things. A brilliant new course was given by Antoine-François Fourcroy, for which all the preparations were carried out by Antoine-Louis Brongniart, who assisted as Fourcroy's lecturer in chemistry.

Antoine-Louis most likely introduced his young nephew Alexandre to many of the learned academicians at the Jardin. He probably also exposed the young man to the practical side of chemistry. Just before the wars of the revolutionary period took him away from his usual occupations, Antoine-Louis Brongniart produced a fascinating text on how to bleach used writing paper to make it serviceable again. Writing paper had become extremely scarce during the Revolution — so much so that the editor of the *Gazette de Paris*, Durozois, and his wife had been guillotined for possessing a supply of paper. Its dearth therefore was a problem worth addressing seriously. Antoine-Louis declared that he had already resolved it, for he had been discussing his solution in his courses since 1768. He entered into correspondence with a "young lady named Françoise Geneviève Masson, artist, living in the rue des Fossés Saint-Jacques," who had tried out her own process with the paper manufacturer Didot, whose production facilities were on the Essone River near Paris. A report by the Consultation Office, dated July 5, 1792, seems to have favored Brongniart's experiments.[17]

From the civil corps of pharmacists, Brongniart's uncle was mobilized into the military corps as a military pharmacist first class in August 1792. He began working at the military hospital in Lyon the following year. Soon afterward he was named to the chair of chemical arts upon the foundation of the Muséum d'Histoire Naturelle in Paris on June 10, 1793; this chair would go to Louis Nicolas Vauquelin upon the death of Antoine-Louis in 1804.[18]

Brongniart's uncle was promoted to chief pharmacist for the Armée d'Italie in 1796, where he came to the attention of Napoleon, who named him chief pharmacist for all armies on 7 Messidor Year 8 (June 25, 1800).[19] The text indicates that Bonaparte had personally singled him out. This might be interpreted as one of the keys to the future success of the young Alexandre Brongniart, whose interaction with Napoleon between 1800 and 1815 was considerable.

Student, Teacher, and Researcher

The most brilliant period in the history of French chemistry began in 1775, with the discovery of the role of oxygen in the oxidation process by A. L. Lavoisier and his disciples in the "chemistry revolution." For some time, historical and pedagogical ties had bound chemistry and natural history together. Treatises were categorized according to the distribution of the three natural kingdoms: animal, vegetable, and mineral. With the publication of his *Traité élémentaire de chimie*, Lavoisier broke with an empirical, even "alchemical," chemistry, to ground himself in analytical logic.[20]

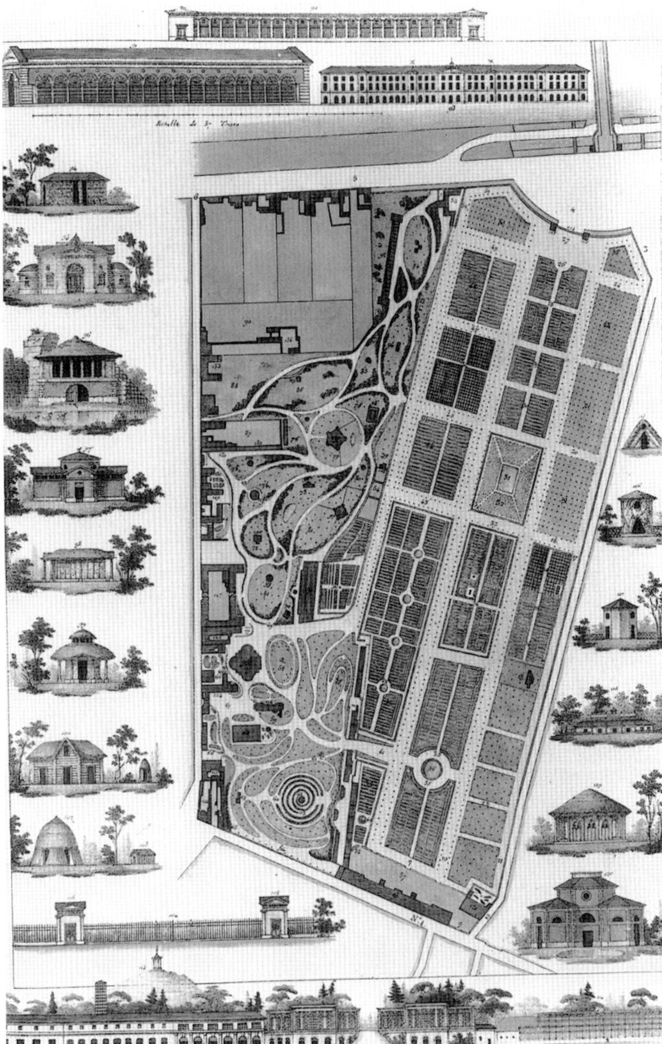

Fig. 2-4. Plan, elevations, and views of the Jardin du Roi, by Thouin, 1823. (Paris, Muséum d'Histoire naturelle, Bibliothèque Centrale)

A doctor by training and a chemist by vocation, Claude-Louis Berthollet had been trained by "phlogistians"[21] and was one of Lavoisier's most active collaborators. Berthollet was the force behind a circle of researchers known in 1807 as the Société d'Arcueil, a precursor of the Société Chimique de Paris. He introduced some of France's greatest nineteenth-century scientists to the world of research: L.-J. Guy-Lussac, L.-J. Thénard, and P.-L. Dulong.

Alexandre Brongniart was unavoidably influenced by such models and "had received, from his earliest youth, as a sort of general sustenance, the strong and durable sense of the unequaled success of Lavoisier's chemistry in illuminating, like a new day, the philosophy of nature. From the very beginning, it opened the way for him, and it continued to serve as his guide throughout his career."[22] From 1786 he attended the courses taught by Sage and Guillot-Duhamel at the Ecole des Mines which, before the Revolution, was housed at the Paris Mint. He also served as a preparer for his uncle at the Jardin du Roi.[23] Despite, or perhaps because of, his age — he was sixteen — he organized a classroom in his father's official living quarters in the Hôtel des Invalides where he worked ardently to propagate the ideas of his father's friend Lavoisier, which were then considered controversial.[24]

Further evidence of his early commitment to the sciences is Alexandre Brongniart's position as one of the founding members of the Société Philomathique, also known as the Amis des Sciences.[25] The goal of this society, which met for the first time at the end of 1788, was mutual instruction: its members read and discussed recent scientific papers. Their motto was "Science et Amitié" (Science and Friendship). The society's founding members were Cuvier, Stéphane Sylvestre Lacroix, Augustin Pyrame Candolle, and José Francisco Corréa de Serra; they were advised by Bertholet, Monge, Laplace, Lacépède, and Fourcroy.[26]

In order to comprehend the novelty and interest of this learned society, it is important to note that when the publication of the papers of the Academy of Sciences was cancelled in the revolutionary turmoil in 1793, Alexandre Brongniart proposed that the Société Philomathique bring them together and publish them. The organization was a sort of refuge for the scientific community during the years of the Revolution.[27]

If Brongniart's precocity and determination were remarkable, the volume of his completed work is no less so. He surprised his contemporaries with his aptitude for the study of mineralogy, which he had begun to teach to the Société Gymnastique.[28] At the same time, probably to please his father, "who would have preferred his son to follow a career in the arts,"[29] he earned a Maître dès Arts diploma in 1789 but thereafter quickly returned to his scientific preoccupations. In 1789 and 1790 he attended courses preparatory to a degree in medicine. It is likely that Brongniart studied with Corvisart, judging by a paper in the archives of the Academy of Sciences: "Certificate of attendance at courses in anatomy, physiology, surgery, and childbirth during the winters of 1789 and 1790, and at courses in clinical medicine and medical material, at the amphitheater of the La Charité Hospital in 1791."[30]

These studies left him enough time to travel to England to examine the collections of the "Prince of Botanists," Carl von Linné, whose classifications were recognized as the most reliable and were, from 1737 to 1810, the most commonly used in scientific study. The Société Linéenne of Paris had been founded in December 1787 and accepted both amateurs and scientists for membership until 1790. The London branch has been active since its founding in 1788.[31] During his trip to England, Brongniart also visited mines and picturesque sites in Derbyshire, noting his observations in an essay on the enameler's art that was his first foray into the vitreous arts.

Brongniart was named a member of the Société d'Histoire Naturelle upon its creation on August 27, 1790. The spirit here was different from that at the Société Philomathique. It was more political and required more initiative, especially to preserve the royal gardens when their existence was jeopardized by the revolutionary government.[32] Brongniart presented a report on "the necessity of establishing a menagerie" in 1792, and made two brief presentations on zoology at the Société Philomathique in 1791 and 1792.[33]

In 1793 Brongniart encountered personal trials as well: arrested while collecting botanical samples in the forest of Fontainebleau in August, he spent five days in jail at Nemours.[34] Soon afterward he joined the corps of military pharmacists, like his uncle, and became an aide to the Armée des Pyrénées de l'Ouest in the Bordeaux-Bayonne region. While there, he studied the local flora and fauna. He encountered some serious trouble after one of his companions, Pierre-Marc Broussonet, a learned botanist from Montpellier, decided to flee to Spain during their excursion together into mountains conveniently near the Spanish border.[35] Brongniart himself was arrested at the start of 1794 because of his acquaintance with Broussonet. The intervention of Fourcroy[36] and probably the fall of Robespierre rescued Brongniart.

Brongniart's Institutional Influences

Brongniart's earliest responsibilities coincided with the remarkable political upheavals of France in the 1790s. It is rare historically to find a social or political ideology in such harmony with the scientific activities of its time. During Brongniart's early career, political upheavals were linked to scientific adventures and the technological evolution. The challenge to scientists and politicians alike was to unite this coexistent mosaic to form a new elite that, sustained by an ideology based on progress through science as well as faith in meritocracy, would administer the country. Thus it was necessary to find new administrators and to provide instruction. The difficulty resided in fitting all the pieces together into a whole.

The curiosity of the Encyclopedists was by no means the prerogative of scholars alone. Encyclopedists believed that an intellectual continuum linked mathematics and the fine arts, creating a union that would in fact be played out in the professional life of Brongniart. The rationalism that was intrinsic to much of the intellectual spirit of the eighteenth century was described by Condorcet in the ninth chapter in his *Esquisse d'un tableau historique des progrès de l'esprit humain* (Outline of a historic picture for the progress of the human spirit). Similarly, Laplace and J.-B. Biot believed in the interconnectedness of the sciences.[37] The sciences had been optional in the colleges during the ancien régime and were taught at extremely varied levels. However, they increasingly became the penultimate point of reference in the hierarchical structure of higher education in the secondary schools (*lycées*) in France. While there was little change in the training offered for medical and pharmaceutical careers, which had been the core of university life before the Revolution, new high-level scientific research institutions had to be created to accompany discoveries and the corresponding new branches of academic disciplines. The innovative sciences had to be assured a privileged place in the national education system then being developed.

At the end of the eighteenth century, chemistry played a very particular role as an intellectual training ground. Chemists, and thus scientists, were in power: they sat on the Comité de Salut Public (Public Health Commission). A particularly innovative new organization was the Ecole Centrale des Travaux Publics, which later became the Ecole Polytechnique. Its aim was to mold the elite by following a generalist and unifying two-step model: first providing a general scientific training, and then refining the student's training in specialized schools such as the Ecole des Mines, which were devoted to applied knowledge in various disciplines.

In the past, the state had called on scientists for short-term military needs and long-term civil ones. This mission was taken over by the Ecole Polytechnique, which trained military and civil engineers.[38] It is noteworthy that Alexandre Brongniart participated in the genesis of this critical body: he would later write, "I was part of the Corps des Mines before the existence of the Ecole Polytechnique."[39]

The law of August 24, 1794, created an Agence des Mines composed of three members who were appointed by the Comité de Salut Public.[40] Under its authority was the Corps des Mines, composed of eight inspectors and twelve engineers, including Alexandre Brongniart, who had been appointed engineer.[41] He immediately conducted numerous inspection tours, of the four Norman districts in particular. From April to October of 1795 he traveled through the areas between Provence and the Alps. He also trained three students during this time and produced several field reports, all of which have been preserved.[42] He continued for some time to write reports for the Conseil des Mines.[43]

During this period, Brongniart's professional activity was prodigious. From 1795 to 1806 he was professor of natural history and of zoology at the Ecole Centrale, located at the Collège des Quatre Nations, one of five such schools in the Département de la Seine.[44] In 1798 and 1799 he was a temporary instructor in physical geography and mineralogy at the Ecole des Mines.[45] At the same time, he gave a course in entomology at the Société d'Histoire Naturelle.[46]

Because the sciences were continually being "popularized" by publications,[47] as well as by encyclopedias and dictionaries — in particular the *Encyclopédie méthodique* published by C. Joseph Panckoucke[48] — specialized publications gradually began to appear.[49] Between 1794 and 1825, naturalists worked almost equally to popularize scientific knowledge and to conduct research.[50] The Muséum d'Histoire Naturelle grew considerably, particularly between 1799 and 1815, a growth that was well documented after 1802 by the *Annales du Muséum*, a periodical that attained, and sustained, a high reputation among European scientists.[51]

It became clear to the Consulate (1799 – 1804) that in order to teach the natural sciences, it would be necessary to see that the works of the best specialists were published. To help decide which texts to use in instruction, the council at the Ecole Polytechnique charged with improving pedagogy soon began asking for written courses.[52] Alexandre Brongniart, who was then assigned to mineralogy, began working with Georges Cuvier to produce a classification system for various zoological and mineralogical subjects. This resulted in several joint publications that strengthened the ties binding the scientific community together. Brongniart and Cuvier jointly wrote the "Essai sur la géographie minéralogique des environs de Paris" (Essay on the mineral geography of the surroundings of Paris), which was published starting in 1808 in the *Journal des Mines* and presented to the Institut in 1811.[53] In it Brongniart revealed the value of fossils, when classed geologically in their order of evolution, in analyzing mineralogical strata. The novelty lay in applying zoology to the problems of mineralogical strata.

Cuvier and Brongniart's continuing collaboration permitted them to use field observations to show the role that fossils could play in the dating and classification of different ground strata. Brongniart also introduced the concept of tertiary soil. He fixed the chronology of sedimentary soils and was then able to determine the relationships between geographic change and the disappearance of the dinosaurs. Through this work, he contributed to the foundation of the science of stratigraphy. He applied the research and classification method developed by Cuvier, who was then occupied with his "Essais sur le règne animal" (Essays on the animal kingdom), to the study of reptiles and in 1797 published his own Classification des Reptiles, a work that would remain the authority in herpetology for some time to come.[54] Brongniart devised the classification of reptiles in four orders — sauria, batrachia, chelonia, and ophidia[55] — a system that was adopted by naturalists world round. In 1817 F. M. Daudin would even name a type of lizard the "Brongniartian".[56]

Brongniart was named professor of natural history at the Imperial University in Paris in 1806. In 1807 he published his *Traité élémentaire de minéralogie avec des applications aux arts* (Elementary treatise of mineralogy with applications to the arts).[57] This work achieved great success due to the breadth of his views and the clarity of his expression. In the same year, he was elected a corresponding member of the Academy of Sciences of the Institut de France. Two years later, he received his doctorate in science and began to teach mineralogy as part of the science faculty. After 1813 he also taught geology as an adjunct professor at the Jardin du Roi.

Traces of tension exist in Brongniart's letters, showing him to be on the defensive when accused of hoarding positions. To understand these attacks, it is helpful to consider the circumstances associated with his election to the Institut. Laplace knew that the hold of convictions on people's minds required both a community and a consensus. He praised the Institut for "the useful influence [which] has dissipated the accumulated errors of our day with an enthusiasm that in another time would have been put to use perpetuating them."[58]

In effect, the Academy of Sciences had been shut down in August 1793. Many scientists during that year lived with the sense "of being in a terrible tempest, surrounded by reefs and the debris of shipwrecks," in the words of the geologist Déodat de Dolomieu.[59] Lavoisier had emphasized the communality of the sciences, however, as far greater than that of the world of letters, and the republic needed scientists for the war effort and for the reorganization of the country. Laplace stressed the usefulness of the academies as venues for the most noble expression of scientific unity.[60] The national Institut was created on October 25, 1795, by the Convention, which resuscitated the old system in an attempt to create "an abbreviated version of the scholarly world." Alexandre Brongniart was elected to it in 1815, to the seat formerly held by Desmarest at the heart of the prestigious first class, in section 6, devoted to natural history and mineralogy.[61] His election was a glorious confirmation of his importance. He served as the Institut's vice-president in 1826 and as president in 1827. He was also the author of "luminous" reports "in which he judged the papers submitted to the Academy with gentleness and fairness."[62]

This distinction angered certain colleagues of Brongniart. When he presented himself to the Muséum d'Histoire Naturelle in 1819 as a candidate for the chair in geology recently left vacant by the death of Faujas de Saint-Fond, he was attacked and his attempt failed. He then proceeded to mount his defense.[63] He ultimately

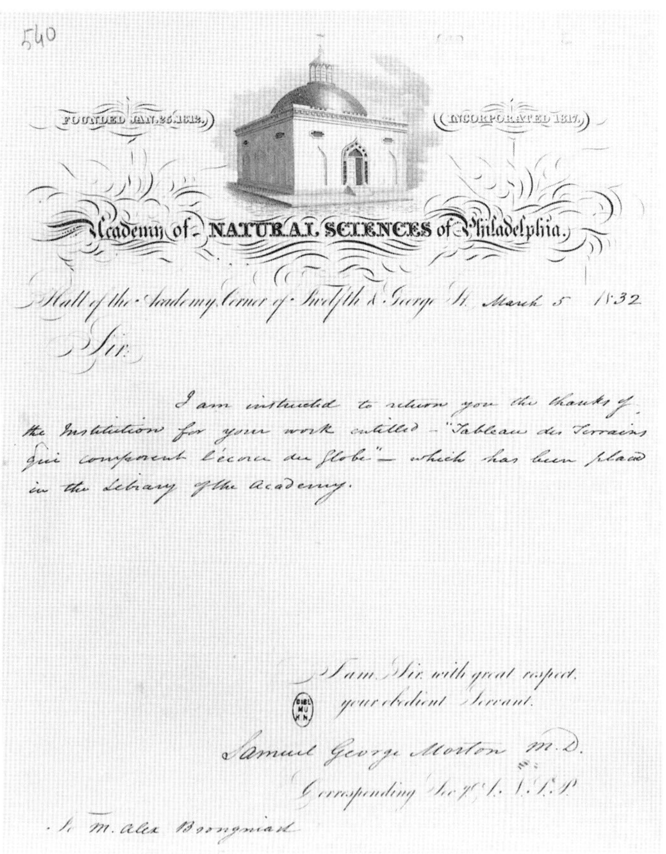
FOUNDED JAN. 25. 1812.
INCORPORATED 1817.
Academy of NATURAL SCIENCES of Philadelphia.

Hall of the Academy, Corner of Twelfth & George St. March 5 1832.

Sir.

I am instructed to return you the thanks of the Institution for your work entitled "Tableau des Terrains qui composent l'écorce du globe" which has been placed in the library of the academy.

I am, Sir, with great respect, your obedient Servant.

Samuel George Morton M.D.
Corresponding Secy A.N.S.P.

To M. Alex Brongniart

Fig. 2-5. Letter dated March 5, 1832, from Dr. Samuel George Morton of the Academy of Natural Sciences of Philadelphia to Alexandre Brongniart. (Paris, Muséum d'Histoire naturelle, Bibliothèque Centrale)

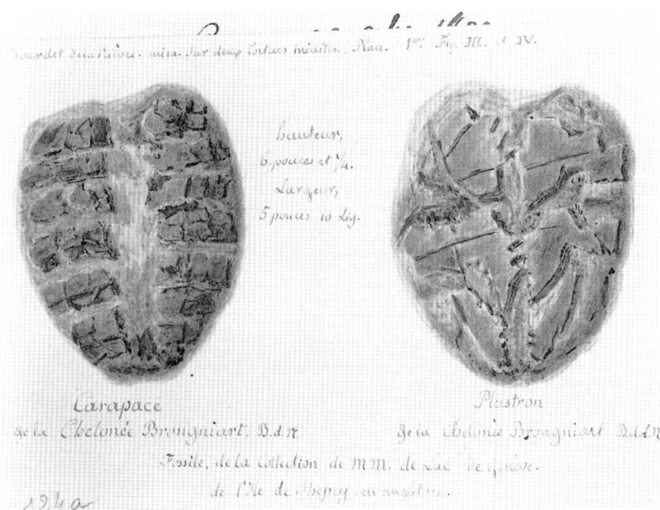

Fig. 2-6. Sketches of the *chelonia Brongniart*, a tortoise fossil whose discoverer petitioned to name it in honor of Alexandre Brongniart. (Paris, Muséum d'Histoire naturelle, Bibliothèque Centrale)

obtained the chair in mineralogy, replacing de Haüy in 1822. From this date until his death, the courses he taught in that capacity enabled him to strengthen his friendships with both Geoffroy Saint-Hilaire and Cuvier. These were "courses in 43 lessons, each of which was one hour twenty minutes at least, and sometimes two hours, with 45 students." There exists in the archives a "list of persons having attended the mineralogy courses at the Jardin in 1827 and wishing to participate in the lesson on the ceramic arts, which will take place at Sèvres on Tuesday, July 25, at precisely 11 o'clock: Azolette, director general of the Quinze-Vingt, Billard, resident student at the central Pharmacy located on the quai de la Tournelle." There are also "Notes on various people who came to my course." For example, in 1828: "Eugène Boch, the son, Charles Wagner, a Pole from Warsaw studying medicine, Marnal, damask preparer, Parent du Châtelet, 28 rue Geoffroy Lasnier,"[64] or in 1829, a few individuals such as, "Barruel, son of the Regent of the Ecole de Médicine, Chenavard, Laperouse, grandson of the Inspector of Mines, Professor of natural history at Toulouse, Ampère, the son, a certain Christie, and Doctor Jaehkel, from Fribourg," and finally in 1832, the twenty-year-old engraver Clerget.[65]

In addition to other administrative tasks, Brongniart fulfilled the role of resident expert at the museum. Whenever there was a donation to be received or an individual piece or collection to be purchased, his opinion was required. When de Haüy's collection was proposed by his nephew, Vuillemot-Hauy, Brongniart wrote a detailed report in which his own interests are in evidence: "this is an extremely precious collection in terms of the history of science, and one of the most useful from the point of view of teaching . . . ." He also examined Cuvier's collections in 1832 and the mineralogical collection of the *chevalier* Gillet de Laumont in 1835.[66]

French academicians at the end of the eighteenth century were part of a European network that traveled and communicated regularly.[67] For example Guyton de Morveau, of the Academy of Dijon, corresponded with the Swede Torbern Bergmann.[68] Paving the way for the considerable development of technical literature, exchanges in journals and publications multiplied.[69] Alexandre Brongniart fit squarely in this line of the conquest of knowledge. To scholars confronted by the mass of his correspondence with people around the world, it becomes apparent that the effect of this dynamic on Brongniart's methods is incontestable. Whether a young friend who was a lawyer in Philadelphia,[70] or his nephew who was French consul in Spain,[71] everyone was pressed into service to retrieve information (see chap. 9). With his letters Brongniart wanted not only to assemble observations about travel, but he was also motivated by the hope of finding samples of every type of pottery made in the world — a project he had conceived early on for the museum at Sèvres.

Over the years, the majority of the letters deal with exchanges of information[72] or of mineralogy samples: of cobalt,[73] of anthracite from Pennsylvania (fig. 2-5),[74] of rocks and animal species,[75] of insects,[76] and of fossil catalogues.[77] He gladly sent books, scholarly journals,[78] and mineral samples to places like New York[79] and Mexico,[80] as well as "two wild pigeons."[81] When they decided to form a "respectable museum" of natural history in Lexington, Kentucky, its administrators wrote to Brongniart, reporting on the institution's progress and asking his advice.[82] A similar request came from the porcelain manufactory in Portugal owned by Duarte

Ferreiro Pinto Basto.[83] There are some very lively and amusing letters that describe rare species or exotic animals, but the collection also chronicles the mores and way of life in places such as Calcutta and New York.[84] One correspondent who signed himself "the traveling naturalist" or "the traveling geologist" asked permission to name a tortoise fossil *chelonia Brongniart*, and included three watercolor sketches along with his request (fig. 2-6).[85]

Brongniart's documents include files pertaining to "Papers relative to requests, receptions, mailings, gifts, acquisitions, and exchanges of minerals, rocks, and fossilized organisms,"[86] as well as manuscripts dealing with his voyages, his contracts with publishers, some lecture sheets, and "Papers relative to the arrangement and cataloguing of my mineral collections."[87] Also to be found are personal observations, scattered sheets for a "Special Physical and Civil Geography of Europe in general, the European lands of Asia, Africa, North America, Colombia or South America, and the Maritime world of Walker."[88] His voyages and inquiries often led to these precise descriptions, sketches, and notes.[89]

The Ties Between Brongniart, the Ceramic Arts, and Sèvres

From 1800 until around 1840 scientific analysis and its methodology constituted a field of research in which cognitive and commercial interests coincided, for science was to be exact, but also useful. For example, Fourcroy disseminated the use of gravimetric analysis with hydrogen sulfide to discover traces of lead in clarified wine or cider. Lavoisier's work on mineral waters was at the intersection of three scientific disciplines: health, geology, and chemistry.[90] Similarly, Alexandre Brongniart moved readily between the investigative methods of the field (travel, analysis, and sampling) and theoretical training (teaching, research, and publication). He also shared Berthollet's opinion that "The arts can only make limited progress when they are directed strictly by a blind practice . . . but if artists are guided by the knowledge of those properties that have been analyzed by physics and its complement, chemistry, there is no limit to the perfection to which they may be brought."[91]

At the end of the eighteenth century, science was perceived as needing to possess a fundamental utility that would place it at the heart of society. Science should also, it was felt, contribute to practical training in the trades — that is, it should be put into the service of a trainee with technical needs linked to the exercise of a profession.[92]

The intervention of the political world into the scientific world occurred to the extent that all decisions concerning teaching and civil careers had to pass before the eyes of the minister of the interior. The Ministère de l'Interieur, created in 1790, was temporarily dissolved but was reestablished in 1795. By 1799, under the first consul, it comprised a number of divisions: agriculture, arts, factories, mines, foundries, interior commerce, trade balance, subsistence, population, religion, public education, and the theater.[93] Lucien Bonaparte, the first consul's brother, inaugurated the reorganization of this imposing agency, and he signed the nomination of Alexandre Brongniart as director of the Sèvres manufactory on 18 Brumaire 1800. Although there is little to document this event, several aspects of the nomination shed light on the choice of Brongniart, a young man of only thirty, for this honor.

An important factor in Brongniart's appointment was the solidarity among Freemasons. Although it is not known whether Brongniart himself was a Mason, both Lucien Bonaparte and Brongniart's father were members. The fellowship of the scientific community, which boasted many Freemasons, would also have aided Brongniart's career. Finally, his powerful family network probably helped to bring about his appointment.[94] It is likely, for example, that First Consul Bonaparte knew Brongniart's father and sisters Louise and Emilie as well as his uncle (see note 19). Napoleon had a passion for the exact sciences, which he placed at the apex of the intellectual hierarchy, and whose leaders were least likely to overstep their limitations and infringe on his then fragile power. There is documented evidence of Bonaparte's interest in science. During the entire first half of 1795, he had remained in Paris, expanding his knowledge of the field. He wrote to his elder brother Joseph: "Classes in history, chemistry, and botany come one after the other." He may have audited classes at the Ecole Normale or attended the lectures of Monge and Laplace at the Muséum d'Histoire Naturelle and the Société Philomathique.[95] Expressions common in Napoleonic language — the rise of the enlightenment, the reign of reason, the progress of the human spirit, the "laboratory of Egypt" — suggest that during this period Bonaparte was aligned in his thinking with the Encyclopedist community to which Brongniart belonged.[96]

There is therefore nothing surprising about the nomination of Brongniart to head the manufactory at Sèvres. His capacity for work, the seriousness and determination he had shown in other areas, and his scientific interests were placed in the service of the ceramic arts. Brongniart's son-in-law would later remark that "his scientific studies, his technical knowledge and the frequent social relations his family had with all of the great artists of the period combined to make him the natural choice for the job."[97]

Starting in 1802, Brongniart inaugurated the program of official annual receptions and exhibitions where the work of the manufactory would be displayed to the government. In April 1802 he initiated a series of annual lectures on the ceramics in the Musée Céramique, after which he conducted tours of the Sèvres workshops for the students. He gladly received visitors at the manufactory, and several of them later sent him observations from their travels abroad.

In 1831 Feuillet de Conches reported to Brongniart on the English manufactories, where painting on large sheets of glass was being developed in response to its growing popularity at the time. As for porcelain, he wrote: "their porcelains are simply copies of the pastes of old Saxony and Japan; either that or they are servile imitations of the old Sèvres porcelains. The house of Davenport and Pontigny, one of the best, has just executed a service for King William: the form and the ornaments are a pastiche of old Sèvres . . . . The paintings executed in the good London houses are not without harmony; but they transgress by their lack of finesse and good taste. None of those pictures of flowers or fruits, none of those landscapes such as are made by your Robert and other artists: the English would never try to compete with you on that field, and if something of the sort appears in their shops, it's something produced by your workshops. At the firm of Spode and Copeland, one of the leading houses, there is a fruit plate from your firm that costs 1000 pounds sterling!"[98]

On February 22, 1844, Brongniart sent the king a red leather-

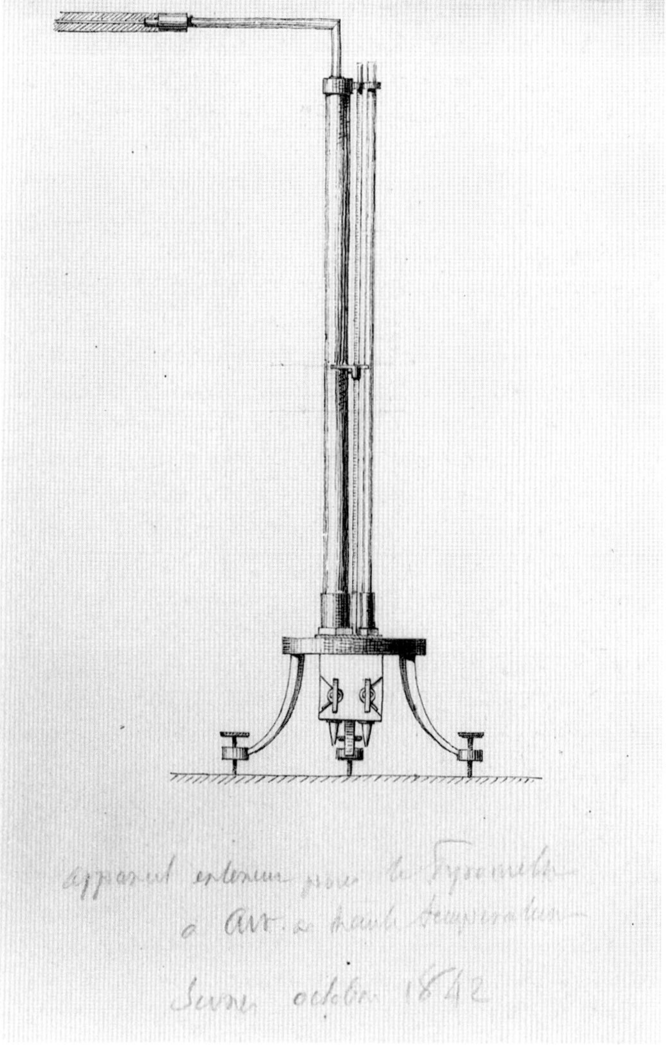

Fig. 2-7. Design for a pyrometer, dated October 1842; watercolor. (Paris, Muséum d'Histoire naturelle, Bibliothèque Centrale)

bound copy of his book *Traité des arts céramiques ou des poteries considérées dans leur histoire, leur pratique et leur théorie* (translated into English as "Coloring and Decoration of Ceramic Wares"). The text of this treatise, which was written between 1830 and 1844, bears witness to the immense work and the methodology of Alexandre Brongniart. He had written to every important person in the field in order to obtain accurate information and precious sources: foreign scholars, friends, the most illustrious as well as the most modest manufacturers, were all consulted.[99] This book brought together Brongniart's research on every aspect of clay, kaolin and colors, his analyses of ceramics and pyrometers (fig. 2-7),[100] and even the results of the galvanographic tests of Fr. de Kobell.[101] The next year Brongniart published a catalogue of the museum at Sèvres, entitled *Description méthodique du musée céramique de la manufacture royale de porcelaine de Sèvres,* which he prepared with Denis-Désiré Riocreux.

During this period Brongniart continued to accrue honors. He was made a knight of the Order of Saint-Michel[102] (1816), and progressed from knight of the Légion d'Honneur (December 26, 1814), to officer (June 7, 1825), and finally commander (April 29, 1845), an honor conferred at the same time on his son-in-law, J.-B. Dumas.[103]

At this date, the Encyclopedist mentality had been in full bloom for some time, but numerous schisms had emerged within the scientific community, often for political and social reasons. As a consequence, scientists later in the century increasingly withdrew into their own individual fields of study, which destroyed the camaraderie that had existed during the Revolution.

Brongniart the Man

Portraits of Brongniart from childhood through his adult years are abundant, from a bust sculpted by Houdon when Brongniart was an infant (see the frontispiece)[104] to later images of the thin, bony face of Brongniart's mature years, which offered a physiognomy that would have been severe were it not for the affability in his eyes.[105]

Following in the footsteps of his father, who was a member of the first municipality of Paris, Alexandre volunteered in the National Guard, under the orders of the prince of Salm-Kyrbourg, on July 14, 1789, the day the Bastille fell. In 1800 he married Cécile Coquebert de Montbret,[106] whose father was a scientist and member of the Institut and who had just been named consul in Amsterdam. From 1802 to 1822 the couple lived with Cécile's parents in a three-story house at 3, rue Saint-Dominique, which Montbret had purchased for the use of various branches of his family, including Hazons, Coqueberts, and Brongniarts. (The house at 3, rue Saint-Dominique became the property of Cécile Brongniart in 1832.) After 1822 Brongniart and his wife occupied the suite in a pied-à-terre at the Muséum d'Histoire Naturelle where de Hauy had lived.[107] It was on the upper floor of a residence at the Jardin des Plantes. J.-B. Dumas, who would later become his son-in-law, lived on the first floor, and professor Valenciennes on the ground floor.

A picturesque description of the life in these dwellings has been left us by Louis de Launay:

> When his sojourns at Sèvres had ended, usually on Saturday evening, Brongniart got into his one-horse cabriolet driven by a coachman from the imperial livery and later the royal livery, and he set off on the trip to the rue Saint-Dominique. This vehicle, whose appearance has been preserved for us in a watercolor by Troyon — who was at that time at the Sèvres manufactory with his father, a porcelain painter under Isabey — had, according to the mocking younger generation, all its pouches and pockets stuffed with minerals and stones, which forced the ladies, according to the customs of the time, to hold themselves rigorously straight, lest their shoulders should come into contact with some uncomfortably-stuffed surface.
>
> Mme Brongniart, as a prudent manager, attempted to insure that this continual commuting did not lead to waste, and so the cook would climb up besides the coach-driver and bring provisions from one residence to the other in a vast basket covered in waxed canvas. The poodle, Médor, accompanied the party, or rather preceded it, going along completely on his own towards home, governed by a invariable ritual, without ever getting lost.

It was thus that the arrival in the rue Saint-Dominique occurred; and there Sunday and Monday would be spent, often after having spent Saturday night participating in Cuvier's weekly reception.[108]

Sunday lunch, traditionally devoted to family and friends, did not prevent Brongniart from receiving visitors in the afternoon who sometimes stayed to dinner. His "day" attracted scientists from all over Europe and even America: George Bentham from London, James Hutton from Dublin, and Mr. Keratry from Philadelphia, for example; and there were artists, including Delacroix, Delaroche, Déveria, Gérard, Isabey, and Ingres, as well as the Sèvres manufactory's esteemed porcelain painter, Marie-Victoire Jaquotot, who knew the Brongniart women well enough to lend them some sheet music and to drop in as a neighbor. Brongniart's colleagues and students were always invited: the Ampères brothers, Dominique Jean Arago, Frédéric Henri Humboldt, Michaël Faraday, and David Brewster. A delightful signed letter, dated December 4 [1842], invites "M. Duperrey, Captain of Hussards, Member of the Institut, rue de Seine," to dine the following Sunday evening "with a few of our colleagues and in particular M. de Humboldt, who has taken a lively interest in our nomination."[109]

His abundant correspondence reveals another aspect of Brongniart's personality. There are numerous letters in which correspondents thank him for the welcome received either during a visit at Sèvres[110] or at a reception, or for his having sent them information.[111] Brongniart was capable of shedding the formal courtesy of his official demeanor and writing with considerable compassion when the circumstances warranted it, as in replying to a widow,[112] a young petitioner,[113] an old member of the Société Philomathique[114] (of which Brongniart was still treasurer in 1819)[115] who had requested a post. He also used a personal tone when gathering and exchanging memories,[116] or inquiring about his correspondent's health.[117] In the latter context, one of his traveling companions in Provence, who had become a pastor in Switzerland and was extremely eloquent about the state of his own health, wrote him a series of letters in which we learn that Brongniart's motto at the time was "Ceci se mange froid" (Revenge is a meal eaten cold) and that up until 1818, he read the Bible to his children.[118]

A personal touch sometimes appears in everyday notes analyzing information or responding to questions: a M. Brard, from the Service des Mines in Nîmes, thanked Brongniart after receiving a "charming sequence of colors on porcelain."[119] The sincerity of many of the notes he received bears witness to the confidence people had in Brongniart. Borson, for example, who was both Brongniart's colleague and a professor of mineralogy at the Academy of Sciences of Turin, in a letter dated May 6, 1817, described his concerns: "So much has happened in the three years, more or less, since our last letter [1813]. Those events affecting this country have, happily, not been damaging to the institution of which I am a part, and after a period of uncertainty and volatility, I have managed to keep my post."[120] There are two letters to the assistant surgeon at the Saint-Louis Hospital, Jules Cloquet, in which Brongniart intervened on behalf of two employees of the Sèvres Manufactory, asking that they be given special care.[121]

Brongniart made the magnanimous gesture of renouncing his pension in 1832, when he learned of a major budget cut. He made this proposition to the director general for the benefit of "furloughed, active, or impoverished inspectors or engineers," in order to help them avoid "the discouraging or too onerous reductions [in the budget of the Corps]."[122] It was not the first time he had made such a gesture. Upon his nomination to the directorship at Sèvres, he had already renounced his benefits as engineer, which were not reinstated until March 10, 1813.[123]

Unanimous admiration such as that given to Brongniart could only be inspired by an *honnête homme*, or a true gentleman, even if Brongniart's own wife, in a letter to their son Adolphe, who was away traveling, wrote that his father might "be a little less rigid."[124] This is somewhat evident in a note written by Brongniart in the corner of a letter he had received from the young Jean-Jacques Ampère, who had requested a literary recommendation: "replied 19 July, giving him my reasons for not giving [him] this sort of recommendation." That did not, however, prevent Brongniart from calling him "dear young traveling companion" in another letter two years later.[125] His often very sharp attitude is evident when dealing with a doctor named Koreff, who Brongniart felt could not be taken seriously as a practitioner, and who wrote complaining of Brongniart's "singular and inexplicable" letter.[126] A dissenting opinion, published in 1841, depicts Brongniart as "haughty, imperious . . . , the head of the grand aristocratic-scientific clique of the Muséum," and adds, "but neither these character traits, nor the fact that he had planted his sons, his sons-in-law, his vassals, all over the place" prevented him from having been a scientist of merit.[127]

Brongniart also had strict standards regarding the education of his sons. A folder containing several family letters includes notes describing his son Adolphe's scholarly program for the years 1818–20. He was to follow J.-B. Biot's courses in physics and those of L.-J. Thenard in chemistry from mid-June until September 1818. In 1819, until November, "the new sciences to be learned [are] anatomy, physiology, mammal and bird zoology; the fields of knowledge to be completed [are] chemistry and physics, Greek, German, English, rhetoric and history; the fields to be reviewed [are] drawing and Latin." As for the winter of 1819 – 20: "botany daily from 6 a.m. to noon, on Sundays and Wednesdays, chemistry from noon to 5, and readings each evening." A little later, the father notes, "weekly, 65 hours including errands and lunch, day off on Sunday, and on Wednesday after 2."[128]

As demonstrated in this letter, Brongniart's interest in his family had an exacting side. His son-in-law Dumas, for example, told the story of how, during an evening at the Palais des Tuileries sometime around 1830, the candles began to give off an acrid, offensive smoke, and Brongniart, diverted from the reception, insisted on studying the problem immediately. Dumas later illustrated and demonstrated for him the phenomenon of substitution.[129]

At all times, the solidarity of the Brongniart family was exemplary. The central registry of contracts, baptismal records, and marriage certificates in Paris contains many notarized documents through which one may catch a glimpse of the family's attitudes when faced with the great crises of life. When his uncle Antoine-Louis died in 1804, Brongniart's parents, "upon learning of the difficult position and distress [of the widow]," loaned her a complete set of furniture so that she could live decently.[130]

Fig. 2-8. View of "Vert-Buisson," Alexandre Brongniart's country house in Normandy; painted on porcelain at Sèvres, ca. 1934. The house no longer exists. (Manufacture nationale de Sèvres, Archives)

The architect Brongniart's financial success was such that he was able to leave each of his children a yearly income of 1,000 livres.[131] The inventory drawn up at the time of his death was carried out by L.-A. Pichon, who was empowered to act for the heirs,[132] who, "wanting to give proofs to Madame, their mother, of their affection," left her "in complete possession of everything left by her husband."[133] It is unnecessary to list other such examples of the confidence and solidarity of the clan, which belie, *avant la lettre*, Balzac's clichés regarding the avarice of families. In 1831 Alexandre Brongniart had a country house built, a Swiss-style chalet, near Gisors in Normandy. Christened *Vert-Buisson* (Green-Bush), it was a place where the whole family could be together (fig. 2-8). The house still existed in 1934,[134] at which time one could read the rather dated maxims that its owner had inscribed upon its walls and a porcelain plaque was made at Sèvres commemorating the chalet.

After Brongniart's death in 1847, his son received a great many testimonial letters. As is usual in such circumstances, they bear witness to Brongniart's prestige, especially within the scholarly community but outside it as well.[135] The minister of public works had the chief mining engineers present themselves at the rue Saint-Dominique residence to represent him in the funeral procession.[136] Alexandre Brongniart was buried in Père-Lachaise cemetery, one of his father's civic works from earlier in the century, in a place with the poetic name *Bosquet de l'île* (Arbor bouquet island; fig. 2-9). Sèvres porcelains were placed in his coffin: two cream jugs and two teacups of the finest quality, to which were added twelve pieces of secondary quality.[137] It is not known whether these pieces represented Brongniart's own choice or that of his family. The first hypothesis would be surprising for a man of science, while the second suggests a symbolic choice in homage to the refinement of the pieces created under Brongniart's guidance. Two years later his widow

Fig. 2-9. Tomb of Alexandre Brongniart in Père-Lachaise Cemetery, Paris, adorned by a *vase 'de Socibius'* that was donated by the manufactory.

informed Brongniart's successor, Jules-Joseph Ebelmen, of her desire to place on her husband's tomb a biscuit porcelain vase from Sèvres, the *vase 'Socibius'.* The director then wrote to the minister to solicit the donation of the vase to the family.[138]

Among the numerous posthumous homages paid Brongniart, the first was offered by the mayor of Sèvres, who informed Jean-Baptiste Dumas that a street in the town of Sèvres was to be renamed the rue Brongniart.[139] The second was the magnificent portrait that was hung at the Société d'Encouragement pour l'Industrie, showing Brongniart seated near a table with his published works and a *vase 'Fuseau'* with a blue ground. This portrait, painted by Brongniart's grandson, Edouard Brongniart, was completed in 1877.[140] Edouard was a student of Picot and Heim, and his work was first exhibited at the Salon in 1859. The date of 1877 probably links the painting to another homage to Brongniart, this time on the part of Salvetat, which occurred on the occasion of the inauguration of some new buildings at the manufactory at Sèvres.[141] The date also connects the portrait to the "Eloge de MM. Alexandre Brongniart et Adolphe Brongniart" (Elegy for MM. Alexandre Brongniart and Adolphe Brongniart), presented by his son-in-law J.-B. Dumas in April of that year at the annual public meeting of the Academy of Sciences.

Fig. 2-11. Jean-Baptiste Dumas who married Alexandre Brongniart's daughter Herminie Caroline. (Paris, Muséum d'Histoire naturelle, Bibliothèque Centrale)

Fig. 2-10. Adolphe-Théodore Brongniart, Alexandre Brongniart's son. (Paris, Muséum d'Histoire naturelle, Bibliothèque Centrale)

Brongniart's Familial Legacy

The careers of Brongniart's son and sons-in-law — even those who went into other sciences — illustrate how the trades of chemist and researcher became respectable careers in France in the nineteenth century. By that time scientific investigation was no longer the "mad passion" that Balzac had described in 1834 in his *Recherche de l'absolu* (Quest for the absolute).[142] New social and mercantile circuits were developing, such as industrial firms and learned societies. The descendants of Brongniart were among the rising generation of scientists who had brilliant careers, and who prospered in the schools and in the highest official functions.

Brongniart's son, Adolphe-Théodore (1801 – 1876; fig. 2-10),[143] was admitted to the Société d'Encouragement pour l'Industrie in 1845, when his brother-in-law, Dumas, was its president. Adolphe-Théodore was known for his seminal work as one of the founders of plant paleontology. He was only nineteen when he published his first paper on natural history. Receiving his license to practice medicine in 1827, he taught for two years at the medical faculty before devoting himself exclusively to paleontology and physiological botany. In 1831 he became the adjunct of Professor Desfontaines, succeeding him in 1834 as professor of botany at the Jardin des Plantes and at the Academy of Sciences of the Institut. He traveled a great deal — with his father to Switzerland, the

French Jura mountains, Italy, northern Europe, Alsace, and the environs of Baden. He and his brother-in-law, Victor Audouin, visited the west of France, where he had sometimes gone with his grandfather, and he and Adrien de Jussieu made a trip to Italy.

Following what might be called family tradition, Adolphe-Théodore Brongniart donated his collections of plant fossils to the Muséum in 1833[144] and gave his father's collection in 1847. The latter occupied 644 drawers in 5 glass cabinets and comprised geological and paleontological samples: 1,500 rocks, 10,000 geological samples, and 7,000 fossils.[145]

In 1826 Alexandre Brongniart's elder daughter, Herminie Caroline (1803 – 1890), married Jean-Baptiste Dumas (1800 – 1884; fig. 2-11), whose father was a painter and later secretary of the municipality of Alais. J.-B. Dumas's brilliant career was defined by the framework of the nineteenth century. He was received as a doctor of medicine in April 1832 and a doctor of sciences a few months later. Along with Péclet, Lavallée, and Olivier,[146] he was one of the founders of the Ecole Centrale des Arts et Manufactures (Central School for the Arts and Manufactured Goods) in 1829. Brongniart taught industrial natural history there. According to Perdonnet, "The Ecole Centrale is the Sorbonne for industry."[147]

True to Brongniart family tradition, Dumas accumulated academic posts: he became professor at the Collège de France in 1835 and a member of the medical faculty in 1839, professor of chemistry at the Ecole Polytechnique in the same year, professor at the sciences faculty in 1841, and ultimately belonged to eighty learned societies. Despite the general neglect of the memory of Lavoisier at the start of the nineteenth century, Dumas took up the cause of improving the reputation of the great scientist, whom he considered a genius, and began directing the publication of the whole of Lavoisier's oeuvre starting in 1836.[148] Minister of agriculture and of commerce (1849 – 51), and then minister of education at the start of the Second Empire, Dumas became permanent secretary of the Academy of Sciences in 1868.

Brongniart's younger daughter, Mathilde (1808 – 1882), married Victor Audouin (1797 – 1841) in 1827. After studying law, Audouin's interests shifted towards science and medicine. In 1823 he was chosen by the four academies to be the sub-librarian at the Institut. With his brothers-in-law, he created the *Annales des sciences naturelles.* In 1832 he founded the Société Entomologique de France and, having substituted for Professor Latreille at the museum since 1826,[149] succeeded him in 1833. In 1838 he was elected to the agriculture section of the Academy of Sciences for, among other projects, his work on grapevine insects, in which he collaborated with Milne-Edwards and Blanchard.

To complete this description of Brongniart's brilliant legacy, one must look at the successor he chose for himself at Sèvres, Jules-Joseph Ebelmen, who was named adjunct director in 1845, and who gave the eulogy at Brongniart's tomb at Père-Lachaise. On that occasion he emphasized all that Brongniart had brought to the manufactory through his indefatigable commitment and energies.[150] A member of an elite that devoted itself to ensuring that science would remain at the service of industry, Ebelmen also had the classic background for an industrialist in the early nineteenth century: he was a graduate of the Ecole Polytechnique and a mining engineer. Ebelmen put his training to good use in helping the manufactory adapt during this period of great progress in iron smelting, for example, which was beginning to employ coal, a material adopted by the Sèvres manufactory in 1847 for the firing of hard porcelain.

* * *

During the eighteenth century, the term *scientist* retained its antiquated meaning as "a man of knowledge" rather than "a specialist in the study of nature." By the end of the century, the image of the good scientist in the employ of the state was illustrated by Brongniart's relative Antoine-Louis Fourcroy, who succeeded Macquer at the Jardin des Plantes and went into politics as an official spokesman. An example of the "scientist-citizen" was Lazare-Carnot, who believed that service to the state required faultless knowledge and competence. His role was important in the reorganization of scientific instruction that was going on at the time. The scientist had become one of the cogs in the new state, with the goal of ensuring progress. No longer an isolated figure, he was rather a member of a tightly knit and coherent group, and it was common to belong to several scientific institutions simultaneously.

Because of the original model of the Ecole Polytechnique, the Revolution witnessed the triumph of its engineers. By the start of the nineteenth century, the status of the engineer and the scientist had become more clearly delineated. Scientists achieved autonomy in their careers, even if it became difficult to pursue both high-level research and a more applied practice at the same time. As the years went by, the ties binding science and the technical world became stronger, as exemplified by the composition of the Institut.[151] The French example was followed throughout most of Europe.[152]

Since the development of technology only began to accelerate during the eighteenth century, the relationship between science and technical practice was greatly altered during the first half of the nineteenth century. The birth of a scientific technical practice required closer relations with the more purely scientific disciplines, but the connections were still hesitant, because although in the realm of chemistry it was often necessary to await scientific discoveries, in mechanics, conversely, technical practice often preceded the scientific explanation.[153]

Brongniart's training in the encyclopedic spirit of the eighteenth century reached its full potential in his position at the manufactory. He belonged, however, to the nineteenth century because he participated in the genesis of several critical institutions that were created simultaneously by the Convention, such as the Ecole Polytechnique and the Conservatoire des Arts et Métiers, which gave special attention to modeling objects and drawing. The need for an industrial school, which he championed, had been recognized: in 1829, the Ecole Centrale des Arts et Manufactures was created, to which almost the entire Brongniart family devoted much of its energy. The Brongniart dynasty played no less a role in the evolution of the Société d'Encouragement pour l'Industrie, which was founded in 1801 and officially recognized as being "of public utility" in 1824, and whose purpose was "the improvement of all branches of French industry."[154] Alexandre Brongniart and his father were founding members.[155]

At the meeting of 24 Ventôse Year II (1803), the secretary took note of the "black pottery executed at Sèvres, following an English process," and in 1836, in the *Notices,* there is his brief paper to the Academy of Sciences from April 25.[156] Brongniart would become a member in 1829, four years after his son-in-law, J.-B. Dumas, had been admitted and the same year in which Dumas would enter the administrative council as a temporary substitute member. The purpose of this council was to reorganize the society, and the presence of his father-in-law can only have been a help for Dumas. Brongniart was elected a member of the Comité des Arts Chimiques in the administrative council only in 1844, replacing Darcet, while J.-B. Dumas was vice-president.[157]

The importance of scientific publications, along with dictionaries and journals, was critical to the shaping of this new scientific world. At the start of the nineteenth century, technical literature was developing rapidly throughout Europe. Industry quickly furnished material for works such as Karsten's *Grundriss der metallurgie* (Elements of metallurgy; Berlin, 1831), although the encyclopedic spirit was not abandoned. As a matter of course, this dissemination of technical knowledge stimulated future progress.[158]

The "engineer" was born not only of the progress made in the final years of the ancien régime, but also of its developments as well. He was no longer just a state employee. Now he was provided with all the knowledge necessary to lead new institutions such as the factories and the vast mining explorations — thus, even more, to direct a large manufactory.

When Brongniart took over the Sèvres manufactory in 1800, it was an example of the classic mechanical and technical facility, where power was based on the use of wood and water. This eventually gave way to the use of coal and steam. The increasing scarcity of wood in Europe had led to a long search for a substitute fuel. Brongniart's *Mémoire sur le terrain houiller de la mine du Treuil à Saint-Etienne* (Essay on the coal fields of the Treuil mine at Saint-Etienne)[159] and the sketches and directions he sent to Duval, a mining engineer based at Grasse in the Midi, for the village of Vallauris in 1843,[160] obviously contributed to the replacement of the old wood-and-water system by iron, coal, and steam — the trio that his successors would know.

Despite his important and multifaceted career, Alexandre Brongniart has remained relatively unknown. In general, only his role as director of the Sèvres manufactory attracted any attention, while the greater part of his work — the decades passionately devoted to ordering the world as he saw it, to publishing, and to taking pride in his mission as a publisher — have been ignored. He still defies one of the definitions of a scientist published in the current *Littré* dictionary — one knowledgeable in a particular field. Rather, he is more aligned with the definition of scientists in the *Grand Robert* dictionary as "those who contribute to the progress of science."

I wish to thank several individuals for their assistance in preparing this text — Daniel Blouin, secretary of the Commission d'histoire et du Bicentenaire de la Société d'Encouragement, researcher, Paris I, Panthéon-Sorbonne, Paris; Monsieur Gérard Emptoz, Professor, Centre François Viete, Histoire des Sciences et des Techniques, Nantes; Madame Pascale Heurtel, Conservator at the Bibliothèque Centrale of the Muséum d'Histoire Naturelle; Madame Maisonneuve, keeper of the old archive of the Ecole des Mines, Paris; Madame Morillon, Conservator in the Département des Manuscrits, Bibliothèque Nationale, Paris; Madame Marie Piketty, Documentaliste at the Bibliothèque Interuniversitaire of the Faculté de Paris; Madame Tamara Préaud, Archivist.

In document citations, the following abbreviations have been used:

AMNS (Archives, Manufacture Nationale de Sèvres);

AN (Archives nationales); AN-MC (Archives nationales, Minutier central);

AN-MHN (Archives nationales, archives du Museum d'Histoire naturelle);

AN-TP (Archives nationales, Travaux publics, Ingénieurs des Mines)

ASE (Paris, Archives de la Société d'Encouragement);

CNAM, Paris, Conservatoire National des Arts et Métiers, Archives du Musée,

IF (Institut de France);

MHN (Paris, Muséum d'histoire naturelle);

MHN-BC (Paris, Muséum d'histoire naturelle, Bibliotheque centrale)

Sources

The papers of Alexandre Brongniart are located in the following archives:

MHN-BC, Coll. d'autographes, Ms 1964 – 1968; Correspondence d'Alexandre Brongniart, Ms 1986, Ms 1989, Ms 1997

MHN-BC, Manuscripts, Papiers et manuscrits d'Alexandre Brongniart, Ms 643 – 653, Ms 659, Ms 2195, Ms 2254 – 2354, Ms 2388, Ms 2674, 2743 et 2754 (few pieces in these boxes)

AN-TP, Personnel, Alexandre Brongniart), F14 27162, Alexandre Brongniart

AN-MHN, AJ15 543, dossier Personnel, Alexandre Brongniart; AJ15 512, dossier Personnel.

AN-MC, étude Quatremère, liasse 744, 31 mars 1789; étude Gauldré Boilleau, liasse 962, 4 ventose an IV, manque; ibid., liasse 1011, 30 brumaire an 14; ibid., liasse 1013, 20 janvier 1806, manque; ibid., liasse 1019, 26 juillet 1806, manque; ibid., liasse 1033, 31 mars 1808 et liasse 1034, 16 avril 1808; ibid., liasse 1061, 16 juin 1813 et liasse 1064, 29 décembre 1813.

IF, Académie des Sciences, archives, dossier A. Brongniart; Archives Bertrand, carton 9, chemise "Géologues, minéralogistes, naturalistes, A à W, autographes".

AN, dossier légion d'Honneur, Alexandre Brongniart LH 371/73 JB. Dumas, LH 842/779, Adolphe LH 371/72

ASE, GEN(éral), dossier 2/25. et GEN(éral), Procès-verbal du Conseil d'Administration, compte-rendu de la séance générale du 27 novembre 1844.

Brongniart family papers are located in the following archives:

AN, O1 836, registre des médicaments délivrés par les apothicaires royaux du 26 juin 1787 au 2 aou?t 1789

AN-MC, étude Vingtain, *acte des 18 et 19 thermidor An XII; acte du 8 ventose An XII. Les meubles et effets furent vendus pour payer les créanciers; le produit de la vente fut de 231, 46 F.*; étude Quatremère, *acte du 31 mars 1789*; étude Gauldré Boilleau, *acte du 22 juin 1813*; *acte du 29 décembre 1813.*

AN-MHN, archives du Muséum, AJ15543, dossier Personnel, A.-L. Brongniart; AJ15509, dossier Personnel, 270, *lettres de nomination par le comte de Buffon*, April 9, 1779, and *lettres de provision de ladite charge*, same date; dossier Personnel, 274, *liste des personnes ayant souscrit au cours de 1777 – 91.*

CNAM, Manuscrits autographes, M. 205, M. 402, M. 442 et M. 493; N S 3 [Bgt]/1.

1. See Hahn, *L'anatomie d'une institution scientifique* (1993).

2. Geognosy is the branch of science embracing the study of rocks (lithology), their natural relationships within the earth's crust (stratigraphy), and the organic remains that they enclose (paleontology).

3. *Alexandre-Théodore Brongniart*, exhib. cat. (1986).

4. Michel-Barthélemy Hazon (1722 – 1822) joined the Academy with the sponsorship of Boffrand. In 1745 he took second prize for a lighthouse design. He was appointed administrator of buildings, gardens, arts and manufacture in 1749. In February 1751 he was named special superintendant of the Ecole Militaire, then controller of Choisy. After the reform of the king's household in 1778 he became superintendant of buildings with Mique and Soufflot.

5. Gallet, *Les Architectes parisiens du XVIIIe siècle* (1995), pp. 260 – 61.

6. IF, Académie des Sciences, archives, dossier Alexandre Brongniart, pamphlet, *Si Gressy-en-France m'était conté*. . ., ed. Raymond Selleret, undated.

7. Alexandre Théodore is recorded in 1778 as a member of the Orient de Paris (the Grand Lodge of Paris); he also belonged to the Lodge of the Social Contract, or Saint Jean d'Ecosse du Contrat Social (Bibliothèque Nationale, Department of Manuscripts, Masonic Archive, records).

8. *Dictionnaire de Biographie française*, vol. 7, pp. 419 – 21.

9. Gallet, *Les Architectes parisiens du XVIIIe siècle* (1995), pp. 93 – 100.

10. Fourcroy was one of the contributors to *Méthode de nomenclature chimique* (1787), along with C. L. Berthollet, L. B. Guyton de Morveau, and A. L. Lavoisier.

11. AN, Légion d'honneur, [dossier missing].

12. Bensaude-Vincent and Stengers, *Histoire de la chimie* (1993), p. 87.

13. AN-AHN, AJ/15/509, dossier Personnel, 270, letters of nomination by the Comte du Buffon, 9 April 1779, letters of confirmation same date; ibid, dossier 271: letter from the Baron de Breteuil announcing a gratuity of 500 *livres* from Louis XVI, dated 4 June 1785. There was "one gold mark to pay for this charge." Also see ibid., dossier 273, May 8, 1779. A.-L Brongniart owed money for the post of Premier Apothecary (ibid., dossier 272, May 3, 1790).

14. Bouvet, "Les apothicaires royaux" (1930), pp. 207 – 8; AN, O/1 836, register of the medicines delivered by the royal apothecaries June 26, 1787 – August 2, 1789; the equipment was borrowed. See also Anchel, "Une famille de pharmaciens" (1933), pp. 563 – 68.

15. Dumas, "Les Brongniart," p. 97; I am grateful to Marie Piketty, at the Bibliothèque Interuniversitaire de la Faculté de Paris who brought this manuscript to my attention. See also AN-AHN, AJ/15509, dossier Personnel, 274, list of persons who subscribed to the course between 1777 and 1791.

16. Hamy, *Les derniers jours du Jardin du roi* (1893), pp. 16 – 18. Gérard Van Spaendonck of the Académie de Peinture became the successor at the Jardin du Roi to Mlle Basseporte (ibid., p. 27 n. 5). "The administrator's salary not having been paid since January, it was possible to deduct from the sum thus made available the allowance for the course that Louis-Antoine Brongniart had been requesting since 1790 in consideration of the rise in the price of drugs and other materials needed for his experiments" (ibid., p. 44). As long as he remained premier apothecary, as he says in his petition of May 9, which survives, "the emoluments of that post covered his expenses and he carried out the work with pleasure. Now that things have changed his income is below average," and he could no longer carry on. His annual deficit being estimated at 400 livres, with the permission of the directors of the Département de Paris he received 1,200 *livres* for the three years 1790, 1791, and 1792.

17. CNAM, Manuscrits autographes, M. 205, M. 402, M. 442 and M. 493.

18. For the history of the museum, see Lemoine, *Le Muséum national d'Histoire naturelle* (1935); *Centenaire de la fondation du Muséum d'Histoire naturelle* (1893).

19. "Bonaparte, 1st Consul of the Republic, with total confidence in the ability and the good conduct of Citizen Antoine-Louis Brongniart, appoints him to the post of Chief Pharmacist to the army; he shall fulfill his functions under the orders of the chief ordnance commissioner of the said army, Paris 7 Messidor, year 8, signed by Cambacérès, seen in Dijon this 24 Messidor, Year 8 [July 13, 1800]" (AN-AHN, AJ/15/543, dossier Personnel, A.-L. Brongniart).

20. Bensaude-Vincent and Stengers, *Histoire de la chimie* (1993), p. 119.

21. The "theory of phlogiston" was promoted by the chemist G.-E. Stahl (1660 – 1734); it was based on a so-called element of fire (phlogiston), which was reputed to impart combustibility. As far as ceramics are concerned, when a metal-bearing earth or oxide is reduced by carbon, phlogiston gives way to earth, which becomes metallic once more and develops its characteristic colors. The theory was refuted by Richard Kirwan; his text was translated into French (*Essai sur le phlogistique*) in 1788.

22. Dumas, *Eloge de MM. Alexandre Brongniart et Adolphe Brongniart*, p.3.

23. The date of the first class has been given as 1783 (Omalius d'Halloy, *Notice biographique sur la vie d'Alexandre Brongniart* [1860], p. 1), but Brongniart himself reported to the Conseil des Mines that "he had assumed the position in December 1786" (AN-TP, Personnel, F/14 2716/2, general notice at the beginning of the document, resumed in 1831).

24. *Les chimistes français du XIXe siècle*, exhib. cat. (1900), p. 24.

25. MHN, Bibliothèque centrale, Manuscripts: Ms 647 — Papers and mss., A. Brongniart. For a discussion of his courses at the Société Gymnastique, held at the Société Philomatique from December 9, 1789, to January 22, 1791, see Elie de Beaumont in *Discours . . . prononcé aux funérailles de M. Alexandre Brongniart* (n.d.), p. 10. The Société Philomatique began in 1788; its aim was mutual instruction, and recent papers relating to science were read and discussed at its meetings. Brongniart was in correspondence with members of the group throughout his life. According to his pupil Beaumont, he was treasurer of the society until his death.

26. M. Duméril in *Discours . . . prononcé aux funérailles de M. Alexandre Brongniart* (n.d.), p. 14.

27. Hahn, *L'anatomie d'une institution scientifique* (1993), pp. 379 – 80.

28. MHN, Bibliothèque centrale, Manuscripts, Ms 647 — Papers and mss. of A. Brongniart (December 10, 1788 – March 20, 1789), opening lecture of the mineralogy course, quoted by L. de Launay.

29. Omalius d'Halloy, *Notice biographique sur la vie d'Alexandre Brongniart* (1860), p. 1.

30. IF, Académie des Sciences, archives, dossier A. Brongniart, certificate "entirely in the hand of Corvisart and signed with the date, 6 August 1793." I am grateful to Mmes Leroi and Davesne for information about the Société de Médecine, one of a number of learned societies in existence at the end of the eighteenth century. It was founded on 22 Pluviose, year 5, in six sections or committees. Brongniart was elected to the Académie de la Société de Médecine on April 11, 1797, into the section concerned with "Natural history and medical matters." For further information, see Rougon, "Les archives de la Société de Médecine" (1882), pp. 80 – 81: J. Couvreur, "Histoire d'une centenaire La Société" (1996), pp. 828 – 31; Thélot, "Précis historique de la Société" (1989), pp. 1 – 2.

31. Blunt, *Linné, le Prince des botanistes* (1986), p. 5. The doctor- naturalists of Montpellier became very excited by Linnaeus's ideas in the middle of the nineteenth century; in spite of lack of support from Buffon himself, Linnaeus was made a member of the Académie royale des Sciences de Paris in 1738.

32. Hahn, *L'anatomie d'une institution scientifique* (1993), p. 235 and note 54.

33. AN-MHN, AJ/15 512, dossier Personnel, "Rapport fait à la Société d'Histoire naturelle de Paris sur la nécessité d'établir une Ménagerie," signed with A.-L. Millin and Pinel on 14 December 1792.

34. Launay, *Les Brongniart* (1940).

35. Dhombres and Dhombres, *Naissance d'un nouveau pouvoir* (1989), p. 20.

36. *Dictionnaire de Biographie française*, vol. 7, col. 419; AN-TP, Personnel, F/14 2716/2. Fourcroy was one of the signatories of the decrees of the Comité de Salut Public, according to the *Extrait du registre des arrêtés et délibérations de la Commission des armes et poudres de la République* (Extract from the register of decrees and deliberations of the Commission on arms and explosives of the Republic).

37. Dhombres and Dhombres, *Naissance d'un nouveau pouvoir* (1989), p. 208.

38. Ibid., pp. 46 – 47.

39. AN-TP, F/14 2716/2, letter of 15 October 1816 from Brongniart to comte Molé, director-general of the Ponts et Chaussées and Mines.

40. Ibid.

41. *Ecole Polytechnique* (1894). The Corps des Mines of the ancien régime was never officially dissolved during the Revolution.

42. AN-TP, Personnel, F/14 2716/2. The students were Remmel, Descotils, and Advenier; some

of the reports were edited by Dieudonné Dolomieu and André Jean Marie Brochant de Villiers.

43. MHN, Bibliothèque centrale, Manuscripts: Ms 650 — papers and manuscripts of A. Brongniart, papers dated January 17, 1821, and March 19, 1832, relating to the installation of blast furnaces, ore cleaners, coal, iron works, nail making, et cetera.

44. In 1802 these institutions, which concentrated on science and design, were replaced by the *lycées*. Also see IF, Académie des sciences, Archives, dossier A. Brongniart, expenses note: "Advances made for the course and the Cabinet d'Histoire Naturelle at the Ecole Centrale des Quatre nations, Nivose, Pluviose and Ventose of year 8."

45. Dhombres and Dhombres, *Naissance d'un nouveau pouvoir* (1989), pp. 84, 858 (n.154).

46. MHN, Bibliothèque centrale, Manuscripts: Ms 648 — Papers and manuscripts of A. Brongniart; AN-TP, Personnel, F/14 2716/2, letter of 15 October 1816, "in 1798, M Hauy, titular professor, who was busy editing his treatise on mineralogy, had requested to be temporarily replaced."

47. The market share occupied by "scientific" books was 14 percent for the period 1798 – 1825, which is considerable.

48. Dhombres and Dhombres, *Naissance d'un nouveau pouvoir* (1989), pp. 367 – 69. The encyclopedia numbered 166 volumes, published between 1781 and 1832.

49. Ibid., p. 376.

50. Ibid., p. 383.

51. Ibid., pp. 212 – 13.

52. Ibid., pp. 575 – 603.

53. It was further reprinted in 1822 and 1835.

54. *La Grande Encyclopédie* (1889), vol. 8, p. 129.

55. Elie de Beaumont in *Discours . . . prononcé funérailles de M. Alexandre Brongniart* (n.d.), p. 4.

56. *Dictionnaire des Sciences naturelles* (1817), vol. 5, p. 348.

57. Brongniart, *Traité élémentaire de Minéralogie* (1807). Bibliothèque de la Faculté de Pharmacie, Rés. 11 547.

58. Dhombres and Dhombres, *Naissance d'un nouveau pouvoir* (1989), p. 403.

59. Ibid., pp. 13 – 18.

60. Ibid., p. 216.

61. IF, Académie des Sciences, archives, dossier A. Brongniart, ampliation no. 712, recorded November 30, 1815, extract from the proceedings of Monday November 20, 1815 with a letter (No. 1849) from the minister of the interior, dated December 1 1815, to Cuvier, permanent secretary.

62. Elie de Beaumont in *Discours . . . prononcé aux funérailles de M. Alexandre Brongniart* (n.d.), p. 9.

63. AN-MHN, AJ/15 543, dossier Personnel, A. Brongniart, dossier "Application for the chair of geology at the Jardin du Roi 3 August 1819 and the chair of mineralogy at the Jardin du Roi June 1822", esp. "Note prepared in case of need, has not been used: no objection had been raised on 9 September 1822." These letters and notes, with their passion and seething indignation, present a side of Brongniart's personality that is rarely glimpsed.

64. MHN, Bibliothèque centrale, Manuscripts: Ms 643/1 — Papers and manuscripts of A. Brongniart.

65. Ibid., Manuscripts: Ms 643/2 — Papers and manuscripts of A. Brongniart.

66. Ibid., Manuscripts: Ms 660 — Papers and manuscripts of A. Brongniart. Meeting of 6 August 1822, proposal by Vuillemot-Hauy and report of 18 February 1823.

67. It is not known whether the collectors and learned owners of *cabinets de curiosité* were connected.

68. Bensaude-Vincent and Stengers, *Histoire de la chimie* (1993), pp. 90 – 91.

69. Gille, ed., *Histoire des Techniques* (1978), p. 730.

70. MHN, Bibliothèque centrale, Autograph collection, Ms 1966-Correspondence of A. Brongniart, Letters from William Keating, 18 III 1837, piece 512. "Correspondence of A. Brongniart" is omitted but implied below in nn. 71 – 86.

71. Ibid., Ms 1966, letters from Théodore Pichon, May 30, 1835 – November 10, 1840.

72. Ibid., Ms 1964 — letters from Ami Boué, from Munich, Vienna, and Berne, 1818 – 29; ibid., Ms 1965, letter from Duckland, on the glass of Oxford, September 8, 1818, piece 169a.

73. Ibid., Ms 1965 — letter from Esmark, [1825], piece 249.

74. Ibid., Ms 1964 — letters of Peter Brown, April 28, 1831, piece 165.

75. Ibid., Ms 1964 — letters from Devaux, Angers, 1822, piece 226.

76. Ibid., Ms 1965 — letters from Dupont, letter of October 12, 1801, piece 243.

77. Ibid., Ms 1965 — letters from J. A. Deluc, Geneva, letter of March 1822, piece 203.

78. Ibid., Ms 1964 — Dupont letters, 1800 – 1802, piece 243a.

79. Ibid., Ms 1965 — letter from Bruce, New York, July 10, 1814, piece 167 (plus list).

80. Ibid., Ms 1964 — letters from José Maria Bustamente, Mexico, December 15, 1824, pieces 173 a and b (acknowledging receipt).

81. Ibid., Ms 1965 — Dupont letters, piece 244a.

82. Ibid., Ms 1964 — letter from Clifford, March 7, 1920, piece 180.

83. Ibid., Ms 1964 — letters from F. d'Almeida, Lisbon, July 18, 1833, piece 14.

84. Ibid., Ms 1964 — letters from Diard, Calcutta, June 5, 1818; ibid., Ms 1964, letters from Dupont; ibid., letters from Amos Eaton from Troy, New York State, September 1830 – 33, pieces 247b and 248a.

85. Ibid., Ms 1964 — letter from Bourdet, Geneva, 12 February 1821, piece 133.

86. Ibid., Ms 644 — Papers and manuscripts of A. Brongniart, from 1818.

87. Ibid., Manuscripts: Ms 644 — Papers and manuscripts of A. Brongniart. For the *Traité de Minéralogie*, written in collaboration with the assistant naturalist De la Fosse and book dealers Roret and Deterville, see ibid., Ms. 646 — bundle "Géognosie-Histoire minéralogique."

88. Ibid., Manuscripts: Ms 645 — Papers and manuscripts of A. Brongniart.

89. Ibid., Ms 646 — Papers and manuscripts of A. Brongniart, Blue bundle: "Notes and diverse extracts from books, museums, voyages . . ." Also see AN-TP, Personnel, F/14 2716/2 (inspections for the department of Mines); ibid., letters of June 20 1817 and June 10, 1824 (travels in the Morvan, the Jura, Switzerland, Burgundy, and the Vosges, as well Sweden and Norway, by invitation of Berzelius). For his correspondence with Berzelius, see Soderbaum and Holmberg, *Jac. Berzelius*, supp. 3.

90. Bensaude-Vincent, "Eaux et mesures Eclairages" (1995), pp. 49 – 68.

91. Sadoun-Goupil, *Le chimiste Claude-Louis Berthollet* (1977), pp. 142 – 43.

92. Dhombres and Dhombres, *Naissance d'un nouveau pouvoir* (1989), pp. 403 – 406.

93. Ibid., p. 747 – 51.

94. Along with the Conseil des Ponts (Council on bridges), a Conseil des Bâtiments Civils (Council on civil buildings) was established in 1795, its members consisting mainly of architects, including Brongniart, Chalgrin, Poyet, and Rondelet. Its mission was to oversee public buildings.

95. Dhombres and Dhombres, *Naissance d'un nouveau pouvoir* (1989), pp. 661 – 62.

96. "Une relation science-pouvoir idéalisé: le laboratoire d'Egypte (1798 – 1801)" in ibid., pp. 93 – 148.

97. Dumas, *Eloge de MM. Alexandre Brongniart and Adolphe Brongniart* (1877), p. 22.

98. MHN, Bibliotheque centrale, autographes, Ms 1965 — Correspondence of A. Brongniart, Letters from F. Feuillet de Conches, London, December, 12, 1831, pièce 274.

99. Ibid., Papers and manuscripts of A. Brongniart, Ms 651/1, Ms 651/2, Ms 652 and Ms 653.

100. Ibid., Manuscripts: Ms 649 — Papers and manuscripts of A. Brongniart.

101. Ibid., Autograph collection, Ms 1966 — Correspondence of A. Brongniart, Letters from Fr. de Kobell, Munich, November 18, 1840 – April 8, 1843.

102. Damien, *Le grand livre des Ordres de Chevalerie* (1991), p. 31. The Order of Saint-Michel was established by King Louis XI on August 1, 1469, and was designed to reward "distinguished merit." Discontinued during the Revolution, it was revived in 1816 and served as a kind of forerunner of the Order of Arts and Letters. It was abolished in 1830 by King Louis-Philippe.

103. AN, Légion d'honneur, dossier LH 371-73, Alexandre Brongniart, with an extract from his birth certificate; ibid., LH 371-72, Adolphe Théodore Brongniart, Commander on 12 August 1864, and on the same day, Officer of the Order of Leopold of Belgium; ibid., dossier LH 842-77, J. B. Dumas elevated to the rank of the Grand Cross on August 14, 1863.

104. There is also a bust by Houdon of Brongniart's sister Louise (also in the Musée du Louvre). Louise became Mme. Novall de Saint-Aubin and then Marquise de Dampierre. Brongniart's second sister, Emilie, known as Ziguette, became Baronne Pichon. Her husband was the trade commissioner and *chargé d'affaires* to the United States.

105. There are numerous portraits, including one reproduced in Lacroix, *Minéralogistes et Géologues français*, vol. 3, *Les Géologues*, chap. 7. Also see IF, Académie des Sciences, archives, dossier A. Brongniart.

106. Charles-Etienne Coquebert de Montbret was a botanist and an active member of the

Société d'Encouragement as was Brongniart's father. Montbret's obituary in the society's *Bulletin* cited examples of his genius including the introduction of statistical research to France and his presidency of the Société de Géographie (Dejérando, 'Notice sur m. Coquebert de Montbret" [1831], pp. 281 – 85).

107. René Just Hauy (1743 – 1822) characterized each mineral species by a fixed polyhedric form and postulated a correlation between the macroscopic and the microscopic properties of a substance.

108. Launay, *Les Brongniarts* (1940), p. 141.

109. CNAM, Archives du Musée, N S 3 [Bgt]/1. See also AMHN, Bibliotheque centrale, Manuscripts, Ms 659 — Papers and manuscripts of A. Brongniart, letters from Duperrey, January 17, 1835 ("Voyage of the Astrolabe"); ibid., letter December 11, 1835, (botanical aspects, "Voyage of La Coquille"). At the time Duperrey was an admiral, peer of the realm, and minister for the Navy and the colonies.

110. AMHN, Bibliotheque centrale, Autograph collection, Ms 1965 — Correspondence of A. Brongniart, letters from F. Feuillet de Conches, London, December 12, 1831, piece 274. "Correspondence" is omitted but implied below in nn. 111 – 14.

111. Ibid., Ms 1966 — letters from F. W. Hoeninghaus, April 14, 1824, piece 464; C. Kersten, member of the council for the royal factories of Saxony, September 28 1830, piece 518; and Kleinschrod, counsellor at the Ministère de l'Interieur, Munich, 14 April 1833, piece 526.

112. Ibid., Ms 1964 — letters from Madame Brochant de Villiers, "his neighbour," 27 September 1840, piece 159.

113. Ibid., Ms 1964 — letter from Nér_e Boubée, 10 December 1830.

114. Ibid., Ms 1965 — letters from A.G. Desmarest, 3 July 1809, piece 218. See also: IF, Académie des Sciences, Archives, dossier A. Brongniart, and invitation from Brongniart to Deleuze to a reception, sent November 9, 1813.

115. MHN, Bibliotheque centrale, Autograph collection, Ms 1966 — Correspondence of A. Brongniart, letters from G.B. Gravenhorst, envoy to Breslau, June 2, 1819, piece 433b."Correspondence" is omitted but implied below in nn. 115 – 20.

116. Ibid., Ms 1964 — letters from Bresson, Berlin, 14 January 1837, piece 157; Ms 1966, letters from C. A. Kuhn, his traveling companion in 1812 in the Erzgebirge, April 13, 1823, piece 538; and letter from Nadaud, Bonn, October 28, 1835, piece 541.

117. Ibid., Ms 1964 — letters from Scipion Breislak, Milan, administrator of explosives and saltpeter to the Kingdom of Italy, May 17, 1823, piece 156.

118. Ibid., Ms 1966 — letters from Louis Gautheron, 28 August 1795 – January 26, 1819, esp. letter of September 17, 1818, piece 398c.

119. Ibid., Ms 1964 — letter of 5 April 1832, piece 145, from Brard.

120. Ibid., Ms 1964 — letters from Borson, Turin, 26 October 1812 to 18 December 1829.

121. IF, Académie des Sciences, fond Archives Bertrand, carton 9, dossier "Géologues, minéralogistes, naturalistes, A à W, autographes, lettres du 9 avril 1830 pour Hiron, premier tourneur en porcelaine et 16 avril 1830 pour Antoine Weismann."

122. AN-TP, Personnel, F/14 2716/2, letter of March 28, 1832. The director general provided him with a pension all the same. Brongiart had been appointed chief engineer, second class, on January 29, 1819, with 4,500F (undated note), and first class on 3 August 1828.

123. Ibid., F/14 2716/2, letter of thanks from Brongniart to Comte Laumond, director general of mines. Brongniart appears to have had problems, but these cannot be identified. A note of April 1, 1817 summarizes his complaints. The dossier contains several letters in which he emphasises his usefulness to the Corps, even at the time when he was busy being administrator of the Sèvres factory.

124. MHN, Bibliotheque centrale, manuscripts: Ms 659 — Papers and manuscripts of A. Brongniart, letter of 19 September 1844, with a postscript from Mme Brongniart to her son.

125. Ibid., Bibliotheque centrale, Autograph collection, Ms 1964 — Correspondence of A. Brongniart, letters from J. J. Ampère, July 11, 1840; IF, Académie des sciences, Archives, dossier A. Brongniart, letter of 15 August from Brongniart to J. J. Ampère.

126. MHN, Bibliotheque centrale, Autograph collection, Ms 1966 — Correspondence of A. Brongniart, letters from Koreff, 19 July 1841, Piece 534.

127. Bouquet, "Petite histoire des membres libres de l'Académie de médecine" (1941).

128. MNH, Manuscripts, Ms 659 — Papers and manuscripts of A. Brongniart.

129. Bensaude-Vincent and Stengers, *Histoire de la chimie* (1993), p. 169.

130. AN-MC, étude Vingtain, acts of the 18 and 19 Thermidor year 12 (August 6 – 7, 1804); also see ibid., acts of 8 Ventôse year 12 (February 28, 1804). The furniture and effects were sold for 231,46 francs to pay his creditors.

131. AN-MC, étude Quatremère, acts of March 31, 1789.

132. Ibid., étude Gauldré Boilleau, act of June 22, 1813.

133. Ibid., act of December 29, 1813.

134. Regnault, "La maison des Brongniart" (1934), pp. 510 – 12.

135. Letters were received from the Intendant Géneral, Montalivet, Becquerel, Bérardin, A. de Jussieu, Bertrand Geslin, François Delisle, Adolphe de Candolle or his cousin, Bout de Breslis, secretary of the Commandements de la Reine, the duchesse d'Orléans, and many others; some of the speeches by students and colleagues survive (MHN, Bibliotheque centrale, Manuscripts: Ms 659 — Papers and manuscripts of A. Brongniart, folder "family letters").

136. AN-TP, Personnel, F/14 2716/2, letter of 8 October 1847.

137. Pieces of Porcelain delivered to private clients and those presented as gifts by order of the Intendant Géneral: "9 October 1847, 27 – 32 A curved cream jug, high-fired blue ground, decorated in gold and platinum 18/258-37 One id. green ground id. 15/8-21 One tea cup with panels (Leloy) no saucer, turquoise ground (immersion), gold band 13/8-16 One tea cup, fluted AB, green ground (immersion), gold band 10/56 Reject store: 1 breakfast cup from Fontainebleau service / 1 Saucer id. / 1 Peyre coffee cup id. / 1 Chinese coffee cup reticulated / 1 Saucer to the above / 1 thin tea cup / 1 Saucer to the above / 1 Fragonard tea cup / 1 Saucer to the above / 1 Plain Peyre milk jug / total: 159, 40f" (AMNS, register Vaa 3, folio 9v).

138. "The cost price of this vase, which has already been produced in the factory and which is adorned with figures and ornamentation in relief requiring all the skills of the potter, is valued at 1,000 francs. I humbly request you, Monsieur le Ministre, to make up your mind that the vase in question will be presented in your name to the family of M. Brongniart. The long administrative service of my venerable and illustrious predecessor, the extremely important services that he has rendered to science and industry during his long and hard-working career seem to me to be worthy of this high mark of your good will, which will I am sure receive the highest praise from all" (AMNS, dossier Ob 2, Personnel, draft of a letter from Ebelman to the minister).

139. IF, Académie des Sciences, archives, dossier A. Brongniart, letter of January 21, 1861, from the mayor of Sèvres to J.-B. Dumas, senator.

140. Edouard-Charles-Franklin Brongniart (1830 – 1905) was an inspector of secondary education and established a curriculum for teaching drawing that was followed in 350 schools in Paris. There are other portraits, by David d'Angers and by M. de Sacy, one of which, *Saint Nicholas Saving a Child*, is in the church of Saint- Nicolas-des-Champs.

141. Salvetat, "Manufacture nationale de Sèvres" (1877), pp. 3 – 17.

142. Bensaude-Vincent and Stengers, *Histoire de la chimie* (1993), pp. 125 – 26.

143. In 1827 Adolphe-Théodore Brongniart married Agathe Boitel (1802 – 1863), whose father was a gilder in the factory (Charles Marie Pierre Boitel) (AMNS, dossier Ob 2, Personnel).

144. MHN, Ms 659 — Papers and manuscripts of A. Brongniart, letter of June 24, 1833, in which Geoffreoy-Saint-Hilaire, A. de Jussieu, Cordier express their gratitude for this legacy.

145. MHN, Bibliotheque centrale, manuscripts: Ms 659 — Papers and manuscripts of A. Brongniart, undated letter (after 1847) signed by the three Brongniart children. There is a reply from the office of the Ministre de l'Instruction Publique et des Cultes, Rouland, dated May 3, 1857.

146. Comberousse, *Histoire de l'Ecole Centrale* (1879).

147. The Ecole Centrale, the first *grande école*, trained industrial civil engineers; its vocation today is still the development of upper management and business executives. The Ecole Polytechnique had served the military, including military engineers, since 1804.

148. IF, Académie des Sciences, Minutes of meetings, Paris and Blois (January 1995), *Il y a deux ans Lavoisier*, pp. 176, 196 – 97, 206 – 20, 279, 310; Dumas and Grimaux, eds., *Lavoisier A.-L.: Oeuvres* (1864 – 93).

149. MHN, Manuscripts: Ms 660 — Papers and manuscripts of A. Brongniart, correspondence between Latreille and Brongniart in May 1826.

150. IF, Académie des Sciences, Archives, dossier A. Brongniart, transcripts of speeches by M. Ebelmen and M. Virlet d'Aoust; M. Chevreul in *Discours . . . prononcé aux funérailles de M. Alexandre Brongniart* (n.d.).

151. Pichon, *Architectes et Ingénieurs* (1988), n.223.

152. Gille, ed., *Histoire des Techniques* (1978), p. 728.

153. Ibid., pp. 726 – 27.

154. For further information see Blouin, "La Société d'Encouragement" (1996), pp. 11 – 21.

155. ASE, GEN(éral), dossier 2/25. Although their names figure in the supplementary list of 1802, Brongniart did not join until 1804. It is not known whether Chaptal's departure motivated this or whether it was Brongniart, who was involved though seldom present. The report of the meeting of October 13, 1847, mentions him as a member of the administrative council, which was honoured to count him as one of its members (*Bulletin de Société d'Encouragement pour l'Industrie nationale* 46 [1847], p. 608).

156. *Bulletin de Société d'Encouragement pour l'Industrie nationale* 2, (1803), p. 11; ibid. 35 (1836), p. 183, respectively.

157. Ibid. (1844), pp. 582 – 83; ASE, GEN(éral), minutes of the Conseil d'Administration, record of the general meeting of November 27, 1844.

158. Gille, ed., *Histoire des Techniques* (1978), p. 731.

159. Dufrénoy in *Discours . . . prononcé aux funérailles de M. Alexandre Brongniart* (n.d.), p. 26.

160. "Near Grasse and in the village of Vallauris a large amount of coarse pottery is made, as well as refractory bricks; the fuel used is largely branches of pine trees and brushwood, but these are becoming scarcer and scarcer and more and more expensive. Near this village for the last two or three years an anthracite mine has been exploited. When this fuel is put in a favourable location it burns well and gives out a lot of heat. And because this anthracite produces no smoke we thought of using it for the firing of pottery" (MHN, Bibliotheque centrale, Manuscripts, Ms. 653 — Papers and manuscripts of A. Brongniart, Letter of 8 March 1843, from Duval to Brongniart). Duval ends the letter by asking "what books would contain the principles of kiln building for use with anthracite?"

Alexandre Brongniart, by Emile Wattier, 1847; oil on canvas. (Manufacture nationale de Sèvres, Archives)

Chapter 3

Brongniart as Administrator

Tamara Préaud

In a letter dated 25 Floréal year 8 (May 17, 1800), Lucien Bonaparte, *ministre de l'intérieur*, announced to Jean-Jacques Hettlinger and Jean-Hilaire Salmon l'aîné, the two directors of the national porcelain manufactory at Sèvres, that there was to be a complete reorganization of the enterprise. The most important feature of the plan was a radical reduction of the workforce from 235 employees to 66, with a promise of pensions for workers at least sixty years of age who had been employed for twenty years or more. The minister added:

> Formerly the Sèvres manufactory was unrivaled when it came to perfection of craftsmanship, but I see with dismay that for some years now it has made little progress in the arts of fabrication; there exist today several private establishments that in certain respects appear to eclipse its glory. It seems to me this inertia should be attributed to several causes. Thus, in reorganizing the manufactory I have set out not only to reduce public expenditures; I also intend to restore its former prosperity and transform it into a school of art. The fabrication of porcelain is fully established in France, and in upholding it at Sèvres my primary view has been to make it an object of emulation for private establishments. Thus any future work undertaken should serve to advance this fabrication; but to implement this project it seemed to me that a chemist should direct the manufactory. You know that the arts pertaining to the manipulation of clay constitute one of the most important branches of chemistry, and Sèvres can only decline if it is not headed by a man well versed in this science. This consideration has prompted me to name as director Citizen Brongniard [sic] fils, author of a highly regarded treatise on enamels . . . Citizen Brongniart will concern himself not only with things pertaining to the fabrication of porcelain; in addition, he will also perform experiments relating to glassware and pottery . . . .[1]

With considerable foresight and anxious not to offend the two directors, who had effectively been demoted, the minister had been careful to justify his selection by detailing the change he judged to be indispensable. The same day he wrote directly to "Citoyen Brongniart fils" informing him of his nomination "in accordance with favorable reports presented to me concerning your morality and your talents" and describing the post's responsibilities in language similar to that used in the above-cited letter.[2]

The Early Years

On 8 Prairial (May 25) Alexandre Brongniart accepted the offer in the following terms: "I promise you to use all the ardor inspired in me by my love of country and by your gesture of confidence in me to fulfill your beneficial views. I will use the knowledge I have acquired and supplement it with that of the famous chemists with whom I have the good fortune to be acquainted to restore to this manufactory the superiority necessary for it to continue to render France the services it has previously rendered. I will do everything within my power to transform it into a veritable school of art. My desires in this regard are absolutely consistent with your intentions."[3]

The Sèvres Manufactory had indeed served as a model and point of reference for all of Europe's porcelain makers throughout the second half of the eighteenth century. The appointment to such a prestigious post of a young man—Brongniart had just turned thirty—who also lacked experience in financial matters, personnel management, and even ceramics was typical of the period. Given the factory's disastrous state at the time, however, the decision was quite daring. After the end of the Revolution, calm had been restored to Sèvres by the establishment of a collective directory on 13 Pluviôse of the year 3 (February 2, 1795).[4] Five years later, when the new administrator began his tenure, the manufactory's coffers were empty, and its workers and suppliers had not been paid for many months. Because the suppliers had halted deliveries, essential materials such as clay, wood, colors, gold, and tools were lacking. Furthermore, various government departments had appropriated countless pieces, emptying the warehouse of its finest pieces without providing compensation. To compound these problems, the manufactory's workforce had just been reduced by 75 percent. Considering all these factors, the difficulty and dimensions of the task confronting Brongniart become clear.

He set to work courageously. The most urgent matter before him was the procurement of funds. On June 17, 1800, he wrote to Lucien Bonaparte describing "the almost complete want of materials and money," observing that the six months' severance pay awarded the dismissed workers had demoralized the remaining staff members who had not yet received monies due them. He called them "men of merit who could have taken their knowledge elsewhere, to the establishment's detriment," and noted that "if the government could pay what it owes this establishment its situation would be much improved."[5]

His plea seemingly fell on deaf ears, and Brongniart was obliged to proceed as best he could on his own. On 9 Messidor year 8 (June 28, 1800) he requested and was soon granted permission to reduce the prices of odd and unfashionable pieces and to organize a sale "of old porcelains that encumber our warehouses and harm the manufactory by suggesting to visitors that it still produces these gothic things."[6] With the help of "citizens Lignereux and Coquille, renowned merchants of *objets de curiosité* and citizen Boileau, certified appraiser," Brongniart set the new prices and managed to sell 26,000 francs worth of old porcelain in outdated forms, much of it to foreign buyers.[7] Additional money was raised by the sale in July of a horse and of ornaments from the chapel,[8] followed by another sale at the Louvre in 1800 that disposed of "objects rendered waste goods by the age of their forms or their flaws" as well as of important pieces "that current taste obliged me to remove from the warehouse."[9] These sales netted another 35,993 francs, which, along with 15,000 francs finally forthcoming from the government, made it possible to pay workers for the last seven months of year 7 (1799–1800) and the first four months of year 8 (1800–1801), to settle small outstanding debts, to purchase gold for gilding, and to satisfy the most important suppliers with partial payments.

In this way Brongniart succeeded in putting the manufactory back to work, but settlement of the debt in its entirety was to take time. A new fiscal arrangement effective 8 Prairial year 9 (May 29, 1801) assured regular operations by guaranteeing a general monthly subsidy of 5,000 francs. In addition, it prohibited the use of current income to settle accumulated debts. Brongniart was careful to point out again that if the government paid for all the pieces it had ordered prior to year 10 (1801–2) the manufactory would be able to settle most of these debts, and that, if not, the government itself should do so.[10] Previously, in January 1801, he had pleaded for a decision to be made "on principle that porcelains ordered by the government are to be sold to it at market price, and that in future it will discharge the value of all articles provided it."[11] His request was granted, at least in theory.

Auctions held in Germinal year 10 (March–April 1802) made it possible to pay backwages to working personnel for the balance of year 8 (1799–1800). In August 1807 Brongniart again requested without success payment of 141,148 francs still due to providers and the dismissed workers—whose pensions had been disbursed very irregularly—from years 7 to 12 (1798–1804).[12] Although on November 18, 1808, he stated that a recent imperial decree stipulated payment of sums due for the years 9 to 12 (1799–1805),[13] it seems that settlement, which was ordered anew by a ministerial decree of November 20, 1816, was not actually effected until 1820 when debts from the years 1798 and 1799 were simply canceled.[14]

Restoring financial solvency and settling accounts were not the only tasks facing the new director. He was also obligated to continue the reorganization effort undertaken by his predecessors, aiming to restore calm and to institute sound management in the aftermath of the Revolution. On 8 Pluviôse year 9 (January 28, 1801), the new *ministre de l'intérieur*, Jean-Antoine Chaptal, granted most of the requests made by Brongniart, including one "to allow the administrator the liberty to hire workers, dismiss them, fix their salaries, and employ them in whatever way he judges fit."[15] Apparently, Brongniart proposed to relinquish the possibility of future government subsidies, and the prudent minister observed: "Events might befall that oblige you to turn to the government and, in moments of distress, you will always find in it a resource of which you should not deprive yourself."[16] The minister further approved plans for experiments with chemical and mechanical processes relating to porcelain fabrication as well as plans to conduct public classes in the art of pottery.

The register in which directorial decisions were recorded indicates that Brongniart began by regulating the distribution of consumable supplies such as firewood and candles in order to reduce expenses.[17] He also introduced order and method in the accounting of raw materials and products in the course of fabrication. He revived the old practice—previously introduced in the mid-1700s when the manufactory had been located at Vincennes—whereby each workshop in the manufactory's system was held accountable for the pieces it received from the workshop that had completed the previous step in the production of the porcelain. Shortly thereafter Brongniart ordered the physical regrouping of pieces by category and state of completion, as well as the establishment of a precise inventory.

Unfortunately, organizational decisions were not the exclusive prerogative of the director. On 15 Thermidor year 10 (August 3, 1802) he received a copy of a decree issued eleven days earlier. A cover letter clarified this "governmental decree which gives a new existence to the Sèvres manufactory." Henceforth production was to be divided into two distinct categories: "ordinary products intended for sale" whose production costs were to be covered by receipts; and luxury objects reserved for the government to be produced in an *atelier de perfectionnement* that was slated to receive 6,000 francs per month. The minister concluded with words that must have profoundly influenced Brongniart, for they are echoed in his own writings until the end of his career: "You will neglect neither the beauty of the forms, nor the richness and stability of the colors, nor the quality of the paste."[18] He also advised the director: "You must never lose sight of the fact that if Sèvres becomes inimitable in the matter of luxury objects, it must also serve as a model for all ordinary objects. Above all you must embrace the idea that a manufactory under immediate government scrutiny will cease to merit its protection the very day on which any other manufactory can compete with it in the matter of perfection."[19] In fact, the proposed system was never practicable and apparently was never implemented.

A major task facing Brongniart was the renewal of the manufactory's production. He diligently sought to dispose of unfashionable pieces that crowded the warehouses. As early as July 1800, exhorting the *ministre des relations extérieures* to remit at least partial payment for pieces delivered to the minister's department, Brongniart emphasized: "You would contribute by this act of justice to the progress of the arts that you love by giving me the means to make in the establishment that I direct . . . changes that purified taste and the perfection of chemical science dictate be brought to bear on fabrication."[20] Even at this early date in his tenure, artistic and scientific considerations were indissolubly linked in his mind. On August 4, 1800, he requested that the *ministre de l'intérieur* do away with *artistes-en-chef* because "the objects they produce will always be in the same genre and it is useful for the productions of a factory to be as various as the taste of the purchasers."[21] Conversely, he requested authorization "to solicit drawings and designs from different artists whose talent is generally acknowledged" as well as permission to involve them in actual production of the pieces, "which would obtain a higher price due to the author's reputation," concluding that "it is by implementing this project that I could with a bit of time renew the forms of the Sèvres manufactory which is reproached for not having kept up with the progress of the arts."[22] On October 29, 1801, he wrote: "I am presently overseeing completion of assorted service and *déjeuner* almost all of which I found to be incomplete . . . . Finally, aided by friendly advice hitherto offered free of charge by artists of my acquaintance, I am beginning to renew or rectify those forms that require it."[23]

On October 23, 1801, Brongniart had issued a publicity statement to the press, informing them that "Sèvres porcelain . . . is much improved over the past year in the purity of its forms, the variety of its ground [colors], and the interest of its subjects and compositions, as much in painting as in sculpture. The greatest possible effort has been made to emulate the antique and keep in step with advancing taste. The advice and work of the most skillful artists in Paris have been turned to account in these different genres."[24] Production was indeed transformed with great rapidity (see chap. 6). Finally, during these early years in Brongniart's tenure, he began to plan a museum of ceramics, first envisioned in Fructidor year 9 (August 1801) in relation to the Enquête des Préfets (see chaps. 9 and 11).

Brongniart and Governmental Agencies

It is not surprising that Brongniart managed to retain his post despite several shifts of government. Such cases were not uncommon in the period, and in any event by the late Empire his managerial skills and scientific abilities had won him acclaim throughout Europe, assuring his position. His relations with his hierarchical superiors, always seemingly positive, were couched in very different styles during the course of his tenure, passing from a quasi-egalitarian republican tone under the Consulate to one of marked civility under the Empire, and finally to the deference that prevailed under the Restauration and the July Monarchy.

The *administrateur,* as he was usually called, was not autonomous, given that the manufactory belonged to the state. Until 1804 it was overseen by the *ministre de l'intérieur,* Lucien Bonaparte, who had appointed the new administrator and his successor, Jean-Antoine Chaptal, who was a passionate advocate of chemistry applied to industry and an audacious entrepreneur open to all novelties. As an excellent administrator, Chaptal was temperamentally well matched with his subordinate Brongniart whom he addressed as "*mon cher Brongniart.*"[25] At times, however, Chaptal was inclined to temper Brongniart's sometimes overheated enthusiasm.[26]

A senatorial decree issued on 28 Floréal year 13 (April 19, 1805) linked the manufactory to the Liste Civile, which provided the emporor's living expenses and so on, and henceforth it became the responsibility of the Intendant Général de la Liste Civile. Between 1805 and 1811 this position was occupied by Pierre Daru, who also organized the emperor's military campaigns and was often obligated, therefore, to delegate his authority in the Paris offices to his brother Martial. Thus, a few days after the battle of Austerlitz (December 2, 1805), Pierre Daru sent Brongniart a long report on the Vienna porcelain factory.[27]

Despite the change in authority the administrator continued to maintain relations with successive *ministres de l'intérieur,* because they oversaw the nation's industry. Jean-Baptiste de Champagny, minister from 1804 to 1807, was anxious to improve the quality of ordinary faience and pottery, including reducing health hazards caused by lead in the glazes, and thus continued the important prefectural inquiry initiated by Chaptal (see chap. 11). Brongniart's advice about new processes was also solicited several times: he was asked his opinion, for example, on Gonord's transfer-printing process in 1805, or on the transparent glazes without metallic oxides developed by "Sr. Kuny de Bude in Hungary" in 1811, or on Monginot's carbon-fueled firing process introduced in 1811.[28]

After the many difficulties of the tumultuous years 1814 and 1815, during which France was invaded by the English, Russian, and German forces and the emperor twice abdicated,[29] Sèvres—still a dependency of the Liste Civile after the second Restauration of the Bourbons in 1815—was overseen by successive ministers of the Maison du Roi. In August 1824 the post of *directeur général des beaux-arts de la Maison du Roi* was established and responsibility for Sèvres shifted to that authority. The appointment of Sosthène, vicomte de La Rochefoucauld, to the position must have pleased Brongniart, for the two men had served together on the ceramics jury of the 1823 "Exposition des produits de l'industrie" (Exhibition of industrial products), held in the Louvre. They seem to have gotten on extremely well,[30] as did Brongniart and the new *inspecteur général du département des Beaux-arts,* the painter Lancelot Théodore de Turpin de Crissé, who became a kind of artistic advisor to the manufactory (see chap. 6).

Sèvres survived two difficult years after Louis-Philippe's accession in 1830, since the Assembly refused to approve the king's Liste Civile for him until April 1832 because of his immense personal fortune. Brongniart sometimes found that his direct relations with the king and the royal family were strained by tensions with the Intendants Général, who were jealous of their prerogatives, but the resulting problems remained manageable.

Brongniart and the Sovereigns

The director of the manufactory often dealt directly with the various sovereigns of France in the first half of the nineteenth century. This occurred primarily when they paid visits to Sèvres. Napoleon came about once a year and was often accompanied by the empress and a few ladies of the court to whom he distributed small gifts. Such occasions were almost always unanticipated, and Brongniart counted himself lucky when he was given a few hours' advance warning. One of these visits almost ended in disaster: on August 18, 1807, when the emperor (or someone in his entourage) thought there might be flaws in the colors and draftsmanship, he threatened to close the manufactory.[31] This was probably mere caprice, for Napoleon did not hesitate to distribute gifts to his companions in the course of the same visit, and when he returned a year later he expressed satisfaction at the progress achieved, despite the fact that there was no real difference between the pieces produced. The emperor seems to have been a demanding and impatient taskmaster; in 1808, when Brongniart was absent from the manufactory, it was reported to him that as a result of delays, Dominique-Vivant Denon feared "that the Emperor might become angry and that the results might be very unpleasant for everyone."[32]

Sometimes the empress Josephine came alone and appropriated objects on the spot, generating impromptu deliveries for which Brongniart subsequently found it difficult to exact payment.[33] Other times the emperor brought foreign guests with him; he evidently took pleasure in showing the establishment to visiting sovereigns and other dignitaries. On 14 Nivôse year 13 (January 4, 1805), for example,

Brongniart sent the mayor of Sèvres a list of those privileged to be invited on the occasion of the pope's visit, including "Monsieur le Curé (solely on condition that he deliver no harangues)."[34]

Among the first visitors Brongniart received following the Restauration was the duchesse d'Angoulême, daughter of Louis XVI and Marie Antoinette, who came to Sèvres on June 22, 1814. Louis XVIII was received next, on August 10, with the comte de Blacas, the minister of the Maison du Roi. This visit prompted Brongniart to write: "His Majesty saw only the warehouse, but . . . I took care to have assembled there the principal pieces whose progress was sufficiently advanced to be judged. His Majesty gave evidence on several occasions of his unequivocal satisfaction. . . . He deigned to address to me in particular words as flattering as they were honorable."[35]

Louis XVIII, like his brother, the future Charles X, had been a faithful client of the manufactory before the Revolution (despite their both being official protectors of their own Parisian porcelain factories at the time) and was thus perfectly capable of judging its progress. The tray from the *déjeuner 'L'Art de la Porcelaine'* (see cat. no. 39) proves that the king returned at least once in 1816, doubtless thanks to the manufactory's proximity to Saint-Cloud.[36]

There were still other occasions for face-to-face encounters. In 1814 Brongniart obtained authorization to revive the tradition of holding annual exhibitions at the Louvre where the manufactory's latest creations were displayed. These had been established by Louis XV at Versailles and were continued at the Tuileries by Louis XVI, after the Revolution had begun.[37] The sovereigns always visited these presentations, where they were escorted by Brongniart, who was also charged with personally presenting gifts to members of the royal family. When this opportunity was denied to him in 1828, he protested vigorously.[38]

Brongniart also made personal presentations of exceptional pieces recently produced at the manufactory. These visits must have been rare under the Bourbons, however, and thus all the more cherished by the director. He became indignant in fact when the talented Sèvres artist Marie-Victoire Jaquotot asked to present her porcelain copy of François Gérard's *Cupid and Psyche* to the king unaccompanied by Brongniart.

The situation changed completely under Louis-Philippe, to whom Brongniart wrote on August 25, 1830, very soon after his accession: "Sire the persons Your Majesty permitted me to introduce to him were for the most part already known to him. This flattering circumstance results from the interest that Your Majesty has kindly evidenced in the Manufactory by the visits and commissions with which he has honored it. Such a favorable predisposition allows us to think that the encouragements which the duc d'Orléans gave to this establishment of art and industry by all the means within his power will not be forgotten by the king of the French."[39] The archival documents even suggest that a familiarity of sorts developed between the ruler and the administrator, who were near-contemporaries. In 1845 Louis Philippe agreed to appoint Jean-Jacques Ebelmen as adjunct administrator to Brongniart, but refused Brongniart's offer to renounce his own salary in favor of the younger man. As the comte de Montalivet, Intendant Général, explained to Brongniart: "His Majesty, by retaining your salary in its entirety, wanted to indicate to you the price He attaches to your venerable and so honorable services and to those that the Royal Manufactory of Sèvres can still expect from your knowledge and your experience."[40]

Financial Management

Most of Brongniart's administrative dealings concerned the management of the manufactory's budget. After the 1805 decree whereby Sèvres was linked to the sovereign's Liste Civile, a fixed annual operational budget was allotted the manufactory. It received the designated sums in regular installments, and in exchange, it turned over to the sovereign the revenues from its sales. In principle, all deliveries to government agencies were taken into account so that these sums were counted as revenues.

The administrative imposition of fiscal constraints on Sèvres posed many problems. Several times under the Empire, Brongniart had to threaten to cease work entirely by the beginning of the following autumn if supplementary funding could not be obtained. Such an occurrence would preclude provision of New Year's gifts for distribution by the empress and would prevent delivery of productions required by the emperor. Furthermore, Brongniart emphasized that such a hiatus might entail the loss of the factory's best artists to private Parisian competitors who were more regular in their payments to employees. Similar discrepancies between orders for work and available funds arose under Charles X, and in 1824 Brongniart wrote to the vicomte de La Rochefoucauld: "I had the honor of telling you on several occasions that I cannot proceed with the activity necessary for such work . . . without exceeding the allotted funds. You were good enough to reply each time that I should carry on and that you would take care of the matter."[41] Such protests usually proved successful, and the indispensable supplementary monies were provided.

Another source of difficulty was the slowness and irregularity of payments, and even the occasional nonpayment. Invoices for the New Year's gifts of January 1, 1813, for example, went unpaid, the result of Napoleon's abdication and the sudden change of government. The manufactory was sometimes unable to meet urgent expenses because it had no control over the release of funds and was not allowed to settle debts with revenues from sales without special authorization. It was very difficult to coordinate payments and orders of essential raw materials that could only be shipped in mild weather. Similar administrative delays in verifying the manufactory's accounts were a constant irritation. In 1821 accounts submitted for the 1812–17 period still had not been examined. Finally, the volume and complication of obligatory paperwork prompted the director to complain vigorously. Because he had resolved from the beginning to purge the staff of "unproductive" personnel, a single *commis* had to deal with this burgeoning task.

Brongniart never tired of explaining to successive official correspondents that before his arrival at Sèvres its bookkeeping had been totally irregular, and that it had been he who had remedied this situation by instituting a series of precise and methodical accounting practices. The overall budget was divided into two parts: one covered the salaries of the permanent staff and the other was for raw materials, equipment, and payments to workers who were not yet on the permanent staff. Early in his tenure, Brongniart had decided to distinguish between two categories of employees: permanent staff (*personnel fixe*) and part-time workers (*en extraordinaire*). The permanent staff members, the more privileged of the two, were accorded various administrative advantages.[42] Workers entered this elite only after having served as workers *en extraordinaire* for at least a year, if by that time they had proven their utility and would move to Sèvres where, when necessary, they could be located rapidly. *Personnel fixe* were distributed among three departments: pastes and kilns, colors and firing, and painters and gilders. Beginning in 1806, weekly meetings were held with the department heads to ensure operational efficiency. Brongniart demanded hard work, unfailing diligence, high production, and quality workmanship of his staff. He also expected them to have irreproachable morals, although it seems he was often disappointed on this last point.

The manufactory implemented a system of bonuses and penalties to guarantee quality. In accordance with widespread eighteenth-century practice, "salaries" were keyed to performance and determined by productivity. As each new object was completed, Brongniart consulted with the department head and other staff members to establish the fee a worker would be paid for his role in production. Workers were paid by the piece on a monthly basis, on the understanding that there was an annual maximum they were not to exceed. This theoretical maximum served as the basis for establishing the overall budget and projecting profits. A set of registers in the Sèvres archives records the amount asked by the artist and the fee actually paid by the administrator for each piece; the former almost always exceeds the latter.

Workers *en extraordinaire* were employed irregularly or did not yet qualify for *personnel fixe* status. Their payments were included in the second part of the budget along with anticipated expenditures for raw materials. Here again Brongniart demonstrated his organizational skills and his will to impose fiscal discipline. Competition between suppliers kept prices down, and each delivery occasioned a series of examinations whose results were recorded and samples of the supplies were deposited in the museum for control purposes. One of Brongniart's ongoing concerns was having an adequate store of supplies. He managed to keep a stock of primary materials on hand despite budgetary constraints, a prudent move that paid off in the difficult years between 1830 and 1832. Maintenance of the facility was the responsibility of the Bâtiments du Roi. In 1811 Brongniart insisted that he be consulted about maintenance costs since they were eventually levied against Sèvres. He carried the day on this point, and after that time no expenditures were permitted unless they had been explicitly authorized by him in advance.

In 1832 Brongniart wrote to Baron Fain, the Intendant Général: "Trusting in my good and firm intentions, I have taken until the present, in the acquisition of materials and products . . . the course I would have followed for myself if the establishment belonged to me."[43] This formulation might appear surprising, but all of Brongniart's superiors readily acknowledged the remarkable qualities he brought to bear in performing his duties: clarity, rigor, exceptional organizational skills, and flawless integrity. Thus it was that Pierre Daru, in rendering the accounts for the year 13 (1804–5) wrote to Brongniart: "It will be a true pleasure for me, Monsieur, to point out to His Majesty that the results of this accounting substantiate the care with which you have conducted your administration, just as its clarity demonstrates the order that you have succeeded in maintaining there."[44] In the same manner, the accountants of 1822 wrote: "it would be difficult to find more order and precision than that which exists in all parts of the administration of the Royal Sèvres Manufactory and . . . in the present circumstance we can only confirm what has already been said on this subject by the former accounting commission."[45]

It is very difficult to judge whether Brongniart's rigorous attention to detail ever allowed the manufactory to be profitable. In the account-books, at least, the value of completed Sèvres pieces remained remarkably stable throughout the period: prices assigned to objects that entered the warehouse in the first years of the century remained unchanged on an inventory drawn up fifty years later.

Conversely, the operating costs increased, although at a slow pace. In 1837 Brongniart estimated that the average annual budget under the Empire was about 295,000 francs; under Louis XVIII, 310,000 francs; under Charles X, 328,000 francs; and under Louis-Philippe, 330,000 francs.[46] These increases were due in part to added personnel, a necessity given the extreme specialization of the workers and their organization into successive workshops. It would have been impossible for Brongniart to operate the establishment with the sixty-six employees who were left on staff when he arrived at Sèvres in 1800. As the financial crisis abated over time, Brongniart gradually rehired some of the workers he had previously let go, first as workers *en extraordinaire* and then as permanent staff. In the year 10 (1801–2) this last category consisted of 78 employees; by 1808 it had risen to 94, and it subsequently stabilized between 110 and 120.[47]

Brongniart insisted from the beginning on retaining the prerogative to hire and dismiss personnel as he saw fit. Nonetheless, he was repeatedly obliged to deflect his administrative superiors when they urged him to hire their protégés. He reminded them—diplomatically but firmly—that he always sought the best-qualified workers and that such recommendations would have no effect on his decisions (see chap. 6).

Salary increases were another factor reflected in the rising figures. These were granted, in Brongniart's words, only "in cases where merit is insufficiently remunerated in comparison with payment generally accorded such merit, or talents acquired since admission to the manufactory. It is impossible to refuse such requests *when they are well founded*, for otherwise only mediocrities would remain in the manufactory."[48] Brongniart further insisted on "the obligation, the real obligation of the royal manufactory to make [products that are] larger and larger, more and more beautiful in response to what is rightfully expected of it."[49] Finally, the director noted that if the budget were reduced, production would have to slow down. This would increase the cost of producing each piece because the general operating expenses would then be divided among a smaller number of objects.[50]

By conventional accounting standards the balance sheets were idiosyncratic, and their necessary organization into discreet annual units inevitably entailed uncertainties. Allowing that the fictive sales to the sovereign were a compensation for payments that effectively functioned as advances, it seems that at least under the Empire the manufactory generated a profit, thanks to a significant proportion of important pieces delivered to the emperor to be used in his household or to serve as gifts.

In 1806, however, Daru refused to believe the figures presented by the administrator for the year 13 (1804–5). True, Brongniart had weighed expenditures (315,000 francs) against the combined total of the sales receipts (314,000 francs) and the assigned value of the overstock (220,000 francs) to obtain a profit figure of 219,000 francs. Nevertheless the sales figure alone almost equaled expenditures.[51] In 1810 Brongniart was able to report a "rather considerable" profit, and in 1811 the figure in the positive column was as high as 57,723 francs.[52]

In succeeding years the accounts became less impressive, as the rulers became increasingly parsimonious. A balance sheet for 1814 to 1820 indicates that the manufactory's aggregate expenditures during that period amounted to 2,189,230 francs while its sales revenues came to only 1,634,782 francs (920,786 from the king and 713,996 from private clients), creating an average annual deficit of about 80,000 francs. Brongniart was quick to emphasize, however, that the figure for receipts did not include the 93,130 francs for the 1813 New Year's gifts that had never been paid. To further ameliorate the picture, he asked that account also be taken of the assigned value of pieces added to the warehouse stock during that period, to the sum of 421,018 francs.[53]

Unfortunately, there are no such balance sheets dating to the time of the July Monarchy. The surviving registers do indicate, however, that, apart from stained-glass windows, Louis-Philippe preferred small and medium-sized porcelains. This resulted in a significant increase in salable stock, dominated by the large pieces Brongniart was obligated to produce for the Louvre exhibitions. Consolidating aggregate revenues and the total assigned value of pieces completed in any given year produced favorable results on paper, but Brongniart himself acknowledged that pieces in stock rapidly lost value as they became unfashionable. There was a discrepancy between assigned value based on the costs implied by the production of a piece and market value, as sadly evidenced by a series of auctions organized by the manufactory to liquidate parts of the stock (see chap. 10).

Commercialization

The establishment of prices was a crucial problem. No documents pertaining to this process in the eighteenth century survive, but discrepancies in prices assigned to different examples of the same biscuit sculpture model during the period suggest that successful firings and the general quality of workmanship were taken into consideration in setting prices. During his tenure, Brongniart gradually introduced a complex evaluation procedure. When a new form was produced, one or two examples were made and glazed. When they entered the stock of undecorated pieces, a first valuation sheet was drawn up noting expenses specifically related to its production. This included the cost of maquettes, drawings, molds, paste, shaping, glazing, and firing. This figure was increased by roughly a third to cover general operating expenses (building maintenance, tools, and so on). On this basis, prices were set for undecorated pieces in accordance with a tiered schedule of qualitative categories: first, second, third, and waste goods. After a piece was decorated, a new valuation sheet was prepared taking into account costs incurred by ground application, painting, gilding, polishing, and bronze mounting. (In the case of ensembles such as *déjeuners* and dinner services, this valuation sheet was drawn up only after the service had been completed.) Again, the figure thus obtained was increased by a third to cover operating expenses, and the result was the net price.

The actual sale price was established in the weekly departmental meetings, in accordance with the piece's quality. Brongniart must have kept track of the pricing practices of his competitors: he considered it normal for private entrepreneurs to show a profit of 100 percent, but at Sèvres he never assigned retail prices that exceeded the net price by more than 30 percent. In 1817 he wrote: "Costs entailed by producing the large pieces that the manufactory makes and ought to make . . . to maintain its character and attain its goals are very considerable and . . . the prices I assign pieces, however high they might seem at first glance, are low in comparison with the care brought to bear on all parts of the fabrication process and the difficulty of their obtaining success."[54] Such calculations were approximate by their very nature. It was impossible to assess and allocate operating expenses accurately, a task that was made even worse when it came to accounting for seconds, wasted time, and other imponderables. Even so, this system was the first attempt to approach pricing methodically. All the pieces valued in this way were intended for sale; sales receipts were meant to balance subvention allotments.

The manufactory's principal client was the reigning sovereign who financed it. He chose table services,[55] dressing-table sets, or furnishings for himself and those close to him or pieces to give as diplomatic and other gifts. The type and value of these purchases varied from government to government during this turbulent period in French political history. Napoleon made ample use of Sèvres for propaganda purposes. He used and presented significant quantities of the manufactory's most beautiful pieces resulting in a relatively small increase in warehouse holdings during his regime. Louis XVIII continued to offer the most beautiful productions to members of his family and his entourage after each annual exhibition, but his purchases for personal use were relatively modest. His infirmities made it difficult for him to move about, and he had no need of a service for each palace. Charles X also pursued a policy of thrift. He made very few important gifts of Sèvres porcelain. He was so frugal in fact that he never even took possession of the table illustrating his own coronation; it was eventually acquired by the king of Spain.[56]

Louis-Philippe made more ample use of Sèvres. He expanded the number of services used in his various residences, and thus placed increasingly large orders of such pieces. All of these objects were rather small, however, and simply decorated, even when intended for the royal table. Similarly, he preferred pieces of medium size to use as gifts and as accessories for the royal household.

Throughout his tenure, Brongniart sought to increase royal purchases. He accomplished this partly by providing luxury productions but also by offering pieces for everyday use such as water jugs, chamber pots, and inkstands. These allowed him to counterbalance his general operating expenses. In 1822, announcing the success of life-size busts of the king and members of the royal family (see chap. 8), Brongniart expressed the hope that these productions, which he affected to be more durable than marble and more seductive than plaster, might be used as furnishings by the sovereign and his principal ministers.[57] He raised this issue again a bit later: "Moreover . . . I cannot let myself weary of repeating, because it is my duty to do so . . . that the flow of the manufactory's products would increase in a manner most favorable to this establishment if the ministers and administrative heads would set an example of good taste and a preference for perfection over manifest opulence by placing among the furnishings of their residences and tables some of the manufactory's carefully fabricated pieces . . . [It would be advantageous] if the minister of foreign affairs instead of using exclusively gold and diamond jewelry as diplomatic gifts also made such use of a certain number of the rich and precious objects of the royal manufactories, notably that of porcelain."[58] He would not have been so insistent on this point if public sales had been sufficient to balance the budget.

The administrator did all he could to promote such sales. Beginning with his first publicity statement to the newspapers, he made skillful use of the press. By about 1830, however, these publications had become more independent, and reviews of the manufactory's annual exhibitions began to be less and less favorable. The Louvre exhibitions were a form of publicity, showcasing Sèvres's most remarkable productions, especially when entry to these exhibits, although open by invitation only, became increasingly easy to come by. Initially organized on an annual basis, the exhibitions became less frequent, however, under Louis-Philippe. They were only worthwhile when a sufficient number of suitable new pieces were on hand, but this type of production was a substantial drain on an already strained budget. In addition, the king's preference for simpler objects made it unlikely that he would buy the larger ones that were part of the exhibition. In a few exceptional cases, artists were permitted to exhibit their work for Sèvres at the salon, but such authorization was granted only after the pieces in question had first been shown with other Sèvres productions.

After 1823 Sèvres ceased to participate in the exhibitions of national industrial products, to avoid the appearance of competing unfairly with private entrepreneurs. Entries in the Sèvres visitors' register, however, indicate that, when the manufactory's museum opened to the public in 1824, the access it afforded to Sèvres production and the historic collections was widely appreciated.

From the moment of his arrival Brongniart had insisted on the importance of a salesroom in Paris itself. When efforts in 1800–1801 to obtain suitable space in a public building proved fruitless, he had to make do with space in a warehouse run by the dealer, or *marchand-mercier*, Lignereux. He was forced to give this up in 1804 when Lignereux decided to move to a location that would be less commercially viable for Sèvres. Brongniart raised the issue again in 1814, explaining that the manufactory's location between Paris and the château of Versailles became remote once Versailles ceased to be the seat of government. He proposed that a Parisian "depot" might be advantageously coupled with a small workshop capable of executing simple decorative schemes on the spot. This would prompt the artists at Sèvres to moderate the prices they asked and would keep the art staff apprised "of refinements invented in the Parisian factories."[59]

A first warehouse was established in the rue de Grammont in 1815; it moved to the rue Sainte Anne in 1817. When this lease expired in 1828 the salesroom set up shop in the rue de Rivoli, but first there was an auction of excess stock as well as pieces from the warehouse at Sèvres. The sale announcement specified that it would include "pieces of different genres and qualities, good and defective, primarily old forms and featuring old decorative schemes, notably flower pieces and a few large vases . . . all colored, painted, and gilded; also a large quantity of undecorated seconds and old forms in both hard and soft paste, and a rather large number of pieces of so-called biscuit sculpture."[60] The results were catastrophic: the total value assigned the offerings in the manufactory's inventories was 159,927 francs, but after expenses the sale netted only some 27,468 francs.[61]

In 1828 Brongniart's request to establish a "school of painting in vitreous colors" in the new Paris salesroom was granted. The school was meant to provide young artists who had completed their preliminary training with the skills needed for specialization in ceramic painting. The insufficient numbers of suitable applicants, however, forced the school to close in 1833. Finally, a decision made by the vicomte de La Rochefoucauld on May 15, 1840, decreed that the Paris salesroom itself be closed. Brongniart admitted on this occasion that the results had never equaled his expectations, although each successive venue had managed to recoup its expenses. Another auction, organized in 1840, was as disastrous as the preceding one: 13,727 pieces, theoretically valued at some 126,777.30 francs, brought in only around 20,299.75 francs.[62] As with the sales organized during his first years at Sèvres, Brongniart was seeking to rid his warehouses of countless undecorated and unfashionable pieces. Unfortunately, however, fakes and genuine undecorated pieces overpainted by independent artists would proliferate in response to the increasing demand for eighteenth-century Sèvres porcelain. It is therefore difficult to understand the director's decision to sell work that would effectively increase the possibilities for such falsification, especially when the financial gains for the manufactory were so insignificant.

Even so, records of sales and commissions (see chap. 6) indicate that the manufactory managed to develop a regular, if relatively small clientele. It consisted of members of the ruling families (especially the duchesse de Berry and the Orléans clan), foreign sovereigns and dignitaries (see cat. no. 64), rich financiers such as the Rothschild family, government administrators, and private individuals. The prevalence of English clients is striking, and many purchases at Sèvres were also made by merchants, including other porcelain producers, who were accorded a slight discount. There were also customers who bought any soft-paste porcelain remaining in stock after Brongniart's early auctions, and there were national and private establishments with an interest in porcelain techniques.

On arriving at Sèvres in 1800, Brongniart had elected not to challenge the organizational status quo, whose workings must have been explained to him by his predecessors, both of whom had been with the manufactory for quite some time (Jean-Hilaire Salmon l'aîné since 1784 and Jean-Jacques Hettlinger since 1785). Operations had proceeded along these lines for more than half a century. The finished objects that resulted were admired and imitated throughout Europe. Brongniart probably considered this to be sufficient proof of the success of this strategy. He adhered to its general principles: projected deliveries of objects in production from one workshop to the next; a clear distinction between the shaping and decoration of forms, with the respective workshops overseen by different supervisors; work remunerated by the piece on the basis of yearly estimates or *en extraordinaire*; and the active involvement of outside artists to provide the models for forms and decorative schemes. On his arrival in 1800, however, he encountered sloppy accounting methods that must have shocked his orderly intelligence. Accordingly, he codified the established practices, introducing modifications and additions over the years, as experience suggested their necessity. More than a revolutionary, Brongniart revealed himself to be a remarkable organizer.

[Ed. note: The documents cited below are from the Archives of the Manufacture Nationale de Sèvres (AMNS).

1. [Autrefois, la Manufacture de Sèvres n'avoit point de rivale pour la perfection du travail; mais j'ai vu avec peine que depuis quelques années, elle n'avoit fait que peu de progrès dans l'art de la fabrication; il existe aujourd'hui plusieurs établissemens particuliers qui semblent à certains égards éclipser sa gloire. Cet état stationnaire m'a paru devoir être attribué à plusieurs causes. Aussi, en

réorganisant la Manufacture, je ne me suis pas seulement proposé de la rendre moins à charge au Trésor public; j'ai encore eu l'intention de lui faire recouvrer son ancienne prospérité, et de la transformer en une école d'art. La fabrication de la porcelaine est parfaitement établie en France, et, en la maintenant à Sèvres j'ai eu surtout en vue d'en faire un objet d'émulation pour les établissemens particuliers. Ainsi, le travail qui se fera à l'avenir devra tendre aux progrès de cette fabrication; mais, pour l'exécution de ce projet, il m'a paru qu'un chymiste devoit diriger la manufacture. Vous savez que les arts qui s'exercent sur les terres forment l'une des branches les plus importantes de la chymie, et Sèvre ne pouvoit que dégénerer, puisqu'il n'avoit point à sa tête un homme versé dans cette science. Cette considération m'a déterminé à nommer pour directeur le Citoyen Brongniard fils, auteur d'un mémoire estimé sur les émaux . . . Le Citoyen Brongniart ne s'occupera pas seulement de ce qui est relatif à la fabrication de la porcelaine; il fera en outre des essais sur les verreries et les poteries . . .] Carton L 1.

2. [d'après le témoignage avantageux qui m'a été rendu de votre moralité et de vos talents] Carton Ob 2, dossier 2 (photocopy of an original now in a private collection).

3. [Je vous promets de mettre tout le zèle que m'inspire l'amour de mon pays et la marque de confiance que vous voulez bien me donner pour remplir vos vues utiles. J'employerai les connaisances que j'ai acquises et j'y joindrai celles des chimistes célèbres avec lesquels j'ai l'avantage d'être lié pour redonner à cette manufacture la supériorité dont elle a besoin pour continuer de rendre à la France les services qu'elle lui a déjà rendus. Je ferai tout ce qui dépendra de moi pour la transformer en une véritable école d'art. Mes désirs sont à cet égard absolument conformes à votre intentions . . .] Carton T 1, liasse 1.

4. The men appointed to this joint directorship were Jean-Jacques Hettlinger (1734-1803), formerly adjunct director, Jean-Hilaire Salmon l'aîné (d. 1805) formerly treasurer, and the chemist François Meyer, who soon resigned. Under the new administration the first two reverted to their former posts.

5. [le dénuement presqu'absolu de matières et d'argent . . .] [hommes de mérite qui auroient pu porter ailleurs leur connoissance et nuire ainsi à l'établissement . . .] [si le gouvernement pouvoit payer ce qu'il doit à cet établissement sa situation seroit plus heureuse . . .] Register Vc 2, fol. 55v – 56.

6. [de vieilles porcelaines qui encombrent nos magasins et qui nuisent à la manufacture en fesant croire à ceux qui viennent la visiter qu'elle fabrique encore de ces choses gothiques . . .] ibid., fol. 56v – 57.

7. Ibid., fol. 69v ff., letter dated 6 Brumaire year 9 (October 29, 1801).

8. Register Vy 12, fol. 189, dated 3 Thermidor year 8 (July 23, 1800) and 189v, dated 7 Thermidor year 8 (July 30, 1800).

9. [objets de rebut par l'ancienneté de leurs formes ou par leurs défauts . . .que le goût actuel m'ordonnoit d'ôter du magasin . . .] ibid., fol. 94v. The Louvre sale was held from 25 Fructidor year 8 to 8 Vendemaire year 9 (September 13 – October 1, 1800).

10. Register Vc 2, fol. 119v – 120, letter dated 13 Ventôse year 10 (March 5, 1802).

11. [en principe que les porcelaines que demandera le gouvernement lui seront vendues au prix marchand, et qu'à l'avenir il acquittera la valeur de toutes les fournitures qui pourront lui être faites . . .] Carton T 1, liasse 1, dossier 1, letter from the *ministre de l'intérieur* dated 8 Pluviôse year 9 (January 28, 1801).

12. Register Vc 3, fol. 105 – 105v, letter dated August 26, 1807.

13. Ibid., fol. 147 – 48, letter dated November 18, 1808.

14. Carton M 4, liasse 1; carton M 5, liasse 4, dossier 2.

15. [de laisser à l'administrateur la liberté de prendre les ouvriers, de les renvoyer, de fixer leurs salaires et de les employer de la manière qu'il jugera la plus utile . . .] Carton T 1, liasse 1, dossier 1.

16. [il peut encore survenir des événements qui vous obligent à recourir au gouvernement et, dans les moments de détresse, vous trouverez toujours en lui une ressource dont vous ne devez point vous priver . . .] ibid.

17. Register Y 4.

18. [. . . vous ne négligeres ni la beauté des formes, ni la richesse et solidité des couleurs, ni la qualité de la pâte . . .] Carton T 1, liasse 3, dossier 1, letter dated August 4, 1802.

19. [vous ne perdrez pas de vue que si Sèvres devient inimitable pour les objets de luxe, il doit encore servir de modèle pour tous les objets courant. Surtout penetres vous de l'idée qu'une manufacture qui va être sous les yeux immédiats du gouvernement cesserait de mériter sa protection du jour même où toute autre manufacture pourrait le (lui) disputer en perfection] Ibid.

20. [vous contriburez par cet acte de justice aux progrès des arts que vous aimez en me donnant les moyens de faire dans l'établissement que je dirige . . . les changements que le goût épuré et la perfection des sciences chimiques ordonnent d'apporter dans la fabrication . . .] Register Vc 2, fol. 60 – 61, letter dated 1 Thermidor year 8 (July 20, 1800).

21. [les objets qu'ils produisent seront toujours dans le même genre et il est utile que les productions d'une fabrique soient aussi variées que le goût des acheteurs . . .] Register Vc 2, fol. 63v ff., letter dated 15 Thermidor year 8 (August 4, 1800); carton T 1, liasse 2, response dated 12 Frimaire year 9 (December 3, 1800).

22. [demander aux divers artistes dont le talent est généralement reconnu des dessins et projects . . . qui acquerront un plus grand prix de la réputation de l'auteur . . .] [cest par l'exécution de ce projet que je pourrai dans quelques temps renouveller les formes de la manufacture de Sèvres à laquelle on reproche de n'avoir point suivi les progrès des arts], ibid.

23. [Je fais compléter dans ce moment les assortiments de pièces de service et de déjeuner que j'ai trouvés tous incomplets...enfin, à l'aide des conseils amicaux et jusqu'à présent gratuits des artistes avec lesquels je suis lié, je commence à renouveller ou rectifier celles des formes qui l'exigeoient . . .] Register Vc2, fol. 69 ff., letter dated 6 Brumaire year 9 (October 29, 1801).

24. [La porcelaine de Sèvres . . . a beaucoup gagné depuis un an pour la pureté des formes, pour la variété des fonds et pour l'intérêt des sujets et des compositions, tant en peinture qu'en sculpture. On a cherché, autant qu'il est possible, à se rapprocher de l'antique et à marcher d'un pas égal avec les progrès du goût. On a profité, dans ces différents genres, des conseils et des travaux des plus habiles artistes de Paris] Carton T 1, liasse 3, dossier 5.

25. Carton T 1, liasse 5, letter dated 13 Germinal year 12 (April 3, 1804).

26. He convinced Brongniart to reconsider his intention to deprive the manufactory of future government subsidies, something for which the administrator must subsequently have been immensely grateful to him. Similarly, in the letter cited in the preceding note he states that establishing a faience and tinted earthenware factory as part of Sèvres would be misguided.

27. Brunet and Préaud, *Sèvres* (1978), 254 – 56.

28. Register Vc 3, report sent on 26 Germinal year 13 (April 16, 1805); register Vc 4, letters dated July 24, 1811 and September 12, 1811.

29. Lechevallier-Chevignard "Le Rachat de la Manufacture de porcelaine" (1907). This author is excessively critical of Brongniart. Aside from the fact that pressure from the extremely reactionary royal administration must have been quite strong, it should be noted that, judging from the lists of works relating to the Bonapartes that were turned over to the Prussian commissioner or destroyed, the administrator managed to save the most important decorated pieces, surrendering primarily busts and medallions of relatively little value.

30. See, for example, a letter from the vicomte de La Rochefoucauld to Brongniart dated August 25, 1826: "The Inspector General of the Department of Fine Arts [Turpin de Crissé] has addressed to me, Monsieur, a report on the visit he has just made to various establishments under my competence. The Sèvres manufactory could scarcely fail to evoke from him lavish praise of the beauty of its products, the talent of its artists and the enlightened zeal of its director. I can only confirm all his flattering comments about it" [M. L'Inspecteur général du département des Beaux-Arts m'adresse, M., un rapport sur la visite qu'il vient de faire des divers établissements placés dans mes attributions. La Manufacture de Sèvres ne pouvait manquer d'être l'objet de tous ses éloges par la beauté de ses produits, le talent de ses artistes et le zèle éclairé de son Directeur. Je ne puis que confirmer tout ce qu'il en dit de flatteur . . .] (carton T 11, liasse 1, dossier 1). On the occasion of the vicomte's appointment, Brongniart wrote to him from Stockholm on September 5, 1824: "Monseigneur. I have just learned . . . that I now have the honor of being under your orders. The relations which it was my benefit to have with your excellency when you presided over the jury for the exposition of 1823 familiarized me with the manner in which Your Excellency views the arts and sciences and will help me to fulfill your intentions more completely" [Monseigneur. Je viens d'apprendre . . . que j'avois maintenant l'honneur d'être sous vos ordres. Les relations que j'ai eu l'avantage d'avoir avec votre excellence lorsqu'elle présidoit le jury de l'exposition de 1823 m'ont fait connoître la manière dont V.E. envisage les arts et les sciences et m'aideront à remplir plus complettement ses intentions . . .] (carton M 5, liasse 3, dossiers 1 – 2).

31. Gastineau "Une menace de suppression de la Manufacture de Sèvres" (1932).

32. [il craint que l'Empereur ne se fâche et qu'il en résulte des choses très désagréables pour tous π. . .] Carton M 1, dossier 7.

33. On March 18, 1807, in a cover letter accompanying a list of pieces carried off in this way, Brongniart wrote: "She [Josephine] even had them placed in her carriage. Her Majesty readily consented to my request for a written order to this effect." [. . . elle (i.e. Joséphine) les a même fait mettre dans sa voiture. S.M. a bien voulu sur ma demande me donner cet ordre par écrit] (register Vc 3, fol. 92vo – 93).

34. [Monsieur le Curé (seulement à condition qu'il ne fera point de harangue) . . .] Carton T 1, liasse 6.

35. [S.M. n'a vu que le magasin, mais . . . j'avois eu soin d'y faire réunir les principales pièces en fabrication assez avancées pour être jugées. S.M. a donné à plusieurs reprises des témoignages non équivoques de sa satisfaction . . . elle a daigné m'adresser particulièrement des paroles aussi flatteuses qu'honorables . . .] letter to Baron Mounier, Intendant des Bâtiments de la Couronne, dated August 11, 1814 (register Vc 4, fol. 104).

36. A letter dated November 4, 1824 from Brongniart to the vicomte de La Rochefoucauld alludes to a visit made by Louis XVIII "last July" (register Vc 7, fol. 48 ff.).

37. Ennès, *Un âge d'or,* exhib. cat. (1991).

38. Letter from Brongniart to the vicomte de La Rochefoucauld dated February 16, 1828: "The king made known his intentions either to his minister or to myself, and in 1826 His Majesty did me the honor of conveying his orders to me directly in his office . . . . Another custom, Monseigneur le vicomte, that I value highly . . . is that gifts of porcelain from the king's manufactory should be transported and delivered directly to the August members of the royal family by the director of this manufactory" [Le Roi faisoit connoître ses intentions soit à son ministre, soit même à moi et S.M. m'a honoré en 1826 de me transmettre directement ses ordres dans son cabinet . . . Un autre usage, auquel, Monseigneur le Vicomte, je mets beaucoup de prix . . . c'est que les présents en porcelaine de la Manufacture du Roi étoient portés et remis directement aux augustes membres de la famille royale par le Directeur de cette manufacture] (register Vc 7, fol. 183v ff.). Brongniart goes on to vigorously protest against the failure to observe this rule, soliciting the reestablishment of his prerogatives, which he deems "too honorable for the director . . . to let fall into disuse" [trop honorables pour le Directeur . . . pour qu'il puisse les laisser perdre] (ibid.).

39. [Sire les personnes que V.M. m'a permis de lui présenter ont la plupart l'honneur d'être déjà connue (sic) d'elle. Cette flatteuse circonstance résulte de l'intérêt que V.M. a bien voulu témoigner à la Manufacture par les visites et les commandes dont elle l'a honorée. Une si favorable prévention nous permet de croire que les encouragements que le duc d'Orléans a donné à cet établissement d'art et d'industrie par tous les moyens qui étoient en son pouvoir ne seront pas oubliés par le Roi des Français . . .] Carton T 12, liasse 3, dossier 3.

40. [S.M., en maintenant le chiffre intégral de votre traitement, a voulu vous donner un témoignage du prix qu'Elle attache à vos anciens et si honorables services et à ceux que la Manufacture royale de Sèvres doit encore attendre de vos lumières et de votre expérience.] Register Vb 5, letter dated April 14, 1825.

41. [J'ai eu l'honneur de vous dire à plusieurs reprises que je ne pourrois donner à ces travaux l'activité nécessaire . . . sans dépasser le crédit accordé. Vous avez eu la bonté de me répondre chaque fois que j'eusse à poursuivre et que vous y pourvoiriez . . .] Carton M 6, liasse 3, letter dated October 21, 1825.

42. Thomas, "Etude du Personnel" (1987/1988).

43. [me confiant dans mes bonnes et fermes intentions, j'ai suivi jusqu'à présent, pour l'acquisition des matières et denrées . . . la marche que je suivrais pour moi-même si l'établissement m'appartenait] Register Vc 8, fol. 139, letter dated September 27, 1832.

44. [. . . ce sera pour moi un véritable plaisir, Monsieur, de faire remarquer à S.M. que les résultats de ce compte prouvent le soin que vous apportés dans votre administration, comme sa clarté prouve l'ordre que vous avez sçu y maintenir . . .] Carton T 2, liasse 1, dossier 1, letter dated 7 Frimaire year 14 (November 29, 1805).

45. [il (est) difficile de trouver plus d'ordre et d'exactitude que ce qui existe dans toutes les parties de l'administration de la manufacture royale de Sèvres et...dans la circonstance présente nous ne faisons que confirmer ce qui avait déjà été dit à ce sujet par l'ancienne commission des comptes . . .] Carton M 6, liasse 1, dossier 1.

46. Carton T 13, liasse 4, dossier 12, letter dated March 9, 1837.

47. Thomas, "Etude du Personnel" (1987/1988), diagram no. 2.

48. [dans le cas où (ce) mérite ne serait pas assez rétribué en comparaison des paiements attribués partout à un mérite semblable, ou de talents acquis depuis l'admission dans la manufacture. Il est impossible de se refuser à des demandes pareilles *quand elles sont réellement fondées,* sous peine de ne voir rester dans la manufacture que des médiocrités . . .] Register Vc 9, fol. 161v ff., letter dated October 25, 1843.

49. [l'obligation, la réelle obligation où la manufacture royale a été de faire de plus en plus grand, de plus en plus beau pour répondre à ce qu'on a le droit d'attendre d'elle] Carton M 9, liasse 2, letter dated October 26, 1838.

50. Carton M 3, liasse 5, cover letter sent with the budget for 1818.

51. Carton T 2, liasse 1, letter from P. Daru dated March 4, 1806.

52. Register Vc 4, fol. 29 ff., letter dated October 14, 1811; carton T 7, liasse 1, dossier 4, letter dated February 21, 1814.

53. Carton T 10, liasse 1, dossier 5.

54. [. . . les frais pour exécuter les grandes pièces que la manufacture fait et doit faire . . . pour soutenir son caractère et atteindre son but sont très considérables et . . . les prix que je porte aux pièces, quelqu'élevés qu'ils paroissent au premier aspect, sont foibles en comparaison des soins apportés dans toutes les parties de la fabrication et des difficultés de leur succès . . .] Carton T 8, liasse 1, dossier 2, letter dated July 1, 1817, to the comte de Pradel.

55. *Versailles et les tables royales,* exhib. cat. (1993 – 94), pp. 216 – 24.

56. Carton T 12, liasse 2, dossier 6, letter dated May 12, 1829.

57. Carton T 9, liasse 3, dossier 2, letter dated September 24, 1822.

58. [Au reste . . . je ne puis me lasser de répéter parce qu'il est de mon devoir de le faire . . . l'écoulement des produits de la manufacture aura plus d'activité et auroit lieu de la manière la plus convenable à son institution si les ministres et les chefs supérieurs de la haute administration vouloient donner l'exemple du bon goût et de la préférence qu'ils accordent à la perfection sur la richesse apparente en plaçant dans l'ameublement de leurs hôtels et de leurs tables quelques pièces soignées de la manufacture . . . si le ministre des Affaires étrangères au lieu de composer ses présents diplomatiques uniquement de bijoux d'or et de diamant y fesoit entrer pour une certaine partie quelques objets précieux et riches des manufactures royales notemment de celle de porcelaine . . .] Register Vc 7, fol. 158 ff., letter dated August 10, 1827.

59. [des perfectionnements inventés dans les fabriques de Paris] Register Vc 4, fol. 109v. ff., letter dated September 13, 1814.

60. [pièces de différents genres et qualités, bonnes ou défectueuses, principalement d'anciennes formes ou d'anciennes décorations notamment des tableaux de fleurs, quelques grands vases . . . le tout coloré, peint et doré; plus une grande quantité de pièces de porcelaine blanche en rebut et d'anciennes formes tant dure que tendre et une assez grande quantité de pièces de sculpture dit biscuit . . .] Carton M 6, liasse 1, dossier 3.

61. In a letter dated January 19, 1827, Paul Noualhier attributed the extent of this failure to "the bad faith and intrigue of all the merchants who worked together to obtain the soft paste and white porcelains at the lowest prices . . . except for the early days of the sale, when they had not had time to reach an understanding among themselves. But thereafter the soft-paste fell to roughly the price of hard-paste" [. . . la mauvaise foi et l'intrigue de tous ses marchands qui se coalisent pour avoir la porcelaine tendre et blanche au plus bas prix . . . eccepté cependant les premiers jours ou on l'a mise en vente et ou ils n'avoient pas eu le temps de s'entendre entre eux. Mais depuis ce temps elle est tombée a peu de chose près au prix de la dure . . .] (carton U 4, liasse 3).

62. The poster for the sale announced: "Groups and figures in biscuit in the Greek, Etruscan, Louis XIV, and Louis XV styles; imitation Woodwood pieces [sic]. White pieces of all kinds; pieces with high-fire grounds of blue, green, and other colors: all ready for decoration" [. . . groupes et figures en biscuit des styles grecs, etrusques et des siècles de Louis XIV et de Louis XV; pièces à l'imitation de Woodwood. Pièces en blanc de toute nature; pièces en fond au grand feu, bleu vert et autres couleurs: le tout préparé pour être décoré . . .] (carton U 4, liasse 4, dossier 2).

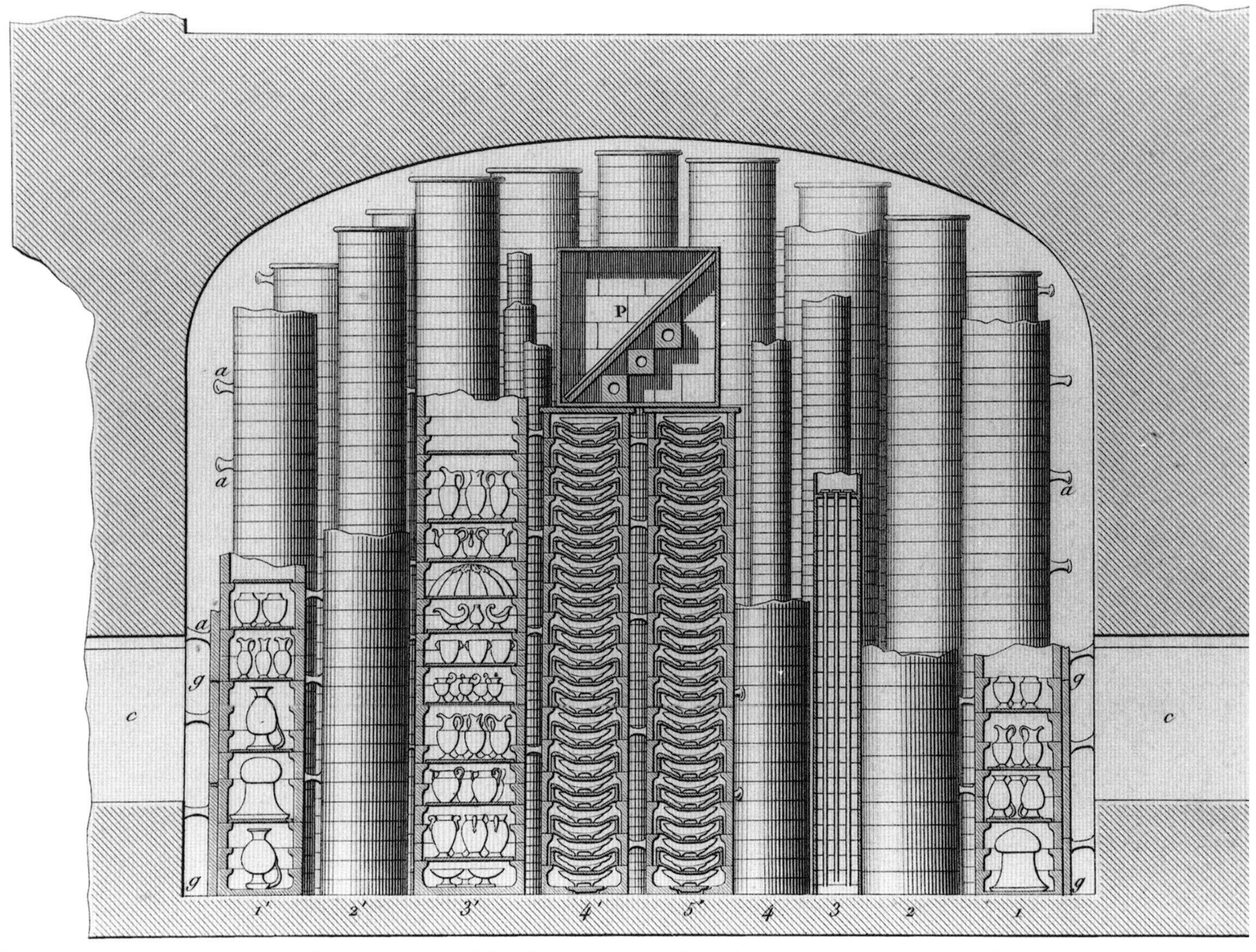

Fig. 4-1. Saggars stacked in one of the kiln chambers before firing. (From Brongniart, *Traité des arts céramiques* [1844], Atlas, pl. 52, detail)

Chapter 4

Brongniart as Technician

Tamara Preaud

One of the factors influencing the selection of Brongniart as director of the Sèvres porcelain manufactory, despite his professional inexperience, was a conviction that only a mineralogist and chemist would possess the knowledge needed to bring about improvements at all stages of porcelain production. This faith in the potential of science, which was typical of the period, was not misplaced in the case of the new Sèvres administrator; Brongniart would take interest in all technical and scientific aspects of the manufactory's operations.

The process of making porcelain came under the aegis of the manufactory's first large subdivision, the Department of Kilns and Pastes. From preparation of the paste to an object's entry into the stock of undecorated pieces, this division oversaw production. It was responsible for the shaping of the clay and the firing of kilns (fig. 4-1), including the first bisque firing and the subsequent glaze, or glost, firings. The department was headed by Jean-Baptiste Chanou l'aîné, who was succeeded in 1825 by Jean-Marie-Ferdinand Régnier. A skillful craftsman, Régnier not only designed several forms and introduced new techniques (fig. 4-2; also see cat. no. 31), but also made important technical innovations and was generally acknowledged by Brongniart as being very ingenious.

One of Brongniart's first decisions with respect to the operations of the manufactory involved this department. It was a decision particularly fraught with consequences. In a report dated 1 Germinal year 9 (March 22, 1801), the new director announced to the entire staff the "provisional" closing of the soft-paste workshop, which was a separate operation from the hard-paste workshop (see chap. 10). Several reasons were given for this extreme measure. Although the soft-paste porcelain had in fact established the excellent reputation of the Sèvres manufactory in the eighteenth century, soft paste unfortunately did not possess the same advantages as hard-paste porcelain made with kaolin. Given the shortage of funding and the staff dismissals, particularly of older workers who had been responsible for soft-paste production, the manufactory could no longer afford to produce two pastes. Soft paste also entailed considerable expenditure, and it sold poorly.[1] The decision was much criticized later in the nineteenth century when eighteenth-century porcelain had returned to fashion and was avidly sought by collectors. Admittedly, the grave circumstances in which the manufactory found itself in 1801 — lacking adequate personnel, sufficient funds, or raw materials — made such a consolidation of resources inevitable. The decision was also doubtless influenced by the fact that neoclassicism was then at its height, and soft-paste porcelain had come to epitomize the aesthetic excesses associated with the rococo.

Fig. 4-2. A cup from the *déjeuner 'Régnier à reliefs',* 1812. Biscuit relief was used against, in this case, a gold ground. (Sèvres, Musée national de céramique)

Despite later shifts in taste that eventually restored the reputation of the rococo and although there were several demands for rococo-style porcelain from the royal administration by the 1830s, Brongniart never seems to have envisioned resuming the actual production of soft-paste.[2] He preferred to devote his energies to hard paste, of which three variants were used: regular hard paste; hard paste for sculpture in biscuit; and a "Chinese" paste developed by Ferdinand Régnier that was much easier to work and was intended for very large pieces. The director's ongoing preoccupation and source of pride was in maintaining a high quality of work despite variations in raw materials from one delivery to the next.

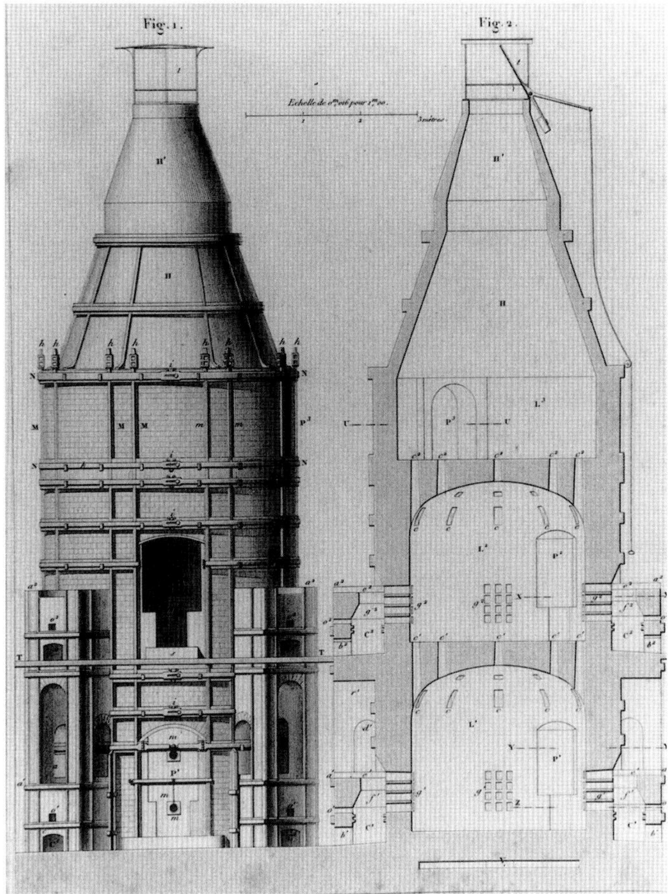

Fig. 4-3. The two-chambered high-fire kiln used at Sèvres during Brongniart's tenure. (From Brongniart, *Traité des arts céramiques* [1844], Atlas, pl. 50)

In January 1828 he decided to compare Sèvres porcelain paste with paste used by Paris porcelain makers which had been deemed "equally beautiful." It was his intention to abandon the manufactory's own paste unless it proved to be "superior to that of Paris." In the latter case, "we would retain the Sèvres manner of fabrication, even if we find no way of improving the success and cost [of our production]."[3] In 1830 he sent the vicomte de La Rochefoucauld a long report on the same subject.[4] He acknowledged that the paste from Limoges, which was used in Paris porcelain, was less expensive, easier to work, and less subject to damage in the course of firing than the Sèvres paste. Its receptivity to colors also allowed for better glazing and less flaking because of its greater fusibility with enamels. Nonetheless, Brongniart listed many qualities that he felt compelled him to retain Sèvres paste: it was whiter and more resistant to changes in temperature, and it produced edges and relief details that were finer and more precise. In addition, its glaze was more acid resistant and its colors and gilding were more durable. Ongoing chemical analysis must have led to improved pastes and enamels, but Brongniart emphasized that the physical condition of the materials, such as the degree of wetness, was just as important as their composition.

Brongniart also took an interest in the kilns used in both biscuit and glost firing. Not content to maintain, improve, and modify traditional kilns, he oversaw the construction in 1842 of a new type of kiln featuring two tiers of firing chambers surmounted by a third space for bisque firing (fig. 4-3). This must have seemed rather audacious, for the following year the porcelain maker Édouard Honoré wrote to him: "I dare not adopt this innovation for the kiln I am constructing . . . . Perhaps I will be bolder after having seen it function."[5]

When it came to combustible fuels, Brongniart had a marked preference for wood over coal and peat that were just beginning to be used for firing ceramics in France in the early nineteenth century. When consulted in 1811 about "Sieur Monginot's proposal to fire porcelain at the manufactory with coal," he responded: "It is possible

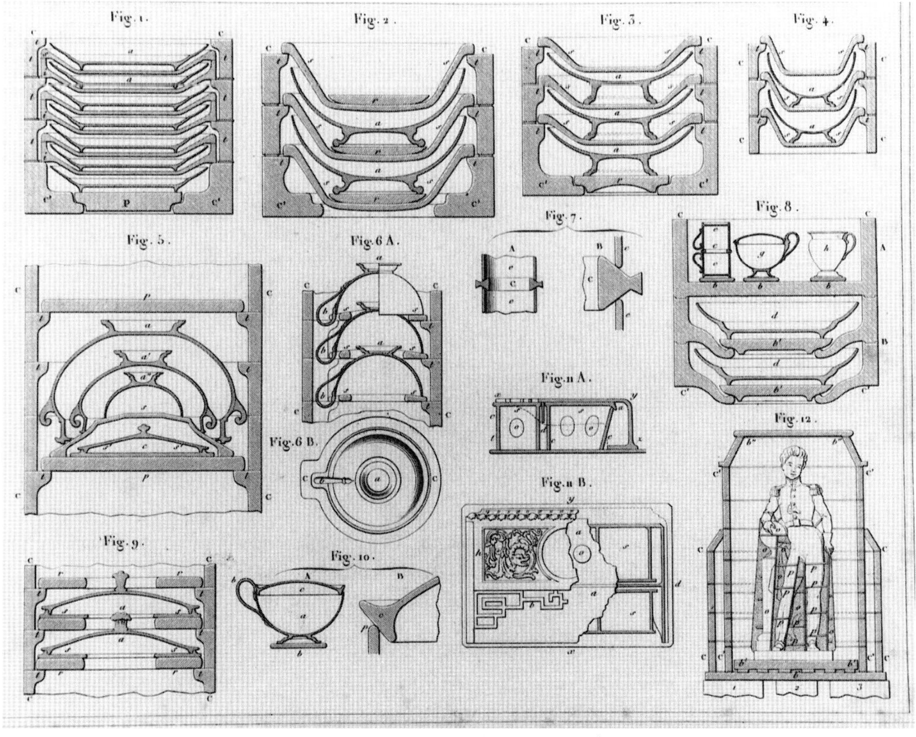

Fig. 4-4. Saggar designs, including those introduced by Régnier (top left), used for a variety of forms, from plates to sculpture. (From Brongniart, *Traité des arts céramiques* [1844], Atlas, pl. 49)

Fig. 4-5. View of the throwing room at Sèvres, from a sketch by Jean-Charles Develly. The worker in the foreground is throwing a vase on a plaster bat attached to his wheel, while the worker in the background uses a metal trimming tool to finish shaping a vase. He refers to the drawing pinned on the back wall as his model. The calipers hanging nearby are used to measure the thickness of the piece. (From Brongniart, *Traité des arts céramiques* [1844], Atlas, pl. 46, fig. 3)

Fig. 4-6. View of the mold-making room, from a sketch by Jean Charles Develly. The worker (A, far right), is rolling out a slab of porcelain paste; another worker (B, left center), positions a slab on a mold for a fluted bowl, and a third worker (C, left), uses a damp sponge to press the paste into every cavity of the mold. Another worker (G, right center), has just removed a handle from the mold and is cleaning it and correcting any flaws before attaching it to the *sucrier*, or sugar server, beside him. (From Brongniart, *Traité des arts céramiques* [1844], Atlas, pl. 46, fig. 1)

and even probable that porcelain could be fired in this way, but it seems to me very likely that despite any precautions taken the porcelain would always be less white than that which we fire with wood."[6] He seems to have kept informed about experiments with coal- and peat-fueled kilns without ever becoming convinced that any savings that might result would be achieved without diminished quality.

Notable progress was made in another aspect of glost firing, namely *encastage*, or firing in saggars. This technique involved placing pieces in enclosed saggars, or containers, that protected them from direct contact with the flames during firing. The saggars were piled up inside the kiln to maximize the use of available space, thereby reducing fuel costs, without compromising the stability of the stacks or impeding circulation of the heated air during the firing. The first improvement was the introduction of *cul-de-lampe*, or concave, saggars which could be stacked more compactly and securely (fig. 4-4). The new saggars seem to have been adopted first at Sèvres in 1814 and were "generally accepted in the factories of Paris" by about 1819.[7] In 1839 Régnier devised a refinement that further maximized the use of space and also reduced the amount of ash falling that could spoil the pieces. For this innovation, Brongniart awarded him a bonus of 2,000 francs[8] and gave Régnier's name to the process, which Brongniart published in the *Bulletin de la Société d'Encouragement*[9] and explained in his own treatise, *Traité des arts céramique* . . . .[10]

Although Brongniart admitted that when it came to shaping the

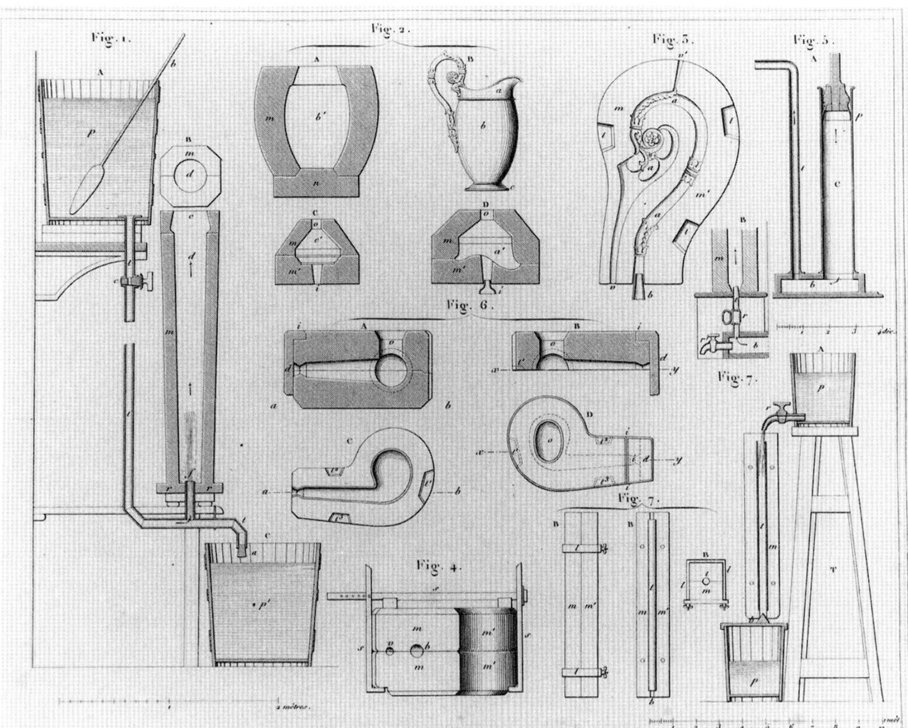

Fig. 4-7: Slip-casting equipment, including molds used to make columns, milk jugs and their handles, and other forms. (From Brongniart, *Traité des arts céramiques* [1844], Atlas, pl. 47)

piece, the Sèvres manufactory was "under an obligation to finish with a care, a perfection, and a brilliance that no commercial consideration should hinder,"[11] he adopted — as supplements to the traditional techniques of throwing on the wheel and using molds (figs. 4-5 and 4-6) — a certain number of new procedures, some of which were intended to lighten the workload of the personnel.

The date of the first attempts at slip casting is not known (fig. 4-7), but it was initially used for plaques meant to embellish furniture or serve as a foundation for painted compositions. In 1824 a pump was used "for the slip casting of clock-candelabra, table legs, and other furnishings."[12] Aside from complicated or large objects, slip casting in plaster molds was used primarily to make laboratory equipment, such as retorts and tubes, which the manufactory produced in large quantities.[13] Thus a memorandum on the staff meeting of November 17, 1821, states that "two small busts made by the slip-casting process represent no improvement in the matter of economy," while the cast tubes "are much improved, they are of perfectly consistent thickness, very uniform and smooth inside."[14]

The jiggering technique was much more difficult to perfect due to the characteristics of the paste. As with slip casting, it seems to have had limited applications: apparently, it was used only for plates. Brongniart saw a jigger in operation at the Imperial Viennese Porcelain Manufactory in 1812,[15] but he seems to have waited for the return of Ferdinand Régnier from Paris in 1820 before trying one out at Sèvres.[16] As a designer, Régnier also contributed to the fabrication of new machinery used at Sèvres. At the meeting of November 17, 1821, the head of the Department of Kilns and Pastes presented "plates made with a jigger which produces a result so satisfying with regard to fabrication and successful outcome to justify Monsieur the administrator's deciding to have a jigger made and to have this mode of fabrication continued by a thrower paid on a monthly basis."[17]

This recommendation was not followed, however, perhaps because of unexpected difficulties. It was probably the enormous quantity of plates needed for the various palaces under Louis-Philippe that revived interest in the process some twenty years later. In August 1841, in response to a query from Charles Pillivuyt, Brongniart acknowledged that jiggering had not yet been perfected,[18] and the first jiggered plates did not appear in the sales inventory until 1842. Once the process had been mastered, however, it was definitively adopted, and all plates made after 1842 bear on their reverse the telltale raised rings left by the jiggering process.

One of the advantages of Régnier's firing in saggars technique was a reduction in the number of pieces spoiled by falling ash in the course of firing. To salvage damaged pieces, however, Brongniart had them polished on a hand-turned lapidary lathe,[19] but he soon replaced this equipment with a motorized lathe (fig. 4-8) developed at Chantilly. This mechanism was also used to remove areas of glaze before pieces were loaded into the kiln. These areas — such as feet or the rims of pieces that were fired upside down — had to be left unglazed to keep the piece from fusing to the saggars or each other during firing and to prevent warping. Once the piece was fired, the unglazed area could be gilded directly if necessary.

Finally, the manufactory perfected the fabrication of double-walled vessels such as the *cafetière 'Chinoise réticulée'* (see cat. no. 76); the outer wall featured openwork patterns and the inner one served as the actual vessel wall. The production of these pieces, each a technical tour de force, was inspired by Chinese models, and the technique was explained and illustrated in Brongniart's *Traité* (fig. 4-9).[20]

Other shaping processes had more ephemeral production lives. One such case is the artificial tulle devised in 1812 by Benoît Chanou for his *Amour assis dans un fauteuil garni de tulle* known as the Lace Cupid. Chanou soaked a piece of lace in slip, applied it to his sculpture, and fired the whole; the fibers burned away but the porcelain retained the lace's shape and openwork pattern. Brongniart thought

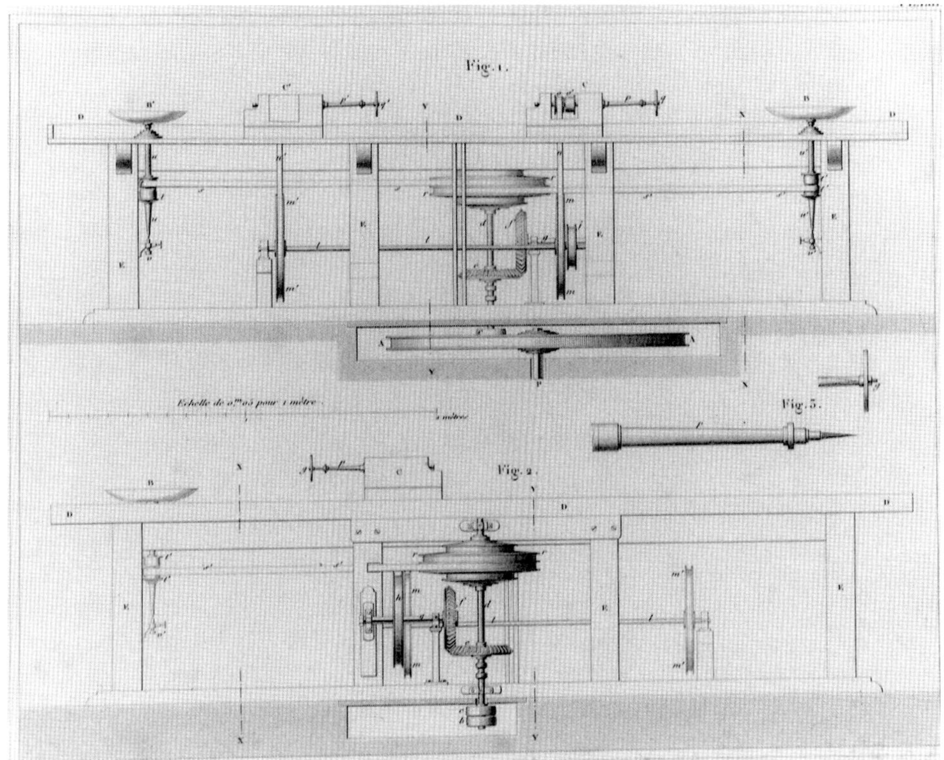

Fig. 4-8. Two views of the polishing lathe used at Sèvres. (From Brongniart, *Traité des arts céramiques* [1844], Atlas, pl. 53)

that the process would have limited applications and that in any event it was unfashionable at that time.[21] Accordingly, he authorized the inventor to produce only enough examples to satisfy market demand. Brongniart's judgment proved incorrect, however; the Lace Cupid became one of the manufactory's most popular items in the first quarter of the nineteenth century.

In 1818 Brongniart acquired from Honoré Boudon de Saint-Amans the right to use his molding process, which employed a special paste developed for cameos to be incorporated in crystal and fixed on the piece under the glaze (see cat. no. 48).[22] It is not clear whether this same mixture was subsequently used for handles and ornaments, but the fact that it is not mentioned in the *Traité* suggests that it was not.

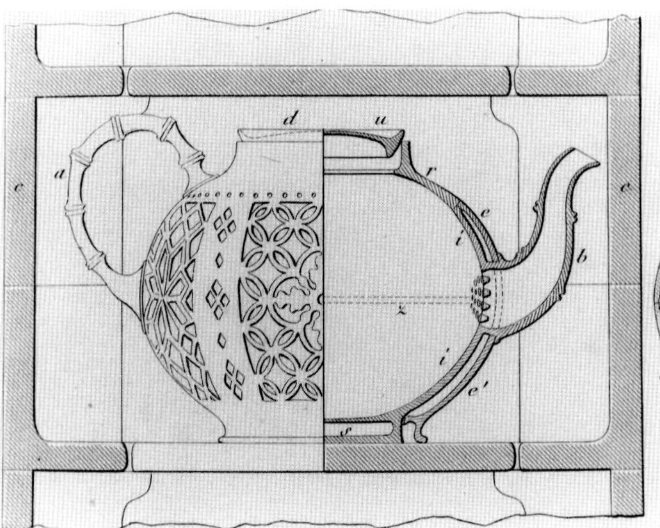

Fig. 4-9. Cross-section of a reticulated teapot called *théière 'Chinoise Réticulée',* in a saggar, showing the double-wall construction of the pot. (From Brongniart, *Traité des arts céramiques* [1844], Atlas, pl. 48, detail)

When asked for advice about the pricing of pieces by the porcelain maker Dagoty, Brongniart wrote: "The merit of porcelain consists primarily in the solidity and beauty of the paste, the selective choice of forms, good taste and composition in the ornament, of whatever kind, the brilliance, solidity, and consistent appropriate glazing of the colors, the talent of true artists who have painted the flowers, landscapes, and figures."[23] This blend of technical and aesthetic criteria remained characteristic of Sèvres work during Brongniart's tenure. Apparently, the quality of the colors was considered just as important as the skill of the artists using them, which explains the establishment of a new department for "the preparation and firing of colors and gilding." It was first directed by Charles-Louis-Marie Méraud, followed by Pierre Desfossés, and Jean-Augustin Bunel, previously a color preparer and ground applier, who beginning in 1841 was assisted by the chemist Alphonse-Louis Salvetat.

Just as he had abandoned soft paste, Brongniart found himself obliged, after a final, fifteen-day firing in November 1801,[24] to give up the remarkable tunnel kiln for the firing of colors and gilding.[25] It had been developed by Claude-Humbert Gérin in 1748 when the manufactory was located at Vincennes,[26] and had been moved to Sèvres in 1756 where it was used until 1801 for the firing of both soft and hard paste. Financial considerations had always made it necessary to wait until a large number of pieces were ready before proceeding with the firing of painted pieces. In the first years of the nineteenth century, economic hardships had reduced the number of painters and gilders, thus making this kiln even more uneconomical. Its continuous firing was quite expensive because it required night labor. Accordingly, the new director chose ". . . a means of firing painting that is simpler, faster, and more economical. The means in question are the small kilns known as muffle kilns."[27] This type of kiln contained an inner box or lining (the muffle), which acted as a large saggar and protected the work from combustion gases and ashfall during firing. Only the large plaques used for copies of paintings and the stained and painted windows ordered by Louis-Philippe posed problems by virtue of their size and shape, necessitating the design and construction of special muffle kilns of unusually large dimensions.

In 1803 the administrator presented the Institut de France with a new pyrometer using silver rather than mercury and capable of measuring the temperatures within these kilns with greater precision. Nevertheless, countless complaints from artists about damage to their work during firing might suggest that technical instruments were still inadequate. That the porcelain painters Abraham Constantin and Marie-Victoire Jaquotot, disappointed by the results of trial firings made at Doccia, Italy, preferred to run the risk of sending their large plaques from Italy to Sèvres for firing is evidence of the manufactory's technical excellence.

At the end of the eighteenth century, the range of colors capable of resisting the high temperatures necessary to vitrify glazes was limited to cobalt blue (its intensity varying according to the thickness of the application), tortoise-shell brown, and combinations of the two. To these Brongniart soon added a brilliant green based on the chrome that had recently been discovered. In the *Traité*, he dates its introduction at Sèvres to 1802[28] but without indicating that he was responsible for it.[29] In fact, this material must have presented certain problems initially, for in a report of 1806 the administrator refers to the "chromium green for glost firing," specifying that it is "an entirely new colored ground."[30] Eventually these colors were supplemented by a titanium-oxide yellow and a uranium-oxide black.

The adoption of a new procedure for applying high-temperature ground colors by immersion in the glaze (fig. 4-10) rather than application by hand prior to glost firing prompted Bunel to develop additional hues. The first attempts were made in April 1831, "in imitation of a small green vase given [to the museum] by a Parisian manufacturer."[31] In October of that year, a few pieces with green grounds achieved through immersion were presented at the staff meeting and judged to have a "rich and brilliant tone."[32] Despite this success, the experiments seem to have been discontinued until 1837 when the manufactory strove to create pieces "in imitation of German cups,"[33] probably because two Parisian porcelain makers — Discry and Hallot — were producing similar colors.[34] Several samples were displayed at the Louvre exhibition on May 1, 1838, when the catalogue specified that the colors had been developed by Bunel; mention is also made there of an applied platinum gray for glost firing developed by the manufactory's colored-ground specialist Paul Noualhier.

By chance, the earlier suspension of these experiments contributed to the development of a new method of decoration. Some of the ground colors that had been prepared for the 1831 immersion experiments had long since dried and had not been used in the 1837 tests. They were, therefore, still available in 1840 for Ferdinand Régnier's "experiments in ornament with colored inlaid paste like that in so-called Henri II earthenware" (made in the sixteenth century and now known as Saint-Porchaire earthenware). He had seen shards of this pottery at the museum. His experiments resulted in inlay decorations which were first exhibited at the Louvre in 1842 in the *vase 'Arabe Dauzats'* (see cat. nos. 91 and 99).

The range of colors for high-temperature firing was limited to metallic oxides capable of resisting very high temperatures. On the other hand, given the glaze's low fusibility, muffle-fired colors (both grounds and painted decoration) tended to flake or were often somewhat matte. To avoid these two drawbacks, Bunel developed a series of colors that he called *demi- grand feu* or *couleurs de moufle dures*, a breakthrough for which he received a bonus of 500 francs.[35] As the

Fig. 4-10. View of the glaze room at Sèvres, from a sketch by Jean-Charles Develly. One worker (left) is passing a plate through the glaze, while another (center left) redips a plate, this time vertically in the glaze. The two women are retouching pieces, either brushing on extra glaze to cover thin spots (center right) or removing glaze from the foot ring (right) to prevent the plate from sticking to the saggar during the firing. (From Brongniart, *Traité des arts céramiques* [1844], Atlas, pl. 46, fig. 2)

Fig. 4-11. Plate from the *service 'des Arts Industriels',* Sèvres, 1835; hard-paste porcelain. The frieze along the border is probably transfer-printed. (Museum of Art, Rhode Island School of Design)

French terms suggest, these colors were fired in muffle kilns but at temperatures that were higher than usual, falling between the customary parameters of glost and muffle firing.

Apparently, Brongniart was not fully satisfied with the available range of background colors. In January 1839 he invited Bunel and Louis Robert, then head of the painting-on-glass workshop, "to try developing colors for both glost and muffle firings like the Chinese ones that the administrator will point out . . .."[36] The request apparently went unheeded. On the other hand, in a dossier devoted to "Chinese red for glost firing," Salvetat noted: "In a written instruction dated January 10, 1845, M. Brongniart called my attention to the richness and brilliance of the singular grounds hitherto found only on Chinese porcelain. At the same time, he had me undertake to study their veritable nature in view of reproducing them."[37] Brongniart died before he could see the first results of these experiments which were made on a piece of hard paste whose glost firing was successfully completed on May 31, 1848.

The range of colors available for muffle firing was considerably wider, and Brongniart devoted special attention to them. Certain nuances, however, could be obtained at Sèvres only with preparations developed by Parisian specialists. In 1826 Bunel wrote to Brongniart: "I . . . hope to assemble a complete assortment, for only three colors are now lacking: indigo blue, deep yellow, and golden yellow."[38] At a staff meeting held on August 30, 1827, "the members . . . , consulted about colors lacking from the collection that might be obtainable in Paris, declared that all that was now lacking for painting with the best means currently available were the following colors: grays for flesh . . . the series of reds for flesh. There are several very good ones but the series is incomplete . . . purple. That of M. Mortelèque is generally more beautiful."[39] Notes from 1830 indicate that in the interim the situation had not changed.

In fact, not all of the formulas in question were the property of Sèvres; some belonged to specialists who marketed them to other clients as well. Pierre Robert, who headed the painting-on-glass workshop prior to his son Louis, had at his disposal a series of colors judged by Abraham Constantin in 1827 to be more complete than Bunel's.[40] Bunel's case was a special one: in addition to the formulas made known to him when he began to work for the manufactory, he knew others "taken from a manuscript I prepared for myself from notes by my father-in-law, M. Weydinger, who was making colors twenty years before I met him, and from those by Meyer communicated by Monginot."[41] He found it normal to be marketing his own property, and Brongniart seems to have authorized this for a time.[42] In 1836, however, Brongniart convinced Bunel to turn over all his formulas for publication in the *Traité.* In any event, each delivery of colors was carefully tested by Denis-Desiré Riocreux and examined in conference with others; samples of all accepted colors were then turned over to the museum to assure the quality control that was crucial to the establishment's reputation.

Gilding techniques, however, remained quite traditional. Precipitated gold had been used on hard paste from the moment this porcelain had been introduced in the 1770s, while gold obtained by

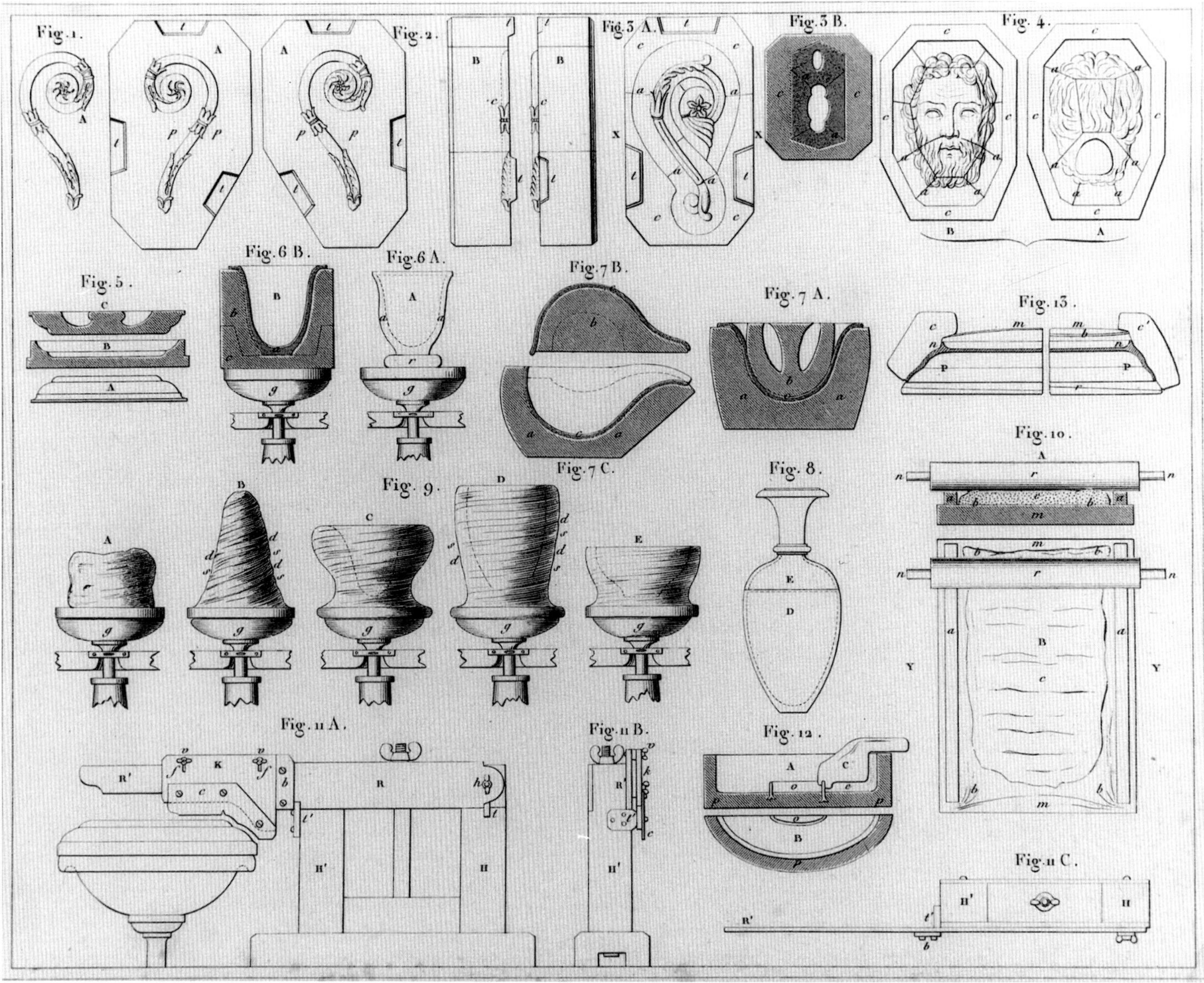

Fig. 4-12. Some of the equipment used at Sèvres during Brongniart's administration included: molds for handles, portrait heads, plates, cups, sauceboats (top two rows); the traditional potter's wheel, in this case demonstrating stages in throwing the body of a vase in two sections, to which other parts would be added (row 3); a slab roller (row 3, right); and the jigger that was used for making plates (bottom row). (From Brongniart, *Traité des arts céramiques* [1844], Atlas, pl. 55)

crushing gold leaf, subsequently known as *en coquille*, was consistently employed for soft paste. There were several periods when in order to improve the durability of gilding, it was applied and fired before pieces were painted.[43]

In addition to the introduction of these technical improvements and innovations, several special workshops were established. The earliest was the transfer-printing workshop which opened in 1806 following an agreement with François-Antoine Legros d'Anizy, an applier of colored grounds at Sèvres since 1802.[44] The porcelain transfer-printing process, effected with etched or engraved copperplates, was initially used solely to print the gold, crowned "N"s (for Napoleon) on services for the imperial palaces; the accompanying myrtle friezes and branches (often used to hide imperfections) were painted by hand. Gradually, its use became more widespread. In 1808 Dominique-Vivant Denon lent the manufactory the copper plates with portraits of Italian artists that he had etched, for printing in brown or sepia on porcelain. Then the first printed ornamental motifs such as stars and filigree appeared, followed by more complex applications. After 1815 Legros's workshop did little more than print identifying manufactory marks on the backs of pieces.

Advances in the use of porcelain transfer-printing continued, however, thanks largely to the gilder Charles-Louis Constans, who was placed in charge of printing friezes (fig. 4-11) and other motifs on table services in 1817. This application was practicable only when the service was sufficiently large to justify the preparation of a plate. Constans was also responsible for printing decorative motifs such as emblems on small vases and other ornamental pieces. The printing was sometimes carried out in brown or black, in which case it was used as a foundation for hand-applied colors instead of gold. Brongniart insisted on repeated tests of the durability of gilding applied in this way before approving the method for general use. Despite the efforts of both Legros and Constans, Brongniart never seems to have developed an interest in lithography as a tool of the manufactory.[45]

Brongniart had always maintained that the manufactory should concern itself with "vitreous and ceramic arts" insofar as they used enamels that were fired, and in 1827 he received authorization to open a workshop for painting on glass (see chap. 7).

Finally, on the occasion of the Louvre exhibition of June 1, 1846, Brongniart devoted a special section of the catalogue to enamels on metal, about which he wrote: "The king desired that we supplement paintings made with vitrifiable colors on porcelain with enamel decorations on metal, which produce a brilliant effect quite distinct from that of colorations on porcelain. His Majesty asked that we renew the fabrication of enameled pieces in the manner of the Limosins, incorporating improvements to be expected in light of advances in the chemical sciences."[46] This represented a return to origins of sorts: Brongniart's essay on enamels on metal, "L'Art de l'émailleur sur métaux,"[47] had been one of the principal justifications for his appointment to Sèvres.

Although this workshop did not open officially until September 1845, there is evidence of experiments along these lines dating from much earlier. On December 16, 1838, Brongniart wrote: "M. Meyer showed me a small black-ground goblet with grisaille flowers and ornament that he made from scratch and that seemed to me a complete success"; he then decided to ask J. C. F. Leloy to design "a footed bowl whose size and disposition I will indicate to him" before paying another visit to Meyer, "who was brought to me by M. Wattier."[48] The results must have been satisfactory, and Jacob Meyer-Heine was permanently engaged in 1840 to head the enamel-on-metal workshop.

As was his custom, and perhaps following the lead of his Parisian competitors, Brongniart began by testing on porcelain the effect produced by white or colored enamels against black grounds (see cat. no. 106), and he might have used the resulting pieces to convince the sovereign to establish the specialized workshop. The latter was in operation from 1845 to 1872[49]; in addition to the pieces inspired by French Renaissance work that were ordered by Louis-Philippe, from the beginning it also produced pieces influenced by Eastern models (see cat. no. 109).[50]

Finally, one last workshop had a very special status. At a meeting held on March 19, 1819, the administrator announced regulations "pertaining to the permanent organization and work of the mounting workshop" provisionally established on January 16, 1815.[51] In an effort to obtain low prices without any compromise in qualiry and to avoid the repeated, perilous transfer of merchandise between Sèvres and Paris, these regulations created a department consisting of "workshops for mounting and garnishing in gilt bronze, iron, copper, and other metals or materials, and for joining and trimming pieces of fired porcelain." Under the terms of an agreement dated March 22, 1819, these workshops were placed under the direction of the modeler and mounter Louis-Honoré Bocquet.[52] He was employed *à l'entreprise*, whereby he was paid a predetermined sum for each job. He then shared this amount with the workers in his employ who were not affiliated with the manufactory. Sèvres commissions were accorded priority, but if these projects did not fully occupy the time of his personnel they could accept outside jobs, having first obtained Brongniart's authorization. This arrangement made it possible for Brongniart to manage the amount of work given to the mount-making department, depending on his budget.

As might be expected, Brongniart was extremely attentive to all technical aspects of production. He was kept informed about new developments in ceramic production in general. If he did not adopt each innovation, it was because he directed a small manufactory with a limited production. Introduction of early mechanized techniques would have been of limited utility and would have led to a backlog of objects in the decoration workshops. In reality, the true beginnings of industrialization in ceramic production date from the second half of the nineteenth century. Brongniart, who died in 1847, did not live to face the choice between mechanization and the preservation of the manual techniques that prevailed in his tenure. Even his most virulent critics never questioned the extraordinary technical quality of the pieces produced under his direction.

Ed. note: The documents cited below are from the Archives of the Manufacture Nationale de Sèvres.

1. Carton M 1 and register Y 4.

2. Surprisingly the first person to object to this decision was Dominique-Vivant Denon, who wrote to Brongniart on April 26, 1807: "Since Etruscan vases are selling so well, why don't you make more of them, and why don't you make them in soft paste? This would be an excellent way to propagate good taste, for in vases that's where it resides exclusively" [puisque les vases étrusques partent avec tant de rapidité, pourquoi n'en faites-vous pas davantage, et pourquoi n'en faites-vous pas en porcelaine tendre? C'est le grand moyen de propager le bon goût puisqu'en vases c'est là qu'il réside exclusivement] (carton T 3, liasse 1, dossier 3).

3. Carton N 1.

4. Register Vc 8, fol. 67v ff., letter dated July 10, 1830.

5. [je n'ose pas adopter cette innovation pour le four que je vais construire . . . Peut-être serai-je plus hardi après l'avoir vu fonctionner] Carton T 14, liasse 4, dossier 15.

6. [Sieur Monginot d'essayer à la manufacture de cuire la porcelaine au charbon de terre . . . il est possible et même probable qu'on pourra cuire la porcelaine par ce moyen, mais il me paroît très probable que, quelque précaution qu'on employe, la porcelaine sera toujours moins blanche que celle que nous cuisons au bois] Register Vc 4, fol. 26v ff. letter to the minister of the interior dated September 12, 1811.

7. Carton U 14, liasse 3, note from Jean-Baptiste Chanou aîné.

8. Carton R 33 (1839), notice of expenditures dated July 31, 1839.

9. *Bulletin de la Société d'Encouragement* 38, p. 308.

10. Brongniart, *Traité des art céramiques* . . . (1844), vol. 2, pp. 312 – 15.

11. [dans l'obligation de fabriquer avec un soin, une perfection et un éclat auxquels aucune considération commericale ne doit mettre d'entrave] Ibid., p. 279.

12. Carton U 15, liasse 3, dossier 1.

13. Until the discovery of deflocculants at the end of the nineteenth century, paste diluted with water was used in slip casting.

14. [deux petits bustes faits par le procédé du coulage ne présentent aucun avantage sous le rapport de l'économie] [présentent une amélioration sensible, ils sont d'une parfaite égalité d'épaisseur, très unis et lisses intérieurement] Register Y 13, fol. 41.

15. Brongniart, *Traité des art céramiques* . . . (1844), vol. 2, p. 281.

16. Régnier was paid in 1820 for "17 days' work on experiments with jiggered plates" [17 jours employés à des assiettes d'essai au calibre] (register Va' 23, fol. 158v). In the first trimester of 1822 Régnier was paid for "two days for designing a machine for jiggering plates" [deux jours pour le dessin d'une machine pour calibrer les assiettes] (Register Va' 24, fol. no. 135).

17. [des assiettes faites au calibre qui donnent un résultat assez satisfaisant sous le rapport de la fabrication et de la réussite pour que Morsieur l'administrateur se décide à faire faire un calibre et à faire continuer cette fabrication par un tourneur au mois] Register Y 13, fol. 41.

18. Letter dated August 17, 1841: "As for plate jiggering, this is a well-known fabrication process used in all the manufactories in Germany, at Chantilly etc. and putting it into practice would be as simple as could be. But such is not the case with the process we've been developing for quite some time without yet achieving the desired results, thinking each time we've gotten it right but never having it . . . . I know well that this is partly due to the character of our paste, but we still don't regard the process as sufficiently perfect to be described publicly. And it is only after the publication of our discoveries that we place them in the public domain. That's the only thing to which the royal manufacture is profoundly attached; to have, *for her honor*, the priority of her useful and new process" [quand au calibrage des assiettes, c'est un procédé de fabrication bien

connu, tel qu'il se pratique dans toutes les manufactures d'Allemagne, à Chantilly, etc. et pour le mettre en pratique c'est la chose la plus simple. Mais il n'en est pas ainsi du procédé que nous poursuivons depuis bien long-temps sans être encore arrivés au résultat que nous désirons, croyant chaque fois le tenir et ne l'ayant jamais . . . . je sais bien que cela tient en partie à la susceptibilité de notre pâte; mais enfin nous ne regardons pas le procédé comme encore assez parfait pour être décrit en public. Or ce n'est qu'après la publication de nos nouveautés que nous les mettons dans le domaine public. C'est la seule chose à laquelle tienne essentiellement la manufacture royale, c'est d'avorir *pour l'honneur* la priorité de ses travaux utiles et nouveaux . . .] (carton T 14, liasse 2, dossier 5).

19. Brongniart, *Traité des art céramiques* . . . (1844), vol. 2, pp. 345 – 48.

20. Ibid., vol. 2, pp. 292 – 93.

21. Carton T 6, liasse 1, dossier 5, letter to the Intendant Général dated February 12, 1812.

22. Carton U 15, liasse 2, dossier 1.

23. Register Vc 4, fol. 7 ff., letter dated April 3, 1811.

24. Register Y 4, decision dated 15 Pluviôse year 9 (February 5, 1801).

25. Brongniart, *Traité des art céramiques* . . . (1844), vol. 2, pp. 663 – 64.

26. Préaud and d'Albis, *La Porcelaine de Vincennes* (1991), p. 223.

27. [un moyen de cuire la peinture plus simple, plus expéditif et plus économique. Ce moyen, ce sont les petits fours nommés moufles] Carton T 1, liasse 6, dossier 5, letter dated 25 Germinal year 13 (April 15, 1805). Muffle kilns were not new and had long been used elsewhere.

28. Brongniart, *Traité des art céramiques* . . . (1844), vol. 2, p. 514.

29. In a report on colors for glost firing, Bunel wrote: "When chromium was discovered, its oxide was used for glost firing, and the first [chromium green] was fabricated at Sèvres by the administrator . . . . I was the administrator's aid on this occasion" [à l'époque de la découverte du chrôme, son oxide fut employé au grand feu, et le premier fut fabriqué à Sèvres par l'administrateur . . . j'étais aide de Mr. L'administrateur à cette occasion] (carton N 3, dossier 2 F). Brongniart was in contact with many chemists prior to his arrival at Sèvres, among them the discoverer of chromium, Louis-Nicolas Vauquelin.

30. Carton Pb 1, liasse 1, dossier 15, "Aperçu des principaux travaux en train au 1er juin 1806."

31. On colors for glost firing, see carton N 3, dossier 2 F, report from J. A. Bunel.

32. Register Y 14, fol. 40v., meeting of October 22, 1831.

33. Carton N 3, dossier 2 F.

34. Ibid. In a letter dating from 1839, Discry writes of immersion-applied glazes, which he had shown to the Société d'Encouragement, and underglaze relief decorations made with ground bisque and sugar, painted in blue on a celadon ground, a process which must have led to the development of the so-called *pâte-sur-pâte* technique (Préaud, "Sèvres: La pâte-sur-pâte" [1992], pp. 46 – 57).

35. Brongniart, *Traité des art céramiques* . . . (1844), vol. 2, pp. 546, 583 – 84; Carton R 93 (1839).

36. Register Y 14, fol. 139v, meeting of January 22, 1839. In a small dossier on remarkable pieces of Chinese porcelain, Riocreux noted "two bottles of a purplish, copper red" [deux bouteilles rouge purpurin de cuivre] seen at the merchant Houssaye's in Paris in February 1836 and a handled bottle made of "richly decorated celadon" [céladon richement orné] seen at Roussel's in September 1831 (carton U 15, liasse 2, dossier 4).

37. [Dans une instruction écrite datée du 10 janvier 1845, Monsieur Brongniart apellait mon attention sur la richesse et le brillant de ces fonds singuliers qu'on n'a rencontrés jusqu'ici que sur la porcelaine de Chine. Il m'engageait, en même temps, à étudier pour les reproduire, leur véritable nature] Carton N 2, dossier "Essais par analyse et synthèse sur le rouge au grand feu des Chinois par Mr. Salvetat."

38. [j'ai . . . l'espoir de réunir un assortiment complet puisqu'il ne faut plus maintenant que trois couleurs: bleu indigo, jaune foncé, jaune d'or] Carton Ob 2, dossier Jean-Augustin Bunel.

39. [les membres . . . , consultés sur les couleurs qui manquent à la collection et qu'on peut ou qu'on a pu se procurer à Paris ont déclaré qu'il ne manque pour peindre avec l'ensemble des meilleurs moyens possédés actuellement que les couleurs suivantes: les gris pour chairs...la série des rouges pour chairs. Il y en a plusieurs de très bons mais elle est incomplète . . . le pourpre. Celui de M.Mortelèque est généralement plus beau] Carton U 15, liasse 5, dossier 3.

40. Brongniart wrote: "M. Constantin finds M. Robert's series of fixed colors much more complete than that of M. Bunel. . . . The mixing yellow of M. P. Robert is an essential color without which M. Constantin could not have made his painting. The red of the alderman's cloak was made with a color from M. Bourgeois. The light gray is from M. Morteleque" [M. Constantin trouve la série des fixes de M.Robert bien plus complète que celle de M. Bunel . . . . Le jaune à mêler de M.P.Robert est une couleur essentielle sans laquelle M.Constantin n'aurait pu faire son tableau. Le rouge du manteau de l'échevin a été fait avec une couleur venant de M. Bourgeois. Le gris clair est de M. Morteleque] (ibid., note dated October 13, 1827).

41. [extraits d'un manuscrit que je me suis fait avec les notes de mon beau-père, M. Weydinger qui faisait des couleurs vingt ans avant que je le connusse et avec ceux de Meyer comminiqués par Monginot] Carton Ob 2, dossier J. A. Bunel, letter to Brongniart dated November 13, 1843. The person in question could be Jean-Léopold Weydinger aîné, born in 1764, painter and gilder at Sèvres (1775 – 96), employed by Pouyat (1818 – 19) after which he requested his retirement pension (carton Ob 11, dossier J. L. Weydinger). Meyer could be the chemist François Meyer, who briefly directed the manufactory (see chap. 3 in this volume), and Monginot, the Parisian decorator Charles Monginot (Guillebon, *Faïence et Porcelaine de Paris*, [1995], pp. 210, 383).

42. Brongniart instructed Bunel to devote all his knowledge and work time to Sèvres without divulging its secrets, adding: "I see no harm, I even see some advantage for the progress of the art that the king's manufactory should foster and propagate, in your communicating procedures that are your own property to persons of interest to you or with whom you might have family or commercial interests" [je ne vois aucun inconvénient, je vois même un avantage pour les progrès de l'art que la manufacture du Roi doit faire avancer et doit propager, à ce que vous donniez aux personnes qui vous intéressent ou avec lesquelles vous pouvez avoir des intérêts de famille ou de commerce, communication des procédés qui vous sont propres] (ibid., letter of August 3, 1827).

43. Records of the meeting of June 24, 1825 note: "Having newly acknowledged the advantage, with regard to the solidity of the gold and the success of the paintings, of firing separately and firmly the gilding on decorated pieces prior to the painting, in future we will follow this procedure which has been neglected" [Ayant de nouveau reconnu l'avantage sous le rapport de la solidité de l'or et sous celui de la réussite des peintures, de cuire séparément et solidement l'or des pièces décorées avant la peinture, on suivra à l'avenir ce procédé qui avoit été négligé] (register Y 13, fol. 95).

44. Préaud, "Transfer-Printing Processes Used at Sèvres" (1997).

45. In September 1819, Legros d'Anizy attempted to print a large frieze on a plate using lithography; the etching process could transfer only linear compositions, with shadows being rendered by stippling.

46. [Le Roi a désiré qu'on associât aux peintures en couleurs vitrifiables sur porcelaine, des décorations en émaux sur métal, d'un brillant tout à fait distinct des colorations sur porcelaine. Sa Majesté a demandé qu'on reprît la fabrication des pièces émaillées à la manière des Limousins, en y apportant les perfectionnements qu'on doit attendre des progrès des sciences chimiques] *Notice sur quelques-unes des pièces qui entrent dans l'exposition . . . 1er juin 1846* (1846), p. 31.

47. Brongniart, "Art de l'émailleur sur métaux" (1791); carton U 15, liasse 2., manuscript dated "London, 1790."

48. [M. Meyer me fait voir une petite coupe fond noir fleurs et ornements grisailles qu'il a faite entièrement et qui me paraît d'une réussite complète] [coupe dont je lui indique la grandeur et la disposition . . . qui m'est amené par M. Wattier] Carton U 15, liasse 3.

49. The catalogue of the 1846 Louvre exhibition states that the studio opened in September 1845. There must have been a delay, for Ebelmen wrote to Brongniart on September 26, 1845: "Work at the enameling workshop has begun. But M. Meyer is not yet completely equipped and must make rather frequent trips to Paris to complete his assortment. His kiln has already been fired up once. The results were very good and probably nothing will need to be changed at his establishment. I think that next week the workshop will be in full operation and I hope that on your return you will already find some interesting executed work" [Les travaux de l'atelier d'émaillage sont commencés. Mais M. Meyer n'est pas encore complètement outillé et il doit faire d'assez fréquents voyages à Paris pour compléter son assortiment. Son fourneau a été allumé déjà une fois. Le Tirage en est très bon et il n'y aura probalement rien à changer à son établissment. Je crois que la semaine prochaine l'atelier sera en pleine activité et j'espère qu'à votre retour vous trouverez déjà quelques travaux intéressants exécutés] (carton Ob 5, dossier Ebelmen).

50. These productions had nothing to do with what Brongniart addressed in a letter to the comte de Montalivet dated February 12, 1845, where, speaking of Meyer-Heine, he wrote: "So they can be entirely the result of the industry and workshops at Sèvres, I am having a kiln and a muffle kiln installed and prepared for him. . . . He will establish his enameling workshop there; the enameled pieces that he makes will be introduced into porcelain pieces that they will enrich with that brilliance particular to enamels on spangles of gold, silver, and even platinum. . . . M. Salvetat . . . will make the necessary colors for the enamel workshop. We hope that in a few months, when all the enamel can be made at Sèvres, it will no longer be necessary to purchase them in Venice or elsewhere" [pour qu'elles sortent entièrement de l'industrie et des ateliers de Sèvres, je lui fais arranger et monter un fourneau et une moufle . . . Il y établira son atelier d'é-

maillage; les pièces émaillées qu'il fera seront introduites dans des pièces de porcelaine qu'elles enrichiront de l'éclat particulier qui appartient aux émaillages sur paillons d'or, d'argent ou même de platine . . . . Mr. Salvetat . . . fera pour l'atelier d'émaillage les émaux nécessaires. Nous espérons que dans peu de mois, tous les émaux pouvant être faits à Sèvres, il ne sera plus nécessaire d'en acheter ni à Venise ni ailleurs] (register Vc 10, fol. 2 ff.).

51. Register Y 13, fol. 2v – 3, meeting of March 19, 1819; register Y 4, fol 170 ff., organizational regulations issued March 18, 1819.

52. Bocquet was a "modeler for the fabrication of porcelain at Dagoty's concern" when Brongniart first took note of him and asked him, in 1811, to produce the model for "Denon" bowl no. 3 (register Vf 61, fol. 13v, payment of September 11, 1811; carton M 5, letter dated April 15, 1823 soliciting his addition to the list of "personnel fixe"). In 1815 Bocquet signed an agreement to direct the mount-making workshop *à l'entreprise,* and in 1823 he became a member of the permanent staff. In addition to mounting bronze fixtures (handles, bases, joints), he continued to produce models until 1860.

Fig. 5-1. *View of the Sèvres Manufactory* (detail) by Fortier and Duparc after A. E. Michallon, n. d.; engraving. (Manufacture nationale de Sèvres, Archives)

Chapter 5

Brongniart and the Art of Ceramics

Tamara Préaud

Alexandre Brongniart began his tenure at Sèvres knowing little of the ceramic arts and techniques, especially the process whereby enamel colors are fired onto ceramics and glass. Very soon, however, these technical aspects became a passionate, lifelong interest, a development that is not surprising given Brongniart's wide and unbiased scientific curiosity. Throughout his career he strove to remain well-informed about the latest processes, and discoveries. Similarly, he made it a policy at the Sèvres manufactory to be generous with colleagues and competitors, not only by encouraging them but in more concrete ways as well, by making the results of his own experiments available to them and even providing them with models and guidance.

Brongniart traveled a great deal to obtain information. In Fructidor year 8 (August – September 1800), a Parisian porcelain maker named Deruelle wrote to him, expressing his opinion that before Brongniart's arrival the manufactory had kept aloof from the outside world: "It was left to you, Citizen, to remedy all these ills. Being the first of this establishment who has been willing to consult with practitioners of the art of porcelain and visit the Parisian factories to communicate with entrepreneurs about their organization, fabrication, firing, preparations, compositions, prices and workers' salaries, fiscal management, the valuation of their merchandise, etc., considering all these matters in comparative terms . . . ."[1]

The administrator's expeditions were not always for the sole purpose of gathering information. On April 1, 1807, he requested authorization to visit the kaolin quarries in the Limousin region of central France. Noting that there were only two suppliers in Limoges (Alluaud and Pouyat) of this essential ingredient for the making of porcelain and that " . . . everyone complained about them," he intended to verify for himself that no viable competitor could be found and that "kaolin clay is as rare in the environs of Limoges as is made out."[2] In the same dispatch he proposed to see "if it would be possible and advantageous to acquire for the manufactory a quarry of good quality" and set out to confirm that other strata of kaolin did not exist toward Bayonne and the Auvergne region. It was probably for similar reasons that he went to Normandy in 1811. Inevitably, he took advantage of these excursions to visit ceramics factories along his route.

His travels outside France were frequent as well. Always methodical, Brongniart kept meticulous lists of the clothing and toiletries — including a sewing kit — needed for trips of varying lengths. He also carefully planned for the storage of the samples he would collect along the way, deciding in which compartments of his carriage he would put them. He collected not only things potentially useful to the manufactory — technical data, prints, ceramics, and glassware — but also geological and botanical samples. He visited mines to gather specimen rocks for the Muséum d'Histoire Naturelle, sought out mounted plant and animal specimens, and made geological notes and sketches.

In 1812 he traveled to German-speaking parts of Europe; in 1817, to Switzerland; in 1820, to the Italian peninsula; in 1824, to Sweden, Norway, and Denmark; in 1835, to Belgium, Holland, and Luxembourg, as well as to regions in Germany; and in 1836, to England and another part of Germany. Wherever he went he investigated special technical processes, sketched unusual machinery, noted prices, and recorded salary levels. Recording data was not always easy, as he indicated in his account of a visit to the Vauxhall factory in England in 1836: "I took as many notes as possible . . . . They must be written down from memory, for it would be suspicious to take them on the spot."[3] Furthermore, he sometimes arrived at inopportune moments. He was obliged to visit the Saint-Amand factory during a work suspension occasioned by a change of ownership, and after touring the Tournai factory without a guide, he wrote: "Thanks to the explanation without operation that Triboulet gave me, and the operations without explanation that I observed in Tournai, I know rather well in general outline how soft-paste porcelain is made in Tournai."[4]

It could also be difficult to gain access to certain factories. The first attempt at an exchange of raw materials and decorated pieces with Meissen in 1808 produced difficulties that prompted Brongniart to write: "I found, like you, that the superintendent of the Saxony manufactory put on too many airs, and with little reason, for granting my request would hardly have divulged any secrets, for the secret of porcelain amounts to nothing, now that it is general knowledge, and if the Meissen manufactory has special processes we can quite well do without them, our porcelain being on a level with that of Saxony."[5]

In 1812 the exchange finally took place, but before departing for Germany, Brongniart took the precaution of writing to the French ambassador to the Saxon court, Baron de Serra: "His Majesty the Emperor has instructed me to visit the principal porcelain factories in Germany. I know how difficult it is to see the inside of the Meissen manufactory. I will not be so indiscreet as to request access to specific workshops or procedures unique to the

Fig. 5-2. *The Exposition des Produits de L'Industrie Française in the Cour Carrée of the Louvre,* artist unknown, 1801; watercolor. (Paris, Musée Carnavalet)

manufactory, but I would like to be received there as favorably as possible. Please be so kind, Monsieur le Baron, as to do what you can to help me obtain this favor."[6] Thanks to this request he was well received by the director, Count Camille Marcolini, and was able to visit the factory.[7]

In addition to taking trips himself, Brongniart profited from those taken by others. Several individuals brought back information and/or objects for the ceramics museum from their journeys. In return Brongniart, with permission from the royal administration, presented them with modest gifts from the manufactory's stock. In 1829 Jules de Blosseville, ship's navigator aboard the *Chevrette*, was rewarded in this way, and in 1835 the future admiral Abel Dupetit-Thouars was similarly recognized for his donation of Peruvian pottery.[8]

While in England in 1836, Brongniart met Sir Alexander Johnston, ". . . who has a son in Macao very well placed to obtain information about the fabrication of Chinese porcelain. I gave him some instructions about research and inquiries that might be pursued there."[9] When presenting the captain of the *Cléopâtre* with some Sèvres porcelain to be offered as gifts during his voyage to the China seas, Brongniart also provided him with "a memorandum listing the Chinese and Japanese porcelains and the information I desire to obtain for the Musée Céramique de la Manufacture Royale, as well as more precise and complete knowledge of the art of porcelain in China and Japan, an art these peoples practiced several centuries before it was introduced to Europe."[10]

This passage demonstrates the degree to which the enrichment of the museum was linked with the development of Brongniart's knowledge. He also noted ". . . information given in March 1843 by Chavagnon, a naval commissioner, who has penetrated China [and among other things] he confirmed to me that the porcelain is glazed immediately after being dried in the sun, in other words without having been bisque fired."[11] By 1844 there had been enough of these gifts for Brongniart to write to Benjamin Jaurès, a ship's lieutenant: "The ceramics museum of the royal manufactory, enriched by gifts from the most distinguished naval officers, has prompted me to place at the king's disposal pieces whose special ornamentation makes them appropriate gifts for His Majesty to offer the officers of this illustrious corps."[12]

Brongniart also sought the help of his personal friends. One of the few files of private correspondence preserved at Sèvres contains a letter dated April 11, 1833, addressed to the economist Frédéric Le Play before his departure for Spain. In it Brongniart asked him to obtain mineral samples for the Muséum d'Histoire naturelle as well as 100 to 150 francs worth of ceramics, ". . . modern as well as old," for the museum. Brongniart enclosed a list of pieces already in the collection, and added: "If M. Sureda, the former director of this factory [La Moncloa], whom I got to know well in Paris, is still alive, try to see him, convey my regards to him, and ask him for information about the fabrication of *porcelain* in Spain."[13] Brongniart's equally good relations with the sinologist Stanislas Julien enabled him to establish contact with Jesuit missionaries in China, who in 1844 submitted a detailed report by Father Joseph Ly about China's porcelain production.

Brongniart was also aided by travels of employees of the manufactory. The painter Jean-François Robert, for example, was summoned to Florence by Grande Duchesse Elisa, Napoleon's sister, and he sent Brongniart a long report in 1813 on the Ginori factory in Doccia,[14] detailing the kinds of paste it produced and describing its rapid firing method, using kindling as fuel.[15] The worker charged with accompanying a musical clock, *pendule 'Turque'* (see cat. no. 102), to be presented to the viceroy of Egypt, Mehemet-Ali, was instructed to bring back samples of modern ceramics as well as animals indigenous to the region.[16] Similarly, a bronze worker was sent with gifts to the bey of Tunis, and Denis-Désiré Riocreux, curator of the ceramics museum, drafted a list of objects to be brought back from the region.[17]

Building the collections and increasing Brongniart's store of information were inextricably linked. This can be seen in the institution of a formal exchange policy between Sèvres and other manufactories. An 1802 study of raw materials and pottery from various French provinces was undertaken with the cooperation of the regional prefects, and this enriched the manufactory with clay samples and artifacts (see chap. 11). This first collection of material probably suggested the idea of a reciprocal exchange agreement with foreign factories (see chap. 9). Initially, the motive for forming the collection was technological, but the objects assumed an increasingly diverse character as consignments sent by other factories began to include whole pieces as well as shards.

By 1824, when the museum opened to the public, its collection included items of historical, artistic, and technological interest, and this development proved seminal to the future of the manufactory. Early signatures in the visitors' register show that glass and ceramics manufacturers of all kinds, both French and foreign, came to the museum to learn about their colleagues' activities. All of them quickly grasped the advantage of contributing their most recent productions to the museum as a way to establish their contributions to the field. This facilitated Brongniart's keeping up with the latest developments.

Typical of changing attitudes toward Sèvres as its collection

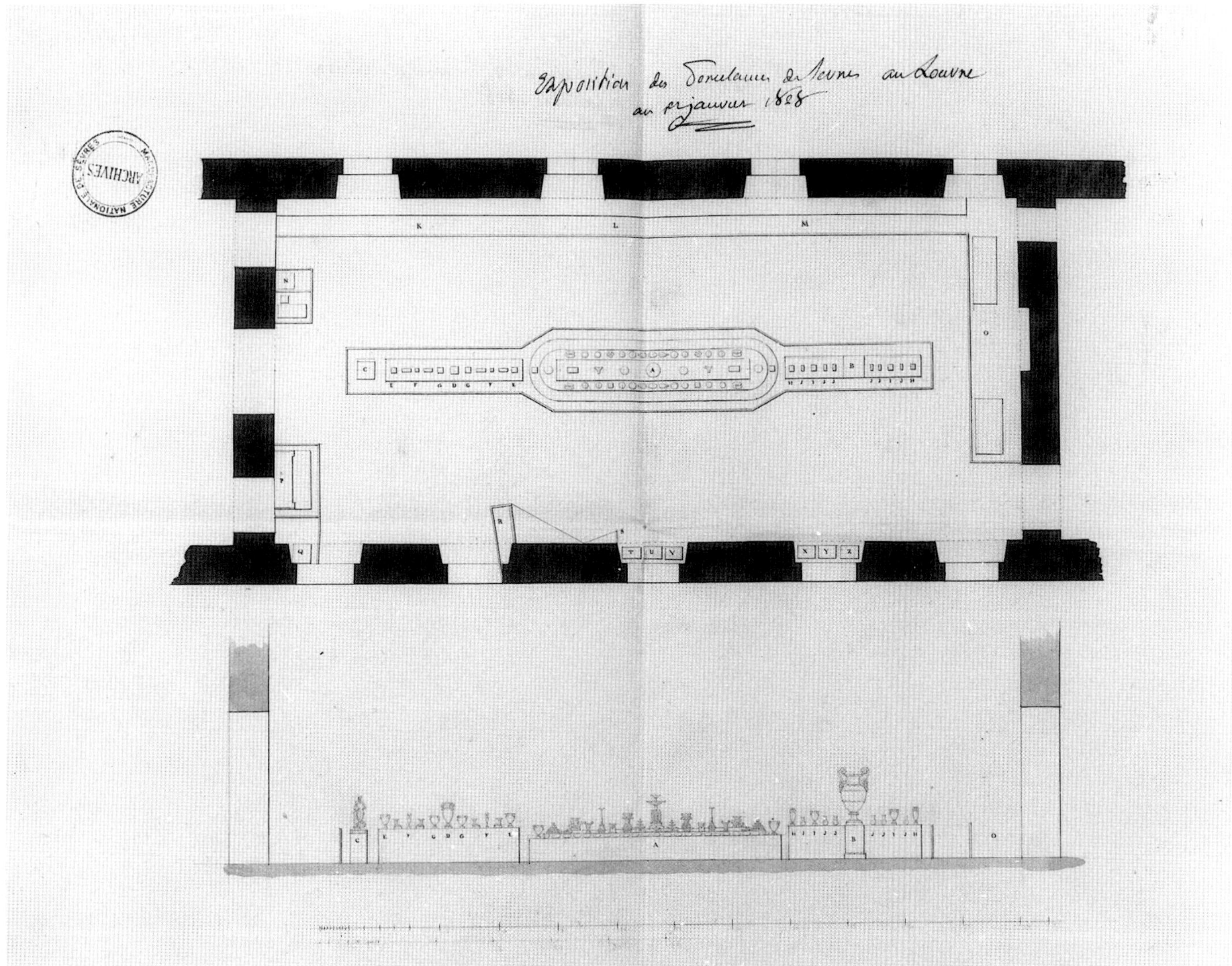

Fig. 5-3. Plan of the Sèvres display at the New Year's Exhibition, Palais du Louve, 1827–28. (Archives of the Manufacture Nationale de Sèvres)

grew are the comments of the painter, designer, and ceramist Jules Ziegler. In 1834 he sent Louis-Philippe a report on the Sèvres manufactory that was quite critical, describing it as an "establishment fallen . . . into discredit in public opinion." A few years later, however, in 1838, he wrote to Brongniart: "I had the honor of speaking to you about my brother Adolphe who makes stoneware and whom I have engaged to try making a few works of art. Wanting to neglect nothing in the matter of his instruction in the ceramic arts, he would like to spend a month or two at Sèvres and profit from the gathering of masterpieces that you have assembled there." In 1839 Ziegler requested casts of the Flemish vases designed by Claude-Aimé Chenavard so that they could be produced in stoneware (see cat. no. 80). Finally, in 1842 Ziegler acknowledged that "this ceramics museum is a refuge from the revolutions of fashion, which takes things up and then drops them; thus I intend to have everything that seems to me of some merit sheltered there."[18]

Brongniart created another source of information through his relationship to exhibitions of industrial products. Initially, the manufactory regularly took part in these expositions. Brongniart displayed everyday objects that were notable for the quality of their paste and elegance of their forms. This prompted criticism; it seemed to his competitors that Sèvres was trying to take business away from the private factories. To avoid future accusations Brongniart requested permission to make the exhibition of 1823 the manufactory's last[19] and henceforth served only as a member of the ceramics jury. Participants thus sent him letters and documents pertaining to their operations and innovations, often accompanied by representative objects.[20] Brongniart made use of this information only at the museum, not in the manufactory itself. Many of the pieces and documents that Brongniart accumulated in this capacity enabled him to construct important elements of his seminal study of ceramics, *Traité des arts céramique* . . . (1844).

Brongniart was interested in the relationship between Sèvres's pricing formula and those used by other porcelain manufacturers, especially in Paris. He also compared pricing on his trips abroad. On 18 Ventôse year 9 (March 10, 1801), he wrote to a client: "As to our prices, I hope you will find them no higher than those of other porcelain factories taking as much care with their products as we do, and that we do not take undue advantage of our manufactory's reputation."[21] A year later he used the comparison to promote the high quality of Sèvres's work: "I should also point out to you that in general our prices are higher than those of the factories in Paris, because our porcelain is more resistant, our forms are purer and more elegant, our gilding is more durable as well, and, finally, the ornaments and flowers are made with a care, a purity of drawing not brought to bear in the other factories."[22] Such competition was an issue only where very simple pieces were concerned, and Brongniart emphasized repeatedly that market conditions were more favorable to the manufactory when it came to large, important pieces. In 1808 he wrote to the Intendant Général: "All the information I obtain, all the research I do proves to me more and more that the Sèvres manufactory is no more expensive than others of equal merit, and that in some cases it is less expensive, especially when it's a question of precious and difficult pieces."[23]

Brongniart was especially well informed about the prices of Parisian porcelain producers during the Empire, because during this period, he was asked several times to verify the prices of pieces that had been sold to the Garde-Meuble or left on deposit as securities against loans. In 1811, for example, he assessed the prices of pieces made by the firms of Dagoty and Darte Frères, and had suggested lowering some of the prices of the latter, observing: "I hope you will note that they apply principally to pieces of everyday use that the Imperial Sèvres Manufactory delivers to the Garde-Meuble de la Couronne at prices less than those of the Dartes."[24] Brongniart must have been quite happy when, after the duchesse de Berry asked him in 1823 to assess the prices of some vases "sold by the porcelain factory on the boulevard Poissonnière,"[25] her maître d'hôtel reported, "I went to see them and pointed out to them that the price they were asking was much too high, and that the Sèvres manufactory, which produced better work in every respect, had fabricated some at my request for a much lower price and, I repeat, infinitely better executed."[26]

Keeping a reasonable parity between Sèvres's prices and those of the private factories was a constant concern, despite the fact that the manufactory was subsidized. In 1822 Brongniart decided that "plates and other pieces with production flaws insufficient to preclude their use, but which make them inferior to pieces fabricated carelessly in the other factories, will be reduced to the highest prices of the Parisian factories."[27] The minutes of a meeting held on February 8, 1825 report:

> The administrator desiring, to the degree permitted by the care and perfection brought to bear in the fabrication of the Royal Sèvres Manufactory, to bring retail prices into line with those used by the Parisian factories for simple pieces with gold edges, arranged for the decoration of sample cups with gold edges from the Paris salesroom and from Sèvres. M. Robert, head of the Paris salesroom presents a series of *'Litron'* cups with gold bands whose production costs are discussed and compared with those of similar cups made at Sèvres. The administrator, after having compared these cups with samples of the same kind acquired on the Paris market and originating from private factories and having listened to the advice of the meeting, set new prices for cups and plates with gold bands.[28]

A similar procedure was followed in 1843, and again the minutes from the meeting, during which samples of plates from Charenton, Chantilly, Champroux, and Foecy were examined, report: "The administrator, wanting to establish new prices for plates made at the manufactory, considering the prices of plates made in the private factories, these plates having been carefully examined and compared with those made at Sèvres, it was acknowledged that in terms of paste quality, fabrication, and purity of form those from the manufactory were much superior to the samples, which could at best be compared with our inferior catagory [third choice] . . . ."[29] A new price structure was decided on this basis. Thus despite the fastidious maintenance of work records that itemized salaries and costs for raw materials, these components were not the sole means of determining the cost of the manufactory's output.

Such concerns about price comparisons could be extreme, as reflected in a passage from the minutes of another meeting, held on February 13, 1841: "The administrator presents for consideration a double-shell butter dish made in Paris whose price is much lower than those produced by the manufactory; it being observed that the form and workmanship of the one made in Paris is much different in terms of merit, it was decided that the molds of the butter dish produced at Sèvres would be turned over to the Parisian producer with a request to have [a sample] cast and finished, and to provide an indication of the price at which this white piece might be sold."[30]

Although Brongniart kept a close eye on his competitors, his dealings with them were customarily quite cordial.[31] He held that it was Sèvres's "noble" role "to preserve and propagate good procedures in the ceramic arts [as well as] provide support and free instruction to all those who practice them or study them."[32] Obviously, other porcelain makers did not hesitate to profit from this generosity. Thus it was that in 1808 the distinguished Parisian porcelain maker Edouard Honoré wrote to Brongniart requesting an explanation of the high-fire chromium-green-ground process.[33] In 1833, having been updated about the use of a jigger, Honoré informed Brongniart that "I will use your procedure in my facility and I think that the nature of our paste will favor its success."[34] In 1834 several of the most important porcelain makers of the period — Nenert Latrille and Ruaud; Edouard Honoré; Pétry and Ronsse; Alluaud père; and Jacob Petit — asked the director to experiment at Sèvres with a new smokeless kiln, with the use of peat and coal as fuel, and with multilevel kilns:

> The solution of these serious questions, you will acknowledge Monsieur, will have the happiest influence on the prosperity of our art. . . . The private industry having already made considerable sacrifices to obtain [them], it is worthy for the Royal Manufactory to participate in what still remains to be done. Your practical experience, the extent and variety of your knowledge in the physical sciences, and your quality as administrator of the Royal manufactory place you in the happiest position to assure the success of the experiments it will be useful to carry out.[35]

In exchange, the administrator did not hesitate to seek his colleagues' help. In May 1836, for example, he asked Régnier and Bunel to try out "the large muffle kiln of M. Darte in Paris" before having one built at Sèvres.[36]

In addition to providing technical information and carrying out experiments, Brongniart also arranged for Sèvres's workers to share their expertise with the competition. In 1840 the Société Discry Talmours et Cie requested the services of Antoine François Toussaint Delacour, "a worker whom you were so good as to hire on the basis of our recommendation,"[37] to throw four large vases.

Despite his privileged position Brongniart seems to have maintained congenial personal relations with other ceramists. In 1828, for example, Arnoux père reminded him that ". . . in January 1825, an earthenware maker from Toulouse had the honor of paying you a visit in Paris and at Sèvres. It was myself who received from you at that time the most obliging reception and [benefited from] the goodwill with which you receive all those who call upon you with the goal of educating themselves."[38] Arnoux also wrote to him in 1845: "Monsieur, you have always received my eldest son with such goodwill that I should not fear appearing overly importunate in introducing to you the bearer of the present [letter of introduction], who is the youngest of my children. Like his brother Léon Arnoux, the director of our pottery factory, the latter comes to Paris to take courses at the École Centrale."[39]

In addition to receiving visitors at Sèvres, where they came to see the ceramics museum, Brongniart also had visitors at his residence in Paris. Edouard Honoré, for example, wrote that he planned to thank Brongniart in Paris "on Sunday, at the hour in which you customarily receive."[40] The names of many of Brongniart's colleagues and competitors also appear on the list of those attending the May 1835 exhibition in the Louvre.[41] One of the most striking manifestations of this support is the cooperation given to the creamware research of Honoré Boudon de Saint-Amans, who was authorized to install an experimental workshop in the manufactory at his expense and even to display its productions at the Louvre exhibition of January 1, 1829. Brongniart defended this arrangement, writing: "The desire to attach the name of the Royal Manufactory to all improvements achieved in the ceramic arts encouraged me to listen to the proposals of M. de Saint Amand although I foresaw increased work and oversight responsibilities for myself. . . . I see no real inconvenience in granting him the authorization he requests; on the contrary, I see instruction for us and some honor for the Royal Manufactory, which will derive satisfaction from having cooperated solely by its protective intervention in the introduction of a pottery much in demand and new to France."[42]

Brongniart was sometimes consulted by people outside the field of ceramics. In 1842, when the use of polychromy in ancient monuments was being much discussed in France, Prosper Mérimée, *inspecteur des monuments historiques*, who had been asked to draft a report with Baron Taylor on the use of painted earthenware in architecture, requested a meeting. Brongniart responded with an extended letter full of technical information. He enumerated the respective advantages of enameling on slabs of lava stone and stoneware and praised the recent advances in stoneware production made by the stove maker Pichenot, who had developed an enamel that was resistant to cracking when frozen.[43]

Brongniart also maintained relations with foreign colleagues, which had been established in the course of reciprocal visits. In 1836, prior to his third visit to Germany, he wrote that he was certain to be allowed to tour KPM, the Berlin manufactory, ". . . in the most complete way; I have just received from M. Frick, the director of this establishment and my travel companion in Germany in 1812, a letter that leaves no room for doubt on this subject."[44]

In the course of this extended trip he subsequently wrote from Munich: "I cannot help, Monsieur le Baron, but remark to you, perhaps with sentiments not without vanity on my part . . . that most of the heads of the ceramic and porcelain establishments in Germany are either mineralogists or attached to the art and the administration of mines."[45]

This sense of professional community had facilitated dialogue and exchange of information since the time he first joined the manufactory. In 1805 Brongniart had already written to the Intendant Général Pierre Daru asking that he forward to his colleagues at the porcelain manufactory in Vienna a series of questions as well as some requests for samples: "I have not at all been afraid of multiplying these questions, or even of posing some that are indiscreet. . . . I consider the imperial and royal manufactories to be unlike the private commercial houses that think they must make a mystery of everything, but like establishments charged with perfecting their art and which should employ, toward this end, the same means of communication used by scientists in making advances in the fields they cultivate."[46]

In return, at Sèvres, Brongniart had occasion to receive colleagues from throughout Europe and allowed them to observe the manufactory's operation. He even granted a request made by the Danish artist Lorents Rasmus Lyngbye to study in some detail "the operation of muffle kilns" as well as "the process of transfer printing that I consider one of the most precious things in the fabrication industry."[47]

These cordial and open relations did not prevent the imperial and royal administrations, any more than the director himself, from trying to maintain Sèvres's preeminence. Pierre Daru, announcing the arrival of a few sample cups sent by the director of the Vienna manufactory in 1805, wrote: "When thanking him for this little present, be sure to tell him that you will be sending him a similar shipment, and I think it would be best if this shipment were more beautiful than his. The manufactory that you direct so ably should have but one aim: that of constantly being the first of Europe in all respects."[48]

Some twenty years later, when discussing the presentation of a service to the French ambassador in Vienna, the vicomte de La Rochefoucauld expressed similar views: "Seeing as the capital to which this gift is to be sent possesses a beautiful porcelain manufactory, it will be essential that the objects . . . be particularly beautiful and capable of proving our superiority in industry of this kind."[49] And on the occasion of a commission for two vases intended for the king of Prussia (see cat. no. 66), the Intendant Général was similarly insistent: "His Majesty . . . has ordered that the Sèvres Manufactory be charged with executing for His Majesty the King of Prussia two vases whose forms and dimensions are to be absolutely identical to those this monarch deigned to send to me, and which were produced in the Berlin workshops. I need not enjoin you to take every care that these two objects be such as to assert the superiority of our industry in fabrications of this kind, and to increase abroad the just renown of the establishment that you direct."[50]

One noteworthy aspect of the relations between Brongniart and other contemporary producers concerns the authorization to make molds of old and new models, which was given quite liberally. Initially, such requests must have come as a surprise to the administrator. In 1828, for example, Brongniart advised against a purchase proposed by the porcelain maker Dihl who was offering to sell his collection of forms and molds prior to closing his establishment. Brongniart wrote: "Furthermore, and it is an unfortunate thing for the arts, most old factory models lose much of their value after a certain time, because they take on an outmoded character that the public tends to reject."[51]

Many producers, however, especially those working in bronze and porcelain, sought authorization to use old Sèvres models. This may have been encouraged by the opening of the manufactory's museum: old Sèvres plasters were exhibited there alongside rock samples and objects from all periods and countries, perhaps playing a role in the revival of eighteenth-century decorative arts. In 1822 the bronze-caster Jeannet asked to borrow modern models. Brongniart agreed on condition that Sèvres's prior use of them be acknowledged. Justifying his decision, he wrote: "One of [the manufactory's] utilitarian goals is to propagate good processes and good models in the arts, or at least what it regards as such, and to promote their progress in this way. One of these means is to offer producers good models that they can *imitate* or *copy* . . . and even sometimes to give them the means to acquire at no expense to them what cost a great deal by permitting them to take molds."[52]

It seems that this intention to use his privileged position to be helpful and serve as a model for the whole of the ceramics profession and perhaps even the wider field of artistic craftsmanship in general, was a determining factor throughout Brongniart's long career.[53] The surviving lists of those requesting the opportunity to use models include the names of both French and foreign porcelain producers in addition to many bronze makers.[54] Although sculpture was most in demand, in 1842 the firm of Talmours et Hurel wrote: "Some time ago we conceived the project of executing the old Sèvres forms for table services, forms that have already been copied by M. Nast."[55] And in 1842 Herbert Minton asked for a series of eighteenth-century vase forms.

These requests indicate a shift in taste, but they scarcely seem to have influenced Brongniart's own inclinations with respect to copying older forms. He wrote Riocreux in 1846 that "the molds are being altered and as we are resuming this fabrication we are obliged to suspend these authorizations."[56] He was referring to a decision he had been forced to make against his better judgment, when members of the royal family requested groups, figures, and services that Brongniart qualified as out-of-fashion (see chap. 10).

One can only wonder at the director's attitude toward the old pieces of eighteenth-century porcelain that remained in the manufactory's stock. There can be no doubt about Brongniart's sincere desire to render service to others, nor about his profound belief in the excellence of the forms devised at Sèvres throughout its history. It is surprising, to say the least, however, that he seems to have been impervious to the fact that his policy of allowing molds to be made directly from Sèvres's originals would inevitably lead to confusion between originals and copies and almost certainly encourage fraud.

With regard to the sale of Sèvres's stock of eighteenth-century soft-paste porcelain, Brongniart authorized private sales of blanks to various tradesmen between 1815 and 1825, and went so far as to organize an auction of old pieces when the Paris salesroom moved in 1827. At that time fakes were already beginning to proliferate, and Brongniart was sufficiently conversant with the problem of post-production decoration to recognize its telltale symptoms with some precision.[57] It is difficult to make sense of his apparent laxity in this matter, fostered as it was by a man whose scrupulous integrity is a matter of record. He may have been so firmly convinced of the superiority of the manufactory's products that he felt confusion on this point was impossible, or perhaps he was too naive to conceive of any eventual deceptions.

Brongniart's approach to ceramics evolved over time. At the beginning of his tenure, he wanted to help pottery manufacturers to improve their production and to reduce the danger of lead in glazes. It was in this spirit that the Enquête des Préfets (prefectural inquiry) of 1802 was made (see chap. 11). Before long, the presence at Sèvres of old plaster models, drawings, and prints, which Brongniart inventoried, primarily in view of establishing their value, as well as the collection of Greek vases acquired from Dominique-Vivant Denon in 1786, suggested to him the idea of assembling a larger collection (see chap. 9). In all likelihood, the growing accumulation of objects from throughout the world impressed upon him the need for a general system of classification, something that had not yet been established. Such a project, indispensable to a specialist in natural history, could not be carried forward without taking into account, at least theoretically, the totality of known ceramics. This generated the idea of bringing together ". . . everything pertaining to the ceramic arts and vitrification in all parts of the globe from the most distant past to the present day."[58]

To a scientific mind, such a collection required that each piece be analyzed historically so that it could be situated correctly. Accordingly, Brongniart assumed the multiple roles of technician, classifier, and historian. It is difficult today to appreciate the originality of such an undertaking, but it should be noted that no other history of ceramics had yet been written. Hence the importance of the *Traité des arts céramique* . . . , published in 1844 but conceived much earlier. In 1830, when requesting authorization for an extensive information-gathering tour of France and the rest of Europe, Brongniart wrote: "Considering as an obligation of the favorable position in which I find myself, the composition of a work on the ceramic arts, I have already planned and drafted the abstract of a general treatise which I intend to complete and publish in the course of 1831 . . . a project on which I have been engaged for more than eight months."[59] In fact the July Revolution of 1830 precluded his traveling beyond Limoges, but he continued to gather notes and information. A few years later, after returning from Germany in 1836, he apparently set to work on his treatise again; following this date he all but ceased publishing in the fields of geology and mineralogy. The *Traité* ultimately consisted of two volumes of text and an atlas of plates illustrating the most interesting technical procedures. The work proved to be a fundamental resource; it presented the first historical overview of ceramics as well as a system for their classification that was so skillfully conceived that it is still used today.

Denis-Désiré Riocreux played a major role in the preliminary research for the *Traité*. Thousands of notes in his small, round hand bear witness to his tireless activity: he drafted abstracts of histories and archival documents, corresponded with local scholars, and visited dealers and salesrooms. His crucial role was acknowledged in 1845, a year after publication of the *Traité*, when a logical complement to it was published; the *Description méthodique du musée céramique* . . . bore his name as well as Brongniart's on the title page. The text described the pieces in the collection according to the classification system established in the *Traité*, indicating, wherever possible, their dates and places of origin. This was accompanied by a table of marks of ceramists throughout Europe and by lists of Sèvres ceramics marks and artists' initials which were published for the first time. A companion volume of plates illustrated a selection of characteristic objects, with considerable space being allotted to productions of the Sèvres manufactory. Henceforth, with these two multivolume works, scholars, collectors, dealers, and others with an interest in ceramics had access to a precise frame of reference for future study, and this development led to a sudden increase in publications in the field.

Brongniart's impartial attention to all types of ceramics influenced future developments in another respect as well. Not satisfied with merely collecting ceramics that had become neglected — work by Bernard Palissy, Hispano-Moresque earthenware, so-called Saint-Porchaire earthenware, and Flemish stoneware—he had them interpreted in Sèvres porcelain (see cat. nos. 79, 80, 85, 91, and 99). Although the results were sometimes awkward, they called attention to little-known masterpieces and undoubtedly helped to bring about a shift in taste among collectors. Along similar lines, he encouraged Charles Avisseau's attempts to rediscover Bernard Palissy's late-sixteenth-century process for making *rustiques figulines*, in which figures of serpents, birds, fruit, and other motifs were made in high relief. Brongniart also promoted Jules Ziegler's experiments in artistic stoneware.[60] These two men, Avisseau and Ziegler, are rightly considered the precursors of the studio potters who proliferated in the second half of the nineteenth century. By championing their efforts, Brongniart assumes his place among those who radically transformed the world of ceramics.

Ed. note: The documents cited below are from the Archives of the Manufacture Nationale de Sèvres (AMNS).

1. [il vous etoit réservé, Citoyen, de remédier à tous ces maux. Etant le premier de cet établissement qui est bien voulut consulter les praticiens dans l'art de la porcelaine, et visiter les manufactures de Paris pour communiquer avec les entrepreneurs sur leurs organisation, fabrication, cuisson, préparation, composition, prix et salaires d'ouvriers, économie, valeur des marchandises etc. vous faisant de tout des objets de comparaison] Carton N 1.

2. [tout le monde s'en plaint] [si les kaolins argileux sont aussi rares aux environs de Limoges qu'on veut le faire croire] [s'il seroit possible et avantageux d'acquérir pour la manufacture une carrière de bonne qualité] Register Vc 3, fol. 94v ff.

3. [j'ai pris aurant qu'il est possible de le faire des notes . . . il faut les prendre de mémoire car il serait suspect de les prendre sur les lieux] Carton M 10, dossier 1.

4. [grâce à l'explication sans opération que Mr. Triboulet m'avait donné et aux opérations sans explication que j'ai vu pratiquer à Tournay, je sais assez bien comment se fair en général la porcelaine tendre de Tournay] Carton M 9, dossier 5 (1835).

5. [j'ai trouvé comme vous que Mr. le commissaire de la Manufacture de Saxe fesoit excessivement le renchéri et avec d'autant moins de raison que l'accession à ma demande ne peut en rien dévoiler son secret, que le secret de la porcelaine est nul puisqu'il est connu de tout le monde et que si la manufacture de Meissen a des procédés particuliers nous pouvons sans vanité nous en passer, notre porcelaine n'etant point au-dessous de celle de Saxe] Carton T 4, liasse 1, dossier 4, letter dated January 24, 1808.

6. [S.M. l'empereur m'a chargé de visiter les principales manufactures de porcelaine de l'Allemagne. Je connois les difficultés qu'on éprouve pour voir l'interieur de la Manufacture de Meissen. Je ne prétends pas porter l'indiscrétion jusqu'à demander à avoir connaissance des atteliers particuliers ou des procédés propres à cette manufacture, mais je désirerois y être recu le plus favorablement possible. Auriez-vous la bonté, Monsieur le Baron, de me faire obtenir cette faveur] Carton T 6, liasse 1, dossier 5, letter dated August 8, 1812.

7. Carton T 6, liasse 1, dossier 5, letter dated September 23, 1812.

8. Carton M 7, liasse 3, dossier 3 (1829); register Vaa 2, fol. 111, October 1835.

9. [qui a un fils à Macao dans une position très favorable pour avoir des renseignements sur la fabrication de la porcelaine chinoise. Je lui ai remis une instruction sur les recherches et questions qu'il y avoit à faire] Carton M 10, liasse 1, dossier 1.

10. [une instruction qui fair connaître les objets de porcelaine chinoise et japonaise et les renseignements que je désire avoir tant pour le Musée ceramique de la Manufacture royale que pour la connaissance plus exacte et plus complète de l'art de la porcelaine à la Chine et au japon, art que ces peuples ont exercé plusieurs siècles avant qu'il fût introduit en Europe] Carton M 12, liasse 2.

11. [renseignements donnés en mars 1843 par M. Chavagnon commissaire de la marine qui a pénétré en Chine] [il me confirme que la porcelaine est mise en couverte immédiatement après la dessication au soleil c.a.d. sans avoir été dégourdie] Carton U 15, liasse 2.

12. [Le musée céramique de la Manufacture royale, enrichi des dons des officiers de marine les

plus distingués, m'a fait penser à mettre à la disposition du Roi des pièces qui par leur ornementation spéciale fussent appropriées aux présents que S.M. voudroit faire à des officiers de cet illustre corps] Carton M 12, liasse 14.

13. [si M.Sureda ansien directeur de cete fabrique et que j'ai beaucoup connu à Paris existe encore, tâchez de le voir, rappellez-moi à son souvenir et demandez-lui des renseignements sur la fabrication des *porcelaines* en Espagne] Carton U 15, liasse 1, dossier Le Play.

14. Carton T 16, liasse 2, dossier 4, letter dated October 3, 1813.

15. In the 1830s Abraham Constantin was sent to Florence to make copies of paintings on porcelain. He had had a sample plaque fired at Ginori's kilns, but the result was so disappointing that he preferred to risk sending his unfired plaques to Sèvres, even for the first firing of the painting. The plaques would then be returned to Florence; they were sometimes transported between cities several times before the work was completed.

16. Brongniart had recommended that this worker seek the aid of a D. Clot-Bey who wrote to Brongniart on September 26, 1846: "Also, I eagerly gathered whatever objects of modern Egyptian and Nubian pottery I could find that are indicated in the note that you delivered to Mr. Couët who communicated it to me, I thought you would also like it if I added some vases fabricated in Yemen and some others from Mutaya in Carmania. All that's lacking is the white, covered Menouf *terraille* (creamware) known as a *Touban,* which I will send you later" [aussi me suis-je empressé de réunir les objets de poterie moderne d'Egypte et de Nubie qu'il m'a été possible de trouver et qui sont désignés dans la note que vous avez remise à Mr. Couët qui me l'a communiquée. J'ai cru vous être agréable en y joignant quelques vases fabriqués dans Yemen et d'autres venant de Mutaya en Caramanie. Il ne manque que la terraille de Menouf à couvercle blanc dite *Touban,* que je vous enverrai plus tard] (carton M 13, liasse 4).

17. Riocreux sought pieces of pottery that were "modern, everyday, with information pertaining to their origins and their prices" [modernes, usuelles, avec les renseignements requis sur leur origine et leur prix]; "pipes that are used in Tunis" [pipes dont on fait usage à Tunis]; "samples of facing tiles, those from ancient monuments, if they can be had, as well as those used on modern structures" [des échantillons de carreaux de revêtement, tant ceux provenant de monuments anciens, s'il peut s'en procurer, que de ceux que l'on peut employer encore dans les constructions modernes] (carton M 13, liasse 3). On January 2, 1847, Brongniart had written to the French consul in Tunis: "I wanted to have the Sèvres ceramics museum profit from our worker's trip by enriching it with special pottery from the realm of Tunis, modern as well as ancient. I gave him instructions accordingly. He will purchase the modern pieces. As for the old ones, that's a different matter; if they are to be of any interest, they must be clearly antique and of old Carthaginian fabrication, that people being renowned for its factories for beautiful pottery" [J'ai voulu faire profiter le musée céramique de Sèvres du voyage de notre ouvrier pour l'enrichir des poteries spéciales du royaume de Tunis, tant des modernes que des anciennes. Je lui ai donné des instructions en conséquences. Les modernes, il les achètera. Quand aux anciennes, c'est différent; il faut, pour qu'elles aient quelqu'intéret, qu'elles soient évidemment antiques et de l'ancienne fabrication cartaginoise, peuple renommé pour ses fabriques de belle poterie] (ibid.)

18. [établissement tombé . . . en discrédit dans l'opinion publique] [j'ai eu l'honneur de vous dire un mot de mon frère Adolphe qui s'occupe de grès et que j'engage à essayer quelques ouvrages d'art. Voulant ne rien négliger pour son instruction dans la connaissance des arts céramiques, il désire aller passer un ou deux mois à Sèvres et profiter de la réunion des chefs-d'oeuvre que vous y avez rassemblés] [ce musée céramique est un azile contre les révolutions de la mode qui adopte et délaisse; aussi je songe à y abriter tout ce qui me paraît avoir quelque mérite] Carton Ob 11, dossier "Ziégler."

19. On December 12, 1833, Brongniart was obligated to reiterate his position on this point to the comte de Montalivet: "The sole object of these exhibitions is to call the attention of the public and the government to factories and producers who have made real advances in their art by fabricating *well* and as economically as possible, which is to say at viable cost. . . . All masterpieces dependent on extraordinary means and individual talents, in other words on qualities that are not transmissible, seem to me inappropriate for exhibitions of this kind, since they are meant to reward the industry and not the manual or intellectual gifts of this or that person as in the fine arts exhibitions. . . . If the royal manufactory is to compete in this exhibition, it should do so only with objects produced by means of *processes* that are more perfect or more economical than those used previously and that, if made public, might then prove useful to art and industry. . . . Thus I should desire, because I think it appropriate, that the royal establishments, which are no longer industrial establishments in the real meaning of the word, not enter into competition with the private establishments, since these will always claim, and perhaps with good reason, that we have an unfair advantage" [L'objet unique de ces expositions est d'appeler l'attention du public et du gouvernement sur les fabriques et fabricants qui ont fait faire des progrès réels à leur art en fabricant *bien* et au meilleur marché possible; c'est-à-dire à un prix qu'on puisse soutenir . . . toute pièce qui est un chef-d'oeuvre dû à des moyens extraordinaires ou à des talents individuels, c.à.d. à des qualités qui ne sont pas transmissibles, me semble étrangère à ce genre d'exposition, car il s'agit d'y récompenser l'industrie et non le talent manuel ou intellectuel de telle ou telle personne comme dans les expositions des Beaux-Arts . . . . Si la manufacture royale doit concourrir à cette exposition ce n'est qu'en y apportant des objets fabriqués par des *procédés* plus parfaits ou plus économiques que ceux qui ont été employés jusqu'alors et qui, rendus publics, peuvent devenir alors utiles à l'art et à l'industrie. . . . J'aurais donc désiré, parce que je le crois convenable, que les établissements royaux qui ne sont plus des établissement industriels dans la véritable acception de ce mot, ne fussent pas appelés à entrer en lice avec les établissements particuliers, car ceux-ci auront toujours à dire, et peut-être avec raison, que nous concourrons avec eux à armes trop inégales] (register Vc 8, fol. 189v ff.).

20. These documents are preserved in the manufactory archives but are scattered among various inventoried cartons.

21. [quant à nos prix, j'espère que vous ne les trouverez pas au-dessus de ceux des manufactures de porcelaine qui fabriquent avec le soin que nous y mettons, et nous n'abuserons point de la réputation dont jouit notre manufacture] Carton T 1, liasse 2, dossier 4, letter to "citoyen Joseph Bernard marchand de crystaux, place d'Armes à Avignon."

22. [je dois vous prévenir également que nos prix sont en général plus élevés que ceux des fabriques de Paris, parce que notre porcelaine est plus solide, nos formes plus pures et plus élégantes, notre dorure plus solide aussi et, enfin, les ornements et fleurs faits avec un soin, une pureté de dessin qu'on n'apporte pas dans les autres fabriques] Register Vc 2 (unpaginated), letter dated 8 Floréal year 10 (April 29, 1802) to "M. Jacques Christian à Stuttgart."

23. [Tous les renseignements que je prends, toutes les recherches que je fais me prouvent de plus en plus que la Manufacture de Sèvres n'est pas plus chère que les autres à mérite égal et que dans quelques cas elle est meilleur marché surtout lorsqu'il s'agit de pièces précieuses et difficiles] Register Vc 3, fol. 145v – 146, letter dated October 15, 1808.

24. [j'espère que vous voudrez bien remarquer qu'elles portent principalement sur des pièces d'un usage ordinaire que la Manufacture impériale de Sèvres livre au Garde Meuble de la Couronne à un prix inférieur à celui de Mrs. Darte] Carton T 5, liasse 2, dossier 3, letter dated November 15, 1811 to Alexandre Desmazis, administrator of the Garde-Meuble.

25. At this time the factory belonged to Edouard Honoré (Plinval de Guillebon, *Faïence porcelaine* (1995), pp. 370 – 74).

26. [J'ai été les trouver et leur ai représenté que le prix qu'ils demandaient était très exagéré et que la manufacture de Sèvres qui faisait mieux sous tous les rapports en avait exécutés à ma commande à un beaucoup moindre prix et je le répète infiniment mieux traités] Carton T 10, liasse 1, dossier 4 (various).

27. [les assiettes et autres pièces qui auront des défauts de fabrication qui n'en empêchent pas l'usage, mais qui les mettent au'dessous des pièces fabriquées sans soins dans d'autres manufactures seront réduites au prix du plus haut tarif des manufactures de paris] Carton M 4, liasse 2, decision made November 8, 1822.

28. [M. l'administrateur désirant se mettre en rapport, autant que peut le permettre le soin et la perfection apporté dans la fabrication de la Manufacture Royale de Sèvres avec les prix du commerce des manufactures parisiennes pour les piéces courantes à filet d'or, a fait établir comparativement à l'atelier du dépôt de Paris et à Sèvres des tasses à filet d'or. M. Robert chef du dépot de Paris présente une série de tasses Litron filet d'or dont les prix de fabrication sont comparés et discutés avec ceux de pareilles tasses faites à Sèvres. Monsieur l'administrateur après avoir comparé ces tasses avec des échantillons du même genre achetés dans le commerce à paris et provenant de manufactures particulières et avoir pris l'avis de la conférence, arrete un nouveau tarif pour le prix des tasses et assiettes à filet d'or] Register Y 13, fol. 88v – 89.

29. [M. l'administrateur voulant établir de nouveau le prix des assiettes fabriquées à la Manufacture eu égard au prix des assiettes faites dans les manufactures particulières (on examina en conférence des échantillons venus des fabriques de Charenton, Chantilly, Champroux, Foecy)]; [Ces assiettes examinées avec attention et mises en comparaison avec celles faites à Sèvres, il a été reconnu que par la qualité de la pâte, la fabrication et la pureté de la forme celles de la manufacture étaient bien supérieures aux échantillons qui ne pouvaient tout au plus être comparés qu'au troisième choix] Register Y 14 bis, fol. 57v – 58, conférence of August 1, 1843.

30. [M. l'administrateur fait voir un beurrier double coquille fabriqué à Paris dont le prix est de beaucoup inférieur à ceux fabriqués à la manufacture; sur l'observation que la forme et le travail de celui fait à Paris offre une grande différence de mérite, il a été décidé que les moules du beurier qu'on exécute à Sèvres seraient remis au fabricant de Paris en le priant de le faire mouler et reparer et d'indiquer le prix auquel cette pièce en blanc pourrait être vendue] Ibid., fol. 23v. The Parisian butter dish in question had doubtless been made by Edouard Honoré, for the latter, when sending an object of this type *en deuxième choix* to Brongniart on February 1, 1841, indicated its price and then added: "In any case, Monsieur, to make a just comparison with those fabricated at Sèvres, account must be taken of the perfection of these latter and the difficulty of working your paste" [toutefois, Monsieur, pour faire une comparaison juste avec ceux qui se fabriquent à Sèvres, il faut tenir compte de la perfection de ces derniers et de la difficulté de travail de votre pâte] (carton T 14, liasse 2, dossier 5).

31. Préaud, "Alexandre Brongniart et les porcelainiers parisiens" (1970), pp. 13 – 19.

32. [la noble destination de conserver et de propager les bons procédés dans les arts céramiques" et de "donner secours et libérale instruction à tous ceux qui les pratiquent ou les étudient] Register Vc 8, fol. 74v. ff., letter to the commissioners in charge of the Liste Civile dated August 10, 1830.

33. Carton T 4, liasse 1, dossier 1.

34. [j'userai chez moi de votre procédé et je crois que la nature de nos pâtes aidera à la réussite]

Carton T 12, liasse 7, dossier 3, letter dated September 28, 1833.

35. [La solution de ces graves questions vous le reconnoitrez Monsieur auroit la plus heureuse influence sur la prospérité de notre art . . . l'industrie particulière ayant déjà fait des sacrifices considerables pour l'obtenir, il est digne de la Manufacture royale de s'associer à ceux qui restent à faire encore. Votre expérience pratique, l'étendue et la variété de vos connaissances dans les sciences physiques et votre qualité d'administrateur de la manufacture royale vous placent dans la plus heureuse position pour assurer le succès des expériences qu'il est utile de faire] Carton U 15, liasse 3.

36. Register Y 14, fol. 104r – 104v, conference of June 4, 1836.

37. [ouvrier que dans le temps vous avez bien voulu prendre sur notre recommandation] Carton T 14, liasse 1, dossier 2.

38. [en janvier 1825, un fabricant de faïence de Toulouse eut l'honneur de vous présenter ses respects et de vous faire sa visite à paris ainsi qu'à Sèvres. C'est moi qui reçu de vous à cette époque l'accueil le plus obligeant et les marques de cette bienveillance avec laquelle vous recevés tous ceux qui s'adressent à vous dans le but de s'instruire] Carton T 11, liasse 2, dossier 10.

39. [Monsieur, vous avez toujours acceuilli avec tant de bienveillance mon fils aîne, que je ne dois pas craindre de vous paraître trop importun en vous présentant le porteur de la présente, qui est le plus jeune de mes enfants. Comme son frère Léon Arnoux, directeur de notre manufacture de poterie, celui-ci se rend à Paris pour suivre les cours de l'école centrale] Carton T 15, liasse 1, dossier 4, letter dated October 10, 1845.

40. [dimanche à l'heure ou vous recevez habituellement] Carton T 14, liasse 2, dossier 5, letter dated April 2, 1845.

41. Carton U 8, dossier "Exposition du 1er Mai 1835." Brongniart cites Nast, Honoré, Neppel, Discry, Denuelle, and Baruch-Weill.

42. [Le désir d'attacher le nom de la Manufacture du Roi à toutes les améliorations qui se font dans les arts céramiques m'a fait écouter les propositions de Mr. de Saint Amand quoique j'y entrevisse pour moi un surcroît de travail et de surveillance . . . Je ne vois pas d'inconvénient réel à lui accorder la permission qu'il demande, j'y vois au contraire de l'instruction pour nous et quelqu'honneur pour la Manufacture du Roi qui aura à se féliciter d'avoir concouru par sa seule intervention protectrice à l'introduction d'une poterie très recherchée et nouvelle pour la France] Register Vc 7, fol. 185ff., letter dated February 18, 1828.

43. Carton T 14, liasse 5, dossier 19.

44. [de la manière la plus complète; je viens de recevoir de Mr. Frick directeur de cet établissement et mon compagnon de voyage en Allemagne en 1812 une lettre qui ne me laisse aucun doute à ce sujet] Register Vc 9, fol. 8 – 10, letter dated April 22, 1836.

45. [je ne puis me défendre, Monsieur le Baron, de vous faire remarquer, peut-être avec un sentiment ou perce de ma part un peu de vanité . . . que la plupart des chefs d'etablissements céramiques de porcelaine sont en Allemagne ou minéralogistes ou attachés à l'art et à l'administration des mines] Carton M 10, dossier 1, letter to Baron Fain, Intendant Général de la Liste Civile, dated October 12, 1836.

46. [Je n'ai point craint de multiplier ces questions ni même d'en faire d'indiscrètes . . . je considère les manufactures impériales ou royales non pas comme des maisons de commerce particulières qui croyent devoir faire mystère de tout, mais comme des établissements chargés de porter leur art à sa perfection et qui doivent mettre en usage pour arriver à ce but les memes moyens de communication qu'employent les savants pour faire faire des progrés à la science qu'ils cultivent] Carton T 2, liasse 2, letter dated 26 Frimaire year 14 (December 17, 1805).

47. [la conduite du feu des moufles . . . le procédé de l'impression que je considère comme une chose des plus précieuses dans l'industrie de la fabrication] Carton Ob 7, dossier Lyngbye.

48. [en le remerciant de ce petit présent, il faudra lui annoncer que vous vous occupés de lui faire un envoi semblable et je crois qu'il convient que cet envoi soit plus beau que le sien. La manufacture que vous dirigés avec tant d'habileté ne doit avoir qu'un objet: celui d'être constamment la première de l'Europe sous tous les rapports] Carton T 2, liasse 1, dossier 1, letter dated 21 Frimaire year 14 (December 13, 1805).

49. [Comme la capitale dans laquelle ce présent doit être envoyé possède une belle manufacture de porcelaine, il sera essentiel que les objets . . . soient particulièrement beaux et qu'ils puissent constater aux yeux des étrangers notre supériorité dans ce genre d'industrie] Carton M 6, liasse 3, commandes du Ministère des Affaires Étrangeres 1825 – 1828, letter dated December 7, 1826.

50. [Sa Majeste . . . a arrêté que la Manufacture de Sèvres serait chargée d'exécuter pour S.M. le roi de Prusse deux vases de forme et de dimensions absolument semblables à celui que ce monarque a daigné m'envoyer et qui est sorti des ateliers de Berlin. Je n'ai pas besoin de vous recommander d'apporter tous vos soins à ce que ces deux objets soient de nature à constater la supériorité de notre industrie dans ce genre de fabrication, et accroître chez l'étranger la juste renommée de l'établissement que vous dirigez] Carton M 6, liasse 4, dossier 2, letter dated November 17, 1826.

51. [d'ailleurs, et c'est une chose malheureuse pour les arts, la plupart des anciens modèles des manufactures perdent beaucoup de leur valeur au bout d'un certain temps, parce qu'ils portent un caractère de cette demi-ancienneté que le public rejette le plus ordinairement] Register Vc 7, fol. 191vff., letter dated May 29, 1828.

52. [un des buts d'utilité auxquels elle tend est de répandre dans les arts les bons procédés et les bons modèles, ou du moins ce qu'elle regarde comme tels, et de favoriser ainsi leurs progrès. Un de ces moyens est d'offrir aux fabricants de bons modèles qu'ils peuvent *imiter* ou *copier* . . . et même de leur donner quelquefois le moyen d'acquérir sans aucun frais ce qui lui a coûté beaucoup en leur permettant d'en tirer des moules] Carton T 9, liasse 3, dossier 2, letter dated March 22, 1822.

53. In 1837, the prefect of the Haute-Vienne had solicited for the city of Limoges "a suite of models of the principal forms, both utilitarian and ornamental, executed by the royal manufactory of Sèvres." Brongniart regretted that the request had remained a dead letter, maintaining that granting it would have been "honorable for the royal manufactory, [and] perhaps useful for both the Limoges porcelain producers and those of other pottery factories" (register Vc 9, fol. 42 – 42v., letter dated September 29, 1837). Similarly, when the royal administration expressed support for a similar request from the bronze-worker Victor Paillard, Brongniart responded: "I thought I would be fulfilling the intentions of the King by rendering His Majesty's manufactory as useful as it could be to private industry, thereby changing into feelings of esteem and good will those of jealousy and envy that some private producers unthinkingly bear towards it. It is by freely providing them with drawings, models, processes, etc. that I have proven that the King's manufactory was an aid to rather than a competitor of private industry. Thus I have always been disposed to receive producers of porcelain, pottery, and bronze, and to aid them in copying and executing the pieces they desire to imitate" (register Vc 10, fol. 43v, letter dated November 23, 1846).

54. [Etat des fabricants tant en porcelaine qu'en bronze, Mds. de curiosités, etc. qui ont obtenu l'autorisation de reproduire des modèles de Sèvres, tant de l'ancienne que de la nouvelle fabrication, comme Figures et Groupes, Vases, etc. au 27 Novembre 1846] and [1842 Mai 21 Etat des anciens modèles de vases demandés par M. Minton] carton T 15, Liasse 1, dossier 1.

55. [Depuis longtemps nous avons formé le projet d'exécuter les anciennes formes de Sèvres pour le service de table; formes qui du reste ont été copiées précédemment par Monsieur Nast] Ibid., letter dated July 7, 1842.

56. Ibid., undated letter.

57. Carton T 13, liasse 4, dossier 12, letter dated January 17, 1837, concerning a plate sold to two Englishmen by "Le Sr. Marlé md. de curiosité."

58. [tout ce qui est relatif aux arts céramiques et (de) la vitrification dans toutes les parties du monde depuis les temps les plus reculés jusqu'à nos jours] Register Vc 8, fol. 3v-5, letter dated March 5, 1836.

59. [regardant comme un devoir de la position favorable ou je me trouve de composer un ouvrage sur les arts céramiques, j'avais déjà fait le plan et rédigé le sommaire du traité général que je compte terminer et publier dans le courant de 1831 . . . travail dont je me suis occupé depuis plus de huit mois] Ibid., fol. 62, letter dated June 5, 1830.

60. In June 1845, he purchased "a large oval platter with reptiles, shells, and plants, in relief; imitation enameled earthenware by Bernard Palissy" for 100 francs from one "Mr. Avisseau modeleur et mouleur figuriste en terre cuite demeurant à Tours rue Saint Maurice no. 41" (carton R 42 [1845] receipt signed July 7, 1845).

Fig. 6-1. *Vase 'Fuseau',* Sèvres, 1806; hard-paste porcelain. (Compiègne, Musée national du château)

Chapter 6

The Nature and Goals of Production at the Sèvres Manufactory

Tamara Préaud

The collapse of the economy in France during the Revolution had far-reaching repercussions. The ensuing shortages of funds at Sèvres forced the manufactory to focus on the production of small objects for the most part during this time. This was the situation when Alexandre Brongniart became administrator in 1800. Throughout his extended tenure, as the manufactory began to recover and reorganize, these small pieces continued to be made, just as they had been throughout the eighteenth century, never entirely giving way to the large showpieces (fig. 6-1) that soon came into production. Attitudes, however, as well as governments, did change, and during the Empire, Brongniart expressed his confidence in the emperor's preference for prestige items, writing to Pierre Daru, the Intendant Général:

> I still have the same opinion as you, Monsieur, regarding the good that the Sèvres Manufactory should perpetually seek to attain and my efforts are constantly directed to this end. It is certain that if one wants to make a factory lucrative, it is necessary to modify the organization of its works and renounce the large pieces that are very costly due to the ongoing losses that they generate. But I think I am sufficiently well acquainted with the generous and large views of the Emperor to be persuaded that he will require of the Sèvres manufactory only that it continue to be an example of good taste, perfection, and emulation for all porcelain factories.[1]

Eventually, the success achieved by Sèvres's production would add to the prestige of other French porcelain makers in the export markets, and this approach justified the policy in the eyes of the administration, as indicated in a statement by Daru: "The Manufactory that you direct with so much skill should have but a single object: that of being consistently the first of Europe in all respects . . . . The Emperor will derive very little profit from the manufactory; but the commerce of France will gain if it meets the perfection of your example, and this view is more noble, more worthy of the Emperor than the calculation of a small profit."[2]

The return to power of the Bourbons in 1814/15 manifestly corresponded to a change in attitudes of the ruling parties toward the arts and art patronage. Threatened with a significant reduction of funding for the manufactory, Brongniart pleaded his case to the new administration by explaining that "the reduction of funding for fabrication . . . would deprive the manufactory of the means to reimburse the crown treasury with revenues from public sales of a large part of the advances made to it . . . . Far, then, from diminishing work activity, I seek to increase it, but I [plan to] give it a new direction by associating with the art and luxury objects that should nevertheless form the distinctive character of the royal manufactory, many useful objects that will be easy to sell."[3] As proof of this orientation, Brongniart exhibited and sold examples of these small pieces at the annual exhibitions of the products of the manufactory at the Louvre, while the prestigious objects continued to serve primarily as gifts to be offered by the sovereign. Similarly, when Brongniart participated in the 1819 "Exposition des produits de l'industrie" (Exhibition of the Products of French Industry) held at the Louvre, he exhibited only everyday pieces notable for the perfection of the forms and the quality of the workmanship.

In the 1823 exhibition, however, threatened with seeing these simple products drown in the mass display of ceramic objects offered by a multitude of makers, Brongniart preferred to exhibit only showpieces. Subsequently, he refused to participate in these exhibitions altogether, a decision influenced by the hostile reaction of Parisian porcelain makers to the Sèvres manufactory. The views of these rivals had also changed: under the Empire their work had often been as luxurious as that of Sèvres. They had been compelled to simplify it, however, in order to survive economically, and they maintained that Sèvres, by selling more standard, everyday ware, became a rival all the more dangerous because of its privileged, subsidized position. This accusation was ill founded. Brongniart himself declared sadly that the Sèvres objects, although "precious by their perfection in every respect, pure forms, severe decoration, well-executed paintings, [nonetheless were] scarcely appreciated by the richest and most exalted people in Paris [because] most rich people . . . attach greater value to things that are striking and fashionable than to things executed with perfection."[4]

To counter the criticisms of his competitors, Brongniart emphasized that Sèvres could assist the ceramics industry as a whole, not only through its prestige but also by sharing the results of technical experiments and research that it was in a position to undertake. At about the same time, Sèvres began to authorize the reproduction of its models, while continuing to share its vast repos-

Fig. 6-2. *Déjeuner 'Chinois réticulé*, Sèvres, 1840; hard-paste porcelain and gilded bronze. This was made for Queen Marie Amélie. (Musée du Louvre)

itory of technical knowledge. In 1830 Brongniart summarized his position to the commissioners charged with establishing the budget before granting a Liste Civile for King Louis-Philippe:

> I will strive to maintain with decorum and moderation the character of perfection, superiority, and general utility that I have tried to impress upon the establishment entrusted to me, and which has seemed to me to have as its noble destination the conservation and propagation of good processes in the ceramic arts, the provision of support and liberal instruction to all those who practice and study them, the offering to the arts of drawing applied to this kind of industry a refuge against the invasions of bad taste animated by fashion, the furnishing of distinguished artists with a means of cultivating an art capable of preserving the beautiful productions of painting, but an art that is very difficult, very costly, and of too limited a productive capacity as a result of its own perfection to be turned over to private industry.[5]

During the 1833 budget negotiations, Brongniart issued a clear, sweeping statement about the manufactory. All of Sèvres's undertakings were to have "as their end result the maintenance of that which is acknowledged to be good, the perfection of that which is already known, the discovery or application of new things or processes."[6]

He established two main categories of endeavor. The first consisted of scientific work. In addition to "the scientific theory of the ceramic arts," on which "the current director and the chemist" were engaged, Brongniart included the replacement of marble statuary "by biscuit porcelain, which is more durable, more reproducible, and less expensive," as well as painting on glass, which still required "perfection of mounting, increased brilliance, and variation in color,"[7] and even enamel painting on lava stone.[8]

The second category included more artistic work. As to the "kinds of production to undertake," he wrote that this would depend "on the use and issue that the King would like to give these productions."[9] He distinguished five subcategories within this genre, each corresponding to specific types of objects: furnishings for the royal residences, including various table services (fig. 6-2), vases, and furniture; allocations for diplomats and diplomatic gifts, such as elaborate services, large vases, and ambitious pieces of furniture; gifts in recognition of services rendered, such as pieces of intermediate size, and busts and portraits of the royal family; pieces for the collection of the Musée Royal des Arts (exceptional pieces);

and pieces for sale to the public or to administrative agencies, which he described as "small pieces of choice form and with decoration in a rational taste."[10]

Apart from the divisions established by Brongniart, a new kind of use was found for the manufactory's output during the final years of Louis-Philippe's reign, initially on such a modest scale that it would scarcely deserve mention. This consisted of pieces given as prizes, donated to museum collections, or presented in recognition of good works.[11] Eventually, however, this category assumed a prominent role in assuring the manufactory's survival during the Second Republic (1848 – 51).

Commissions

It has been widely assumed that the manufactory worked primarily on state and private commissions, but in reality these were relatively few in number, at least when it came to specific orders. The first state commissions date to April 21, 1806.[12] Some of the objects in this commission were indeed executed: the *table 'des Maréchaux'* (see cat. no. 16); another table, with portraits of great warriors of antiquity; a third table representing the Musée Impérial (see cat. no. 44)[13]; pedestals for large vases (see cat. no. 17); and plates bearing portraits of the sovereign's favorite horses. Other projects were not realized: the biscuit models of the Palais des Tuileries and the Arc de Triomphe du Carrousel, for example, or a table illustrating the imperial family (see cat. no. 26).

The emperor accompanied his orders with specifications concerning the decoration of everything that the manufactory produced for him. In the same 1806 order, for example, he made several recommendations: "Place on the services . . . views of the Adige, of Venice, of Genoa, and of the Realm of Italy, more interesting and more historical than those to be found elsewhere"; for diplomatic gifts, "use portraits, views of Paris and of different imperial palaces"; and "finally, replace all the figures of nude women and insignificant landscapes . . . with things that are known and historical."[14] Napoleon also demanded a list of the "great men of the last century . . . of whom there are models,"[15] referring to the Grands Hommes series of figures that Sèvres had initiated in 1782 and reserving for himself the choice of those to be placed in his apartments. On May 16, 1806, he announced his selection as well as the names of several figures he would like to have added.[16] On November 4, 1807, at the emperor's direction, the Intendant Général, Pierre Daru, ordered a new table service, which was ultimately designated the *service 'de l'Empereur'* (fig. 6-3; see cat. no. 20).[17] On January 3, 1812, the duc de Cadore transmitted Napoleon's instructions for two *déjeuners*, one featuring portraits of the ladies-in-waiting of the court and the other decorated with portraits of the empress's sisters and sisters-in-law.

These few orders represent the only specific imperial commissions. Compared to the bulk of pieces manufactured during this period, they do not amount to much in terms of production. There were virtually no commissions from Louis XVIII, unless it was he who ordered the coffer for his snuffbox with a series of covers featuring portraits painted by Marie-Victoire Jaquotot.[18] Orders from Charles X were almost as scarce. By contrast, Louis-Philippe and Marie-Amélie, who commissioned many stained-glass projects, also made numerous requests for all manner of objects, but without specifying the decorative schemes, themes, or motifs to be applied

Fig. 6-3. Plate decorated with a view of the obelisk of Mont Genèvre from the *service 'de l'Empereur'*; hard-paste porcelain, 1808. (Fondation Napoléon)

to the pieces they ordered. From the various administrations Brongniart also received many requests that were vague and imprecise, noting only object type, value, and quantity. On 10 Nivôse year 13 (December 31, 1804), for example, the *intendant général de la Liste Civile* asked for "the most beautiful objects from the manufactory, and the most fitting to be distributed tomorrow by Her Majesty the Empress as New Year's gifts."[19] In 1809 the comte de Frioul announced that the emperor wanted to present the king of Saxony "with beautiful vases larger than those he can obtain at home," and the queen of Westphalia with "something gallant."[20] In 1840 it was made known that the king had stipulated that production should consist primarily of medium-sized vases, *déjeuners*, tazza, and table services,[21] and in 1844 the comte de Montalivet wrote: "the King desires that a certain number of porcelain *déjeuners* be composed for a price of between three and six thousand francs."[22]

In addition to commissions placed directly by the sovereign, the manufactory was obliged to respond to orders from various official agencies — the Garde-Meuble, the *officiers de la bouche*, who were in charge of everything relating to meals in the royal household, and the *officiers des appartements* for the various residences — as well as from government ministries. Finally, private individuals and dealers could also place orders. In most cases, these were for table services decorated with monograms and coats-of-arms.[23]

The known commissions and orders reveal the great extent of the director's responsibilities. He alone was in a position to estimate future demand and to set production levels accordingly. He was called on to explain his calculations in this regard on several occasions. On 24 Brumaire year 13 (November 15, 1805), for example, protesting against being obligated to empty his warehouses to furnish the Château de Fontainebleau, he wrote that: "when establishing the vases in question, I reflected on the uses for which they might be intended, and I assessed their beauty and value such that some might be appropriate for decorating the palaces of the Tuileries and Saint-Cloud, which have almost none, and others might be offered as gifts by the government, and, these two goals having been fulfilled, a sufficient number would remain to furnish the other palaces."[24]

Somewhat later, he described his general approach: "The porcelains I put into production have no particular destination except when they are ordered for some special purpose. In the ordinary course of work, these are intended to enrich the warehouse with all the pieces that can be requested for the service of the Emperor or bought by the trade . . . . It is in accordance with my experience of these rather frequent requests, the nature of the pieces that are preferred, the high value expected of them, and the rapidity with which they must be delivered, that I direct the work at the manufactory."[25]

After having vainly requested specifics as to the number and size of the pieces that Charles X might want to bestow as gifts at his official coronation at Notre Dame in 1825, Brongniart had to decide on his own and noted that "it is precisely by responding to such extraordinary needs in all regards, which is to say unexpectedly yet with magnificence and propriety, that the manufactory . . . gives proof of its utility in different respects."[26]

Apart from Brongniart's involvement with production levels, it also fell to him to determine what was produced. Each year he established a chart listing the pieces that were to be made, stipulating their categories, and numbering them. Each object was then assigned to one or more painter-gilders, and additional summary lists were drawn up for each artist to assure that all of them were kept busy.[27] This made it easier to allocate the work loads properly and to use the available personnel to the best advantage. The administrator also had to take into account production capabilities, weighing the reuse of extant models against the obligation to create new ones.[28] For all objects and ensembles of any importance, progress sheets or files were prepared and annotated as work advanced.

With the exception of certain "political" subjects the decorative schemes on pieces were also largely selected by Brongniart. The choice of ornamental motifs featuring landscapes, flowers, plants, and animals was left entirely to his discretion, as was that of most figural compositions, which were still popular. The traditional ranking of categories within the arts, upon which academic art was based, retained much of its authority during Brongniart's tenure. This system, which placed history painting at the top of the hierarchy, had been established in the seventeenth century by the Académie Royale in Paris. Whatever the motif, however, the administrator issued precise instructions that left the decorators very little freedom, as in his directives to Fragonard for porcelain plaques (see cat. no. 46). In most cases, Brongniart probably stipulated the choice of subsidiary motifs as well, for these had to be stylistically and thematically consistent with the principal ones.

Artists and Consultants

Brongniart sometimes had less independence when it came to selecting artists, both those serving purely in an advisory capacity and those who were his true collaborators, producing forms, executing decorative schemes, and painting compositions. Only two men were ever named to supervisory positions officially above his own, and, while he did not select either of them, he seems to have gotten along quite well with both of them.

The first, Dominique-Vivant Denon, bore the title, "director of the Louvre, of the Mint, and of the Sèvres Manufactory," but this is somewhat misleading. Denon indeed made recommendations about the production and selection of what was then called Etruscan and Egyptian forms. He also influenced the choice of certain artists and subjects, occasionally acting as an intermediary between Sèvres and some artists, and he oversaw work during Brongniart's absences, but this was the full extent of his involvement in the manufactory's operations. Despite Brongniart's many ties to the artistic world, dating to his youth, it is likely that the young scientist would have been delighted to have so benevolent an advisor as Denon at his disposal.

In the same manner, Lancelot Théodore Turpin vicomte de Crissé, named an *inspecteur* in the *département des beaux-arts de la Maison du Roi* in 1825, had nothing but praise for the director of Sèvres. He not only offered advice about forms such as the *vase 'Etrusque Turpin'*, but also served as an intermediary in dealings with artists — assessing and guiding their work and negotiating fees — and made several acquisitions at auctions for the Musée Céramique. During this period, Brongniart certainly had no need for a moral authority to support him, but the existence of an official advisor can scarcely have displeased him, given that he had always sought the counsel of others.

When, in 1807, there was a possibility that the manufactory would be closed because the emperor thought he detected faults in the colors and poor draftsmanship,[29] Brongniart explained how he went about assessing the work performed there: "Although I have devoted myself more to the sciences, notably chemistry and mineralogy, than to the arts, I do not think myself a stranger to them. Even so, I cannot delegate to myself the right to judge and to have the drawing of an artist who passes for being talented altered, but I can only choose them well and to base my judgment on their merit, I have used a means that seemed to me suited to eliminate prejudice. Often and repeatedly I show to artists of acknowledged merit, such as Gérard and others, work by painters who work for the manufactory, and in accordance with the judgments that they make separately and on several occasions, I appraise rather impartially the merit of the various persons."[30]

In 1826 he wrote to the vicomte de La Rochefoucauld, *directeur général des beaux arts de la Maison du Roi*: "I will maintain, as you kindly encourage me to do, the course I have followed, which is to adopt no artist exclusively but to consult with and listen to all those who, having a well-deserved reputation for their work, can never be completely wrong, and to choose among their counsels, when these are not unanimous, those which seem to me the best, for with such good guides I can be assured of following various paths without straying far from the good route, at least not for very long."[31]

One of Brongniart's principal advisors was apparently François Gérard, who gave opinions about the work of others on a regular basis and lent his own works to Sèvres for copying on several occasions, from portraits of the emperor to such works as *Cupid and Psyche*. He even made a drawing specifically for the manufactory entitled *Homer with the Potters of Samos.* The list of artists who visited the Louvre exhibition of Sèvres products on May 1, 1835, indicates that Brongniart must have maintained particularly close relations with official artists and members of the Institut de France, to which he also belonged.[32]

In addition to being asked to offer advice regarding the choice and selection of pieces, many artists were actively involved in the process of creation and execution. On his arrival, Brongniart had requested and obtained permission to abolish the *artiste-en-chef* positions, an action meant to encourage more variety in the production than at that time existed.[33] The need for variety was generally acknowledged. Denon, for example, urged: "The more such people we have, the better they will perform. The result will be a variety of taste that will benefit the manufactory."[34] Brongniart was determined to employ at Sèvres not only varied talents but, above all, those that were the best. In 1808 he could announce to the Intendant Général with pride: "The manufactory has never possessed a more complete gathering of distinguished artists and workers. Not only does it have without *any exception* the best porcelain figure painters that exist in Paris, it has also taught several distinguished artists how to paint on porcelain, by this means increasing the number of painters in this genre."[35]

Brongniart was constantly obligated to defend his freedom of choice in the face of countless recommendations made by members of the court. On one such occasion, he justified his independence, writing: "Discrimination in the choice of artists and workers, a choice determined solely by their talent and independent of all other considerations such as high or powerful protection, adversity, need for a livelihood, a situation worthy of support, services rendered, etc. etc., all of which are admissible as qualifications when what is in question is not a manufactory in which it is a constant necessity to make objects of art and industry better than anyone else, this severity in making choices, I say, is one of the fundamental principles of the success of our work."[36]

He even maintained that such recommendations were a disservice to their intended beneficiaries: "Please be persuaded, Monsieur le Vicomte, of this rule that will rarely deceive you: all porcelain artists who solicit recommendations for positions at the king's manufactory indicate by this very [action] that they are mediocre talents with whom neither producers nor enlightened amateurs want anything to do. Skillful persons, on the contrary, the only persons worthy of working for this royal establishment, are almost always busy as a result of their talent and ask for nothing. I have been compelled to seek out almost all the skilled artists and workers that make the honor and reputation of the manufactory."[37]

Brongniart had precise ideas as to the type of artist he sought to recruit: "Sèvres needs either persons of remarkable talent capable of sustaining the reputation of the king's manufactory, contributing to the merit, value, and interest of very large and very expensive pieces that the manufactory produces, or persons with fluent and agreeable talents in a position to decorate small utilitarian and ornamental pieces in a tasteful and seductive manner."[38]

Aspiring figure painters were by far the most numerous applicants seeking employment at the manufactory, and Brongniart established a demanding criteria for their selection: "When it is a question . . . of hiring a figure painter for this establishment, my choice should fall on he or she whose *talent is the most elevated, the most complete, and the best suited to our work.* No other considerations, of whatever kind, should have the slightest influence over me. . . . When a painter-copyist is in question, as the manufactory should produce only copies of paintings of the first merit, he must have the talent to render the original *perfectly* and *completely*, for of what use is an expensive copy if it does not fulfill these necessary conditions perfectly?"[39]

Reliance on painters also employed by rival Parisian producers sometimes caused difficulties, if freelance painter Moïse Jacobber is to be believed. In a letter to Brongniart, he wrote: "The effect of the second firing on my plates is one of the disadvantages that results from doing the same kind [of work] in two ways so contradictory to one another, since by doing work alternatively for Paris and for you, the latter must necessarily be affected by the carelessness required by the first, and this incompatibility is also prejudicial against me, for having completed the work for you, I cannot subsequently summon the hastiness required by the fees [I receive] for my work for Paris."[40]

The role of the head painter was defined quite clearly by Brongniart to two candidates being considered to replace Claude-Charles Gérard as *chef des peintres* in 1825:

> I sent both of them a written description of the principal responsibilities and obligations; I tried to acquaint them with the qualities necessary properly to fill the post . . . . I tried to convey to them that it would be necessary, without ceasing to be just, to be the man of the manufactory and not of the artists and workers attached to their department; that precise knowledge of all color and firing processes was required, along with that of the value and [necessary] quantities of the materials used; that without being an artist of the first rank, it would be good for them to possess a certain amount of talent so that they would be respected, and that they must have sufficient skill and drawing ability to decorate ordinary objects with taste, reflection, and decorum. That the decoration of large pieces often being carried out in accordance with designs provided by the most distinguished artists, it was necessary to know how to direct their execution with discernment as regards their success and even from the point of view of economy, which here consists of achieving perfection by the shortest and surest route; finally, that in addition to [possessing] all this expertise they would be obliged to oversee [the work] actively and at every moment.[41]

Relations between the administrator and the artists selected by him were not always free from problems. In order to convince them to give priority to their work for Sèvres, Brongniart used a "mixture of firmness and respect, [exercising] much moderation in order not to alienate and lose skillful artists, small in number, very useful, and difficult to replace."[42] He affirmed elsewhere: "I do not want . . . to be disobeyed at Sèvres, and for that reason I order only what I have the right to order and the power to implement."[43] Despite his goodness, he was sufficiently convinced of the eminence of the royal manufactory to be severe with turncoats. In a letter to a former Sèvres painter named Langle, he wrote:

> I thought, Monsieur, that the Sèvres manufactory was a royal

establishment sufficiently remarkable by its reputation and importance for some honor to follow from attachment to it, and for continued affiliation with it to be incumbent upon no conditions. I have never accepted any such from anyone, and I will not begin today by entertaining those from a person who has no title to demand even such distinctions as might rightfully be claimed by a great talent. . . . I remind you, Monsieur, what I have always maintained and have said to you, namely that when one leaves the manufactory in this way one will never return to it as long as I remain there, and that the note placed in the register will certainly engage my successors to adhere to the same rule.[44]

One of the main areas of friction between artist and administrator was the setting of fees and remunerations. The series of registers that record descriptions of work completed, the sums requested by the artists, and the fees finally accorded by the administrator, bears witness to frequent disagreements. The father of Josse François Joseph Swebach was undoubtedly expressing a widely held view when he wrote: "I am not surprised that you found my son's vases too expensive. I am used to your haggling, and I think that if I asked six francs for a work that is worth fifty, force of habit would lead you to offer me five francs."[45]

Despite such conflicts, documents as well as objects indicate that, overall, Brongniart had a good relationship with his workers. He managed to maintain considerable variety by using artists of quite diverse talents, and because his acute sense of his own obligations was countered by genuine benevolence, he was able to maintain an atmosphere sufficiently harmonious to foster a remarkably high quality of production.

Sèvres Production under Brongniart

The richness and variety of the Sèvres porcelain preclude any general characterization. Even so, there are a few general principles that apply. Brongniart's attitudes toward the proper overall style for the manufactory's products seem to have changed over his long career. At the beginning, he avoided adherence to fashion, writing to the Intendant Général in 1815: "I try to maintain in the forms and modes of decoration the principles of a style exempt from the influence of fashion. The happy position in which the manufactory finds itself provides it with the means to shelter itself from this influence pernicious to good taste and the arts. I also try to use on the pieces only subjects of some historical or literary interest, and I avoid as much as possible subjects that are insignificant or completely invented."[46]

In 1826 the vicomte de La Rochefoucauld encouraged Brongniart to retain these views: "If the Sèvres manufactory is the first in Europe, it owes this . . . to the care you have taken to avoid everything that might offend against taste and appear to be a product of fashionable caprice."[47] The situation changed considerably after 1830, when sources of inspiration began to multiply, but Brongniart continued to insist on the necessity of strict rules even in the context of the new eclecticism. In 1831 he wrote: "I desired to show that these works exemplified all styles and all genres susceptible of acceptance by men of taste, whatever style or genre they might prefer. I sought to make the manufactory's products monuments to the history of the arts in their different phases, and while seeking to have them attain this double goal I sought to have them please the mind as much as the eye."[48]

The principal characteristic of Sèvres in all periods is the extraordinary variety of its production. This results, first of all, from the use of many different forms for each type of object. During the first half of the nineteenth century, new designs for ninety-two different vases and eighty-nine different cups were produced, including the variations in their handles and feet. These forms did not displace one another. As new models were added, older ones continued to

Fig. 6-4. Casket called *coffret 'la Toilette des femmes dans les cinq parties du monde'*, Sèvres, 1842; hard-paste porcelain. This piece was presented by King Louis-Philippe to Queen Victoria. (Royal Collection, Her Majesty Queen Elizabeth II)

be made, if only to accommodate replacement orders. As a result, the diversity of production at any given moment was impressive.

The range of objects produced is equally astonishing. Dinner services consisted of soup or bouillon dishes and/or dinner plates, butter dishes, salad bowls, sauceboats with stands, and gravy jugs with stands; to these were sometimes added soup tureens, saltcellars, dishes, and casseroles. For dessert services, there were smaller plates, compotes, dishes, table-sugar bowls, ice-cream coolers, fruit bowls, and baskets. Each object existed, of course, in many versions which could be combined in a multitude of ways. Some pieces could be sold either as part of a service or separately, for example egg cups, jam pots, and broth bowls. Very few changes were introduced into the ensemble of the eighteenth-century *déjeuner*, which included cups and saucers, cream or milk jugs, sugar bowls, and tea or coffee servers. The specialized cups for tea, coffee, and chocolate began to take on distinct characteristics, and low-footed dishes and trays were eventually added. Toiletry articles did not change; they included water jugs, washbasins, round and oval chamber pots, and various jars and boxes. Other functional pieces included sewing thimbles, inkstands, lamps, and pipes. Some porcelain plaques bore copies of paintings, while others were incorporated into furnishings of various sizes: jewel caskets (fig. 6-4), consoles (see cat. no. 46), clocks, tables, and *guéridons*. Because variations were based on existing forms, there were actually few real additions made to the line. In fact, very few additions of any kind were made to the existing catalogue of objects, that had been produced in porcelain in the eighteenth century. These additions included etagères, melon dishes, ice-cream cups, pots for herbal teas, zarfs, compotes and stands, comfit dishes, and breakfast trays with a central vertical handle.

A process of revitalization began with Brongniart's appointment as director, and gradually thereafter the rhythms of creation slowed, except around 1823 – 25 and after the accession of Louis-Philippe in 1830. Most of the polystylistic tendencies of the era appeared as early as the Empire, and these developed subsequently at varying rates. Neoclassicism gradually lost ground to the regional and historical forms of exoticism fostered by Romanticism.

A similar diversity characterizes the sources that were used for forms and decorative schemes. Inspiration was derived from ancient ceramics borrowed from the Louvre, the Musée Céramique, or private collections; contemporary objects made by foreign ceramic producers[49]; and ancient or contemporary works from France or abroad of widely varying character, including paintings, prints, or other graphic works, both specially commissioned and otherwise, as well as medals and other diverse objects.

Decorative schemes fell into two basic categories. There were those adhering to the system developed during the years that the manufactory was at Vincennes (1740 – 56). They consisted of a colored ground, gold ornament often heightened with platinum during the first half of the nineteenth century, and cartouches (or reserves) bearing painted compositions in polychrome or cameos. In the decoration of these reserves, Brongniart again remained faithful to the academic hierarchy of painting genres. The second category consisted of purely ornamental schemes, which sought to free decorative motifs from the tyranny of the cartouche. This approach was intentional. Denis-Désiré Riocreux, describing Parisian decorative schemes inspired by Limoges enamels in grisaille, wrote in 1840: "This decoration makes hard-paste porcelain

Fig. 6-5. *Vase 'Jasmin Cornet à anses'*, Sèvres, 1844; hard-paste porcelain. (Fontainebleau, musée national du Château)

emerge from the circumscribed resources within which it seemed obliged to be contained."[50] The diversity of decorative systems explored to this end is remarkable: bichromatic color schemes (fig. 6-5; blue and gold, white and gold, red and black); scraping the ground to expose the porcelain body and applying contrasting color; adding colored ornament in relief; inlaying colored paste into the porcelain body; and imitating enamels applied on a metal surface.

In most cases, the surface decorations at Sèvres were typical of those available during the first half of the nineteenth century. There was a striving for stylistic and thematic consistency between decorative schemes as a whole and the forms to which they were applied, but variety was also a constant preoccupation. The same forms were often decorated with different ornamental schemes; such pieces cannot be considered unique. Nonetheless, the coordination of the principal subject matter and its ornament was always carefully calculated.

Finally, one of the most characteristic manifestations of Brongniart's methodical frame of mind appeared very early in his administration, namely his preference for coherent, thematically linked ensembles of objects. The *service 'á vues de Suisse'* (1804) was

Fig. 6-6. Fruit bowl called *jatte à fruits 'sirènes'* from the *service 'des Petites chasses'*, Sèvres, 1821; hard-paste porcelain. (Sèvres, Musée national de céramique)

something of an innovation at Sèvres. It featured depictions of real landscapes as they appeared in a series of prints. Logical groupings of pieces of this sort came to dominate most of Sèvres's production during Brongniart's tenure, as demonstrated by matching vases and other decorative objects, programmatic *déjeuners* and table services, and coordinated central and subsidiary decorative motifs. Brongniart explained his views on this point in an 1834 letter: "I have always sought to give a kind of interest to ornamental and service pieces issuing from the manufactory's workshops by attaching the principal idea to the ensemble of these objects or to their various parts, by forming suites linked by a kind of program or by devotion to a quality, a use, or to some other idea or principal condition."[51]

First Empire. Brongniart began his administration by clearing the warehouses of outmoded pieces. Admittedly, most of the service pieces in question dated from the end of the Vincennes years in the early 1750s; but not everything was rejected. The illustrated form books indicate that neoclassical designs by Louis-Simon Boizot and Jean-Jacques Lagrenée survived the purge, as did the classic *tasse 'Litron'.* Limitations in staff and financial resources necessitated the gradual development of new forms, each of which required a long gestation period.

The earliest of the new forms were designed by Brongniart's father (architect Alexandre-Théodore Brongniart) and Charles Percier, both of whom favored severe profiles inspired by antique models for vases — such as the *'oeuf'*, *'fuseau'* and *'étrusque'* vase forms — as well as tableware, as in the *déjeuner 'Pestum'* (see cat. no. 113). Denon, for his part, recommended the use of "Etruscan" models, either from the Musée Napoléon or from the collection of ancient ceramics that he himself had assembled and then sold to Louis XVI in 1786 (see cat. nos. 114, 115). There were also countless "Egyptian" models borrowed from Denon's own drawings made during Napoleon's Egyptian campaign in 1798 (see cat. no. 116). There are a few instances of more fantastic forms (fig. 6-6), often of naturalistic inspiration, for example, an inkstand (1810) and a sugar bowl (*écritoire* and *pot à sucre 'Argonaute'*, 1813), accurately modeled after seashells, and a *théière 'Oeuf et Serpent'* (1805; see cat. no. 32)

Fig. 6-7. Tabletop, *table 'des Maréchaux'*, Sèvres, 1810; hard-paste porcelain. (Châteaux de Malmaison et de Bois Préau)

and accompanying pieces, as well as even more ambitious objects the first of which was the candelabrum presented to the pope in 1805. It was also during the years of Brongniart's tenure that the manufactory produced elements for its first large pieces of furniture, tables, and columns.

With regard to iconography, Brongniart had no choice but to focus on imperial propaganda of various kinds, including: portraits of the sovereign and members of his family and entourage; celebrations of Napoleon's military victories, as in a vase commemorating the battle of Austerlitz (see fig. 6-10 and cat. no. 14), or another vase bearing a copy of Jacques-Louis David's *Napoleon Crossing the Saint-Bernard* (1810). There were evocations of court life including hunting scenes (see cat. no. 25) and allegories such as those found on objects celebrating the birth of the emperor's son, the future king of Rome (see cat. no. 30). Even depictions of great figures from antiquity were linked to the sovereign; for example, a table commemorating ancient military leaders (1812) was commissioned at the same time as the *table 'des Maréchaux'*, honoring the marshals who served under Napoleon (fig. 6-7; see cat. no. 16).

While some genre subjects also evoked Napoleonic themes — such as *A Conscript Departing the Paternal Farm* by Jean-Louis Demarne, which was copied on a *vase 'Clodion'* — others were solely anecdotal, for example Swebach's grisaille depictions of various craftsmen which appeared on the two *services 'Encyclopédique'*.

Landscapes also tended to be linked to the life of the emperor, if only indirectly, the most obvious case being the *service 'de l'Empereur'*, his personal service (fig. 6-8; see cat. nos. 20, 21). In some cases, however, figural compositions were free of all contemporary allusion, as in the mythological scenes on the *service 'Olympique'*, which had been started, however, before the Empire.

Flower painting, which was rather scorned at the beginning of the period by Brongniart, subsequently returned to favor, largely because it served to demonstrate the broad range of the manufactory's palette. Examples include gold, ornamental friezes of stylized flowers designed by Brongniart père for use on tableware, ornamental pieces, and small vases. Various polychrome motifs, among them flowering plants, bouquets, floral insets, and rich floral wreaths encircling vases were also used during this period.

Fig. 6-9. One of a pair of ice pails called *glacières 'Chimères'* from the *service 'de la Chevalerie'*, Sèvres, 1834; hard-paste porcelain and gilded silver. (Manufacture Nationale de Sèvres, Archives)

Fig. 6-8. Plate decorated with a view of the Palais des Tuileries and the rue de Rivoli, from the *service 'de l'Empereur'*, Sèvres, 1808 – 10; hard-paste porcelain. (Château de Fontainebleau, musée Napoléon)

A few approaches that were to be exploited more fully in later years made their first appearance in this period. Such was the case with historicism: in Germinal year 13 (April 1805) Swebach executed a "gothic painting"; in 1807 a *service 'de l'Histoire de France'* was begun (fig. 6-9; see cat. no. 71); and in 1808 two *vases 'Floréal'* were decorated with polychrome figures of Jeanne Hachette and Seigneur de Bayard, accompanied by military attributes, possibly suggesting imperial propaganda. Doubtless this was also true of the *vase 'Cordelier'* bearing a copy of Demarne's *Henri IV Returning from the Battle of Joyeuse* (1809).

Florentine micro-mosaics and pietra dura inspired a mode of decoration that first appeared in 1806 and reached a peak between

Fig. 6-10. *Vase 'à bandeau';* Sèvres, 1806; hard-paste porcelain. (Châteaux de Malmaison et de Bois Préau)

1811 and 1814, after which it quickly disappeared (see cat. no. 24).

The eighteenth-century brand of exoticism, typified by *turquerie* and chinoiserie, became more varied. The influence of the Egyptian survey expedition was intensified at Sèvres as a result of Denon's advisory role there. Aside from the *service 'Egyptien'* (see cat. no. 13), with its monumental centerpiece (1807 – 8), many déjeuners with forms and ornamentation inspired by the same source were produced, as were vases decorated with "Mameluke" motifs. There are also references to "Indian" motifs, schemes in the "Japanese taste" (1808 – 09), and "Cashmere borders" accompanied by "Persian" motifs (1812 – 13), probably inspired by the shawls that had become fashionable. Such terminology was indiscriminately applied; a teapot commissioned by the banker Etienne Delessert in 1812, for example, was sometimes described as "Japanese" and sometimes as "Turkish" (see cat. no. 37).

Another new source reflects a general shift in taste. Instead of copying works by seventeenth-century Flemish masters or by contemporaries, as had been done in the eighteenth century, the best Sèvres painters began to take their inspiration from Italian Renaissance artists. In 1809, for example, Jaquotot copied Raphael's portrait of Joanna of Aragon and Leonardo's *La Belle Ferronière*; Antoine Bérenger reproduced Raphael's *School of Athens* on a déjeuner tray begun in 1814, and on another tray begun the same year, Jaquotot copied Leonardo's *La Belle Jardinière.*

In addition to these transcriptions, there were other developments in the approach to decoration. Within the traditional framing and blocking scheme, remarkable advances in the palette of colors — probably the result of Brongniart's training as a mineralogist — led to a proliferation of antique cameos of trompe l'oeil sardonyx, agate, carnelian, and other hard stones (see cat. nos. 8, 23). These were far more convincing that the pale imitations sometimes found on eighteenth-century pieces. Brongniart's interest in mineralogy might also explain a parallel development — the increasingly prevalent use of trompe l'oeil marble and hardstone as ground treatment.

Several modes of decoration that had been used briefly in the preceding century were brought back into production. Most of these had relatively simple palettes. Red and black schemes in the Etruscan style were not new to Sèvres (they had first been used there in 1785), but they now met with unprecedented success. Discussing the *vase 'd'Austerlitz'* (fig. 6-10), Brongniart wrote: "This sort of painting is not rich, but it is severe, monumental, and the only kind that can be executed quickly."[52] Despite the administrator's customary rigor, the archaeological accuracy was not always perfect. Thus one finds a "rectangular plaque [of a] Greek subject executed in Etruscan [style]," dating from 1805, and an "Egyptian sugar bowl [with] Etruscan decoration in red and black," dating from 1810.[53]

Figures painted in gold against a blue ground with incised outlines were also reintroduced at this time. The process had been used for a type of decoration called *figures étrusques* that had first been used in 1782. In its revival, however, it also evolved; outline incisions were replaced first by shadows painted in brown, then by shadows in burnished gold. Similarly, grounds that had been blue in earlier works could be rendered as tortoise shell or chromium green.

Another technique that began to be used again was the scraping away of areas of the colored ground to accommodate painted motifs. Previously, it was used in the 1760s for setting polychrome flowers against a blue ground known as *bleu Fallot.* In 1807 it was used again for pieces with the new chromium green ground, first for figures and then for floral motifs. At that time, Brongniart wrote of vases that Jean Georget had painted with this technique: "It is a new genre and should produce quite an effect."[54]

There were no real innovations in the area of relief decorations set against colored grounds. Sèvres, like Wedgwood in England, had begun to use this technique in the 1780s.[55] In addition to the traditional white-against-pale- blue scheme that continued to be used for vases, pieces produced during the Empire also featured gold reliefs set against red and blue grounds as in elements of the centerpiece ensemble for the *service 'Olympique'* and a sumptuous white against gold, further enriched by contrasts between the glazed and matte areas (see cat. nos. 19, 31). The taste for antique sculpture reflected in such decorations also explains the rare paintings imitating reliefs in faux bronze (see cat. no. 1).

Finally, new decorative techniques were also perfected and used under the Empire. The transfer-printing process was introduced (see chap. 4), and the Sèvres archives also contain mysterious references to "pâte-sur-pâte" which apparently produced results resembling the *molette* technique whereby a rolling pin carved with a motif is used to impress a frieze of repeated motifs into the surface of the malleable porcelain. The process was patented by Jean-Népomucène-Herman Nast. References are also made to an "inset stone" technique, which involved either a trompe l'oeil painting of a stone or real stone insets; both the latter two types of decoration seem to have enjoyed a brief heyday at the end of the Empire and the beginning of the Restauration (see cat. no. 40).

The Restauration. There was neither a stylistic nor a significant political rupture between the successive reigns of Louis XVIII (1814 – 24) and his brother Charles X (1824 – 30), which allows the Restauration period to be considered as a whole. Fewer new forms were created during these years than under the Empire; the dominant creative figure in the period was Alexandre-Evariste Fragonard. Most of the pieces continued to be based on the same sources that had been used during the previous regime. Stylistically, neoclassicism continued to dominate production, although in a less severe mode than previously, as seen in many designs, such as in the *vase 'Etrusque Turpin'* (1825) and the *vase 'Grec de Luynes'* (1828), as well as pieces for *déjeuners* such as the *pot à lait 'Campanien'* (1825), or pieces for the table such as the *compotier 'Clarac'* (1824), *compotier 'étrusque de 1825'* (see cat. no. 119), or the *compotier 'à Quatre Pieds'* (see cat. no. 65), among others. The most imaginative, inventive work of the period was in designs for table services. An entirely new type of object was introduced: the *porte-compotier*, described on the occasion of the January 1826 exhibition at the Louvre as a "kind of little table, made like those used by the ancients."[56]

Naturalism, which had been used at the factory during the Empire, continued to develop in every area of production. It can be seen in such objects as a *vase 'Jasmin Treillis'* (see cat. no. 43); an inkstand called *'Navire'* (1814), an ice-pail called *'Madrepore'* (1817); a sugar bowl called *pot à sucre 'Mélissin'* (see cat. no. 51); and a shell-shaped butter dish called *beurrier 'Simple Coquille'* (see cat. no. 120). The Gothic style, previously but a timid presence in the Sèvres decorative vocabulary, began to manifest itself in such forms as a *vase 'Anthophore'* (1822, see cat. no. 57), *coupe 'Diatrète'* (1819; see cat. no. 48), *tasse 'Gothique'*, *vase 'Gothique Fragonard'* (1824), and *guéridon 'Gothique'* (1829). Exoticism made a tentative spontaneous reappearance in such designs as a teapot called *'Chinoise'* (1818; see cat. no. 47) and was subsequently reinforced by specific commissions such as those for cups designated *tasse 'Turque'* and *tasse 'Japonaise'* (1816), or pieces called *'Persan'* (1825; see cat. no. 64). Similarly, forms created in the early years of the century continued to be produced but with revised decorations.

Monarchical propaganda replaced that which had aggrandized the emperor; although the approach taken was similar, the percentage of such pieces in the overall production declined. In addition to portraits of the rulers and family members, there were evocations of military exploits, as in the *vase 'Etrusque AB'* (1825, see cat. no. 59) commemorating the duc d'Angoulême's triumphal entry into Paris; and a paie of *vases 'Medici'* decorated with incidents from the French campaign in Spain, which were painted by Jean-Charles Develly. Allusions to dynastic events were made in the decoration of a jewelry case commemorating the wedding of the duc de Berry (1817) and the vases celebrating the birth of the duc de Bordeaux (1820). Charles X apparently became less interested in representations of this kind, however, because after the pieces made to commemorate his accession and coronation, few if any were produced. Less direct evocations continued to appear in the form of landscapes linked to members of the royal family or their ancestors, particularly Henri IV, who became the object of a veritable cult. Depictions of him were by no means limited to the manufactory,[57] but he figured in many of its productions, notably a *déjeuner* (1818) decorated with his apotheosis, vases (1819, 1820) representing the transport of the new bronze statue of him and its installation on the Pont-Neuf, and a *guéridon* (see cat. no. 55) commemorating the public celebration marking this occasion, all of which compositions were devised and painted by Develly.

Neoclassical subjects, which had been used during the Empire to suggest aggrandizing parallels, became more autonomous. Some were depicted as cameos by Louis-Bertin Parant; two *vases 'Medici'*, for example, bear Parant's compositions, *The Meeting of Hannibal and Scipio* (1816) and *Alexander at the Tomb of Achilles* (1820). Others were painted in polychrome within cartouches, as on two *vases 'Etrusque Cylindre'* decorated by Antoine Béranger showing *Aristotle Receiving the Gifts of Alexander* (1821) and *Herodotus in Egypt* (1822). Gold figure painting against a blue ground did not entirely disappear: Fragonard himself used it to paint *Antique Wedding* and *Antique Meal* on the *vase 'grec de Luynes'* (1828). Smaller vases decorated with incised or painted Etruscan ornaments were also produced.[58] A more amiable neoclassical note was struck by many mythological subjects, as in a *vase 'Medici'* decorated by Leguay with *Diana's Nymphs Battling Putti* (1824); a secretary decorated by the same artist with *The Muses on Parnassus* (1827) as well as by Anacreontic compositions such as those for the *déjeuner 'des Peines et plaisirs de l'Amour'* (1817), or the *déjeuner 'des Amours de divers caracteres'* (1824).

Genre scenes met with great success during this period. Their most productive practitioner was Develly, who used them on many *déjeuners*: *'L'Art de la porcelaine'* (1816, see cat. no. 39); *'Les Sens'* (1817); *'Les Jeux les plus remarquables de différents peuples de l'Europe'* (1818). He also used them on table services, the most famous being the *service 'des Arts Industriels'* (see cat. no. 67), and furnishings such as a clock called the *pendule 'Geographique'* (1821) and a *guéridon* (1829) with decoration inspired by Milton's *Paradise Lost*. Other painters also worked in this vein. There is, for example, a *déjeuner* with a composition by Jean- Baptiste Isabey entitled *The Tasks and Milestones of a Farmer's Life* (1817). In another example, a vase (1826) is decorated with representations of the senses painted by Adelaïde Ducluzeau after oil studies by A.-E. Fragonard.

The ceramic arts themselves were already being represented in various ways. In addition to the *déjeuner 'l'Art de la Porcelaine'* (1816), the subject was also evoked on the cover plaque of a snuff-box (1819 – 20) for Louis XVIII, on a vase commemorating the various skills associated with the *département des beaux-arts* (see cat.

no. 66), and on a clock painted in 1830 by Jean-Auguste-Edouard Liénard. Other ceramic materials were alluded to on the *vase 'Cordelier'* (1819) which was dedicated to famous potters, and on the *vase 'de Socibius'*, which was inspired by an ancient vase in the Musée Royal and bore reliefs representing the "arts and sciences competing for the perfection of ceramics," personified as ancient potters (1824).[59]

It is difficult to determine what stylistic vocabulary was used for some of the programs typical of Brongniart such as the one described as "subjects with allegorical figures painted in sepia representing Time allowing the agreeable arts to pass while retaining the frivolous arts,"[60] executed by Isabey on a *vase 'Medici'* (1818).

The most accomplished figure painters at Sèvres devoted themselves to an activity which now began to assume increasing importance, namely the copying of famous paintings onto porcelain. Brongniart and his circle intended these copies to safeguard for posterity works that were fragile and perishable in their original state. Photography was then undergoing its protracted birth and porcelain's long-term stability had not yet come into question.[61] In addition to reduced copies on tableware and ornamental pieces, there was also an increase in plaques of large dimensions, made possible by improved slip-casting techniques. Interest in such projects was considerable.

In 1817 the comte de Forbin, director of the Musée Royal, allocated work space for freelance artists engaged in producing such pieces. He even agreed to lend certain paintings to Sèvres so that resident personnel could copy them there. Abraham Constantin was charged with copying paintings by Raphael in Florence (*Madonna del Granduca*, 1824). A clear preference was developing for works by Raphael; other copies after him include the *Madonna with a Carnation* (copied by Jaquotot in 1817 – 18), the heads of the Virgin and Child from the *Madonna of the Fish* (copied by Jaquotot, 1818 – 19), and the head of the Virgin from the *Holy Family* (copied by Constantin, 1818 – 19). In 1820 additional examples from the Italian school include Leonardo's *Mona Lisa* (copied by Ducluzeau), Correggio's *Mystic Marriage of Saint Catherine* (copied by Constantin), and Titian's supposed portrait of his mistress (copied by Jaquotot). Works by Flemish masters that were copied include a Van Eyck Virgin (copied by Sophie de Bon, 1818), Gerard Dou's *Dropsical Woman* (copied by Georget, 1822), Carel Dujardin's *Wooded Grove* and *Cart with a White Horse* (copied by Pierre Robert, 1821 and 1826), Rubens's *Portrait of Richardot* (copied by Béranger, 1826), and Anthony Van Dyck's *Self-Portrait* (copied by Jaquotot, 1826). Earlier French artists were also transferred to porcelain: Hyacinthe Rigaud's *Portrait of Louis XIV* (copied by Leguay, 1818 – 19) and Nicolas Poussin's *Assumption of the Virgin* which was represented on two *vases 'Etrusque Caraffe'* (copied by Sophie de Bon, 1821; the other by Aimée Perlet in 1828); Poussin's *Diogenes* was copied on a plaque by Jean-Baptiste-Gabriel Langlacé in 1829. A few contemporary artists were also deemed worthy of such preservation, above all François Gérard: *Cupid and Psyche* (copied by Jaquotot, 1824); *The Entry of Henri IV into Paris* (copied by Constantin, 1827); and *Saint Theresa* (copied by Ducluzeau, 1829). Works by other artists included: Anne-Louis Girodet-Trioson's *Atala* (copied by Jaquotot, 1830), Antoine-Jean Gros's *Francis I and Charles V Visiting the Tombs at Saint Denis* and Gros's *Bust Portrait of Francis I* (both copied by Georget, 1820); and Paul Delaroche's *The Prince of Carignan at the Siege of the Trocadéro* (copied by Constantin, 1829). The comte de Forbin's *Evening Prayer* was copied on a *vase 'Etrusque AB'* by Achille Poupart in 1825.

Traditional landscapes continued to be fashionable. There were a few monumental pieces with landscapes such as the table called *table 'des Châteaux Royaux'* (1817) and a clock called *'Geographique'* with a turning face (1821). In addition, landscapes figured on countless vases, *déjeuners*, and table services, notably the *service 'Voyage pittoresque de l'Europe'* (1828) and the *service 'des Departements'* with its many views of France (see cat. no. 63). A growing taste for exotic motifs is reflected in *vases 'Clodion'* with views of Africa by Develly (1817), a table service decorated with views of sites outside Europe, principally India (1821 – 22), *vases 'Cordelier'* with views of Brazil, and a *déjeuner* featuring views of Egypt (1824).

Flowers, plants, and other natural elements were omnipresent, from modest garlands decorating simple toiletry articles to ambitious still-life paintings executed by Jean-François Philippine on plaques incorporated into a secretary called *'Les Productions de la nature'* (1826). Brongniart always insisted on scientific precision when it came to representations and inscriptions. Floral species of all kinds — none of them imaginary — were depicted during Brongniart's administration in a multitude of formats, including bouquets, garlands, and wreaths; baskets, fruit, and shells were also frequently depicted. Groupings could be based on color, species, as in the *service 'des Roses'* and the *service 'Lileaceous'* (see cat. no. 49), or themes such as edible plants (*service 'des plantes comestibles'*, 1817) and horticulture (*service 'de la culture des fleurs'*, 1822). Sometimes allusions were less direct, as in a console (see cat. no. 46), in which the three phases of plant life were represented on plaques after compositions by A.-E. Fragonard. The intermittent employment of Pauline Knip as outside painter (1808, 1817 – 26) probably explains the rare pieces decorated with birds painted with ornithological precision, such as the *service 'des Oiseaux de l'Amérique méridionale'* (1820) and *vases 'Floréal'* (1822 and 1824).

One of the period's most original developments was the emergence of Gothic Revival, which made itself felt in all the decorative arts.[62] Although the vogue had begun tentatively at Sèvres during the Empire, under the Restauration it became a full-fledged phenomenon. In addition to new forms, there were many decorative, Gothic Revival schemes, the finest of which were produced by Jean-Claude Rumeau and Joseph Vigné. Here again, such decorations were used on simple individual cups (see cat. no. 62) and medium-sized vases (see cat. no. 57). Small furnishings were also made in this idiom: a Gothic clock with motifs taken from the life of the sixteenth-century French hero, Pierre du Terrail de Bayard (by Rumeau, 1821); a Gothic bookcase (1826); and a jewel casket bearing a portrait of the duchesse de Berry (see cat. no. 70). Some larger pieces of furniture also exist, notably the *'Paradise Lost' guéridon* (1829), whose "Gothic style" incorporated grisaille medallions "heightened with gold in the manner of Limoges enamels" around the central composition.[63]

The attraction of other cultures, already noted in connection with a few landscape subjects, also manifested itself sporadically in ornamental schemes, depending partly on diplomatic relations. In 1816 Leroy and Breguet commissioned a series of *tasses 'Japonaises'*

Fig. 6-11. Cup called *Tasse 'Litron'* and saucer from the *déjeuner 'Du Guesclin et Clisson'*, Sèvres, 1835; hard-paste porcelain. (Sèvres, musée national de céramique.

and *tasses 'Turques'*; two of the latter were delivered to the Persian ambassador in 1819.[64] There may be some connection between this delivery and an 1825 commission from Prince Abbas-Mirza of Persia (see cat. no. 64). In 1817 the manufactory inaugurated a series of deliveries to the ministry of foreign affairs for the pasha of Cairo with a *déjeuner* decorated with views of Paris identified in Turkish characters, some tobacco pots (in fact, ad hoc adaptations of previously extant forms, including two ice pails called *Seaux à glace 'Egyptien'*) and a teapot called *théière 'Turque'* (see cat. no. 37).[65]

As always, the most intense fascination was with China, but during the Restauration it took a new perspective, no longer centering on a fantastic East but rather on the attentive observation of genuine ceramic productions. In 1826 Brongniart requested a special allocation of funds to purchase at the sale of the Sallé collection "several pieces of Chinese porcelain remarkable with regard to technical processes and that are lacking in this part of the manufactory's collection."[66] It could be that the purchases made on this occasion prompted a reprise, with new decorations, of the *théière 'Chinoise'* designed by Fragonard in 1818 (see cat. no. 47). The administrator justified his interest in such pieces in these terms: "The Chinese and the Japanese, who have practiced this art for more than two thousand years, have introduced to it a variety of pastes, colors, and applications that Europeans still have not been able to obtain after exercising it for, at most, a hundred years. Thus it seems to me as useful as it is interesting to bring together successively in our collections all the pieces that acquaint us with the processes and results of which we still don't possess samples."[67] This enthusiasm was not without later consequences.

Aside from the popularization of transfer printing that came from the systematic, increased use of the technique for repetitive friezes (see cat. no. 49) and small motifs, there were few technical advances in this period. Elements in burnished gold were often replaced by painting in shaded platinum (see cat. nos. 59, 61, and 62). Inset or painted stones were rapidly abandoned, except for a short-lived variant: in 1807 there had been an attempt to incorporate "*clichés d'or*" (possibly a thin gold medal under the glaze), encouraged by Denon, and in 1816 Mme Desarnaud had worked to encase porcelain cameos in crystal under the glaze. Both attempts had failed. Brongniart, however, realized several prototypes — never put into production — using processes developed by Honoré Boudon de Saint Amans. Thus in January 1821 he was able to exhibit at the Louvre the only objects successfully embellished in this way: two *vases 'Théricléens'*, decorated with medallion portraits of Bourbon rulers, and a *coupe 'Diatrète'* (see cat. no. 48).

These few excursions into other areas of decoration were definitely exceptions and the manufactory otherwise continued to exploit decorative techniques perfected during the Empire period.

The July Monarchy. The year 1830 marked a profound rupture in the world of Parisian decorative arts, ushering in an age of Romanticism. Furthermore, the brief July Revolution of 1830 resulted in the removal of the Bourbons in favor of Louis-Philippe, a member of the Orléans family. His title "king of the French" indicates a significant political shift. The slowness with which the new administration settled into place explains the manufactory's failure to exhibit at the Louvre before December 1832. During this time, Brongniart's views changed considerably, coming to encompass a much broader range of stylistic resources. The catalogue of the 1832 exhibition cites Greek, Renaissance, Gothic, and Egyptian models. In 1835 Flemish ones were added to the list, and in fact quite a few more can be seen. This eclecticism was probably encouraged considerably by the proliferation of illustrated books made possible by advances in lithography. As in the past, many of

Fig. 6-12. *Table 'Renaissance'* by Claude-Aimé Chenavard. (From Brongniart and Riocreux, *Description méthodique du musée de la manufacture* [1845],P, pl. 5)

the stylistic terms were applied quite freely: "Gothic," for example, was used to describe the rigorous lancet arches of Jean-Charles-François Leloy (fig. 6-11; see cat. no. 82) as well as the exuberant compositions of Alexis Etienne Julienne (see cat. no. 97), and "Renaissance" was associated with a wide variety of aesthetic idioms (fig. 6-12).

The new period was also marked by a shift in the type of objects produced, with medium-sized pieces becoming more prevalent (see chap. 3). Finally, there was a notable change in the dominant colors: brownish purple grounds came to prevail over the traditional blue and green, and there was also a gradual reappearance of white porcelain, which prior to this time was almost always masked.

The forms and decorations of the July Monarchy period were very closely linked. The most important designers of new models were ornamentalist Claude-Aimé Chenavard, architect Léon Feuchère, and, beginning in 1842, Jules Peyre.

Propaganda pieces did not disappear completely. Countless vases, plaques, and other objects bore portraits of members of the ruling family — or, in the case of landscapes, were linked to the royal family through choice of subject matter, as in a *déjeuner* (1834 – 37) featuring both portraits of royalty and views of the château and park at Neuilly and, in another example, a casket (1841) decorated with views of royal châteaus and an interior view (Queen Marie Amélie's study in the Tuileries). Designers at the manufactory also depicted celebrations of dynastic events, such as the wedding of the duc d'Orléans, which was shown on a cabinet (1838), or military deeds such as the maritime exploits of the prince de Joinville, represented on a coffer (1844 – 46). There were more oblique allusions, reconciling members of the royal Bourbon and Orléans families (*déjeuner 'Princes et princesses des maisons royales de France'*, 1845). Vases also depicted the royal hunts of the French court (see cat. no. 100)).

The neoclassical style did not entirely disappear. Although the large biscuit *vase 'Medici'* dedicated to Phidias (1823 – 1832) and the *vase 'Etrusque à rouleaux'*, showing the physical education of the ancient Greeks, were begun during the preceding reigns, several new forms in a similar vein were introduced, such as vases called *vase 'Hyacinthe'* (1830); *vase 'Turbiné'* (1831) and *vase 'Lagène'* (1831); or a sugar bowl called *pot à sucre 'Grec'* (1837); and another vase called *'des Vendanges antiques'* (1839 – 44). Decorative schemes were also devised in the same spirit. Some were relatively faithful to their models, such as a small teapot called *théière 'étrusque plate'* (1832), which had an "incised Etruscan decoration in a black ground covered with red," and a cream jug called *pot à lait 'cornet Fragonard'* and matching basin called *cuvette 'Athenienne'* with a white ground, decorated with a red Etruscan decoration (1833). Other designs took more liberties with the originals. In the 1832 Louvre exhibition catalogue, Brongniart wrote of the *vase 'd'Achille'*, which featured a blue ground and Etruscan figures against a purplish ground; he maintained that Fragonard had introduced "a little more correction into the figures" but had "nonetheless sought not to stray at all from the style of the period and of the people."[68]

Colors that are scarcely antique are encountered again in the *vase 'Etrusque Turpin à gaudrons'* (1833) which was decorated with gold fluting heightened with green and had fretwork in carnelian red. A little later, preference seems to have been given to paintings from Herculaneum, imitated for example on a clock, the *pendule 'Les Repas Antiques'* (1839 – 43), which had been commissioned by the king to harmonize with the stucco work in the "Greek style" designed by Percier for a dining room at the Château de Saint-Cloud. An Anacreontic sensibility is also apparent in a *déjeuner 'Eloge de la Rose'* (1835), which featured a tray decorated with a painting by Leguay after a composition by Girodet illustrating an ode.

Countless decorative pieces, suitable for use as either furnishings or gifts, bore portraits of writers, artists, and craftsmen, from antiquity to the modern periods, as well as representations of various divinities and allegorical figures. Develly's genre scenes were still much appreciated. He continued to produce table services such as the *service 'Agronomique'* (1832 – 34) and ornamental pieces such as a clock called *pendule 'des Trois Horloges à Paris'* and a jewelry casket depicting women of different nationalities at their toilettes (see cat. no. 98).

A place of honor was still reserved in this domain for the celebration of the ceramic arts. In addition to portrait vases honoring potters and to the rediscovery of Bernard Palissy, this is demonstrated by the *déjeuner 'des Potiers Anciens'* (1835 – 40) and the *dejeuner 'de l'Art Céramique'* (1832 – 41), which featured a tray depicting the peoples of various nationalities presenting their ceramic productions in the garden in front of the manufactory. Its pieces were decorated by Develly with depictions of ceramics workshops at Sèvres, in China, and in the land of the "Boshuanas" women. On a *coupe 'de Benvenuto Cellini'* (1843), Develly painted a "figured chart of the ceramic and vitreous arts from ancient times until the sixteenth century."

All these examples suggest the difficulties Brongniart probably encountered in his ongoing efforts to find new ideas for the manufactory's decorative programs. This necessity led to the pragmatic reuse of patterns, which sometimes resulted in strange compositions. One can only wonder how the artist would have interpreted instructions for a design (1839 – 44) in which the "genius of the sciences of the nineteenth century" was to be represented by an allusion to the use of electricity for the galvanic, or plating, process. This and another subject, the "genius of industry" discovering the steam engine, were to be treated "in the genre of the paintings of Herculaneum," the artist having been instructed to "try to idealize it as much as possible."[69]

Copies of paintings on porcelain plaques continued to be produced in relatively large numbers. The copyists did not hesitate, however, to alter their models a bit. They sometimes sought, for example, not to depict the work as it was, but rather as it had appeared at the moment of its completion. In describing a copy by Langlacé of Jacob von Ruysdael's *Ray of Sunlight*, the comte de Turpin wrote, "In accordance with the very rational system of Mme Jaquotot, M. Langlacé has *reestablished* in the azure of the sky the tone that it must have been before the old varnish yellowed and rendered it almost green; but he has not proceeded in precisely the same way for the mass of clouds, [and] as a result . . . the clouds are a hundred years old while the azure is eight days old."[70]

Copying one of Raphael's frescoes in the Vatican Stanze presented Constantin with problems of another kind. He felt obligated to alter its perspective. The original had been conceived to be seen from a distance and from below, not up close, as was then the case with easel paintings. In addition, there were extended discussions between Constantin and Brongniart regarding the best way to handle an area occupied by a window in the actual fresco. Such difficulties, however, did not prevent either Constantin or Jaquotot from traveling to Italy on several occasions to copy works by Raphael, a favorite painter. Constantin reproduced *The Mass at Bolsena* and *The School of Athens* (both 1830 – 34) and *The Deliverance of Saint Peter* (1838 – 42); while Jaquotot made copies of *Madonna with a Veil* and *Portrait of Joanna of Aragon* (1830 – 34), *Saint Cecilia* (1837 – 40), *Self-Portrait* (1837 – 42), and *Portrait of Julius II* (1840 – 42). Sèvres painters copied other Italian masters as well. Ducluzeau reproduced Domenichino's *Ascension of Saint Paul* on a *vase 'Etrusque Caraffe'* (1831 – 34). Titian's supposed portrait of his mistress was copied by Béranger (1833 – 35) while Titian's *Man with a Red Beard*, was copied by A. Ducluzeau (1840 – 42).

The work of Flemish masters also provided inspiration for Sèvres copyists during the July Monarchy. These included: flower paintings by Van Huysum and Van Spaendonck (copied by Moise Jacobber, 1829 – 32 and 1835 – 38); Van Dyck's *Self-Portrait* (copied by Ducluzeau, 1833 – 35); Van Dyck's *Charles I* (copied by Marie Pauline Laurent, 1838 – 42); Ruysdael's previously mentioned *Ray of Sunlight* (copied by Langlacé, 1834 – 39); and Gerrit Dou's *Portrait of the Artist's Family* (copied by Victorine Tréverret, 1836 – 40). Pauline Laurent made two copies after Terborch on *vases 'Floréal'* (1844 – 46).

Fig. 6-13. *Vase 'Egyptien B'* or *vase 'Champollion'*, Sèvres, 1831 – 32; hard-paste porcelain and gilded bronze. (Compiègne, Musée national du château)

A few contemporary artists were also copied. Jean-Auguste-Dominique Ingres's *Portrait of the duc d'Orléans* was reproduced by Ducluzeau (1842 – 44); François-Xavier Winterhalter's *Portrait of Prince Albert* was copied by Beranger (1846), while Winterhalter's *Portrait of Queen Victoria* was copied by Ducluzeau (1846). The interest in artists was also expressed in portrait vases and in furnishings such as a *guéridon* table dedicated to Raphael.

Landscapes continued to appear on countless table services, such as the *services 'Vues pittoresques de l'Europe'* (1827–33); *'Vues d'Italie'* (1830–34); *'Forestier'* (1834–37); *'des Pêches'* (from 1840). On *déjeuners* the Sèvres artist Jules André painted views of Rouen (1837) and of the park at Saint-Cloud (1844). Landscapes were used on furnishings, such as a *guéridon* (1843) decorated with views of sites along the Seine between Paris and Rouen. Some of these landscapes had royal associations (see cat. no. 90). Somewhat uncharacteristically, Louis-Philippe, who usually left the choice of subject to Brongniart, stipulated the inclusion of crown properties on table services featuring European views—where they would not be out of place—as well as on services decorated with views of Italy. One can easily imagine Brongniart's reluctance to authorize such jumbled programs.

Floral motifs were still used to decorate innumerable small and medium-sized pieces, and even some beautiful vases and table services. Flowers appeared in groups and bouquets as well as in wreath and arch formats, often sorted by species or color. There was a marked preference for simple species, such as hawthorne, violets, and eglantine. This same taste prompted the development of several more or less naturalistic forms, among them the *vase 'Aromaphore"* (1837–38) designed by Leloy to satisfy a royal commission. The relief ornaments on this potpourri represented various scented plants.

Some of the new forms conceived during this period are difficult to classify stylistically. A few are truly novel, such as two "ribbed" *déjeuners* (1830 and 1840); plates "with relief gadrooning" (1842); "lobed" table and coffee services by Peyre (1842). With others it is all but impossible to make sense of their varied sources of inspiration. A typical example of the latter category is the *surtout 'des Comestibles'* (1834 – 36), which centered on themes of food and dining, designed by Fragonard in accordance with a program devised by Brongniart (see cat. no. 84). When exhibited it was described as being in the "Greek style," probably because of the presence of divinities and ancient forms, but its excess of ornament makes it very much at odds with the idea of neoclassicism.

The taste for exotica, discernible in the preceding political periods, increased considerably. Ancient Egyptian sources continued to be used, but in a different spirit. Instead of the gold hieroglyphs against a blue ground that were faithful to illustrations published by Denon and the Commission d'Egypte (see cat. no. 13), as well as consistent with the imperial aesthetic, Brongniart and Jean-François Champollion, the decipherer of the Rosetta Stone, approved vases with more fantastic shapes and more brightly colored palettes (fig. 6-13; see cat. no. 72), all the while professing respect for the renderings made by Champollion in the actual tombs at Thebes.

France's interventionist policies in North Africa and the Middle East most likely explain the proliferation of "Arab" and "Moorish" forms, subjects, and motifs. With regard to forms, an Hispano-Moresque vase in the Alhambra inspired a large *vase 'Arabe'* that was produced at Sèvres from drawings provided by Adrien Dauzats in 1838. This form found an echo on a more modest scale in a *vase 'Arabe'* designed by Léon Feuchère (see cat. no. 99) and a cooler called *glacière 'Arabe'* by the same artist. Commissioned by Louis-Philippe for presentation to Mehemet-Ali, the viceroy of Egypt, a musical clock, the *pendule 'turque'* (see cat. no. 102), features refined openwork panels, possibly inspired by filigree work of a kind that reappears on other pieces of similar inspiration, for example a *zarf 'Reticulé'* (1844) and a *vase 'Pyriforme'* (1845 – 46). Painted and gilded ornament in the so-called Moresque style was used to decorate the *guéridon 'Arabe de l'Alhambra'* (1830 – 35), as well as the *service 'Moresque'* (1826 – 36) which also bore portraits of famous Arabs. Most of these pieces demonstrate a concern for consistency between forms and decoration. The "Persian" decoration said to have figured on a dessert service in 1844 seems to have been similar in character.

North African and Middle Eastern influences were also discernible in the first productions of Sèvres's enamel-on-metal workshop (see cat. no. 109). The everyday life of these regions was evoked by Develly on two *déjeuners* (1832 – 35 and 1838).

China continued to fascinate Brongniart. His early scientific interest was in its technical processes for porcelain, particularly ones used there for centuries to achieve remarkable ground colors. The Chinese pieces with double walls that he had admired at the Sallé sale of 1826 probably explain the production at Sèvres of the *déjeuner 'Chinois Réticulé'* (see cat. no. 76), whose first pieces were exhibited at the Louvre in 1832, at the same time as the *théière 'Chinoise Ronde'* designed by Fragonard (see cat. no. 75). All of Sèvres's collaborators competed with one another in this genre. In 1833 – 34, Leloy designed a paneled *déjeuner* called *'Chinois à pans'*, decorated with depictions of different tea plants, the various utensils used to prepare the beverage, and the aromatic plants used to heighten its perfume. In 1832 Chenavard began work on a *guéridon 'Chinois'* (see cat. no. 81) that was to be accompanied by a *déjeuner* for which he only had time to design the coffeepot. It seems likely that the pure, restrained forms of the "rose" and "violet" vases designed by Leloy in 1840 were influenced by his study of Eastern originals. The cabinet-on-stand called *'Chinois'* (see cat. no. 101) conceived by Léon Feuchère was one of the last manifestations of the style; it features panels decorated with scenes from Chinese life paraphrasing original paintings executed on the spot by Auguste Borget. Everyday life was also evoked by Develly on a *déjeuner* celebrating tea, "it's harvest, preparation, and use in China" (1835).

Other foreign venues and customs were also surveyed. There were two editions of a *déjeuner* (1833 and 1835; and see cat. no. 83), decorated with scenes detailing the harvest of cocoa and chocolate as well as with Mexican motifs. Théophile Fragonard's project for two *vases 'Océaniques'* was equally exotic. It was "modeled after pottery from the Viti [Fiji] Islands" and meant to be decorated with "subjects taken from the customs of the still savage tribes of those parts."[71]

Subject matter was not inspired solely by exotic locales. Increasingly, models were sought in different eras of the past. The Gothic Revival became more expansive (see cat. no. 97), but it was used rather infrequently. Earlier medievalism was also represented, for example, in a casket called *coffret 'Roman'* (see cat. no. 105), in the *vase 'Adelaïde'* (1844), which was devoted to famous medieval painters (1844), and, especially, in productions made by the manufactory's stained-glass and painting-on-glass workshop (see chap. 7).

It was Renaissance models, however, that exerted the strongest stylistic influence at the manufactory during this period. To some degree this was a function of contemporary fashion, perhaps reinforced by Louis-Philippe's interest in the Château de Fontainebleau, but it also seems likely that Brongniart's predilection derived in large part from his study of old pieces assembled in the museum, which suggested ways to renew production.

Brongniart was especially drawn to the work of Bernard Palissy or what was then liberally attributed to him, often simply because his was the only ceramist's name from the period to survive, probably because of Palissy's scientific writings. These may have played a role in whetting Brongniart's interest, but it is also possible that Palissy's fossil research became known to the administrator at an early date. In 1822 Brongniart complained that the museum owned no examples of Palissy's work.[72] At the time, objects of this kind rarely passed through the auction rooms and were known only to a few devotees. The revolution of 1830 prompted a resurgence of interest in Palissy, who was newly presented as a national treasure, a political martyr, and an overlooked popular hero — in sum, as a figure who was tailor-made to rally disappointed republican sentiments. Apparently, Brongniart did not immediately grasp these political implications, and Sèvres actively participated in the process of glorification. At the salon of 1831, Auguste Vatinelle exhibited a painting on glass, after an oil by Fragonard, representing the famous episode in which Palissy burned his furniture to complete a firing of his kiln. This same incident was depicted again, this time from a painting by Charles Alexandre Debacq which had been exhibited at the salon of 1837 and was copied on a tray from the *déjeuner 'des Potiers Célèbres Modernes'* (1840) as well as on the central plaque of an ornamental frame (1846).

Explicit reference was made to Palissy on the occasion of the exhibition of the *vase 'de la Renaissance Chenavard'* (fig. 6-14; see cat. no. 79), which was first shown at the Louvre in 1832; clearly, it was the rich polychrome reliefs on the piece that prompted the comparison. Not surprisingly a number of other works featuring the same kind of decoration were also seen as related to Palissy. They were produced in relatively large numbers because they achieved effects as novel as Palissy's at a rather low cost. Examples include Chenavard's *surtout 'des Comestibles'* (see cat. no. 85) and the *déjeuner 'de François Ier'*, designed by Fragonard (see cat. no. 78).

Less typical ornamental reliefs, some of them closer to Renaissance models than others, are found on quite a few objects, many of which were conceived by Chenavard, including a table base (see cat. no. 92) and a vase (1839). Many others were by Hyacinthe Régnier: ornamental plates (see cat. no. 88); a *coupe 'de Benvenuto Cellini'* (1838); a *coupe 'Cassolette'* (1839); and *caisse 'à fleurs hexagone'* (1840). The effect of sculpted motifs was sometimes undermined by the use of color; accordingly, the white/gold and matte/polished contrasts that had originally been developed to complement antique revival reliefs were used again on the *vase 'de la Renaissance Fragonard'* (1835) as well as on Fragonard's centerpiece in the "Greek style."

Many painted schemes evoke other celebrated figures of the period, either individuals such as Benvenuto Cellini, whose name was attached to the *coupe* already mentioned and who was also commemorated in a *déjeuner* (1838 – 42), or anonymous types such as "famous knights" or "famous personages of the sixteenth century" who were celebrated in vase decoration.

Finally, during this period several kinds of ornament associated with the "Renaissance style" were used, among them grounds that resembled niello and damascene. These were almost ubiquitous, often in conjunction with inappropriate forms and themes, as for example in a *vase 'Coupe'*, whose form was inspired by models from antiquity, which also bore portraits of members of the royal family and decorated with "Renaissance" motifs.

Pieces attributed to Bernard Palissy were not the only ceramics from the Renaissance to be used by Brongniart. It was probably at Brongniart's initiative that Chenavard modeled three vase forms after sixteenth-century Flemish stoneware (see cat. no. 80). A vase named after a model published by Léon Feuchère in *L'Art Industriel*[73] was described when it was first exhibited in 1846 at the Louvre as having a form and decoration in the style of sixteenth-century stoneware vases from Germany.

Fig. 6-14. *Vase 'de la Renaissance Chenavard'*, designed by Claude-Aimé Chenavard, Sèvres, 1830 – 32; hard-paste porcelain. (Château de Fontainebleau)

It seems impossible that the design of the *coupe 'Chenavard'*, dating from 1835 (see cat. no. 91), did not result from a close study of what was then called Henri II earthenware, now known as Saint-Porchaire earthenware, despite the fact that such models were explicitly mentioned only in connection with a *coupe 'Henri II'*, which was issued six years later, in 1841. Curiously, the inset paste technique was first used not in imitation of pieces of this type, but rather on a *vase 'Arabe.'* It reappeared, however, on another *coupe 'Henri II'*, dating from 1846.

During the early nineteenth century, Italian earthenware had remained relatively unknown in France, which probably explains the fact that it was imitated only quite late. The first forms to be inspired by it were two ewers called *buires 'ovulaire'* (1845) and *'cylindroïde'* (1846), both designed by Hyacinthe Régnier. The first decorations described as "in the genre of Italian earthenware" appeared only in 1846.[74]

Another category of Renaissance design that was influential at Sèvres was the grisaille enamel work heightened with colors and gold against black grounds, which had been produced in the workshops of Limoges. Initially these enamels were imitated in painting on porcelain; as in medallions surrounding the central composition of the *guéridon 'Gothique'* paying homage to Milton's *Paradise Lost* (1830). In a subsequent phase, these paintings covered the entire surface of the vase, notably in the series of *vases 'Adelaïde'* painted by Jacob Meyer-Heine beginning in 1841. Finally, in 1845 the manufactory created a special workshop for enamel on metal, which Louis-Philippe himself charged with reviving the tradition of Limoges enamels.

Given the openness of mind manifest in his use of a wide variety of sources, it is surprising that Brongniart did not participate in the renewed interest in eighteenth-century rococo works. His resistance could be a function of his early art education in the 1780s and 1790s, at which time such works were increasingly being discredited. Despite the influence of collectors, who often came to him for advice,[75] and a growing demand for casts of his old models, he seems to have been reluctant to undertake such reeditions without specific royal commissions. The ones he received concerned decorative sculpture and service pieces. On August 31, 1846, Madame Adélaïde, Louis-Philippe's sister, ordered a *surtout* composed of figures and groups from the eighteenth century.[76] On October 9 of the same year the duc de Nemours requested a reedition of the subsidiary figures from the *surtout 'du Triomphe de Bacchus'*, to be enriched with bronzes "according to a drawing that will be conveyed by M. Lamy,"[77] and on November 4 the duc d'Aumale ordered a complete *surtout 'des Chasses'*.[78] Similarly, on June 6, 1846, the duc de Nemours, after examining a series of drawings, models, and examples, chose a series of forms attributed to Duplessis père, also ordering the creation of a new tray for a saltcellar called *salière 'Vaisseau'*, the whole ensemble to feature blue grounds, floral ornament, and gilding "imitating as much as possible the gilding against a blue ground on old soft paste."[79] This decision was rapidly imitated by his brother Aumale, who ordered plates of a different model, although still dating from the Vincennes period, as well as some reliefs entirely gilded in green gold.[80]

The extent of Brongniart's artistic responsibilities are clear. He alone decided what work was to be undertaken and by which artists. He was also responsible for determining the decorative programs to be used. There are even a few suggestions in archival records that he was the originator, or at least the instigator, of certain forms. A register entry dating from 1805 records the arrival in the warehouse of "1 water jug and its basin ewer form by M. Brongniart fils."[81] A list of projects undertaken by Leloy in 1818 includes "June 1 Basket Vase composition by M. Brongniart refined in small."[82] Discussing the *corbeille 'Palmier'* of 1820, the administrator himself noted that it was "after an idea and sketch by myself and a design or sketch by Mr. Fragonard."[83] Given this evidence, there is reason to suspect that he may also be responsible for at least the basic idea of forms designated in the documents by the initials "AB",[84] especially since for models designed by Denon, some are clearly marked "Denon" and others simply marked "D."

The work produced at Sèvres consistently met with a favorable response by successive sovereigns. Such was not the case with critics, however, and during Brongniart's extended tenure he was taken to task at various times for different and sometimes contradictory reasons. Prior to 1830, these attacks were relatively restrained, for Sèvres's pieces were in harmony both with the production of Parisian porcelain makers and with the prevailing taste for a tempered neoclassicism. The revival of interest in soft-paste porcelain was just beginning, and no one would have dreamed of criticizing Brongniart for no longer producing it. At most, there were occasional objections to overly fantastic forms and to choice of themes and subject matter (see cat. no. 66). The situation changed considerably after the 1830 revolution. Primarily for political reasons, the opposition press began to question the very existence of the royal manufactories. Unfortunately for Brongniart, one of the most influential republicans, Victor Schoelcher, was also the son of a porcelain producer; on the other hand, Aimé Chenavard, who was the manufactory's finest designer, was claimed by the ranks of the opposition, and this rather complicated the task of left-wing critics. At the same time, taste in general had evolved, and as a result Brongniart increasingly found himself out of harmony stylistically. His outmoded neoclassical sympathies were vigorously attacked, along with his indifference to the newly fashionable rococo revival.

Very early on, a few journalists began to focus on even more fundamental issues,[85] drawing attention, beginning in this period, to a problem that was to assume increasing importance in the following one, namely the inappropriateness of using miniature painting on curving surfaces. They insisted on the incompatibility between works in two and three dimensions, on the ineffectiveness of decorative programs with uniform tonal values, and on the necessity of replacing these with ornamental compositions better adapted to ceramic forms and calculated to be legible at a glance. This was precisely the program that was to be taken up by the manufactory in the second half of the nineteenth century, after the death of Alexandre Brongniart.

The archival documents cited below are from the Archives of the Manufacture Nationale de Sèvres (AMNS).

1. [J'ai toujours la même opinion que vous, Monsieur, sur le bien que la Manufacture de Sèvres doit perpétuellement chercher à atteindre et mes efforts sont constamment dirigés de ce côté. Il est certain que si l'on vouloit faire une fabrique lucrative, il faudroit en modifier l'organisation de ses travaux et renoncer aux grandes pièces qui sont très dispendieuses par les pertes réitérées qu'elles occasionent. Mais je crois connoître assez bien les vues généreuses et grandes de l'Empereur pour être persuadé qu'il n'exigera de la Manufacture de Sèvres que de continuer à être un exemple de bon goût, de perfection et d'émulation pour toutes les fabriques de porcelaine] Register Vc 3, fol. 47v ff., letter dated January 1, 1806.

2. [la manufacture que vous dirigés avec tant d'habileté ne doit avoir qu'un objet: celui d'être constamment la première de l'Europe sous tous les rapports . . . l'Empereur n'en retirera que peu de profit; mais le commerce de France y gagnera s'il ne reste pas en arrière de la perfection dont vous avés donné l'exemple et cette vue est plus noble, plus digne de l'Empereur que le calcul d'un petit bénéfice] Carton T 2, liasse 1, dossier 1, letter dated 21 Frimaire year 14 (December 12, 1805).

3. [la diminution des fonds appliqués à la fabrication...ôteroit à la manufacture les moyens de rembourser le trésor de la couronne par les produits de la vente au public d'une grande partie des avances qu'il lui fait . . . Loin donc de diminuer l'activité des travaux, je cherche à l'augmenter

mais je lui donne une nouvelle direction en associant aux objets d'art et de luxe qui doivent néanmoins toujours faire le caractère distinctif de la manufacture royale beaucoup d'objets d'usage et d'un débit facile] Register Vc 4, fol. 164 ff., letter dated November 17, 1815.

4. [précieux par leurs perfections sur tous les rapports, des formes pures, des ornements sévères, des peintures bien faites . . . à peine appréciés par les gens les plus riches et les plus élevés en dignité de Paris . . . la plupart des gens riches . . . mettent plus de prix aux choses éclatantes et en vogue qu'aux choses exécutées avec perfection] Register Vc 7, fol. 153 ff., letter dated July 10, 1827. Instructions sent to the *chef des peintres*, Claude Charles Gérard, concerning such simple pieces bear witness to Brongniart's preoccupation with quality: "He should see to the decoration, always careful and salable, of medium-sized vases, *déjeuners*, table services, and individual pieces of the 2nd and 3rd categories. . . . To arrive at this goal . . . [he should] determine the sale price in advance with the director and decorate the pieces in accordance with these indications, as richly but as economically as possible, a [result] he will obtain by choosing ornaments that produce an effect without being difficult to execute. He should always take care to avoid everything that is in bad taste, as things in good taste are no more expensive than others. . . .carefulness of execution, especially as regards solidity, must never be neglected" [Il doit s'occuper de faire décorer en courant soigné et vendable, des moyens vases, des dejeuners, des services de table et des pièces détachées prises dans le 2me et le 3me choix . . . pour arriver à ce but . . . determiner d'avance les prix de vente avec le directeur et orner d'après cette donnée les pièces agréablement, le plus richement et cependant le plus économiquement possible, ce qui l'obtiendra (sic) en choisissant des ornements qui produisent de l'effet sans être d'une exécution difficile. Il doit avoir toujours soin d'eviter tout ce qui est de mauvais goût, les choses de bon goût n'étant pas plus chères que les autres . . . le soin dans l'exécution et surtout dans ce qui a rapport à la solidité ne doit jamais être négligé] (Carton M 3, liasse 1, note dated January 25, 1814). In a similar vein, Brongniart provided Chenavard with the following guidelines regarding the design of forms for tableware: "Generally speaking, it is necessary 1. that one or several fingers be able to pass between the handle and the piece, according to its size and weight 2. that the piece have a base sufficiently broad to prevent its falling over at the slightest shock 3. that it pour well etc." [il faut in général 1. qu'un ou plusieurs doigts suivant la grandeur et la pesanteur de la pièce puissent passer entre l'anse et la pièce 2. que la pièce ait assez de base pour ne pas tomber au moindre choc 3. qu'elle verse bien etc.] (Carton Ob 3, dossier Chenavard).

5. [Je m'efforcerai de maintenir avec convenance et mesure le caractère de perfection, de supériorité et d'utilité générale que j'ai tâché d'imprimer à l'etablissement qui m'est confié et qui m'a paru avoir pour noble destination de conserver et de propager les bons procédés dans les arts céramiques, de donner secours et libérale instruction à tous ceux qui les pratiquent ou les étudient, d'offrir aux artistes distingués un moyen de cultiver un art conservateur des belles productions de la peinture, mais un art très difficile, très dispendieux et trop peu productif par suite de sa propre perfection pour être livré à l'industrie particulière] Register Vc 8, fol. 74v ff., letter dated August 10, 1830.

6. [pour but et pour résultat le maintien de ce qui est reconnu bon, le perfectionnement de ce qui est déjà connu, la découverte ou l'application de choses ou de procédés nouveaux] Carton T 12, liasse 7, dossier 1 ("Affaires arriérées à traiter au 14 Janvier 1833").

7. [théorie scientifique des arts céramiques]; [le directeur actuel et le chimiste]; [par de la porcelaine en biscuit plus durable, plus multipliable et moins chère]; [perfection dans la monture, augmentation dans l'éclat et variation dans la couleur] Ibid.

8. Regarding the technique of painting on lava, he specified that it was a "means of replacing mosaics with productions in unlimited dimensions, more effective, easier to make, more durable, and twenty times less expensive. All these qualities are presumable. Experimentation alone can verify them or modify them. It is up to the royal manufactory to perform these rather costly experiments" [moyen de remplacer la mosaïque par des productions d'une dimension sans limites, d'un effet meilleur, d'une exécution plus facile, d'une durabilité plus grande et d'un prix 20 fois inférieur. Toutes ces qualités sont présumables. L'expérience peut seule maintenant les constater ou les modifier. C'est à la manufacture royale à faire cette expérience assez dispendieuse] (ibid.).

Brongniart was consulted by the comte de Montalivet in 1841 with regard to a proposal made by Achille Deveria to "execute a large painting on lava in vitrifiable colors [to] show the advantages the arts might derive from this genre of painting in buildings or parts of buildings exposed to sun, rain, and humidity" [exécuter un grand tableau sur lave en couleurs vitrifiables pour montrer le parti que les arts pourraient tirer de ce genre de peinture dans les édifices ou parties d'édifices exposés au soleil, à la pluie ou à l'humidité] (Register Vc 9, fol. 121 ff., letter dated August 21, 1841). After summarizing the history of the technique and expressing an interest in it, Brongniart concluded that he did not have sufficient funds to undertake the project at Sèvres.

9. [genre de production à faire]; [cela dépendra de l'emploi et de l'écoulement que le Roi voudra donner à ces productions] Carton T 12, liasse 7, dossier 1 ("Affaires arrièrées à traiter au 14 Janvier 1833").

10. [petites pièces de formes choisies et de décoration d'un goût raisonné] Ibid.

11. Register Vb 5, letter of October 24, 1845 (order to send a series of portrait medallions depicting members of the royal family to the museum in Bourges); ibid., letter of July 27, 1846 (authorizing a prize for a boat race organized at Sèvres); ibid., letter of February 8, 1847 (authorizing prizes for a raffle benefiting the poor of the town of Sèvres).

12. Carton T 2, liasse 1.

13. In 1815 after the fall of the Empire, the museum was renamed the Musée Royal.

14. [placer dans les services . . . des vues de l'Adige, de Venise, de Gênes et du Royaume d'Italie, plus intéressantes et plus historiques que celles que l'on va chercher ailleurs]; [mettre des portraits, des vues de Paris et des différents palais impériaux]; [remplacer enfin toutes les figures de femmes nues et paysages insignifiants . . . par des choses connues et historiques] Carton T2, liasse 1.

15. [grands hommes du siècle dernier . . . dont on a les modèles] Carton T2, liasse 1.

16. Ibid. The figures to be added were William the Conqueror, Duguesclin, Gustav Adolf, Friedrich II, Caesar, Hannibal, Homer, Virgil, Tasso, Christopher Columbus, the first Medici, and Prince Eugène.

17. Carton T3, liasse 1, dossier 1.

18. Lajoix, "Marie-Victoire Jaquotot" (1990), pp. 153 – 71.

19. [les objets de la manufacture les plus beaux et les plus convenables pour les étrennes que S.M. l'Impératrice doit distribuer demain] Carton T 1, liasse 6, dossier 1.

20. Carton T 4, liasse 2, dossier 1, letter dated December 1, 1809.

21. Carton U 8, dossier "Exposition de 1840."

22. [le Roi désire que l'on fasse composer un certain nombre de déjeuners en porcelaine dans les prix de trois à six mille francs] Carton M 12, liasse 4, letter dated May 10, 1844.

23. Fortunately, there were also more interesting commissions. Many of these were for decorated table services, including one intended for the Landgrave of Hesse, a few pieces from which were exhibited at the Louvre in 1830, and another ordered for the viceroy of Egypt, Mehemet-Ali, by the baron de Saint Joseph and the Maison Pastré Frères of Marseilles in 1832 (Register Vtt 3, fol. 151v – 152). There were also some instances of bronze-makers having vases made to their own designs, with simple blue grounds, for mounting, as well as a few commissions for porcelain pieces produced using specific techniques. There were also some more poetic projects, for example a *vase 'Anthophore'* decorated with bouquets of flowers chosen so that the first letter of each flower spelled the name "Gabrielle," ordered by one M. de Luppé (Vtt 1, fol. 107, February 1820).

24. [en faisant établir les vases dont il est question j'avois réfléchi aux usages auxquels ils pouvoient être destinés et j'en avois gradué la beauté et la valeur de manière à ce que les uns puissent servir à décorer convenablement les palais des Thuileries et de Saint-Cloud qui n'en ont presque point, que les autres puissent être donnés en présent par le gouvernement et que ces deux objets remplis il en resta encore assez pour l'ameublement des autres palais] Carton T 1, liasse 6, dossier 5.

25. [Les porcelaines que je fais établir n'ont de destination particulière que lorsqu'elles ont été demandées pour un objet spécial. Dans le cours ordinaire des travaux, elles sont destinées à assortir le magasin de toutes les pièces qui peuvent être demandées pour le service de l'Empereur ou enlevées par le commerce . . . c'est d'après l'expérience que j'ai de ces demandes assez fréquentes, de la nature des pièces qu'on préfère, de la haute valeur qu'on veut qu'elles aient et de la rapidité avec laquelle il faut les livrer, que je dirige les travaux de la manufacture] Carton T 2, liasse 2, letter dated April 29, 1806.

26. [c'est précisément en répondant à de tels besoins extraordinaires en tout c.a.d. en temps imprévu, en magnificence et en convenance que la Manufacture fait preuve des ses différents genres d'utilité] Carton M 6, liasse 3, letter dated August 10, 1827.

27. Another incentive, devised to assure that artists were never without work between important commissions was the creation of so-called *services perpétuels*, table services that were always in production, the most famous of which is the *service 'marli d'or'*.

28. Such recycling was standard procedure. In 1808 excess columns made for the *service 'Olympique,'* for example, were converted into candelabra clocks, while other tall pieces from the same ensemble were used in a service "with red ground, flowers, and butterflies" delivered to Fontainebleau (carton Pb 1, liasse 1, dossier 17, travaux de 1808). In addition, the series of *guéridons* was intended to make use of preexisting balusters, and salvageable portions of flawed, large plaques were incorporated into clocks.

29. Gastineau, "Une menace de suppression . . ." (1932), pp. 3 – 7.

30. [quoique je me sois livré beaucoup plus aux sciences et notamment à la chimie et à la minéralogie qu'aux arts, je ne crois pas y être étranger. Je ne puis cependant m'arroger le droit de juger et de faire changer le dessin d'un artiste qui passe pour avoir du talent, mais je ne puis que les bien choisir et pour établir mon jugement sur leur mérite, j'ai employé un moyen qui m'a paru propre à eloigner tout esprit de système. Je fais voir souvent et à plusieurs artistes d'un mérite bien reconnu, tels que Gerard et autres, les ouvrages des peintres qui travaillent pour la manufacture et d'après le jugement qu'ils en portent séparément et à plusieurs reprises j'apprécie avec assez de justesse le mérite des diverses personnes] Carton T 3, liasse 1, dossier 5, letter dated

August 3, 1807. Apparently, this indignant letter was never sent, for Brongniart noted on it, "non enregistré."

31. [je me maintiendrai comme vous voulez bien m'y encourager dans la route que j'ai suivie, qui est de n'adopter aucun artiste exclusivement mais de consulter et d'écouter tous ceux qui ayant une réputation justement acquise par leurs travaux ne peuvent jamais errer complètement et de choisir entre plusieurs bon conseils, quand ils ne sont pas unanimes, celui qui me paroitra le meilleur assuré qu' avec de si bons guides je pourrais suivre des routes assez variées sans craindre de m'écarter beaucoup de la bonne voie n'y de m'en écarter longtemps] Register Vc 7, fol. 105 ff., letter dated August 28, 1826.

32. The list included: Louis Pierre Henriquel-Dupont, who made a pencil portrait of Alexandre Brongniart; François Gérard; one of the Deveria brothers, probably Achille, who made some stained-glass designs for Sèvres; Horace Vernet; Carle Vernet; and Charles Percier, who also did some work for the manufactory (Carton U 8, dossier "Exposition du 1er Mai 1835").

33. Register Vc 2, fol. 63v ff., letter dated 15 Thermidor year 8 (August 3, 1800). One of the consequences of the granting of Brongniart's request was an agreement executed on 1 Thermidor year 10 (July 20, 1802) with his father, the architect Alexandre-Théodore Brongniart. Brongniart père committed himself to visit Sèvres once a week to indicate current decorative schemes and oversee their execution, and he also agreed to provide, each month, one drawing of a piece and his proposed decor for it. In exchange he received 1,200 francs per year, with additional drawings being paid for separately. But such contracts seem to have been rare (Register Y 4).

34. [plus nous aurons de ces messieurs et mieux ils feront. Il en résultera d'ailleurs une variété de goût qui tournera au profit de la manufacture] Carton T 5, liasse 1, dossier 2, letter dated June 11, 1810.

35. [La Manufacture . . . n'a jamais possédé une réunion plus complette d'artistes et d'ouvriers distingués. Non seulement elle a sans *aucune exception* les peintres de figures sur porcelaine les plus forts qui existoient à Paris mais elle a instruit plusieurs artistes distingués à peindre sur porcelaine et elle a par ce moyen augmenté le nombre des peintres de ce genre] Carton T 4, liasse 1, dossier 4, letter dated July 21, 1808.

36. [la sévérité dans le choix des artistes et des ouvriers, choix déterminé uniquement par leur talent et indépendant de toute autre considération telle que haute ou puissante protection, infortune, besoin de vivre, position digne d'intérêt, services rendus etc. etc. toutes choses qu'un peut admettre comme titres lorsqu'il ne s'agit pas d'un établissement où il faut faire constamment mieux que tout autre des objets d'art ou d'industrie, cette sévérité dans les choix, dis-je, est un des principes fondamentaux des succès de nos travaux] Register Vc 8, fol. 138 ff, letter dated September 26, 1832.

37. [Veuillez bien, Monsieur le vicomte, être persuadé de cette règle qui vous trompera rarement; c'est que tous les artistes sur porcelaine qui sollicitent des recommandations pour être occupés par la manufacture du Roi, prouvent presque toujours par cela même qu'ils ont un talent médiocre dont ne veulent ni les fabricants ni les amateurs éclairés. Les personnes habiles au contraire par conséquent les seules personnes dignes de travailler pour cet établissement royal, sont presque toujours occupées par suite de leurs talents et ne demandent rien. J'ai été obligé d'aller chercher presque tous les artistes et ouvriers habiles qui font l'honneur et la réputation de la Manufacture] Carton Ob 1, dossier Clarisse Arnaud, letter dated January 6, 1825.

38. [Il faut à Sevres ou des personnes d'un talent remarquable capables de soutenir la réputation de la manufacture du Roi, contribuant au mérite, à la valeur et à l'intérêt des pièces très grandes et très chères que la manufacture exécute ou des personnes d'un talent facile et agréable qui soient en état d'orner avec goût et d'une manière séduisante des petites pièces d'usage et d'ornement.] Register Vc 7, unpaginated, letter dated September 26, 1826.

39. [lorsqu'il s'agira . . . d'attacher un peintre de figures à cet établissement mon choix devra tomber sur celui ou celle dont le *talent sera le plus élevé, le plus complet et le plus convenable à nos travaux.* Aucune autre considération de quelque genre qu'elle soit ne devra avoir sur moi la moindre influence ... S'il s'agit d'un peintre copiste, comme la Manufacture ne doit faire que des copies de tableaux de premier mérite, il faudra qu'il ait le talent de rendre *parfaitement* et *complètement* l'original car à quoi servirait une copie dispendieuse si elle ne remplit pas parfaitement cette condition de rigueur] Carton Ob 9, dossier Madame Paulinier.

40. [l'effet que le second feu a fait sur mes assiettes est un des inconvénients qui résulte de faire le même genre de deux manières si opposées car en faisant alternativement l'ouvrage de Paris et le vôtre, celui-ci doit nécessairement se ressentir du peu de soin qu'exige le premier et cette incompatibilité est aussi à mon préjudice car en sortant de faire votre ouvrage, je ne puis de suite me livrer à la promptitude qu'exigent les prix de mes travaux pour Paris] Carton T 8, liasse 3, dossier 3, letter dated November 9, 1819.

41. [Je leur ai communiqué à l'un et à l'autre l'état écrit de leurs principaux devoirs et de leurs obligations; j'ai tâché de leur faire bien connoitre quelles étaient les qualités qu'il falloit posséder pour remplir convenablement la place . . . je leur ai fait sentir qu'il falloit sans cesser d'être juste être l'homme de la manufacture et non celui des artistes et ouvriers attachés à leur départment; qu'il falloit une connaissance exacte de tous les procédés d'emploi des couleurs et de leur cuisson, celle des pièces, des valeurs et des quantités des matières employés; que sans être artiste de premier rang, il etoit bon qu'ils eussent un talent qui les fit considérer et qu'il falloit qu'ils eussent en outre l'art et des moyens de dessins suffisant pour disposer avec goût, réflexion et convenance la décoration des objets ordinaires. Que la décoration des grandes pièces étant faites sur des dessins fournis souvent par les artistes les plus distingués, il falloit savoir en diriger l'exécution avec discernement sous les rapports du succès et même de l'économie qui consiste ici à arriver à la perfection par la voie la plus courte et la plus sûre; qu'il falloit enfin outre ces connoissances une surveillance active et de tous les moments] Carton T 10, liasse 3, dossier 3, letter dated February 17, 1825.

42. [avec beaucoup de modération afin de ne point éloigner et perdre des artistes habiles, peu nombreux, très utiles et qu'il seroit très difficile de remplacer] Carton T 6, liasse 1, dossier 5, letter dated October 15, 1812.

43. [Je ne veux . . . pas être désobéi à Sèvres et pour cela je n'ordonne que ce que j'ai le droit d'ordonner et le pouvoir de faire exécuter] Carton U 8, dossier "Exposition de 1832 – 1833," letter dated January 8, 1833, responding to an article by Ferdinand Charles de Lasteyrie published in *Le Temps* on January 1.

44. [Je croyois, Monsieur, que la Manufacture de Sèvres étoit un établissement royal dans une position assez remarquable en réputation et en considération pour qu'on tînt à quelqu'honneur à lui être attaché et qu'on ne lui fît aucune condition pour y rester. Je n'en ai jamais accepté de qui que ce soit et je ne commencerai pas aujourd'hui à en recevoir d'une personne qui n'a aucun titre même pour demander les distinctions auxquelles les grands talents peuvent avoir droit . . . . Je vous rappele, Monsieur, ce que j'ai toujours déclaré et ce que je vous ai dit, c'est que quand on quitte ainsi la manufacture on n'y rentrera jamais tant que j'y serais et la note mise sur les registre engagera certainement mes successeurs à suivre à cet égard la même règle] Carton Ob 7, dossier Langle, letter dated October 29, 1844.

45. [Je ne suis pas surpris que vous trouviez trop chers les vases de mon fils. Je suis abitué à vous trouver marchandant, et je crois que vous demendants 6 francs d'un ouvrage de 50 la force de l'habitude vous ferois m'offrire 5 francs] Carton T 3, liasse 1, dossier 3, letter dated October 15, 1807.

46. [Je tâche de maintenir dans les formes et le mode de décoration les principes d'un style exempt de l'influence de la mode. La position heureuse dans laquelle se trouve la manufacture lui donne les moyens d'être à l'abri de cette influence pernicieuse au bon goût et aux arts. Je tâche aussi de ne placer sur les pièces que des sujets qui aient quelqu'intérêt historique ou littéraire et j'éloigne autant qu'il m'est possible les sujets insignifiants ou de pure invention] Carton T 7, liasse 2, dossier 4, letter dated April 13, 1815.

47. [si la Manufacture de Sèvres est la première de l'Europe elle le doit . . . au soin que vous avez pris d'en écarter tout ce qui pourrait blesser le goût et paraître produit par les caprices de la mode] Carton T 11, liasse 1, dossier 1, letter dated August 25, 1826.

48. [j'ai désiré faire voir que ces travaux présentaient des exemples de tous les styles et de tous les genres susceptibles d'être admis par les hommes de goût quelque soit le style ou le genre qu'ils affectionnent. J'ai cherché à faire des produits de la manufacture des monuments de l'histoire des arts dans leurs différentes phases, et tout en cherchant à leur faire atteindre ce double but, j'ai tâche qu'ils puissent plaire à l'esprit autant qu'aux yeux.] Register Vc 8, fol. 104 – 104v, letter dated September 3, 1831.

49. When first recorded in January 1811, an oval *déjeuner* tray with a smooth edge is described as being a "forme de Vienne" (Carton Pb 2, valuation of January 30, 1811; Register Vu 1, fol. 107v, no. 267.9). There are also references in the documents to a "Corbeille Berlin" (1822) and a "Wedgwood" *théière* (see cat. no. 126).

50. [Cette décoration fait sortir la porcelaine dure des ressources bornées dans lesquelles elle paraissait devoir être limitée] (Carton U 15, liasse 2, note of October 13, 1840).

51. [j'ai toujours cherché à donner une sorte d'intérêt aux pièces d'ornement ou de service qui sortent des ateliers de la manufacture en attachant l'idée principale à l'ensemble de ces objets ou de leurs diverses parties, en formant des suites liées par un sorte de programme ou de consécration à une qualité, à un usage ou à toute autre idée ou condition principale.] Register Vc 8, fol. 204 – 204v, letter dated May 29, 1834.

52. [Ce genre de peinture n'est point riche, mais il est sévère, monumental et le seul qui puisse s'exécuter avec promptitude] Carton T 2, liasse 2, letter to Pierre Daru dated 26 Frimaire year 14 (December 17, 1805).

53. [plaque quarré sujet grec exécuté en étrusque] Carton Pb 1, appréciation du 18 Frimaire year 14; [sucrier égyptien décor étrusque en rouge et noir] Register Vu 1, folion 17, No. 257 – 8, entry dated August 1, 1810.

54. [c'est un genre nouveau et qui doit produire beaucoup d'effet.] Carton Pb 1, liasse 1, dossier 16, travaux de 1807.

55. Dawson, "Copiers or Competitors?" (1983).

56. [espèce de petite table, faite à la manière de celles qui étaient en usage chez les anciens] *Notice sur quelques-unes des pièces . . . 1.01.1826*, no. 37, p. 22.

57. Jones, "Henri IV and the Decorative Arts of the Bourbon Restauration" (1993), pp. 2 – 21.

58. These Etruscan ornaments were sometimes used on neoclassical forms such as a *vase 'Etrusque à larmier'* (1819) with "green ground all-over Etruscan decor in gold and platinum" and

a *vase 'Etrusque Turpin'* (1826) with "gray ground Etruscan decor incised in the ground," but they also appear on a *vase 'Jasmin Japonais'* (1824) with "brown ground and red Etruscan ornaments incised in the ground."

59. This vase was chosen for the tomb of Alexandre Brongniart.

60. [sujets de figures allégoriques peints à la sépia représentant le temps faisant passer les arts agréables et retenant les arts futiles] Carton Pb 4, appréciation of May 20, 1818.

61. Lajoix, "Alexandre Brongniart et la quête," nos. 1 and 2 (1992/1993).

62. *Le "Gothique" Retrouvé avant Viollet-le-Duc.* exhib. cat. (1979 – 80).

63. [en grisaille rehaussée d'or à la manière des émaux de Limoges] *Notice sur quelques-unes des pièces . . . 1er janvier 1830*, cat. no. 5.

64. Register Vbb 5, fol. 382v, April 15, 1819; Register Vz 3, fol. 151 – 151v, May 28, 1819. The Persian ambassador had just purchased fifty plates with floral decorations (Register Vz 3, fol. 146v, May 1819).

65. Register Vz 3, fol. 63v, May 28, 1817. A *déjeuner* service with floral decor was also delivered to the ministry of foreign affairs for presentation to the Egyptian pasha (Register Vbb 7, fol. 31, October 19, 1827). Finally, in 1830 the viceroy of Egypt was presented with a new series of pieces, including the service with landscapes of Egypt of 1824 (Register Vbb 8, fol. 11v ff., February 25, 1830), not including the direct orders of Mehemet-Ali (see n. 16 above).

66. [plusieurs pièces de porcelaine de la Chine remarquables sous le rapport des procédés techniques et qui manquent à cette partie de la collection de la Manufacture] Register Vc 7, fol. 95v ff., letter dated April 10, 1826.

67. [Les Chinois et les Japonais qui pratiquent cet art depuis plus de deux mille ans y ont introduit une variété de pâtes, de couleurs et d'applications que les Européens n'ont pu encore obtenir depuis cent ans au plus qu'ils l'exercent. Il me paraît donc aussi utile qu'intéressant de réunir successivement à nos colletions toutes les pièces qui nous font connaître des procédés ou des résultats dont nous ne possédons pas encore d'échantillons] Register Vc 8, fol. 19 ff., letter dated April 24, 1829.

68. [a cherché néanmoins à ne point s'écarter du style de l'époque et du peuple] *Notice sur quelques-unes des pièces . . . 27 decembre 1832*, no. 14, pp. 15 – 16.

69. [dans le genre des peintures d'Herculanum]; [tâcher de l'idéaliser autant que possible] Carton Pb 10, Vases 1838 – 44 (1839 no. 17).

70. [suivant le système très rationnel de Madame Jaquotot, Monsieur Langlacé a *rétabli* dans l'azur du ciel le ton tel qu'il devait être avant que le vernis vieilli l'eut jauni et rendu presque verd; mais il n'a pas suivi tout à fait la même marche pour la masse de nuages, il en résulte . . . que les nuages ont cent ans et l'azur huit jours] Carton Pb 8, liasse 2, dossier 7, letter dated March 23, 1838.

71. [tirés des poteries des îles Viti]; [sujets tirés des usages des peuplades encore sauvages de ces parages] Carton Pb 4 (travaux 1844 – 48), liasse 1, vases, 1846, no. 19.

72. Carton T 9, liasse 3, dossier 2, letter dated February 15, 1822.

73. Feuchère, "L'Art industriel" (1842), p. I, pl. 3.

74. [dans le genre des faïences italiennes] Carton Pb 11bis, appréciation of May 9, 1846.

75. See, for example, a letter from Count Anatole Demidoff dated January 25, 1838, requesting authentification of a plate made of "old Sèvres soft paste," and asking Brongniart "what was formerly the most highly regarded of old Sèvres work, [whether it was the] colors *bleu turquoise*, *bleu de Roi*, green, or rose" (Carton T 13, liasse 5, dossier 16a). I would like to thank Robert Wenley of the Wallace Collection, London, for having confirmed my reading of Count Demidoff's signature.

76. Register Vtt 6, fol. 43.

77. [d'après le dessin qui sera remis par M. Lamy] Ibid., fol. 43v.

78. Ibid., fol. 44.

79. [imitant le plus possible la dorure sur bleu de l'ancienne pâte tendre] Ibid., fol. 42v.

80. Ibid., fol. 43v, November 4, 1846.

81. [1 Pot à l'eau et sa jatte forme Buire de Mr. Brongniard fils] Carton Pb 1, record of entry into sales inventory on 19 Messidor year 13 (July 8, 1805).

82. [Juin 1 Vase Corbeille composition de Mr. Brongniart mis au net en petit] Carton Pb 4, travaux de 1818.

83. [D'après une idée et croquis de moi et un dessin ou esquisse de M. Fragonard] Carton Pb 8, liasse 1, Sculpture.

84. The list of pieces so identified is as follows: *tasse 'à chocolat AB'* (1813); *glacière 'AB'* (1816); *tasse 'AB à reliefs'* (1817); *ecuelle 'à bouillon AB' avec soucoupe* (1818); *pot à crême 'AB'* and *beurrier 'AB'* (1829); *déjeuner 'AB à côtes'* with *plateau tétramère'* (1830); *ecritoire 'AB'* (1838); and *déjeuner 'AB à côtes'* (1840). There is also a *vase 'Etrusque AB'* of uncertain date; the plaster model as revised in 1825 carries the mention "imité de l'Antique," and Brongniart may have done nothing more than indicate what model was to be used.

85. See, for example, Théophile Gautier's review of an exhibition held at the Louvre at which products from royal manufactories were displayed (*La Presse* [June 21, 1844]).

Fig. 7-1. *Bouquet of Flowers*, by Hyacinthe Régnier, 1839; gouache, ink, and pencil on paper. This cartoon for a sacristy window in the chapel of the château d'Eu was later painted on glass by Eglée Riocreux. (AMNS, Section D, § 11, 1839)

Chapter 7

The Stained-Glass and Painting-on-Glass Workshop at Sèvres, 1827 – 1854

Karole Bezut

After a decline of about two centuries, the art of stained glass experienced a revival in France in the beginning of the nineteenth century. This coincided with a renewal of interest in the Middle Ages and the restoration of the Catholic faith encouraged by the clergy and monarchy after 1815. Thanks to Alexandre Brongniart, the porcelain manufactory at Sèvres played a prominent role in the rediscovery of stained glass. Under Brongniart's direction the manufactory established an important glass workshop, which came to be widely celebrated.

The Decline of Stained Glass

The precipitous decrease in the use of stained glass in Europe had begun in the sixteenth century, in the wake of the Council of Trent (1545 – 63). The Catholic Church, advocating greater involvement among the faithful in its services, criticized the inclusion of stained-glass windows in places of worship, maintaining that they caused church interiors to be unduly darkened and were distracting to the faithful. The importance once attached to such windows as privileged elements of ecclesiastical decor had increasingly shifted to large altarpieces.

Throughout the seventeenth and eighteenth centuries, translucent white windows with simple decorative borders were used in church architecture, notably the chapel at Versailles which was erected between 1689 and 1707. Its windows were decorated only with the cipher of Louis XIV and painted borders of alternating gold fleurs-de-lys and florets. In most Medieval churches as well, stained glass was replaced with plain windows. Few houses of worship were spared, and as a result many irreplaceable examples were lost forever. In 1741, for example, the canons of Notre Dame de Paris instructed the *peintre-verrier* (glass painter) Pierre Le Vieil to remove all of the cathedral's earlier stained glass except for its three rose windows.[1]

In addition stained-glass makers, faced with a declining number of commissions, gradually became simple glaziers who did little more than make minor repairs. They often replaced damaged areas of glass with pieces salvaged from other windows sacrificed to save those considered to be more significant or in a better state of repair. Eventually, the skills of glass painters were almost completely lost, and glass workers were no longer capable of painting the necessary replacement pieces, much less of producing comparable original works.

By the eve of the Revolution, the French art of stained glass was being kept alive by a handful of craftsmen, among them Le Vieil, a member of the venerable family of *peintres-verriers* from Rouen. He was also the author of *L'Art de la peinture sur verre et de la vitrerie* (The Art of painting on glass and stained glass; 1774), which was the last French painting-on-glass manual to appear until the nineteenth century.

The Rebirth of Painting on Glass

In the early years of the nineteenth century new demands initiated the revival of glass painting. Bonaparte's policy of reconciliation between the state and the Roman Catholic Church, formalized by the Concordat in July 1801, required the replacement of stained-glass windows that had been vandalized or destroyed during the aggressive secularization of church property beginning in 1789. The restored churches and various properties would then be returned to the Catholic hierarchy. The Catholic Church in France, having regained its power, was also determined to restore religious practices that had largely been abandoned during and after the Revolution. The pictorial stained-glass window, laden with moral overtones, was considered more effective as a "catechism-in-images" than easel paintings, which tended to be difficult to read in darkened interiors, obscuring their allegorical and iconographical elements.[2] Windows were perceived as a perfect instrument of propaganda for the French clergy in this new "age of faith," which saw the cult of saints assume a special prominence. Members of the clergy stressed connections between members of their congregations and the saints who shared their names. The renewal of the art of stained glass can also be attributed in part to the pan-European Romantic movement, which encouraged a rediscovery of the Middle Ages and its artistic heritage and techniques.

The first attempts to revive painting on glass were made in Paris between 1798 and 1800 at the initiative of Christophe Dihl, a ceramist-enameler of German extraction. The technique involved painting on the backs of sheets of crystal glass which were then protected by attaching another sheet of glass to the back after firing. Although these works of art were well received,[3] they were expensive, and the technique used in their fabrication proved unreliable as the glass was prone to cracking during firing.

The process was soon replaced by an "enameled glass" technique developed by Ferdinand Mortelèque. This was a more direct approach; it involved painting directly on the outer surface of the glass without using a second sheet or, later, using tinted glass. Mortelèque's 1816 painted-glass *Christ on the Cross* made for the church of Saint-Roch, Paris, was the first large painted-glass window to be produced in France since the Concordat of 1801.

The work of French craftsmen was paralleled by that of two English glass painters, Warren White and Edward Jones, who came to Paris at the invitation of the comte de Chabrol, prefect of the Seine. Beginning in 1826, the two Englishmen executed windows depicting Saint John the Baptist, Saint Joseph, and John the Evangelist for the church of Sainte-Elisabeth, as well as a Marriage of the Virgin for Saint-Étienne-du-Mont.

There were thus many attempts in the first thirty years of the century to restore stained glass to its previous luster. Given the paucity of commissions and the inadequate financial support, however, only a handful of individuals embarked on such projects. They worked alone, lacking the means to establish anything remotely resembling a painting-on-glass workshop. They were also confronted with a major technical impediment to the production of true stained glass, which was not used until the late 1820s when chemists were able to employ copper oxides to produce red stained glass (an elusive color). Although blue and green stained glass had been obtainable prior to that time, it was not until after the establishment of the workshop at Sèvres in 1827 that nineteenth-century stained glass as an art form began to be explored seriously.

The Painting-on-Glass and Stained-Glass Workshops

When Alexandre Brongniart was appointed director of the Sèvres porcelain manufactory in 1800, he was already interested in developing new coloring agents for porcelain. His research culminated in a lecture delivered to the Institut de France in 1802 — "Essai sur les couleurs obtenues des oxydes métalliques et fixées par la fusion sur les différents corps vitreux" (Essay on colors obtained from metallic oxides and fixed by fusion on various vitreous bodies).[4]

Brongniart's principal goal in his essay was to make chemists aware of recent advances in the field of vitrifiable colors, which were used for painting on both porcelain and glass. His text reveals that very soon after his arrival at Sèvres, he was investigating painting on glass, an activity hitherto unknown at the manufactory. Having studied the writings of earlier stained-glass craftsmen — Neri, Kunckel,[5] and Le Vieil — to learn about pigments appropriate for use on glass, he complains in his essay that their descriptions of the relevant processes are imprecise and recounts that he collaborated with Charles Méraud, the preparer of colors at Sèvres, to produce a palette suitable for use by glass painters.

At the same time, Brongniart initiated the first trials of painting on glass at Sèvres. In 1801 – 2 the manufactory was responsible for producing the image of a lion using a technique devised by Méraud[6], and two bouquets of flowers[7] painted on glass. In 1809 Charles-Etienne Le Guay depicted an image of Sapho using Dihl's double-glass technique. A paucity of commissions, however, caused Brongniart to discontinue Dihl's technique at Sèvres.

Meanwhile, in Paris, Mortelèque achieved great public success with his displays at the "Expositions des produits de l'Industrie" (Exhibitions of Industrial Products) which were held intermittently. In the 1819 event he exhibited an enameled head on glass of Henri IV for which he won a bronze medal. In 1823 Brongniart, irritated by the favorable reception accorded Mortelèque's enameled glass windows in that year's exposition,[8] resolved to draw attention to Sèvres's pioneering role in the reintroduction of stained glass. Accordingly, he ordered the resumption of trials under the direction of Pierre Robert. A painter by training and manager of the manufactory's Paris salesroom, Robert executed several windows between 1823 and 1826, some made entirely of painted glass and others featuring a combination of tinted and painted glass. In 1825 Robert exhibited a bouquet of flowers painted under his direction by Louis Schilt on a single sheet of glass. Brongniart was especially enthusiastic about this work. The subject matter had not been used before in stained glass, and Brongniart, who planned to promote such windows for use in secular buildings, thought it especially appropriate for domestic interiors.

Brongniart also hoped to dispute claims that the old stained-glass techniques had been lost and that modern examples came nowhere near equaling the beauty of the earlier works. In 1825 he had Pierre Robert make exact copies of four early panels from Sainte-Chapelle in Paris. These small leaded windows, composed of tinted glass with hand-painting include *The Archangel Michael Weighing Souls, The Sacrifice of Abraham, Virgin and Child,* and *Judith Showing the Head of Holofernes to the People of Bethulia.* They were presented to the public at the annual exhibition of the manufactory's products and then entered the collection of the Musée Céramique at Sèvres. Robert also made a reproduction on glass of *The Virgin of the Green Cushion,* a celebrated painting by Andrea Solario in the Louvre. These samples were insufficient to convince the prefect of the Seine, still committed to English glass painters, to commission a window from Sèvres. Brongniart, however, did not give up. Indeed, after viewing the Paris church windows painted by the two Englishmen White and Jones, he was more convinced than ever that French artists could produce work of comparable if not superior quality.[9]

In 1826 Brongniart's convictions finally had an impact; a report he had drafted on the question convinced the vicomte de La Rochefoucauld, director of the Departement des Beaux-Arts, that it was necessary to establish a painting-on-glass workshop at Sèvres. He also convinced the comte de Chabrol to commission six windows from Sèvres for the new church of Notre-Dame-de-Lorette in Paris.[10] The early months of 1827 were spent raising the funds to set up a workshop and subsidiary facilities at the manufactory. Both the workshop and the laboratory required many casement windows to provide the natural illumination needed for making stained-glass windows. The furnishings were kept simple: Brongniart specified only a few large worktables and a corner cabinet for storing paints and other necessary materials.[11] In the laboratory, Brongniart called for the construction of three muffle kilns in which glass panels painted with vitrifiable colors could be fired; one of the room's walls was lined with tubs for mixing colors.

In May 1827 Pierre Robert was named head of the painting-on-glass workshop, which was officially established on July 4, 1827 by order of King Charles X after authorization of a special credit line of 26,000 francs.

Personnel in the Workshop. From 1827 to 1854, the workshop was directed successively by three men. The first was Pierre Robert, who died in the 1832 cholera epidemic, only a few years after his appointment. His successor was Auguste Vatinelle, one of the figure painters in the workshop, who served as director until March 1837, when he resigned after a financial disagreement with the administration. His departure caught Brongniart unprepared. It was no easy matter to find someone capable of assuming all the responsibilities incumbent upon the head of a painting-on-glass workshop. Brongniart drafted a list of the necessary qualifications, and they were formidable.[12] According to this list, the position required competence in all matters pertaining to the production of stained glass, both aesthetic and technical. It demanded an ability to oversee the execution process, assuring that the pieces fit together and budgets were not exceeded. Other administrative talents included an ability to allocate work both to students and to workers, assessing their ability as well as their conduct. The head of the workshop had to judge the quality of the raw materials, of glass and colors, as they were delivered to the workshop. He was required to keep abreast of developments in the field through close contact with the scientific community, sharing with them advances made at the manufactory. In addition, Brongniart maintained that the head of the workshop should be an artist, capable of participating in the actual painting. Over and above these essential technical qualifications, he must have a character that was both agreeable and beyond reproach, to avoid compromising the manufactory's impeccable reputation.

In 1837 because no one in the manufactory fit this demanding bill, Brongniart decided to head the workshop himself, with the assistance of Frédéric Bonnet, one of its glass painters, and Louis Robert, the son of its founder and a chemist by training. This provisional arrangement continued until April 1839, when Louis Robert was officially named head of the painting-on-glass workshop, a post he occupied until the department closed in 1854.

The manufactory never had a large permanent staff of glass painters. Each year there were no more than five or six painters, both for figures and ornament, at any given time. For rush projects and very large paintings on glass, however, painters who usually worked in the porcelain workshop collaborated with their colleagues in the glass workshop. In 1837, for example, King Louis-Philippe asked Sèvres to make a large stained-glass window for the chapel of the château de Compiègne. Entitled *The Church and Faith*, and after designs by Jules Ziegler, it measured 21 1/4 by 8 1/4 feet (6.50 x 2.50 m). The workshop's entire staff at the time — Frédéric Bonnet and Pierre Doré — as well as two students — François Favre and François Fialeix — were mobilized to paint the borders. The main subjects, two allegories representing the Church and Faith, were the work of Antoine Béranger, one of the manufactory's finest painters of figures on porcelain. Although not a permanent member of the staff, Béranger was associated with the stained-glass workhop beginning in 1829. To assure that the project was completed in time three porcelain painters and gilders were also employed.[13] It was not unsual for painters to move between the departments. After the fall of the July Monarchy in 1848, when the painting-on-glass studio's existence was threatened, and the staff had to be reduced, some glass painters were kept on as porcelain painters. Paul Roussel, a glass painter, for example, worked on porcelain projects for the manufactory between 1850 and 1871.

In all some thirty-eight glass painters worked at one time or another in the Sèvres workshop during its existence: sixteen ornamental painters, sixteen figure painters, three landscape painters, and three flower painters. The figure painters required the greatest skill and were often considered the "noblest" of the artists working on glass. Generally they did not execute borders, which was the province of the ornamental painters. There were far fewer landscape and flower painters, for the motifs in which they specialized appeared only rarely in religious and historical compositions. Nonetheless, the Sèvres manufactory was fortunate to employ two notable specialists in flower painting: Louis Schilt, who worked during the tenure of Pierre Robert in the years 1823 – 25, and Eglée Riocreux, daughter of Denis-Désiré Riocreux and wife of Louis Robert. Between 1840 and 1845 she composed and painted bouquets on several windows and painted mirrors (fig. 7-1).

As for technical personnel, the workshop began with a single person performing the functions of glazier, came-worker (responsible for assembling the lead framework), general workshop assistant, and laboratory assistant. An official glass cutter, François-Xavier Schaerdel, and a second workshop assistant were subsequently added to the staff. Finally, beginning in 1844, a third technician was employed to oversee and operate the muffle kilns.

The Workshop Budget. Compared to other Sèvres workshops, painting-on-glass was a small operation receiving a minuscule portion of the manufactory's overall budget. Under the July Monarchy (1830 – 48), the salaries of its staff averaged only 12,000 francs, which was 5.5 percent of the manufactory's total payroll.[14] Expense records relating to the purchase of the raw materials needed for the workshop are only available for the years 1827 to 1830, during which time they averaged 4,000 francs annually.[15]

Like all the administrative personnel, the head of the workshop received an annual salary equal to that of other workshop heads and ranged between 3,000 and 4,000 francs. The glass painters, were paid in accordance with the "maximum" system (see chap. 3). At the beginning of each year, the administration established a production schedule and determined the maximum amount of work to be allotted each painter. If the total fees for work actually done in the course of the year exceeded this maximum, the balance was carried over into the next year's fees. Workers could, however, increase their earnings by taking on freelance projects, or work *en extraordinaire*, for the manufactory. In addition, Brongniart continued to honor the traditional hierarchy in the manufactory's salary schedules: figure painters were paid more than ornamental painters who, in turn, received higher salaries than technical workers. There was, however, one notable exception to this rule: the glazier and came-worker Schaerdel, an excellent collaborator, received a salary that equaled and sometimes exceeded the pay of ornamental painters. Occasionally the most favored figure painters, such as Paul Roussel, received salaries even higher than that of the workshop's head.[16] Only rarely were Brongniart's professional relations with the workshop's staff disturbed by financial disagreements.

The Fabrication Process

The design and production of stained-glass windows at the manufactory's workshop followed a deliberate routine. It began with the making of cartoons. Brongniart required that his designers provide a full-scale grisaille cartoon and small color sketch in oil or watercolor for each window. The cartoons indicated precise contours as well as linear treatments of such details as fabric folds and any trompe l'oeil modeling that was necessary (fig. 7-2). The placement of the leading and the surrounding structure of the window were also clearly indicated. In any case, there was no need for the artist to provide a finished oil painting of the design, but an oil or watercolor sketch was essential as a guide to the colors required for the different parts of the

Fig. 7-2. *Saint John*, by Alexis Apoil; charcoal and red pencil on paper. This was used as a cartoon for a window in the chapel at Amboise. (AMNS, Section D, § 11, undated)

composition (fig. 7-3). Traditionally, the sketch was one-tenth the size of the grisaille cartoon.

Brongniart's designers included some of the most admired artists of the day: Jean-Auguste-Dominique Ingres, Eugène Delacroix, Achille Devéria, Hippolyte Flandrin, and Horace Vernet, as well as the architect Eugène Viollet-le-Duc. In many cases they were chosen directly by King Louis-Philippe, not by the director. These artists produced original designs specifically conceived for stained glass, as well as slightly modified copies of existing canvases.[17] Brongniart's relations with these prestigious figures were not always easy: he often had to hound them for delivery of cartoons, which were late due to other obligations such as travel, exhibitions, and other commissions. The resulting delays sometimes brought the workshop's activity to a halt. Furthermore, financial disagreements were more frequent with the artists providing cartoons than with the manufactory's own staff. Despite the logistical problems, Brongniart maintained fruitful collaborative relationships, especially with Ingres, Viollet-le-Duc, and Devéria.

The Sèvres workshop turned to outside suppliers for some of its primary materials. White and stained glass as well as crystal glass were obtained from the principal French glass (and mirror) factories, notably Choisy-le-Roi, which was directed by Georges Bontemps and celebrated for its beautiful copper-sulphide – based red glass. Other suppliers included Saint-Gobain, Cirey, and Saint-Quirin. In 1843, for example, Brongniart collaborated with Saint-Quirin when Louis-Philippe commissioned the Sèvres workshop to make six large paintings on crystal glass illustrating the Passion of Christ for the funerary chapel at Dreux. This dependence on outside suppliers sometimes caused serious problems. The workshop might exhaust its supply of glass due to unforeseeable delays in delivery.[18] Quality control was another problem. There were often discrepancies between glass supplied at different times but intended to be the same color. Such inconsistencies sometimes resulted in unintentional variations in colors in a single window, which compromised the unity of the composition.[19]

Although the Sèvres workshop, like the earlier stained-glass makers, made use of large pieces of monochrome glass, these served primarily for the principal masses of compositional forms, such as draperies and backgrounds. For the folds, shadows, and faces, white glass was hand-painted with enamel colors. This composite technique was used, for example, in the windows made after cartoons by Ingres for the chapel of Notre-Dame-de-la-Compassion in Neuilly: the figures of Saint Louis and Saint Philip were executed entirely in true stained glass, while the tunic worn by Archangel Raphael was painted on glass in a bluish enamel with rose-mauve shadows, and Saint Helen's white-and-gold embroidered dalmatic was also painted in enamel,[20] the preferred medium in the Sèvres workshop. According to Brongniart, the technique of using vitrifiable colors on white glass represented "true painting on glass, an art scarcely known to the ancients and one that has already attained a high degree of perfection since the discoveries of modern chemistry have come to its aid."[21]

Vitrifiable colors, or enamels, consist of a colorant — usually a metallic oxide — and a flux, composed of borax, sand, and lead-oxide, which would bond with the glass by fusion when fired. During the nineteenth century, the palette of enamels was continually being enriched, and in 1843 Brongniart drafted a list of some thirty colors used in painting on glass in the Sèvres workshop.[22] This was not an exhaustive list; the known hues could be changed by altering the amount of binder used.

The minerals arrived at the manufactory in a raw state. They were finely ground and melted in a crucible in a furnace in the workshop's color laboratory. Impurities rose to the surface and were skimmed off when cool. The enamels were then ground again to a fine powder in special mills. When a color was needed for painting, the enamel powder was mixed with a thickener to prevent its running on the glass during application and which kept it in place prior to firing. Before application, enamels could also be diluted, either with water (to produce a lighter tint) or with turpentine or lavender water (to produce a more opaque tint).

The actual painting was transcribed from a transparent-paper tracing taken from the cartoon. If the painter was working on white glass, he placed the glass over the cartoon; the transparency of the glass allowed the contours and shadows to be visible. The enamels were applied with brushes made from animal hair or bristle — sable, polecat, badger, or pig — the size and kind of hair depending on how much surface was to be painted.[23]

After the application of enamel colors, the glass was fired in a muffle kiln made of fire-proof clay and heated with wood or coal as fuel. The pieces of glass were slid into the kiln on sheets of heat-resistant tôle or lava stone. At Sèvres, Louis Robert had recommended the use of lava from the Auvergne region, which was first coated with chalk diluted with water and allowed to dry.[24] During the firing, the temperature was gradually increased until it reached 1300° to 1460° F (700° to 800° C) which occurred within 5 1/2 to 6 hours. To monitor the firing, the operator placed in the kiln special test tubes containing small pieces of glass painted with enamels known to melt at precisely 1150° (620° C). When these enamels were sufficiently vitrified in the test tubes in both the upper and lower ducts of the kiln, the furnace could be emptied of fuel and the kiln left to cool. Although the actual firing lasted a total of 6 1/2 or 7 hours, the glass sheets could only be removed after another 10 hours or so, the time required for the kiln to return to room temperature.

In 1843 Brongniart decided to build a new muffle kiln measuring 74 7/8 inches high, from the floor to the top of the ceiling arch, by 63 inches wide by 78 3/4 inches deep (190 by 160 by 200 cm). It would be used solely for firing the large painted crystal glass commissioned by Louis-Philippe for the funerary chapel at Dreux. In 1844, as soon as the kiln was operational, Louis Robert began to experiment with paintings on crystal glass. The chemical composition of crystal glass was different from that of regular glass, and the enamel reacted differently with it, requiring more firing time than regular glass to reach the fusion temperature. Robert reported that the process required twenty-five hours at low temperature followed by six hours at high temperature.[25]

Firing glass was always risky: breakage could be caused by careless handling, excessively high temperatures, precipitous cooling, or other factors. Some colors could vaporize in a second or third firing. As a result every successful glass firing at Sèvres was considered an occasion for celebration and was immediately reported by Robert and his successors to Brongniart, who in turn informed the comte de Montalivet, Intendant Général de la Liste Civile under Louis-Philippe. In September 1846, for example, Louis Robert proudly announced the successful firing of a window representing Christ on the Mount of Olives, which had been painted by Alexis Apoil and

Fig. 7-3. *Faith*, by Antoine Béranger, 1830; pencil and gouache, partially varnished, on paper. This color sketch was for a window in the chapel of the château de Randan (AMNS, Section D, § 11, 1834)

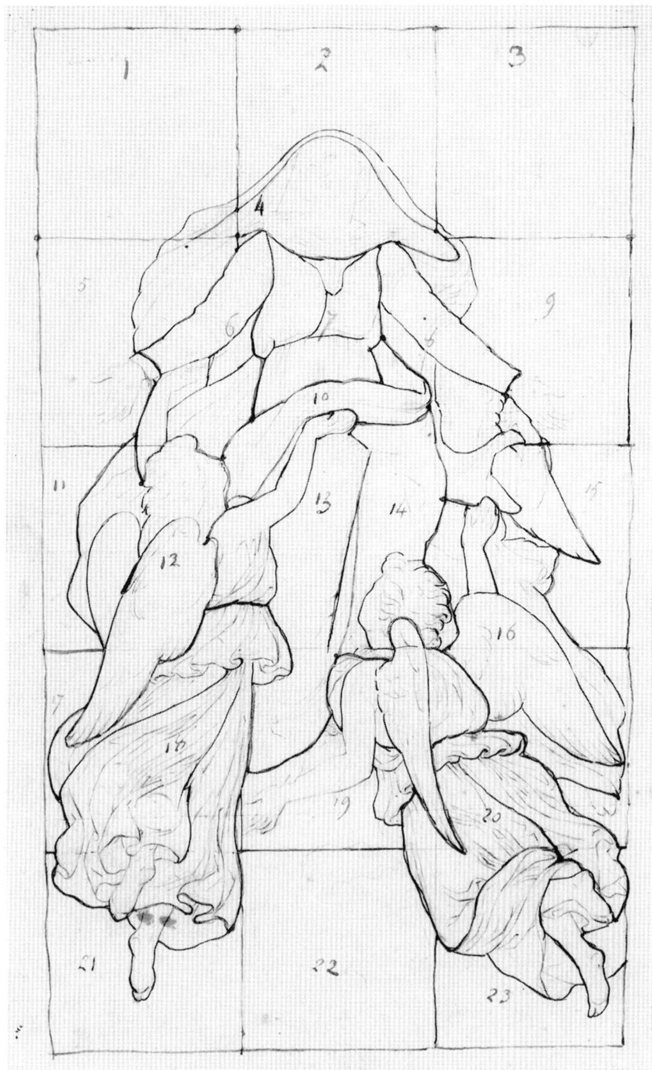

Fig. 7-4. *The Assumption of the Virgin,* by Hippolyte Lebas; pencil and black and red ink on paper. In this squared schematic drawing after a composition by Pierre-Paul Prud'hon, which was destined for a window in the church of Notre-Dame-de-Lorette, Paris, the indications of the came pattern are clearly marked. (AMNS, Section D, § 11, 1827)

Fig. 7-5. Window ornaments by Claude-Aimé Chenavard, 1837; watercolor and ink on paper. This cartoon was made for a panel in the middle of the window at the entrance of the church at Eu. (AMNS, Section D, §11, 1837)

Fig. 7-6. Sections of a rose-campion frieze design by Louis Schilt, 1834; ink and gouache, partially varnished, on paper. This design for transfer-printing was inspired by a print in the *Album de l'ornemaniste* by Claude-Aimé Chenavard. (AMNS, Section D, § 11, 1834)

Jules André for the chapel at Dreux. He commented that "the violent red tones that so worried the king were, as I anticipated, moderated by the heat and are very satisfying; the sky in the landscape has turned out very well."[26]

Once the firing was completed, the pieces of glass were leaded together. Stained-glass windows from previous eras featured veritable webs of leading; Brongniart, however, thought that too much leading compromised a window's legibility. He advocated a different approach at the Sèvres workshop whereby windows had as little leading as possible and instead were made of constituent pieces of glass that were much larger than those used in earlier periods (fig. 7-4).

The Marketing of Sèvres's Stained and Painted Windows

Windows made in the Sèvres workshop were extremely expensive. The high fees paid the workshop's glass painters made production costs much higher than at private establishments. The cost was also inflated by the many operational expenses that were absorbed by the manufactory and which Brongniart estimated to be one-quarter the total production cost. These sums were incorporated into the net price, or estimated production expenses, of the windows, which served as the basis for calculating their official sale price and, in principle, included a profit for the manufactory. In fact this figure was insufficient to cover production costs completely, for it did not include outlays required for the window designs and the cames and overall frame, none of which figured in the manufactory's calculations. The cartoons and sketches were often the work of renowned artists who commanded high fees for their services.[27] The mounts, too, were often quite costly depending on the complexity demanded by the design.

Given these additional outlays, it was common for the cost of producing and installing a Sèvres window to amount to more than double the manufactory's asking price for the piece. In one extreme case, the window representing Saint Amélie, which was commissioned by Louis-Philippe in 1831 for the chapel at the château d'Eu, entered the manufactory's inventory on December 1832, with an assigned sale price of 6,500 francs. This figure only covered the execution of the painting on glass and the leading used to assemble the window.[28] Another 1,500 francs were paid for the color sketch of the overall composition by Claude-Aimé Chenavard and 4,000 francs for Paul Delaroche's original oil painting and related drawings, paid previously by Louis-Philippe. Finally, 2,100 francs were paid for a special iron frame that was prepared by Sèvres's specialist for such constructions. Thus, the total expenses came to 14,100 francs, to be paid by the client. Given such conditions, only the wealthiest clients, primarily the royal family, could afford to place commissions.

In the hope of winning a larger and less affluent clientele, Brongniart developed a technique for printing decorative motifs, such as borders, by mechanical means that reduced time and costs. This process, basically the same transfer-printing technique used on porcelain and glassware, made it possible to repeat decorative motifs rapidly and inexpensively, thereby considerably reducing the sale price of the windows. The motif itself was either etched or engraved on a copperplate, with special care being taken to vary the depths of the marks to assure tonal variety. The marks also had to be sufficiently distinct to preclude smudging. The plate was inked with a mixture of linseed oil, a vitrifiable color, and a binder, and the image

Fig. 7-7. *Agnès Sorel*, by Emile Wattier, 1836; gray and pink pencil, black lead, wash and white highlights on paper. This window cartoon was commissioned by M. Pescherard of Loches. (AMNS, Section D, § 11, 1836)

was then printed on thin, dampened, unsized paper. This paper was carefully pressed against the glass, which was then fired at a moderate temperature so that the binder and ink did not vaporize. The paper burned away, leaving only the decoration. In theory this was the end of the process, but in practice it was usually necessary for ornamental painters to retouch the motifs by hand, because the amount of enamel on the paper transfer was often too small to produce the desired effect.[29]

Brongniart found models for friezes, borders, and other motifs in tapestry albums as well as the *Album de l'ornemaniste* by Claude-Aimé Chenavard, an ornamental painter and designer. Brongniart much admired Chenavard and often had him collaborate on window projects (fig. 7-5). Before long the painting-on-glass workshop had produced a sizable assortment of windows featuring transfer-printed borders, rosettes, and representational elements (fig. 7-6). The manufactory sold many pieces of glass with printed borders to private clients through its salesroom in Paris, and it also received commissions for entire windows with transfer-printed designs. Two such windows were executed by Hyacinthe Fontaine in 1833: the first, described as an "ornamented window with printed and colored

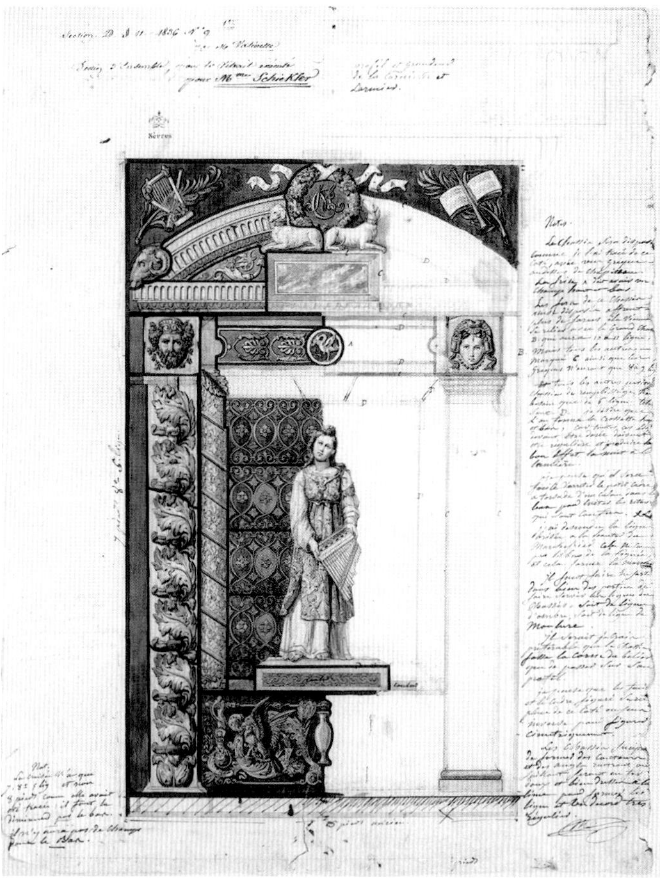

Fig. 7-8. *Saint Cecilia*, by Auguste Vatinelle, 1836; watercolor, gouache, pencil, and ink on paper. This window design was commissioned by a Mme Schickler. (AMNS, Section D, § 11, 1836)

motifs," was sold for 150 francs; the second, "lancet window with a mosaic of rosettes, printed and colored," for 50 francs.[30]

Financial records at Sèvres reveal that the total annual production cost for work completed by the painting-on-glass workshop during its existence seems to have exceeded its annual sales revenues: between 1830 and 1856 the discrepancy averaged some 14,000 francs annually. This situation was not due to unscrupulous clients failing to collect finished work but rather to Brongniart's insistence that the staff produce uncommissioned work when it was otherwise unoccupied. Most such pieces were sent to the salesroom in Paris, where they were used as display samples and were sometimes sold.

Projects Realized by the Workshop

Ecclesiastical Commissions. In 1829 Brongniart, determined to obtain commissions for the workshop, appealed to church and civil authorities, but with disappointing results. The high cost of Sèvres's productions netted only two, one in Reims and the other in Besançon. The first was for the chapel in the palace of the archbishop in Reims, which the architect Robelin had begun to renovate five years earlier, for the coronation of King Charles X. He asked the Sèvres workshop to make glass borders decorated with fleurs-de-lys for the thirteen windows in the Salle des Rois.[31]

Robelin also oversaw the second Sèvres commission, initiated by the archbishop of Besançon for the cathedral in 1829. This was a more important project. In addition to colored borders for nine windows, it involved five windows in the choir, depicting each of the Four Evangelists and the Assumption of the Virgin.[32] After several delays, the five main windows, each measuring 16 1/3 by 4 feet (5 x 1.2 m), were eventually delivered in 1834. The five figures stand out clearly on a blue background. The total cost of the work for Besançcon amounted to 10,000 francs.[33]

Private Commissions. Most of the workshop's private commissions involved colored windows for the private chapels of members of the French nobility and the prosperous middle class. Such was the case with one M. Delisle, for example, who in 1835 commissioned four casement windows representing saints Amélie, Theresa, Peter, and John for a chapel in the town of Sèvres.[34] A similar commission was placed in 1836 by the marquise de Chaponnais, who ordered two windows representing a total of four figures — the Virgin and saints John, Peter, and Simon — for a chapel under construction at Beaulieu, her property near Lyon.[35] Secular stained glass was still rare at this time, but the manufactory did receive a few such commissions. In 1835 a certain M. Pescherard from Loches ordered five painted-glass medallions bearing his initials as well as portraits of Charles VII and Agnès Sorel (fig. 7-7).[36]

Wealthier individuals could afford windows with figures, usually saints (fig. 7-8),[37] Christ, the Virgin, or God the Father. There were also religious motifs for those with more modest resources. In 1837, for example, a M. Delaporte ordered a "roundel with yellow ground and blue letters forming the initials [AM] of Ave Maria,"[38] while in 1838 a M. Mathon commissioned a "painted- glass roundel representing the inscription Jehovah within a glory [halo]."[39]

The high cost of Sèvres's windows often prompted clients to scale back ambitious projects. Some clients abandoned plans for several windows and made do with only one. Mme Eyre from Metz, for example, initially envisioned a series of windows for her chapel: a choir window culminating in a trefoil, six lateral windows, and a three-panel rose window above the portal. After receiving the cost estimates, however, which were very high, she ordered only the choir window featuring two figures of saints.[40] Even so, the bill came to 1,500 francs, a sum well beyond the reach of many potential clients, especially for a single window.

Less wealthy individuals contented themselves with windows decorated with transfer-printed borders, which were far less expensive than windows with figurative painting. It was not unusual, in fact, for the workshop to be commissioned to make nothing more than a simple coat-of-arms,[41] a cipher,[42] or a small roundel. Such small projects did not bring much revenue to the manufactory, but they demonstrated that the workshop's productions need not be the exclusive province of a wealthy elite. In any event, private clients fortunate enough to acquire a Sèvres window took considerable pride and satisfaction in their purchases, basking in the manufactory's prestige. In 1837 Brongniart asked a Mme Schickler to lend her Saint Cecilia window to a small exhibition at the manufactory, but her architect responded that she could not comply because she was planning a soirée at precisely the same time, "in the gallery of her home, where she intended to show off her painted windows."[43]

Private commissions were relatively numerous in the work-

Fig. 7-9. *Scene from the Life of Saint Amélie*, by Emile Wattier, 1835; thin gouache and pencil on paper. This window design was for the chapel at the château de Fontainebleau. (AMNS, Section D, § 11, 1835)

Fig. 7-10. *Scenes from the Life of Francis I,* by Jean Alaux, watercolor and pencil on paper. The individual scenes include *Portrait of the King* (top); *Mary Stuart Kneeling before Charles V* (center); and *A Tournament Viewed by Francis I and Charles V* (bottom). The window was installed in the Pavillon de l'Horloge at the Palais du Louvre. (AMNS, Section D, § 11, 1839.

Fig. 7-11. A lobed ornament by Eugène Viollet-le-Duc, 1840; gouache and pencil on paper. This was used on the four lancet windows featuring the three virtues and a guardian angel in the chapel at Dreux. (AMNS, Section D, § 11, 1840)

shop's first decade but dwindled after 1840, when this workshop of the manufactory was overwhelmed by an uninterrupted series of royal commissions during the years of the July Monarchy.

Royal Commissions. There can be no doubt of Louis-Philippe's appreciation for the art of stained-glass. His personal and political attachments to the church and his deep interest in art and the Middle Ages coalesced in the medium of stained and painted glass windows. He placed no fewer than thirty-eight important commissions with the Sèvres painting-on-glass workshop over a period of almost twenty years. A demanding patron, the sovereign kept close watch on the progress of each of these projects. He paid frequent visits to Sèvres and was unsparing in his criticism when something displeased him, insisting upon hiring or dismissing designers and even modifying programs that he himself had devised. These alterations occasionally caused difficulties for the workshop, which sometimes found itself saddled with useless panels.[44]

The king was not the only member of the royal family with a taste for stained glass. His sister Madame Adélaïde placed several commissions with the Sèvres workshop for Randan, her property in the Auvergne. And his daughter Marie, a student of the painter Ary

Scheffer and a sculptor as well, supplied preliminary cartoons for the windows of the chapel of Saint-Saturnin at the château de Fontainebleau.[45]

Throughout his reign Louis-Philippe was devoted to the renovation of the royal residences, both prestigious palaces, such as Fontainebleau, and the smallest residences, such as Bellevue, as well as those at Pau and Amboise which had been neglected by French sovereigns for decades. These architectural projects inevitably included the installation of stained-glass windows commissioned from Sèvres: Fontainebleau in 1836 (fig. 7-9), Compiègne in 1837, the Louvre and the Grand Trianon in 1838, Pau in 1841, Bellevue in 1846, and Amboise in 1847.[46] With the exception of the Louvre commission, which was intended for the Pavillon de l'Horloge (fig. 7-10),[47] a secular space, these windows were for the king's private chapels.

Louis-Philippe also commissioned work for residences belonging to his family, namely the châteaux of Eu, Bizy, and Carheil, as well as the funerary chapel at Dreux.[48] The Dreux project represents the most important series in the history of the Sèvres workshop. Between 1839 and 1845 five commissions for this chapel and its crypt resulted in the production of forty windows and paintings on crystal glass at a total cost of some 170,000 francs.

The first Dreux commission, placed on September 24, 1839, called for five windows for the chapel of the Virgin (fig. 7-11) representing the Virgin of Sorrow and the theological virtues, all after designs by Ziegler, as well as a guardian angel after a design by Devéria. The second commission (May 15, 1841) called for the production of eight windows for the ambulatory representing subjects from the life of Saint Louis after designs by several artists, including Eugène Delacroix, Horace Vernet, Hippolyte Flandrin, and Emile Wattier (fig. 7-12). The third commission (July 20, 1843) was the largest of the series. The chapels near the entry were to receive four windows designed by Charles de Larivière: *Christ on the Cross, Christ in the Garden of Olives, Saint Adélaïde Distributing Alms,* and *Saint Arnoul Washing Pilgrims' Feet,* while the transept bays of the funerary chapel were decorated with windows featuring twelve figures of saints by Ingres and ornamental frames by Viollet-le-Duc.

Finally, for the north aisle and south crypt of the funerary chapel, the king also ordered five paintings on crystal glass measuring 5 2/3 x 5 1/4 feet (1.7 x 1.6 m), depicting scenes from the Passion of Christ, after cartoons by Julien Gué and Larivière. These paintings on crystal glass were executed on large individual sheets of glass without caming. Installed in the crypt about 6 2/3 feet (2 m) above the floor, they were intended to be seen from up close. The proximity of large windows, located at regular intervals along the aisle gallery, illuminated these paintings on glass, which were unique in the Sèvres production.[49]

The fourth commission (July 13, 1844) called for decoration of the chapel's apse with a large window, *The Apostles and the Virgin Receiving the Holy Spirit,* again after a composition by Larivière. The fifth commission (July 15, 1845) called for two lancet windows and two ornamental grisaille rose windows for the chapel's crypt.

In mourning, Louis-Philippe also turned to the Sèvres workshop. When his eldest son, the duc d'Orléans, died in a carriage accident, he commissioned seventeen windows for his son's final resting place in the chapel of Notre-Dame-de-la-Compassion in Neuilly.[50] The king requested cartoons for the windows from Ingres, who had been a close friend of the duke. Ingres completed the preliminary nude and clothed figure drawings in a matter of weeks and by late August 1842 was ready to undertake the full-scale cartoons. The Sèvres workshop began to translate these into glass the following September. The windows, which depict the theological virtues as well as various saints, were all installed by July 1, 1843, shortly before the official consecration of the chapel. They met with the entire royal family's approval.[51]

When asked, the king and queen also donated Sèvres windows

Fig. 7-12. *Scene from the Life of Saint Louis,* by Emile Wattier, 1844; watercolor, pencil, and white gouache highlights on paper mounted on cardboard. Inscribed "Saint Louis departing for the Holy Land confers the regency on his mother, 1248," this color skecth was for a window in the funerary chapel at Dreux. (AMNS, Section D, § 11, 1844)

Fig. 7-13. *Saint Denis l'Aréopagite*, window in the chapel of the Saint-Sacrement, church of Saint-Roch, Paris; designed by Achille Devéria and executed on glass in 1850 by François Favre (figure) and Gabriel Robert (ornament).

to churches that otherwise could not afford them, for example Saint-Roch (fig. 7-13) in Paris and the cathedral of Saint Louis in Versailles.[52]

The iconographic programs commissioned by Louis-Philippe were consistent with the spiritual tenor of the age and centered on the mysteries of Christ, notably the Passion (at Dreux), Christ among the Elders (the chapel at the Château of Compiegne), and some of the Marian devotional themes pervasive in the nineteenth century, namely the Assumption (chapels at the Trianon and the cathedral in Versailles), the Nativity (the chapel at the residence at Pau), and the Holy Family (the Bizy chapel). The iconography of some of the windows commissioned by Louis-Philippe concerned the Church, alluding to representations of the Trinity (the church at Eu) and the sole figure of God the Father (chapel at the Château de Compiègne). The king also selected allegorical subjects such as a guardian angel (funerary chapel at Dreux) and the various theological virtues, whose moralizing character made them especially appealing in the period (the property at Randan, the château and the church at Eu, the funerary chapel at Dreux, and Notre-Dame-de-la-Compassion at Neuilly).

The dominant thematic content of the windows commissioned by the royal family, however, was unquestionably hagiographic. There is nothing surprising in this, for the iconography of the lives of the saints was of particular interest in the nineteenth century. Every church made it a priority to obtain, if not an entire cycle depicting episodes from the life of its patron saint, then at least a single window portrait. Furthermore, the programs chosen by Louis-Philippe were conceived in accordance with a double agenda: they were meant to exalt both the Christian faith and the royal family. This explains the presence of saints Louis, Philip, and Amélie (the queen's name saint) at Eu, Dreux, Fontainebleau, Sèvres, and Neuilly. These associations were made especially explicit in Neuilly, where the patron saints of the royal children were also rendered in stained glass. The ties

Fig. 7-14. *Saint Helen*, window in the chapel of Notre-Dame-de-la-Compassion, Neuilly; designed by Jean-Auguste-Dominique Ingres and executed on glass in 1843 by Frédéric Bonnet (figure), François Favre, Achille Mascret, and Félix Bastide (ornament).

between the royal family and their patron saints were further emphasized when Ingres borrowed the features of the king and queen and the duc d'Orléans and his widow, Hélène of Mecklenburg-Schwerin (fig. 7-14)[53] for the faces of saints Philip, Amélie, Ferdinand, and Helen.

The king also instructed designers at Sèvres to incorporate national figures into their window compositions. Sometimes these were saints, for example Saint Flour, whose life is illustrated in the windows designed by Viollet-le-Duc for the cathedral of Saint-Flour (fig. 7-15), Saint Lawrence of Dublin, depicted in the portal window of the church at Eu, and saints Gilda and Mathurin, represented in the Breton chapel in Carheil. Other windows paid homage to secular heros, such as Rollon, William the Conqueror, and Philip Augustus in the church at Eu, and earlier French kings — Clovis in the chapel at Carheil, and Charlemagne, Dagobert, and Pépin le Bref in the Palais du Louvre.

The exceptional iconographic diversity and richness of the windows commissioned by Louis-Philippe provide ample proof of the remarkable vitality of the art of stained and painted glass in the nineteenth century.

The End of the Sèvres Stained-Glass Workshop

After flourishing for twenty years, the Sèvres painting-on-glass workshop was undermined by two successive events: the death of Alexandre Brongniart on October 7, 1847, and the fall of the July Monarchy in February 1848.

The manufactory's new administrators, Jacques Ebelmen and Victor Regnault, were less committed to the workshop than Brongniart had been; they had not devoted twenty years of their lives to it. And the end of the July Monarchy marked the virtual end of royal commissions, which had represented almost all of the workshop's most important commissions. With the royal family in exile in England, the Second Republic authorized the workshop only to complete work already in progress, notably the windows ordered for the church of Saint-Roch in Paris and the cathedral of Saint-Louis in Versailles.

After the advent of the Second Empire in 1851, Napoleon III showed little interest in the workshop and did not place any important commissions. The minister of the Maison de l'Empereur simply disregarded numerous requests for windows. In the early 1850s only the cities of Bordeaux and Tours were granted imperial stained-glass.

During this same period the manufactory was bitterly attacked by proponents of a more historically correct approach to stained-glass window design, who criticized both the high cost of the workshop's windows and their troubadour style, which dated to earlier in the century and was denigrated by later historians. Brongniart's efforts to reduce expenses through transfer printing had not been as successful as anticipated, and the workshop's productions continued to be well beyond the budget of most private clients, who gave their patronage to one of the several more reasonably priced private stained-glass workshops in Paris and the provinces.

In addition, archaeologists and historians promoted the notion that the highest art of stained glass meant emulating thirteenth-century models, which were executed entirely in individual pieces of stained glass that were joined by intricate networks of leading. They invariably represented scenes from the Bible in medallions of various forms. As this manner of design and production became more widely adopted, the attacks against Sèvres's compositions, that translated large paintings into colored glass became increasingly vigorous.

Fig. 7-15. *Scene from the Life of Saint Flour: Baptizing the Infidels*, by Eugène Viollet-le-Duc, 1844; gouache, ink, and wash on paper. This drawing was for a window medallion in the cathedral of Saint-Flour. (AMNS, Section D
§ 11, 1844)

The most prominent advocate of the true Medieval approach was Adolphe-Napoléon Didron père who disseminated his views about Christian art in the *Annales archéologiques*, a journal started in 1844. As early as 1839, he had collaborated on the design of the period's earliest imitation thirteenth-century window for the Church of Saint-Germain-l'Auxerrois, depicting the Passion of Christ. Didron's convictions came to be shared by the directors of the other important French stained-glass workshops, notably Émile Thibaud and Étienne-Hormidès Thévenot in Clermont-Ferrand, Charles-Laurent Maréchal in Metz, and Antoine Lusson in Le Mans. It was these establishments, not the manufactory at Sèvres, that were given the period's most important commissions for restoring Medieval stained-glass windows at the cathedrals of Clermont-Ferrand and Bourges, at Sainte-Chapelle and Notre-Dame in Paris, and at the abbey of Saint-Denis.

Being criticized and passed over for important commissions, as well as losing personnel, the workshop was increasingly threatened. Its fate was sealed in December 1853, when the minister of the Maison de l'Empereur, Achille Fould, proposed to the Sèvres administrator, Victor Regnault, that the workshop be dissolved. In Fould's view, Sèvres's stained-glass production was inferior in quality to that of private industry, and, seeing as it no longer served as a model for independent producers, he found it impossible to justify further state expenditures to support it. Regnault managed to obtain a one-year reprieve to enable the workshop to complete two commissions, but a definitive closure date was set for the end of 1854. At that time a portion of the stained and painted glass in the manufactory's stock was delivered to the Musée Céramique of the manufactory, becoming part of its collection.

Without the support of the government, the Sèvres painting-on-glass workshop could not continue. The Bourbon and Orleans families had believed that they legitimized their authority through their alliances with the Roman Catholic Church, and this was expressed, in part, through the creation and donation of stained glass. The Second Republic had no need for such claims, and the Second Empire under Napoleon III, which was created through a plebescite, did not require church approval in any significant manner.

In its glory, under Alexandre Brongniart's direction, the Sèvres workshop embraced the ideal of the *vitrail-tableau*, or stained-glass window conceived along the lines of an ambitious painting, collaborated with the most prestigious artists, who responded with remarkably rich designs, and was committed to refining the palette and increasing the intensity of vitrifiable colors. Never had the Sèvres manufactory contented itself with the servile imitation of old models. It took a highly original approach to the art of colored glass and played an essential role, as the first important nineteenth-century workshop, in the rebirth of the medium in France.

Note: The documents cited below are from the Archives of the Manufacture Nationale de Sèvres (AMNS) and the Archives Nationales (AN).

1. Perrot, "Vitraux et leur destin" (1980), pp. 34 – 39.

2. Brisac, "Repères pour l'étude de l'iconographie du vitrail" (1986), pp. 369 – 76.

3. Alexandre Lenoir was enraptured by "these paintings on mirrors, which are real pictures, which have the brilliance of and produce as many effects as those executed in oils" [ces peintures sur glace, [qui] sont de véritables tableaux, qui ont l'éclat et qui produisent autant d'effets que ceux qu'on traite à l'huile] (*Traité historique de la peinture sur verre* [1856], p. 144).

4. See *Journal des Mines* 12 (no. 67), pp. 53 – 80.

5. D'Holbach, *Art de la verrerie de Néri, Merret et Kunckel* (1752).

6. "A painting on prepared glass, executed in the year 10, using the technique of M. Mèrault [sic], chemist specializing in vitrifiable colors at the manufactory. In the center, a lion; border of transparent yellow arabesques against an azure ground. Sides 60 cm in length" [une vitre en peinture d'apprêt, exécutée en l'an X, par les procédés de M. Mérault, chimiste en couleurs vitrifiables de la Manufacture. Au centre, un lion; bordure d'arabesques en jaune transparent sur fond d'azur. Largeur de côté 60 cm.] Brongniart and Riocreux, *Description méthodique du Musée céramique* (1845), p. 377, no. 251.

7. An article published in *Le Moniteur* on 29 Nivôse year 10 reported that "citizen Brongniart, director of the National Porcelain Manufactory at Sèvres, presented . . . two bouquets of roses painted on glass whose colors are so well preserved that, although only one of them was fired, it was impossible to discern the slightest alteration, even in their subtlest nuances" [le citoyen Brongniart, directeur de la Manufacture nationale de porcelaine de Sèvres, a présenté . . . deux bouquets de roses peints sur verre et dont les couleurs sont tellement bien conservées que, bien qu'un seul d'entre eux ait subi l'action du feu, il était impossible de distinguer la plus légère altération, même dans leurs nuances les plus tendres] (cited in Levey, *Histoire de la peinture sur verre* [1860]).

8. Mortelèque's work is the subject of a notation by Héricart de Thury, the director of public works in Paris (AN, F13 960, notation dated September 15, 1823).

9. In a workbook entry dated August 14, 1826, Brongniart commented on the colored-glass window representing the marriage of the Virgin, executed in 1826 by White and Jones for the church of Saint-Etienne-du-Mont in Paris: "the red drapery of Saint Joseph is beautiful. The blues are pale. The greens are poor. The flesh tones are wan" [la draperie rouge de saint Joseph est belle. Les bleus sont pâles. Les verts sont mauvais. Les carnations sont blâfardes de ton] (AMNS, Pb 21, liasse 2).

10. In a letter dated February 27, 1827, the comte de Chabrol commissioned Sèvres to produce these six windows, at a total cost of 30,000 francs, for the church of Notre-Dame-de-Lorette. The first of these works, *The Assumption of the Virgin*, after a painting by Pierre-Paul Prud'hon, was delivered in 1830.

11. AMNS, Pb 22, liasse 2, dossier 3.

12. Ibid, letter dated March 3, 1837 from Brongniart to M. de Montalivet, Intendant Géneral de la Liste Civile.

13. Ibid., "stained-glass windows" entry in sale inventory no. 3, April 29, 1837; AMNS Vp 2, projects register for painting on glass, 1834 – 37.

14. AN, O4 2740, O4 2741, and O4 2742, payment authorizations for the various departments of the Sèvres manufactory, 1831 – 47.

15. AN, O3 1571: budgets of the Manufacture de Sèvres during the creation of the painting-on-glass workshop (1827 – 30).

16. According to the archives, in 1842 the aggregate payroll for the staff of the painting-on-glass workshop broke down as follows: Louis Robert (head), 3,000 francs; Bonnet (figure painter), 2,121 francs; Roussel (figure painter), 4,500 francs; Mascret (ornamental painter), 1,450 francs; Favre (ornamental painter), 1,200 francs; Schaerdel (glass cutter), 1,629 francs; and Rousseau (workshop assistant), 1,020 francs (AN, O4 2741).

17. In a letter dated April 21, 1842, concerning the second commission for the Orléans funerary chapel at Dreux, Brongniart asked the artist Charles Bouton to alter the proportions of the architecture in the composition of his painting, *Saint Louis Prisoner of the Infidels* (then at the château de Fontainebleau), which the king wanted copied for the chapel (AMNS, Pb 21, liasse 3, dossier 13).

18. In a report to Brongniart dated October 10, 1835, Louis Robert noted that the workshop was about to run out of red and green glass and suggested that more might be obtainable from suppliers in Paris and Choisy-le-Roi (AMNS, Pb 22, liasse 2, dossier 4).

19. In a report on an August 1843 trip to Germany, Louis Robert, told of visiting the royal painting-on-glass workshop in Munich, where he noted the problem of color inconsistency had been avoided by keeping on hand a stock of identically hued glass that came, in each case, from the same producer (AMNS, U20, liasse 1).

20. See F. Gatouillat, "Les Vitraux d'Ingres" in *Actes du colloque international Ingres* (1980), pp. 147 – 55.

21. Brongniart, *Mémoire sur la peinture sur verre* (1829).

22. This list includes formulas for mixing enamels of white, black (three), blue (three), green (four), yellow (eight), red, brown (six), purple (two), and violet (AMNS, Pb 22, liasse 2, dossier 3).

23. Bontemps, *Guide du verrier* (1868).

24. AMNS, Pb 22, liasse 2, dossier 4, trials with coatings on sheets of lava, July 1834.

25. AMNS, Pb 21, liasse 1, account by Louis Robert of a crystal glass firing on April 6, 1845.

26. [Les ton rouges violents qui effrayaient tant le roi ont donné, comme je l'avais prévu, leur part au feu et sont d'un ton très satisfaisant; le ciel du paysage est très bien venu], AMNS, Pb 22, liasse 1, dossier 5.

27. In a letter to the comte de Montalivet dated July 15, 1835, Brongniart informed him that Jules Ziegler had asked for a total of 6,000 francs for work on the Compiègne window, of which 4,000 francs covered the original composition — which included two full-length figures and a half figure of God the Father. Brongniart considered this to be reasonable in light of Ziegler's "high reputation," but found the additional 2,000 francs demanded for cartoons, models of the borders, and framing elements, and for visits to Sèvres to oversee the work in progress to be excessive. He offered the artist 1,000 francs for these services, but Ziegler was insistent. In the end the king authorized payment of the full 6,000 francs (AMNS, Pb 21, liasse 3, dossier 12).

28. AMNS, Pb 22, liasse 2, sales inventory entry no. 3 on December 12, 1832.

29. Roussel, "Impressions sur verre" (1989), pp. 28 – 33. The problem remained essentially unresolved until 1862, when Charles-Laurent Maréchal of Metz developed a transfer-printing technique using deeply engraved plates and organic inks that vitrified without distortion.

30. [Fenêtre d'ornements avec attributs imprimés et coloriés. Fenêtre en ogive, avec mosaïque à rosaces, imprimées et coloriés], AMNS, Pb 22, liasse 2, sales inventory entry nos. 7 and 7 bis on December 28, 1833.

31. AMNS, Pb 21, liasse 1.

32. AN, F19 7643, proposal to restore nine bays of Besançon cathedral sent on April 3, 1829 by Robelin, architect, to the duc de Rohan, archbishop of Besançon.

33. AMNS, Registry Vcc, no. 6, August 9, 1834.

34. AMNS, Pb 21, liasse 1.

35. Ibid.

36. AMNS, Vcc, register of objects delivered from the painting-on-glass workshop to the sales inventory, 1828 – 38.

37. The saints represented include Amélie, Theresa, Cecilia, Peter (twice), John (twice), Simon, George, and Charles.

38. [Rond avec un fond jaune à auréole et lettres en bleu formant les initiales d'Ave Maria], AMNS, Vcc, sheet no. 7, August 19, 1837. This window was assigned a sale price of 18 francs.

39. [Rond en verres peints, représentant l'inscription Jéhovah dans une gloire], ibid., sheet no. 6, May 15, 1838. This panel was assigned a sale price of 15 francs.

40. AMNS, Pb 21, liasse 1, letter from Mme Eyre to Brongniart dated September 2, 1839.

41. Coat-of-arms sold to a M. de Syon on April 15, 1833 for 50 francs (AMNS, Vcc, sheet no. 1).

42. Cipher in yellow against a gray ground sold to a M. Bellocq on June 1, 1838 for 15 francs (ibid., sheet no 3).

43. [Dans la galerie de sa maison, où elle souhaite justement faire admirer sa fenêtre en vitraux peints], AMNS, Pb 21, liasse 1, letter dated April 16, 1837.

44. Lacambre and Lacambre, "Les Vitraux de la chapelle de Carheil" (1970) p. 88. The king's first project, which dates from August 27, 1844, envisioned four windows for the sanctuary and tribune, each with a single saint, but a revised project dating from December 18, 1845 called for the execution of four windows with *two* saints each. As a result of these changes, the framing elements designed by Hyacinthe Régnier had to be reconceived, as did the figures, whose original dimensions were too large for the new configuration. For evidence of a similar revision of another of Louis-Philippe's window commissions, at the chapel at Eu, see cat. no. 95 in this volume.

45. AMNS, Pb 21, liasse 3, dossier 4.

46. For the Compiègne commision, see ibid., dossier 12; for The Louvre, ibid., dossier 14; the Grand Trianon, ibid., dossier 5; Pau, ibid., dossier 16; Bellevue, ibid., dossier 21; and Amboise, ibid., dossier 9.

47. See Ennès, "Les Vitraux du pavillon de l'Horloge" (1992), pp. 56 – 74.

48. For the château d'Eu, see AMNS, Pb 21, liasse 3, dossier 1; for Bizy, ibid., dossier 24; for Carheil, AMNS, Pb 22, liasse 1, dossier 5; for Dreux, AMNS, Pb 21, liasse 3, dossier 13.

49. *Notice explicative des fenêtres peintes . . .* (1847).

50. AMNS, Pb 21, liasse 3, dossier 18.

51. See F. Gatouillat, "Les Vitraux de la chapelle Saint-Ferdinand," in *Mécénat du duc d'Orléans* (1993), pp. 158 – 65.

52. Louis-Philippe decided to pay for the more expensive of two windows requested by Versailles, namely, the Assumption of the Virgin after a cartoon by Achille Devéria; its projected cost was 5,500 francs (AMNS, Pb 21, liasse 3, dossier 11).

53. Ingres used the same process for the figures of saints Louis, Philip, and Amélie which he designed for the transept windows at Dreux.

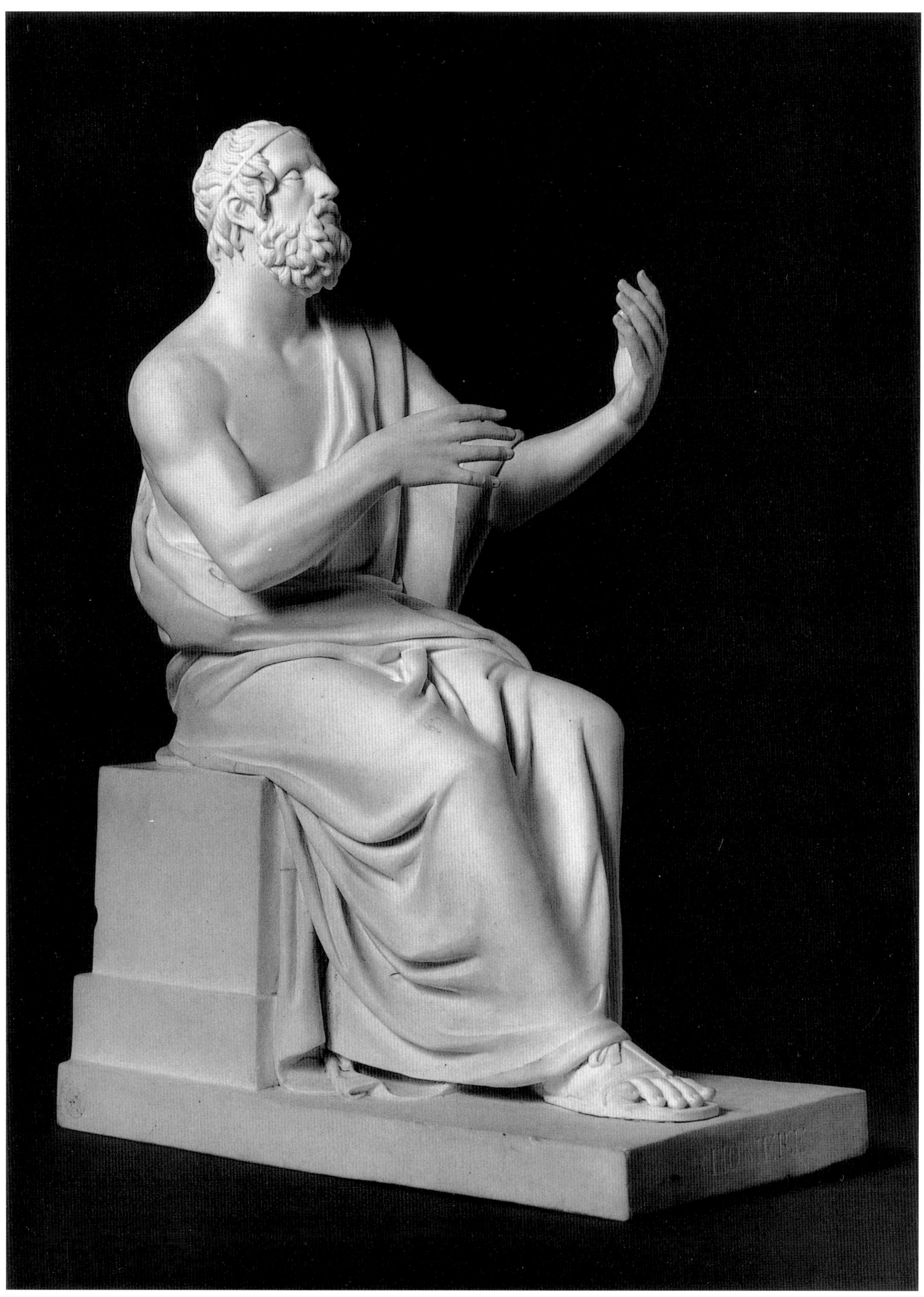

Fig. 8-1. Figue of Homer, model Callamard, 1807; hard-paste porcelain. (Sèvres, Musée Nationale de Céramique)

Chapter 8

Sculpture at Sèvres During the Brongniart Administration

Tamara Préaud

In the middle of the eighteenth century, the porcelain manufactory at Vincennes-Sèvres began to use unglazed porcelain, or biscuit, for the production of small-scale sculpture. This brought about a completely new category of European ceramics, one that remained relatively intact into the beginning of the nineteenth century. Beginning in the 1830s, however, the introduction of glazed and colored sculpted elements and other innovations again transformed sculpture at Sèvres, resulting in a highly original body of work. Unlike the manufactory's other genres, sculpture cannot be easily divided according to political periods in France, and for this reason it has been discussed here in a separate chapter. With the exception of *surtouts* (centerpieces)[1] and a few other forms or specific works of the Empire period,[2] Sèvres's works of sculpture have been largely overlooked by art historians. In this area, however, as in other areas of production at Sèvres, Alexandre Brongniart made many significant contributions.

The Persistence of Eighteenth-Century Models

For both practical and economic reasons, eighteenth-century sculptural forms and models at Sèvres continued to be used into the nineteenth century. Soon after Brongniart began his tenure at the manufactory, he was asked to provide sculpture for both table and interior decoration. Because there had not yet been time to have new models developed, he exploited the existing stock of figures and sculptural groups in the warehouse. The models continued to be used because once an ensemble of table decorations had been put into service at one of the royal palaces such as the Palais des Tuileries, for example, it was often necessary to replace pieces that were broken or lost.

Until the end of Louis-Philippe's reign, therefore, the manufactory continued to produce groups of figures that had been either created around 1800, or were already somewhat old, even at that date. These included: *The Abduction of Oreithyia* and *The Rape of Proserpine* (1786); ornamental baskets (1773); *The Four Seasons* (1787), the Muses and Divinities (1780s), as well as more recent works, such as *The Sacrifice of Iphigenia* (1797), *Hector's Farewell to Andromache* and *Paris' Farewell to Helen* (1797), *Ovid Consoled by Love and Hope* and its pendant *Anacreon Served by Love and Cypris* (1801), dancers and musicians (1801), and figures from *The Four Parts of the World* (1801). In addition there were requests for casts of eighteenth-century models that bear witness to a growing interest in the manufactory's groups and figures. Only gradually, however, did the Sèvres administration seem to have taken any real notice of this trend in the market (see chap. 5).

Orders and Commissions

Specific orders for sculpture from the Sèvres manufactory are extremely rare. Most decisions to produce such works were made by Brongniart alone. One of the few direct commissions was made by Napoleon, in a letter dated April 26, 1806 (see chap. 6),[3] in which he requested biscuit reproductions of the Arc de Triomphe du Carrousel and the Palais des Tuileries. Brongniart succeeded, however, in convincing the emperor to drop his request, surmising that the technical challenge of replicating rectilinear architecture in biscuit would be too great for the manufactory and that it would also be too difficult to simulate the vast expenses of the palace's glass windows in the model.

In the same letter, the emperor asked for a list of available figures from the Grands Hommes series that had been begun in 1782 under the comte d'Angivillier. He wished to make a selection for reissue and to suggest new figures to augment the series. On May 17, 1806, the emperor indicated twelve famous men to add to the series.[4] His choices included some French subjects, but most were from beyond French shores: William the Conqueror, Bertrand DuGuesclin, Gustav Adolf, Friedrich II, Julius Caesar, Hannibal, Homer (fig. 8-1), Virgil, Tasso, Christopher Columbus, the first Medici, and Prince Eugène. Only three, based on models by Charles-Antoine Callamard, were actually executed at Sèvres during the Empire: Homer (1807), Virgil (1807), and Tasso (1809).

Among the occasional private orders for Sèvres sculpture were several from Dominique-Vivant Denon who had some porcelain impressions made from a plaster model of the hand of Pauline Bonaparte[5] and also commissioned busts of himself as well as medallions with his own portrait.[6] Another client, the "comtesse d'Aunay, née Colbert," ordered several small busts of Colbert in 1830,[7] and a woman identified as "Lady Rood" provided a model of a medallion representing a "Major Rennel," requesting that several copies be made.[8]

Toward the end of Louis-Philippe's reign, various members of the royal family commissioned centerpieces composed of works originally modeled in the eighteenth century. For the king's sister Madame Adélaïde[9] and for his son the duc de Nemours,[10] the manufactory used elements that were in production. The duc d'Aumale, however, was more original. He epitomized the emer-

Fig. 8-2. *Joan of Arc*, Jean-Charles-Nicolas Brachard aîné after designs by Alexandre Evariste Fragonard; plaster. (Sèvres, Manufacture Nationale, Archives)

gent antiquarian taste of the 1840s by choosing from the *surtout 'des Chasses'* which had been out of production for nearly half a century.[11]

Otherwise, Brongniart rarely received orders for sculpted works, and the few that he did were often extremely vague. For example, in 1801 the *ministre du trésor public* requested figurines for a *surtout*: "I should like them all to be mythological subjects, or something of the sort . . . . [A]ny figural nudity must be within the bounds of decency."[12] The demand for propriety continued throughout the period. In 1810 M. Ertault, the *quartier-maître du palais*, noted that "the Apollo will not do, on account of the nudity; it will have to be replaced."[13] Similarly, in 1821 the duchesse de Berry specified that she wanted "no nudity whatsoever."[14] The orders placed by the *service de la bouche*, which was responsible for the king's table, usually specified merely the size of the pieces to be replaced, leaving open the choice of model.

Political or dynastic events may also explain the appearance or popularity of certain subjects: medallions of the Duke of Wellington, for example, appeared after 1815; busts and medallions of the duc de Berry were made in 1820 after his assassination, and busts of Alexander of Russia were introduced after his death in 1825. Similarly, when the remains of Napoleon were returned to France for reburial in les Invalides in 1840, busts of the emperor were reissued.

Official Portraits

Representations of the sovereign and his family were among the most active areas of production for the manufactory paid for by the Liste Civile. Brongniart had no qualms about the propagandist role played by the manufactory and did not hesitate to promote the Sèvres portrait work. In 1822 he wrote to the *ministre de la Maison du Roi* about some life-size busts in biscuit then being executed, and at the same time he somewhat exaggerated the merits of Sèvres porcelain:

> these busts . . . have . . . all the éclat of white marble, they . . . have the perfection and merit of it when the model has been made by able hands. And since they are an exact cast of these models and not a copy, they have all their perfection when they are not altered by the fire, which is rarer than one might think. They are much harder than marble, absolutely invulnerable to atmospheric alteration, and, I do not hesitate to state, less fragile.[15]

Napoleon was the subject of the largest number of portraits. There were busts of him as a general, as First Consul (by Louis-Simon Boizot), and as emperor (by Antoine-Denis Chaudet); these were nude (1805) or draped with cloth (1811), with or without a crown, in porcelain or bronze, and in various sizes.[16] And there was an equestrian figure based on a design by Carle Vernet (1801 and 1804).[17]

There were also busts of Empress Josephine (by Chaudet in 1808 and François-Joseph Bosio in 1809) and of Empress Marie-Louise (Bosio in 1810).[18] Various representations of the emperor's infant son, the king of Rome, were also made: busts after models by Henri-Joseph Ruxthiel (1811, 1812) and a figure seated on a lion skin by Bosio (1812). Innumerable medallions showed sovereigns and members of the royal family and its circle. The destruction of a large portion of the corresponding models and molds during the invasion and occupation of France in 1815 explains a certain confusion in their classification, nor were they ever precisely described in the Sèvres records.

Equally, during the Restauration, the principal members of the royal family were represented in busts of varying sizes, beginning with Louis XVIII (life size) and his brother the comte d'Artois who was also later depicted when he became Charles X (life size) and whose wife and two sons — Louis-Antoine de Bourbon, the duc d'Angoulême, and Charles-Ferdinand de Bourbon, the duc de Berry (life size) — and their wives were also represented. The duc and duchesse d'Angoulême became the dauphin and dauphine in 1824. In addition there were Sèvres representations of the children of the duc de Berry, including his son, Henri-Dieudonné, the duc de Bordeaux, also known as "the miracle child." The duc de Bordeaux was the only one to be represented in a full-length figure portrait; it was based on a model by Pierre-Sébastien Guersent.[19]

With the return of the Bourbons to power, portraits of ancestral members of the dynasty began to reappear with increasing frequency. Busts and medallions of Louis XVI and Marie-Antoinette, which had survived the destruction of the Revolution and its aftermath, were complemented by new creations. There was a series of equestrian figurines (1817 – 18) of the kings of France, attributed to Brachard père: Charles V, Francis I, Henri IV, Louis IX, Louis XII, and Louis XIV. Before long, busts based on these statuettes were being produced separately and became very popular — especially Henri IV and Francis I.

After 1830, under the July Monarchy, royal propaganda became much more discreet. Only a relatively small number of busts of Louis-Philippe were produced. These were based on the model by Jean-Marie-Ferdinand Régnier which was shown at the Salon of 1817 and had been made when the king was still the duc d'Orléans. Another model, adapted by Charles Fischbach in 1835 from a work by James Pradier, is known only from written evidence and may never have been produced. Portraits of members of the king's large family were probably only produced as medallions based on models by Jean-Auguste Barre.

Nonroyal Portraits

Although Napoleon had envisioned a continuation and enlargement of the Grands Hommes series, only three of the great men he chose were in fact created during his reign. Other sculptural works, however, may be considered almost as part of the series, notably four full-length statues modeled after drawings by Alexandre-Evariste Fragonard: the duc de Crillon (1818); Jean Dunois (1820); Joan of Arc (1820; fig. 8-2 and see cat. no. 54); and Du Guesclin (1818), who was the only one on the emperor's original list. The first three were modeled by Brachard père and the fourth, by Guersent. Despite the pronounced romantic style of these figurines, their sizes and prices, which were identical to others in the Grands Hommes series, suggest that in Brongniart's mind they were part of the same cycle. A final echo of the series might be recognized in the figure of Joan of Arc at Arms (1840) modeled at Sèvres by Charles Fischbach. It was based on a work by Louis-Philippe's daughter Princesse Marie, herself a talented sculptress.

Famous men of different eras were also celebrated in small busts and/or medallions. In 1801 Charles Percier and Pierre-François-Léonard Fontaine ordered several medallions representing writers, which were integrated into panels at the First Consul's library at Saint-Cloud. The order itself does not specify the writers,[20] and the extant models at Sèvres seem to indicate that they represented a wide chronological range.

In sending busts of the military commanders Desaix, Kléber, and Latour d'Auvergne to the *ministre de l'intérieur*, Brongniart wrote in 1801: "I felt that it was the duty of the National Porcelain Manufactory of Sèvres to have various busts of famous men, and especially great warriors lost to the country in recent times, executed in porcelain . . . ."[21] Despite the minister's favorable response, Brongniart seems to have quickly recognized that such a series appealed neither to the sovereign nor to the public; he soon abandoned the project.

The representations of contemporaries were very few. A bust of the archchancellor Jean-Jacques Régis de Cambacères (by Philippe-Laurent Roland, 1806), made him the only dignitary of the Empire thus memorialized. There was also a bust of Albert de Haller (by Chaudet, 1804), as well as a medallion (1822), and a bust (1840) of Georges Cuvier, one of Brongniart's friends from his youth. In addition to busts of figures from antiquity — Hippocrates (1807), Aesculapius (1819), Cicero (1820), and Demosthenes (1820) — there were representations of Frenchmen from the recent past, more or less: the comte de Buffon, André-Ernest-Modeste Grétry, and Jean de La Fontaine were represented in busts in 1823. Religious figures, sometimes with plinths bearing bas-reliefs of scenes from their lives, were especially favored: Saint Vincent de Paul (1818), Saint Charles Borromée (1819), François de La Mothe-Fénelon (1822), and Jean-Baptiste Massillon (1822). Most of the models for these works are attributed to Brachard père, although the sources are not known.

Allegory and Anecdote

Allegorical statuary, which had been popular in the eighteenth century, did not disappear altogether. A sculptural group, *Peace Led by Victory*, by Boizot was made in 1802, and two versions of *The Guardian Angel of the Children of France*, one by Charles Cumberworth and the other by James Pradier, were released in 1844. Anecdotal sculpture was represented by *Paul and Virginie* by Chaudet, made in 1801, and by *L'Amour dans un fauteuil garni de Tulle* [*Love Seated in an Armchair Trimmed with Tulle*], which is known as the Lace Cupid, by Benoît Chanou (1812).

Chanou's sculpture must have annoyed Brongniart, because, when Chanou requested permission to give one of the first examples of the Lace Cupid, a technical tour de force, to the king,[22] Brongniart could not refrain from remarking: ". . . the applications of this fabrication process are extremely limited. The present taste, purified by the study of the masterpieces of the sculpture of antiquity, is at odds with this sort of use of the materials."[23] Despite Brongniart's disapproval, this piece ultimately became one of the best-selling works offered by the manufactory during the period, its popularity lasting until the end of the 1820s.

Sculptural Innovations at Sèvres

Surtouts. There were two main categories of sculpture at the manufactory at this time: pieces made as decoration for domestic interi-

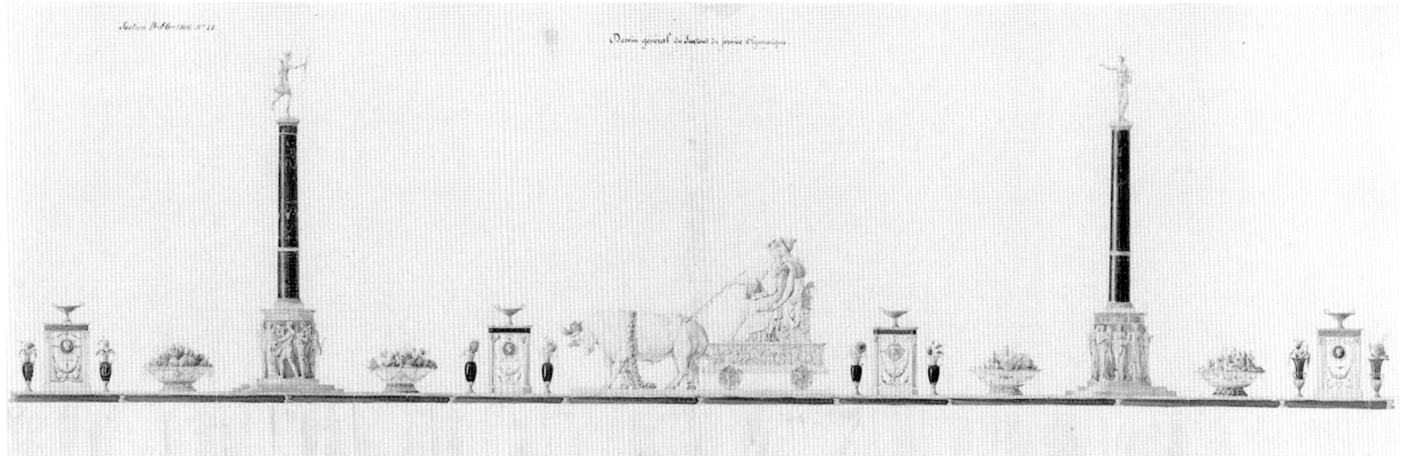

Fig. 8-3. General view of the *surtout 'Olympique'*, 1806; watercolor and ink on paper. (Manufacturer Nationale de Sèvres, Archives)

ors and objects made as part of a *surtout* (centerpiece). This distinction often had more to do with the client's preferences than with the object itself. In many cases, the same objects served both purposes.[24] A sharp distinction may be made, however, between the concepts governing the design of *surtouts* dating to the eighteenth century and those made at the beginning of the nineteenth century. The earlier centerpiece groupings were composed in an often erratic manner with pieces that bore little or no iconographic connection to one another[25]; these groupings were often composed of pieces that were available at the time of purchase or delivery. The most important *surtouts* made during the Empire relied on a coherent concept that reinforced the themes and motifs of the accompanying dinner service. The design and fabrication of *surtouts* was a very active part of the manufactory's production between 1804 and 1814. During that time, Sèvres created *surtouts* for the *services 'Olympique'* (figs. 8-3 and 8-4), *'Egyptien', 'de l'Empereur',* and *'des Saisons'.*[26]

Fig. 8-4. Column called Collone du Surtout 'Olympique', 1803–4, Sèvres; plaster model (Manufacture Nationale de Sèvres)

Nevertheless, some of the individual elements from these *surtouts* were integrated into the ongoing production of the manufactory. *The Three Graces*, for example, from the *surtout 'Olympique'* sometimes was used as table decoration and other times formed the support of a clock. Figures after the antique from the *surtout* for the *service 'de l'Empereur'* were also issued separately. These were so successful that before long they were being produced in two sizes. Other elements from the *surtout 'de l'Empereur'* were transformed into individual or simpler models, such as the candelabra *'antique'* and a tripod *'d'Apollon'.*

Period illustrations indicate a predetermined arrangement of the pieces on the table that went beyond stylistic or thematic coherence (see cat. no. 22). In reality, however, this rigor may have been more theoretical than real. There is, for example, a table plan detailing the precise placement of the various elements of the *surtout* for the *service 'Olympique',*[27] which had been given to the Russian tsar Alexander I in 1807. In the same year, the marquis de Caulaincourt, the French ambassador to the Russian court, had been provided with a *service 'marli d'or'* and his own *surtout 'Olympique'* but the centerpiece could not be arranged according to the table plan because it lacked two columns and twenty-eight of the original forty vases designed for the original *surtout.*[28]

Similarly, Brongniart had specifically noted that the centerpiece of the *service 'de l'Empereur'* "must be accompanied by neither vases nor flowers nor any accessory piece [because] that would weaken its effect . . . ."[29] This table service was finished just in time for the celebration of the wedding of Napoleon and Marie-Louise in 1810. A painting by Casanova of the Grand Couvert dinner (fig. 8-5) held on that occasion, however, reveals that Brongniart's instructions were not followed.[30] The principal pieces of the emperor's Grand Vermeil (silver-gilt) service were placed on the table with the *Figures after the Antique* from the porcelain *surtout* of the *service 'de l'Empereur'* and with Sèvres flower vases.

Later, individual elements from different *surtouts* were used together: the table service given in 1826 to the French ambassador to Vienna comprised a *Chariot of Bacchus and Cérès* and two examples of *The Three Graces* created for the *surtout 'Olympique'* as well as two candelabras *'Antiques'*, which had been simplified, based on those created for the *service 'de l' Empereur'*.[31]

Surtouts evolved during the period, amply illustrated by the Empress Josephine's rejection of a famous Sèvres service. In 1810, with credit that Napoleon had set up for her at Sèvres as part of their divorce settlement, Josephine ordered a *service 'Egyptien'*, with its full *surtout*. When the *surtout* was presented to her two years later, in May 1812, however, she found it to be too severe[32] and ordered a replacement, designed by her architect, Louis-Martin Berthault, which was composed entirely of ornamental baskets.[33]

This commission inaugurated a new fashion, and in subsequent years Sèvres introduced several basket models in different sizes (fig. 8-6; also see cat. no. 45). For these table decorations Sèvres's artists created a wide array of fanciful forms, freely combining sculptural works with baskets to create *surtouts*.[34] This return to more arbitrary groupings may have been a reaction against the requisite cohesiveness of designs for *surtouts* during the early years of the Empire. There is nothing, however, to explain Brongniart's decision two decades later to revive the concept of a cohesive *surtout* when in 1833 – 34 he ordered designs for two totally different *surtout 'des Comestibles'*, which celebrated food and the art of dining. One was by Alexandre-Evariste. Fragonard (fig. 8-8; also see cat. no. 84) and the other, by Claude-Aimé Chenavard (see cat. no. 85).

Biscuit. Traditional creations in biscuit did not totally disappear. Apart from the ones already mentioned, there were, for example, two figurines designed for clocks: *Uranie*, modeled in 1806 by Auguste Taunay and based on a painting from Herculaneum which had been noted by Dominique-Vivant Denon, and the *Génie des Sciences*.[35] Another clock-case in biscuit, designed by Percier in 1813, was decorated with bas-reliefs on the theme of the sun and seasons.[36]

There were also, and more importantly, innovations in the use of biscuit, primarily by the integration of sculpture, whether freestanding or in bas-relief, into ornamental compositions. In some cases, figurines were conceived to be a part of a larger, complex object. For example, four figurines wearing crowns made of fruit associated with each of the four seasons support the *corbeille 'Canéphore'* designed by A.-E. Fragonard and executed by Guersent (1818). Six other figures represented the principal cities of France (Paris, Lyon, Bordeaux, Marseille, Rouen, Strasbourg). Created by Guersent they were meant to surround the pedestal of a table decorated with scenes from the coronation of Charles X painted by

Fig. 8-5. *Le Grand Couvert, or Marriage Banquet of Napoleon and Marie-Louise in the Playhouse at the Palais des Tuileries,* by Casanova, 1812; oil on canvas.

Fig. 8-6. Flower or fruit basket called *Corbeille 'aux Cygnes'*, decorated by Pierre-Louis Micaud, Sèvres, 1823; hard-paste porcelain. (The Metropolitan Museum of Art, New York. Purchase, Gift of Mr. and Mrs. Charles Wrightsman, by exchange, 1985)

Jean-Charles Develly in 1826. These same figurines may have been used at the base of a central element in the *surtout* of the *service 'des Départements'* (1827; see cat. no. 63). Later, freestanding figurines and other elements, still in biscuit, were used to decorate complex polychrome objects, such as a mantelpiece at Fontainebleau (1835 – 37; see cat. no. 87), a cabinet (1837 – 38) celebrating the marriage of the duc d'Orléans,[37] the coffer (1844 – 46) of the Maritime Acts of the prince de Joinville,[38] or the *pendule 'des Quatre Saisons'* (1844 – 45).[39]

Low- and middle-relief were more frequent than freestanding sculpture, and traditional medallions saw new uses. In addition to the portrait medallions integrated into the library of the first consul at Saint-Cloud, biscuit medallions were set into crystal (see cat. no. 48).

Vases incorporating bas-relief biscuit porcelain plaques had been made in great numbers in the 1780s. Many new versions were made during the Restauration, and the vase *'de Socibius'*, exhibited at the Louvre in 1825, was one of the most spectacular of these forms. Inspired by an antique marble of the same name in the Musée Royal, it replaced the original figures of the gods with "allegorical figures of the arts and sciences, who contribute to the perfection of the art of ceramics. . . . "[40] Even more monumental was the vase *'de Phidias'*, which was over 78 inches (200 cm) high. On it was a bas-relief by Guersent in which the Greek sculptor Phidias presents the full-size model of his statue of Jupiter, to his most eminent contemporaries.[41]

Even at this date there were a few pieces ornamented with bas-reliefs in white biscuit on a blue background, an aesthetic introduced at Sèvres in the beginning of the 1780s. In 1843 – 45 a vase by Henri de Triqueti used this technique for bas-reliefs and ornaments that evoked antique grape harvests.[42]

In an elegant variation, white biscuit bas-reliefs were set against gilded backgrounds, sometimes with subtly contrasting matte and brilliant surfaces. This treatment seems to have originated in the designs of Auguste-Pierre Famin (see cat. no. 19). It was used again for pieces of the *déjeuner 'Régnier'* (see cat. no. 31), for elements of the *surtout 'des Comestibles'* by A.-E. Fragonard (see cat. no. 84), and on a vase *'de la Renaissance'* (1834 – 35) by the same artist.[43] The pedestal of the table *'des Maréchaux'* designed by architect Percier in 1806 (fig. 8-9) is encircled by biscuit porcelain figures on a gold ground.

Polychrome sculpture. The most original development in the sculpture workshop at Sèvres involved the revival of polychromy in the 1830s. This work was hardly new in ceramics, but when the manufactory of Vincennes-Sèvres adopted white, matte biscuit around 1751 – 52,[44] it had made a break with the past and at the same time had challenged its contemporaries with something new. By the July Monarchy, Sèvres would again prove itself to be an innovator by reviving polychrome ceramic sculpture.

Alexandre Brongniart's interest in the history of ceramics most likely played a determining role in the revival of multicolored sculpture. The first evidence of any renewed interest in polychromy at Sèvres appeared very early, in 1804, with the rhytons and columns of the *surtout 'Olympique'*.[45] The rebirth of polychromy, however, began in 1830 with the design of a vase *'de la Renaissance'*

Fig. 8-7. *Cornet d'abondance*, one of a pair, presented to Tsar Alexander I, 1806, Sèvres; hard-paste porcelain. (Palais des Armures du Kremlin, Moscow)

Fig. 8-8. Designs for elements in a *surtout* by Claude-Aimé Chenavard. (From Brongniart and Riocreux, *Description méthodique du musée de la manufacture royale de porcelaine de Sèvres* [1845], P, pl. 11)

by Chenavard, which had relief elements modeled by Antonin Moine (see cat. no. 79). By the Louvre exhibition of May 1, 1838, this kind of work had peaked in the manufactory's production. At the Louvre, the Sèvres display included the new *surtout 'des Comestibles'* by Chenavard with its sculptural pieces (see cat. no. 85), a table with an enameled porcelain base (see cat. no. 92), and two coupes (cat. no. 91) also designed by Chenavard. The technical tour de force of the display, however, was the coupe *'de Benvenuto Cellini'* by Hyacinthe Régnier, which had reliefs on both the inside and outside of the vessel. Sèvres also exhibited a cabinet which was made for the wedding of the duc d'Orléans as well as the mantelpiece from Fontainebleau both of which also had ornamental elements in white biscuit porcelain, which contrasted with the elements that were polychrome.

The vases *'Flamand'* by Chenavard (fig. 8-11; also see cat. no. 80) and the *déjeuner 'de François I'* by Fragonard (see cat. no. 78) are other emxamples of Sèvres polychromy, but the manufactory's sources of inspiration were not limited to the Renaissance period. The *vase 'Aromaphore'* by Jean-Charles-François Leloy (1837) depicts flowers and seeds used in the preparation of the potpourri for which it was designed. The *caisse à fleur hexagonale* (1840) is one of many creations by Hyacinthe Régnier that was inspired by a Middle Eastern aesthetic.

Brongniart searched for the right balance between traditional production of white biscuit, modeled in the round or in bas-relief, and more original works, which were probably inspired by the pieces he collected for the Musée Céramique. Within a few years, other European manufacturers were to explore both types of figure production. It would be hard to maintain, for example, that the Parian wares so common to English ceramic manufactories of the second half of the nineteenth century were not inspired by Sèvres biscuit. At the same time, the richly multicolored, historicist fantasies by Fontainebleau ceramist Jacob Petit or the majolicas by English ceramist Herbert Minton may have been inspired in part by

Fig. 8-9. The *table 'des Maréchaux'*, Sèvres, 1810; hard-paste porcelain. (Châteaux de Malmaison et de Bois Préau)

visits to the Sèvres collections.[46] Finally, it could even be suggested that the renewed taste for color in the ceramic arts played a part in the revival of polychromy in European statuary in the late nineteenth century.[47]

Note: The documents cited below are from the Archives of the Manufacture Nationale de Sèvres (AMNS).

1. Arizzoli-Clementel, "Les Surtouts impériaux" (1976).

2. Brunet, "Contribution à l'iconographie Napoléonienne" (1954), pp. 456 – 67; idem, "En marge des Napoléonides" (1957), pp. 281 – 83; idem, "Pendule en biscuit de Sèvres" (1979), pp. 162 – 64; Gastineau, "Rude à la manufacture de Sèvres" (1932), pp. 181 – 86; idem, "Les travaux de la Manufacture de Sèvres" (1934), pp. 270 – 89; Grandjean, "Deux remarquables souvenirs napoléoniens" (1974), pp. 323 – 30; idem, "Du nouveau sur les collections de Joséphine à Malmaison," (1987), pp. 175 – 79.

3. Carton T 2, liasse 1, dossier 1.

4. Ibid.

5. Brunet, "En marge des Napoléonides" (1957), pp. 281 – 83. It is possible that the order placed by Denon on April 2, 1822, corresponds to the same object: "two hands in biscuit porcelain sculpture paste molded from plaster models provided by M. Denon and turned over to the chief of kilns in good condition . . . please do a cost-evaluation right away that includes the cost of the molds etc. for the two hands in question" [deux mains en porcelaine biscuit pâte de sculpture moulées sur les modèles en plâtre donnés par Mr. Denon et remis au chef des fours en bon état . . . en faire de suite l'appreciation en faisant supporter les frais de moules etc. aux deux mains commandés] (register Vtt 2, fol.13 v.). If this were simply a reedition, there would probably have been no need for new molds (assuming that the original ones had not been destroyed in 1815).

6. A bust was introduced in 1822 and a medallion in 1825. The artist responsible for the models is not known.

7. Register Vz 5, fol. 44v.

8. Register Vbb 10, fol. 222v.

9. An order of August 31, 1846, lists four groups of *The Four Parts of the World* as well as figures of Ganymede, Hebe, Mars, and Minerva (register Vtt 6, fol. 43). Delivery was made on May 13, 1847 (register Vbb 11, fol. 15).

10. An order of October 9, 1846, lists two groups of three caryatids, eight figures of fauns, bacchants, Flora and Zephyr with corbeilles; it specified that "the bronzes are to be executed by M. Bocquet, following the design to be provided by M. Lamy [Eugène-Louis Lamy]" [les bronzes devront être exécutés par M. Bocquet d'après le dessin qui sera remis par M. Lamy] (register Vtt 6, fol. 43v) Delivery was made on March 20 and 25, 1847 (register Vbb 11, fol. 15v).

11. An order of November 4, 1846 specified two groups of *The Deer Hunt*, two groups of *The Boar Hunt* and *The Wolf Hunt*, two *Hunters' Grooms with Horns*, four *Hunters' Grooms with Rifles*, and two each of the two kennelmen (register Vtt 6, fol. 44). Delivery was made on May 10, 1847 (register Vbb 11, fol. 16).

12. [Je désire qu'elles soient toutes de sujets mythologiques, ou d'un genre analogue . . . la nudité des figures doit être décente] Carton T 1, liasse 3, dossier 2, letter of 29 Brumaire year 10 (November 20, 1801).

13. [l'Appollon ne pouvant servir à cause de sa nudité, à remplacer . . .] Carton T 5, liasse 1, dossier 4, letter of January 25, 1810.

14. [ne veut point de nudité] Carton T 9, liasse 2, dossier 4, letter of July 13, 1821.

15. [ces bustes . . . ont . . . tout l'éclat du marbre blanc, ils . . . en ont la perfection et le mérite lorsque le modèle a été fait par des mains habiles. Enfin, comme ils sont une empreinte exacte de ces modèles et non une copie, ils en ont toute la perfection lorsque le feu ne les a pas altérés, ce qui est beaucoup plus rare qu'on ne le pense. Ils sont beaucoup plus durs que le marbre, absolument inaltérables par les météores atmosphériques et, je ne crains pas de l'affirmer, moins fragiles] Carton T 9, liasse 3, dossier 2, letter of September 24, 1822.

16. Gastineau, "Les Travaux de la Manufacture de Sèvres" (1934), pp. 270 – 89.

17. Brunet, "Contribution à l'iconographie Napoléonienne" (1954), pp. 456 – 67.

18. The bust of Marie-Louise by François-Nicolas Delaistre was only produced by Sèvres in 1967.

19. The figure was exhibited in Paris at the Louvre on January 1, 1828, (no. 15 in the catalogue of the exhibition). During the final work on the model, vicomte Turpin de Crissé wrote to Brongniart, "this figure has been judged unacceptable . . . . [T]he figure was found to be meager, and weak of form; the head looks old, tired, ugly; the extremities little, the pose mannered" [cette figure a été jugée non recevable . . . on a trouvé que la figure étoit maigre, pauvre de forme; la tête vieille, fatiguée, laide; les extremités petittes, la pause (sic pour pose) maniérée . . .] (carton T 11, liasse 2, dossier 5, letter of December 4, 1827).

20. The order covered ninety-six medallions, of which forty-eight were to be in white biscuit on a blue background, twenty-four painted in colors, and twenty-four painted "in the Etruscan manner" (carton T 1, liasse 3, dossier 2, order of 8 Brumaire year 10 [October 30, 1801]).

21. [J'ai cru qu'il etoit du devoir de la manufacture nationale de porcelaine de Sèvres de faire executer en porcelaine les bustes des hommes utiles et surtout des guerriers recommandables que la patrie a perdus depuis peu . . .] Carton T 1, liasse 2, dossier 4, letter of 21 Ventôse year 9 (March 10, 1801).

22. The child seated on the chair raises a tulle veil that envelops the whole. In order to obtain the effect of tulle in porcelain, Chanou soaked real tulle in porcelain slip and placed it on the group before firing. When it was fired, the cloth burned away leaving its form in porcelain.

23. [l'application de ce procede de fabrication est extrêmement borné. Le goût actuel purifié par l'etude des chefs-d'oeuvre en sculpture de l'antiquité ne s'accorde guère avec l'emploi de pareils ajustements] Carton T 6, liasse 1, dossier 5, letter from Brongniart to the Intendant Général, February 12, 1812.

24. Some figures from the *'Quatre Saisons'* were delivered on 24 Brumaire year 13 (November 15, 1804) for a centerpiece for Fontainebleau, while others were part of a gift for M. de Segur on June 30, 1806, among the "pieces for apartments" (register Vbb 2, fol. 2, and Vy 17, fol. 18 and 18v).

25. The only exception seems to have been the surtout designed for the wedding of the dauphin, the future Louis XVI (Ennès, "Le surtout de mariage en porcelaine de Sèvres du Dauphin" (1987), pp. 63-73. The Russian Parnassus , created by Boizot for the service ordered by Empress Catherine II in 1777/78, had no iconographic connection with the groups that accompanied it.

26. Arizzoli-Clementel, "Les Surtouts impériaux" (1976), fig. passim.

27. Ibid., fig. 10, pl. 3.

28. Delivered on December 31, 1807 (register Vbb 2, fol. 77v).

29. [ne doit recevoir ni vases ni fleurs ni aucune autre piece accessoire [car] cela nuiroit à son effet . . .] Carton T 5, liasse 1, dossier 8, letter dated February 26, 1810.

30. Arizzoli-Clementel, "Les Surtouts impériaux" (1976), fig. 33, pl. 10.

31. For delivery, see Register Vbb 7, fol. 27.

32. Arizzoli-Clementel, "Les Surtouts impériaux" (1976), p. 25.

33. The only one produced before the death of Josephine in 1814 was the *corbeille 'aux Cygnes'.*

34. For example, the service delivered to the marquis de Latour-Maubourg, ambassador to Constantinople, on September 7, 1821, was accompanied by ten figures after the antique (reduced-scale versions of the ones from the *service 'de l'Empereur'*) with a large *corbeille 'Palmier'* and "two *corbeilles* Lion for the sides" (register Vbb 6, folios 8 and 30v). Also, as late as 1842, a centerpiece was delivered to the château de Bizy that contained a *corbeille 'Canéphore',* two *corbeilles 'Corinthiennes',* two *corbeilles 'Coupe Fragonard',* with two groups of *The Three Graces* and two tripods *'d'Apollon'* (register Vbb 9, fol. 103).

35. Twentieth-century catalogues have wrongly entitled the *Genie* as *The Night* (Les Oeuvre de la Manufacture de Sèvres, T1, no. 484, pl. 47)

36. Brunet, "Pendule en biscuit" (1979), pp. 162 – 64.

37. Sculptures by Jean-Louis-Nicolas Jaley; see Chevallier, *Musée national du château de Fontainebleau* (1996), no. 75, pp. 106 – 9.

38. General composition by Léon Feuchère, reliefs by Combette, and bronzes by Armand Feuchère; see *Notice . . . June 3, 1844* (1844), no. 5.

39. General composition by Ferdinand Régnier and figurines in biscuit porcelain by Jean-Baptiste-Jules Klagmann; see *Notice . . . June 1, 1846* (1846), no. 5.

40. [figures allégoriques des arts et des sciences qui concourent à la perfection de l'art céramique . . .] *Notice . . . January 1, 1825* (1825), no. 20. This vase, with a composition by A.-E. Fragonard, was chosen by Alexandre Brongniart's widow for her husband's tomb at Père-Lachaise cemetery in Paris.

41. This work, whose classicism contrasts with everything else in the exhibition, was conceived and undertaken starting in 1822; see *Notice . . . December 27, 1832* (1832), no. 6; Chevallier, *Musée national du château de Fontainebleau* (1996), no. 56, pp. 84 – 86.

42. *Notice . . . June 3, 1844* (1844), no. 11.

43. *Un âge d'or* (exhib. cat., 1991), no. 144, pp. 275 – 77.

44. Préaud, "La Sculpture à Vincennes" (1992), pp. 30 – 37.

45. Arizzoli-Clementel, "Les Surtouts impériaux" (1976), figs. 9 and 11, pl. 3.

46. The names of various members of the Minton family appear regularly in the museum's visitor register as well as those of many foreign and French manufacturers (serie Vs, vol. 1 – 5). There is also correspondence reflecting the long, cordial association between Brongniart and Léon Arnoux, who was responsible for Minton's majolicas (carton T, *passim.*). Jacob Petit wrote to Brongniart on January 18, 1844: "I just recently had the occasion to visit the museum of the Royal Manufactory at Sèvres, where I was so very agreeably surprised" [J'ai eu dernièrement l'occasion de visiter le musée de la Manufacture Royale de Sèvres, dans lequel j'ai été bien agréablement surpris], and he went on to request permission "to sketch certain objects" [de dessiner quelques objets] and even "to take a cast of some of them" . . ." [prendre le moule de divers d'entre eux] (carton T 14, liasse 5, dossier 19).

47. Blühm, *The Colour of Sculpture 1840-1910*, exhib. cat. (1996 – 97).

Fig. 9-1. Crater vase, Apulian geometric style, 300 B.C.; terracotta. This was originally part of Dominique-Vivant Denon's collection which was acquired in 1786. (Sèvres, Musée national de céramique, MNC 62)

Chapter 9

Brongniart as Taxonomist and Museologist: The Significance of the Musée Céramique at Sèvres

Sylvie Millasseau

In 1800, when Alexandre Brongniart was appointed director of the Sèvres porcelain manufactory, among the first initiatives he undertook was the inauguration of a study collection of ceramics. To this end, he began the aggressive acquisition of samples of raw materials and examples of contemporary work, many in the neoclassical idiom, which would be added to an existing assemblage of ancient ceramics in the possession of the manufactory. By the 1830s, however, his mission had expanded considerably. He recognized the need for a scientific classification of ceramics, and the Sèvres collections came to include a considerable array of historical pieces. By Brongniart's death in 1847, the museum had become one of the first encyclopedic collections of ceramics in the world. This endeavor also influenced Brongniart's own evolution as a scholar, culminating in the publication of his seminal *Traité des arts céramiques* (1844) and *Description méthodique du musée céramique* (1845), a catalogue of the Sèvres collection, written in collaboration with Denis-Désiré Riocreux.

The concept of establishing a museum of ceramic arts, crafts, and techniques in the early nineteenth century might not seem surprising in itself, especially given the museological fever that was sweeping Europe at the time. Even Brongniart's success in mobilizing scholars, researchers, and manufacturers to share their knowledge might be seen simply as evidence of the intellectual openness and spirit of cooperation that prevailed in the European scientific community in the first half of the century. The actual acquisition of material, however, more than 3,800 objects entering the collection through what often amounted to bartering, is unusual and of much greater significance.[1]

Although Brongniart claimed to have followed strict guidelines in assembling the collection, as outlined in the catalogue (1845),[2] by the time of his death the range of the collection had changed considerably. It encompassed everything from pre-Columbian vases to eighteenth-century Meissen porcelain animals (acquired through an exchange with the Palais Japonais in Dresden), from raw materials to all manner of studio equipment including a kiln. The rarity and beauty of some of the objects also belied Brongniart's claims to have followed rigid, formal criteria.

The Genesis of the Sèvres Museum

Beginning in the mid-eighteenth century, the need for museums in France was discussed at great length in philosophical, artistic, and even political circles. As private collections began to proliferate, there was growing criticism of this appropriation of significant artistic achievement, especially because of the constraints placed on public access to art. As was often noted, the restrictions often made it impossible for young artists to learn by studying and copying the most illustrious works of the past.[3] As early as 1747, La Font de Saint-Yenne published a pamphlet in which he advocated exhibiting in the Louvre "all the immense and unknown riches" of the royal collections, "arranged systematically."[4]

In the decorative arts, a growing resolve to improve the quality of production through technical instruction and the study of models led to the establishment of tuition-free drawing schools, the first of which was founded in Rouen in 1741 by the painter Jean-Baptiste Descamps. These schools assembled study collections from which future museums would develop.[5] Thus, in 1766, when the painter Jean-Jacques Bachelier, who had been artistic director of the Sèvres manufactory since 1751, proposed that such an institution be founded in Paris it was part of a larger phenomenon.[6]

From this beginning, the Musée Céramique eventually emerged. In a similar spirit, the many plates illustrating artisans' workshops in Denis Diderot and Jean d'Alembert's *Encyclopédie, ou Dictionnaire Raisonné des Sciences, des Arts et des Métiers* (1751 – 72) were meant to broaden knowledge about the decorative arts and crafts as well as to encourage appreciation of their importance.[7]

By the final decade of the eighteenth century the revolutionary government in France found itself confronted with the vexing problem of how to manage the immense patrimony of the transformed French nation. Much of this consisted of the confiscated property of the clergy (November 2, 1789), the émigres (November 9, 1791), and the crown (August 10, 1792). Deliberating the disposition of this vast array of buildings, paintings, sculpture, artifacts, and other objects, two opposing camps soon emerged: one, smaller and ultimately less powerful, advocated the destruction of the symbols of a detested regime; the other called for the preservation of these "monuments of the arts and sciences," which were deemed the heritage of "a regenerated France."

Soon after the opening of the Muséum National des Arts on August 10, 1793, the abbé Grégoire, an inveterate opponent of the destruction of property, submitted a report dated 8 Vendemaire year 3 (September 27, 1794) to the National Convention calling for the establishment of a Conservatoire des Arts et Métiers.[8] His plan was approved, leading to the establishment of the first European museum of science and industry. And thanks to the efforts of

Alexandre Lenoir, a depository of confiscated church possessions was set up in the convent of the Petits Augustins, in Paris; it became the Musée des Monuments Français.[9] Ultimately, the preservationists prevailed, but only after an explosion of iconoclastic violence wrought irreparable damage to the material remains of the monarchical and ecclesiastical past.

It was at this propitious moment that Brongniart was appointed director of the Sèvres manufactory. When he arrived, on March 24, 1800, he found himself at the head of a ruined institution that had lost two-thirds of its personnel. As part of his plan to restore it to operation and, above all, to obtain much-needed revenues, Brongniart envisioned opening a retail establishment in Paris. To raise the necessary funds, he proposed to the *ministre de l'interieur* that he be permitted to auction off outdated pieces from the manufactory's stock (see chap. 10).[10]

A porcelain painter named Jullien, son of one of the directors of the Bourg-La-Reine factory, then advanced an even more audacious plan. In a letter dated 18 Fructidor year 8 (September 6, 1800) to the Conseil des Mines, a copy of which was sent to Brongniart on 22 Fructidor (September 11), Jullien first expressed his approval of the council's intention to place on exhibit "beside the white soil of the Département de la Haute Vienne, the industrial products that had been made from it."[11] This idea of displaying raw materials alongside objects made from them would form one of the key approaches to collecting adopted by Brongniart.

Jullien also suggested that this initiative be widened to include pieces made in the capital of Paris, whose porcelain makers had become "the most considerable branch of the industry," and that examples of contemporary porcelain be shown with other pieces made previously in Saint-Cloud, Vincennes, Mennecy, and elsewhere, as well as with "those that successive chemists at the Sèvres manufactory . . . might offer to the friends of the nation's art and industry." This would constitute "a complete collection for the use of scientists and researchers, who could perhaps fill whatever gaps they encountered in the way of degraded tints and increase the number and beauty of their original colors."[12] Jullien's notion of including older work was ahead of Brongniart's thinking at the time. Brongniart became interested in historical pieces for the Sèvres museum more than a quarter of a century later.

Jullien further impressed upon the Conseil des Mines the need for rapid action, "especially as regards the [pieces] from the Sèvres manufactory . . . . The auction of porcelains previously fabricated by this establishment is to take place on the 21st of this month . . . . Someone must be delegated to put aside that morning a few pieces which, in his judgment, might be consistent with the council's proposed goals."[13]

Jullien was a staunch preservationist, but with an important difference. Most other preservationists considered sculpture, painting, and other works to be worthy of presentation in a museum, while the decorative arts were judged to be minor by comparison and of monetary value only. Jullien disagreed, and this view was shared by Brongniart. A combined preoccupation with very real fiscal concerns however, and a prejudice against the rococo may have erased any scruples Brongniart might have had about selling off "these old porcelains that encumber our warehouses." He dismissed them as "ces choses gothiques."[14]

Jullien's enlightened position outlined in his letter is aligned with the period's preoccupation with issues of pedagogy, with the mission of making museums serve the higher goal of the *progrès des arts.* His stance is unusual, however, for including even those artifacts from the past, then being sold at auction, which were made exclusively for pleasure and in a stylistic idiom no longer fashionable. Unfortunately, there is no record of Brongniart's ever having mentioned this letter or acknowledging that it had influenced him in any way.

At the beginning of a long and carefully worded letter to Jean-Antoine Chaptal, the *ministre de l'interieur,* dated 10 Thermidor year 9 (July 30, 1802), Brongniart set forth his reasons for wanting to establish a study collection: "I believe it will be useful to the progress of the ceramic arts and their history, to assemble in a methodical way, in the national establishment that was previously a school of one of this art's branches and which ought to be that of the art as a whole, all the objects of art and science that might serve the history of fine and ordinary pottery."[15] He pointed out that, although the activity of the manufactory was "languishing," it possessed "precious materials" that might serve as the embryo for such a collection, namely:

> a beautiful series of Etruscan vases;
> a rather beautiful series of flower, fruit, and animal studies by different masters, notably Desportes and Oudry;
> a series, interesting for the history of the progress of taste, of models for all the ornamental and utilitarian vases made by the manufactory since its inception;
> a rather large quantity of clay and [other] raw materials from various places and of various kinds used in the fabrication of pottery.[16]

He complained, however, about the disorder and the neglect that existed in the collection.[17] Noting the gaps in the material he suggested that it be supplemented by the addition of "samples of all pottery clays, both French and foreign, [and] a set of specimens of all known porcelains and potteries."[18] Aware that his superiors would be concerned about the costs of expanding the museum, he proposed that the ministry collaborate with him in organizing an official survey called the Enquête des Préfets (see chap. 11), which he argued would serve his purposes, but at minimal government expense. This would involve the prefects' "sending to Sèvres samples of all the pottery clays from their districts either in use or usable. Twenty livres would suffice."[19] Completed pieces from the various factories and manufactories would be obtained on an exchange basis. As to the space needed to house these materials, he explained that the establishment of the retail shop in Paris had freed a few rooms at the manufactory, which if properly refurbished, might house the museum.

Brongniart's plan bears a strange resemblance to the one elaborated by the Conseil des Mines a year or so earlier, and he may have had a hand in the latter's conception. Chemist, mineralogist, and scientist to the core, he insisted above all on the utility of such a collection as an educational tool for students of the applied sciences. Brongniart also voiced another motive, one consistent with views that were widely held at the time. Since the Treaty of Vergennes (1786), the French market had been flooded with

English creamware, which, being both attractive and inexpensive, was quite popular. According to Sèvres's new director, the development of a competitive French product was nothing less than a national obligation.[20]

The systematic assembly and organization of "unknown riches" envisioned by Brongniart could only further this goal. The dissemination of technical knowledge might lead to the necessary discoveries, thereby contributing to the "progress of art,"[21] in this case, of the ceramic arts and affiliated industries. The collection of the future museum began to grow as gifts wewe made and other opportunities for acquisitions presented themselves.

The Organization of the Museum

In 1812, after samples collected under the auspices of the Enquête des Préfets and porcelains from other principal European producers were in hand, Brongniart began to structure the collection "from a technical point of view," a scientific perspective he preferred throughout his career.[22] He reformulated the collection's parameters to include "all objects produced by firing,"[23] which meant that it would include glassware, enamel work, mosaics, and even common bricks. To assure that the collection had "all the didactic interest"[24] to which he aspired, he had explanatory labels attached to the pieces, making sure in particular that they specified the name of the donor. The labeling of everything that entered the collection was essential.

He was admirably assisted in this project by Denis-Désiré Riocreux, who began his career at the manufactory as an ornamental painter.[25] Obliged to abandon porcelain painting due to serious vision problems, he was placed in charge of experiments with vitreous colors. Brongniart had more important plans for him, however, and by the end of 1817 Riocreux was made *de facto* curator of the manufactory's growing collection, with instructions to label the pieces, register them, and "oversee all correspondence with the publishers in the field."[26] This directive required Riocreux to make certain that government agencies sent the manufactory all new publications on ceramics and related topics. Riocreux brought to his task an artist's sensibility as well as considerable insight. The museum's archives contain countless notes detailing discoveries made by Riocreux, all of them countersigned by Brongniart who either approved or rejected them. In 1829, five years after the museum had opened to the public, Riocreux was officially named its curator.[27]

Information about the physical appearance of the museum is scarce. It was situated on the second floor of the manufactory, above the painting workshops.[28] Apparently its furnishings were modest, for in 1834 Brongniart complained that the waxed floor was dangerously slippery, presenting a danger to visitors, and called for the installation of walkways covered by "carpeting, oil-cloth, or even plain cloth."[29] That, however, is the extent of documentation of the premises. It is not known when the decision was made to draw up an inventory. By 1817 at the latest, Riocreux was responsible for drafting all the entries in the inventory. In fact, two different inventories were drawn up. The first adhered to the classification schema later used by Brongniart in both the *Traité des arts céramiques* and the *Description méthodique du musée céramique*. However, Riocreux eventually abandoned this typological system in favor of an approach based on acquisition date.

The government was hesitant to underwrite purchases. In principle Brongniart had to obtain special authorization for such expenditures, and his superiors were not above reprimanding him when they felt he had neglected this duty.[30] When the collection had reached a certain stage of development, however, the only way for Brongniart to fill some of its gaps was to venture into the art market. In 1825 he made his first request to the vicomte de La Rochefoucauld, then *directeur général des beaux arts de la Maison du Roi* and his direct superior, for an annual "special fund of 1,000 francs" for the acquisition, over and above whatever works and models were needed for the manufactory's workshops, of "all sorts of primary materials and ceramic products, from the most commonplace pottery to the most precious, from all periods and all nations."[31] In 1826 Brongniart requested "special funds" for the acquisition of some Chinese porcelains at the Sallé sale.[32] Given the scarcity of available funding, it is not surprising that Brongniart developed the habit of obtaining pieces he wanted for the museum by offering samples of modern Sèvres production in return. Riocreux kept a register of all such "gifts" offered in exchange for donations to the collection.[33]

The Collection of Ancient Ceramics

During the second half of the eighteenth century, many wealthy, educated, and socially prominent people became interested in archaeological excavations, an activity that would indirectly prove to be quite beneficial to the Sèvres museum. In the nineteenth century this pastime became increasingly popular. As a zealous antiquarian, Dominique-Vivant Denon had amassed, during his sojourn in the Kingdom of the Two Sicilies, a considerable number of ancient ceramics, which he sold to Louis XVI in 1786. They account for the first 292 numbers of Riocreux's inventory.[34] Most date to the Hellenistic period and were made by Greeks working in Southern Italy: Apulian, Campanian, or Lucanian red-figure vases, notably a striking black figure askos (MNC 109) decorated with a female profile linked to a large palmette. Denon's collection also includes geometric yellow-slip kraters (MNC 62; fig. 9-1) and kantharitic jars.[35] Also from the Hellenistic period, but in the Attic style, are a few polished completely black pieces of unusual form (MNC 99), some Attic black figure vases (MNC 57, 100), and, in the same group, two kantharitic goblets (MNC 258.1, 244).[36]

Denon's example may have later inspired M. Gaspary, the French consul in Crete, who "offered" — unsolicited and in exchange for ready cash — the pieces he had collected in 1828 on the island of Milo.[37] His audacity forced Brongniart's hand a bit, but a small hydra (MNC 1496.6) and a skyphos (1495.4) in the geometric style typical of Milo entered the collection.[38] Beginning in 1828, a naval officer named Jules de Blosseville gave the museum its most significant pieces in this manner.[39]

Indeed, the many scientific missions organized under the Restauration and the July Monarchy presented Brongniart with choice opportunities for collecting pieces from outside of France. As a result, many unusual objects found their way into the museum's displays: notably oenochoës (MNC 1419.3, 1419.4, 1419.6) with dark red geometric decoration painted on white slip; double tumblers (MNC 1419.8) with white geometric decoration, a kernos (MNC 1419.9) that Brongniart reproduced in his catalogue of the museum, and finally some large kraters (MNC 1419.2) with polished black decoration.[40] In 1842 these were joined by two small objects from the Hellenistic period representing a goat and a duck. Excavated in Athens, they were obtained by the captain of the sloop *Embuscade* and presented to the manufactory by Dubuc, *directeur des dépenses des bâtiments de la couronne*.[41]

In the 1820s the international archaeological community was electrified by the discovery of several tombs in the Etrurian region of Chiusi, most especially at Vulci.[42] In 1828, by means unknown, Riocreux managed to acquire the first piece from these excavations to enter a French collection: a small black-clay kantharitic vase with handles (MNC 1075), of Etruscan origin. As the result of an exchange with a dealer named Toppi, an Italian living in Paris, this piece was joined a year later by a chamfered and spouted black-polished oinochoë (MNC 1163.4).[43]

In 1836 the collection was considerably enriched by the purchase of seventy pieces of ceramics, for 1,500 francs, at the second sale of the Durand collection.[44] Riocreux, to whom Brongniart had delegated his authority during his absence in England and Germany, faced stiff competition. The other bidders included the comte de Clarac, curator of antiquities at the Louvre; Raoul Rochette, curator of the Cabinet des Médailles et Antiques of the Bibliothèque Royale; as well as various scholars (notably an antiquarian named Brönstedt),[45] wealthy collectors (including the comte de Pourtalès), and at least one rival manufacturer, Godard de Baccarat, the director of the firm of Baccarat.[46]

It is difficult to match entries on the purchase list prepared by Riocreux with actual pieces in the collection,[47] because the descriptions are too generic. Number 166 from the sale, however, may correspond to a superb dark green Attic oinochoë (MNC 2035) with incised decoration. Riocreux spent the considerable sum of 200 francs for this piece, which he described as: "Greek vase, white and violet paintings with gold embossed ornament."[48] The Durand sale also occasioned the acquisition of the collection's first Corinthian pottery: two alabaster vases (MNC 2047, 2048) decorated with animal friezes and featuring a ground color that Brongniart judged to be quite rare.[49] The Etruscan part of the collection was also enriched. Pieces bearing secure attributions included, for example, a kantharitic vase (MNC 2054) of smoked and polished clay with incised decoration[50] and an unusual four-footed goblet (MNC 2055) with relief decoration, reproduced in the volume of plates that accompanied the *Description méthodique du musée céramique*.[51]

It was also through Toppi that the first Egyptian piece entered the collection, a funerary statuette (MNC 1185) found in excavations outside Thebes. In 1830 this object was joined by pieces sent by an envoy of an archaeologist named Lenormant, notably an earthenware scarab also from Thebes. The museum was indebted for many of its Egyptian artifacts to the inveterate traveler Baron Taylor, whose donations included a canopic jar (MNC 1475) from Tanis capped the head of the deity Hapi (New Kingdom).[52] In 1846 Victor Schoelcher, son of the ceramics producer Marc Schoelcher, contributed several Egyptian pieces, notably a long handleless bottle (MNC 3600.2) dating from the Middle Kingdom.[53]

In January 1836 John Robison, secretary of the Royal Society of Antiquarians in Edinburgh, sent Sèvres a glazed ornamental brick that, according to him, had been taken from Babylon. After countless peregrinations it finally arrived but unfortunately was broken.[54] In 1847, when sculpture from Khorsabad arrived at the Louvre, Sèvres received more bricks from Babylon through the intermediary of the French consul in Baghdad.[55]

Gallo-Roman and Celtic Pottery

There were many Roman and Gallo-Roman ruins in northwestern Europe that had long aroused the curiosity of both professional and amateur antiquarians. In the nineteenth century, the proliferation of urban construction sites led to the discovery of many more such remains. Not surprisingly, the museum's donors include an engineer from *Ponts et Chaussées* (the department responsible for bridges and roads); an architect from the department of public works; and even an architect in charge of restoring the Luxembourg palace. Accounts of these discoveries proliferated as amateur and professional archaeologists widened their searches to excavate tombs and burial mounds. Gradually, however, interest shifted to the remains of other cultures, and by 1847 Celtic pottery increasingly became a part of the museum's collection.

The first donation of Gallo-Roman pottery fragments (MNC 641) was sent in 1809 by M. Ramond, prefect of Puy-de-Dôme; he claimed they had been found at the Gergovie plateau, near Clermont in central France. The next acquisition came only in 1822, when an antiquarian named Schweighaeuser residing in Strasbourg, donated fragments of pottery molds and pieces with impressed decoration (MNC 773, 774) that he had found at Heiligenberg and Rheinzabern on the Rhenish frontier.[56] In 1824, thanks to the generosity of Grignon, head of the ironworks in Bayart, some pieces formerly in the collection of the abbé de Tersan, a famous eighteenth-century amateur-collector, entered the collection. These fragments (MNC 829), some of which bear the maker's name, had been discovered in 1772 in Champagne.[57]

In 1829 an appeals lawyer named Michelin, at the Cour des Comptes, turned over vase fragments (MNC 1209, 1210) found on the site of the Palais de Justice on the Île de la Cité in Paris.[58] To relieve the boredom of life in a small town, Renaud de Saint-Amour, a colonel in the third regiment of hussars garrisoned at Lauterbourg, began excavations in its environs. In 1831 he discovered several potters' kilns in Rheinzabern that were quite well preserved. He sent plans of them to Brongniart, as well as three complete terracotta molds (MNC 1383.1, 1383.2, 1383.3), for which he received in exchange several pieces of Sèvres porcelain.[59]

Beginning in 1828 the Roman cemetery near Bordeaux known as Terre-Nègre was excavated by a professor named Jouannet from the local academy. He donated several small cups (MNC 1054.1, 1054.2) and goblets (MNC 1572.2) in good condition as well as a small amphora (MNC 1572.4) and an oinochoë (MNC 1572.5) made of reddish clay.[60]

In Orléans M. Jollois, a local civil engineer, undertook similar excavations in the Roman cemetery of that city. His finds included a small red vial (MNC 1630.6) with a polished surface and an oinochoë (MNC 3139.1) with a double-pointed handle.[61] Work at the Luxembourg palace overseen by an architect named Gisors led to the discovery of the ruins of a pottery in its gardens. Cups and shards of red-clay pottery (MNC 2287.18, 2287.10) from this site, some of them bearing a potter's name, found their way to Sèvres.[62]

The most remarkable Roman pieces entered the collection in 1836 via the comte d'Espine, the surgeon-dentist of the king of Sardinia. He donated several objects discovered in excavations at

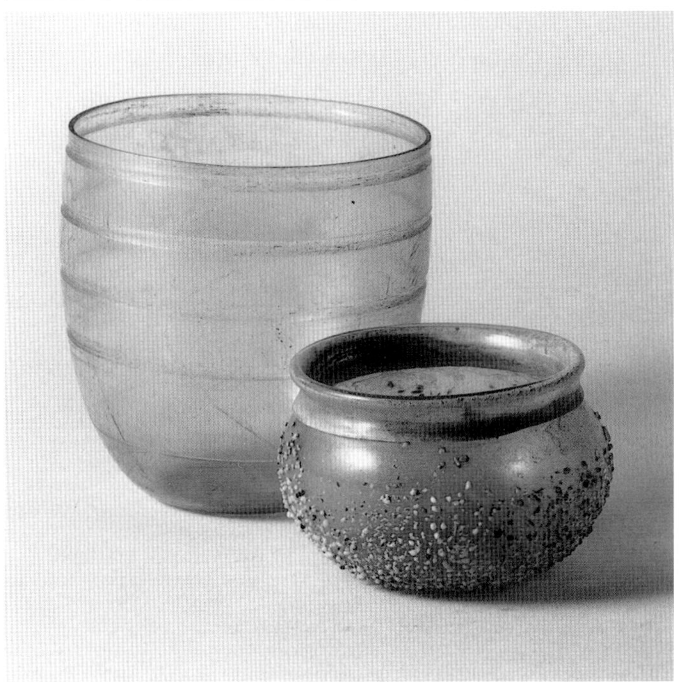

Fig. 9-2. Glass bowls, Roman. 300 B.C. These were donated by César de Saluces in 1836. (Sèvres, Musée national de céramique, MNC 2265)

Pollentia, in Piedmont.[63] These included amphoras, lamps, and some magnificent glass goblets, one of which is covered with raised decoration (fig. 9-2).

Until this time, gifts and exchanges had brought the collection only small pieces or fragments. Not surprisingly, when Brongniart learned of the discovery of fourteen amphoras, each more than seventeen *pieds* high at the Gallo-Roman site of Mons- Selencus in the Alps, he asked the mayor to contribute one of them to the museum.[64]

Increasingly in the nineteenth century, those interested in ancient history widened the scope of their studies to include the ancient, indigenous civilizations of France. A burial mound in Dieppe, which was excavated in 1843, yielded early fragments. Deville, the curator of the Musée d'Antiquités in Rouen, wrote that "these crude pottery remains seem to predate the invasion of Julius Caesar, or at the least to be contemporary with it."[65] Another excavator, Delanoue, in sending a donation of pieces, recounted the circumstances of their discovery: "Pottery fragment found .50 meters below the surface along with human bones in diluvial deposits in the grotto of Rancogne."[66] Even the curate of Sèvres, the abbé Bainvel, became a disciple of this new archaeological passion and offered the museum a "druid" vase from a dolmen near Ploemeur.[67]

Brongniart's carefully cultivated relations with the European scientific community led to the acquisition of many examples of Germanic pottery. In 1837 Alexander Baron von Humboldt, the esteemed German naturalist, donated a hand-shaped cup (MNC 2285) made of polished yellow clay.[68] In 1838 Forschammer, a German archaeologist, contributed two gray clay cups, a goblet of yellow polished clay, and some vase fragments (MNC 2570.2 – 2570.7) excavated in what is now Denmark.[69] Finally in 1844 Olfers, curator of antiquities to the king of Prussia, sent fourteen Germanic vases from the warehouse of his own museum, most of which came from Brandenburg.[70]

Acquisitions from Travelers

Part of the collection reflects the adventurous individuals who, in the first half of the nineteenth century, turned their passion for travel into a recognized profession. In this period the Muséum d'Histoire Naturelle, acting in cooperation with the French government, organized many expeditions to other regions. Brongniart, who maintained close ties with those individuals at the museum, did not hesitate to ask its mineralogists, naturalists, and geographers to act as his agents as well. Before they departed, he gave them instructions and a few crates that he hoped would be filled en route with materials for the museum. He had dealings not only with ships' captains and lieutenants but often with the surgeons, doctors, dentists, and other personnel who accompanied the expeditions. Members of the diplomatic corps were also pressed into service.

Although many of these individuals possessed little or no knowledge of ceramics, surprisingly, they appear to have made few mistakes. Perhaps the explanation for this lies in the instructions Brongniart gave them. He directed them to purchase pieces only from the districts that they visited, to make these purchases from knowledgeable sources, or to retrieve pieces recently excavated from archaeological digs. He also directed them to gather samples of both ancient and contemporary pottery, preferably complete pieces, but fragments would suffice. They were to record to the best of their ability the place of acquisition, the materials used in the fabrication process when possible, and whether or not a potter's wheel had been employed. Sketches were to be made of the kilns, and all samples were to be carefully wrapped and labeled.[71] Everyone taking part in these efforts was provided with 200 francs to cover related costs. Sometimes these efforts were for naught, for the hazards of navigation were such that collected materials did not always reach their intended destination.[72] In many more cases, however, the museum at Sèvres benefited significantly.

The Americas. In 1827 thanks to the efforts of a chief surgeon named Busseuil aboard the frigate *Thétis*, the collection acquired its first piece of pre-Columbian pottery, an entire black Chimu stirrup vase (MNC 979).[73] The naturalist Dessalines d'Orbigny made an exploratory voyage to South America that lasted from 1826 to 1834. During that time, he sent back pottery made by two indigenous tribes, the Guaranis of Paraguay and the Corrientes of Argentina, and upon returning to France he delivered to the museum what Brongniart termed a "curious group" of Incan pieces.[74] This included a vase in the form of a reclining llama (MNC 1762), a spherical pitcher (MNC 1761) with geometric decoration found in Bolivia, and, most notably, several pre-Columbian objects of very high quality, among them a stirrup vase (MNC 12249) in the shape of a bird and a vase (MNC 1768) decorated with the figure of a large cat, a vase (MNC 1763) with geometric decoration from Chile (Atacama), and an Aztec figure (MNC 1773, damaged by exposure) from Teotihuacán in Mexico.[75]

The French consul Barrot left for the Americas in 1835 and later sent a case of Peruvian antiquities from Manila. It reached Sèvres in 1838 and contained, among other things, a lovely Mochica

Fig. 9-3. Mochica stirrup-vase, 1000–1200 A.D.; terracotta. It was part of a shipment sent by Consul Barrot from Manila and was inventoried in 1838. (Sèvres, Musée national de céramique, MNC 2547-1)

stirrup vase with a body shaped like two parrots (MNC 2547.1; fig. 9-3) and a zoomorphic Chimu vase (MNC 2546.3).[76] Admiral Dupetit-Thouars managed to obtain several Central and South American vases for the museum. Most were Incan, but they also included a superb Chimu vase (MNC 2797) decorated with a frieze of opossums.[77]

In 1837 a mineralogist named Stokes, who lived in London, corresponded with Brongniart and donated some pre-Incan pieces he had gathered in Peru, including several crudely modeled statuettes (MNC 2417.1, 2417.2, 2418.6).[78]

The first piece from French Guiana to enter the collection, a newly made orange-colored cup (MNC 794), was donated in 1823 by Jean François Robert, a painter at the manufactory, who had obtained it from a ship's purser.[79] Thanks to the comte de Clarac, it was joined by another cup from Guiana in 1830. And in 1843 the intrepid ceramicist Victor Schoelcher contributed a number of important pieces and fragments from the Caribbean, including a mask (MNC 3646) from Puerto Rico.[80]

North American productions were also represented. A brown clay vase (MNC 1326) was donated by Professor Duméril, in 1830,[81] but most of the North American acquisitions were obtained through the efforts of one of Brongniart's former students, a man named Ducatel, who had become a professor of chemistry in Baltimore. In 1837 he sent a number of fragments found near the city of Marietta in Ohio.[82]

Coastal Regions of Africa, the Indian Ocean, and the Pacific. No one knows why the miniature painter Chapon went to Madagascar, but he returned to France in 1829 with an apodal water pot (MNC 1076) and a vase (MNC 1085) made of a grayish paste covered with a graphite-based glaze. Africa was poorly represented in the collection at the time. In 1836 Brongniart noted in his instructions to Captain Laplace, who was embarking for Africa, that the museum possessed "no samples of pottery from southern and eastern Africa" and that according to the travel account of one Daniel, "the Hottentots made pieces of pottery that are quite varied and rather large."[83] The captain duly obliged Brongniart by penetrating the South African interior in search of jars and other pottery made by the Bantu, but his efforts were in vain.[84] Brongniart did not give up, however, and in 1838 he provided a surgeon major named Ackermann, who was departing for Madagascar, with a similar set of instructions, but again to no avail.[85] The explorer Rochet d'Héricourt was more successful. In the course of his expedition to Abyssinia, he managed to obtain two vases and a bottle (MNC 3751.1, 3751.2) in the Choa kingdom, all featuring polished black surfaces with incised decoration, which he brought back in 1845.[86]

The coastal areas of the subcontinent were explored with increasing intensity in the second quarter of the nineteenth century. This region of the globe was scouted for Brongniart by Jules de Blosseville, who in 1828 sent back twenty-seven objects (MNC 1059 – 1062), including glazed pottery from Calcutta and polychrome figures from Chandernagor. In 1833 the naturalist Lamare Picquot brought back from Bengal some goblets, coolers, and an incense burner (MNC 1551 – 1554). In 1837 in Pondicherry Laplace acquired some vases for everyday use as well as "some modeled figures which give an idea of the talent of Indian potters," to which he added: "the workers are miserable . . . ; their trade barely provides them with the wherewithal to survive."[87] He also obtained some pieces in Ceylon, a small assortment of Malaysian pottery, and even some glazed pieces from Cebu in the Philippines (MNC 2857 – 2864).[88]

In 1840 explorations in the Fiji Islands acquired some crude pottery coated with a gummy, resinous glaze; a sample (MNC 2898) was collected by a hydrographic engineer named Dumoulin, aboard the *Astrolabe*, during a round-the-world voyage. In 1846 a ship's captain named Bérard brought back from New Caledonia two cooking pots (MNC 3672) coated with a vegetal glaze.

The Mediterranean Basin and the Arab World. When the eminent chemist Jean-Pierre Joseph Darcet departed for Egypt in 1829, the precise set of instructions Brongniart gave him included an excerpt dealing with pottery from Denon's *Voyage dans la haute et basse*

Egypte (1802) as well as a few lines from a "Mémoire su l'industrie de l'agriculture de l'Egypte" (Memorandum on Egyptian Industry and Agriculture) by a certain Girard (undated).[89] According to these texts, the terracotta pottery production was essentially limited to Upper Egypt between Dendera and Thebes, a kind of potstone was its predominant material, and the pieces were baked in the sun.

It was another donation, brought back in 1830 by Lenormant, an archaeologist who accompanied Jean-François Champollion to Egypt in 1828, however, that most intrigued Brongniart. Chemical analysis revealed the glaze on these fragments to be composed of tin and lead. According to information gathered by Lenormant, they dated from the ninth century A.D., making them the earliest examples of stanniferous glazes then known.[90] Other fragments, made from siliceous paste, resembled those made in ancient Egypt.

In 1832 Baron Taylor compounded this stupefaction by bringing back mosaic tesserae (MNC 1449) from the wall of the Jerusalem mosque. In the words of Brongniart, "its paste is so sandy, it is so similar to sandstone that I suspect it is stone . . . that has been enameled."[91]

When the archaeologist Botta was appointed French consul in Mossul in 1835, he was expressly reminded not to forget the museum.[92] By and large, Sèvres did well by Botta, but all he could obtain in San'a, Mecca, and Djedda was everyday contemporary pottery (MNC 2748 – 2756). Following Baron Taylor's example, he also took an enameled tessera (MNC 2757) from a wall of the tomb of Mohammed in Medina. This zeal, however misplaced, had its reward, pushing back the documented date of the Arab community's knowledge of alkaline silicate glazes by a full century.[93] Tin glazes were in use by the ninth century and alkaline silicate glazes by the eleventh.

Brongniart was especially anxious to obtain materials from the Ottoman Empire. In 1830 Virlet, a member of the Morea Commission, sent him a large consignment of modern pottery from the Dardanelles region along with some pipes from Constantinople and some vases from Smyrna (MNC 1328 – 1334).[94] In 1843 Brongniart asked Diran, assistant director of the mint in Constantinople, to contribute "some raw and prepared materials used in the fabrication of [your] pottery."[95] In 1847, Viquesnel, a member of the *Société Géologique,* sent some samples along with a cover letter describing ceramics production in Sule Burgas.[96]

There is a handwritten copy of an excerpt of Jean Chardin's *Journal du voyage du chevalier* (1711), an account of a trip to Persia, among Brongniart's papers at Sèvres.[97] According to Chardin, "so beautiful are [the] glazes" of the porcelain made in Persia that the work was virtually indistinguishable from that of China. This impression was subsequently confirmed by many others, notably the comte de Milly in his book *L'Art de la porcelaine* (1771).[98] Brongniart sought a scientific explanation for this, but a definitive answer long eluded him. A beautiful coupe (MNC 449) that entered the collection in 1806 with a group of Chinese porcelains was decorated with large blue-flowered rinceaus against a white ground and with highlights in what Brongniart and Riocreux, in the *Description méthodique du musée céramique,* termed an "aureo-coppery" luster. Riocreus characterized it in his inventory as "earthenware imitating porcelain," adding the query: "Persian?"[99]

So strong was the desire for Persian porcelain that Brongniart, like many others, was tempted to ascribe such origins to seventeenth-century Nevers earthenware covered in tinted enamel.[100] In 1829 when Brongniart agreed to an exchange with Toppi that netted the collection a Chinese blue enamel plate with an overlay white decoration, he had already received the shards sent by Lenormant. When Riocreux recorded the exchange, however, he resorted to a language of equivocation frequently encountered in contemporary documents dealing with such artifacts: "an ordinary blue-enameled earthenware plate called Persian porcelain."[101] The object in question is illustrated in the *Description méthodique du musée céramique* among "oriental" ware.[102] Riocreux repeated the error in 1843, when Jules Ziegler, a stoneware maker, donated a small bottle (MNC 3129) "in the oriental style" featuring a decoration of white flowering branches against a yellow enamel ground; it was also included in the same plate of "oriental" wares.[103]

In 1835 in instructions to Botta, Brongniart expressed doubts about the existence of a true Persian porcelain: "I do not know of any, and I don't even think pottery of this kind was made in Persia but they did make, and may make still, earthenware . . . remarkable for the beauty of its vivid azure blue enamel."[104]

That same year Brongniart acquired from a Parisian dealer named Poirier a superb blue Iznik bottle (MNC 1842) that Brongniart thought was Persian (fig. 9-4).[105] During a trip to

Fig. 9-4. Iznik bottle, second half of the 16th century; silaceous pottery. Purchased by Brongniart from a Paris dealer in curiosities named Poirier, it entered the inventory in 1835. (Sèvres, Musée national de céramique, MNC 1842)

Nuremberg the following year he purchased a jug (MNC 2134) decorated with pinks and eglantine, described in the inventory as "white paste [earthenware] simulating porcelain, attributed to the workshops of Persia." [106]

Brongniart also had his share of bad luck. A case sent in 1843 by Sir John MacNeil, English envoy to the shah of Persia, never arrived. This was unfortunate, for it contained a tile from the Shiraz mosque, another from the Isaphan mosque, and some wall plaques from the mosques in Tabriz and Rhei.[107]

A gift presented in 1844 by the captain of the *Despointes,* however, certainly must have helped to solve the question of attribution. This was an extraordinary Syrian cup (MNC 3292) covered with a lapis blue glaze and decorated with a gilded arch motif. The circumstances of its discovery left no doubt of its origins: it had been found in a well along with similar cups and an Arabic manuscript. It appears in the *Description méthodique du musée céramique,* in the chapter devoted to glazed pottery and is described in the inventory as an "Arabic production of the ninth century."[108]

At the De Guignes sale of 1846 Brongniart purchased a Persian soft-paste cup made with a rice-grain technique that must have assured him that the Persians had developed a porcelain body, but by then the *Traité des arts céramiques* and the *Description méthodique du musée céramique* had already been published.[109] Perhaps he remained skeptical, because Riocreux, describing the piece in the inventory, vacillated once again, adding the query: "Persian porcelain?"

The Far East. In 1806 the museum acquired a large number of Chinese porcelains, and in his preparatory notes for the *Description méthodique du musée céramique,* Brongniart identifies the donor of this collection as Pierre Daru, the Intendant Général.[110] In a letter to Daru dated January 21, 1808, he identifies Denon as having contributed the first pieces of what was thought to be Japanese porcelain.[111]

Most of the 107 pieces acquired in 1806 had been porcelains with blue underglaze decoration in the form of figures or floral motifs, but they also included: a "Compagnie des Indes" cup bearing a mythological subject painted in grisaille; some pieces with Imari decoration; others featuring gold decoration against a blue ground; and a small pot (MNC 380) with a green vermiculated ground and salamanders in relief.

Prior to the advent of scholarly, methodical research on Far Eastern ceramics, analysis of this work was just as difficult as it had been to comprehend Persian porcelain.[112] It was especially difficult to distinguish between Chinese and Japanese porcelain, a situation that persisted throughout the century in varying degrees. Only one written source for Chinese ceramics was available to Brongniart, and he used it extensively: *Lettres édifiantes* had been written between 1712 and 1722 by a Jesuit missionary to China named Père d'Entrecolles. With respect to Japanese ceramics, Brongniart had to rely on a few lines devoted to the subject in a 1732 book [113] and on the counsel of a German-born acquaintance, a naturalist and doctor named Siebold, who had lived in Japan for seven years.

The inventory does not offer precise indications as to when this porcelain entered the collection, and Riocreux's vocabulary was understandably too limited in this domain for him to provide anything other than summary visual descriptions. Porcelain that was classified as "Compagnie des Indes," or export porcelain, made for the East India Company, was not distinguished from other Chinese porcelain. Dating was practically nonexistent. The first timid attempts were made on the occasion of the public sale of cargo from the *La Fayette* in Le Havre in 1844. The museum apparently purchased a Wan-Li vase (MNC 3401.2).

Brongniart's subsequent purchases reflect more clearly his preoccupations as the director of a porcelain manufactory; they exemplify technical processes that he sought to master. As he explained to Consul Barrot, who was about to embark on a voyage that would likely take him to China, "the Chinese apply colors to their porcelain that are varied and quite bright, very thickly and with a relief we cannot approach in Europe."[114] Similar technical considerations prompted him to request special acquisition funds for the 1826 Sallé sale where he purchased four pieces with openwork panels, a small flask with double panels, and three small cups made of agatized glass.[115]

In 1827 Brongniart acquired six Chinese pieces from a Parisian dealer named Leblanc, including a "purple red enamel" and another blue enameled piece (MNC 906 and 907). In 1839 he negotiated an exchange with the *perruquier-coiffeur* of the town of Sèvres and acquired a very beautiful Chinese ewer (MNC 2603) lacking its handle — a fortuitous absence, which, as noted in the inventory, demonstrated that "the Chinese painted on unfired paste." In addition, he was always on the lookout for one of the large vases that only the Chinese seemed to produce. In 1837 Brongniart, despite the parsimonious government budgets, paid a London dealer named Baldock 1,165 francs for such a vase (MNC 2420), this one 51 1/4 inches (130 cm) in height[116]; remarkably, it survives intact in the museum storerooms.

Although Brongniart increasingly sought to acquire Chinese pieces from all periods, he specifically asked his agents abroad to obtain modern pieces "of known date, within ten years," to select pieces showing the variety of colors used in China and "never seen in Europe," and to record their Chinese names.[117] In 1840 Captain Laplace adhered admirably to this brief. He sent back from Cochin China several pieces of glazed pottery and stoneware (MNC 2858 – 2860) indicating their names and intended use wherever possible. In Canton he obtained "a large bowl or washbasin" (MNC 2870), some 23 5/8 inches (60 cm) in diameter, for a mere 135 francs, this low price being due to a slight crack in the bottom.[118]

A Sinologist named Callery, who served as an interpreter on the French mission to China in 1844, acquired some thirty pieces of modern porcelain (MNC 3423, 3424), carefully selected for its variety. But it was a Father Ly who, in 1846, surpassed Brongniart's highest hopes by sending a group of contemporary porcelains from "Kin Te Ching" and, more importantly, some samples of raw materials carefully packed in a stoneware vase (MNC 3663) to assure their safe arrival. The previous year Brongniart had obtained from a Parisian dealer named Houssaye in exchange for goods worth about 3,000 francs, a porcelain model of the tower of Nankin (MNC 3624, now in the collection of the Musée Guimet), which soon took its place in the museum alongside eight other pieces.[119]

Chinese glass production also intrigued Brongniart. As he wrote to Barrot and Laplace, he had never encountered, either on the market or in a private collection, glassware or crystal from the

Far East. In 1829, three years after acquiring agatized cups at the Sallé sale, he made an exchange with Toppi and obtained another small cup (MNC 1180) made of the imitation jade glass known as *pâte de riz*, or rice paste. By 1838, although that year a botanist named Gaudichaud brought him two bracelets (MNC 2542) made of the same material, the collection still possessed no ordinary glassware.

The pieces donated by Denon in 1808 could not be attributed to Japan with any degree of certainty. In 1829 Cailleux, the director of the warehouses of the Musée Royal, presented the museum with fourteen plates (MNC 1201) made of "porcelaine du japon," which were in fact Chinese plates with Imari decoration. The same year, Jules de Blosseville sent Brongniart a large stoneware jar (MNC 1120) he had acquired in Batavia, supposedly of Japanese origin and intended "for the storage of water aboard junks."

In 1823 Dr. Siebold had been sent to Japan on a medical mission. Upon his return to Paris, he presented Brongniart with a cup (MNC 1966) and a small goblet (MNC 1967) "in the extra-thin porcelain known as eggshell" as well as another goblet (MNC 1968) "made of porcelain paste fired *au dégourdi*" or in the middle temperature range. These were the only pieces that Brongniart considered to be authentically Japanese.

Contemporary Work. Contemporary ceramics and glassware were well represented in the museum's displays from the beginning. Brongniart's aim was to classify "the ceramic arts . . . of all places and all times," and such pieces were indispensable if he was to succeed in explaining "the progress of the art" to its visitors. He was fascinated by technical advances of all kinds, whatever their origin, and he opened the establishment's doors wide to the work of independent producers. As a result, the museum became a window onto the most audacious and ingenious developments in the field in the first half of the nineteenth century. To this end, Brongniart took advantage of the Enquête des Préfets, a nationwide investigation into the ceramic arts (see chap. 11), and the industrial exhibitions in Paris to cultivate relations with other European producers and manufactories. During his European travels, he also gathered objects that were appropriate to his goals for the museum. Beginning in 1802, the pieces entering the collection reveal Brongniart's taste and preferences.

His long-term fascination with English creamware and stoneware, which were inexpensive and thus highly competitive, began soon after his arrival at Sèvres. One of the first pieces to enter the collection after the 292 objects of the 1786 Denon acquisition was a fine stoneware teapot, numbered 295 in the inventory. It features white relief ornament against a black ground and was probably acquired by Brongniart during his 1802 trip to England, although the inventory does not confirm this. The same year, an imitation-bronze stoneware goblet (MNC 316), made by Chanou at Sèvres, also entered the collection. It was an "attempt to imitate English production," as it was described in the inventory, and further represents the technical ingenuity and imitative skill so characteristic of the nineteenth century.

In 1800 the Institut de France, concerned about the many technical issues within French industry, including the effects of sudden changes of temperature, porosity, and the use of toxic lead glazes in ordinary French pottery, offered a prize for the successful development of an inexpensive pottery that addressed these issues.[120] In 1801 the prize was awarded to the French scientist Jacques Fourmy for a new material christened *hygiocérame* (from the Greek *hygeia*, "health"), and in 1802 Brongniart added two examples of it (MNC 312 and 313) to the museum's collection.

The Enquête des Préfets. This survey ultimately made a significant contribution to the collections of the museum, but the prefects' response to Brongniart's requests for materials was less than enthusiastic. After the initial questionnaire campaign of 1806, Brongniart complained to the *ministre de l'intérieur* that only four perfects had bothered to respond and those incompletely (deliveries were supposed to include finished pieces and samples of the raw materials used in their fabrication). Somewhat earlier, in 1802, however, Brongniart may have obtained some fine stoneware (MNC 310, four pieces) produced by Bosc in Musigny (Côte d'Or) through the survey. In 1804 he received some earthenware (MNC 324) with delicate blue decoration from the Boch factory in Septfontaines as well as two white earthenware vases (MNC 320) from the Creil factory. A fine piece of stoneware (MNC 334) from the Utzschneider factory in Sarreguemines was in the collection by 1806. During the brief period of Napoleonic conquest in the early nineteenth century, France extended its boundaries considerably. As a result, the prefect Chabrol was able to send some fine earthenware from Savona and pottery from Albissola, while Merlet obliged with earthenware from Cologne.

By the time the survey ended, hundreds of pieces had entered the collection. Most were inventoried in 1808, assigned nos. 511 to 636 and nos. 639 to 661. Many of these represented several objects sharing an inventory number.[121]

The Industrial Products Exhibitions. The earliest exposition in France took place in 1798; two others followed in 1801 and 1802, and the third to be organized under the Empire, in 1806, lasted twenty-four days and featured no fewer than 1,400 exhibitors.[122] Subsequent political and military developments brought this rush of enthusiasm to an end: it was not until 1819, during the reign of Louix XVIII, that the next exhibition occured. Thereafter, however, one was organized every four years. These provided an incredible windfall for the museum, and an enormous number of objects entered the museum directly from the exhibitions.

Beginning with the 1823 exhibition, Brongniart consistently served as a member of the jury. In a letter to the comte de Montalivet dated December 1833, he described the priorities that shaped his judgment on these occasions. "The sole object of these exhibitions," he wrote, "is to draw the attention of the public and the government to the factories and producers who have made real progress in their art by producing quality work at the lowest possible price."[123] In his view, then, it was not their primary purpose to honor unique showpieces produced at extravagant cost. As he observed to Saint Cricq-Cazaux, a ceramics producer in Creil, "the difficulty consists of making something as beautiful and fine as possible at the lowest possible price."[124]

Brongniart made notes during the exhibitions assessing the various products on display. He was always curious about the quantities of pieces produced, the materials used in their fabrication, the particulars of their firing, and the number of workers used

Fig. 9-5. Inkwells, ca. 1823; stoneware; produced by François-Paul Utzschneider of Sarreguemines. The one on the left is in trompe l'oeil porphyry; the other, tilted to show the inventory label, represents petrified wood. These entered the collection from the Exposition des Arts Industriels, held at the Louvre in 1823. (Sèvres, Musée national de céramique, MNC 770-1)

to produce them. He sometimes visited the warehouses in Paris to obtain supplementary information.

At the close of each exhibition, Brongniart sent letters to the exhibitors whose work had impressed him with its quality and originality, requesting approval to appropriate some of their pieces for the museum and specifying that, if they agreed, the objects would be "placed prominently, dated, and labeled with the name" of the producer.[125] Exhibitors responded positively to these requests.

The honor of being represented at Sèvres could come at a price. Some of the pieces underwent a variety of tests or were put into use before finding their way to the showcases. The inventory informs us, for example, that two fine earthenware plates (MNC 673) from the Creil factory "were subjected, the one to the action of potassium hydrosulfide for half a day, the other to vinegar evaporation." A porcelain coffee jug (MNC 687) made by the Parisian producer Desprez was "used daily for two years," during which time it was "exposed to heaters and hearth fires." A refractory pottery crucible (MNC 808) from the Lamontagne factory in Limoges was subjected to "the trial of feldspathic fusion at high temperature in the porcelain kiln." More prosaically, a plate (MNC 1671) from Montereau "was used for two years at the table of Monsieur Dumas, professor at the Royal Academy of Sciences."[126]

Many manufacturers subsequently donated examples of technical developments at their own initiative, independent of the exhibitions. In such cases Brongniart always requested that they indicate the prices, for in his view "the judgment of commercial objects must be based on price as well as quality."[127]

The production of fine earthenware made from indigenous materials that would rival English creamware was something of an obsession among all French manufacturers during the early nineteenth century. In this domain, the intervention of Boudon de Saint-Amans was decisive. In the course of several stays in England he had become thoroughly acquainted with the processes used there, and in 1827 Brongniart allowed him to undertake some trials at Sèvres.[128] The development of transfer printing held out the promise of attractive, brightly colored tableware for a large public. In the same period, decorative ewers and jewelry caskets began to proliferate in many bourgeois households. The vitality of this kind of production seemed limitless: encouraged by technical advances, its practitioners devised a steady stream of variations on old themes, which they sincerely believed represented marked improvements.

Creamware, or *faïence fine*, from Creil (Oise) and Sarreguemines (Lorraine) was selected from the 1819 exhibition, as were pieces of *hygiocérame* made by the Parisian producer Desprez. Brongniart also singled out work realized by François-Antoine Legros d'Anizy at Sèvres, specifically a porcelain plaque (MNC 705) decorated with figure compositions in muffle-fired colors and a Sèvres porcelain plate (MNC 712) decorated with "a frieze of palmettes printed in gold by the lithographic process." Legros d'Anizy had also experimented with his transfer-printing techniques on creamware produced in Creil, a sample of which (MNC 713) was added to the collection.

Brongniart was extremely interested in everything having to do with glazes, including luster glazes. A Parisian craftsman named Girard had covered a hard-paste porcelain lid (MNC 703) with a platinum ground glaze.[129] Sèvres had set a precedent in this regard by producing two *vases 'fuseau'* with platinum grounds as early as 1814.[130] Ten pieces of *faïence fine* (MNC 671) from the Utzschneider factory made with marbled paste or covered with a glossy black glaze were also added to the museum's collection.

The most idiosyncratic pieces at the 1819 exhibition were made by the prolific Boudon de Saint-Amans. Something of a ceramics polymath, at that time he was interested in the fabrication of sulphides, a technique with which he experimented at the Mont-Cenis crystal works near Creusot. Some of the results entered the museum, namely a glass quoit inset with a painting on porcelain imitating precious stones and several other pieces decorated with depictions of famous people (MNC 694, 8 pieces).

Nast's productions exemplified the highest standards of the Parisian factories. Brongniart singled out a white porcelain vase (MNC 688.1) with biscuit relief ornament.

Donations from the exhibitions were sometimes supplemented by purchases elsewhere to increase the collection of modern pieces. Concerned about the quality of the French products available to the public, Brongniart often made such purchases on the open market, sometimes buying pieces without ornament or with the simplest of decoration. A typical example is a cup (MNC 780) decorated with a gold fillet, acquired in 1822 from an itinerant salesman in the park at Saint-Cloud.

In 1821 Legros d'Anizy was employed at the Sarreguemines factory, where he experimented with gold glazes on *faïence fine*. He donated one of these to Sèvres: a baluster vase, or *vase 'Medici'* (MNC 770.1), entirely covered in gold.

The 1823 exhibition revealed the full creative genius of the ceramist François-Paul Utzschneider, who had developed a technique for giving fine stoneware the appearance of semiprecious stones and other materials. From his submissions Brongniart selected two inkwells (MNC 809), one of them imitating porphyry and the other petrified wood (fig. 9-5).

Although eventually glassware was well represented in the collection, Brongniart began to acquire it slowly. In 1819 the Chagot brothers, who were based in Creusot, exhibited a masterly pair of candelabra with sixteen glass shades,[131] but in 1823 Brongniart chose only a few crystal goblets (MNC 813) for the museum. He selected similar pieces (MNC 814) from those placed on display by Godart of Baccarat.

In 1824 Brongniart placed on exhibit at the museum the principal colors available for painting on hard-paste porcelain made by Mortelèque (MNC842), a Parisian chemist, as well as a plaque (MNC 843) bearing fired samples of the main colors used at Sèvres.

In 1826 Boudon de Saint-Amans was in Creil carrying out experiments in hopes of developing a fine stoneware "like that of the English." His success is evident in a variety of pieces (MNC 944.1); neoclassical in form, they are black with spare relief ornament.

Fouque of Toulouse is a small manufactory near Choisy and Creil, but nonetheless examples of its plates (MNC 994) with printed decoration over much of their surfaces, were selected for representation in the museum. Bureaux of Paris was similarly honored for his submissions made of an opaque porcelain called *faïence porcelaine* (MNC 997), a new variation of *faïence fine.* Brongniart was also interested in the porcelains made with pure alumina and silica by Guignet (MNC 1017 and 1018), whose factory was situated in Giez, near Aujon. Andot of Septvieilles donated eight terracotta pieces (MNC 981) modeled with the aid of a mechanical press.

The first milk-glass also entered the museum's collection in 1827 (MNC 966). These objects were selected from the many flower vases and jewelry boxes made of the material, some combining several colors, exhibited by the Bontemps factory in Choisy-le-Roi. Paste, artificial pearls, and imitation gemstones produced by Lançon of Septmoncel (Jura) and Bourguignon of Paris were also deemed worthy of the museum (MNC 1035 and 1036).

In 1828 a factory at Bercy on the outskirts of Paris donated several examples of their production. In addition to a set of crystal glasses of sturdy but elegant form, it presented a mantelpiece vase made to resemble red marbled stone (MNC 1070) as well as many decorative decanters and jewelry caskets of various colors. Of greater significance, however, the factory also sent the first pieces of imitation cut glass produced with a metal pressure mold (MNC 1069). In 1829 the Creil factory revealed an Asian influence in their production when they donated a cooler made of fine paste, of a yellow color called "Nankin," decorated with painted flowers in earth tones (MNC 1149.2).

Charles de Bourgoing, who was secretary of the French delegation to Saint Petersburg, registered a patent for the production of lithophanes in 1826 and worked to further their development at Montreuil-sous-Bois. In 1828 the Société d'Encouragement awarded him a bronze medal for the invention. Several of his efforts entered the museum the following year (MNC 1157).[132] He and Baron Alexis du Tremblay went into partnership in 1827, opening a factory at Rubelles, but production did not get underway until 1838 – 39.

In 1830 Brongniart became interested in molded glass decanters shaped like tortoises, bouquets of flowers, and even the Fontaine des Innocents in Paris (fig. 9-6). He acquired several examples (MNC 1317) directly from one "M. Blottière, *maître-faïencier* in Paris," who claimed to have originated the idea, but the pieces had been produced at the factory in Landel in 1830.

Fig. 9-6. Molded-glass flasks, ca. 1830; produced at the Landel glassworks. Representing (from left) a turtle, fountain, and bouquet of flowers, these were donated to the museum by a Paris faïence-maker named Blottière in 1830. (Sèvres, Musée national de céramique, MNC 1317)

Experiments conducted in 1817 by Saint-Amans at Sèvres led to the development of a new material: opaque porcelain. An improved version of *faïence fine,* it was made with nontranslucent kaolin paste. Possessed of the nontoxic qualities so enthusiastically endorsed by the Institut, it was soon adopted by other producers, and it triumphed at the 1834 exhibition. In addition to fine earthenware and stoneware, the Creil factory donated some specimens of *faïence fine* covered with transfer-printed "Chino-English" motifs (MNC 1667). The Sarreguemines factory again distinguished itself with stoneware of high quality, this time with colored paste decoration (MNC 1681).

In 1836 the Montereau factory experimented with the application of red pigments on opaque porcelain by means of transfer printing. Among these colors were a stannous chrome red glaze called "pink-color," a red prepared in the Sèvres laboratories by Malagutti. An "English" red provided in 1805 by the Tournai-based producer Bettignies, and another developed by Gratien Milliet, the director of Montereau, were also used. The museum received an example of each attempt (MNC 2002).

Additional innovations were introduced by master glassmakers, such as Bontemps of the Choisy-le-Roi works and Godart of Baccarat. They presented pieces with pressure-molded decoration resembling diamond cutting (MNC 1725). Some of the Baccarat pieces featured arabesque motifs in relief set against rough-grained grounds (MNC 1717). Seiler of the Saint-Louis glassworks presented an array of similar objects, some of which found a place in the museum's collection (MNC 1718). The imaginative work of Jacob Petit, a porcelain maker, was admired by Brongniart, and many bibelots produced by him also became part of Sèvres's collection (MNC 1589 and 1695).

Also in 1836 several examples of glasses produced by the baron

Fig. 9-7. Cup and saucer decorated with Egyptian motifs, ca. 1804; produced and donated by the KPM Manufactory, Berlin, in 1806. (Sèvres, Musée national de céramique, MNC 492-5)

de Klinglin in collaboration with the Sèvres painting-on-glass workshop (see chap. 7) entered the collection (MNC 2021); some of them were painted by Louis Robert, who headed the workshop from 1839 to 1854. Another glass (MNC 2722.6), this one with flat sides and made to resemble agate, was donated by Seiler of the Saint-Louis glassworks.

A professor named Chevreuse, who had previously taught chemistry at the school of artillery engineering in Metz, had established a factory in nearby Bordes for the production of tiles that looked like slate. In 1838 he proudly donated three samples, which had been hollowed in a way devised by him to prevent warpage, or "the buckling caused by firing." At that date, however, he was still having difficulty producing a uniform slate color economically.[133]

A porcelain maker named Halot, in an attempt to reduce production costs, began to use a decorative process developed by Noualhier whereby the ground color was brushed on the porcelain by hand before the high-temperature firing. To document his efforts, he donated several pieces, including a small brownish coffee cup with a faceted body (MNC 2519.3).

At the 1839 exhibition, the ceramist Utzschneider presented several objects of unusual sophistication. Brongniart succeeded in obtaining one of these baluster vases made of stoneware resembling jasper with inlaid decoration consisting of a reddish paste (MNC 2686.1). After it was fired, the piece had been polished on a lapidary lathe.[134] David Johnston, director of a newly established factory in Bordeaux, donated some imaginative stoneware designs made from paste of various colors, including a teapot in the shape of a beehive (MNC 2683.2). Discry, a Parisian porcelain maker, displayed pieces with blue decoration under immersion glazes that were greatly admired and were duly solicited for the collection (MNC 2700.5). Du Tremblay contributed several enamel wall tiles (MNC 2701) from the new Rubelles factory.which he had launched in partnership with Bourgoing.

The 1830s saw many technological advances in the field of ceramics production at Sèvres, and in the ensuing decade a new generation of manufacturers was able to survive on this remarkable inheritance often without pursuing comparable initiatives of its own. Especially noteworthy were the submissions of Bonnet of Apt, who produced *faïence fine* from a marbled paste that could be used for delicate relief work (MNC 3024, entered the collection in 1842). Ziegler donated a large number of stoneware pieces of Moorish and Gothic Revival inspiration in 1842, all produced in his factory in Voisinlieu.[135] In 1844 Creil presented objects made of a new ceramic material, a hard earthenware called *pétrocérame* (MNC 3325), and that same year Gosse sent cups "made of reinforced porcelain for use by café-keepers."[136]

Glassmakers continued to experiment with color in hopes of renewing their decorative vocabulary, looking to Venice for guidance. After the 1839 exhibition at the Louvre, a glass with a stem resembling a twisted cord, made by Bontemps, was accessioned by the museum. A year later Bontemps sent a water jug whose entire surface was covered with filigree work, and in 1843 Nocus and Bredghem of the Saint-Mandé glassworks donated a stemmed cup (MNC 3079) whose thin walls were also decorated with filigree. At the 1844 exhibition Bontemps exhibited a goblet made of millefiori (MNC 3555.1), and in 1846 Seiler of the Saint-Louis works donated another millefiori piece (MNC 3637). Baccarat followed suit by presenting an elegant ewer decorated with blue and white filigree (MNC 3727).

Exchanges with Foreign Manufactories. Brongniart had no intention of allowing France's borders to limit the museum's assembly of contemporary ceramic and glass production. From the beginning, he established working relationships with other European manufactories to facilitate exchanges. The cooperation of these establishments was contingent upon favorable political circumstances, but overall they proved extremely worthwhile, resulting in the museum's acquisition of some remarkable pieces. A spirit of scientific enquiry was to govern the exchanges. As in the Enquête des Préfets, the participants were asked to fill out a questionnaire prepared by Brongniart. The transactions involved both finished work and raw materials.

In December 1805 Brongniart submitted to the Vienna manufactory a set of twenty-six questions about their sources of kaolin, procedures for cleaning it, the grinding of feldspar, the preparation of clay for saggars, the wood fuel used, the composition of the pastes, glazes, and colors, techniques for making relief ornament in gold and other materials, and the problems usually encountered with painted and gilded decoration. He also requested drawings of kilns, samples of all colors in raw and fired states, and information about payroll management (he wanted to know whether they paid their workers by the day).[137]

Although some manufactories, such as Meissen, were not receptive to such invasive inquiry,[138] others, such as the manufactory at Vienna, responded cordially. To some extent, this may have been influenced by Brongniart's previous demonstration of good faith. In 1804 through chevalier Landriani, he had sent two samples of metallic oxide to Vienna for use in preparing a rose porcelain glaze.[139] Perhaps because of this, Matthias Niedermayer, director of the Vienna manufactory, obligingly answered Brongniart's questionnaire and, beginning in July 1806, sent two deliveries.[140] The first consisted of raw materials, namely clay samples, and the second contained twenty pieces of Vienna porcelain. He also complied with Brongniart's request for samples, sending enamels and metallic lusters used in the manufactory's workshops (MNC 470.20). The shipment also contained a painting on a porcelain plaque by Joseph Nigg (MNC 470.18) after a flower painting by Van Huysum, some small coffee cups (MNC 470.1 and 470.2) showing Middle Eastern influence, a few flawed blanks, and two cups and saucers, one with ultramarine grounds and silver decoration and the other with a new yellow-orange ground.[141] Sèvres reciprocated in 1808 with a delivery of sixteen pieces, among them a small vase with a glost-fired black ground and Chinese decoration, a cup with a green ground color that had a low luster, a soup cup on which all of Sèvres's available colors and gilding were systematically displayed, and several cups painted by Sèvres's best painters: Jacquotot, Drouet, and Swebach.[142] Some thirty years later, in 1838, Baumgartner, the director of the Vienna factory, sent more pieces and another set of samples of the colors and metallic lusters used there (MNC 2517).

In November 1805 Brongniart met Friedrich Philipp Rosenstiel, who was director of the Berlin manufactory from 1802 to 1832 and had come to Paris to present some vases being given to the empress Josephine by Luise, queen of Prussia.[143] In late December 1805 Brongniart prepared a few pieces for Rosenstiel in reciprocation for those that had been presented to Sèvres.[144] This was not the end of the exchange, however, for early in 1806 Rosenstiel sent a case containing fifteen pieces made in Berlin.[145] The delivery included several cups and saucers (MNC 492.2) painted to resemble pietra dura, a superb conical cup decorated with an Egyptian landscape set against an imitation mosaic ground, with a gilded interior (MNC 492.5; fig. 9-7), a cup and saucer with gold and silver decoration, several soft-paste pieces, and some examples of hygioceramics.[146]

In November 1808, thanks to the efforts of "M. Schwerin, member of the Central Council of Bavarian Mines," Brongniart received samples of raw materials and completed pieces from the manufactory in Nymphenburg.[147] Of the twenty-eight objects in this delivery, the most notable were a cup and saucer (MNC 486.9) decorated with baskets of flowers signed "Reis," a cup (MNC 486.7) with glost-fired black ground decorated with a gold frieze, several cups (MNC 486.11, 486.12, 486.13) bearing medallion portraits of members of the Bavarian royal family, some biscuit pieces and even a paperweight shaped like a sphinx and covered with a copper luster.

By contrast, Brongniart's requests were little appreciated by the Meissen porcelain manufactory. Annoyed by the terse reply from the manufactory, he wrote to the Intendant Général, observing that "the secret of porcelain amounts to nothing now that it is general knowledge."[148] He refused to admit defeat and rerouted his request through Steinhauer, the minister of Saxony. This strategy proved successful, and the eagerly awaited delivery arrived in early January 1809.[149] It included samples of kaolin and clay for saggars as well as a total of twenty-three pieces of glazed and biscuit porcelain, many of them dating to the late eighteenth century. Several of the cups (MNC 469.15) were decorated only with sprays of flowers or flowered wreaths, maximizing the effect produced by the brilliant white paste. A hot-chocolate cup featured a novel dark brown ground with a mosaic decoration, and two other chalice cups (MNC 469.16, 469.17) had handles resembling coiled snakes.

From the Fürstenberg manufactory, Brongniart received a delivery in 1807 consisting of several cups with glost-fired blue grounds and an impressive assortment of seventy-six biscuit busts of Greek, French, and German philosophers, Roman emperors, mythological heroes, and reigning European monarchs and emperors as well as Johann Winckelmann, Henri Le Léon, and Anton Mengs, among others. At the conclusion of the Treaty of Vienna (1814), the duchy of Brunswick sought reparation for the seizure of these goods.[150] When Captain Mahner, Brunswick's representative, came to Sèvres, Brongniart made a point of explaining to him the disinterested nature of the exchanges, but he also made it clear that he would readily surrender most of the busts, for in fact they had taught him nothing. In the end he retained eight of them.[151]

Initiating exchanges with Russia required much more effort and patience on Brongniart's part. In 1810 he had made known his intentions directly to Prince Alexei Kuratin when the latter visited the Sèvres manufactory, but nothing came of this. In 1824 Brongniart sent a detailed request to the administration of the imperial manufactory in Saint Petersburg and was sent some clay samples but nothing more.[152] In September 1830 the secretary of the French embassy to Russia, Charles de Bourgoing, sent Sèvres a few pieces from the Poskachina factory as well as some vases, teapots, cups, and white porcelain from the Saint Petersburg manufactory.[153] In 1837 Brongniart wrote directly to Baron Meyendorf, advisor to the Russian state, asking that he arrange for the delivery of some recent productions of the Saint Petersburg manufactory. Brongniart noted that during a visit to Potsdam he had seen some of its vases in a palace and been impressed by their high quality.[154] Nine objects from Saint Petersburg finally arrived in 1839, notably a vase (MNC 2815.1) with a glost-fired blue ground and gold decoration, a plate (MNC 2815.3) with a landscape painted by Pierre Stechetine after a composition by Moucheron as well as a gold frieze in relief on its rim, and an inkwell (MNC 2815.17) in the form of a shell and two pieces of coral. Brongniart's difficulties were not yet at an end, however, as he was severely reprimanded by the Intendant Général for having negotiated directly with Russia without going through appropriate channels. An official named de Wailly of the *intendant's* office chided him with the statement, "relations with the Russian court are so very delicate . . . ."[155]

Brongniart as Collector. Brongniart, as a mineralogist and the director of the preeminent porcelain manufactory, was very much at ease with the technological ferment of the first half of the nineteenth century. Wanting to investigate new processes and mechanical inventions that interested him first-hand, he became an avid European traveler, beginning with an 1802 trip to England. The fact that many directors of European porcelain-producing establishments, especially in Germany, were either also mineralogists or affiliated with the mining industry tended to work in his favor, making them more receptive to his requests for access, information, and samples.[156] Brongniart also attended scientific congresses, never forgetting the museum and always doing his best to gather suitable objects for the collection.

On these trips Brongniart made extensive records of everything that interested him. Paste-making materials, the number of pieces per firing, retail prices, the size of the staff needed for various fabrication processes were all duly noted. He also made sketches of tools, kilns, and innovations and was equally curious about everything pertaining to the history of the manufactories that he visited.

In 1812 Brongniart left for the German duchies and principalities. His primary purpose was to learn about firing processes used in Berlin — "very different from those at Sèvres" — as well as about kilns in Bohemia that ostensibly used less fuel.[157] At Meissen, thanks to the cooperation of its director, Count Camille Marcolini, Brongniart was able to visit the workshops and kilns.

In 1820 on a tour of Italy, Brongniart obtained a porcelain plate (MNC 730.1) decorated with a plum-tree branch, which had been produced at the Ginori factory in Doccia. He also brought back some fine earthenware from Vicenza and Le Nove. He was interested in soft-paste porcelain produced by the Cozzi factory in Venice, which had closed eight years earlier, and acquired a sample (MNC 764).

In 1824 Berzelius, the secretary of the Academy of Sciences in Stockholm, invited Brongniart to Sweden.[158] While en route he visited the royal manufactory in Copenhagen, where he selected fourteen pieces of hard-paste porcelain (MNC 834), mostly decorated with twigs painted in blue underglaze colors. In Denmark he obtained some black pottery (MNC 832) given a high luster by burnishing and some glazed pottery (MNC 833) from the island of Bornholm. At the Rörstrand factory in Sweden, he chose fourteen pieces of fine earthenware exemplifying the range of ground colors used there. It was probably also in Sweden that he found eight pieces of stoneware (MNC 872) identified as having been produced in "Helsinborg in Scania" as well as three small refractory pottery crucibles (MNC 873) intended for use by goldsmiths.

Invited to a "gathering of all the scientists in Germany" scheduled to begin in Bonn on September 16, 1835, Brongniart planned to visit Strasbourg, Mayence, and Stuttgart as well as to make a brief quick trip to Holland.[159] He also took advantage of the opportunity to visit large-scale operations like those of Boch-Buschmann in Mettlach and Utzschneider in Sarreguemines (Lorraine). In all likelihood, it was this stopover at Sarrequemines that prompted Utzschneider to donate to the museum another precious Medici form vase (MNC 1945.2) made from paste resembling granite that had been cut and polished on a lapidary lathe as well as a pair of candelabra torcheres (MNC 1936.13) entirely covered with gold luster. The Boch-Buschmann firm was generous as well, adding to the collection a twenty-piece creamware service with transfer-printed decoration (MNC 1941).

Brongniart made many purchases in Frankfurt and Bonn, especially Bohemian glassware, whose rich colors were the envy of French producers. A cordial meeting with a man named Steigerwald, the brother of the director of the Hayda glassworks in Bohemia,[160] resulted in another donation of Bohemian glass. A purplish red champagne glass (MNC 1982.1), a chalice glass (MNC 1922.9) in a delicate shade of rose, and an amethyst-colored decanter (MNC 1982.6) were sent to Sèvres, along with several trays (MNC 1978) decorated with a variety of cut patterns.

While in Frankfurt, he acquired a plate (MNC 1969) with the ridged decoration typical of recent Meissen work. In Bonn, he found a teacup (MNC 1970) produced at the Gotha factory decorated with a view of Bonn within a reserve as well as a cup and saucer (MNC 1972.5) from Ravenstein decorated with purple "Chinese" motifs.

In 1836 Brongniart decided to visit London and Staffordshire with return trips through Berlin, Dresden, Bohemia, and Bavaria.[161] On arriving in London, he was received at the Royal Society and obtained letters of recommendation from many of its scientist members prior to visiting the Staffordshire ceramic factories. He also stopped at "most of the porcelain, earthenware, and stoneware shops" in the capital "to get an idea of the character of the products." Accompanied by the Reverend W. Buckland, a professor of mineralogy and geology, he went to examine the Worcester porcelain factory. Thomas Grainger gave him some samples of raw materials used in his factory, which Brongniart found to be particularly interesting because they confirmed the English use of crushed bone in their paste. En route to Birmingham he took a side trip to Stonebridge to see its stoneware factory. In Derby, at the Wood factory in Burslem, he was amazed by the large quantities of ware produced.[162] Back in London, he made several purchases intended for the collection: six Wedgwood creamware plates (MNC 2139.7), a Davenport plate (MNC 2151) with an "Indian decoration in green and pink-colour," and several Davenport cut crystal glasses (MNC 2260 and 2259), which were sometimes tinted.

Returning to the Continent, Brongniart proceeded to the Fürstenberg factory to examine recent advances made there. From there he traveled to Berlin, where, guided by von Humboldt and warmly received by Christoph Georg Frick, director of the Royal Porcelain Manufactory, he made a large selection of porcelain for the museum: forty-eight pieces, including tableware — notably a saucer with stamped heart motifs against a gray glaze-fired ground — as well as laboratory equipment and even some tobacco pipes. He also made a point of visiting a factory near Berlin that produced hygioceramics.[163]

The next stop on Brongniart's itinerary was Meissen, where he met with Kühn, the director of the manufactory and also a mining engineer. There he was able to examine the new jigging machines for the shaping of plates.[164]

In Dresden he was accompanied by Klemm, the curator, through the Palais Japonais, and he paid an extended visit to the Messerschmidt pottery and stove factory. He acquired a few pieces of utilitarian pottery made by local craftsmen near Pirna.[165] In Silesia he made a stop at the Carlstahl factory, where he obtained several cut glass goblets as well as a test tube (MNC 2175.1) about 19 3/4 inches high (50 cm).

In the environs of Carlsbad he found many porcelain and earthenware factories. The former were of special interest because they produced porcelain without using feldspar.[166] In Elbogen he chose to visit the factory run by the Haïdinger brothers, where he obtained several pieces, notably a small deep-blue coffee cup (MNC 2249.16). While in Hammer he visited the factory operated by Fischer,[167] a fellow mineralogist and geologist, and acquired a small octagonal tray (MNC 2250.5) for playing Boston, a card game that was popular at the time.

In Ratisbonne, he selected for the museum a hot-chocolate cup (MNC 2259.19) on three claw feet and decorated with a view of the principal church of the city from the Schwerdtner factory.

He remained longer in Munich, where he toured the Nymphenburg porcelain factory accompanied by Schmitz. He managed to obtain samples of its raw materials,[168] but the high point of the visit was the local porcelain, earthenware, and pottery fair. In a letter to Sèvres, he noted that ceramic production was "often quite bizarre in this part of Germany," continuing with manifest satisfaction: "you can imagine what a harvest I gathered."[169]

Scientists as Collectors. These acquisitions were not sufficient to fill the museum's showcases, and they certainly did not quench Brongniart's curiosity. He was always seeking individuals who shared his interests, and he found many natural allies among those who taught the sciences. Mieg, a professor of chemistry and physics in Madrid, for example, was especially energetic on Sèvres's behalf. He collected a considerable number of objects from all over Spain for the museum. In addition to earthenware and pottery from Valencia, Alcora, and Talavera de la Reyna, he sent examples of glazed pottery (MNC 1091 – 1113) from Andalucia and Estramadura, and he also arranged for the royal manufactory at Moncloa to deliver some pieces (MNC 1116 and 1118), which were produced, "like opaque French porcelain," with "kaolin clay from Galapagar." In 1834 Wöhler, a professor of chemistry in Kassel, arranged for the delivery of samples of local ceramics production, including terracotta architectural ornaments (MNC 1743).

Brongniart solicited the aid of a professor of chemistry named Walter, who was in Cracow, to obtain examples from that area of eastern Europe, which was not yet represented in the collection. In 1841 Walter sent thirty-four pieces of earthenware, ordinary pottery, and glassware that he had obtained in Cieszyn, Lublin, Frywald, and many other localities.[170] From Krasnoyarsk in 1844, a professor of chemistry named Hann, at the Polytechnic School in Warsaw, sent a goblet (MNC 3399) made of dark blue glass and two small glass burettes (MNC 3400) for applying oil.

The United States. In 1826 Brongniart received a delivery of materials from the United States, sent by Chanou. This superb gift included "white clay suitable for the fabrication of saggars found at Cape Hope in Massachusetts, clay for the fabrication of stoneware from South Amboy, New Jersey, materials for the production of earthenware from Burlington County, New Jersey, clay for ordinary pottery from Chester, Pennsylvania, etc."[171] Also included were some porcelain blanks (MNC 911) made in New York with local materials by Ducasse and Chanou himself. To complete this part of the museum's collection, Brongniart appealed to a former student named Ducatel, who had studied the basics of mineralogy at the Collège Duplessis.[172] In 1836 Ducatel, who was by then teaching chemistry in Baltimore, sent his former professor six cases overflowing with raw materials and finished pieces.

The first case contained red bricks made with a presser; Ducatel apologized for having been unable to obtain the design of the machine, known as "Willard's Patent Brick Presser." The second case contained refractory bricks that, by his report, were "considered superior to the English bricks from Stourbridge." The third case contained various stoneware articles, such as a gallon jar, a quart jar, and a cider jug. The fourth case was completely filled by a large stoneware cask intended for use in taverns (capacity 43 gallons). The fifth case contained chamber pots, flower vases, coffee pots, jugs of various kinds, and some hospital bedpans. The sixth case contained window glass; all attempts to produce glassware and crystal in Baltimore, however, had failed.[173]

In 1836, Brongniart sent a letter to a professor of chemistry named Silliman at Yale University, describing his goals for the Sèvres museum and asking him to collect whatever objects he could for the collection and to encourage others to do the same. Silliman decided that the most efficient way to handle Brongniart's request would be to publish excerpts from his letter; these appeared in the October issue of *The American Journal*.[174] As for Silliman himself, he sent some examples of hard-paste porcelain made in Philadelphia (MNC 2422).

In a letter dated January 6, 1837 to a mineralogist named Keating in Philadelphia, Brongniart hinted at a certain resignation and moderated his demands. Opting for realism in the face of the vastness of the American territory, he said he would content himself with information about "the most notable [ceramics factories] in the northern and southern United States."[175]

Historical Pieces

For a quarter of a century the growing collection of the Sèvres museum corresponded quite closely to the program described by Brongniart in his letter of 10 thermidor year 9 (July 30, 1802) to the *ministre de l'intérieur*.[176] The two principal elements of the collection were, at that early date, an ensemble of antique vases and another of far eastern productions. Its originality resided in its presentation of modern porcelain of prestigious provenance but also, and above all, in that of ordinary pottery.

During the time of Brongniart's early education, neoclassicism had been the dominant aesthetic expression and the rococo had become outdated. This background later may have made him insensitive to the charms of the rococo and often indifferent to the qualities of earlier European productions. Historical pieces, however, gradually entered the collection, not on the basis of their various aesthetic merit but rather as evidence of the evolution of technical processes.

Brongniart's acquisition policies as well echoed tendencies then pervasive in French culture. The development of the Louvre's collection after the end of the Empire indicates a renewal of interest in indigenous production. In 1824 the first Durand collection was acquired by the Louvre in its entirety for the sum of 480,000 francs. It consisted of many ancient pieces; the second installment of the sale consisted of some 97 pieces of Italian earthenware, 114 objects attributed to Bernard Palissy, some Limoges enamels, and some stained-glass windows.[177]

In 1828 Charles X authorized the Louvre to acquire the collection of the painter Pierre Révoil, which consisted largely of medieval and Renaissance artifacts. In addition to plates and other glazed pieces attributed to Palissy, it also boasted some examples of the richly inlaid "Henri II" earthenware that significantly enriched the museum's collection.[178] In the nineteenth century there was a tendency to consider any French enameled platter or other pottery artifact with relief elements to be products of the workshop of Bernard Palissy. Works by him, or in the style associated with him, were quite popular at the time, largely due to the continuing interest in his writings.

As for what was then known as "Henri II" earthenware (now attributed to Saint-Porchaire), its origins were unknown, a fact

Fig. 9-8. Platter in shell form, Delftware, 17th century. This was acquired as part of an exchange with a dealer named Toppi on May 27, 1830. (Sèvres, Musée national de céramique, MNC 1266.

that, coupled with its manifest quality, surrounded it with an intriguing aura of mystery. It was both fragile and rare,[179] which meant that the few extant copies were especially coveted by collectors. As early as 1812, Héricart de Thury, an inspector of mines and member of the Académie Royale des Sciences, donated a Limoge enamel plate painted by Suzanne Court (MNC 348).

At the Denon sale of 1827 Brongniart acquired a large oval platter (MNC 965.1) by Bernard Palissy decorated with fish and reptiles.[180] In 1829 he made two purchases from the dealer Leblanc: a superb Niderviller platter (MNC 1126) bearing the factory's mark on the bottom and decorated with a composition of shepherds in a rustic landscape, and a large Flemish beaker (MNC 1128) decorated with lion heads which he thought to be of Venetian origin.

The provenance of six pieces of majolica (MNC 738 – 743) that entered the collection in 1820 is not clearly documented, but it seems likely that they were obtained by Brongniart during a trip to Italy. Consisting of four plates, a bowl, and a salt cellar entirely covered with figural decoration, they exemplify the virtuosic *istoriato* pottery for which Urbino was famous.

The first piece of soft-paste porcelain to enter the collection (MNC 651), a figurine of a Chinese man in a long polychrome robe, was acquired in 1812 as a donation from Brongniart's mother. It was produced at the Mennecy factory, but the inventory attributed it to Saint-Cloud. In 1824 a former painter at the manufactory named Caron, who was the son of a potter at the Saint-Cloud factory, donated two objects produced at Saint-Cloud: a large earthenware jug (MNC 867) decorated with a blue floral motif and a small soft-paste cup and saucer (MNC 868) decorated with a lambrequin decoration.

Exchanges between 1829 and 1833

Brongniart significantly enlarged the collection's historical holdings through exchanges made with four dealers: Hairon, Vachée, Collot, and Toppi. Negotiated between 1829 and 1833, these acquisitions included ancient pottery, Chinese pieces, and some Nevers plates thought to be of Persian origin. They were obtained in exchange for pieces of eighteenth-century Sèvres soft-paste porcelain that were duplicates or, more often, were flawed.[181] Brongniart obtained several other pieces—notably a round Palissy platter, a Limoges enamel cup, and an Etruscan sarcophagus—at some cost to himself, ceding in exchange twelve white plates and two fruit bowls from his personal service as well as two small rectangular trays from his office. The same agreement called for the delivery of 400 round lids from the manufactory's inventory.[182]

Transactions effected in 1829 with Vachée[183] resulted in the acquisition of an albarello (MNC 1183; exchange of September 23, 1829) decorated with a man's profile made by Masseot Abaquesne as well as a Nevers flask (MNC 1167, exchange of August 4, 1829) with grips shaped like ibexes and decorated with figures on two sides. Two Delft plates with characteristic cobalt blue figures (MNC 1193, exchange of September 23, 1829) also entered the collection, preceded by a mother and child figure (MNC 1165, exchange of August 4, 1829) from the Avon factory. An exchange with Hairon brought to the collection a small German bottle (MNC 1169, exchange of August 12, 1829) of white glass decorated with cobblers's attributes.[184]

Between 1830 and 1833 several exchanges negotiated with Toppi resulted in various acquisitions[185]: a remarkable Delft tray (MNC 1266, exchange of May 27, 1830) shaped like a shell (fig. 9-8), a large lobed platter (MNC 1379, exchange of October 11, 1831; fig. 9-9), from Rouen decorated with cornucopias, and a wine cooler (MNC 1477 exchange of July 9, 1832) decorated with Chinese fishermen from Strasbourg. The most significant gains for the museum, however, were in the domain of eighteenth-century French porcelain. These included a small wine cooler (MNC 1278, exchange of June 15, 1830) decorated with polychrome bouquets from the Chantilly factory, another wine cooler (MNC 1303, exchange of June 15, 1830) with flowering branches in relief from Saint-Cloud, and a small Chantilly spitoon (MNC 1416, exchange of March 15, 1832; fig. 9-10) decorated with dragon motifs.

As for the exchange with Collot, it resulted in the acquisition of the museum's first Moustiers platter (MNC 1524). This piece was decorated with a tiger hunt after a composition by Antonio Tempesta.

Subsequent Acquisitions

Majolica. Italian majolica was much admired in this period; it was the first earthenware to be represented in the collection, and Brongniart continued to acquire it throughout his tenure. When traveling, he did not content himself with inspecting factories and

Fig. 9-9. Platter, eighteenth century, Rouen; earthenware. This was acquired in the Toppi exchange of October 11, 1831. (Sèvres, Musée national de céramique, M.N.C. 1379)

Fig. 9-10. Spittoon, soft-paste porcelain, eighteenth century, Chantilly; part of the Toppi exchange of March 15, 1832. (Sèvres, Musée national de céramique, MNC 1416)

acquiring contemporary pieces but also sought to obtain older objects from dealers at reasonable prices. In Nuremberg, for example, he bought six pieces (MNC 2109 – 2112 and MNC 2132); one was a plate made in the Urbino workshops and the others were Faenza work with *a berettino* or *a compendiario* decoration. At an auction held in 1837, he acquired five pieces (MNC 2470) decorated in the luster technique produced at the Gubbio and Deruta workshops, which were previously unrepresented in the collection. One of these (2470.1) bore the mark of Maestro Giorgio on the bottom.[186] In 1838 at another auction, he acquired a gadrooned bowl (MNC 2489) with a *quartieri* ornament whose well was decorated with an image of Saint Sebastian as well as a large Castelli platter (MNC 2487) decorated with a battle scene. This factory was to be well represented in the collection thanks to a donation made in 1840 by the duc de Luynes. Consisting of twelve pieces for domestic use (MNC 2905 and 2906), such as cups and a sugar bowl, as well as ten plaques, it offered a representative sample of Castelli's eighteenth-century production. Lucca della Robbia was as celebrated and well known in nineteenth-century France as Bernard Palissy. A tabernacle (MNC 3108) made by him was acquired for the museum in 1843 at the Didier-Petit sale.

Delft Wares. Delft earthenware was absent from the collection prior to the Vachée exchanges of 1829. During his 1835 trip to Holland Brongniart hoped to obtain additional pieces of high quality, but at prices lower than those current in France.[187] To his great surprise, the best old pieces were to be had not in Delft but in The Hague. He acquired twelve objects in all, notably an earthenware vase (MNC 1931.7) decorated with peonies in the style of *famille rose*, a water pot (MNC 1931.8) completely covered with landscape motifs, and a box (MNC 1931.9) shaped like a bunch of grapes. The following year in Nuremberg he added to the collection a gadrooned teapot (MNC 2131) decorated with a large floral motif.

German Wares. It was some time before German earthenware was adequately represented in the collection. Brongniart's first interest was fine German stoneware. In 1829 he acquired two jugs (MNC 1055 and 1056) from Leblanc, one of which featured characteristic relief ornament heightened in violet. In Nuremberg, many dealers sold wares in the public squares, and there Brongniart purchased four glazed stove tiles for much less than he would have had to pay in Paris.[188] He also found a jug (MNC 2119) decorated with an openwork star (illustrated in the *Description méthodique du musée céramique*)[189] and a draining plate (MNC 2123) bearing the mark of Höchst on the bottom.

English Wares. Boudon de Saint-Amans donated a quantity of contemporary English creamware and stoneware to the museum which was also indebted to him for several earlier English pieces. In 1820 he presented a small sulphur-yellow cup (MNC 760) from Burslem decorated with a printed quatrain, and in 1830 a Staffordshire creamware fruit bowl (MNC 1050) decorated with a cross-bar openwork pattern. That same year he also donated a coffee cup (MNC 1243) dating from the first half of the eighteenth century decorated with reliefs of strawberries and cabbage leaves. Brongniart's trips abroad proved crucial in this domain. In The Hague he found several old pieces, notably a ravishing marbled teapot (MNC 2001; fig. 9-11) in the form of a shell. In 1836 he was surprised to learn that "old" Wood had established a museum. From this collection he obtained a Wedgwood creamware plaque (MNC 2136) decorated with a relief depicting a stork drinking at a fountain, as well as a coffee pot (MNC 2138) from the Daniel Bold factory decorated with gilded in-glaze letters.[190] In London Brongniart purchased some early English soft-paste porcelain, including an oval Chelsea goblet (MNC 2174.3) decorated with floral bouquets in the style of Meissen. Albert Way, secretary of the London Society of Antiquarians, expanded this part of the collection in 1843 and 1844, when he donated several pieces of soft-paste porcelain from Chelsea and Worcester (MNC 3212, 3213, 3457 – 3459).

Spanish Wares. The Carlist Wars caused havoc in Spain. Church properties as well as countless art objects were confiscated by the government and sold at auction. Between 1835 and 1837 Baron Taylor was able to take advantage of these circumstances. He was in charge of assembling a collection of Spanish paintings for Louis-Philippe, and he also obtained objects for Sèvres. These included floor tiles from such prestigious sites as the Alcazar Palace in Toledo (MNC 2382) and the Monastery of San Francesco in Barcelona (MNC 2381), which was slated for demolition. The large Hispano-Moresque platters so admired by Brongniart, however, were not represented in the museum's collection until 1843, when two examples were acquired at the Didier Petit sale. One bore the emblem of Blanche of Navarre (MNC 3107.1) and the other that of Castille (3107.2).

French Wares. Many items attributed to Bernard Palissy figured in the dealer exchange agreements of 1829 – 33. Brongniart regarded such attributions with circumspection. A reading of Palissy's writings had alerted him to the discrepancy between the reality and the myth of the famous potter's achievement, and in the *Traité des arts céramiques* Brongniart went so far as to maintain that he had learned nothing about pottery-making and enamel technique from these texts.[191]

In 1843 he acquired a Palissy platter (MNC 3145) from the antiquarian Beurdeley for the sum of 500 francs, but the following year he refused a similar piece on the grounds that it was not by Palissy.[192]

The high prices of "Henri II" ware had long placed it out of Brongniart's reach. In 1837, however, an exchange agreement with the seasoned collector Préaux netted the museum two such pieces, a basin cup (MNC 2447.1) with the pendant necklace of the Order of the Holy-Spirit depicted on its interior as well as a broken lid (2447.2).

With respect to Rouen earthenware, Brongniart had the extraordinary luck to discover a fountain and matching basin with lambrequin decoration (MNC 1564) in a shop in Gisors, in Normandy; he acquired it for twelve francs. In 1837 he visited the factory of Amédée Lambert, on which occasion the producer gave him four pieces of old Rouen pottery (MNC 2437): an octagonal wine cooler with lambrequin ornament (subsequently determined to be from Lille), a tray with a similar decoration, a patronymic jug, and a plate decorated with polychrome flowers. That same year, Garneray, the former director of the museum in Rouen, sold Brongniart thirteen pieces made in that center of pottery production for forty-six francs. Many were decorated with the cornucopias typical of such wares, but they also included a large segmented vase (again, subsequently determined to be from Lille), two plates, and a large platter (MNC 2469) decorated with blue lambrequins highlighted in iron red. It was Riocreux who, in 1843, donated the first piece of blue Rouen ware (MNC 3130), described by him as "violet earthenware by Louis Poterat."[193]

In 1832 Brongniart acquired from the print dealer Valardi a yellow and green glazed plate (MNC 1413) from the Beauvais region with an engraved decoration and bearing an inscription along the rim. This important center of pottery production came to be well represented in the collection thanks to numerous donations from Jacques Boucher de Crève-coeur de Perthes, the father of French archaeology. In the course of excavating around Abbeville he discovered Stone Age remains as well as later pottery artifacts, including not only shards of bottles and other objects but a complete blue stoneware flask (MNC 3090) with fleurs-de-lis motifs, discovered in the bed of the Somme in 1835.

It was perhaps thanks to a confusion with Nevers pottery that Saint Jean du Désert work first entered the museum's collection. At the Didier-Petit sale, Brogniart acquired a superb large circular platter (MNC 3108) whose entire surface was covered with a battle scene executed in blue cameo.

Sèvres Porcelain. Sèvres's own production was incorporated into the collection rather late in Brongniart's life. Brongniart had all of the manufactory's previously produced molds and models at his disposition, but the public's antipathy to its earlier productions may have caused reservations about placing them on display.[194] A cup and saucer (MNC 698) dating from 1787 entered the collection in 1819, but it was a special case. The pieces were decorated with neoclassical motifs of arcades, incense burners, and a cantharus lamp. In 1823 Brongniart exhibited two cups called *coupes 'Jasmin'* (MNC 819) with gold and platinum decoration dating from 1814, and a year later a teacup (MNC 839) with a red-orange ground was also put on display. In 1826 a milk jug (MNC 961.3) dating from 1804 with glost-fired blue ground and silver decoration was inscribed in the inventory, where it is described as an "historical specimen illustrating the use of various metals in porcelain decoration."[195]

Fig. 9-11. Teapot, marbled earthenware, eighteenth century, England; purchased by Brongniart at The Hague in 1835. (Sèvres, Musée national de céramique, MNC. 2001)

It was not until 1835, therefore, that a substantial number of Sèvres pieces entered the collection, beginning with fifty-four hard-paste pieces (MNC 1787) characterized in the inventory as a "sample set of historical shape and decorations."[196] Even these, however, were only from the early years of Brongniart's tenure; they had been selected from various Sèvres table services dating from 1804 or later. Some of them had remained in the manufactory's possession because of slight flaws that had rendered them unsuitable for delivery.

Most generously represented was the *service 'Marli d'Or'*, which had been begun in 1805 and remained in production into the Restauration. The painters who had worked on it had since become widely popular: they included Nicolas-Antoine Taunay, Piat-Joseph Sauvage, Martin Drölling, Caron, and J.-F. Robert. In contrast, Brongniart could display only three unfinished pieces from the *service 'Olympique'*, a single plate from the first *service 'Egyptien'*, painted in 1806 by Josse François Joseph Swebach, and another plate from the second *service 'Egyptien'*, also painted by Swebach in 1810. There were similarly modest holdings in other services as well. The manufactory had kept only three plates from the *service 'Iconographique Grec'*, including one decorated with a profile of

Fig. 9-12. Plate from the *service 'Iconographique Grec',* hard-paste porcelain, 1813, Sèvres. The profile of Venus was painted by Degault. One of the first Sèvres pieces to enter the museum collection, it was inventoried in 1835. (Sèvres, Musée national de céramique, MNC 1809)

Fig. 9-13. Bowl, eighteenth century; soft-paste porcelain; produced by the Sèvres manufactory when it was located at Vincennes. It is decorated with a view of the Château de Vincennes, perhaps showing the side in which the original pottery was located. This piece was donated by a dealer named Beurdeley in 1846. (Sèvres, Musée national de céramique, MNC 3657)

Venus by Degault (fig. 9-12), four plates from the *service 'de l'Empereur'* and a single plate, painted by Bouillat in 1808, from the *service 'Vues d'Italie'.*

Between 1810 and 1813 Béranger decorated a scroll vase with a superb composition depicting the arrival in Paris of the many Italian art treasures seized by the French in the wake of Napoleon's victorious campaign. This showpiece had not found a buyer prior to the emperor's fall from power, which meant that it remained in the manufactory's possession. It, too, entered the museum inventory in the 1830s (MNC 1823). Despite its quality, it could not be displayed until the political passions associated with the Italian campaign had cooled. In fact, Brongniart had barely saved it from destruction after the installation of the Restauration government.

At about the same time Brongniart also placed on exhibit a figure of Bacchus (MNC 1830) holding a bunch of grapes. This was among the earliest pieces made at the manufactory with kaolin from the deposits in Saint-Yrieix near Limoges, the first source of this crucial ingredient of hard paste to be discovered within French borders.

Perhaps the most significant development of 1835 was Brongniart's long-delayed decision to exhibit soft-paste porcelain. Unfortunately, by this time the manufactory's holdings had been severely depleted by exchanges and auctions. What remained were primarily pieces dating from between 1770 and 1790. Many were flawed blanks, such as a glass cooler (MNC 1854) from the service made for Catherine II of Russia in 1778. All that remained from the Vincennes years were three plates (MNC 1870 – 1872) in the Saxon style decorated with motifs in relief, a coffee cup (MNC 1878) with a "wolf's-teeth" decoration, and a few of the polychrome floral bouquets (MNC 1895) that had been instrumental in establishing the manufactory's reputation.

Having made the decision to include this work in the museum, however, Brongniart began adding to this part of the collection. A plate from the *service 'des Arts Industriels'* (MNC 2011), decorated with a view of the old mill, was placed on view in 1836 and was joined four years later by two more plates (2872.1 and 2872.2) from the same service, featuring views of the sculpture and painting workshops. In 1838 Espine donated a small Sèvres pommade jar dating from 1760 (MNC 2593). Brongniart, in his letter acknowledging the gift, expressed regret about having ostracized such pieces for so long, stating that if he had acted otherwise "this patriarchal part of our museum would not be so impoverished."[197]

In 1846 the antiquarian Beurdeley donated a Vincennes bowl (MNC 3675; fig. 9-13). In a letter sent with his gift, he apologized for its modesty but noted that it had a certain interest because it was painted with "the château de Vincennes, probably the side on which the manufactory was located."[198]

The Exchange with Dresden. As early as 1830, in a letter to the vicomte de La Rochefoucauld outlining a travel itinerary, Brongniart wrote: "I would like above all to see once again in Dresden the famous Japanese Palace in which an immense collection [of porcelain] has long been assembled."[199] Brongniart had been obliged to return to Paris soon after his departure because of the outbreak of 1830 revolution. It was not until 1835 and 1836 that these travel plans were ultimately realized. His hopes for Dresden were more than met. "I was sure I would find in this residence . . .

all the elements of a history of European porcelain . . . . I spent a great deal of time studying this collection group by group."[200] Brongniart even asked Lindenau, president of the Council of Saxony, to authorize Klemm, the curator of the Japonais Palais, to donate a group of duplicates in the collection to Sèvres. His request was well received, at least initially, and an exchange was negotiated. Six large animal figures from the Palais Japonais were set aside for the Sèvres collection, including a peacock, rhinocerous, bear, pelican, and the celebrated chimera (MNC 2274.35; fig. 9-14).[201] Also pledged were ten early pieces of Böttger stoneware. Some had unblemished reddish brown surfaces decorated with pressed relief ornament while others had been polished on a lapidary lathe or covered with a brown lacquer glaze decorated with gold, and still others featured engraved decoration (MNC 2272). A small seated Chinese magus (MNC 2272.1; fig. 9-15) was also donated. This remarkable assemblage was to be completed by forty-one more pieces, including thirty-three porcelains from Meissen with Korean decoration dating from 1720 – 30 (MNC 2274), which were to be sent after Brongniart's departure.

Fig. 9-14. Chimera, produced at Meissen, 1731–32; porcelain. This was one of the duplicates of pieces in the collection of the Palais Japonais, Dresden, given to Sèvres in an exchange negotiated by Brongniart in 1836. (Sèvres, Musée national de céramique, MNC 2274-35)

Fig. 9-15. Chinese magus 1713; stoneware; made by Böttger. The Sèvres museum acquired this piece in 1836 as part of an exchange with the Dresden museum. (Sèvres, Musée national de céramique, MNC 2272-1)

Before the exchange could be completed, however, there was a diplomatic dispute over the contents. The Saxon government decided to withhold delivery until the reciprocal French gift was safely in their hands. More importantly, because they estimated the total value of the pieces being ceded to Sèvres at 4,000 francs, they insisted on French objects of comparable overall value. Brongniart was quite annoyed by these developments and wrote, not entirely in good faith: "I do not know how they arrived at such a value, given that the things are mostly defaced and flawed."[202]

It proved difficult to assemble objects produced at Sèvres worth such a figure with the warehouses virtually bare. To make up the difference Brongniart turned to the manufactory's holdings in ancient pottery, ceding fifteen pieces from the former Denon collection, a vase from the island of Milo, two Etruscan pieces from Volterra, and two small vases sent from Bordeaux by Jouannet. He also sent five vases from Tchanakale in Smyrna and even some stoneware jars, a jug, and a coffee pot from Baltimore.[203] This assortment was still insufficient, however, and he acquired pieces of opaque porcelain from Montereau, Creil, and Choisy and had some Chinese reticulated pieces made expressly at Sèvres for the delivery.[204] He also located a soft-paste soup tureen and stand produced at Sèvres in 1795 as well as a wine cooler dating from 1798. The group was completed by an imperial wash basin with gold frieze from 1813, a wash bowl from 1815, several pieces of tableware in Etruscan form with gadrooned decorations, a richly embellished coffee pot from the *déjeuner 'François I'*, two plates from the *service 'Marli d'Or'* painted by Schilt and Jacobber, and a plate with shell ornaments painted by Philippine.[205]

The Museum and the *Traité des arts céramiques*

The character of the museum was inseparable from Brongniart's other great project, his treatise on ceramics, the *Traité des arts céramiques.* Influenced by the example of Linnaeus in the realm of botany, Brongniart set out to apply a taxonomic approach to the ceramic arts. In 1830 he informed La Rochefoucauld that he had already drawn up a plan for the work.[206] All the museum's resources were brought to bear on its publication, as was the information obtained through correspondence and during his many travels. This data made it possible for Brongniart to fill many of the lacunae in earlier texts dealing with the subject. As seen, Chardin's publication of 1711 was full of misinformation that Brongniart had difficulty deciphering, and Passeri's book on majolica (1775) was nothing but a paean to the achievements of Pesaro's craftsmen.[207] Brongniart, by contrast, undertook a rigorous classification of ceramics based on a careful examination of the various materials used in their production. No serious history of the ceramic arts could be undertaken until such a system had been developed. Through the close study of individual artifacts assembled in one place one could determine whether a potter's wheel had been used, and a careful analysis of glazes and other surface treatments would serve, through comparison, as a basis for postulating the communication of ceramics techniques from people to people. The publication bearing the fruit of all this research and reflection, consisting of two volumes of text and an additional volume of plates, appeared in 1844.

The next year, a companion work entitled *Description méthodique du musée céramique,* a catalogue of the museum's collection, was published. It had been written with Denis-Désiré Riocreux and adhered to the classification system developed in the treatise, proposing short but concise descriptions by Riocreux of each piece in the collection.

The huge step forward effected by these two works becomes clear when they are compared with publications only slightly earlier in date. One of these, the catalogue of the royal collection in Dresden, written by Klemm and published in 1834, surveys ceramics production from the ancient Egyptians to the contemporary period in a mere sixty-six pages and then describes the museum's holdings on a room-by-room basis.[208] Two years later, De Witte, in his sale catalogue of the Durand collection, decided to follow an iconographic classification according to the subjects depicted on the pieces: mythological, heroic, mystical, civilian, and so on.[209]

Brongniart and Riocreux's *Description méthodique du musée céramique* is vastly different both in scope and approach. In 454 pages of text they analyze the entirety of the museum's collection on the basis of Brongniart's new taxonomic classification system and provide a careful listing of all the marks and signatures found on the pieces (compiled by Riocreux). This was the first time any such compendium had been attempted. The accompanying volume of plates contains fifty-five devoted to ceramic and vitreous productions dating from antiquity to the time of publication, thirteen more plates to Sèvres pieces dating from between 1830 and 1845, and an additional ten plates of the manufactory's glass-painting workshop.

Together, these publications — the *Traité des arts céramique* and *Description méthodique du musée céramique* — represent the culmination of a life devoted to the ceramic arts. During his tenure at Sèvres, Brongniart strove to initiate advances in current production techniques and, more importantly, to improve the understanding of ceramic materials and their historical evolution. It had always been Brongniart's intention to assemble a collection of pieces of all kinds, dating from all periods, that were significant "from a technical point of view." His fundamental priorities were never aesthetic: on the contrary, he sought to bring together simple, unprepossessing pieces that offered evidence about the development of fabrication techniques. His determination to encompass the full range of ceramics production made it possible for the Sèvres museum to present a surprisingly eclectic collection at a very early date. With only limited means at his disposal, Brongniart succeeded in assembling a remarkable array of artifacts tracing the medium's historical development. To a considerable degree, the museum was conceived as a platform to support Brongniart's scientific investigations, but it was also the first such institution in France to be devoted exclusively to a single branch of the decorative arts. It quickly took on a life of its own, but the history of its acquisitions in this formative period offers a fascinating glimpse of the changing values and interests of learned French society during the first half of the nineteenth century.

Note: The documents cited below are from the Archives the Manufacture Nationale de Sèvres (AMNS), the Archives of the Musée de Sèvres (AMS), and the Musée National de Céramique (MNC). In the essay text, the MNC numbers, given in parentheses, represent the museum's inventory numbers; unattributed quotations have been taken from the inventory notations made by Riocreux.

1. There are 3,800 entries in the inventory, but since many of these include several pieces, the number of actual pieces in the collection is much higher. The numbers assigned by Riocreux continue to be used today.

2. "These are neither art objects notable for their form, composition, design, etc., . . . nor historical objects notable for what they represent, nor archeological objects notable for their inscriptions; none of these considerations led us to assemble them. Without being formally excluded, [such pieces] were valuable to us only insofar as they contributed to our knowledge of the history of the ceramic arts . . . [and] finally to the [material] progress of art" [Ce ne sont ni des objets d'art sous le rapport des formes, des compositions du dessin, etc. . . . ni des objets historiques, sous celui des objets représentés, ni des objets archéologiques sous celuis des inscriptions, ce n'est aucune de ces considérations qui nous les a fait recueillir; sans être formellement exclues, elles n'ont eu de valeur pour nous qu'en contribuant à nous faire connaître l'histoire des arts céramiques . . . enfin le progrès de l'art] (Brongniart and Riocreux, *Description méthodique du musée céramique* [1845], preface).

3. Central to this debate was the perceived need to revive the *grand genre* of history painting. See La Font de Saint Yenne, *Reflexions* (1747).

4. Ibid., p. 40.

5. The collection of the school in Rouen boasted "plaster casts, prints, an écorché by Houdon, and a few paintings belonging to the director" (Edouard Pommier, "La Naissance des musées de Province," in Nora, ed., *Les Lieux de mémoire* 2 (1986), pp. 451 – 90, quotation p. 457.

6. Bachelier's school opened on September 10, 1766. See Leben, "New Light on the Ecole Royale Gratuite de Dessin" (1993), pp. 99 – 118; Birembaut, "Les Ecoles gratuites" (1964), pp. 441 – 70.

7. Shackelton, "The Enlightenment and the Artisan" (1980), p. 56 ff.

8. Mercier, *1794: L'Abbé Grégoire et la création du Conservatoire* (1989); Marot, "L'Abbé Grégoire et le vandalisme" (1980); Bergdoll, "Le Progrés des arts réunis et l'abbé Grégoire," in Rabreau and Tollon, eds., *Le Progrés des arts réunis,* (1992), pp. 159 – 67.

9. Haskell, *History and Its Images* (1993), pp. 236 – 52; Dominique Poulot, "Alexandre Lenoir et

le musée des monuments français," in Nora, *Les Lieux de mémoire, La Nation* (1986), vol. 2, pp. 496 – 531 (esp. p. 497 ff.).

10. AMNS, Register Vc 2, letter dated 9 Messidor year 8 (June 28, 1800).

11. [À côté de terres blanches du département de la haute Vienne, les produits industriels qu'il a fourni] AMNS, Carton U 1, liasse L 1, dossier 3.

12. [est devenue à l'égard de Paris, la branche de l'industrie la plus considérable]; [celles des chimistes qui se sont succédés à la manufacture de Sèvres . . . on pourrait offrir aux amis des arts et de l'industrie Nationale, une collection complète dont on se sert, les savants en la consultant pourraient peut-être remplir les lacunes qui se rencontrent dans quelques dégradations de teintes ou augmenter le nombre et la beauté des couleurs primitives] Ibid.

13. [surtout à l'égard de celles de la manufacture de Sèvres . . . la vente des porcelaines anciennement fabriqués dans cette maison doit avoir lieu le 21 de ce mois . . . il faudrait le matin de ce jour que quelqu'un fut chargé de mettre à part quelques unes des pièces qu'il pourrait juger convenir au but que se propose le conseil] Ibid.

14. The passage from his letter reads, "Il serait peut-être encore un moyen de nous procurer quelques fonds pour payer les frais d'établissement, ce serait de faire une vente à l'encan d'un grand nombre de vieilles porcelaines qui encombrent nos magasins et qui nuisent à la manufacture en faisant croire à ceux qui viennent la visiter qu'elle fabrique encore de ces choses gothiques" (AMNS, Register Vc 2, letter dated 9 Messidor year 8 [June 28, 1800]).

15. [Je crois utile aux progrès de l'art de la poterie et à son histoire de rassembler d'une manière méthodique dans l'établissement national qui a été l'école d'une branche de cet art, et qui doit être celle de l'art entier, tous les objets d'art et de science qui peuvent servir à l'histoire de la poterie fine et commune] Ibid., letter dated 10 Thermidor year 9 (July 29, 1801). Even the title of the catalogue, *Description méthodique du musée céramique*, as well as its preface, emphasizes a systematic, didactic approach.

16. [une belle suite de vases étrusques]; [une assez belle suite d'études de fleurs, de fruits et d'animaux de différents maîtres et notamment de Desportes et d'Oudry]; [une suite intéressante pour l'histoire des progrès du goût des modèles de tous les vases d'ornement et d'usage que la manufacture a fait depuis sa création]; [une assez grande quantité d'argile et de matières premières de divers lieux et diverses natures propres à fabrication de la poterie] Ibid. The Etruscan vases were part of the Denon collection of ancient pottery, which Louis XVI had acquired in 1786. Shortly thereafter, d'Angiviller, the king's minister of works, transferred these pieces to the Sèvres manufactory for use as models. See Massoul, *Corpus vasorum antiquorum* (1934).

17. "The objects are scattered throughout the workshops, and even in the attics. They are in a disorderly jumble, without indications as to place [of origin] or date [of acquisition], in the end they are useless riches that will acquire value only by becoming useful" (AMNS, Register Vc 2, letter dated July 29, 1801).

18. Ibid.

19. Ibid.

20. "You realize that it is only by discovery of a suitable clay or mixture of various clays that we will manage to produce white pottery as beautiful as that of the English" (ibid.).

21. Brongniart and Riocreux, *Description méthodique du musée céramique* (1845), preface.

22. Ibid.

23. Ibid.

24. Ibid.

25. Milet, *Notice sur Riocreux* (1883).

26. AMNS, Register Vc 8, letter dated March 2, 1829, from Brongniart to the comte de La Rochefoucauld. Riocreux was also placed in charge of the manufactory's books, prints, drawings, paintings, medals, and models (wax, plaster, and bronze).

27. Ibid, letter dated May 20, 1829, from Brongniart to Riocreux.

28. Milet, *Notice sur Riocreux* (1883).

29. AMNS, Register Vc 8, letter dated January 3, 1834, from Brongniart to the vicomte de Montalivet.

30. "I noticed a bill in the amount of 200 francs . . . You should submit special proposals for acquisitions of this kind" (AMS, Carton 1, Liasse 1, dossier 18, letter dated August 30, 1834, from Montalivet to Brongniart).

31. AMNS, Register Vc 7, letter dated November 22, 1825, from Brongniart to the vicomte de La Rochefoucauld.

32. Ibid., letter dated April 10, 1826, from Brongniart to the vicomte de La Rochefoucauld. Sallé was an artist and antiques dealer; the auction of his collection was held on April 11, 1826.

33. AMS, Carton 1, Liasse 3, 89 bis.

34. Massoul, *Corpus vasorum antiquorum* (1934), preface.

35. Ibid., (askos) pl. 40, figs. 2 and 3; (kraters) pl. 31, fig. 11.

36. Ibid., (hellenistic pieces) pl. 23, fig. 26; (black-figure vases) pl. 15, figs. 8 and 10; pl. 16, figs. 4-6, 7-9; (goblets) pl. 17, figs. 2-4, 8-9.

37. AMS, Carton 1, Liasse 1, dossier 18, letter dated February 1, 1832, from Gaspary to Brongniart.

38. Massoul, *Corpus vasorum antiquorum* (1934), pl. 11, figs. 12 and 13.

39. Ibid., preface.

40. Ibid., (oinochoe) pl. 11, figs. 3, 5, 7; (tumblers) pl. 11, fig. 2; (kernos) pl. 11, fig. 9; (kraters) pl. 12, fig. 1.

41. AMNS, Carton 1, Liasse 1, dossier 17, letter dated February 21, 1842, from Dubuc to Brongniart, Paris; Massoul, *Corpus vasorum antiquorum* (1934), pl. 23, figs. 34, 35.

42. For the rediscovery of Etruscan civilization, see Pallotino, *Les Etrusques et l'Europe*, exhib. cat. (1992).

43. Massoul, *Corpus vasorum antiquorum* (1934), pl. 28, fig. 4; (oinochoe) pl. 28, fig. 27.

44. Edmond Antoine Durand was a merchant who began to collect antiquities in 1799 while traveling in Italy. His first collection was bought in its entirety by the Louvre in 1824. The second collection was sold at auction in 1836, after Durand's death; it consisted primarily of Greek vases and other pieces that had been removed from excavations in Vulci and Nola in Italy.

45. Brönstedt was the author of a memoir entitled *Voyage et recherches en Grèce* (nd). No more information on this source is available.

46. AMNS, Register U 15, Liasse 1, dossier 4, letter dated May 30, 1836, from Riocreux to Brongniart, Sèvres.

47. AMS, Carton 1, Liasse 1, dossier 28.

48. Ibid.; Massoul, *Corpus vasorum antiquorum* (1934), pl. 25, figs. 3, 5, 6.

49. AMS, Carton 1, Liasse 1, dossier 28; Massoul, *Corpus vasorum antiquorum* (1934), pl. 14, figs. 19, 23.

50. Massoul, *Corpus vasorum antiquorum* (1934), pl. 26, figs. 11, 16.

51. Ibid., pl. 28, no. 5; Brongniart and Riocreux, *Description Méthodique du musée céramique* (1845), vol. 2, pl. 28, fig. 5.

52. Massoul, *Corpus vasorum antiquorum* (1934), pl. 1, fig. 19; Maingot, *Le Baron Taylor* (1963).

53. Massoul, *Corpus vasorum antiquorum* (1934), pl. 1, fig. 9.

54. AMS, Carton 1, liasse 1, dossier 28.

55. Ibid., dossier 26, letter dated September 30, 1847, from Lavé to Brongniart, Paris.

56. Massoul, *Corpus vasorum antiquorum* (1934), pl. 57, figs. 8, 13. The place names used in this essay are spelled as they were in the nineteenth century.

57. Ibid., pl. 55, figs. 6-25, 28; pl. 56, fig. 2.

58. Ibid., pl. 55, fig. 9.

59. AMS, Carton 3, liasse 16, letter dated November 16, 1831, from Renaud de Saint-Amour to Brongniard, Lauterbourg; ibid., letter dated December 7, 1831, from Brogniard to Baron Fain, Sèvres; Massoul, *Corpus vasorum antiquorum* (1934), pl. 57, figs, 1, 2, 3.

60. Massoul, *Corpus vasorum antiquorum* (1934), (small cups) pl. 56, figs. 4, 5, 7; (goblets) pl. 56, figs. 11, 12; (small amphora), pl. 58, fig 31; (oinochoe) pl. 58, fig. 32.

61. Ibid., (vial) pl. 56, fig. 26; (oinochoe) pl. 58, fig. 54.

62. Ibid., pl. 56, figs. 20, 25.

63. AMS, Carton 1, liasse 2, dossier 36, letter dated December 10, 1836, from d'Espine to Brongniart plus a little note unlocated.

64. Ibid., dossier 51, letter dated January 29, 1840, from Brongniart to Larchan, Sèvres.

65. Ibid., dossier 65, letter dated October 8, 1843, from Deville to Brongniart.

66. AMS, Carton 3, letter dated January 1839, from Delanoue to Brongniart.

67. Pomian, *Anticomanie* (1992), pp. 59 ff.

68. Massoul, *Corpus vasorum antiquorum* (1934), pl. 60, fig. 23; Carton 1, liasse 2, g9.

69. Massoul, *Corpus vasorum antiquorum* (1934), pl. 60, figs. 4, 5, 6, 7, 8.

70. AMS, Carton 1, liasse 2, dossier 71, letter dated May 5, 1844, from Olfers to Brongniart, Berlin.

71. For examples of Brongniart's instructions, see AMS, Carton 1, liasse 1, 2, to Mazinski, dated February 12, 1830; ibid., liasse 2, dossier 6, to lieutenant of the vessel Laplace; Carton 2, liasse 1,

dossier 1, to Viquesnel.

72. AMS, Carton 2, liasse 1, dossier 1, Barrot mission.

73. Reyniers, *Céramiques américaines,* (1966), p. 110, fig. 193

74. AMNS, Register Vc 8, letter dated May 29, 1834, from Brongniart to the vicomte de Montalivet,

75. Reyniers, *Céramiques américaines,* (1966), (llama vase) p. 144, fig. 282; (spherical pitcher) p. 145, fig. 283; (stirrup vase) p. 114, fig. 206; (cat vase) p. 115, fig. 209; (geometric vase) p. 131, fig. 251; (Aztec figure) p. 60, fig. 81.

76. Ibid., p. 195, fig. 81; AMS, Carton 2, liasse 2, dossier 5, letter dated December 27, 1837, from Barrot to Brongniart, Manila.

77. Reyniers, *Céramiques américaines* (1966), p. 117, fig. 215.

78. Ibid., pp. 142 – 43, figs. 275, 278, 279.

79. Ibid., p. 164, fig. 317,

80. Ibid., p. 101, fig. 186; AMS, Carton 1, liasse 3, dossier 75, letter dated March 5, 1843, from Schoelcher to Brongniart, Paris.

81. Reyniers, *Céramiques américaines,* (1966), p. 169, fig. 329.

82. Ibid., p. 170, figs. 330, 331; p. 171, figs. 332, 333; AMS, Carton 1, liasse 2, dossier 32; ibid., Carton 1, liasse 3, dossier 4.

83. For Brongniart's instructions to Laplace see AMS, Carton 2, liasse 2, dossier 6.

84. Ibid, letter dated December 20, 1837, from Laplace to Brongniart, Cape of Good Hope.

85. Ibid., dossier 7, Ackerman mission.

86. Ibid., dossier 6, letter dated October 28, 1841, from Brongniart to Rochet d'Héricourt.

87. Ibid., letter dated August 28, 1837, from Laplace to Brongniart, Madras.

88. Ibid., letter dated October 29, 1838, from Laplace to Brongniart, Canton.

89. For Brongniart's instructions to Darcet see ibid., dossier 7.

90. Brongniart, *Traité des arts céramique* (1844), vol. 2, pp. 90 – 91.

91. Ibid., p. 97.

92. AMS, Carton 3, liasse 46, Botta mission.

93. Brongniart, *Traité des arts céramique* (1844), vol. 2, p. 92.

94. AMS, Carton 1, liasse 1, dossier 13, cover letter dated May 18, 1830, from Virlet, Modon.

95. For Brongniart's instructions to Diran dated August 9, 1843, see AMS, Carton 2, liasse 2, dossier 1.

96. AMS, Carton 1, liasse 3, dossier 81, letter dated November 27, 1847, from Visquesnel to Brongniart, "Sulé Bourgas."

97. AMS, unpaginated manuscript.

98. Comte de Milly, *L'Art de la porcelaine* (Paris, 1771), p. xxj.

99. [Faïence mimo porcelaine] Brongniart and Riocreux, *Description méthodique du musée céramique* (1845), vol. 1, p. 187, caption to no. 240.

100. Slitine, "La céramique orientale dans les ventes publiques" (1996).

101. [Une assiette faïence commune émaillée en bleu dite porcelaine de Perse] AMS, Carton 1, liasse 1, dossier 12, Toppi exchange.

102. Brongniart and Riocreux, *Description méthodique du musée céramique* (1845), vol. 2, pl. 39, fig. 15.

103. Ibid., vol. 2, pl. 39, fig. 14. Jules Ziegler (1804 – 1856) began his career as a history painter before becoming a potter who worked in stoneware in Voisinlieu, in the Beauvaisis.

104. AMNS, Carton 3, liasse 46, Botta mission, 1835.

105. Brongniart and Riocreux, *Description méthodique du musée céramique* (1845), p. 187, no. 240a.

106. Ibid., p. 187, no. 240b.

107. For a note from Riocreux attesting the loss, see Carton 2, liasse 3, dossier 1.

108. Brongniart and Riocreux, *Description méthodique du musée céramique* (1845), p. 158, no. 190.

109. Soustiel, *La céramique islamique* (1985), pp. 292 – 93.

110. AMS, Carton 3, liasse 2.

111. AMNS, Register Vc 7.

112. Slitine, "La Céramique orientale dans les ventes publiques" (1996).

113. Kaempfer, *Histoire naturelle* (1732).

114. AMS, Carton 2, liasse 2, dossier 5, Barrot mission, instructions of December 1835 (several pages written by Brongniart).

115. [Il se présente] plusieurs pièces de porcelaine de chine remarquable sous le rapport des procédés techniques] AMNS, Register Vc 7, letter dated April 10, 1826, from Brongniart to La Rochefoucauld.

116. AMS, Carton 2, liasse 2, dossier 6, Toppi mission to London.

117. Ibid., dossier 5, Barrot mission (instructions); ibid., dossier 6, Laplace mission (instructions).

118. Ibid., dossier 6, Laplace mission.

119. AMS, Carton 3, liasse 1, Houssaye exchange.

120. Labit and Lassère, "Le chevalier Boudon de Saint Amans" (1973).

121. For further information on the Enquête de Préfets, see chap. 11 in this volume.

122. Plinval-Salgues, "La céramique française aux expositions industrielles" (1961).

123. AMS, Register Vc 3, letter dated December 12, 1833, from Brongniart to the comte de Montalivet.

124. AMS, dossier Creil, letter dated October 5, 1823, from Brongniart to Saint Cricq-Cazaux, Paris.

125. For the prototype letter to producer, see AMS, Carton 3.

126. MNC 678 [avaient été soumises, l'une à l'action de l'hydrosulfure de potasse pendant une demi-journée, l'autre à l'évaporation du vinaigre]; MNC 687 [servi journellement pendant deux ans exposé au feu de poële ou de cheminée]; MNC 808 [subir l'épreuve de la fusion du feldspath au grand feu du four à porcelaine]; MNC 1671 [avait fait l'usage pendant deux ans du service de table de M. Dumas profeseur à l'Académie Royale des Sciences].

127. AMS, Carton 1, liasse 2, dossier 5, letter dated December 10, 1841, from Brongniart to Tissot.

128. Register Vc 7, letter dated February 16, 1828, from Brongniart to the vicomte de La Rochefoucauld.

129. The language in the inventory describes the piece as being entirely covered with a luster, a new technique at the manufactory at this time.

130. Alcouffe, Dion-Tenenbaum, and Ennès, *Un âge d'or,* exhib. cat. (1991), p. 35.

131. Ibid., pp. 133 – 35.

132. Ravel d'Esclapon, *La Faïence de Rubelles* (1988); AMS, dossier 182.

133. AMS, Carton 1, liasse 2, **dossier** 88, Chevreuse donation.

134. Brongniart and Riocreux, *Description méthodique du musée céramique* (1845), vol. 2, pl. 44, fig. 7; Alcouffe, Dion- Tenenbaum, and Ennès, *Un âge d'or,* exhib. cat. (1991), p. 350.

135. AMS, Carton 1, liasse 3, letter dated June 7, 1844, from Gosse to Brongniart, Paris.

136. AMS, Carton 1, liasse 2, dossier 56, Ziegler donation.

137. AMS, Carton 1, Vienna dossier.

138. AMNS, Register Vc3, letter dated January 21, 1808, from Brongniart to the Intendant Général.

139. AMS, Carton 1, Vienna dossier, letter dated April 1, 1804, from Chevalier Landriani to Brongniart.

140. AMNS, Register Vc3, letter dated July 24, 1806, from Brongniart to the director of the Muséum d'Histoire Naturelle.

141. AMS, Carton 1, Vienna dossier.

142. Ibid.

143. AMNS, Register Vc3, letter dated November 17, 1805, from Brongniart to Denon.

144. Ibid., letter dated December 31, 1805, from Brongniart to the Intendant Général.

145. Ibid., letter dated February 5, 1806, from Brongniart to Rosenstiel.

146. AMS, Carton 1, liasse 1, dossier 1, Berlin donation.

147. AMNS, Register Vc3, letter dated November 18, 1808, from Brongniart to the Intendant Général.

148. Ibid., letter dated January 24, 1808, from Brongniart to the Intendant Général.

149. Ibid, letter dated January 12, 1809, from Brongniart to the Intendant Général.

150. AMS, Carton 1, liasse 1, dossier 4, Fürstenberg exchange, letter dated October 5, 1815, from the comte de Pradel to Brongniart.

151. Ibid.

152. AMS, Carton 1, liasse 1, dossier 7, Russian exchange.

153. Ibid.

154. AMS, Carton 1, liasse 2, dossier 44 bis, letter dated November 24, 1837, from Brongniart to Meyendorf.

155. Ibid., letters dated November 4, 1839, from the Intendant Général to Brongniart and from de Wailly to Brongniart, both Paris.

156. AMNS, Carton M 10, dossier 1, letter dated August 12, 1836, from Brongniart to Baron Fain, Munich.

157. AMNS, Register Vc4, letter dated September 9, 1812, from Brongniart to the Intendant Général, Berlin.

158. AMNS, Carton M 5, liasse 3, dossier 1, letter dated March 23, 1824, from Brongniart to the marquis de Lauriston.

159. AMNS, Register Vc8, letter dated August 7, 1835, from Brongniart to the comte de Montalivet.

160. AMNS, Carton M 9, dossier 5, letter dated October 5, 1835, from Brongniart to Vautrin, Carlsruhe.

161. AMNS, Register Vc9, letter dated March 5, 1836, from Brongniart to Baron Fain, Sèvres.

162. AMNS, Carton M 10, dossier 1, letter dated June 5, 1836, from Brongniart to Baron Fain, Sèvres.

163. Ibid., letter dated July 11, 1836, from Brongniart to Baron Fain, Berlin.

164. Ibid., letter dated August 12, 1836, from Brongniart to Baron Fain, Munich.

165. Ibid.

166. For Brongniart's interest in feldspar-free porcelain, see ibid., letter dated July 11, 1836, to Baron Fain, Berlin.

167. Ibid.

168. Ibid.

169. AMNS, Carton U 15, liasse 5, dossier 4, letter dated August 15, 1836, from Brongniart to Sèvres, Innsbruck.

170. AMNS, Carton 1, liasse 2, dossier 51.

171. For delivery from Chanou, see AMS, Carton 1, liasse 3, dossier 32.

172. For delivery from Ducatel, see AMS, Carton 1, liasse 2, dossier 33.

173. Ibid., letter dated June 4, 1836, from Ducatel to Brongniart, Baltimore.

174. AMS, Carton 1, liasse 2, dossier 32, letter dated July 27, 1836, from Silliman to Brongniart, New Haven.

175. Ibid., letter dated January 6, 1837, from Brongniart to Keating, Sèvres.

176. AMS, Register Vc 2.

177. Courajod, *La Collection Durand* (1888).

178. Courajod, *La Collection Révoil* (1886).

179 In 1844 Brongniart knew of thirty-seven such pieces in private collections (Brongniart, *Traité des arts céramique* [1844], vol. 2, p. 175).

180. AMNS, Carton T ll, liasse 2, dossier 6, letter from Turpin de Crissé to Brongniart.

181. [Les pièces en biscuit n'étant susceptibles d'aucun emploi sans être restaurées et sont d'aillleurs toutes de rebut, il en reste deux fois autant] AMS, Carton 1, liasse 1, dossier 12, Toppi exchange of May 27, 1830.

182. Ibid., Toppi exchange of October 17, 1829.

183. AMS, Carton 1, liasse 1, dossier 11, Vachée exchanges.

184. AMS, Carton 1, liasse 1, dossier 12, Hairon exchange.

185. Ibid., Toppi exchanges.

186. The Debruge and Soulages sale.

187. AMNS, Carton M 9, dossier 5, letter dated September 13, 1835, from Brongniart to Vautrin, Amsterdam.

188. AMNS, Carton M 10, dossier 1, letter dated August 12, 1836, from Brongniart to Baron Fain, Munich.

189. Brongniart and Riocreux, *Description méthodique du musée céramique* (1845), vol. 2, pl. 37, fig. 5.

190. AMNS, Carton M10, dossier 1, letter dated June 5, 1836, from Brongniart to Baron Fain, Yorkshire.

191. "Of the twenty-five or thirty sections making up this collection . . . only one concerns pottery and enamel . . . [and] it teaches us nothing" (Brongniart, *Traité des arts céramiques* [1844], vol. 2, p. 62).

192. AMS, Carton 3, dossier 9, letter dated June 7, 1844, from Brongniart to Brond, Sèvres.

193. [faïence violette de Louis Poterat] inventory, MNC 3130.

194. "All these forms and groups, which five or six years ago were regarded with such distaste that one had to pass by the shelves supporting them in haste to avoid the criticisms that they habitually evoked, now began to be admired and sought after" (Brongniart and Riocreux, *Description méthodique du musée céramique* [1845], preface).

195. [Spécimen historique d'application des divers métaux à la décoration des porcelaines] inventory, MNC 961.3.

196. [Suite d'échantillons historiques de forme et décoration] inventory, MNC 1787.

197. Brongniart continues, "If only thirty-eight years ago I had possessed the experience of age, which teaches that whatever is rare is deemed valuable" [Ah que n'avais je, il y a 38 ans, l'expérience des vieux qui apprennent qu'on ne fait grand cas que de ce qui est rare] (AMS, Carton 1, liasse 2, dossier 36, Letter dated December 30, 1838, from Brongniart to Espine, Sèvres.

198. [le bol a peu de valeur mais ce qui est curieux c'est au fond d'y voir peint le château de Vincennes et probablement le côté où se trouvait la manufacture] Ibid., dossier 72, letter dated August 16, 1846, from Beurdeley to Brongniart, Paris.

199. AMNS, Register Vc 8, letter dated June 15, 1830, from Brongniart to the vicomte de La Rochefoucauld, Sèvres.

200. AMNS, Carton M 10, dossier 1, letter dated August 12, 1836, from Brongniart to Baron Fain, Munich.

209. AMS, Carton 1, liasse 2, dossier 30, Dresden exchange.

210. [Je ne sais comment on aura fait l'évaluation de choses la plupart frustres et défectueuses] AMS, Carton 1, liasse 2, dossier 34, letter dated December 30, 1836, from Brongniart to Montalivet, Sèvres.

211. Ibid.

212. AMS, Carton 1, liasse 2, dossier 30, letter dated June 27, 1837, from Brongniart to Klemm, Sèvres.

213. AMS, Carton 1, liasse 2, dossier 34, Dresden exchange.

214. [Ce travail dont je suis occupé depuis plus de huit mois] AMNS, Register Vc8, letter dated June 15, 1830, from Brongniart to La Rochefoucauld, Sèvres.

215. Passeri, *Histoire de la peinture sur majolique* (1775), reprinted in Italian in 1838 (*Istoria delle pitture in majolica*).

216. Klemm, *Die königliche sachsische porzellan-und gefasse- sammlung* (Dresden, 1834).

217. De Witte, *Description des antiquités . . . Durand* (Paris, 1836).

Fig. 10-1. Ice pail, Sèvres, 1778; soft-paste porcelain. Soft-paste porcelain production was halted by Brongniart soon after he became director of the manufactory. This piece, part of a service sent to Catherine the Great, also exemplifies the neoclassical idiom sometimes used at Sèvres in the eighteenth century, (Wallace Collection, England)

Chapter 10

Two Controversial Decisions by Alexandre Brongniart

Antoine d'Albis

Historians have been generous in assessing Alexandre Brongniart's administration. Only rarely, and then with considerable deference, have they criticized his forty-seven-year tenure at Sèvres. With the benefit of hindsight, however, two of his principal decisions were made very early and appear to have been highly unusual: the liquidation at auction of a large stock of pieces, mostly soft-paste, that had accumulated in the manufactory's warehouse; and the elimination of the manufactory's production of soft-paste porcelain in 1801 (fig. 10-1).

The Liquidation of Flawed Pieces

Most of the pieces auctioned between 1800 and 1802 were undecorated blanks, but a few had fired ground colors. Many of the forms were no longer fashionable, or were flawed in some technical way, and therefore not commercially viable in the open market. As might be expected, however, many of these objects ultimately became the prey of independent decorators, once they were sold at auction.

Porcelain objects possessing what is known in French as a *surdécor*, a painted decoration executed without the authorization of the original manufactory, began to appear soon after the first auction authorized by Sèvres. Many of these pieces feature an authentic colored ground, executed by the factory while the blank was still in its possession. The production of such redecorated works would generate considerable confusion with respect to provenance,[1] and they proved detrimental to the reputation of the manufactory for some time afterward.

In this case, Brongniart's passion for order and organization ultimately worked against the establishment's interests. His apparently innocuous and reasonable decision to clear the warehouse of useless, outmoded pieces spawned a host of objects with *surdécors* of dubious quality that often damaged Sèvres's high esteem.

There is, however, reason to moderate this trenchant indictment against Brongniart. In the first place, there was a precedent at the manufactory for such a sale of flawed blanks and probably of pieces with colored grounds and unfinished, flawed decoration. When the manufactory moved from Vincennes to Sèvres in 1756, they had staged the first such auction, and others followed. Rather than destroy valuable works, the factory's administrators chose this means of clearing out the inevitable accumulation of flawed objects.

As for the Louvre sales of July 1800 and April 1802, history has tended to view them uncharitably. This is hardly surprising: most accounts of these sales describe auctions that were duly advertised in the press, at which entire lots of blanks and partly decorated pieces were made readily available to independent decorators. The buyers were more far-sighted than Brongniart, recognizing the profits that could be made by completing and retailing such objects in a transformed state. Under close examination, however, this analysis is superficial at best, and the truth is considerably more complex.

Under Brongniart, the manufactory's prime mission was to explore the most recent artistic and technological developments in porcelain production. Accordingly, Brongniart gave a far lower priority to the retailing of old models than to the creation of new ones which would be consistent with changing tastes and circumstances.

Furthermore, the auctions in question took place between 1800 and 1802, following a decade of administrative turmoil and near inactivity that had depleted the manufactory's stock of most blanks suitable for decoration. During this troubled period, Sèvres's painters, gilders, and other decorators had little choice but to complete whatever pieces were available to them, and it is reasonable to assume that they chose to work with those with the fewest imperfections. The establishment had a tendency to keep even badly flawed pieces instead of destroying them, and it becomes clear that many of the examples in the warehouse when Brongniart became director must have been of very poor quality.

Most of the surviving independently decorated "Sèvres" pieces that can be so identified were so seriously flawed to begin with that it is obvious that they could not have been painted by the manufactory's own workers. These pieces probably should have been destroyed as blanks, but they were delivered to the warehouse all the same, where they were to remain, undecorated, until the time they would be rejected. At the beginning of the nineteenth century, the accumulated stock of blanks must have consisted almost entirely of these unusable pieces, except for a few unmatched singles. It is easy, therefore, to understand Brongniart's decision to liquidate stock, especially given the manufactory's dire financial straits. He needed to raise funds immediately to keep the manufactory operational. He may have felt that outright destruction of these assets was not a reasonable option.

The End of Soft-Paste Production

The decision to discontinue the production of soft-paste porcelain was made in 1801. It was far more momentous than the decision to sell old work. It effectively doomed an entire body of expertise. In the second half of the nineteenth century serious attempts were made by Victor Regnault and Charles Lauth to revive the relevant skills, reestablish supply networks, and return to old formulas, but it was too late. The knowledge needed for success had been relegated to oblivion. The body of work that had been the foundation of Sèvres's prestige both at home and abroad in the eighteenth century proved impossible to duplicate.

The Composition and Properties of Soft Paste. Kaolin, an aluminum silicate clay, is a primary ingredient of true hard-paste porcelain. Before the discovery of their own indigenous deposits of this material, French porcelain makers, unlike many of their German counterparts, had been obliged to use a substitute known as "soft paste." The usual formula consisted of sand, soda of alicante,[2] sea salt, and saltpeter. This composition expanded when exposed to high temperatures in the kiln. Consequently, any glazes applied to it had to have the same properties in order to remain fixed to the body when fired. In practice, this meant a flux rich in alkaline oxides. This family of substances had a particular effect on oxide-based glaze colors. In an alkaline glaze, copper, for example, produces a turquoise or sky blue, cobalt produces a luminous blue (*beau bleu*), and manganese results in violet. When a conventional flux is used these same oxides produce quite ordinary greens, blues, and maroons.

It was the absence of kaolin in the formula for soft paste, therefore, that determined the chemical conditions underlying the singularly beautiful ground colors found on Vincennes-Sèvres soft-paste porcelain. At once transparent and crystalline, the glaze has a shimmering quality in the light, a rare effect produced by the combination of their lead and alkaline ingredients.

The enamel colors used for painted ornament on soft-paste porcelain also had idiosyncratic chemical properties, determined by the necessity that they conform to the glaze when fired. As it happens, these results, too, had uniquely appealing visual qualities. Like the enamels used on hard paste, they were for the most part opaque to make it easier to create lines and shadows in the decoration. When used on hard paste, there was tendency for thickly applied colors to flake off in the kiln. The only way to avoid this problem was to employ enamels with heavy concentrations of stain.

In the case of soft-paste porcelain, however, this problem did not arise. When fired, the painted decoration readily bonded with the lead-based glaze that softened slightly in the heat of the kiln. This made it unnecessary to resort to heavy concentrations of colors: contrasts between lights and darks could now be obtained by applying thicker coats of enamel, allowing artists to achieve the characteristic relief effects that soften the severity of the ornamental elements and forms. In addition, since these enamel colors fuse with such radiant glazes, they never have the dry, matte surfaces so typical of painted decoration on hard-paste porcelain.

Gold decoration could also be thickly applied to soft-paste porcelain with its lead-based glazes and even more thickly to copper-based grounds. Whenever it was thought advisable to enliven an ornamental scheme, the gilders could richly "model" gold with their brushes, often creating a relief element on these motifs. The workers responsible for post-kiln burnishing could then accentuate this delicate modeling by judiciously working the surface, creating juxtaposed matte and polished areas and then adding delicate tooling.

Successful firing of these beautiful alkaline-based grounds and enamels required special handling. Many decorative compositions painted on soft-paste required seven or eight firings. These decorations were prone to liquification under heat, however, and could easily devitrify during requisite later firings. In a normal muffle kiln they would have run uncontrollably.

To solve this problem, in 1748 Claude Humbert Gérin devised a kiln that fired so rapidily that the crystals which triggered the devitrification process did not have time to form, spread and consequently, obliterate the decoration. Because of the impractical nature of this kiln, however, it was abandoned in 1801. Before its destruction, Brongniart had it carefully documented.[3] Thanks to his prudent directive, the firing methods for soft-paste porcelain are known. The pieces were positioned on metal supports in the kiln to assure that the right temperature for each piece was attained as precisely as possible.

Gérin was also responsible for developing the astonishing whiteness and translucency of the Sèvres soft paste. He had most likely read the letters of the Jesuit missionary François-Xavier d'Entrecolles, who in the 1720s had described the processes used by Chinese porcelain makers.[4] D'Entrecolles's scattered observations, however, offered little guidance when it came to determining the primary materials used in China. He had attempted to determine the mineral ingredients of the mysterious substances that the Chinese called "tsekao," "kaolin," "petuntse," and "hoatse," but his calculations proved unreliable. Using them as a guide, Gérin came to the mistaken conclusion that kaolin and alum were one and the same.[5]

Alum had long been used for medicinal purposes, primarily to cauterize wounds. A mixture of aluminum and potassium, it took the form of crystals resembling sea salt. When heated in a crucible to about 800° C it became a fine fluffy white powder. It was this material that, when added to conventional soft paste, gave Vincennes-Sèvres porcelain its radiant whiteness.

The preparation of soft-paste to be used in the Sèvres workshops occurred in two stages. First the chemicals were fired to about 1,150° C. at which temperature they vitrified, becoming what is known as a frit. This frit was then ground and mixed with other ingredients to make the actual paste.

Soft-paste Porcelain Formula, 1740-1801

1. Frit

Salpeter	21.7%
Salt	7.2
Alum	3.7
Alicante soda	3.7
Gypsum from Montmartre	3.7
Sand from Fontainebleau	60.0
	100.0%

2. Paste

Frit (above)	75.0%
Chalk	16.7
Marl from Argenteuil	8.3
	100.0%

As can be seen from its composition, Sèvres's soft-paste porcelain contains only 8.3% marl (a white clay) from Argenteuil. This very low percentage of plastic material, for some reason, makes the body nevertheless relatively easy to work. The complexity of the forms made with this soft paste bears eloquent witness to this fact.

Unlike hard paste, soft paste was bisque fired to a higher temperature (probably between 1,100° and 1,200° C.) than its later glaze firings. The bisque firing was left to "soak" for three to five days.[6] It was this initial exposure to extreme heat that determined the definitive qualities of the soft paste. In the kiln the pieces were often supported by small struts, also made of porcelain, to prevent gross deformation of the vitrified paste.

After successful completion of this firing, an enamel glaze was applied. Before its application, however, the pieces were carefully polished smooth with sandstone to assure their luster and brilliance. They were then immersed in a thick glaze.

Glaze Formula for Soft-Paste Porcelain

Lead oxide	38.5%
Sand from Fontainebleau	28.8
Calcined flint	9.6
Potash	12.8
Sodium carbonate	10.3
	100.0%

After the pieces were glazed, they were fired again to a temperature of 900 to 1,000° C. At this low temperature the glaze coat melted and became transparent; the high lead content gave it a very even and brilliant surface, like crystal. The low temperature of the second firing eliminated further risk of deformation, which meant that at this stage the most complicated pieces could be realized. In 1752 it was discovered that a novel effect could be produced by leaving the white sculpture polished and undecorated after the first firing. The result, called biscuit, had a seductive fine-grained surface suggestive of marble.

Soft-paste porcelain was not without its drawbacks. Glazes applied to it were prone to streaking, and gilded ornament had a vexing tendency to flake off. Reports of another problem are difficult to confirm: it was reputedly much more susceptible to damage caused by sudden changes in temperature than hard-paste porcelain.

Within a short time after the arrival of Brongniart the decision was made to discontinue the production of soft paste. Any soft-paste porcelain pieces that remained in the warehouse, most of which were flawed anyway, were no longer fashionable. Furthermore, by 1800 all of the other great European manufactories — Berlin, Saint-Petersburg, Vienna, Nymphenburg, and Meissen — had shifted to hard-paste porcelain.

Brongniart's goal for the Sèvres manufactory was to restore its prestige. That meant, in part, glorifying France and its military conquests under Napoleon. The icy precision of hard paste was the ideal material for conveying such imagery, and the decision to shift production was a logical one. Once the step was taken to eliminate the production of soft paste, however, a fragile technological equilibrium was destroyed: neglect having done its work, it has proven impossible to revive soft-paste production.[7] In an effort to justify this decision, it is often said that soft paste is difficult to shape, but the considerable variety of complex forms successfully fashioned from the material at Sèvres amply refutes such assertions.

Hard-Paste Porcelain at Sèvres

Despite the very high quality and popularity of the soft-paste porcelain made at Vincennes, from the time that the manufactory was established in 1740 its scientists were actively engaged in unraveling the secrets of true porcelain. Soft paste was then being characterized by many critics as "artificial," or even "fake" because it was a mixture of substances. Hard-paste porcelain, on the other hand, was found in a natural state and therefore was termed "good," "genuine," and durable. Such were the philosophical considerations then encouraging its use.[8]

As early as 1747, "secrets" concerning the composition of the new material were being traded among the pottery workers at Vincennes. In 1752 J. R. Boileau, director of the manufactory, unsucessfully requested that two pottery workers from Flanders sell him their secret. In 1754 he summoned a painter from Germany, C. D. Busch, with the same intention. Five years later he was still pursuing this elusive goal. He held discussions with Paul Hannong, a manufacturer of hard-paste porcelain in Frankenthal, hoping to learn the process he used. These negotiations were cut short by Hannong's death, but in 1761 Boileau approached Hannong's sons, Joseph and Pierre-Antoine. He hoped to take advantage of a family dispute between the two brothers by encouraging competition between them that would ultimately benefit Sèvres.

Pierre-Antoine Hannong was invited to the manufactory to carry out a series of tests in 1762. China clay, or kaolin, was imported from Passau in Austria, and in 1763 Hannong succeeded in producing a few pieces. The museum in Sèvres has a cup made of true porcelain, alleged to have been produced by him in 1765.[9]

In 1768 kaolin was discovered on French soil at Saint-Yrieix la Perche, near Limoges. The location was kept secret, and the discovery soon became a political affair. An apothecary from Bordeaux, Marc-Hilaire Villaris, acting as an intermediary between Limoges and Sèvres, attempted to obtain the highest possible price from Sèvres. He argued with such energy and stubbornness that negotiations came to a halt.

The same year Pierre-Joseph Macquer, a Sèvres chemist and member of the Académie des Sciences, set out to find the location of the mysterious quarry and by November, had succeeded in doing so. He sent 800 pounds of the clay to Sèvres, where it was analyzed and discovered to be the finest china clay in Europe.[10] On returning to Sèvres, Macquer immediately began the task of transforming the china clay into porcelain, and by the end of 1769 he had produced between two and four hundred pieces in hard-paste porcelain. Macquer had the pleasure of presenting his discovery to the king on December 29, at the annual exhibition of Sèvres porcelain at Versailles. By about 1775 and from then to the end of the eighteenth century, the quantity of hard-paste porcelain produced at Sèvres almost equaled soft-paste porcelain.[11]

The Composition of Hard-Paste Porcelain. Hard-paste or true porcelain is composed mainly of kaolin, a clay to which sand and flux are added. As can be seen from the formulas, the composition of the nineteenth-century body is very close to the one used under Brongniart's directorship.

Hard-Paste Porcelain, 1781	
Clay (kaolin) from Saint-Yrieix	65.0%
Sand from Aumont	19.0
Chalk	8.0
Feldspar sand	8.0
	100.0%

Hard-Paste Porcelain, 1839	
Clay from Saint-Yrieix	68.0%
Feldspar sand	22.0
Chalk	7.0
	100.0%

Kaolin particles are small and flat, Giving the clay plasticity and resistance to deformation when it is fired. Unlike soft-paste porcelain, true porcelain is given a first firing, called a bisque firing, or *degourdi*, at a lower temperature (900° C.) than the glaze firing. The bisque pieces thus obtained, are somewhat hard and extremely porous. They are then glazed with a composition quite different from that used for soft paste.

The first formula used at Sèvres depended on a high quantity of fired hard porcelain. Beginning in 1778, however, and continuing to the present, the glaze has consisted almost entirely of a single type of feldspathic rock.

Hard-Paste Glaze, 1769 – 78	
Fired hard porcelain	48.0%
Sand from Fontainebleau	40.0
Chalk from Bougival	12.0
	100.0%

Hard-Paste Glaze, from 1778 to today	
Pegmatite from Marcognac	90.0%
Quartz	10.0
	100.0%

Pegmatite alone, which is a natural mixture of feldspar and quartz, is the essential component of this glaze. It can be applied thinly and used as a glaze; it fires to a fine transparent layer.

The Sèvres glaze fuses readily with the hard paste with its high kaolin content, giving the Sèvres porcelain a particular appearance that has been consistent for two centuries. Its color is clear and rich, not dull or milky, and the glaze itself is smooth and glossy, like porcelain of the eighteenth century. Since its introduction in 1778, this glaze has been used at Sèvres, its ingredients still supplied by the quarry at Marcognac. Because of this, the manufactory has been compelled to use the same basic formula for the porcelain clay body, in spite of problems caused by its high kaolin content.

The Sèvres porcelain was not difficult to throw or mold, but firing it successfully was problematic at best. Warpage and other deformations; stains, gritty surfaces, and marks made during throwing; shrinkage of glazes and coloring materials; drips and crawls; buckled plates that fused to the saggars; firing equipment that melted, broke, or warped; uneven firing, scorching, gray stains appearing during the biscuit firing; problems with the clay, bubbling enamel, underfiring, overfiring — all these and more were problems faced daily by manufacturers of hard porcelain. Finding solutions was a challenge that promised an enormous reward, and in 1836 Brongniart decided to conduct a systematic investigation of the composition of hard paste.

However carefully the purification process had been carried out at the kaolin quarry at Saint-Yrieix, the kaolin, or china clay, that was shipped to Sèvres was still bewilderingly inconsistent in composition, and porcelain made from it had widely varying translucency, unpredictable shrinkage, and was subject to possible deformation during the firing process.

Brongniart began this study by sampling and analyzing the best hard porcelain produced in Sèvres since 1770. He calculated a standard average composition and insisted that henceforth the composition of the china clay be chemically adjusted to eliminate variations. His decision was implemented rigorously. Consequently, a number of faults that had routinely been blamed on the clay body were discovered to have other origins.

Appropriately, Brongniart proposed three hard-paste formulas for use in the different workshops and for different purposes. One paste was for making table services. It contained a large proportion of kaolin with high plasticity. The second paste, for sculpture, had been in use since 1774 and was continued unchanged. It had a slightly lower kaolin content. It was somewhat more fusible than the table-service paste and produced a smoother biscuit. The third formula was developed by Jean-Marie-Ferdinand Régnier who called it "Chinese paste." Grayish in color, like porcelain made by the Compagnie des Indes, it was a hard paste enriched with very malleable clay appropriate to use for large pieces.[12] Despite their differences, these clay bodies were still compatible with the glazes in use at Sèvres.

Firing Hard-Paste Porcelain. Hard-paste porcelain is fired to higher temperatures than soft-paste porcelain: it is brought to 1,400° C in reduction. The glaze and paste are fired to the same temperature at which the porcelain begins to vitrify and the glaze melts completely. In the eighteenth century it was considered that if the glaze coated evenly and was brilliant, the paste was adequately fired.

Brongniart recognized that in order to fire 800 kg of porcelain, more than 13 tons of necessary auxiliary material — the saggars and other kiln equipment — also had to be heated to the firing temperature. In making this calculation, he further noted that he "had not included the other materials to be raised to this temperature each time, namely the materials used in the construction of the kiln,

Fig. 10-2. Vase, Sèvres, 1813; hard-paste porcelain with polychrome enamels and gold, gilt-bronze mounts. (Museum of Fine Arts, Boston)

including the roof and the floor."[13] Firing the high-fire kiln was an extraordinary and costly undertaking.

In 1837 more efficient saggars were introduced, saving considerable space in the kiln (see chap. 4).[14] Although not apparently particularly revolutionary in concept, they allowed pieces to be stacked more tightly and efficiently.

Another innovation was introduced in 1842 when a three-story kiln was constructed. Apparently, however, it was not considered a significant improvement because the design was not used again when a new factory was built in 1874. No real progress in kiln design was made until 1880, when reversed-flame kilns were constructed to designs bought from the English ceramist Herbert Minton. From the eighteenth century to 1880, therefore, circular kilns based on a design by Jean Etienne Guettard, which was sold to Sèvres in 1769, were used.

In firing hard-paste porcelain, supports or struts could not be generally used as they had been with soft porcelain, because the high temperature would cause the glaze to melt and fuse the struts to the pieces. As a result the rims and wells of plates often bowed and sagged as vitrification took place. The high temperatures and need for carefully controlled conditions also demanded kilns and firing equipment that were able to withstand high temperatures. Their development was a challenge to technicians and engineers of the eighteenth and early nineteenth centuries. The reversals and disappointments endured by these technicians can well be imagined.

The Decoration of Hard-Paste Porcelain. Pieces that survived the high-fire intact were then sorted for decoration. The low-fired colors that were used for painted decoration require firing to 900° C, at which temperature the high-fire glaze onto which they are applied does not melt. The composition of the colors is very different from the composition of the glaze, and the tolerance between the two materials therefore is much less assured than it was in soft-paste porcelain production. They fuse less completely and are often matte. When hard-paste was being developed in the eighteenth century, at a time when the taste for the antique was increasing, this matte appearance of the painted surface was considered especially attractive. It made the pieces resemble antiquities found during archaeological excavations. To avoid flaking after pieces have been fired, the colors have to be applied very thinly.

Hard-paste gilding is very different from soft-paste gilding. As the glaze does not soften in the low-fire decoration kiln, it does not dissolve the very fine gold particles. One can use gold transformed into powder by chemical process. The layers of gold are consequently much thinner, making this a much more economical method. This process was introduced in Sèvres in 1770 by which time it had already been used in Meissen for half a century. Under Brongniart, gilding acquired greater solidity, thanks to the replacement of the lead silicate flux used until then with sub-nitrate of bismuth that fired at a higher temperature. A special burnishing process produced gold grounds of exceptional quality.

The ground colors could be fired at low or at high temperature, depending upon the color and the desired surface. At low temperature the result was generally a matte surface. To achieve an attractive brilliance, colored oxides were mixed with the base glaze and fired at high temperature. Around 1775 the celebrated Sèvres background browns, blues, and black, fired this way, were introduced.

Some of the most important developments made during Brongniart's directorship of the factory were made in this area of production. Although by 1778 – 80 the high-fired colored grounds, some of the colored pastes, and the colors used for painting were already of excellent quality, under Brongniart each color, meaning every shade of every color, was brought to a state of perfection through persistent experiment.

An addition to the range of high-fired colored grounds a new green ground color based on chrome oxide, which was discovered in 1798 by the French chemist Louis-Nicolas Vauquelin, was introduced. It was used for the first time in 1802 at Sèvres for *grand feu* green grounds. Although a range of semi–high-fire colors was developed, improvements to the low-fire colors most occupied the factory chemists.

In order to effect change, the firing temperature of the enamel colors and gold had to be measured precisely. Brongniart identified seven different temperatures that were required to finish various pieces, including the application of matte gold and a second application and firing of color.[15] No reliable pyrometer for measuring very high temperatures existed until the end of the nineteenth century. Instead, Brongniart used a simple, effective method, based on a system of test pieces (*montres*). These consisted of carmine red on a gold base derived from purple of Cassius that was dispersed in a flux containing silver. As it is heated, the test piece changes color at different temperature, from dingy yellow when underfired to translucent purple when overfired. When the correct temperature is reached, the test piece turns a beautiful rose pink.

For each firing, a few test pieces were placed inside the kiln. They were withdrawn when exact information about the temperature was required. When gold was being fired, for example, the trial piece had to be violet. When pieces were being retouched with color, the test piece had to be pink where it was applied thinly and yellow where it was thicker.

Large pieces, such as copies of paintings onto porcelain plaques, always have one or more spots of purple hidden on them somewhere as test areas. All color experiments were carried out in the same way. No new color was put into production without Brongniart's approval. Each of the experimental pieces used as models of porcelain painting contains one or two purple trial areas. This became standard procedure in 1818.[16]

In order to have an even more accurate detail of the temperature inside the kiln, a thermometer was created that could measure the dilation of a band of silver. From this Brongniart made fairly accurate estimates of the temperature. Although not accurate on absolute values, this device gave valuable information about the speed at which the temperature rose.

Brongniart used a scale invented for mineralogists by A. G. Werner from Saxony to classify low-fire colors. At Sèvres this range of sixty-five colors, all carefully chosen, is still today a model of its kind. All the colors are necessary for the decoration of the porcelain. They are mixed to produce half tones, or colors with no specific name (known as "broken" colors), used for painting landscapes, distance views, rocks or flesh tones. From the lightest to the darkest shade, they remain stable and fire true, never becoming muddy.

During Brongniart's tenure many new shades were created, including greens based on chromium oxide. Chromium oxide is heat resistant and a variety of very stable colors which mix easily with other colors can be made from it. The range of yellows was enriched by an orange-yellow based on uranium oxide. This was brighter than any previous yellow and very glossy when fired. It was used mainly as a ground color. An lead-chromate orange was introduced as a ground color in 1830.

* * *

To assess the contribution, made more than a hundred and fifty years ago, to a field of study by a scientist is not a task to be undertaken lightly. Brongniart's contributions to the analysis and further development of the clay body and the colors used at Sèvres for glazes and decoration are unparalleled. To have speculated, as Brongniart did, about the correspondence between a chemical compound and a collection of constant physical properties reveals a mind and personality that were well in advance of their time. To have established the physical properties of the hard paste of Sèvres by combining different components according to the results of analyses of deliveries of kaolin, in the first half of the nineteenth century, certainly demonstrates exceptional originality and boldness. Brongniart's color classification is still in use at Sèvres today.

When Alexandre Brongniart was appointed director of the Sèvres manufactory in 1800, he took over an establishment that had suffered considerably from ten years of national political and economic disruption. With the manufactory's finances in disarray, the manufactory's clientele scattered, with general worker morale at a low level and severe shortages of basic materials, Brongniart was beset with serious difficulties. Over the next five decades, he worked closely with various government agencies, encouraged new aesthetic expressions at the manufactory, and fostered technological investigation. By the time of his death in 1847 the Sèvres manufactory had not only survived but was a thriving establishment on the brink of making further significant contributions to the industry in the second half of the nineteenth century.

1. Even specialists sometimes find it difficult to detect the presence of a *surdécor*, especially when the piece has an authentic colored ground produced by Sèvres.

2. Soda of alicante is derived from a plant that grows in the region of Alicante. The plant was reduced to ash and then used in the composition of soft-paste porcelain at Sèvres.

3. Brongniart, *Traité des arts céramiques* (1844), vol. 2, chap. 2.

4. Entrecolles, *Lettres* (1811).

5. Albis, "Le secret" (1988).

6. "Soak" is a ceramics term meaning to maintain the kiln at a high temperature for a specified length of time, in this case three to five days.

7. By 1816, soft-paste might have been more acceptable aesthetically because of the growing revival of interest at that time in the eighteenth century. By then, however, it was already too late to bring it back to its former glory. One of the essential ingredients of the frit, Alicante soda, which had become virtually unobtainable because of political events, had been replaced by an artificial substance that did not possess the same properties. Even more decisive, perhaps, was the destruction of Gérin's rapid-firing kiln which had been the cornerstone of soft-paste production. Without it, pieces fired would witness the devitrification of their ornament.

8. Albis, "Les débuts de la porcelaine dure à Sèvres" (1996).

9. Albis, "La manufacture de Vincennes-Sèvres" (1995), pp. 48-63. The cup (MNC 22 598) was decorated by Rosset.

10. Albis, "La découverte du kaolin de Saint-Yrieix" (1993). This kaolin was used at Sèvres until the quarry was exhausted in about 1930.

11. Albis, "Les débuts de la porcelaine dure à Sèvres" (1996).

12. Brongniart, *Traité des arts céramiques*, vol. 2., class 3, chap. 1.

13. Ibid., vol. 2, p. 367.

14. Ibid., p. 5. They were designed by Régnier and remained in use in Sèvres until 1965.

15. Ibid., vol. 2, class 3, chap. 3.

16. Ibid., p. 676.

Fig. 11-1. Clay and soil samples, including a kaolin sample from the Pieux in the département de la Manche, acquired through the Enquête des Préfets, 1809. (Sèvres, Musée National de Céramique)

Chapter 11

Clay, Pedagogy, and Progress: The History of the Enquête des Préfets, 1805 – 1810

Béatrice Pannequin

The Enquête des Préfets, or prefects' investigation, was a broad examination of the ceramics industry in France and French territories. Its goal was to gather information about the skills and techniques pertaining to the fabrication of ceramics, by distributing questionnaires and collecting ceramics, shards, and samples of raw earth and clay (fig. 11-1). The results were to be analyzed by chemists and engineers working at the Sèvres manufactory under the direction of Alexandre Brongniart. This ambitious project was consistent with a longstanding tradition of methodical explorations undertaken by centralized governments throughout Western history. In the early nineteenth century, as French bureaucracy became more complex, political authority became increasingly centralized.

In the past, the objective of such sweeping investigations was usually the collection of quantitative information within a particular region, often for the purpose of improving taxation procedures.[1] In medieval France, information gathering was considered essential for monitoring an increasingly complex society. The 1328 census of parishes, leaseholds, and stewardship (*L'état des Paroisses et des feux de baillage et Sénéchaussées de France*), for example, set an important precedent for more ambitious investigations later undertaken by Louis XIV's minister Jean-Baptiste Colbert, notably a project called *L'Etat des provinces* (the state of the provinces) which was launched in 1664. The king's military engineer, the marquis de Vauban, followed Colbert's example and drafted a set of census-taking instructions (*Méthode générale et facille pour faire le dénombrement des peuples, 1686*). The data collected — the size and distribution of the population — in addition to soil samples from various regions, served as the basis for recommendations regarding increased agricultural production, then the principal economic resource. Over a century later, in 1802, the Enquête des Préfets would revive the procedure of gathering soil samples, but with a different goal.

In 1780 a growing fiscal crisis prompted Louis XVI's chief financial officer, Jacques Necker, to gather a range of critical data relating to the deteriorating finances of France. The results of this survey would serve as the basis for formal intervention to improve the nation's unstable economy and generate revenue for the government. The project was implemented by regional officials appointed by the central government who were analogous to the prefects of the revolutionary, Directory and Consulate, and Empire periods.

While censuses were meant to be exhaustive, *enquêtes*, or investigations, had more limited application and goals. They made possible the extrapolation of specific data that facilitated the development of statistics and their analysis in the nineteenth-century sense of the term. Under the Revolution, the authorities found such enterprises especially appealing. The government undertook investigations of demographics, health, agriculture, commerce, and industry. While the *enquêtes* demonstrate an eagerness to present a positive image offsetting the period's more chaotic aspects in the eyes of posterity, they also indicate a resolve by the authorities to improve the quality of the nation's output through scientific progress.

In 1802 Jean-Antoine Chaptal, *ministre de l'Intérieur*, called for the organization of separate *enquêtes* to collect data relating to French commerce and industry which had suffered many setbacks during the Revolution. In a letter dated 10 Thermidor year 9 (July 10, 1801) Brongniart signaled to Chapal his readiness to supervise such an investigation along the lines suggested by the minister. In the same letter, in the hope of obtaining the government's support and encouragement, Brongniart discussed his plan to develop a museum at Sèvres. He wrote, "I believe it will be useful to the progress of the ceramic arts and their history, to assemble in a methodical way . . . all the objects of art and science that might serve the history of fine and ordinary pottery."[2] Brongniart anticipated concerns regarding the expenditures involved: "I ask only that you authorize me to assemble in one place, to facilitate their methodical classification, the precious materials possessed by the manufactory and those which it might be able to gather easily and at little expense."[3]

With the cooperation of the prefects, it would be easier to obtain samples from potters in the various regions, and perhaps to discover previously unknown indigenous deposits of suitable clay "as white as that of the English." This reference to English creamware, which was extremely popular in the international marketplace at the end of the eighteenth century, reveals Brongniart's pragmatic side as he searched for a "*faience fine*" that would be competitive.

Given Sèvres's government affiliation and financial support, the manufactory was uniquely placed to undertake such an *enquête*. Brongniart's reputation and his boundless enthusiasm and intellectual curiosity propelled the project. He patterned it on surveys of the eighteenth century, while making it distinctly original in its

Fig. 11-2. Examples of ceramics tools, including horns from Martincamp, which were used as slip-trailers; a crucible from the département du Beauvaisis (collected in 1809); and plate jiggers from Creil in the département de l'Oise. (Sèvres, Musée National de Céramique)

Fig. 11-3. Glazed pottery from the département de l'Allier, acquired through the Enquête des Préfets, 1809. (Sèvres, Musée National de Céramique)

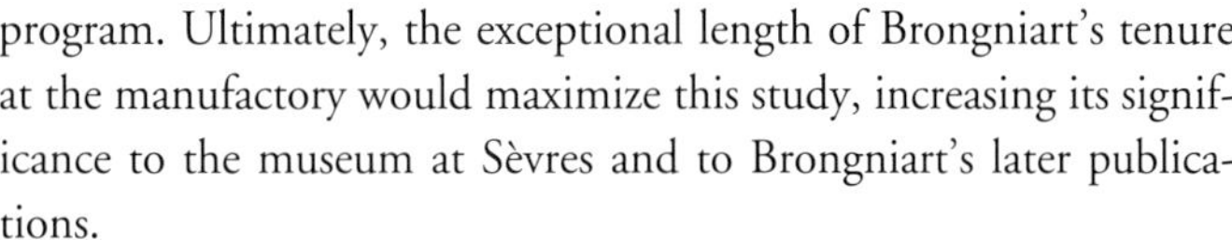

program. Ultimately, the exceptional length of Brongniart's tenure at the manufactory would maximize this study, increasing its significance to the museum at Sèvres and to Brongniart's later publications.

The Questionnaire

The project was launched with an initial set of requests in 1806. A questionnaire was sent by the prefects to potters and ceramics producers working within their districts. The quantitative and technical orientation of the questions, which were applicable to all kinds of ceramics but focused on lead-glazed earthenware in particular, place the inquiry squarely in the tradition of Colbert's and Vauban's information-gathering programs. The questionnaire read:

- What are the various kinds of earthenware and pottery that you produce and for which you use different clays, either pure or in combination? Send: a small earthenware vase and two or three other pieces of each kind of pottery, and attach labels to them with numbers indicating what kind they are (should you use different glazes on pottery of the same kind, please send samples of each glaze); thirty livres of each kind of clay used in the fabrication of your pottery in its purest form, unmixed and untreated. Please attach a numbered label to each sample corresponding to the number you placed on the samples of pottery made from this clay.

- How do you treat your clays before using them?

- In the mixtures you prepare, what proportions of each numbered clay sample do you use in making each numbered variety of pottery?

- What different kinds of glazes and varnishes do you use on your pottery?

- How do you go about preparing each glaze or varnish?

- Where do you obtain the substances contained in each glaze? Send samples of the various sands, pebbles, etc. that you use in preparing the glazes and that can be found in your environs and your department.

- What is the form of the kiln you use to fire the various potteries you make?

- How long does it take to fire each kind properly?[4]

Most potters, lacking analytical skills or even the formal education, could not respond to the questionnaire with the requisite precision. Some did not take it very seriously and others did not bother to respond at all, despite repeated requests from the authorities. Nevertheless, between 1806 and 1810, responses arrived at the Sèvres manufactory from thirty different districts, accompanied by finished pieces and clay samples for analysis.[5] The finished ceramics in these deliveries served—along with 292 Greek vases (acquired from Dominique-Vivant Denon by Louis XVI in 1786) and an assembly of German porcelain—as the core collection of the Musée Céramique that Brongniart had envisioned and proposed.

The materials and data gathered through the questionnaire were sent by the prefects to the *ministère de l'intérieur*, which oversaw the project closely until 1810. All four ministers during the 1802–10 period—Chaptal, Jean-Baptiste Champagny, Emmanuel Cretet (comte de Champenol), and Jean-Pierre Bachasson (comte de Montalivet)—were convinced that technical advances were crucial to the well-being of France. Like Brongniart these powerful political figures were men of the Enlightenment who embraced the idea of the *Encyclopédie,* Diderot's great work of the eighteenth century. In their view, the kinds of analyses and discoveries envisioned by the *enquête* were almost certain to improve the daily life of the population. They wholeheartedly supported the project until the Empire began to disintegrate in 1812.

Many potters and producers did not cooperate wholeheartedly. Some were reluctant to surrender the closely guarded materials, formulas, and techniques that distinguished their work and which had cost them time and effort to develop. Even so, the data collected was richly informative about many potters' habits and materials (fig. 11-2). The actual pieces gathered offered an unparalleled overview of regional French ceramics production. The quality of the responses was largely a function of the interest taken by each prefect in the project, for this determined their persistence in implementing it.

The districts that provided the most complete responses and

Fig. 11-4. Glazed pottery from the département de l'Aude, acquired through the Enquête des Préfets, 1809. (Sèvres, Musée National de Céramique)

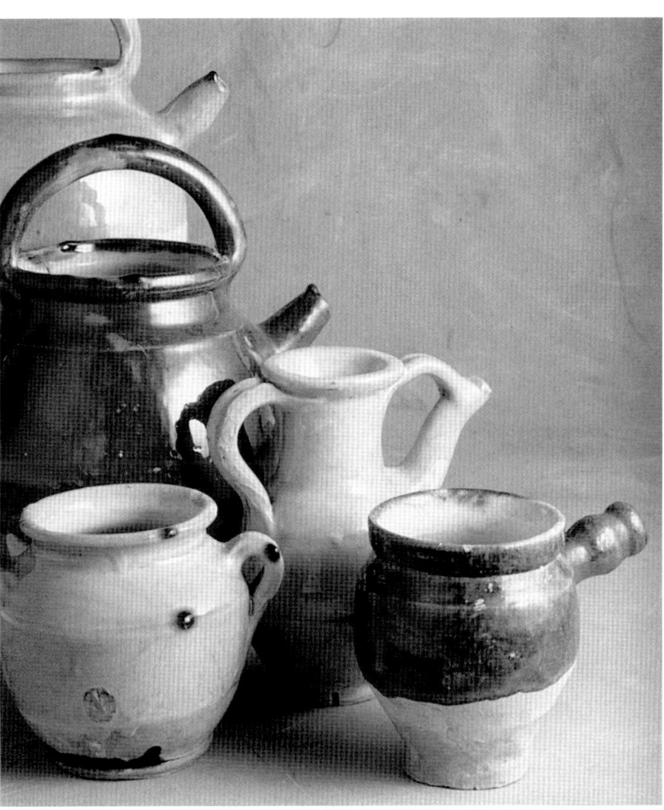

Fig. 11-6. Glazed earthenware from the département du Gard, acquired through the Enquête des Préfets, 1809. (Sèvres, Musée National de Céramique)

Fig. 11-5. Stoneware bottles from the département du Finistère, acquired through the Enquête des Préfets, 1809. (Sèvres, Musée National de Céramique)

Fig. 11-7. Stoneware from the département de la Manche, sent by the prefect Louis Costaz in response to the Enquête des Préfets, 1809. (Sèvres, Musée National de Céramique)

Fig. 11-8. Glazed earthenware sent by M. Chabrol from Albissola in the French territory of Montenotte, Italy, in response to the Enquête des Préfets, 1809. (Sèvres, Musée National de Céramique)

Fig. 11-10. Glazed earthenware dish and stoneware pitcher from Martincamp, département de la Seine-Inférieure, acquired through the Enquête des Préfets, 1809. (Sèvres, Musée National de Céramique)

Fig. 11-9. Glazed earthenware, decorated with slip-trailing, from the département du Puy-de-Dôme, acquired through the Enquête des Préfets, 1809. (Sèvres, Musée National de Céramique)

Fig. 11-11. Creamware bowl from the Delavigne factory in Le Havre, département de la Seine-Inférieure, acquired through the Enquête des Préfets, 1809. (Sèvres, Musée National de Céramique)

numbered samples included the Allier (fig. 11-3), the Aude (fig. 11-4), Finistère (fig. 11-5), Gard (fig. 11-6), the Manche (fig. 11-7), the territory of Montenotte (fig. 11-8),[6] Puy-de-Dôme (fig. 11-9), and the Seine-Inférieure (figs. 11-10 to 11-12). The written responses and clay samples were inventoried, while the objects intended for the future museum were classified by Denis-Désiré Riocreux, who later was made curator of the museum at Sèvres.

The Results

One of the better responses to the questionnaire, from the Départment de la Manche, will serve as a representative example. Because Louis Costaz, the prefect of the Manche district, was intensely interested in the ceramics production of his region, Brongniart wrote to him directly in 1806, requesting clay samples and examples of finished pieces. Brongniart also asked for information about the kaolin deposits known to exist in the area, complaining about the monopoly of the kaolin suppliers in Limoges. "I know that there are quarries of this clay near Valognes," he wrote. "Even though I have been assured that its quality is inferior to that of Limoges, I want to give it a try. You understand that I desire to know rather precisely what this kaolin would cost if delivered to Sèvres, in order to calculate on a sound basis the advantages and disadvantages."[7]

Costaz's eventual response to this inquiry took the form of a memorandum, addressed by the director of the Valognes factory to the subprefect of his district: "I will not provide details of the composition of my porcelain pastes, which are based primarily on white clay from the Pieux, because, being father of a large family, I need to retain for a time exclusive use of the important discoveries made in this line."[8] Having thus safeguarded the secret of his clay formula, the director of the factory went on to boast about his porcelains, both soft and hard paste. He provided information about his prices and described a potter's wheel he had invented that was turned by a "simple mechanism easy to operate." He also sent some porcelain pieces and samples of the precious kaolin from the Pieux region of the district.

Brongniart had this kaolin analyzed at the manufactory and he described it nearly forty years later in his *Traité des Arts céramiques*: "Kaolin from the Pieux, west of Cherbourg, is rich in clay, frequently even plastic, mixed with pink ferrous veins and readily discernable quartz grains throughout."[9] An unbroken chain of information linked the original *enquête* questionnaire of 1806 to results published in Brongniart's *Traité* in 1844.

The Museum

As already noted, the *enquête* would add many pieces to the collection of the museum (see chap. 9). These were all clearly datable, having been obtained from contemporary production. Their modest character, however, did not detract from their significance as artifacts. Brongniart's aim for the museum encompassed both the display of beautiful objects and the presentation of an educational ensemble, in which shards, clay samples, and finished pieces all served to broaden the viewer's understanding of the history and complexities of the ceramic arts. As he envisioned it, the museum was to provide an ordered survey of ceramics techniques "considered in terms of their history, their practice, and their theory."[10]

In hindsight his vision is perhaps regrettable insofar as it often tended to neglect the full richness of forms and colored glazes being explored in contemporary production. As a result the survey bequeathed to posterity many pedestrian pieces instead of the more sumptuous work that was being produced in France, especially by the Paris porcelain makers devoted to the luxury trades. Brongniart's priorities were logical rather than aesthetic, calling for the clear presentation by "order" and "class" of the material at his disposal, complete with identifying labels.

To help realize the museum project Brongniart turned to Denis-Désiré Riocreux, a member of the manufactory's staff, whose dedication to the project continued after Brongniart's death in 1847. Riocreux started at Sèvres as a flower painter, but the loss of an eye forced him to abandon this occupation in 1817. Thereafter, he was the de facto curator of the museum, charged with safeguarding, registering, and classifying its growing collection, although he was not officially named to this position until 1829. The delay was caused by Brongniart's budgetary scruples combined with his reluctance to create a position that "does not contribute directly to the fabrication of porcelain."[11] As always the manufactory came first.

Consistent with Brongniart's program, Riocreux devised oval labels, written in a script of exemplary clarity which is still legible today (fig. 11-13). He recorded provenance, attribution, date, and donor's name, inserting question marks when information was either incomplete or judged possibly incorrect.

The organization and growth of the museum proceeded somewhat in tandem with the manufactory's production (see chap. 9). The practice of exchanging Sèvres vases for comparable pieces from other establishments continued throughout the nineteenth century. This occurred indirectly in 1861, for example, when sixteenth-century stoneware tiles with engraved cobalt decoration from Massy-Brémontier[12] and from the residence of Jehan Ango in Dieppe entered the collection through two intermediaries — the abbé Cochet (archaeologist and author of *Répertoire d'Archéologie de la Seine-Inférieure*, 1871) and M. Mathon (curator of the Musée de Neufchâtel in Bray), in exchange for a pair of Sèvres vases presented to the city of Dieppe.

Riocreux also carried out his own experiments in an effort to develop new aesthetics and production processes for the manufactory. He was responsible for the *pâte-sur-pâte* technique introduced at Sèvres by Jean-Jacques Ebelmen, Brongniart's successor as director of the manufactory. It was inspired by both Chinese porcelains and indigenous pieces from the Lezoux and Auvergne regions which had been obtained through the *enquête*. As Brongniart noted in the *Traité*, "the white of the birds depicted on these pieces . . . is a clayey white and not a tinny white, evidently having been fired at high temperature with the lid."[13]

Technical Research: Jacques Fourmy

An important part of the *enquête* was the analysis of the various

Fig. 11-12. Creamware plates from the Delavigne factory in Le Havre, département de la Seine-Inférieure. (Sèvres, Musée National de Céramique)

Fig. 11-13. An example of the labels prepared by Denis-Désiré Riocreux for objects acquired through the Enquête des Préfets, 1809. (Sèvres, Musée National de Céramique)

samples sent to Sèvres. It was hoped that this might lead to improvements in the quality of production. Brongniart assigned several chemists and engineers to do this work. Notable among them was Jacques Fourmy who focused on analyzing the chemical content of glaze samples and the elimination of toxic lead oxide from glazes. The quest for a substitute for lead oxide and the search for new kaolin deposits were the key preoccupations of Brongniart's research collaborators.

Fourmy, the son of a potter from Nevers, was trained as a geologist and chemist. Interested in the ceramics of all cultures, he began his career as an independent porcelain producer in Nantes but soon turned his attention to research. He was familiar with late-eighteenth-century clinical reports about the toxic effects of improperly fired lead glazes. He was also aware of the government's anxiety, after the Revolution, over the cost of increasingly scarce primary materials. The *ministère de l'interieur* was eager to avoid importing essential glaze ingredients, especially lead from England and tin from Spain. Fourmy undertook to resolve both of these problems.

Extremely critical of French as well as foreign productions, Fourmy drafted a memorandum proposing a set of normative standards applicable to all everyday ceramics for domestic use. These standards were based on affordability, durability, resistance to sudden changes of temperature, and the use of nontoxic glazes. Fourmy emphasized that most lead-glaze ceramics, notably the remarkably popular and inexpensive creamware (then known as "queen's ware" in England and as *faïence fine* in France), were insufficiently fired. As a result the glazes used on them were not completely vitrified, and the lead oxides in the glazes were "vulnerable even to weak solvents, [causing them to] mingle with the food, wreaking havoc with the workings of the body — all the more difficult to discern because of the slowness with which it becomes manifest."[14]

Fourmy embarked on a series of experiments to remedy these health hazards and serious economic problems. He eventually developed a new lead-free material, known as "hygioceramics" (word coined by a geologist named Haüy), which was introduced in 1801. Fourmy believed that his new hygioceramics should be used instead of glazed pottery. Brongniart analyzed this substance in his *Traité*, and primarily on the basis of the high temperature at which it had to be fired, he described it as something between stoneware and porcelain.

In recognition of his achievements, Fourmy was awarded gold medals at the prestigious French industrial products exhibitions of 1801 and 1806. His invention never entered the mainstream, however, probably because of the increased production cost of its lengthy firing process, which consumed considerable amounts of combustible fuel. Aesthetics also played a role in the failure of hygioceramics. In Brongniart's view, this failure confirmed the general public's preference for brilliantly colored pottery: "Although the dual result of salubrity and economy was attained, the people, the great consumer of brilliantly glazed pottery, long opted for the latter in favor of the prior qualities, even at comparable prices."[15]

Similar research was being conducted by Jean-Marie Darracq, a chemist working in the Landes, Basses Pyrénées, and Hautes Pyrénées districts, which had failed to respond to both the 1806 and 1809 questionnaires. Aware of the toxicity of lead glazes, another chemist had developed an alternative ceramics formula, this one based on pumice stone. It too proved to be a failure economically.

Despite the commercial failure of hygioceramics, the invention made Fourmy famous in the early nineteenth century. His reputation prompted Brongniart to appoint him to an adjunct position at the manufactory in 1808, placing him in charge of analyzing the clay samples forwarded by the departmental prefects. In June 1809 Fourmy and Brongniart outlined a program of research whose primary goals were to improve glazes and increase the heat resistance of crucibles.[16] It was quite ambitious and in fact never achieved the desired aims, but many of the experiments performed under its auspices led to improvements in the production process. Fourmy never completely severed his connection to the manufactory and Brongniart; he taught ceramics at the Muséum d'Histoire Naturelle and continued his research independently.

The Enquête de Préfets ultimately failed to provide a comprehensive overview of the French ceramics industry that would enable administrators to elevate the overall quality of French ceramics production. Nevertheless it contributed greatly to Brongniart's later reputation. From much of the information and objects garnered from this survey, Brongniart was able to fashion a portion of the core collection of the Musée Céramique at Sèvres and also to conceptualize elements of his most significant publication, the *Traité des arts céramiques et vitriques*. Without the knowledge acquired through the *enquête*, Brongniart might never have made these enduring contributions to the ceramic arts.

Note: The archival documents cited below are from the Archives of the Manufacture Nationale de Sèvres (AMNS).

1. The Sumerian civilization (ca. 3000–2000 B.C.), which had highly developed accounting and recording techniques, organized the first known general census, in an effort to improve the efficiency of tax collection. A similar enterprise was initiated by the Roman emperor Augustus.

2. [Je crois utile aux progrès de l'art de la poterie et à son histoire de rassembler d'une manière méthodique . . . tous les objets d'art et de science qui peuvent servir à l'histoire de la poterie fine et commune] Register Vc 2.

3. [Je vous demande seulement de m'autoriser à réunir dans un même lieu, pour les y classer méthodiquement les materiaux précieux que possède la manufacture et ceux qu'elle poura rassembler par des moyens faciles et nullement dispendieux] ibid.

4. [Quelles sont les diverses espèces de faïences et poteries que vous fabriquez et pour lesquelles vous employez des terres différentes soit pures, soit mélangées? Envoyez: un petit vase de terre et deux ou troix morceaux de chacune des espèces de poterie et y mettre une étiquette portant le numero pour chacune des espèce différentes (pour le cas où vous employeriez pour une même espèce de poterie différente plusieurs sorte de couvertes, vous voudrez bien envoyer des morceaux pour échantillon de ces différentes couvertes). / Trente livres de chaque espèce de terre employée à la fabrication de vos poteries dans sa plus grande purté et sans mélange ni préparation. Vous voudrez bien mettre—pour chaque terre une étiquette qui portera un numéro correspondant à celui que vous aurez mis sur l'échantillon de l'espèce de poterie fabriquée avec cette terre. / Quelles sont les préparations que vous faitez subir à vos terres avant de les employer? / Dans les mélanges que vous faites, quelle est la proportion dans laquelle chaque terre désignée sous telle numéro entre dans la fabrication de l'espèce de poterie désignée sous tel numero? / Quelles sont les différentes espèces de couvertes ou vernis que vous employez pour vos poteries? / Quels sont les procédés que vous employez pour la composition de chaque couverte ou vernis? / D'où tirez-vous les substances qui entrent dans la composition de chaque couverte? Envoyez une portion de chacun des différents sables, cailloux, etc. que vous employez dans la composition des couvertes et qui se trouvent dans vos environs ou dans le département. / Quelle est la forme du fourneau dont vous vous servez pour faire cuire les différentes espèces de vos poteries? / Combien ce temps faut-il pour donner à chaque espèce le degré de cuisson convenable?] Brongniart, *Traité des arts céramiques* (1844).

5. The archives of the Enquête des Préfets as well as the ceramics and clay and soil samples collected under its auspices are now in the Musée National de Céramique, Sèvres (publication forthcoming).

6. The Territory of Montenotte, also known as the Ligurian Republic, encompassed the Italian communes of Albissola and Savona and was annexed by Napoleon in 1805.

7. [Je sais qu'il y a près de Valognes des carrières de cette terre, quoiqu'on m'ait assuré qu'elle étoit d'une qualité inférieure à celle de Limoges je voudrois l'essayer . . . Vous sentez que je désire savoir assez exactement ce que coutera ce kaolin rendu à Sèvres afin de calculer sur des bases certaines les avantages et les inconvénients] AMNS, Enquête des Préfets, Registre de réception no. 33, letter dated March 21, 1806.

8. [Je n'entrerai point dans le détail de la composition de mes pâtes à porcelaine dont l'argile blanc des Pieux fait la base principale parceque père d'une famille nombreuse j'ai besoin pendant quelques temps de conserver l'usage exclusif des découvertes importantes faites dans cette partie] Ibid.

9. [Kaolin des Pieux, à l'Ouest de Cherbourg. [Ce kaolin] est très argileux, souvent même plastique mêlé de veines rosâtres et ferrugineuses et de grains de quartz très apparents dans plusieurs points] (Brongniart, *Traité des arts céramiques* [1844], vol. 1, p. 47).

10. [considerées dans leur histoire, leur pratique et leur theorie] Register Vc 2.

11. [ne concoure pas directement à la fabrication de la porcelaine] Register Vc 8, letter from Brongniart to Riocreux dated May 3, 1823.

12. Massy-Brémontier is near Neufchâtel-en-Bray in the district of the Seine Inférieure, in Normandy.

13. [Le blanc des oiseaux . . . est un blanc argileux et non un blanc d'étain ayant été évidemment cuit au grand feu avec la couverte] (Brongniart, *Traité des arts céramiques* (1844), vol. 1, p. 426); also see Brongniart and Riocreux, *Description méthodique* (1845), vol. 2, pl. 50, fig. 5.

14. [attaquable par les dissolvans le moins actifs, alors il se mêle aux alimens, et porte dans l'économie animale, des ravages d'autant plus difficiles à prévoir qu'ils sont lents et imperceptibles dans leurs commencemens] Fourmy, *Mémoire* (1802), p. 84.

15. [Lors même qu'on atteindrait ce double résultat, la salubrité et l'économie, le peuple, grand consommateur de Poterie à vernis brillant, préfèra longtemps, même à prix égal, cette dernière qualité à la première] Brongniart, *Traité des arts céramiques* (1844), vol. 1, p. 291; ibid. vol. 2, p. 2.

16. The research on crucibles was carried out primarily by Russinger.

Political Chronology

The Ancien Régime

The Monarchy. . . . . to 1789
Constitutional Monarchy 1789–92

The Republic

The First Republic. 1792–95
Directory. 1795–99
Consulate 1799–1804

The Empire

Napoleon. 1804–14

The Restauration

Louis XVIII 1814–15

The 100 Days

Napoleon. . . . . March–June 1815

The Restauration

Louis XVIII 1815–24
Charles X. 1824–30

The July Monarchy

Louis-Philippe 1830–48

Catalogue of the Exhibition

Tamara Préaud

The drawings presented in this catalogue and the exhibition were chosen in accordance with several criteria. They represent work produced at Sèvres during each of the political periods while Alexandre Brongniart was director of the manufactory. A wide array of objects was made at Sèvres. Some are primarily decorative, such as elaborate vases and centerpieces, while others are more functional, including a variety of pieces for table services. In addition to traditional forms, the manufactory added some new ones, such as the zarf, a kind of cup holder. Sèvres also broadened its repertoire at this time to include paintings on glass, stained glass, and furniture, such as secretaries and small tables known as *guéridons*. One unusual project involved the design of a piano.

This selection of drawings presents the rich assortment of ornamental patterns explored by the manufactory during this period; these included neoclassical, Gothic Revival, Renaissance revival, and Middle and Far Eastern motifs. Representative examples of the working drawings submitted by the many artists, architects, and designers are also included.

Around 1814 Alexandre Brongniart established a much-needed classification and inventory system for the manufactory's large collection of works relating to the ceramic arts—from ancient prototypes to plaster models and molds, from paintings to works on paper, including prints and drawings. This system was applied to the works produced at the manufactory itself and all of the accumulated works, including the drawings that follow, were assigned inventory numbers after the fact, sometimes with erroneous dates. At the same time, Denis-Désiré Riocreux, who was later appointed curator of the Musée Céramique, was instructed to organize and preserve those drawings that were no longered needed in production, a task that he implemented intermittently and slowly, sometimes introducing further mistakes into the records.

Throughout this catalogue, various documents relating to the organization of the work carried out at Sèvres are discussed and cited. At the start of each year, Brongniart drew up a list of anticipated work, organized by object category. During the Empire (1804–1814/15), he sent quarterly reports on work-in-progress to his superiors. As decorated pieces were completed, the production costs and sale prices were recorded on *feuilles d'appréciation*, or valuation sheets. Initially these were hand-written documents and were often incomplete, but beginning in August 1810 they were printed.

In 1820 Brongniart instituted the practice of compiling sheets or files recording the progress of the manufactory's most important projects. In addition to the valuation sheets, which are sometimes less than completely reliable, a register was kept in which objects were listed with the date of their entry into the sales inventory. The numbers assigned them at that time, consisting of the folio number within the register followed by the sequential number accorded to each object on the same page, became the object's permanent reference number. Finally, two sets of registers recorded the removal of each object from the sales inventory, based on its sale by either credit or by cash sale. There are no further documents at the manufactory that track the later history of the objects. Wherever possible, however, in this catalogue the drawings have been related to the piece or ensemble for which they were conceived.

These sketches, however appealing they are on their own, are actually working drawings, the preliminary steps in the long process of producing finished pieces. The designs were subsequently transformed by the purity of the porcelain, the brilliance of the enamel colors, the rich glow of gilt ornament, and the technical acumen of the artists and artisans at Sèvres.

Author/editor's note: Because the documentation available in the archives is often fragmentary, the drawings are arranged in chronological order, on the basis of the date of their receipt, the remittance of payment to the artist, or the beginning of work on the actual piece. Occasionally, bookkeeping idiosyncracies entailed by the "maximum" system (see chap. 3) led to apparent inconsistencies in dating.

In the entry headings, under "inscriptions," neither the inventory numbers inscribed on the drawings nor those inscriptions that were clearly added by later hands have been included. The simplest inscriptions, such as those giving dates or artists, names, are left in French; more complicated inscriptions, especially technical instructions, are translated just before the footnotes accompanying the entry. In the footnotes, the documents cited are from the archives of Manufacture Nationale de Sèvres. Other references are cited by the author's last name, an abbreviated title, and the year of publication. For those, full references will be found in the bibliography. For the dimensions, height precedes width, or diameter in some cases.

The figure references within the entries refer to comparative illustrations, many of which are found in a separate section beginning on page 383.

1.

Design and Decoration for a Vase, 1801 Called *Vase 'Jasmin'*

Alexandre-Théodore Brongniart
Watercolor and pencil on paper
15 1/8 x 12 in. (38.3 x 30.6 cm)
Inscriptions: [verso] *Le 3 fructidor an 9 (1801) / P.f. N° 18 / N° 78;* [recto, middle left, in pencil] *il faudra isoler la terasse de la / moulure en or, et y mettre la teinte / du vase entre la terasse et le filet d'or;* [recto, middle right] [signature and date] *3 fruc. an. 9 / Bt.*
Inv. no. § 8 1801 No 6

Trompe-l'oeil paintings of bronze and various stones — marble and porphyry, sardonyx, or onyx — were made at Sèvres as early as 1800, and they may reflect the new director's interest in metals and mineralogy. A lack of precision in the ledgers makes it impossible to determine with absolute certainty when this *vase 'Jasmin'* entered the sales inventory, but a list of "pieces in the warehouse on 1 Vendemiaire year 14" (September 23, 1805) includes "2 *vases Jasmin* rose ground, bronze figures," priced at 200 francs each, which might correspond to the design shown here.[1] One of the two was delivered on June 6, 1808 to the Château de Compiègne for the *salle des bains.*[2] A description of a similar decoration ("rose ground, bronze figure[s]") appears in the inventory in connection with a cup that was listed on 22 Prairial year 13 (June 1804).[3]

This vase form was among the first created at the initiative of Alexandre Brongniart in his new role as director of Sèvres. Its decoration was designed by his father, an acclaimed architect and designer. Charles-Louis Décoins, one of the manufactory's throwers, worked on the form in Frimaire year 9 (November-December 1800).[4] Initially, there were two versions: the vase could be thrown either as a single entity or in two pieces (a cylindrical vessel with a pierced bottom and a base). The concept for the second version resembled the *vase 'Hollandais'* which was first made at Sèvres in the mid-eighteenth century. Apparently, this version was soon abandoned, but the first continued to be produced, with various ground colors and decorations, until the early 1820s. It was realized in several variations, all notable for their ornamental restraint (see cat. nos. 4, 12, 43).

The details of grapes and scrolling leaves (sketched in pencil immediately below the base of the vase) and the leaf (drawn at the right) were meant to clarify the forms of the frieze on the base, here painted in dark brown against light brown. The small, colored sketch to the left indicates, as specified by the inscription, the precise placement of the strip of ground (*la terasse*) beneath the figures. It was to be situated slightly above the gold molding, doubtless to counter the heaviness of the original scheme.

Inscription: ["Isolate the field of the / gold escutcheon and put in the colour/ of the vase between the field and the thin gold line"]

1. Register Vu 1, fol. 7v.
2. Register Vbb 2, fol. 82v.
3. Carton Pb 1, liasse 2 (appreciations . . . an XIII)
4. The earliest examples appear in the firing registers in Nivôse year 9 (December 1800 – January 1801; two sizes are specified), and two were sold to Madame Gorgerat in Ventôse year 9 (February 1801) (Registers Vc' 5 and Vy 12, fol. 210v)

2.
Design and Decoration for a Teapot, 1801 Called *Théière 'Pestum'*

Alexandre-Théodore Brongniart
Watercolor, ink, and pencil on paper
7 7/8 x 11 3/8 in. (20 x 28.7 cm)
Inscriptions: [verso] *Recu le 4 Ventose an 9 / P.f. N°18 / N°70*; [recto, upper left, in pencil] *ornemens en brun sur or / avec attribut gravé dans le milieu*; [bottom center, in pencil] *un cabaret de deux tasses*; [signed and dated lower right, in ink] *Brongniart Arch. / vent. an 9*
Inv. no. § 3 1801 No 3

This signed drawing is characteristic of the elder Brongniart's style when designing for the manufactory: befitting an architect, the draftsmanship is precise and elegant but a bit dry. This may also reflect a need to communicate clarity of detail, further demonstrated by the overhead view of the cover (right) and the specifications regarding the second reserve and the various decorative motifs, which include leaves for the neck frieze and dolphins in the half-lozenges. The restrained color scheme is typical of the late eighteenth/early nineteenth century.

The history of the "Paestum" cabaret service is somewhat difficult to unravel: the water jug and sugar bowl are mentioned in the work allocations for the year 9 (1800 – 1801) along with a *tasse à thé 'Pestum'*, which may subsequently have been renamed *tasse à thé coupe*. The *théière 'Pestum'* seems to have been made somewhat later, since the first example of the teapot was not fired until 29 Ventôse year 13 (March 1803).[1] The ensemble, which is sometimes referred to in manufactory documents as the *cabaret 'Brongniart'*, reveals the new director's resolve to develop new forms as quickly as possible. Its name, taken from Paestum, the ancient city in southern Italy where ruins of Doric temples are found, reflects the dominant influence of antiquity.

This drawing might represent a preliminary idea for the shape: when it was realized, however, the base was eliminated, and the lid's pinecone knob, a feature frequently found on late eighteenth-century neoclassical vases, was replaced by a smooth shape that was easier to make and, therefore, less expensive.

Inscription: ["ornaments in brown on gold / with attributes engraved in the middle"]; ["a cabaret of two cups"].

1. Registers Va' 15, dossier 1 (year 9) and Vc' 5.

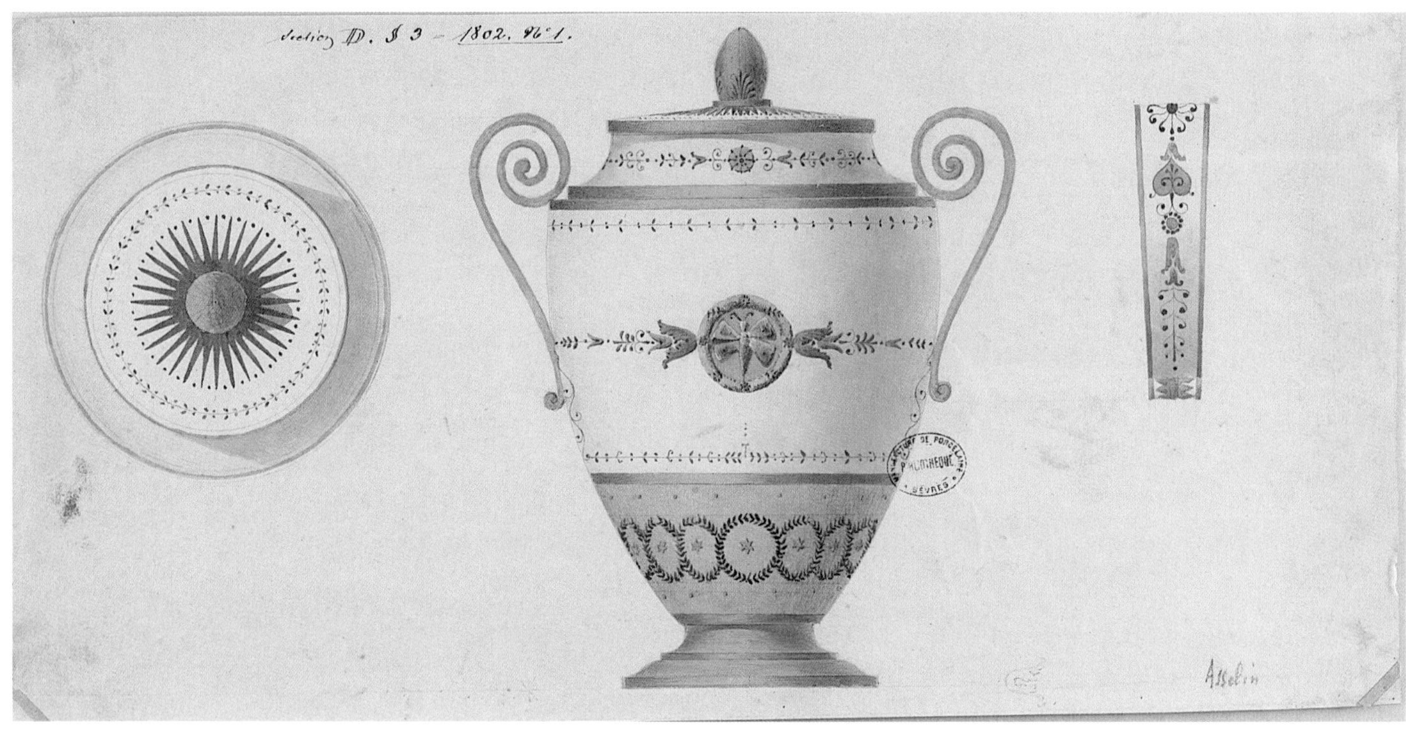

3.

Design and Decoration for a Sugar Bowl, 1801

Called *Pot à Sucre 'A pied anse volute'*

Artist unknown
Watercolor and pencil on paper (cut-out silhouettes glued to sheet)
6 5/8 x 13 1/2 in. (16.8 x 34.4 cm)
Inscription: [verso]: *P. f. N°18 / N° / Recu le* [blank] *frimaire an 10*
Inv. no. § 3 1802 No 1

The precise style of this drawing, with its careful shading to suggest depth, is more suggestive of the work of Brongniart père than that of Charles Eloi Asselin, whose name was inscribed in the lower right corner by a later hand. Because the old inventory does not confirm this attribution, however, the authorship of this delicate ornamental design remains a matter of conjecture. Although the original plaster model for the handle bears the date 1802, the inscription on the verso of the sheet is confirmed by archival documents, which note the firing on 2 Messidor year 9 (June 21, 1801) of sixteen "volute sugar bowls" (*pots à sucre volute*).[1] The form does not seem to have been used after 1815. A variation of the design, made from the beginning, featured lion heads, which were similar to those on the more frequently produced *pot à sucre 'Pestum'*, instead of the volute handles.

1. Register Vc' 5.

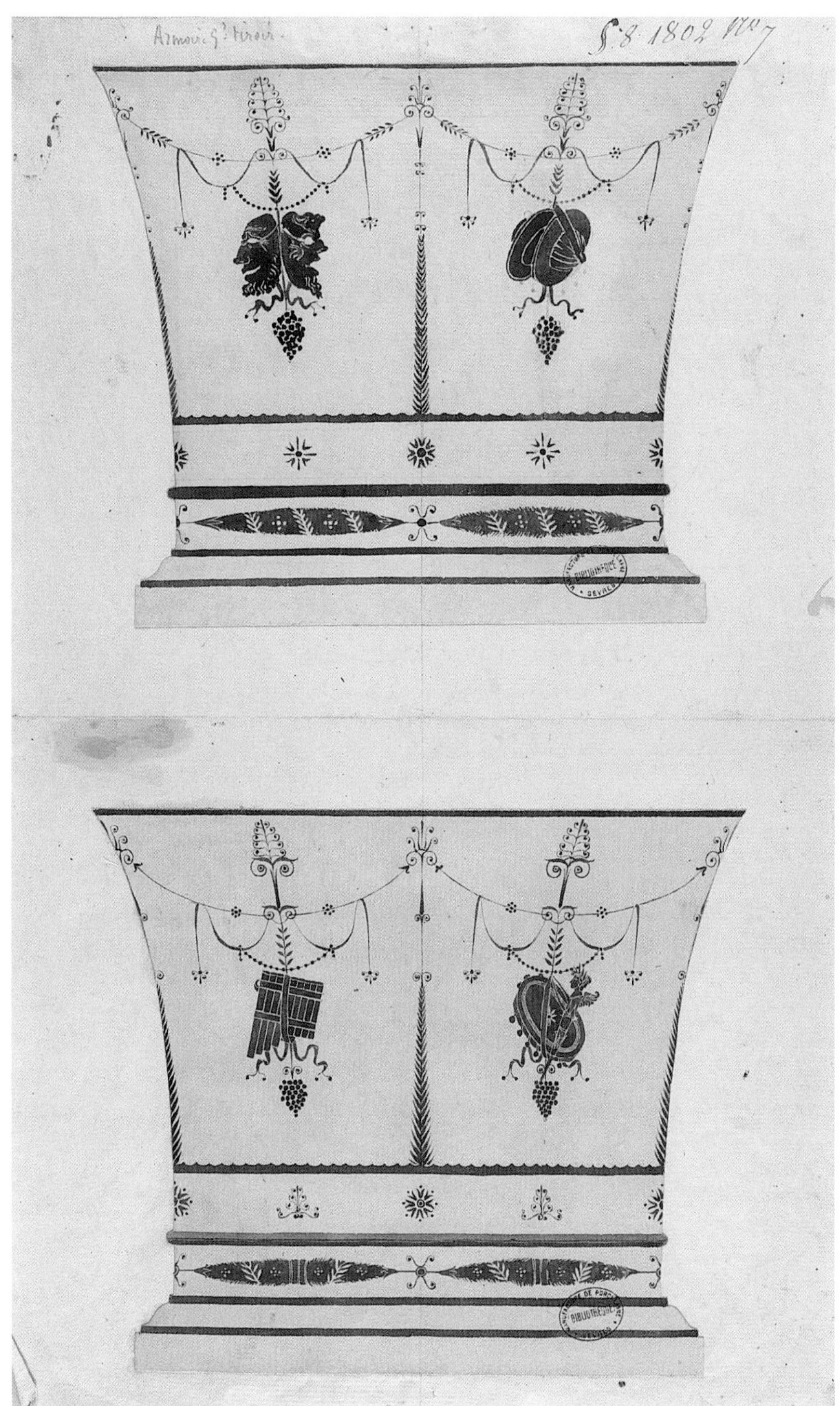

4.
Decorations for Vases, 1802
Called *Vases 'Jasmin'*

Artist unknown
Watercolor on paper (cut-out silhouettes glued to sheet)
16 1/8 x 10 in. (41 x 25.3 cm)
Inscriptions: [verso] *P.f. n° 18. Reçu le 28 (29) fructidor an 10 (1802) / N° 118* [also on verso, an architectural drawing in pencil]
Inv. no. § 8 1802 N° 7

Although the inscriptions on this sheet do not identify the designer, the dry precision of the drawing suggests that it may be the work of Brongniart père. The palette indicated here may have been followed in the execution of some of these vases, but another palette — gold against a gray ground — was employed for a similar decorative scheme on a pair of *vases 'Jasmin'* that are now in the Petit Trianon (see fig. 4a).[1] Assuming that the ground color was indeed retained on some examples, the present design may correspond to the two *vases 'Jasmin'* with *nanquin* ground colors that entered the inventory on 7 Ventôse year 12 (February 1804) and were sold on the 10th of the same month to one M. Thibault.[2]

1. D. Ledoux-Lebard, *Inventaire général du Musée* (1975), p. 47.
2. Carton Pb 1, valuation of 7 Ventôse year 12: "*Jasmin fond nanquin*" (net cost set at 47 francs, of which 18 were for the undecorated blank and 13.5 for the painted decor; sale price set at 72 francs) (Sale Register Vy 16, fol. 40, "2 Jasmins fond nankin et peinture", 144 francs).

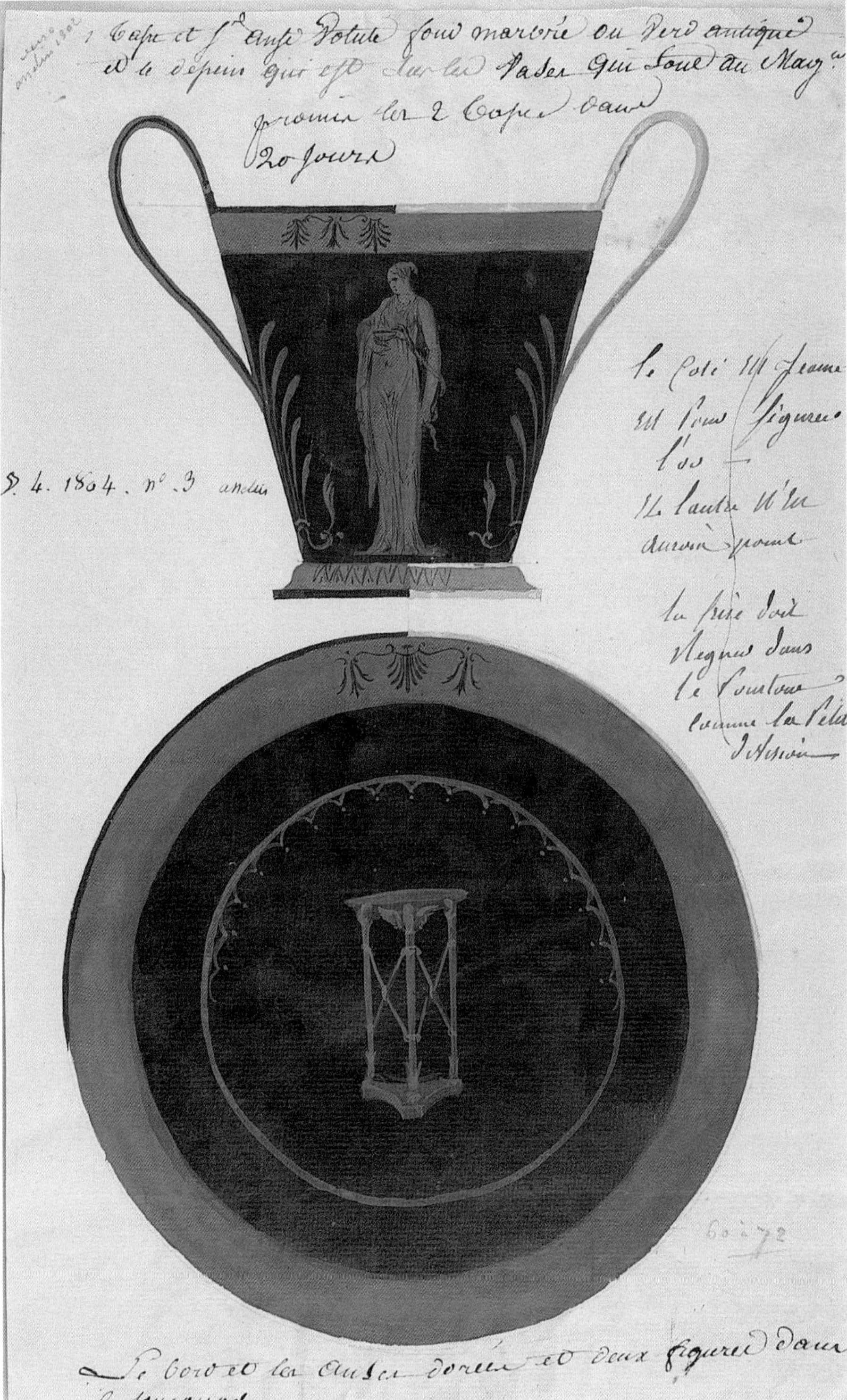

5.

Design and Decoration for a Cup and Saucer, 1802
Called *Tasse 'Conique à deux anses'*

Charles-Eloi Asselin
Watercolor and ink on paper
11 5/8 x 7 1/4 in. (29.5 x 18.3 cm)
Inscriptions: [verso] *Asselin 1802*; [recto, top in ink] *tasse et s(oucoup)e anse volute fond marbré ou verd antique / et le dessein qui est sur les vases qui sont au mag(asin) / promis les 2 tasses dans / 20 jours*; [recto, center right in ink] *le coté en jeaune / est pour figurer / l'or / Et l'autre n'en / aurois point / la frise doit / Regner dans / le Pourtour / comme la Petite / division*; [recto, bottom right in pencil] *60 à 72 fr(ancs)*; [recto, bottom in ink] *Le bord et les anses dorées et deux figures dans / la soucoupe*
Inv. no. § 4 1804 No 3

The elegant neoclassical style of this design, still very much in the spirit of the ancien régime, is typical of the work of Charles-Eloi Asselin, the figure painter who was appointed chef de l'atelier de peinture in 1800. On 18 Brumaire year 12 (November 9, 1803) Brongniart recommended that he receive a bonus for having "made for the manufactory in the year 11 (1802 – 3) a large number of designs."1 The precise annotations make it clear that this drawing was produced to fulfill a commission for two separate cups, and it may well correspond to a transaction noted in the sales registers involving a client named M. Bredert and dated 12 Fructidor year 10 (August 1802): "101-19 1 Cup and saucer Etruscan decoration, 84 francs. 101-18 1 ditto volute handle marbled ground, 48 francs."2 Clearly the use of gold ornament in "Etruscan" ornamentation was considered no more avant garde in 1802 than in 1785, when such decorative schemes were introduced.3

Surviving evidence makes it impossible to establish a secure date for the creation of the tasse 'conique' design, which resembles several eighteenth-century models. It could be produced with one or two handles, and other documents indicate several variations for the design of its foot.

Inscription: ["cups and s(aucer) handle scroll with ground marbled or antique green / and the design that is on the vases that are in the shop / the two cups promised in twenty / days; center right (ink): the side in yellow is to receive the gold design / And the other will / have none / the frieze shall predominate in the circumference / like the small division; . . . the edge and the handles gilded and two figures in / the saucer"]

1. Carton T 1, liasse 5, dossier 5.
2. Register Vz 1, fol. 35.
3. See the letter from Hettlinger to the comte d'Angiviller, dated May 24, 1785, concerning a cup "with Etruscan painting executed after a model provided by Mr. de Lagrenée black ground with red figures (*à figures rouges aurore*). . . . It seems to me it would have been better not to have used the gold fillets"

6.
Design and Decoration for a Vase, 1803 Called *Vase 'Cassolette'*

Attributed to Alexandre-Théodore Brongniart
Watercolor and pencil on paper
11 1/2 x 12 3/4 in. (29.3 x 32.5 cm)
Inscriptions: [verso] *Reçu le 10 Messidor an XI / P.f. N°18 / N°138*; [recto, from top beginning beside frieze detail, in pencil] *au collet / décoration en or sans fleurs coloriées / en or / nul / en or*
Inv. no. § 8 1803 No 13

Although this sheet is unsigned, the handwriting seems to confirm what the style suggests, namely that it is the work of Brongniart's father. It has not been possible, however, to date the entry of this design for a perfume brazier into the sales inventory, "two *vases cassolette*, butterflies etc." priced at 200 francs per pair were delivered to the Château de Compiègne on April 1, 1810.[1] Two others with a slightly lower price — 160 francs per pair — were delivered to the Palais de Trianon on July 2, 1811 (see fig. 6a).[2] Surviving examples show that the decoration of the neck was indeed modified as recommended by the artist.[3]

Because the records are somewhat vague, only the prices make it possible to distinguish this piece from the *sucrier cassolette 'à dauphins'* that was designed for the *service 'Olympique'* and featured the same decoration of butterflies and insects against a pale blue ground. Several additional examples of this sugar server entered the sales inventory priced at 350 francs each, and one of these was delivered to the Château de Compiègne with the two *vases cassolettes*.[4] The same elements recur on a dessert service, described as "red border floral wreath on gold ground butterflies etc.," which entered the sales inventory on October 11, 1809, before being delivered to the Château de Fontainebleau for the emperor's use.[5]

Birds, butterflies, and insects were favored motifs in all of the European decorative arts during the first years of the nineteenth century; they introduced a note of gaity into the prevailing neoclassical idiom, which could be severe at times. As a devoted naturalist, the director had studied insects and fossils, and his interest might have prompted him to encourage their use as motifs at Sèvres.

Inscription: ["at the collar / decoration in gold without colored flowers / in gold / nothing / in gold"]
1. Register Vbb 2, fol. 108.
2. Register Vbb 4, fol. 51, "2 vases forme cassolette fond rouge papillons etc."
3. D. Ledoux-Lebard, *Inventaire général du Musée* (1975), p. 47 and Ducrot, *Musée national du château de Compiègne* (1993), no. 24, p. 79.
4. Register Vbb 2, fol.108, "1 Cassolette fond rouge papillons etc."; another "Vase Casolette fond rouge" priced at 350 francs was sold to a M. Edwards in June 1817 (Register Vz 3, fol. 67), its reference number indicating that it had entered the sales inventory in 1807.
5. Entry in sales inventory: Register Vu 1, fol. 83v, no. 243-18. Delivery: Register Vy 18, fol. 96.

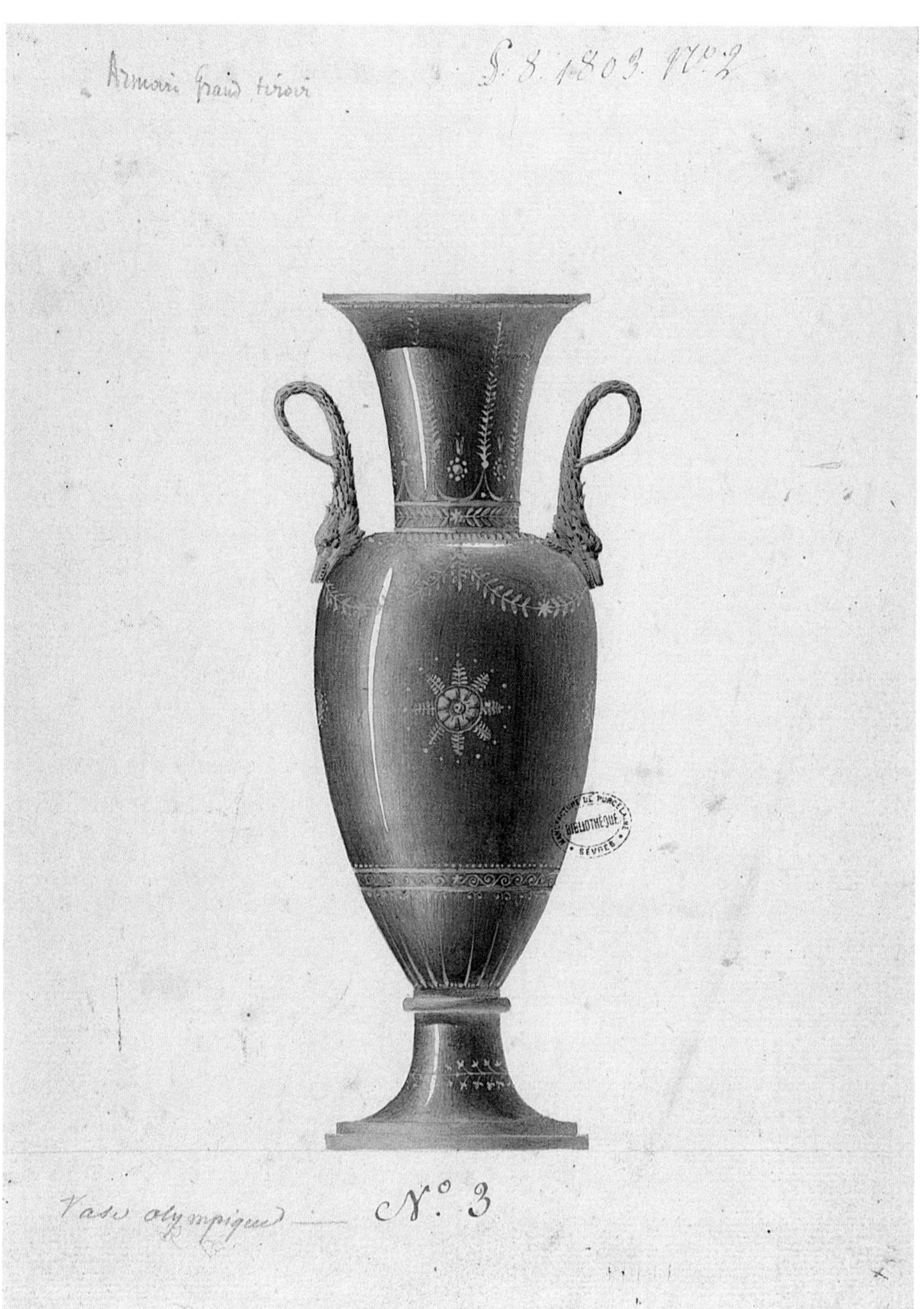

7.

Design and Decoration for a Vase, 1803
Called *Vase 'Olympique No. 3'*

Artist unknown
Watercolor and pencil on paper
11 7/8 x 8 3/4 in. (30.2 x 22.2 cm)
Inscriptions: [verso] *P. Feuille N° 18 / Reçu le 17 Nivose an XI / N° 124*; [recto, below the drawing, in ink]
N° 3
Inv. no. § 8 1803 No 2

Soon after Alexandre Brongniart assumed the directorship of Sèvres, he sought to revitalize the ambitious table services which the manufactory had produced from its inception. The *service 'Olympique'* (see cat. no. 18), for which this vase was destined, was begun in 1803,[1] a date inscribed on some of the drawings. It was designed entirely by Brongniart's father. The service was novel for the time, in that it featured a sculpted and decorated centerpiece, or *surtout*, consisting of several pieces meant to be arranged according to predetermined plan. In addition to a large biscuit group, which included the "chariot of Bacchus and Ceres," two cornucopia, two columns whose bases were encircled by female dancers modeled in high relief by Clodion, and four basins of flowers supported by groups of the Three Graces conceived by Antoine-Denis Chaudet, the *surtout* consisted of "40 small vases with dolphin handles "*beau Bleu*" ground etc. in four forms" each of which cost 72 francs.[2]

Realization of the complete service and its *surtout* took three years. The ensemble was recorded in the sales inventory on December 31, 1806; it was delivered to the Palais des Tuileries in August 1807 and subsequently sent to Tsar Alexander I by Napoleon.[3] In May 1806, a payment of ten francs was authorized to Charles Christian Marie Durosey for the gilding of each "No. 3 vase from the *service 'Olympique'*."[4]

This drawing probably served as a guide for both the form and decoration. It is related to a plaster model bearing the inscription "*Vase 'Olympique' No 2*." The plaster is 8 5/8 inches (22 cm) high, which is slightly larger than the drawing, suggesting that this sheet indicates how the porcelain was to be decorated after it had been fired. The plaster model lacks handles, but it is possible that they were to be executed in bronze.

1. Carton Pb 1, valuation of 28 Germinal year 11 (April 1803), first plate of the *service 'Olympique'*, price not yet determined.
2. [40 petits vases à anses dauphin fond b. Bleu etc. de quatre formes]. See Arizzoli-Clementel, "Les Surtouts imperiaux" (1976); Gavrilova, *Le Service Olympique* (1979); Baca, *Napoleon, Russia and the Olympian Gods* (1996); Baca and Gorbatova, "Le 'Service Olympique'" (1996).
3. For the entry in sales inventory, see register Vu 1, fol. 33, no. 193-1; for deliveries, see register Vy 18, fol. 16v; and register Vy 18, fol. 30.
4. Carton Pb 1, valuation of April 1806.

8.
Decoration for a Plate, 1803
Called *Assiette 'Unie'*

Artist unknown
Watercolor and pencil on paper
7 1/8 x 9 5/8 in. (18.1 x 24.6 cm)
Inv. no. § 5 1803 No 9

The identity of the draftsman who produced this drawing is not known for certain, but the delicate rendering suggests that it might have been Charles-Eloi Asselin. An entry in the sales inventory, made on 29 Prairial year 9 (June 18, 1803), concerns "three plates with wreaths and heads in gray," whose sale price was set at sixty francs each[1]; other entries for the same year mention "sardonyx" and "brown" profiles, descriptions suggestive of the cameolike paintings that subsequently enjoyed long-lasting success at Sevres.

Apparently, a complete service with this decoration was never produced, but on 24 Brumaire year 13 (November 24, 1804), "Monsieur de Lucay, Premier Préfet du Palais de Sa Majesté," chose a service for the Château de Fontainebleau that was quite similar — described as "service Nankeen ground, low relief figures garland of flowers" — and its plates were priced at sixty-three francs each.[2] Another delivery to the emperor, this one made on 14 Frimaire year 13 (December 5, 1804), consisted of "seventy-two plates tortoise-shell ground imitation bronze figures etc.," priced at fifty-four francs each.[3]

Smooth-rimmed round plates produced at Sèvres during the first thirty years of the nineteenth century were based on a model initially devised for the service commissioned from Sèvres by Catherine II of Russia in 1776 – 77. Unlike the more usual plate designs, which specified lobed rims, plates with rims that traced a perfect circle were very difficult to produce without warpage and other defects that destroyed the symmetry of the circle. Their successful production marked a step forward in the chronology of forms. For this design, the plate's profile and thickness, as well as the firing methods, were constantly being altered in hopes of reducing the considerable percentage of waste pieces and seconds.

1. [trois assiettes à couronne et têtes en gris] carton Pb 1, valuations for year 11.
2. Register Vbb 2, fol. 2; see *Versailles et les tables royales*, exhib. cat. (1993 – 94), ill. p. 221. and Chevallier, *Musée national du château de Fontainebleau* (1996), pp. 210 – 211.
3. Register Vbb 2, fol. 6v; see Verlet, Grandjean, and Brunet, *Sèvres* (1954), pl. 101.

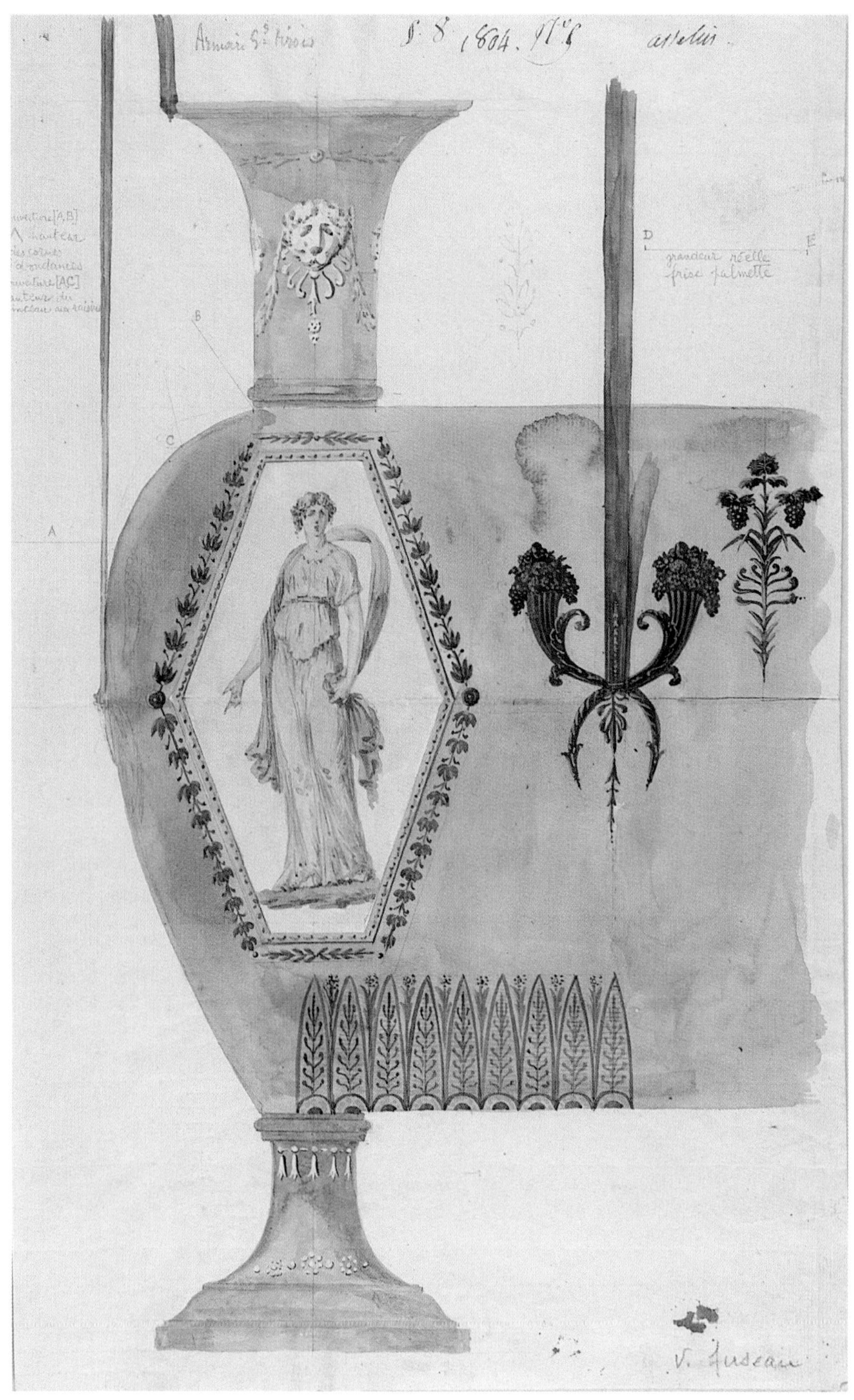

9.
Decoration for a Vase, 1804
Called *Vase 'Fuseau'*

Charles-Eloi Asselin
Watercolor, gouache and pencil on paper
15 3/8 x 9 5/8 in. (39 x 24.3 cm)
Inscriptions: [recto, upper left in pencil] *ouverture (A,B) / hauteur des cornes / d'abondances / . ouverture (A,C) / hauteur du / rinceau aux raisins*; [upper right] *DE / grandeur réelle / frise palmette*; [verso, three sketches for friezes]
Inv. no. § 8 1804 No 5

The female figure within the hexagonal reserve in the drawing was inspired by Pompeian frescoes; classical motifs also appear on the surrounding surfaces and the neck. Similar decorative schemes appear on two *vases 'Fuseau'* with lilac grounds that were delivered to the Palais de Trianon on June 21, 1805;[1] these pieces have flowering plants in the secondary reserve on the opposite side of the vase. Similar reserves, with figures and trees but with different decorative motifs, are found on two additional *vases 'Fuseau'* which were delivered to the Château de Compiègne on June 6, 1808 (see fig. 9a).[2]

Several drawings of this form bear the inscription, "Brongniart vase copied from the original . . . Frimaire year 9" (November – December 1800), accompanied by recommendations for changes in size. The date places it among the first models created for Sèvres by Alexandre-Théodore Brongniart; it was put into immediate production in various sizes. It could be embellished with handles of various kinds, featuring heads, dragons, serpents, or dolphins that were executed in bronze or porcelain. The form was extremely successful: it was produced in at least four different sizes, was constantly modified throughout the nineteenth century, and was often decorated with official portraits or scenes.

Inscription: ["aperture (A,B) / height of the horns / of plenty / aperture (A,C) / height of the vine with grapes; upper right: DE / life size / palmette frieze"]

1. D. Ledoux-Lebard, *Inventaire général du Musée* (1975), p. 168
2. Ducrot, *Musée national du château de Compiègne* (1993), no. 9, pp. 60 – 61.

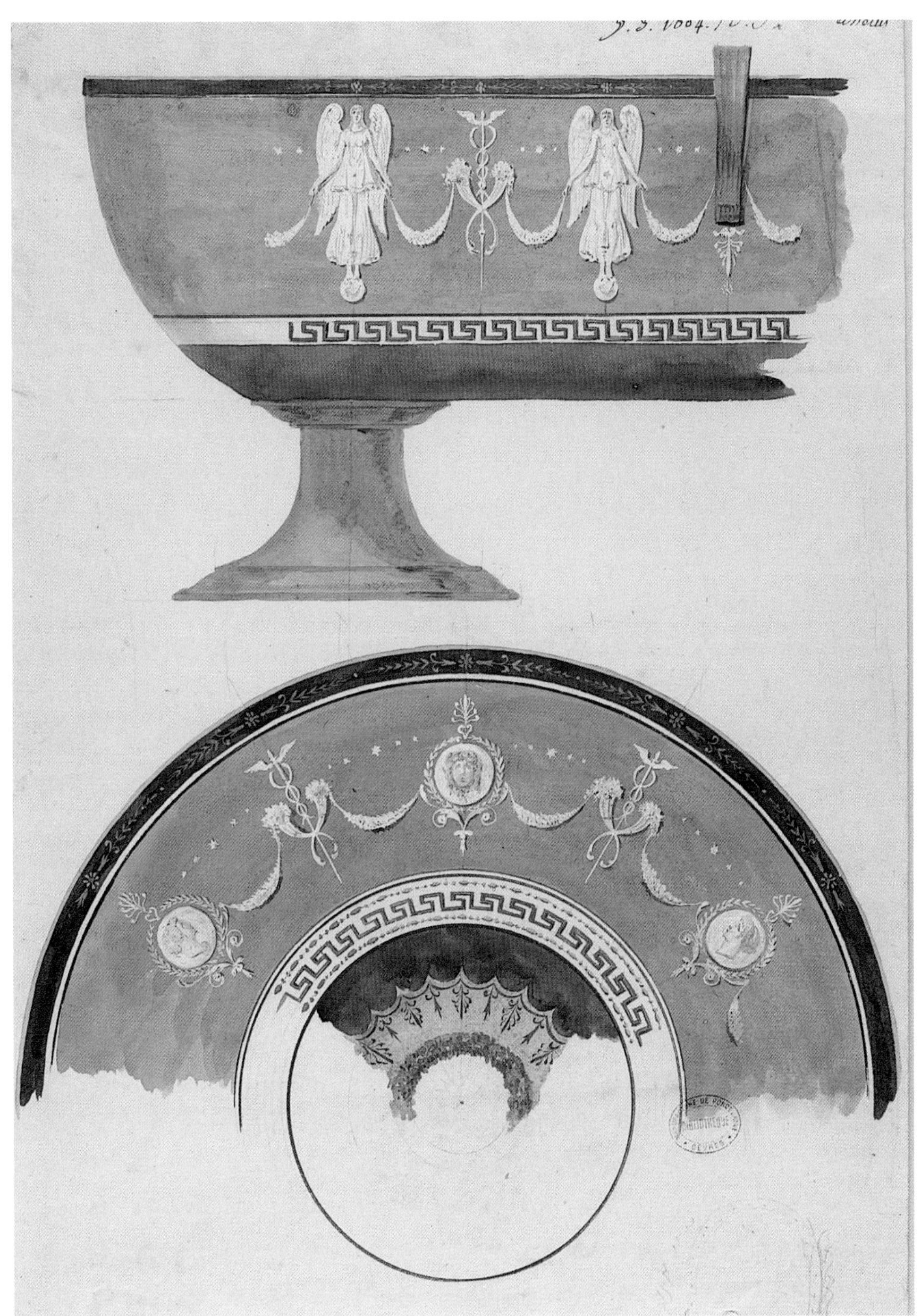

10.
Decoration for a Bouillon Cup and Saucer, 1804
Called *Coupe à bouillon 'Hémisphérique'*

Charles-Eloi Asselin
Watercolor, gouache and pencil on paper
13 1/2 x 9 1/2 in. (34.2 x 24.2 cm)
Inv. no. § 3 1804 No 3

Prior to his appointment as head of the painting studio in 1800, Charles-Eloi Asselin had been primarily a figure painter at Sevres, but thereafter he proved himself a gifted originator of ornamental schemes. Although the themes varied, all were marked by a delicate grace that was becoming out-of-date, as an appreciation for more archeologically correct forms and colors increased in the early years of the nineteenth century. Because there is no way of knowing whether the decoration on this *coupe* was executed against a colored ground or a gold one, it is difficult to match it to a specific entry in the archival documents. It might correspond, however, to an entry on a valuation sheet dated 22 Prairial year 12 (June 12, 1804): "1 soup bowl, gray cariatid[s] against gold ground etc. by Gérard."[1]

The earliest drawing for the form of this standing cup bears the inscription "bouillon cup and saucer with two molded handles year eleven, Ventôse [Coupe à bouillon et sa soucoupe à deux anses a moulures an XI mois ventose]; February – March 1803). Apparently, it was only later that it received the more precise name *coupe 'à bouillon hémisphérique'*, which was meant to distinguish it from later forms. Small decorative pieces such as this one were popular as state and private presentation gifts.

1. Carton Pb 1, valuations for the year 12. The artist named is probably Claude-Charles Gérard, who was appointed head of the painters's workshop in 1804, after the death of Asselin.

11a.
Design and Decoration for a Teapot, 1804
Called *Théière 'Etrusque B'*

Artist unknown
Watercolor, gouache, pencil and ink on paper
8 1/8 x 12 1/8 in. (20.5 x 30.7)
Inscription: [verso] *P.f. Nº18 / reçu le 9 Germinal an XII / Nº151 . . . année 1804*
Inv. no. § 3 1804 No 10

These two designs were sent to the painting department together. They date from the year the shapes were created, and may represent proposals for the forms and decorations of a new déjeuner. The red and black "Etruscan" motifs shown here were not new to Sèvres by 1804 (see cat. no. 5), and would continue to be used throughout the century.

On 18 Frimaire year 14 (December 1805) an important ensemble with "Etruscan shapes, ground and ornaments" painted by Louis Victor Godin aîné was recorded, with a "*pot à lait etrusque*" and a "*théyere bec de dragon.*"[1] It could be part of the "17 piece cabaret service with Etruscan ground and decoration" priced at 1,015 francs, which was entered in the sales inventory beginning on 1 Vendemiaire year 14 (September 23, 1805). This service was eventually presented, on the emperor's orders, to Louis-Philippe de Ségur in June 1806, in recognition of his role as *maître des cérémonies* at the wedding of Princesse Stéphanie, the emperor's niece, who mar-

11b.
Design and Decoration for a Milk Jug, 1804
Called *Pot à lait 'Etrusque B.'*

Artist unknown
Watercolor, gouache, pencil, and ink on paper
11 1/4 x 7 3/8 in. (28.5 x 18.7)
Inscription: [verso] *N° P.f.18 / Reçu le 9 Germinal an XII / N°148*
Inv. no. § 3 1804 No 6

ried the Grand Duke of Baden.[2]

Given that another teapot designed in 1808 is alternately called *Théière 'Etrusque D'* or *Théière 'Etrusque Denon,'* it seems possible that this teapot and milk jug bearing the notation *'Etrusque B'* could have been designed by Brongniart's father. The first forms for a so-called '*Etrusque*' *déjeuner* appear as early as 1781, and several versions were designed under the Empire. It was some time before stylistic consistency became an aesthetic concern, for an "Etruscan" teapot was sometimes used in *déjeuners* that were decorated with hieroglyphs and views of Egypt.

In the 1770s in England, Josiah Wedgwood produced pieces inspired by ancient prototypes using a material known as "black basalt," which he had specially devised to imitate the matte surfaces of the originals. This work was embellished with red encaustic ornament. At Sèvres, however, porcelain with a high-gloss glaze was long the only medium for such replicas; only around 1850, and then very briefly, was polychrome painting used on biscuit. Transpositions of this kind were not unique to Sèvres, for they are also found in pieces produced at the royal manufactory in Naples in the first years of the nineteenth century.[3]

1. "Forme fond et decord [sic] etrusque" (Carton Pb 1, valuations for year 14).
2. "Cabaret de 17 pièces fond et décoration étrusque" (Register Vu 1, fol. 7; Register Vbb 2, fol. 53v).
3. Gruber, *L'Art décoratif en Europe* (1995), ill. p. 116.

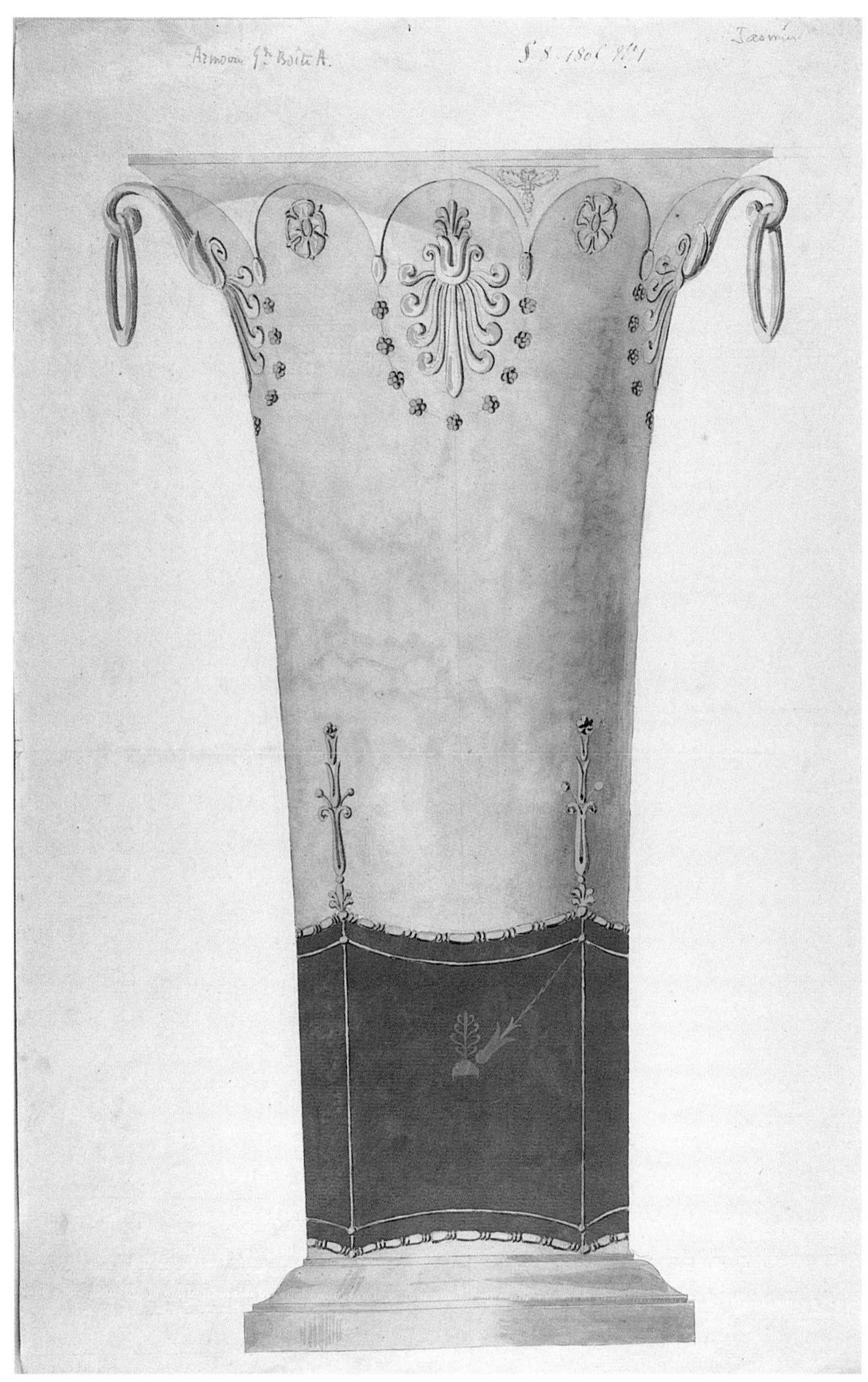

12.
Design and Decoration for a Vase, 1805
Called *Vase 'Jasmin'*

Alexandre-Théodore Brongniart
Watercolor and pencil on paper
21 3/4 x 14 1/8 in. (55.3 x 35.8 cm)
Inscriptions: [verso] *Reçu le 28 Nivose / an 13 / 1805 – Manufacture Imperiale de Porcelaine de Sevres / N°20. de Mr. Brongnart Père;* [verso, architectural drawing in pencil] *maison Veze . . . coupe sur les pt appartemens;* [verso, sketch of section of a vase form] *dans les gravures de / Percier*
Inv. no. § 8 1805 No 1

The use of vivid color contrast and the creation of visual tension suggested by the convex vase form and the concave appearance of the drapery decoration are remarkable even today.

With its cylindrical form and slightly flared lip, this vase is a variation on a form known at the time as the *vase 'Jasmin Japonais'*, which has a simple square plinth base instead of the slightly stepped, circular foot seen here, but is otherwise identical in shape. One of the surviving form drawings bears the inscription "Japanese Jasmine Vase first size corrected by Brongniart fils in April 1808."[1] It seems likely, therefore, that this is a preliminary design antedating the definitive version by three years.

Louis Victor Godin aîné was allotted 18 francs for "1 *vase 'Jasmin'* violet decoration with gold highlights and red ground" in the work allocations of March 1805.[2] The piece in question could well be one of two "large Jasmines dairy form agate ground, base with red ground and gold decoration Godin the elder" that were assigned a price of 225 francs each when they entered in the sales inventory on 14 Prairial year 13 (June 1805).[3]

Inscription: ["Veze house . . . section showing the small apartments] / (verso) among the drawings of / Percier"]

1. "Vase Jasmin Japonais Iere grandeur rectifié par M. Brongniart fils en / avril 1808." Tiroir B IV.
2. "1 Vase Jassemin [sic] decore violet rehaussé d'or et fond rouge" (Carton Pb 1, valuation dated 20 Ventôse year 13).
3. "Grands Jasmin forme Laitrie fond agathe, le bas en fond rouge et le decord en or Godin aînée" (Carton Pb 1, valuations of year 13).

13.
Decoration for a Plate from the *Service 'Egyptien'*, 1805

Alexandre-Théodore Brongniart
Watercolor, pencil, and ink on paper
9 1/2 x 10 in. (24.2 x 25.4)
Inscriptions: [recto, upper left in ink, in the hand of D. D. Riocreux] (Brongniart architecte) [within the design] *CONTRA LATOPOLIS*; [verso] *Reçu le 18 Nivose an 13 – Manufacture Imperiale de P(orce)laine de Sèvres / N° 11 de Mr Brognart Père / an 13*
Inv. no. § 5 1805 No 3

Judging from surviving correspondence and other documents, the *service 'Egyptien'* was the fruit of a collaboration. Brongniart's father was responsible for the selection of forms and the ornamental composition of each piece and Dominique-Vivant Denon was indirectly responsible for the decorative motifs. The views as well as the painted hieroglyphics and other motifs in the gold and faux-relief borders are rigorously faithful to illustrations in Denon's 1802 publication *Voyage dans la Basse et la Haute Egypte*. At the very least, this book may have inspired the idea for such an ambitious service.[1]

The first plates for the service, with views of Egypt painted in sepia cameo by Jacques-François Swebach, entered the manufactory's inventory on 28 Brumaire year 13 (November 1804),[2] but it was not until December 31, 1806, that the first complete service was recorded.[3] This was, however, presented as a gift to Tsar Alexander I in October 1808, a year after the *'service Olympique'* (see cat. no. 7).[4] The price assigned each of its seventy- two plates was 200 francs.

Two editions of the *service 'Egyptien'* were produced; the second was ordered in 1810 by Josephine as partial settlement for her divorce from Napoleon the previous year. When it was delivered in 1812, however, she found it too severe and refused to accept it. The service remained in the inventory of the manufactory until 1818, when it was given by Louis XVIII to the Duke of Wellington for his assistance in restoring the Bourbons to the throne of France.

1. *Versailles et les tables royales,* exhib. cat. (1993), pp. 358 – 64.
2. Carton Pb 1, valuations of the year 13.
3. Register Vu 1, fol. 32v, nos. 192 – 43.
4. Register Vbb 2, fol.88 and Carton T 4, liasse 1, dossier 1, letter from the duc de Frioul dated August 22, 1808 specifying Tsar Alexander as recipient.

14.
Allegory of the Battle of Austerlitz, 1806

Pierre-Nolasque Bergeret
Ink and watercolor on paper
13 3/4 x 21 5/8 in. (35 x 55 cm)
Inscriptions: [recto] *VIENNE HULMM; BATAILLE / DES TROIS / EMPEREURS; VENI / VIDI / VICI; P. BERGERET INV. F. 1806*; [verso in ink, post-1815 notation in the hand of D. D. Riocreux] *Manufacture Royale de Sèvres* (followed by inventory number)
Inv. no. F § 4 1832 No 20

In 1806 Pierre Nolasque Bergeret received 300 francs for his "Etruscan drawing of the conquest of Germany" and 288 francs for having painted a frieze for "a large vase with an allegory of the conquest of Germany executed in the Etruscan style."[1] This was the large *vase 'à Bandeau'* (see fig. 14a) that entered the sales inventory on April 21, 1806,[2] and was delivered to Château de Saint-Cloud for the Emperor a few weeks later, on May 4.[3] The net price was set at 3,334 francs — including 1,000 francs for the undecorated vase and 1,800 francs for the bronzes — and a sale price of 4,500 francs was established. The lack of painterly nuances found in this manner of decoration explains the artist's remarkably low fee.

P. N. Bergeret exhibited his paintings for the first time at the 1806 Salon. On 9 Floréal year 13 (April 30, 1805), Sèvres had paid him for three "Egyptian" designs, and he continued to work for the manufactory sporadically until 1814, after which time he apparently renounced painting on porcelain.[4]

The faded condition of this drawing is probably the result of exposure to natural light. Bergeret's composition is emphatically linear, a style that had gained popularity through the line drawings and engravings of John Flaxman. This idiom was generally admired for its austerity, but when used in detailed compositions with many figures and overlaps, as here, the results could be difficult to decipher. The slightly jumbled effect of overt imperial propaganda is compounded by the contrast of the archaic, heroic treatment of most of the figures with the more realistic handling of the fleeing soldiers at left, whose uniforms and standards are accurately rendered. The vase itself is now in the Musée de Malmaison.

In the inventory of models, a distinction is made between the '*vase à Bandeau*' of 1806 and earlier forms bearing the same generic name.[5]

Inscription: ["Vienna Hulmm; Battle / the three / emperors / veni / vidi / vici / P. Bergeret inv. F. 1806 / (verso) Manufacture Royale de Sèvres"]

1. Register Vj' 13, fol. 10.
2. Register Vu 1, fol. 19, no. 179-1.
3. Register Vbb 2, fol. 50.
4. Register Vf 55, folio 26.
5. Carton U 3 (inventory § 1 1806 no 1).

15.
Decoration for a Vase, 1806
Called *Vase 'Oeuf'*

Alexandre-Théodore Brongniart
Watercolor and ink on heavy paper
13 5/8 x 8 3/4 in. (34.5 x 22.3)
Inscriptions: [verso, on a glued strip of paper, in ink] *N° 88 an 14 Manuf(ac)ture Im(péria)le de Porcel(ai)ne de Sèvres / par Mr Brongniart Pere Arch(itec)te Dess(ina)teur*; [verso, light pencil sketches of frieze motifs]
Inv. no. § 8 1806 No 4

Apparently, this decorative scheme was first used, with slight modifications, on a pair of *vases 'Medicis'* (see fig. 15a).[1] A list of work allocations beginning July 1, 1810, includes "no 2 – 2 Vase Oeuf fish handles 3rd size garlands of flowers, thyrses, cameos, and ornaments – Sisson Degault."[2] These vases are again mentioned in the allocations of 1811, with the notation: "damaged one to be replaced by another." In effect, on June 17, 1812, when the first two vases entered the sales inventory, the net price for the pair was set at 2,332 francs, the sale price of the first at 2,500 francs, and that of the second, said to be damaged (possibly cracked), at 1,500.[3] On October 14, 1812, a third vase of similar description also entered the sales inventory with a price of 2,500 francs.[4] In December 1814, the two good vases were shown at the annual exhibition of the year's most beautiful productions (an eighteenth-century custom revived by Louis XVIII at the suggestion of Alexandre Brongniart). The identity of their eventual owner, who acquired them just after the exhibition, is unknown.[5]

This 1806 date of the design reflects the early introduction of a nineteenth-century style notable for its rigidity and systematic decorative schemes. The manufactory was compelled to propagate this idiom which promoted formal characteristics that supported the Empire. Its artistic advisors included some of the principal developers of the new imperial decorative vocabulary. In addition to Brongniart's father, who was also Inspecteur du Garde-Meuble Impérial during the period, they included Dominique-Vivant Denon, director of the Musée Napoléon, and Charles Percier, the emperor's favorite architect.

The *vase 'Oeuf'* form, used throughout the first half of the nineteenth century, was introduced at Sèvres by Alexandre-Théodore Brongniart in 1802 and was produced in several different sizes from its inception. It was essentially a variation on eighteenth-century forms of similar profile and was repeatedly modified after 1850.

1. Ducrot, *Musée national du château de Compiègne* (1993), no. 27, p. 84.
2. Carton Pb 2, liasse 2 ("Attelier de peinture, travaux à dater du 1er septembre 1809"). The painters in question are Jean-Marie Degault, a specialist in cameo painting, and Jacques-Nicolas Sisson, a flower painter.
3. Register Vu 1, fol. 131v, nos. 291 – 17 and 291 – 18.
4. Ibid., fol. 136, no. 296 – 17.
5. Register Vbb 5, fol. 2v.

16.
Decoration for a Tabletop, 1806
Called *Table 'des Maréchaux'*

Charles Percier
Watercolor, gouache, and ink on paper
10 3/8 x 13 7/8 in. (26.4 x 35.2 cm)
Inscriptions: [recto, clockwise from top in white gouache] *Dienerstein – Vienne – Brunn – Austerlitz – Presbourg – Wertingen – Ausbourg – Memmiengen – Elchigen – Ulm – Wernek – Lintz*; [within central medallion] *Napoleon Empereur Roi*; [along the perimeter, clockwise from top in gold] *Gal Duroc – M^{l} Bernadotte – M^{l} Soult – M^{al} Davoust – M^{al} Ney – M^{al} Lannes – M^{al} Augereau – M^{al} Berthier – M^{al} Bessière – M^{al} Mortier – Cte Marmont – Gal Caulaincourt*; [bottom left in ink, in later hand] *Table des Maréchaux de France*; [bottom right, in ink, in the hand of Alexandre Brongniart] *par Mr. Percier architecte*
Inv. no. § 10 1806 No 7

On April 26, 1806 Pierre Daru, Intendant Général de la Maison de l'Empereur, sent Brongniart a set of instructions regarding pieces commissioned by Napoleon, among them: "2: make a table having in its center a portrait of the Emperor surrounded by those of the generals commanding the seven corps of the Grande Armée, Marshall Berthier, and the Emperor's two principal officers,"[1] he also stipulated that all projects and designs relating to these tables were to be submitted to Napoleon for his approval. Very soon thereafter, Brongniart forwarded his report, entitled "Execution of Commissions Specifically Made by His Majesty the Emperor," suggesting that the table be "composed of colored portraits linked by appropriate ornament; it would consist of a single piece and be about one meter in diameter. The pedestal would be of porcelain, with the figures carved in white against a pale blue ground (see the enclosed drawings[s] of the top and pedestal by M. Percier)."[2] This design was probably the first of these drawings, for which architect Charles Percier was paid 240 francs.[3] To execute the portraits, Brongniart turned to the miniaturist Jean-Baptiste Isabey, warning Daru on July 21, 1807, however, that "this artist had never painted on porcelain."[4]

The table, a technical tour-de-force, entered the sales inventory on October 10, 1810, where it was described as "One round table one meter in diameter representing the portrait of H.M. the Emperor, those of the principal leaders of the Grande Armée during the campaign of 1805, and of the two principal officers of the House of His Majesty, all painted in miniature by Isabey; rich gold ornaments after a design by Percier. The foot also in porcelain forming a truncated column with gold ground and biscuit relief figures representing the martial virtues; rich bronze mounts with a circular glass cover. Price for the government 35,000 francs."[5] It was delivered to the Emperor at the Palais des Tuileries on the following November 18, and Napoleon loaned it to the Salon of 1812 so that Isabey could exhibit it under his own name.[6] It subsequently passed through several hands and is now in the collection of the Musée de Malmaison. (See figs. 16a and 16b.)

1. Carton T 2, liasse 1, dossier 1.
2. Carton Pb 2, liasse 2.
3. Register Y 21, fol. 65 "composition et dessin en petit avec quelques developpement de la table des marechaux et de son pied (§ 10 1806 No 7)."
4. Register Vc 3, vol. 134 v.
5. "1 Table ronde de 1 m. De diamètre representant le portrait de S. M. L'Empereur, ceux des principaux chefs de la grande armée lors de la campagne de 1805 et des deux principaux officiers de la maison de S. M., tous peints en miniature par Isabey; riches ornements en or d'après le dessin de Percier. Le pied également en porcelaine formant une colonne tronquée en fond d'or avec des figures en relief en biscuit representant les vertus guerrieres; riche monture en bronze avec glace formant couvercle. Prix pour le gouvernement 35,000 francs." Register Vu 1, fol. 100v., no. 260 – 34.
6. Salon of 1812, no 501.

17.
Design and Decoration for a Pedestal, 1806

Alexandre-Théodore Brongniart
Watercolor and ink on paper
11 3/4 x 9 1/4 in. (30 x 23.6 cm)
Inscriptions: [verso] *2me Serie. N° 41. Année 1806. / Manf^{ture} Imp^{le} de Porcelaine de Sevres / Par Mr Brongniart Pere Arch^{te} Dessi^{teur};* [verso] [pencil drawing of similar pedestal];[recto, beneath the drawing, in pencil, in the artist's hand] *pour les trois grands vases de La Gallerie / a St Cloud. / scavoir Le grand vase et Les 2 Cordelier,* [scale]; [lower right in ink, in the hand of Alexandre Brongniart]: *Par M Brongniart architecte*
Inv. no. § 10 1806 N° 14

The set of commissions placed by Daru on April 26, 1806 (see cat. no. 16), included two series of pedestals for the Château de Saint-Cloud.[1] Each series consisted of three matching pedestals. Those to be based on this design were intended as supports for three Sèvres porcelain vases. One was a large eighteenth-century *vase 'Medicis'*, which had biscuit reliefs designed by Louis-Simon Boizot and bronze fittings by Pierre-Philippe Thömire. This example had been shown at the annual Louvre exhibition of 1783. The two other vases were brought to Saint-Cloud from the museum. Made of imitation pietra dura, they featured bronze fittings representing children and ropes or cords, hence their name, *vases 'Cordelier'*.[2]. The idea of placing these three pieces on similar pedestals may have originated in 1803; at least this is suggested in a letter from Jean-Jacques Hettlinger to Brongniart, who was in England at the time: he wrote, "Monsieur Fontaine [Pierre-François Fontaine] envisions marble pedestals for the large vases that will be inset with porcelains for which he will provide the designs."[3]

Judging by the date of this drawing, it was probably the one forwarded by Brongniart to the imperial administration with his report of 1806, in which in wrote: "Enclosed you will find a proposed drawing for one of these pedestals. The three visible sides will consist of porcelain plaques, either single ones or several joined by bronzes. The corner fittings, cornices, bases, etc. will be of wood and gilt bronze. Finally, I propose that these three pedestals be identical except for the heads, which should be different."[4]

A drawing of January 1808 "for the pedestal of the Medici Vase in the gallery at Saint-Cloud" shows that there had been a change of plan, and that two different types of pedestal were envisioned. Those for the *vases 'Cordelier'* were delivered on June 21, 1810, "each consisting of three plaques [ ] in diameter representing the subjects of medals struck on the occasion of the Prussian and Polish campaigns, treated in the cameo genre, and a dozen corner fittings in biscuit representing military trophies in relief and in biscuit, the whole fitted together and mounted in green bronze also with rich ornaments in matte gilt bronze"; they had entered the inventory on the preceding June 6.[5]

By contrast, it was only during the reign of Louis-Philippe that the sculptor Honoré de Triquetti designed a pedestal with white biscuit reliefs to support the large *vase 'Medicis'*.[6] None of these objects corresponded precisely with this first project, which is similar to a design for a clock case produced by Charles Percier around 1800.[7]

Inscription: [. . . "for the three large vases in the Gallerie / at Saint Cloud / i.e. the large vase and the two Cordelier vases].

1. The other series was for the Emperor's cabinet and not in the gallery as the inscription indicates. In a report, Brongniart wrote: "these three pedestals could be produced within a month or six weeks, counting from the day His Majesty approves the design, and for a very reasonable price if the drawing I have the honor of sending you is adopted. These pedestals will be in black marble [amended from: black ebony] with white porcelain reliefs against a blue ground framed by gilt-bronze borders . . . each pedestal will cost 2,200 [francs]." (Carton Pb 2, liasse 2.) This was indeed the price specified when the three pedestals entered the sales inventory on August 31, 1807 (post-facto, for they had actually been delivered on August 18). The selection of a scheme consisting of white biscuit medallions against a blue ground may have been dictated by the fact that the pedestals should match a commode delivered for the emperor's cabinet in 1805 (Samoyault, "Les Remplois de sculptures et d'objets d'art" [1971], p. 165).
2. Samoyault, "Les Remplois de sculptures et d'objets d'art" (1971).
3. Carton M 1, letter covering the period from 11 to 21 Vendemaire year 11.
4. Carton Pb 2,liasse 2, "Rapport sur l'execution des commandes particulieres faites par S.M. l'Empereur et Roi."
5. For delivery, see Register Vbb 2, fol. 112v; for entry into the sales inventory, see Register Vu 1, fol. 94v., no. 254 – 39 (net price 10,600 francs, sale price 12,000 francs). The porcelain plaques on these two pedestals were removed in the nineteenth century and are now in the Département des Objets d'Art, Musée du Louvre, as are the modified pedestals, which are still used as supports for the *vases 'Cordeliers'*.
6. Alcouffe, Dion-Tenenbaum, and Ennès, *Un âge d'or,* exhib. cat. (1991), no. 144, pp. 275 – 77.
7. Ottomeyer and Pröschel, *Vergoldete bronzen* (1986), vol. 1, p. 318.

18.
Design and Decoration for a Fruit Bowl, 1806
Called *Jatte à Fruits du Service 'Olympique'*

Alexandre-Théodore Brongniart
Watercolor, gouache, and ink on heavy paper
12 1/4 x 14 1/8 in. (31 x 35.8 cm)
Inscriptions: [damaged when the sheet was cut down prior to mounting]
Inv. no. § 6 1806 No 8

In a production report covering the trimester beginning in Germinal year 12 (March 1804), Brongniart stated that the *service 'Olympique'* had been "underway for more than a year" and that all its forms were "new, very elegant and very rich," without noting that they had all been designed by his father.[1] Aside from a few changes inevitably introduced in the course of shaping, this design was honored in all respects in production.[2] Its decoration was altered: the scheme with gold motifs against a dark blue ground, used for the wide central band, was replaced by one featuring birds and butterflies in flight against a sky blue ground and interrupted by vertical bands; while the lip lost its band of ribboned flowers in favor of gold ornaments against a dark ground.[3]

Although this form was later christened the *jatte à fruits 'cyrène'* (sic), a name inspired by the mythological creatures represented by its four feet, it was simply designated as *Jatte à 'sirène'* when the *service 'Olympique'* first entered the sales inventory.[4] In documents pertaining to the establishment of the plaster model, it is called the "*Jatte à crème 'Olympique'* (with four chimeras)."[5] This design was included in a few table services produced in the 1820s.[6] (See fig. 18a.)

1. Carton Pb 1, liasse 1, dossier 4.
2. The sheet was cut down prior to mounting; as a result, inscriptions in the hands of the artist (right center) and of Alexandre Brongniart (left center and lower right) were eliminated.
3. Gavrilova, Le Service Olympique (1979), ill. p. 3 and pl. 2.
4. See cat. no. 7.
5. Carton Pb 1, work allocations for the atelier de perfectionnement for Floréal and Messidor year 11.
6. Nouvelles acquisitions, exhib. cat. (1989), no. 252, pp. 178 – 79.

19.
Design for a Bowl, 1808
Called *Jatte 'Famin No. 1'*

Auguste-Pierre Famin
Watercolor and ink on paper
7 3/8 x 12 3/8 in. (18.7 x 31.4 cm)
Inscription: [recto, in ink, in the hand of D. D. Riocreux, obscured by the passe-partout] *Jatte Faim. N° 1*
Inv. no. D § 3 1808 No 1

Auguste-Pierre Famin, one of the emperor's architects, was responsible for the Château de Rambouillet. In 1808 the manufactory asked him to supply a view of the château for use on the *service 'de l'Empereur'* (see cat no 20),[1] as well as "three designs of milk bowls" for which he was eventually paid 120 francs on January 5, 1809.[2] The three drawings survive; they represent bowls featuring pale gray figural motifs against a gold ground. Their profiles and motifs vary, but in every case the motifs carry imperial associations. A comparison of this drawing, which is number one in the series, with the only known bowl to have survived reveals that the profile of the original design was retained, despite the presence of a much more complicated drawing of a form bearing the same name in the form book[3]. The ornament was produced in white biscuit relief against a matte gold ground; the antique profiles were replaced by portraits of members of the emperor's family; and finally, the bowl was accompanied by an underplate that is not depicted on this drawing.[4]

Although the drawings date from 1808, the designs here and Number 3 were not produced until 1812, and apparently design Number 2 was never produced, for no trace of it exists in the registers. The first two examples were intended to serve as New Year's gifts. They entered the sales inventory on December 28, 1812[5] and were presented to the comtesse de Luçay and the duchesse de Bassano.[6] Two others, which entered the inventory on November 26 and December 24, 1813,[7] were presented to the comtesse Marmier and the comtesse de Noailles.[8]

The *Jatte 'Famin No. 3'* must also have featured portraits of members of the imperial family. The two that were produced were among the "porcelains relating to the Bonaparte family delivered on instructions from Prussian Commissioner Kupsch,"[9] who in 1815, after Napoleon's defeat at Waterloo, was collecting victory trophies. The documents are inconsistent in naming these objects, sometimes calling them bowls and sometimes dishes. Finally, the ornamental scheme seen here may well have inspired the one used for the *déjeuner 'Regnier à relief'* (see cat. no. 31).

The drawing is rather awkward: shadows produced by the curving surfaces are duly depicted, but there is no acknowledgment of the curve of the bowl as seen in the depiction of the flat medallions and the flanking tripods and griffons.

1. Carton Pb 2, liasse 2, letter dated April 7, 1808.
2. Register Vf 59, fol. 1.
3. Carton Y 22, Livre-Tarif, fig. 5, pl. 12.
4. Du Pasquier and Georget, *L'Aiglon,* exhib. cat. (1993), cat. no. 45.
5. (Register Vu 1, fol. 139v., no. 299-16). [Deux Coupes Famin fond d'or mat riches ornements en porcelaine en mat, portraits en camée de porcelaine relief de la famille impériale, avec globe de verre] "Two Famin bowls gold matte ground rich porcelain matte ornaments, cameo portraits in porcelain relief of the imperial family, with glass globe. Net price 549 francs, sale price 665 francs."
6. Register Vbb 4, fol. 12.
7. Register Vv 1, fol. 10v., no. 62 and fol. 12v., no. 11. Beginning in January 1813, the reference numbers assigned to individual objects consisted of the folio number of the register in which their entry into the inventory was recorded followed by the order number assigned it on the same page.
8. Register Vbb 5, fol. 1v.
9. Ibid., fol. 8v. At the time of the valuation of the undecorated pieces, they are described: "No.1 with portraits and ornaments"... (No.2 ?) Caduceus, paddles, winds, laurels and N...No. 3 with crosses of honor, laurels, N and anchors" (Carton Pb 16)

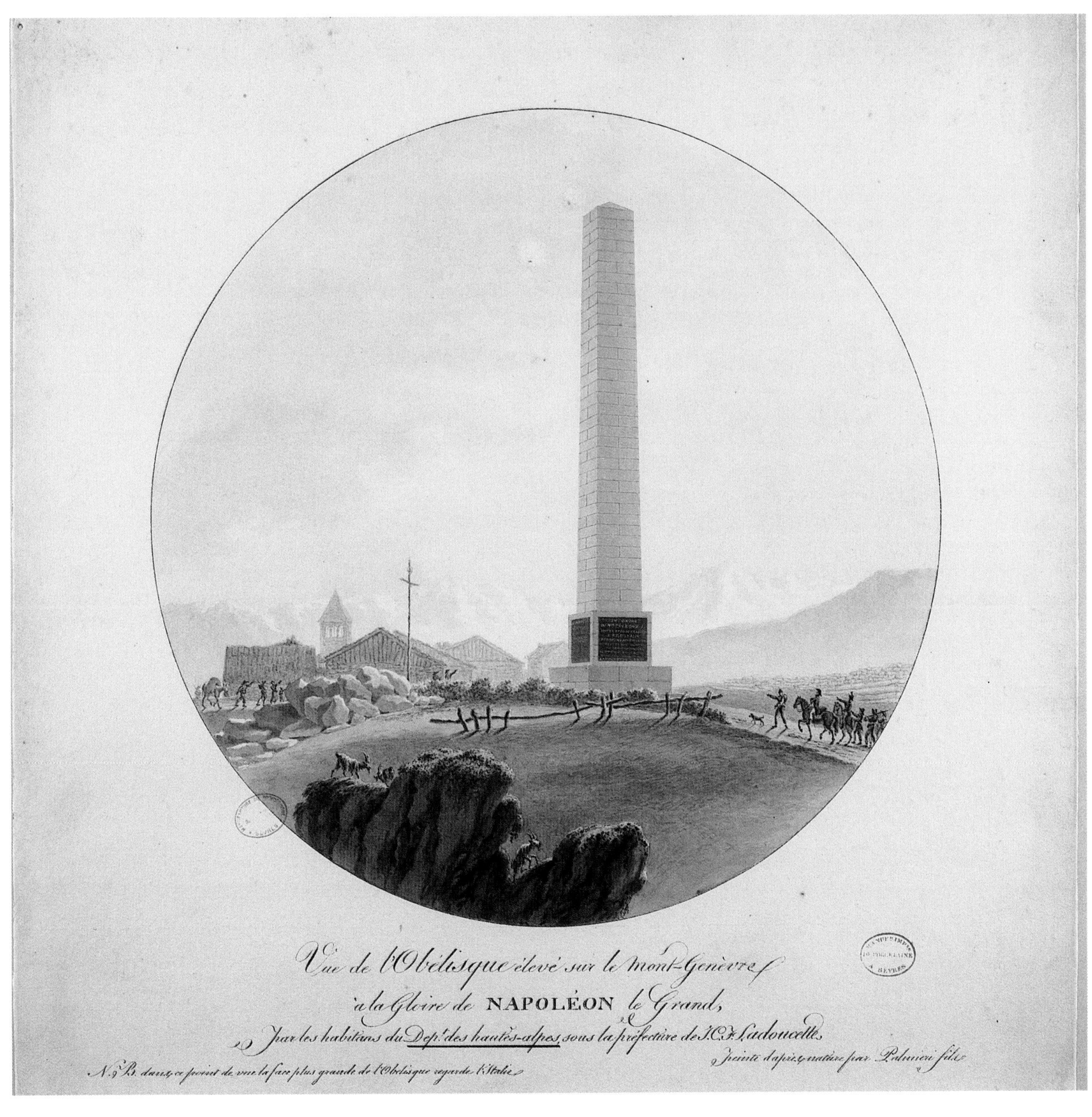

20.
View of the Obelisk on Mount Genèvre, 1808

Pierre Palmieri fils
Watercolor and ink on paper
15 3/4 x 15 1/2 in. (40 x 39.5 cm); drawing diam. 11 3/8 (29 cm) Inscription: *Vue de l'obélisque élevé sur le Mont-Genèvre / à la gloire de NAPOLEON le Grand, / par les habitans du Dept des hautes- alpes, sous la préfecture de J.C.F. Ladoucette – / N.B. dans ce point de vue la face plus grande de l'Obelisque regarde l'Italie – peinte d'après nature par Palmieri fils*
Inv. no. P § 1 No 15, année 1808

On November 4, 1807, Pierre Daru, Intendant Général, wrote to Brongniart from Berlin during its occupation by the French: "His Majesty orders that a new service be made for Him in a very special genre for which the drawings should be very beautiful, none being insignificant. It is his intention that there be no battles or names of men among these drawings, but that, on the contrary, instead the subjects should feature very indirect allusions stirring agreeable memories."[1] Enclosed with the letter was a preliminary list of subjects chosen by the emperor, with a recommendation that Dominique-Vivant Denon be consulted in selecting the others. These instructions were consistent with a more general directive, forwarded earlier with a list of official commissions in April 1806, recommending that the manufactory "place on the services being completed, as well as those made subsequently for the service of His Majesty, views of the Adige [River], of Venice, of Genoa, and of the Kingdom of Italy, more interesting and more historical than those that might be sought elsewhere. Finally, replace all figures of nude women and insignificant landscapes . . . with subjects that are known and historical."[2]

Once a list of subjects consistent with these instructions had been drawn up, renderings of the various sites had to be obtained. On April 7, 1808, Brongniart wrote to the Ministre de l'interieur asking that he commission the execution a painting for plate no. 67 in the service. It was to feature a "view of the new Italian route by Mount Genèvre with the obelisk."[3] Subsequently, his request was forwarded to the prefect of the Hautes-Alpes district, where Mount Genèvre was located, and on July 24, the prefect sent the rendering, "due to the talent of M. Palmieri, a young artist from Turin who went to Mount Genèvre to make it," along with a long letter from the artist.[4] The watercolor arrived at Sèvres on August 4 and on August 22 was given to the manufactory's landscape painter, Jean-François Robert, who received sixty francs for copying it onto a plate that was fired on January 3, 1809. In April 1809, Palmieri was paid 300 francs for the drawing he had provided.[5] Brongniart reacted heatedly to such an excessive sum being paid by a prefect because the manufactory was obligated to reimburse him.

The component pieces of table services were always held until the entire set had been completed, at which time they were inscribed in the registers as an ensemble. Accordingly, the emperor's private service was recorded as having entered the sales inventory on March 31, 1810[6] but in fact it had been delivered to the Palais des Tuileries four days earlier, on March 27.[7]

Inscription: ["View of the obelisk on Mount Genèvre / to the glory of NAPOLEON the Great / from the inhabitants of the Départements des Hautes-Alpes, under their Prefect J. C. F. Ladoucette – N.B. in this view the largest side of the obelisk faces out over Italy – painted from life by Palmieri fils"]

1. Carton T 3, liasse 1, dossier 1.
2. [Recommander à la manufacture de Sèvres de placer dans les services de Sa Majesté des vues de l'Adige, de Venise, de Gênes et du Royaume d'Italie, plus intéressantes et plus historiques que celles que l'on va chercher ailleurs. Remplacer enfin toutes les figures de femmes nues et paysages insignifians . . . par des choses connues et historiques] Carton T 2, liasse 2.
3. Carton Pb 2, liasse 2, travaux de 1810, service de l'Empereur.
4. The beginning of this letter reveals Palmieri's artistic license: "I have the honor of sending you the drawing of the Mount Genèvre obelisk. I have used a color scheme that is agreeable without being too striking; I have contrasted the grayish cast of the obelisk, which it should have due to its being in shadow, with a sky that is cloudy and a bit intense; I did the meadow in various greens, and rather dark, to provide the obelisk with a solid background; finally, Monsieur, to give the idea of an elevated site, I was obliged to introduce some steep rock faces to indicate that there is a very deep valley to the left of the pyramid from this point of view." [J'ai l'honneur de vous adresser le dessin de l'obélisque du Mont-Genêvre. J'y ai fait Regner un coloris agréable, sans Être trop Éclatant; j'ai opposé à la Teinte grisâtre de l'obélisque, ainsi qu'il doit l'avoir, Étant dans l'ombre, un ciel vaporeux, et un peu Chaud; j'ai fait la prairie d'un verd varié, et un peu sombre, pour donner une base solide à l'obélisque; enfin, Monsieur, pour donner l'idée d'un site élevé, j'ai Été obligé d'introduire des pointes de rochers très escarpées, pour indiquer qu'un vallon très profond existe à la gauche de la piramide dans ce point de vue] (Carton Pb 2, liasse 2, travaux de 1810, service de l'Empereur).
5. Register Vf 59, fol. 7v, April 7, 1809.
6. Register Vu 1, fol. 91v - 92, nos. 251 – 62 and 252 – 1.
7. Register Vbb 2, fol. 110v. For a detailed history of this service, see Samoyault, "Les assiettes de dessert" (1990).

Fig. 20a. Plate decorated with a view of the obelisk of Mont Genèvre from the *service 'de l'Empereur'*, Sèvres, 1808; hard-paste porcelain. (Fondation Napoléon)

21.
The Rue de Rivoli along the Tuileries, 1808

Pierre-Joseph Petit
Ink, sepia, and pencil on paper
11 7/8 x 15 3/4 in. (30 x 40 cm)
Inscription: [verso] *Manuf[actur]e Roy[al]e de p[orcelai]ne de Sèvres*
Inv. no. P § 1er N° 2 / année 1811

This drawing was also executed to serve as a rendering for the emperor's private service (see cat. no. 20); it was one of several compositions for the service commemorating projects undertaken by Napoleon to improve the capital city of Paris. On April 15, 1808, Brongniart sent Denon a list of subjects requiring drawings.[1] One of these was a view of the Muséum d'Histoire naturelle, about which Brongniart wrote: "I remind you that we agreed I should ask M. Petit to execute this last drawing, and that if you were happy with it you would give him others to do in the same genre."

At the Salon of 1808, Pierre-Joseph Petit had exhibited an *Allée in the Forest of Fontainebleau Painted on Porcelain* which had not been executed for the Sèvres manufactory. This work may have caught the attention of Denon and resulted in the assignment. Denon seems to have been satisfied with Petit's subsequent first effort for Sèvres, since in 1810 Petit was paid 100 francs each for three views of Paris — the Pont d'Austerlitz, the Jardin des Plantes, and this drawing — as well as for a painting on porcelain of the Jardin des Plantes.[2] The plate with the view of the rue de Rivoli (see fig. 21a) was painted between September 14, 1808 and January 3, 1809, by Nicolas-Antoine Lebel and repeated by the same artist in 1811, Napoleon having presented the first version to his new parents-in-law, the emperor and empress of Austria.[3]

The drawing offers a perspective of the new rue de Rivoli, with the arcaded façades of the buildings (left) and the iron fence (right) surrounding the gardens in front of the Palais des Tuileries, visible in the background. The palace was destroyed in 1871. In fact, given the date of the drawing, this must be an ideal view based on the elevations of the architects, Percier and Fontaine. Despite the favorable terms offered potential investors by the government they were reluctant to build in accordance with pre-established plans, and as a result the uniformly aligned façades were not completed until several years later at the end of the Empire.[4]

1. Carton Pb 2, liasse 2, travaux de 1810.
2. Register Vj' 15, fol. 121.
3. Samoyault, "Les assiettes de dessert" (1990).
4. Biver, *Le Paris de Napoléon* (1963), pp. 64 – 66.

22.
Plan and Elevation for a Centerpiece, 1809
Called the *Surtout du service 'de l'Empereur'*

Alexandre-Théodore Brongniart
Ink on paper
17 7/8 x 22 7/8 in. (45.4 x 58 cm)
Inv. no. § 6 1809 N° 2

The tradition of biscuit *surtouts* (centerpieces) for table services dates from the middle of the eighteenth century when the manufactory was founded. Initially, they were more or less disparate ensembles of pieces that could be arranged in various compositions or configurations, with the notable documented exception of the one created for the marriage of the future Louis XVI.[1] There were set positions for its elements. In 1800, when Brongniart began his tenure at Sèvres, the conception of the porcelain surtout evolved: the pieces were conceived to harmonize with the themes of the accompanying service and were assigned specific places on the table.[2]

This drawing is probably one of two designs for which Brongniart's father was paid the total sum of 100 francs in 1809.[3] It includes an elevation of half of the sequence of pieces, and a schematic plan indicating the placement of the various objects. Because the arrangement of the right half of the *surtout* replicated that of the left half, it was not included in this rendering.

In a preliminary report on the *service 'de l'Empereur'*, Brongniart wrote: "The centerpiece will be entirely in the white porcelain known as biscuit, and consist of sixteen figures and antique objects modeled on pieces in the Musée Napoléon. It is a design for a centerpiece that I devised last year, and if His Majesty approves it, this will accelerate the execution of his service, since several models for it have already been begun. M. Denon has kindly given me advice concerning the choice of figures and other pieces in the centerpiece. As there is no antique group that would be appropriate for the center, we thought that a chariot with two horses driven by a Victory and bearing the Genius of the Arts, identified by the attributes and crowns that it holds, would be a group all the more appropriate because it would recall that it is to victory that we owe the most beautiful objects in the Musée Napoléon, and those composing the centerpiece. There would be no small vases or inconsequential figures in this centerpiece. The enclosed sketch gives some idea of it."[4]

The *surtout* was delivered at the same time as the service (see cat. nos. 20 and 21).

1. Ennès, "Le Surtout de mariage en porcelaine de Sèvres" (1987).
2. Arizzoli-Clémentel, "Les Surtouts impériaux" (1976).
3. Register Y 21, fol. 65v., "dessin general au trait, id. lavé et coloré du surtout des monuments" (general line drawing, id[em] shaded and colored of the centerpiece of monuments).
4. Carton Pb 2, liasse 1, travaux de 1810.

23.
Variations on the Decoration for a Plate from the *Service 'Iconographique'*, 1810

Claude-Charles Gérard
Watercolor, gouache, and pencil on paper
10 1/2 x 7 1/8 in. (26.7 x 18.2 cm)
Inscriptions: [recto, along outer perimeter] *N° 1 adopté*; [along inner border, outside] *N° 1 adopté*; [inside] *N° 1 adopté*; [along perimeter of central medallion] *peint en salis d'or*
Inv. no. § 5 1810 N° 2

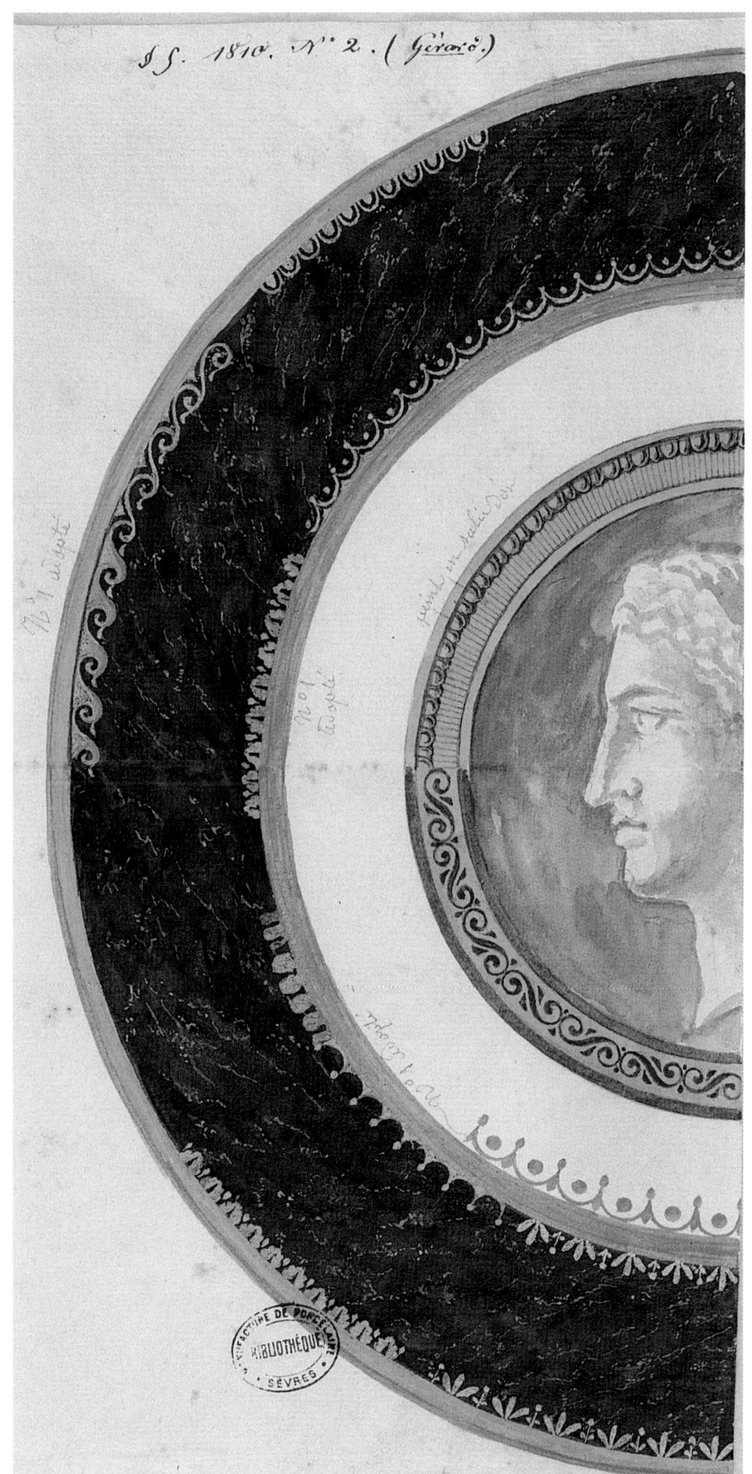

The fashion for engraved antique stones or cameos, pervasive since the eighteenth century, coupled with Brongniart's special interest in mineralogy, probably explains the number of services that were painted with imitation cameos. The two earliest examples featured plates whose borders were decorated with gray laurels painted against a gold ground.[1] In August 1808, an anticipated payment to Jean Georget of 48 francs was entered in the price register for "one plate of a service with antique heads imitating engraved stones."[2] The painters must have objected to this fee as being too low, for Brongniart subsequently wrote: "I beg M. Gérard not to let the service plates with heads languish, and to tell the persons who hesitate because of the fees that, often being allocated finer work, it is only just that they should also make purely utilitarian objects."[3] Number 7 on the list of work allocations commencing on January 1, 1811, concerns an "iconographic service lapis blue border gold ornament and subjects after medals and engraved stones."[4] On January 21, 1811, Brongniart asked the Intendant Général to send the manufactory the volumes of Ennio Quirino Visconti's *Iconographie Grecque*, adding: "At this very moment I am having a very beautiful iconographic service produced that is intended for the service of His Majesty at the Château de Saint-Cloud."[5] In fact, the service officially registered in the sales inventory on August 14, 1811, had already been delivered to Cardinal Fesch, the emperor's uncle, on July 13.[6] A second, identical service, begun in 1813, entered the inventory on May 8, 1817, and was delivered "for the court of Rome" on September 17, 1819.[7]

Claude-Charles Gérard had been named head of the painter's workshop in 1804, on the death of Charles-Eloi Asselin; in this capacity he was charged with designing the gold decoration that frames the central medallions.

Inscription: ["No. 1 adopted (repeated twice) / painted in gold salicylite"]

1. The first of these services, entered in the sales inventory on December 31, 1808 (Register Vu 1, fol. 69, no. 229-16). It was presented to the tsar's ambassador, Count Romanzoff, on February 11, 1809 (Register Vy 18, fol. 70). The second, was officially inscribed in the sales inventory on December 31, 1809 (Register Vu 1, fol. 86v., no. 246-39). It was presented to the king of Wurtemberg on December 29 of the same year (Register Vy 18, fol. 98).
2. Register Y 21, fol. 3.
3. Carton M 2, liasse 2, dossier 1, May 24, 1808.
4. Carton Pb 2, liasse 2.
5. Carton T 5, liasse 2, dossier 3.
6. For entry in sales inventory, see Register Vu 1, fol. 117, no. 277-6; for delivery, see Register Vbb 4, fol. 3v.
7. For entry in sales inventory, see Register Vv 1, fol. 87, no. 26; for Delivery, see Register Vbb 5, fol. 383.

24.
Decoration for a Plate from the *Service 'Médailles'*, 1810

Théodore-Alexandre Brongniart
Watercolor, gouache, and ink on heavy paper
7 3/4 x 10 in. (19.7 x 25.5 cm)
Inscriptions: [recto, central medallion] *CLEMENCE DE L'EMPEREUR*; [verso] *Année 1810. par Mr Brongniart père / Arch^{te} et Dess^{tr}*
Inv. no. D § 5 1810 N° 3

In 1810 a payment of sixty francs was authorized for a "drawing of a plate in mosaic with cameo medallion subjects etc. § 5 1810 No 3,"[1] which clearly corresponds to this design. This piece was intended for a service described as "*service médailles* plate border in colored stones with ornament in the manner of mosaics,"[2] mentioned in the work allocations from 1810 to 1812 and subsequently abandoned. The notation is the earliest in the Sèvres archives to describe this kind of ornament, which was meant to evoke Florentine micro-mosaic work. This treatment enjoyed a short-lived success at the manufactory.

The subject of the central medallion depicts Napoleon pardoning the traitorous prince de Haatzfeld after his wife, the princesse de Haatzfeld made a plea for mercy. The subject was illustrated by several painters since the Salon of 1808[3] and belongs to imperial propaganda. Several of the border cartels illustrate fables by La Fontaine. Decorative schemes with mosaic decoration may have been inspired by porcelain produced by the Berlin manufactory with this trompe-l'oeil effect as early as 1802.[4]

Inscription: ["Imperial Pardon"]
1. Register Y 21, fol. 65v.
2. Carton Pb 2, liasse 2.
3. Salon of 1808, no. 332 (by "[Louis] Lafitte, élève de M. Regnault").
4. Faÿ-Hallé, and Mundt, *La Porcelaine Européenne* (1983), ill. 92, p. 69.

25.
The Emperor Hunting at Choisy-au-Bac, 1810

Jean-François Robert
Ink and watercolor on paper
7 7/8 x 10 1/4 in. (20.2 x 26.2 cm)
Inscriptions: [recto, lower left] *Robert f.*; [center] *Chasse de L'Empereur* [word crossed out] *prise du cerf dans La Rivière d'oise a Choisy au Bac / à une lieue de Compiegne (Oise)*; [verso] *Manf*[ture] *Imp*[le] *de Por*[lne] *de Sèvres / Année 1810 – fait par Mr Robert à Compiegne le 28 mars 1810*
Inv. no. P § 1er N° 1 / année 1810

On March 29, 1810, Pierre Daru, Intendant Général de la Maison de l'Empereur, acknowledged that in the course of the emperor's visit to the manufactory "His Majesty seemed to take pleasure in paintings on porcelain representing landscapes in the environs of Sèvres, St-Cloud, and other imperial palaces, decorated with His Majesty's promenades and hunts."[1] It may have been Napoleon's favorable response that prompted Brongniart, on March 19, to request authorization for the painter Jean-François Robert to accompany the imperial hunts. The date of this drawing indicates that approval was granted immediately.

The work planned for the period beginning July 1, 1810, lists among the vases to be produced: "No 29 2 Medici Vases blue ground[,] colored cartel compositions. View of Compiègne and of a hunt. Robert."[2] The first of these vases, decorated with the *Hunt of the Emperor at Choisy le Bacq* [sic] *near Compiègne*, was entered in the sales inventory on April 16, 1811; the second, showing a *Hunting Luncheon of the Emperor at Buc*, was inscribed in the register on the following July 5. Both vases were delivered to Cardinal Fesch on July 13, 1811.[3]

Jean-François Robert executed both the preliminary paintings and the finished works on porcelain.

Inscription: ["The Emperor's hunt (word crossed out) capture of the stag in the River Oise at Choisy au Bac / one league from Compiègne (Oise)"]

1. Carton T 5, liasse 1, dossier 1.
2. Ibid., liasse 1, dossier 8.
3. For entry in sales inventory, see Register Vu 1, fol. 111, no. 271-1 and fol. 115, no. 274-48; estimated net price 3,699 francs; sale price set at 4,500 francs. For delivery, see Register Vbb 4, fol. 3v.

26.
Design for a Secretary, 1811

Alexandre-Théodore Brongniart, Alexandre Brongniart, and Jean-Baptiste Isabey
Watercolor and ink on paper
18 1/8 x 11 1/2 in. (46 x 29.3 cm)
Inscription: [recto] *Par la manufacture Imperiale de Porcelaine de Sèvres*
Inv. no. D § 10 1811 N° 1

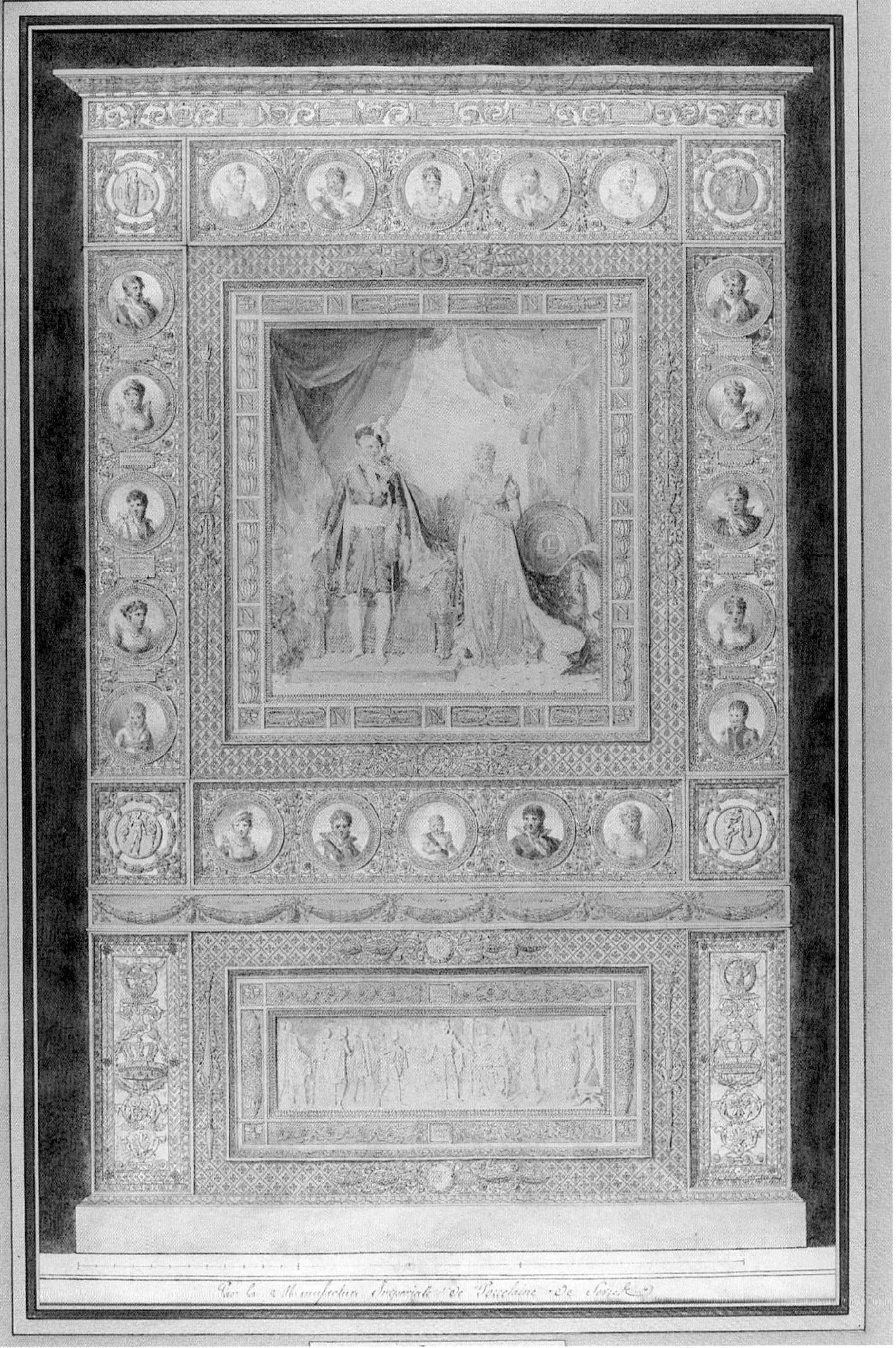

The first object mentioned in an official commission of April 26, 1806 (see cat. no. 16), was "a table as large as possible with portraits of all of the imperial family, as it presently exists. The Emperor and the Empress are to be placed in the center." In a preliminary report on this commission, Brongniart proposed "a round table on which all the members of the imperial family will be represented full-length and in color," specifying that he intended to request the composition from "M. [Louis-Léopold] Boilly painter of unchallenged reputation" who "would receive from M. [François] Gérard the original portraits and all the useful artistic information which the latter might be able to provide him."[1]

On November 14, 1806, Brongniart sent Boilly's sketch to the emperor, and on April 22, 1807, he informed the artist that it had been approved. Shortly thereafter, however, the death of Prince Napoléon-Louis of Holland[2] necessitated a complete revision of this commission, and on June 11, 1807 Boilly requested permission to withdraw.

On the pretext that he had more urgent business, Brongniart postponed this project which, in any event, seems scarcely to his taste. In a report to the Intendant Général of June 4, 1811, he discussed at length the problems posed by such a portrait table and went on to request permission to produce instead a secretary, enclosing a design "devised by my father, Monsieur Isabey, and myself."[3] Isabey had taken some pains with it, for he wrote to Brongniart: "You will easily see that this was not a design to make in eight days, as I thought." On June 9 the Intendant Général responded to the request, observing dryly that "His Majesty wants a table and not a secretary." A table design was duly sent on September 11 and approved on November 29, but there is now no trace of it in the Sèvres archives, and apparently it was never produced.

Although this drawing bears a label attributing it to Charles Percier, the inventory does not identify him as its creator, and the above-cited letter of Alexandre Brongniart states clearly that the design resulted from a collaboration. In general conception, it resembles the preliminary design for a "military secretary whose principal porcelain plaque was to represent the Battle of Marengo etc.," mentioned in the work allocations of 1804. The design corresponding to that project is unsigned, and the documents provide no indication of its author's identity. Like this design, it does not seem to have been produced.

1. Carton Pb 2, liasse 2, dossier "Table de la famille impériale."
2. The young prince, the son of Napoleon's brother Louis and step-daughter Hortense, was designated heir to the throne prior to the birth of Napoleon's own son, the Prince of Rome, who was born in 1811.
3. Carton Pb 2, liasse 2, dossier "Table de la famille impériale."

27. Interior Elevation of the Trianon Dairy, 1811

Artist unknown
Watercolor, pencil, and ink on paper
8 1/4 x 12 3/8 in. (21 x 31.4 cm)
Inscription: [recto, top] *Laiterie de Trianon*
Inv. no. § 6 1811 Nº 4

Soon after her marriage to Napoleon in 1810, Empress Marie-Louise set out to refurbish the elaborate dairy that the architect Mique had constructed at the Petit Trianon at Versailles for her great aunt, Queen Marie Antoinette, in the 1780s.[1] On August 12, 1811, Brongniart sent Alexandre Desmazis, the administrator at the Mobilier Impérial who was overseeing the project, a series of drawings of "porcelain vessels that seemed necessary to my father and me." The ensemble could not be completed until March 17, 1814, which was too late: Napoleon had abdicated for the first time. The pieces were later sold individually.

Comparison of the list of pieces in the sales inventory with this drawing reveals that Brongniart had selected many models which were already in production, sometimes assigning them new uses, such as washbasins that were used as milk bowls.[2] Others were altered slightly as in the *lampe 'Argonaute'*, which, with a cover added, became a sugar bowl. The one notable exception is the large pail resting on the floor, a recycled, undecorated piece originally conceived for Marie-Antoinette's other dairy, at Rambouillet, in 1786.[3]

Of the objects in the drawing, the only one not included in the final list is the large *vase 'Medicis'* in the niche between the windows. The design proposed here is sober and severe, decoration being restricted to gold ornament against a white ground. This is quite distinct in spirit from the Rambouillet dairy where the pieces had supple arabesques and antique figures set against refined background colors, which accentuated the extreme sophistication of the trompe-l'oeil depiction of pine used for the dairy's butter dishes and pails.

1. Grandjean, "Une création . . . Sèvres" (1957).
2. Ibid., p. 183. Recognizable are, from right to left: two *jattes de déjeuner 'Brongniart'* "for cream or cheese" (form devised in 1810 but shown here without the foot that appears in the Livre-Tarif; carnet Y 22, pl. 12, fig. 8). The bowls flank a *vase 'Jasmin Japonais'* with a similar foot as in cat. no. 12. Four *tasses à thé 'Percier'* (forms designed in 1803) stand two on either side of a *sucrier 'Argonaute'* (the lamp and inkstand versions of the form date from 1810, but the sugar bowl is first mentioned in 1813, which suggests that it was developed for this ensemble). A *Lavabo 'ordinaire'* (designed in 1806, named to distinguish it from the *Lavabo 'impérial'* of 1806, also designed "for the use of the Emperor in which the feet can be washed at the same time" (Carton Pb 1, liasse 1, dossier 15, chemise: "*service de l'Empereur*, an 14 et 1806). The second, smaller version of the *lavabo 'ordinaire'* was the one selected for use here as cream bowls (far left). On either side of the central *vase 'Medicis'* are two *pots à lait 'Etrusque à bec cannelés'* which was designed in 1806, when it was recorded that "there are fluted and smooth versions of this same form." Thereafter the same objects recur in reverse sequence, although flanking the *vase 'Jasmin Japonais'* are two *tasses 'd'Hancarville'*. The form of these pieces date from 1810 and were inspired by an illustration in the *Collection of Etruscan, Greek and Roman Antiquities from the Cabinet of . . . Wm Hamilton . . .* published with a preface by d'Hancarville and acquired by Sèvres in 1786).
3. Schwartz, "The Sèvres Porcelain Service for Marie Antoinette's Dairy at Rambouillet" (1992). Two gilded pails were proposed as possible gifts for the Dauphine in January 1829 (Carton U 7, liasse 3, dossier 2, total price 2,000 francs), and one was delivered directly from the manufactory to the museum in April 1839 (Register Vaa 2, fol. 72, 1,000 francs).

28.
View of the Palace of Stupinigi, 1811

Attributed to Louis Reviglio
Gouache on cardboard
Diam. 13 1/4 in. (33.5 cm)
Inscription: [recto, in white gouache] *Vûe de Stupinis / du côté de Turin au Nord*
Inv. no. P § 1 1811 N° 17

When subjects were being considered for the plates in the *service 'de l'Empereur'* (see cat. no. 20), Brongniart and Denon considered the palace of Stupinigi near Turin, where Napoleon had resided briefly in 1805.[1] In the preliminary list of the subjects that had been selected for this service, the only model of Stupinigi available to Brongniart was a scale model located at Saint-Cloud.[2] Although no plate with a view of Stupinigi appears in either the lists drawn up by Brongniart and Denon or the definitive list that has been compiled,[3] the subject may have been used elsewhere. A document dating from 1811 mentions this view in connection with a cup decorated with a "view of Stupinigi painted by Jean-François Davignon," that was part of a *déjeuner* composed of "imperial views . . . taken from the Emperor's service."[4]

The porcelain painter Davignon could have used a new source acquired for a different project. In 1811 Brongniart had begun work on a table to feature representations of nine imperial palaces, including the

Tuileries, Saint-Cloud, Rambouillet, Compiègne, Fontainebleau, Trianon, as well as the Château de Marac near Bayonne, the Quirinal Palace in Rome, and Stupinigi. It is possible that the existing model for the porcelain painting of Stupinigi did not please Brongniart, and he asked Daru to commission a new one.[5] In response he received nine gouaches of palaces in the environs of Turin, including two of Stupinigi.

The painting of the table itself, assigned to Jean-François Robert, was carried out over an extended period. In a report dated April 1, 1814, after the beginning of the first Restauration period, Brongniart states that the first firing of the decoration had not yet taken place. In the same document, the director describes the table as "very beautiful in its dimensions as well as its paintings and ornament," adding that "all the famous houses of all periods can remain. But as various scenes taken from the Emperor Napoleon's everyday life were added to the foregrounds, these should be replaced by scenes of a more anonymous nature."[6] In a report drafted the following year, Brongniart asks whether he "should leave the palace of Stupinigi and the Quirinal Palace or remove them."[7] In fact, the views of Marac, Stupinigi, and the Quirinal were replaced by those of Meudon, Versailles, and Saint-Germain.[8]

Because Brongniart sought to maximize the use of the sources at his disposal, the views of Stupinigi were also painted in 1812 on a plate for the *service 'Marli d'Or'*,[9] and again in 1816 for the *service 'à Vues Diverses'*.[10]

Although the two drawings of Stupinigi are not signed, unlike the other views of residences in the environs of Turin (identified on the gouaches as "Montcailler," "Le Valentin," "La Venerie," "la Vigne de la Reine," "Rivoli," and two views of "Raconigi"), the inventory attributes the entire set of drawings to the painter Louis Reviglio. In his initial request, Brongniart had specified that "if there are any trees close to the palaces, [the artist] must be sure to include them in the drawing in order to avoid the monotony of views that depict nothing but buildings."[11]

The table is now in a private collection.

1. Samoyault, "Les assiettes de dessert" (1990).
2. Carton Pb 2, liasse 2, travaux de 1810.
3. Samoyault, "Les assiettes de dessert" (1990).
4. Register Vq' 3, fol. 20, December 1812. The *déjeuner* was assigned the number "16"; it was entered in the inventory lists as an ensemble on December 28, 1812 (Register Vu 1, fol. 140, no. 300-3), but in fact it arrived the same day at the Tuileries for presentation to the emperor of Austria as a New Year's gift (Register Vbb 4, fol. 11).
5. Préaud, "Un fonds méconnu" (1976).
6. Carton Pb 3, liasse 2.
7. Ibid., liasse 3.
8. The table finally entered the sales inventory on April 24, 1817 (Register Vv 1, fol. 85v, no. 86) and was presented by Charles X to the king of Naples on January 14, 1825 (Register Vbb 7, fol. 1).
9. Register Vq' 3, payment to Lebel in October 1812. The plate was delivered to Louis XVIII after the New Year's Exhibition of 1814 – 15 at the Louvre (Register Vbb 5, fol. 2v).
10. The plate entered the sales inventory on December 27, 1816 (Register Vv 1, fol. 77v, no. 28) and most likely was among thirty-six delivered to the king after the New Year's exhibition of 1816 – 17, along with three small cases, probably to be presented as three gifts consisting of a dozen plates each (Register Vbb 5, fol. 12).
11. Register Vc 4, June 7, 1811.

Fig. 28a. Plate with a view of the palace of Stupinigi from the *service 'à vues diverses'*, Sèvres, 1816; hard-paste porcelain. (Musée des Arts décoratifs, Paris)

29.
Decoration for a Vase, 1812 Called *Vase 'Floréal'*

Paul Abadie
Gouache and pencil on paper
19 5/8 x 13 5/8 in. (50 x 34.6 cm)
Inscription: [verso] *Année 1811 p^r Mr Abadie*
Inv. no. D § 8 1811 N° 11

On June 11, 1810, when Brongniart required an artist to compose a frieze representing the marriage of Napoleon and Marie-Louise, Denon suggested "Monsieur Delabadie [sic], who I do not know but about whom I have received many favorable reports."[1] Before the year was out this artist, probably Paul Abadie, was paid 180 francs for two designs, a *vase 'Etrusque à rouleaux'* and a *vase 'Etrusque cylindre'*.[2] Later, in February 1812, he was paid 240 francs "for three designs, namely a *vase 'Clodion'* green ground gold decoration for Monsieur Demarne [and] two *vase 'Floréal'* gold ground hunt trophies on one, flowers and birds on the other." In return for another design, this one for a "table of the imperial family" (see cat. no. 26), he sought 192 francs but received only 150 francs.[3]

Three vases were decorated after this design, and the sole known example[4] indicates that Abadie's scheme was significantly altered before it was put into production. The first two vases entered the sales inventory on November 11, 1813, and the third was registered on March 17, 1814.[5] All three featured birds painted by Christophe-Ferdinand Caron, as well as flowers painted by Gilbert Drouet, and were fitted with bronze handles made by Pierre-Philippe Thomire.[6]

A reference to these vases in the work allocations for 1813 is annotated with a margin note indicating that they were intended "for the palace in Rome." In fact, the first two were delivered on the orders of Louis XVIII in December 1814, but the recipients are not identified.[7] The last one remained in the warehouse for some time and was eventually included in a presentation to the viceroy of Egypt in 1830.[8]

The form of the *vase 'Floréal'*, designed by Alexandre-Théodore Brongniart in 1805, was used throughout the nineteenth century with different handles in different periods.

1. Carton T 5, liasse 1, dossier 2. The artist in question is probably Paul Abadie père, a student of Charles Percier.
2. Register Vj' 17, fol. 183v.
3. Register Vq' 3, fol. 2v, February 1812.
4. Boston Museum of Fine Arts (inv. 1991.439).
5. Register Vv 1, fol. 10v, no. 50 and fol. 16v, no. 34.
6. For "fifteen birds including one larger than the others painted against the gold ground above the flowers," Caron eventually received the 500 francs per vase that he sought (Register Vq' 1, fol. 22v., January 1813), whereas Drouet — who had also requested 500 francs — obtained only 460 francs "for flowers along the lower strip and a garland of mountain ash berries" (Ibid., fol. 18v, December 1812). Thomire was paid "for squared gilt-bronze ear-of-wheat ferrule handles and the mount," but the amount paid for each piece is not specified (Register Vj' 20 (1813), fol. 177v and Vj' 21 (1814), fol. 216.
7. Register Vbb 5, fol. 2v. The reference number provided here (no. 16-34), is erroneous: it corresponds exclusively to the third vase.
8. Register Vbb 8, fol. 12v, February 25, 1830.

30.
Decoration for a Footed Bowl, 1812
Called *Coupe à bouillon 'Hémisphérique'*

Claude-Charles Gérard
Watercolor, gouache, pencil, and ink on paper
13 1/8 x 11 1/4 in. (33.4 x 28.6 cm)
Inscription: [verso] *Manuf^ture Imp^le de Porce^lne de Sevres / Année 1812 / par Gd.*
Inv. no. § 3 1812 N° 1

This drawing might have been intended for a footed bowl commemorating the nomination of Napoleon's newborn son as king of Rome by the French legislature. It includes portraits of Napoleon and the child holding the imperial insignia; on the matching underplate, there is a depiction of a gold mirror and silver serpent, emblems of the senate which nominated the child for the royal position.[1] This footed bowl, called *coupe 'à bouillon hémisphérique'* (see cat. no. 10), entered the sales inventory on December 31, 1812, and was immediately presented to the comtesse de Marmier.[2]

Anticipating things to come, Alexandre Brongniart made preparations before the birth of Napoleon's son for the production of an object celebrating the arrival of the imperial heir. The event occurred on March 20, 1811, and just two months later, on May 22, a covered bowl entered the inventory. Slightly reminiscent of a baptismal present, the bowl was accompanied by an underplate and both were decorated with allegorical cameos and a scattering of bees, a Napoleonic emblem, against a purple ground.[3] Once the child's health was assured, Brongniart ordered the production of a second covered bowl called *ecuelle 'Gérard'*,[4] as well as a cup bearing a portrait of the newborn.[5]

1. "Sénat," in Tulard, ed. *Dictionnaire Napoléon* (1983)
2. For entry into the sales inventory, see Register Vu 1, fol. 141, no. 301-1, "1 Coupe à bouillon et plateau fond d'or camées portraits de LL. MM. l'empereur, l'imperatrice et le Roi de rome etc.," net price 716 francs, sale price 1,000 francs; for delivery, see Register Vbb 4, fol. 12v.
3. The piece entered the sales inventory on May 22, 1811 (Register Vu 1, fol. 113, no. 273-15) and was presented by the emperor to Marie-Louise when they visited the manufactory on June 10, 1811 (Register Vbb 4, fol. 2).
4. Entered in the sales inventory on December 31, 1811 (Register Vu 1, fol. 122v., no. 282-35) and presented to the comtesse de Beauveau (Register Vbb 4, fol. 6v).
5. Entered in the sales inventory on December 31, 1811 (Register Vu 1, fol. 123v, no. 10) and presented to the duchesse de Dalmatie (Register Vbb 4, fol. 6v).

31.
Design and Decoration for a Cup and Saucer from the *Déjeuner 'Régnier à reliefs'*, 1813

Jean-Marie-Ferdinand Régnier
Ink and pencil on paper
14 5/8 x 9 1/4 in. (37.1 x 23.7 cm)
Inscription: [verso] *Année 1813*
Inv. no. § 3 1813 N° 16

It is not certain if this drawing is actually by Régnier, but there is no doubt that he designed the form itself. In 1813 a Mr. Bodson was paid eighteen francs each for several pencil drawings "of the rich ornament for the pieces of the Régnier Déjeuner."[1] Its teapot, sugar bowl, and milk jug seem to have been conceived from the beginning in two variations: one with antique-inspired decoration in relief, as seen here, and the other with painted decoration instead of raised ornament. There may have been a third option for the cup and saucer, one that included imitation cameo portraits of the members of the imperial family, not painted but executed in relief; the idea for this *déjeuner* may have been suggested by the similar ornament, including the portrait medallions, of the *jatte 'Famin'* (see cat. no. 19). The cups may have been designed first; for the earliest mention of their firing dates from December 26, 1812,[2] and an example with "gilded ground and inner surface" entered the sales inventory on January 28, 1813.[3] By the end of 1813, a *déjeuner* with white biscuit relief decoration against a matte gold ground had been completed.[4] This format was reversed on another with "gold relief decoration against a white ground," which entered the sales inventory on July 21, 1814.[5] (See fig. 31a.)

This model is designated in the contemporary documents as tasse 'Régnier à Reliefs', or, alternatively, the tasse à chocolat 'Régnier à Reliefs'. Apparently the variant with relief ornament, so typical of severe early nineteenth-century neoclassicism, soon ceased to be produced, but the smooth version was still being made in the early 1840s.

J. M. F. Régnier worked for the Parisian porcelain maker Nast before joining the Sèvres staff in 1812.[6] He left the manufactory in 1814 to work for yet another Parisian porcelain maker, named Lefebvre. In a rare exception to his general policy, Brongniart agreed to rehire him in 1820, a strong endorsement of Régnier's abilities. On that occasion Brongniart asked the comte de Pradel, *ministre de la maison du roi*, to come to a special agreement with this "porcelain sculptor, modeler, molder, and thrower, also a machine specialist [who] . . . gave the manufactory the process making it possible to engine-turned porcelain . . . and several elegant form models . . . that bear his name and are consistently successful."[7] Régnier was placed in charge of the Department of Kilns and Pastes in 1826 and also gave his name to a firing process using saggars. This process considerably increased the available space in the kiln and was more economical for the manufactory (see chap. 4).

1. Register Vj' 10, fol. 130v (August 9).
2. Register Vc' 7.
3. Register Vv 1, fol. 1v, no. 29. Clearly this was a smooth example.
4. For entry in sales inventory, see Vv 1, fol. 12v, no. 7, December 24, 1813; for delivery to the duchesse de Castiglione for New Year's Day 1813 – 14, see Register Vbb 5, fol. 1.
5. For entry in sales inventory, see Register Vv 1, fol. 22v, no. 42; for delivery on August 11, 1814, see Register Vbb 5, fol. 2.
6. Plinval de Guillebon, *Faïence et porcelaine de Paris* (1995).
7. Carton Ob 10, dossier Régnier.

32.
Designs for Elements in a *Déjeuner*, 1813
Artists unknown

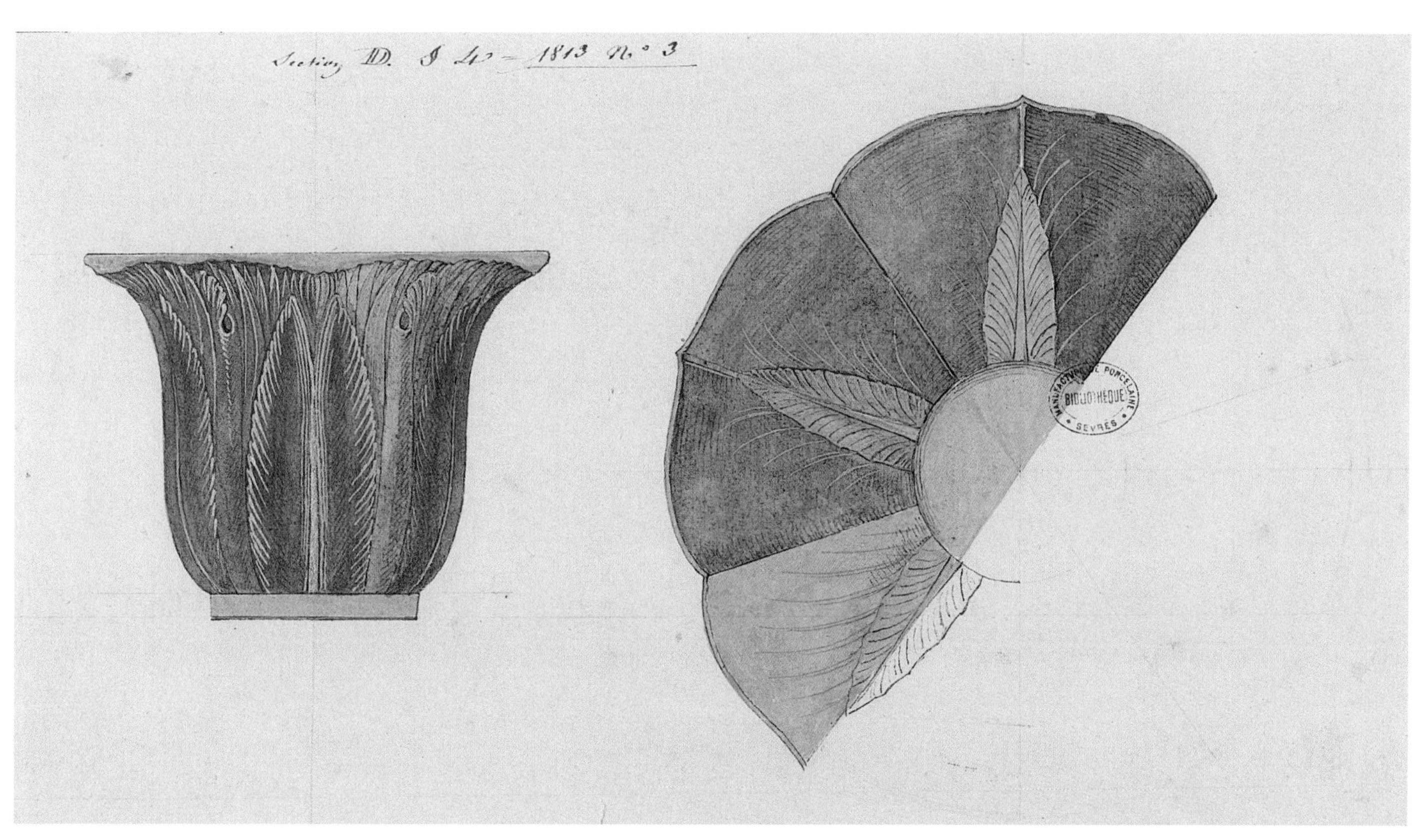

32a.
Cup called *Tasse 'Cobea'* and *Soucoupe*

Watercolor, gouache, ink, and pencil on paper
6 5/8 x 11 7/8 in. (16.7 x 30.2 cm)
Inv. no. D § 4 1813 N° 3

In 1813 Brongniart decided to produce a *déjeuner* incorporating the *Théière 'Oeuf et Serpent'* which had been designed in 1803.[1] The work allocations for 1813 – 14 include a reference to "*déjeuner* no. 29 in imitation forms," probably meaning the botanical and zoomorphic designs seen here. The entry was accompanied by the note: "On September 8 Monsieur Régnier completed the model for the cream jug. I am giving him designs for the sugar bowl and the cup."[2] Unfortunately, the drawings here are unsigned, the inventory does not give an attribution, and there is no record of any payment having been authorized for them.[3] A complete *déjeuner*, to which a round tray had been added, entered the sales inventory on December 24, 1813, and was presented to the comtesse de Beauveau on New Year's Day 1813 – 14 under the name *déjeuner 'de formes variées'*.[4] Composing a single *déjeuner* with naturalistic elements, such as the cup and sugar bowl, and elements such as the teapot and cream jug, seems remarkably bold. Apparently, this was the only full ensemble using these pieces. Some of the individual objects from the service were made and sold separately. The sugar bowl was produced with a gold ground at least once,[5] and a somewhat stiffer version of the cream jug, called *pot à creme 'tête de vache'*, was devised by Alexandre-Evariste Fragonard in 1816. The teapot, called *théière 'oeuf et serpent'* (not shown), had a longer life: it was produced with various ground colors into the 1830s, as was the *tasse 'Cobea'*, evidence of the enduring popularity of some Sèvres designs.[6] The regular structure of the plant form on which the cup was modeled had previously prompted its inclusion in colored or gold-painted friezes on several less elaborate pieces.[7]

1. The first example entered the sales inventory on 26 Frimaire year 13 (December 1804), Carton Pb 1, liasse 1.
2. Carton Pb 3, liasse 3, *Déjeuners* 1813 – 14.
3. The drawings here may, however, correspond to those of "1 pot à creme, 1 pot à sucre, 1 Tasse soucoupe composé par Mr. Brongniart" that are mentioned in December 1813 in the list of work allocated to "M. Leguay doyen aide du chef dessinateur," probably meaning P.- A. Le Guay. (Register Vj' 20, fol. 2).
4. For entry in sales inventory, see Register Vv 1, fol. 13, no. 8; for delivery, see Register Vbb 5, fol. 1v.
5. For entry in sales inventory on December 31, 1813, see Register Vv 1, fol. 14, no. 18. For sale to the dealer Grandcher on May 31, 1814, see Register Vbb 5, fol. 131.
6. In a long explanatory notice accompanying the *Service 'de la Culture des Fleurs'*, plate no. 24 is annotated as follows: "The *Cobea*. The coldframes and the cloches covering the young plants indicate the care they require before becoming sufficiently developed to grow like garlands along cords stretched over considerable distances; the shape of the flower might suggest to a young boy that a cup could be made out of them" (Carton Pb 5, liasse 2 (1), travaux de 1822, services de table).
7. See for example Ducrot, "La Collection des porcelaines et terres" (1993), pp. 62, 78. Note that this plant species had only recently been introduced to Europe where its arrival on the continent is dated 1792 (Pinault-Sorensen, *Dessiner la Nature*, exhib. cat. [1996], p. 27).

32b.
Cream Jug called *Pot à Crême 'Tête de Bélier'*

Watercolor, gouache and ink on paper
10 x 8 1/8 in. (25.3 x 20.7 cm)
Inscriptions: [recto, in the hand of Brongniart] *Pot a creme / tete de Belier*; [verso, cut off] . . . *Imp*[le] *de Porcelaine de Sèvres / . . . n 1813*
Inv. no. D § 3 1813 N° 6

32c.
Sugar Bowl called *Pot à sucre 'Ananas'*

Watercolor, gouache and ink on paper
8 5/8 x 5 7/8 in. (22 x 15 cm)
Inscriptions: [recto, in the hand of Brongniart] *Pot a Sucre ananas*; [verso] [illegible]
Inv. no. D § 3 1813 N° 7

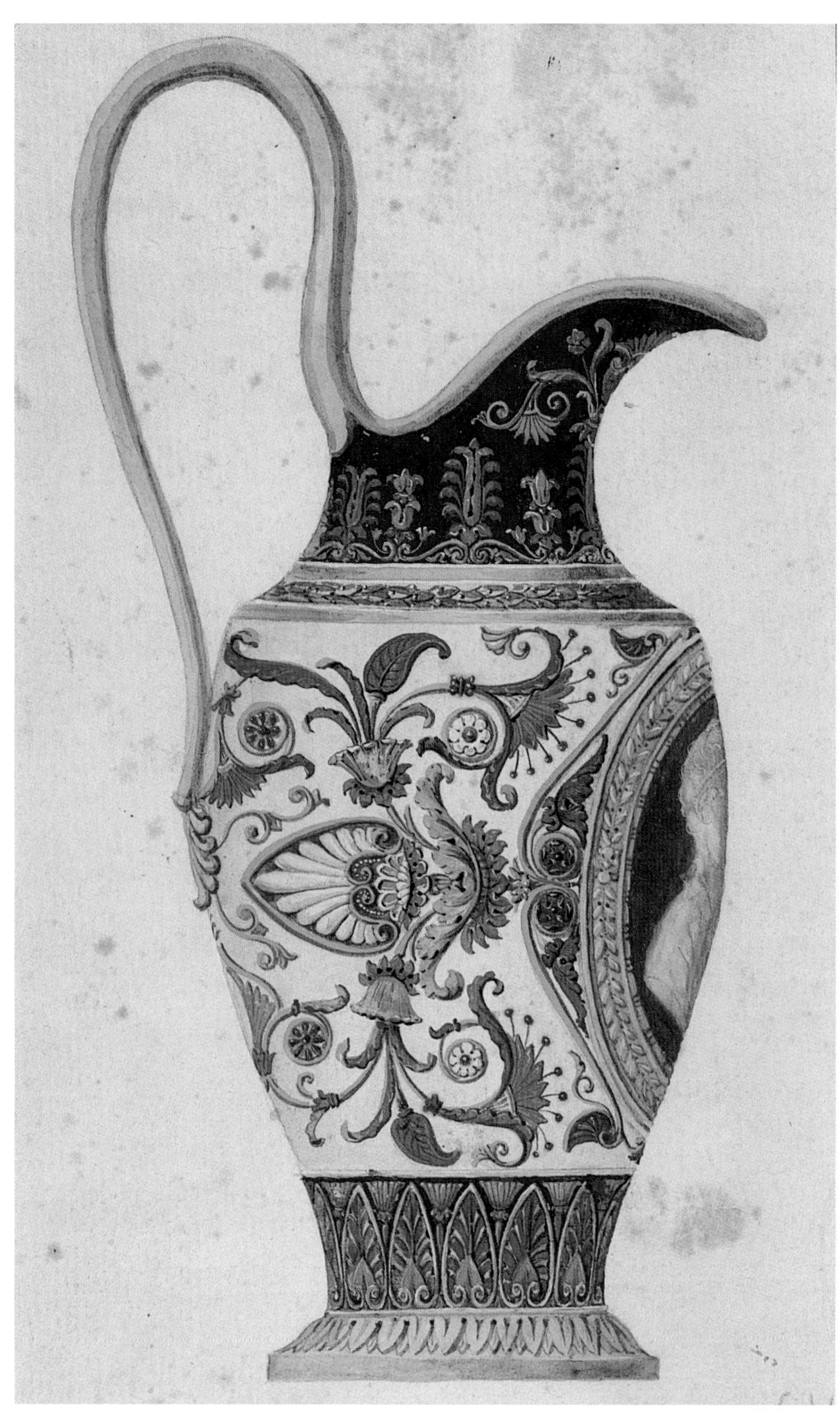

33.
Decoration for a Milk Jug, 1813
Called *Pot à lait 'Grec'*

[?] Bodson
Gouache and pencil on paper
9 1/2 x 6 1/2 in. (24 x 16.4 cm)
Inscription: [verso] *par M. Bodson juillet 1813 – Manuf^ture Imp^le de Porc^le de Sevres*
Inv. no. § 3 1813 N° 4

This precise drawing with its rather formal decorative scheme might have been intended for one of the cameo portrait *déjeuners* proposed in 1813. On July 15, 1813, Brongniart noted: "M. Bodson brought me a great many sketches of forms and decoration. It was agreed that he would finish eight of them in color and would leave the others with me, for a total fee of 300 francs."[1] The list of these drawings mentions two designs for milk jugs.[2] Although none of the extant 1813 *déjeuners* features a decorative scheme identical to the drawing here, some are quite close.[3]

Somewhat earlier, on June 24, Bodson had delivered to Sèvres a series of decorative designs for the pieces of a *déjeuner* "No. 17," which featured rich ornamental schemes incorporating portraits of famous Italians and included a *pot à lait* 'Grec'.[4] Given that this *déjeuner* had a blue ground[5] which was scraped away to accommodate painted decorations, it cannot correspond to this design.

1. Carton Ob 2, dossier Bodson.
2. Register Vj' 20, fol. 130v.
3. Dahlbäck Lutteman et al., *Porslin från Sèvres* (1982), no. 116; Foster, "Cameos and Coffee: Two Sèvres Porcelain Déjeuners" (1994).
4. Carton Ob 2, dossier Bodson.
5. The *déjeuner* entered the sales inventory on December 24, 1813 (Register Vv 1, fol. 11v., no. 24) and was delivered to the comtesse Talhouet for New Year's Day 1813 – 14 (Register Vbb 5, fol. 1v.).

34.
Strength at Rest or *Hercules Asleep,* 1813

Antoine Béranger
Ink with white gouache highlights on tinted paper
15 5/8 x 17 7/8 in. (39.7 x 45.5 cm)
Signature: [recto, lower left] *Béranger*
Inv. no. F § 5 N° 535

On July 21, 1808, Brongniart wrote the *Intendant Général de la Maison de l'Empereur* describing Antoine Béranger as a "young man little known but already possessed of talent and promising of more in the judgment of artists who have seen his work. Yet another [advantageous] hiring [for us]."

Apparently, the director's favorable expectations proved warranted; in 1812 he asked the artist to design two secondary figures for an ambitious vase that he had just agreed to produce.[1] The central scene depicted the emperor's camp before the Battle of Wagram, which was copied by Jean Georget from a painting by Adolphe Roehn. This was to be complemented on the opposite side by two allegorical figures, *Silence* and *Strength at Rest,* that flanked a trophy of arms. Béranger was paid twenty- four francs for each of these designs,[2] which were actually painted on the vase in highlighted gold by Jean-Baptiste Zwinger.

The decorative frieze was being completed when the Empire ended with Napoleon's abdication in 1814, and work on the vase was abandoned. It was probably the peaceful character of Béranger's figures on the back of the vase that kept it from being destroyed when the Bourbons returned to power. After languishing in the warehouse for many years, the vase was resurrected in 1847. New foot, neck, and handles with ornaments originally conceived by Claude-Charles Gérard were added, and it finally entered the sales inventory on October 26, 1848; it was delivered to the residence of the President of the French Senate in 1852.

Béranger had a brilliant career at the manufactory as a porcelain painter. He also exhibited genre paintings at the annual Salon on a regular basis.

1. Préaud, "Le Vase du Sénat," in Sèvres (1993).
2. Register Vq' 3, fol. 5, April 1812.

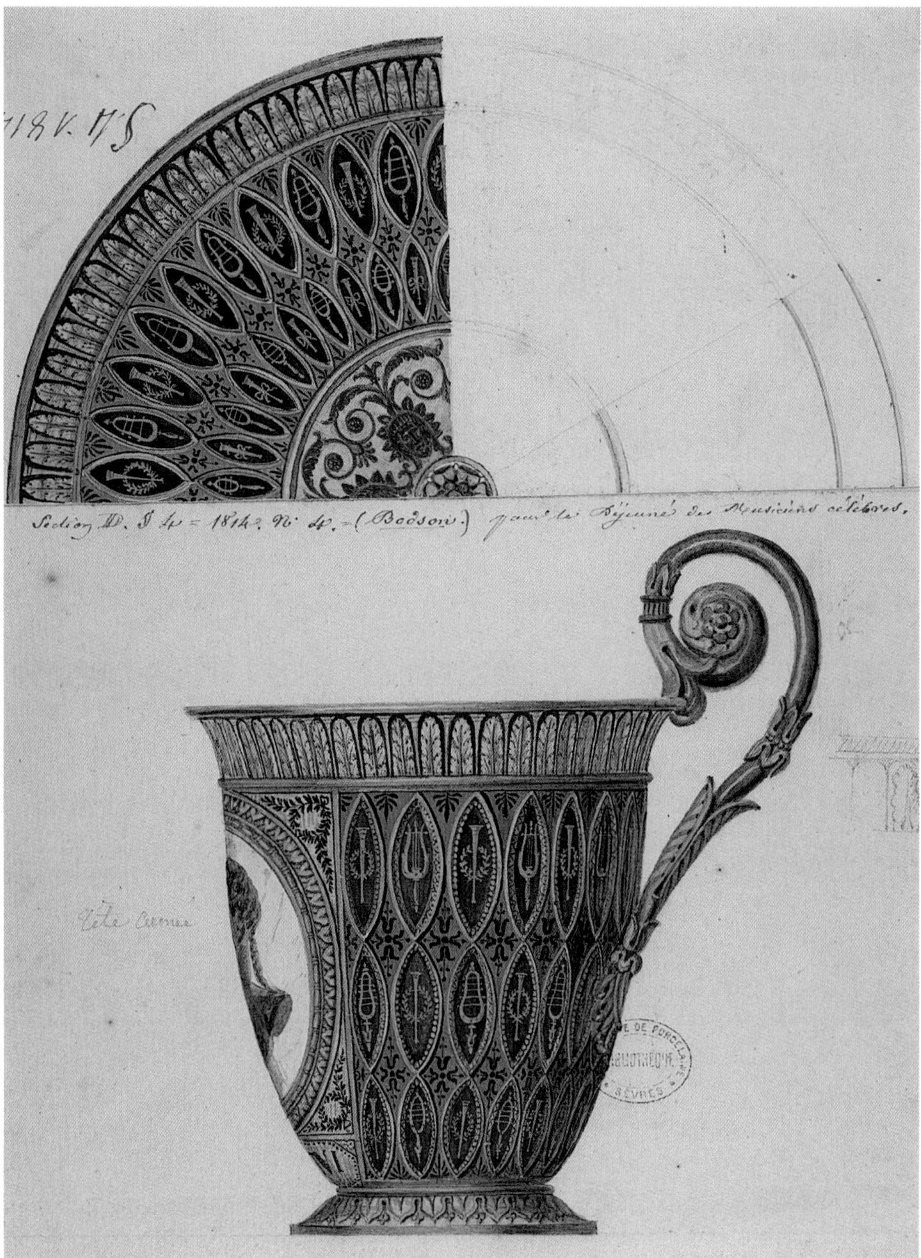

35.

Decoration for a Cup and Saucer from the *Déjeuner 'des Musiciens célèbres',* 1814
Called *Tasse 'A.B.' et Soucoupe*

[?] Bodson
Gouache and pencil on paper
9 x 6 3/4 in. (23 x 17.2 cm)
Inscriptions: [recto, to the left of the cup, in pencil] *tête camée*; [to the upper left of saucer, in ink] *§ 4 1814* [illegible]; [above the cup, in the hand of D. D. Riocreux] *Section D § 4 1814 No 4 (Bodson) pour le déjeuné des Musiciens célèbres*; [verso] *Manufture Royale de plne de Sevres / Année 1814 – 64. année 7bre 1814*
Inv. no. D § 4 1814 N° 4

In January 1814 Bodson was paid twenty-four francs for "a colored drawing of decoration [for the] tasse 'AB' and saucer from the famous musicians [set] blue ground mosaic ovolo motifs and attributes."[1] In effect, the work allocations for 1813 mention a *déjeuner 'des Musiciens célèbres'* (no. 24), but production of this ensemble was abandoned the following year, at least in its original form.[2]

In April – July of 1814, Bodson used the design, however, on a *tasse 'Jasmin'* of the first size, and in April – September on a *tasse à thé 'coupe'* of the first size.[3] It is not clear whether he did this specifically for the first design or simply to make sure that a design that had been payed for did not go unused.

The form seen here is that of *tasse 'AB',* which was created in 1813. It is not known whether the initials indicate that Alexandre Brongniart was the actual designer or were meant simply as a gesture of homage to the director. In any event, this cup was included in *déjeuners* quite regularly until the end of the July Monarchy.

1. Register Vj' 21, fol. 182.
2. A *déjeuner* using this theme was eventually produced but with white ground and gold and colored ornament; it entered the sales inventory on September 22, 1821 (Carton Pb 5, valuation sheets for 1821).
3. "Juillet. rendu 1 tasse et scpe Jass. 1ere fd. beau bleu (d'avril 1814) pour un decore mosaïque or et platine" [July. Rendered one cup and saucer *Jasmin* first "beau bleu" ground (of April 1814) for a mosaic decoration gold and platinum] (Register Vj' 21, fol. 182). "Septembre. Rendu 1 tasse et S. à thé Coupe 1ere gr. fd. b.bleu (d'avril 1814) pour un decor mosaique en navettes avec petits attributs en or et platine doublée d'or et le brunissage de tout, 80 francs [September. Rendered one *tasse à thé coupe* and saucer first size *beau bleu* ground (of April 1814) for a mosaic decoration *en navette* with small attributes in gold and platinum gold interior and the whole burnished, 80 francs] (ibid., fol. 217).

36.
View of the Sèvres Manufactory, 1814

[?] Le Guay
Watercolor on paper glued to cardboard
8 3/8 x 13 1/4 in. (21.4 x 33.8 cm)
Inscription: [recto, beneath the drawing, in ink, in the hand of D. D. Riocreux] La Manufacture Royale de Porcelaine de Sèvres
Inv. no. P § 1 1814 N° 14

This unsigned drawing is attributed to a member of the Le Guay family in the inventory register, but unfortunately no first name is given. By 1814 the artist in question could be either Etienne-Charles Le Guay or his elder brother, Pierre-André. Both were primarily figure painters, but between 1808 and 1812, the same inventory assigns several other landscapes to "Le Guay".[1] Given the ambiguity of these documents, it is impossible to determine which painting was used as a model for each of the many pieces recorded as having been made at Sèvres featuring views of the manufactory. In any case, this drawing was copied by the painter Jean-François Robert on a *tasse 'Jasmin'* (now in the Musée National de Céramique in Sèvres; see fig. 36a),[2] and he probably had the same composition in mind when he executed a drawing for Charles Constans who created a lithograph from it, judging from the similarity of the two works.[3] Brongniart may have used both this lithograph and an etching after a drawing by Achille-Etna Michallon (published by Osterwald) of the building's main façade as seen from the other end.[4]

1. *The Prater in Vienna* (1808); *View of the Château d'Eau from the Ourcq River (Paris)* (1812); *Bacharach, Left Bank of the Rhine* (1812); and *Salmon Fishing near the Rock of Lurcy* (1812).
2. Faÿ-Hallé, Préaud, and Fourest, *Porcelaines de Sèvres au XIXe siècle* (1975), no. 140 (ill). The cup entered the sales inventory on August 4, 1815 (Register Vv 1, fol. 41, no. 32) and apparently part of the composition was copied onto one of the plates of the *service 'Historique'* intended for Fontainebleau (Chevallier, *Musée national du château de Fontainebleau* [1996], no. 281, p. 267).
3. An example now in the archives at Sèvres bears the inventory date 1823.
4. Pinot de Villechenon, *Sèvres: Une collection de porcelaines* (1993), p. 12, ill. 4.

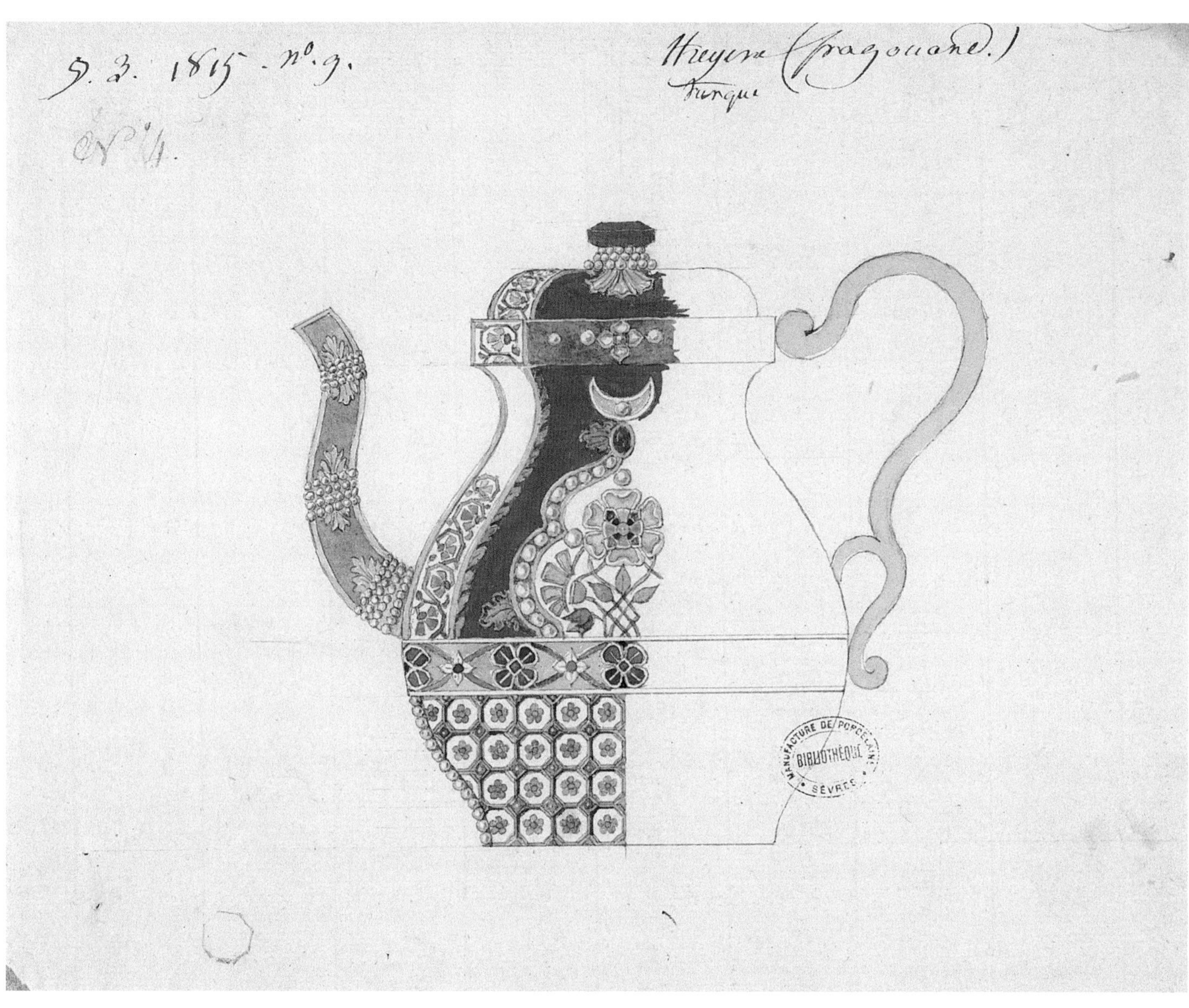

37.
Design and Decoration for a Coffeepot, 1815
Called *Theière 'Turque'*

Alexandre-Evariste Fragonard
Watercolor and ink on paper
7 3/8 x 9 1/4 in. (18.7 x 23.5 cm)
Inv. no. § 3 1815 N° 9
Inscriptions on recto: upper left (ink, in the hand of Brongniart): *§.3.1815.No.9 / No 4*; upper right (ink): *Theyere (fragonard) / turque*;

On August 31, 1815, Augustus, duke of Saxony-Gotha and Altenburg, sent instructions to Brongniart for a new commission. The order was as long and full of stipulations as the one he had sent in 1809, which had not been realized because of the duke's endlessly changing demands.[1] Among several requests, he wrote: "Choose for me a small coffeepot of Turkish form, impressed earthen russet ground, dark brown, to contain only two cups of filtered coffee, with bronze handles gilded four times and Turkish arabesques, baroque color, price 125 – 130 francs."[2]

On October 11, Brongniart sent a detailed memo to A.-E. Fragonard, asking him to develop an appropriate design. A pencil sketch in the margin of the memo indicates that Brongniart initially envisioned the piece as a vessel made of two separate parts. On September 20, 1816, Brongniart sent instructions for completion of this commission to Claude-Charles Gérard, head of the painter's workshop, specifying as number 4, "Turkish coffeepot after the design by Fragonard § 3 1815 n° 9 to have done immediately by [Charles-Antoine] Pain."

On October 2 Brongniart wrote to Treutlinger, the consul from Saxony-Weimar in Paris, informing him that the commission was almost completed, adding: "in order to satisfy him completely by sending only what suits him, I have decided first to send him drawings of the proposed pieces that are made or are ready to be made . . . N° 4 a Turkish two-cup coffeepot. This form was modeled after a design sent from Turkey,"[3] anticipating that its price would be 240 francs.

On March 20, 1817, the duke sent back the drawings with lengthy comments. He wrote that he wanted the Turkish coffeepot to be "as Turkish as the *Grand Seigneur* with brown ground, small ormolu arabesques with enamel, stone, and paste insets and a thousand colors as singular as they are exotic." On November 5, 1817, having received an order for eighteen supplementary cups accompanied by a query on the progress of the earlier commission, Brongniart responded that "several of the pieces already begun . . . [are not] consistent with Your Highness's intentions [and are] not suitable . . . the Turkish teapot has been sold two times because the crescent . . . did not suit Your Highness; if you desire to have a similar one, we could make it without the crescent."[4] Finally, three *théières 'Turque'* officially entered in the sales inventory in July 1818, one of which had in fact been sent to the duke the previous month with the remainder of the commission, on the understanding that he need retain only those pieces that pleased him. To Brongniart's great satisfaction, he kept them all.[5]

1. Préaud, "Alexandre-Théodore Brongniart à la Manufacture de Sèvres" (1986).
2. [Une petite caffetière de forme turque, fonds terre sigillee mordoré, carmelite foncé, qui ne contienne que deux tasses de caffé filtré, à anses bronze quatre fois doré, à arabesques turques, couleur baroque prix 125 – 130 francs] Carton T 8, liasse 3, dossier 6, which contains correspondence and notes pertaining to this commission.
3. The drawing in question could have been one of those provided by the banker Etienne Delessert on November 20, 1812. Although the register of commissions lists a "teapot with Japanese form consistent with the drawings and instructions provided" (Register Vtt 1, fol. 9v), it was a "Turkish teapot lilac ground floral bouquets etc. the whole consistent with instructions provided" that was sold to him in March 1813 (Register Vz 2, fol. 50v). Brongniart made the following annotation on the valuation sheet: "this piece [was] specially made [and its price must cover] models, molds, seconds, doubles, changes etc. (Carton Pb 3). It is possible that a Middle-Eastern model was used, for the general form resembles that of several known examples from the region that were also used in the eighteenth century at Meissen and elsewhere (Rückert, "Wiener und Meissener porzellangeschirr" [1995]).
4. A first "Turkish teapot, Turkish design by Fragonard" entered the sales inventory on December 6, 1816 (Register Vv 1, fol. 75, no. 21; sale price set at 240 francs). Unfortunately, it was "broken during transfer from Sèvres to Paris," as noted in a valuation sheet of March 26, 1817 (Carton Pb 4). A second, similar teapot, which entered the sales inventory on April 24, 1817 (Register Vv 1, fol. 86, no. 1), was part of a delivery to the ministry of foreign affairs for presentation to the pasha of Cairo, along with a *déjeuner* featuring views of Paris captioned in Turkish characters, some tobacco jars, and two vases (Register Vbb 5, fol. 382, April 5, 1817). Yet another entered the inventory on July 3, 1818 (Register Vv 1, fol. 108, no. 14), and two others on the following July 17 (ibid., fol. 108v, no. 70). One of the two that remained was sold for cash in April 1822 (Register Vz 4, fol. 76).
5. Register Vbb 5, fol. 183v.

38.
Decorations for Cups, 1815

[?] Bodson
Gouache and pencil on paper
19 5/8 x 25 5/8 in. overall (50 x 65 cm)
Inv. no. § 4 1815 N 2, 13 to 20 (two numbers 15), 22, and one unregistered

In March 1815 Bodson received 45 francs for "eighteen drawings for cup decorations in color (2 1/2 francs each)." These sketches are typical of the decorations used on services and ornamental pieces that were produced both individually or grouped in *déjeuners* and table services. On January 17, 1814, Brongniart had informed the Sèvres staff that "His Majesty the Emperor might want the manufactory to cover more of its expenses through sales revenues." A few days later, on January 25, he sent instructions to Claude-Charles Gérard, writing that Gérard "should occupy himself with the production of decorative schemes that are carefully executed and saleable on medium-sized vases, *déjeuners*, table services, and individual pieces of the second and third choice . . . to arrive at this goal . . . [he should] determine in advance the sale price with the director and decorate the pieces in accordance with these given as agreeably, as richly, and yet as economically as possible, which [end] he will achieve by choosing ornaments that produce an effect without being difficult to execute. He should always be careful to avoid everything in bad taste, things in good taste being no more expensive than the others . . . care in execution and above all with respect to solidity should never be neglected."[1]

These productions made possible a more equitable distribution of basic operating expenses, which could be divided among a greater number of pieces, something Brongniart was compelled to explain countless times to successive administrations. He stressed the importance of the ruling families taking from Sèvres not only exceptional showpieces but also simpler objects, which would help assure the manufactory's continued operation.

Documentary references concerning work undertaken in 1815[2] indicate that the decorative schemes seen here were used on various cup forms, on several *déjeuners*, and even on some small vases.

1. Carton T 7, liasse 1, dossier 4.
2. Carton Pb 3, liasse 3.

1. The kaolin quarry

2. The pugging mill (*moulin*)

39.
Scenes for the *Déjeuner 'L'Art de la Porcelaine',* 1816

Jean-Charles Develly
Gouache on paper
Largest view 6 1/4 x 9 in. (16 x 23 cm)
Inv. no. Mp § 5 1817 N° 1

As was his custom, Jean-Charles Develly both painted the gouaches here and executed them on the 1816 *déjeuner* (no.9), known as *'L'Art de la Porcelaine.'* The files concerning the project reveal that Brongniart's idea was to represent the various workshops at Sèvres being visited by different groups. He devised this scheme just as he was planning to open to the public the collection of ceramics that he had been assembling since 1800.

The list of scenes to be represented reads: "Sugar bowl — The mill and a visit of students from the Ecole des Mines. The quarries and a visit of mineralogists. 'Paestum' Milk Jug First Size — The large kiln at the conclusion of a firing. 'Paestum' Milk Jug Third Size — The muffle kilns. One cup — The throwers; workshop for

3. Walking the paste

4. The sculptors

making of large pieces [with the] visit of makers. Saucer — Sculptors [with] visit of the interested public. One cup — Painting workshop [with] visit of artists. Saucer — Painting workshop, differently occupied than on the cup, with visit of interested laypeople. Tray — on the rectangular cartel: The sales room and the visit of the King in 1814. The King will be seated, with various pieces being presented to him. On the end medallions: Views in sepia of the two façades of the manufactory."[1]

It is not known whether Develly indeed added visitors to his original compositions when he painted them on porcelain. The page recording the service's entry into the sales inventory on December 27, 1816, however, indicates that the central scene had been replaced by a depiction of the royal visit of June 25, 1816.[2] The complete ensemble was exhibited at the 1816 – 17 New Year's exhibition at the Louvre and was subsequently presented, by order of King Louis XVIII, to the duchesse d'Angoulême, his niece.[3]

For decorations, the manufactory frequently used subjects inspired by the ceramic arts. In addition to vases and *déjeuners* fea-

5. The throwers

6. Molders and repairers

turing portraits of ancient and modern ceramists (such as cat. no. 86), both painted and in relief, the operations of the manufactory itself were represented on at least two other ensembles: a series of plates from the *service 'des Arts Industriels'* (see cat. no. 67), and a *déjeuner 'L'Art Céramique'* which was begun in 1832 and completed in 1841. Although the latter was listed as complete in the catalogue of the Louvre exhibition of May 1, 1840, in fact only the tray was exhibited. This tray was decorated with an imaginary composition depicting people of different nationalities presenting their ceramic productions within the quinqunx of the manufactory. The other pieces in the service bore representations of porcelain being produced at Sèvres and in China, as well as a depiction of "Boshuana women making earthware."[4] All of these compositions were conceived and painted by Develly.

1. Carton Pb 3, travaux de 1816, *Déjeuners.*
2. Carton Pb 3, valuation sheets for 1816; Register Vv 1, fol. 77, no. 4.
3. Register Vbb 5, fol. 12.
4. The tray entered the sales inventory on April 25, 1840 (Register Vv 3, fol. 69, no. 3). The remaining pieces were registered on April 13, 1841 (ibid., fol. 86, no. 8). The ensemble was presented by the president of the Third Republic to the shah of Persia in 1873 (Register Vbb 12, fol. 65v).

7. Attaching handles, spouts, and other elements

8. Glazing

9. Carrying unfired pieces to the kiln

10. Putting pieces into saggars

11. The high fire kiln (*le grand feu*)

12. Preparation of the colors

13. Applying the ground color

14. Painters

15. The muffle kilns

16. Burnishing

17. View of the manufactory, side entry on the Cour Royale

18. View of the manufactory, main entrance

19. The visit of King Louis XVIII to the salesroom at Sèvres

40.
Decoration for a Cup, 1816

Pierre Huard
Gouache and pencil on paper
4 x 6 1/2 in (10.2 x 16.4 cm)
Inv. no. D § 4 1816 N° 19

In October 1816 Pierre Huard was paid for "seven decoration drawings for various forms of cups on white paper.[1] They can hardly be considered highly innovative, however, given that ornamental schemes using "brilliant stones" had first appeared at Sèvres in 1814.[2] The technique in question involved either the painting of trompe l'oeil precious and semiprecious stones or the setting of actual jewels into the porcelain by drilling holes through the vessel wall.[3] These techniques were used for a few years and then almost entirely abandoned, although mounted stones were occasionally used in later pieces, for example the *vase 'de la Renaissance Chenavard'* (see cat. no. 79).[4]

Huard was one of the manufactory's finest ornamentalists, but he seems to have done less design work under Louis-Philippe than during the preceding regimes.

1. Register Vj' 23, fol. 48v; ten francs for each drawing.
2. The first series of pieces to be decorated in this way entered the sales inventory on December 26, 1814 (Register Vv 1, fol. 29v, nos. 34 and 47; fol. 30, no. 23; fol. 30v., no. 47). This manner of decoration has nothing to do with the "jeweled" porcelain produced at Sévres during the 1780s.
3. There is a reference to the "setting of precious stones" (*sertissure de pierres précieuses*) in the work allocations of 1814 (Carton Pb 3, travaux de 1814). At least during its first years, such work was carried out by the goldsmith Pierre-Noël Blaquière (Ennès, "Un fournisseur de la manufacture de Sèvres, l'orfèvre Pierre-Noël Blaquière" [1995]).
4. On August 7, 1839, the manufactory delivered to Hussein Pasha, the Persian ambassador, on the king's orders, "1 Tasse à thé Coupe Iere fond vert imitation de pierreries" (one teacup first [size] green ground imitation gems) priced at 250 francs, but this was one of the pieces entered in the sales inventory on December 26, 1814 (see n. 2, above).

41.
View of Niagara Falls from the Canadian Side, **1816**

Charles-Alexandre Lesueur
Pencil and ink on paper glued to cardboard
7 x 11 1/4 in. (17.7 x 28.5 cm)
Inscriptions: [recto] [within the composition] *prairie et massif de grands arbres / qui chachent la chute*; [under the title, in ink] *Goat Island*; [lower left, below the drawing] *C. A. Lesueur 1816*
Inv. no. P § 1 1818 N° 9

In December 1813 Denon forwarded a request from the Emperor to which Brongniart replied: "His Majesty desires that there be made, for the use of the King of Rome, plates on which will be represented subjects from Roman history, French history, geographic maps, and various animal species. I have the honor of proposing seventy subjects . . . I sought to include those which seemed to me appropriate, simultaneously, to be expressed in painting, to interest a child, to excite his curiosity, and to adorn his memory."[1]

One of the geographic subjects proposed was Niagara Falls. Political developments, primarily the abdication of Napoleon, precluded realization of this project, but the subject was considered interesting enough for the manufactory to decide to acquire a sketch that might serve as a model.

Although Niagara Falls could not figure in the first list of subjects for the *Service 'des Vues hors d'Europe'*, which was drawn up in 1818,[2] it was precisely in that year that payment was authorized for this drawing.[3] Perhaps as a result of this acquisition, it appears on a new list of proposed subjects for the same service, where it is specified that the model to be used was to be found in the portfolios of the manufactory.[4] In the end, a decision was taken to replace this view with one of "Ryacotté in the Baramahl" copied from a printed source.

Oddly, the subject is mentioned again in a list of views projected for the *service 'Historique de Fontainebleau'*,[5] which was eventually realized as a series of plates set into the paneling of the château's Salle des Fêtes. They are still in situ.

Charles-Alexandre Lesueur, a draftsman and naturalist, executed many drawings on vellum for the Muséum d'Histoire Naturelle. He probably produced this landscape (one of three views of this site) as part of a set of drawings made during a trip to the United States with the geologist William Maclure which began in 1815. Brongniart had to have known the young Lesueur before his departure for the United States since the drawings were sent to Brongniart by the artist's father, to whom Brongniart wrote, "The sum I think I can give for the views of the Niagara. . . . I have done what I could to get him a commission in America."[6]

Inscription: ["meadow and clump of large trees / which hide the waterfall"]
1. Carton Pb 3, liasse 2, travaux de 1814.
2. Carton Pb 4, travaux de 1818.
3. Register Vf 68, fol. 26 ("December 12, paid to M. Le Sueur for drawings of Niagara Falls, 49.75 francs).
4. Carton Pb 5, liasse 2 (1), travaux de 1821.
5. Carton Pb 8, liasse 2, dossier 1, service historique de Fontainebleau (1833 – 36). It was decided to use a print from a book rather than one of the manufactory's three drawings of the site by Lesueur (Chevallier, *Musée national du château de Fontainebleau* [1996], no. 283, p. 269), perhaps following the example set by another plate from the same series depicting the "Chute de Genesse Etat de New Yorck [sic] (Ibid., no. 307, p. 291).
6. This information has been kindly provided by Jacqueline Bonnemains, curator of the LeSueur Collection in the Muséum d'Histoire Naturelle, Le Havre. Also see Pinault-Sorensen, *Dessiner la Nature*, exhib. cat. (1996), p. 13.

42.

Decoration for a Vase, 1817
Called *Vase 'Medicis'*

Alexandre-Evariste Fragonard
Gouache, watercolor and pencil on paper
21 1/4 x 16 1/8 in. (54 x 41 cm)
Inscriptions: [recto] [below the drawing, in ink, in the hand of Alexandre Brongniart] *Decoration du Vase Medicis 2e gr. no.16.de 1817. par fragonard*
Inv. no. D § 8 1817 N° 4

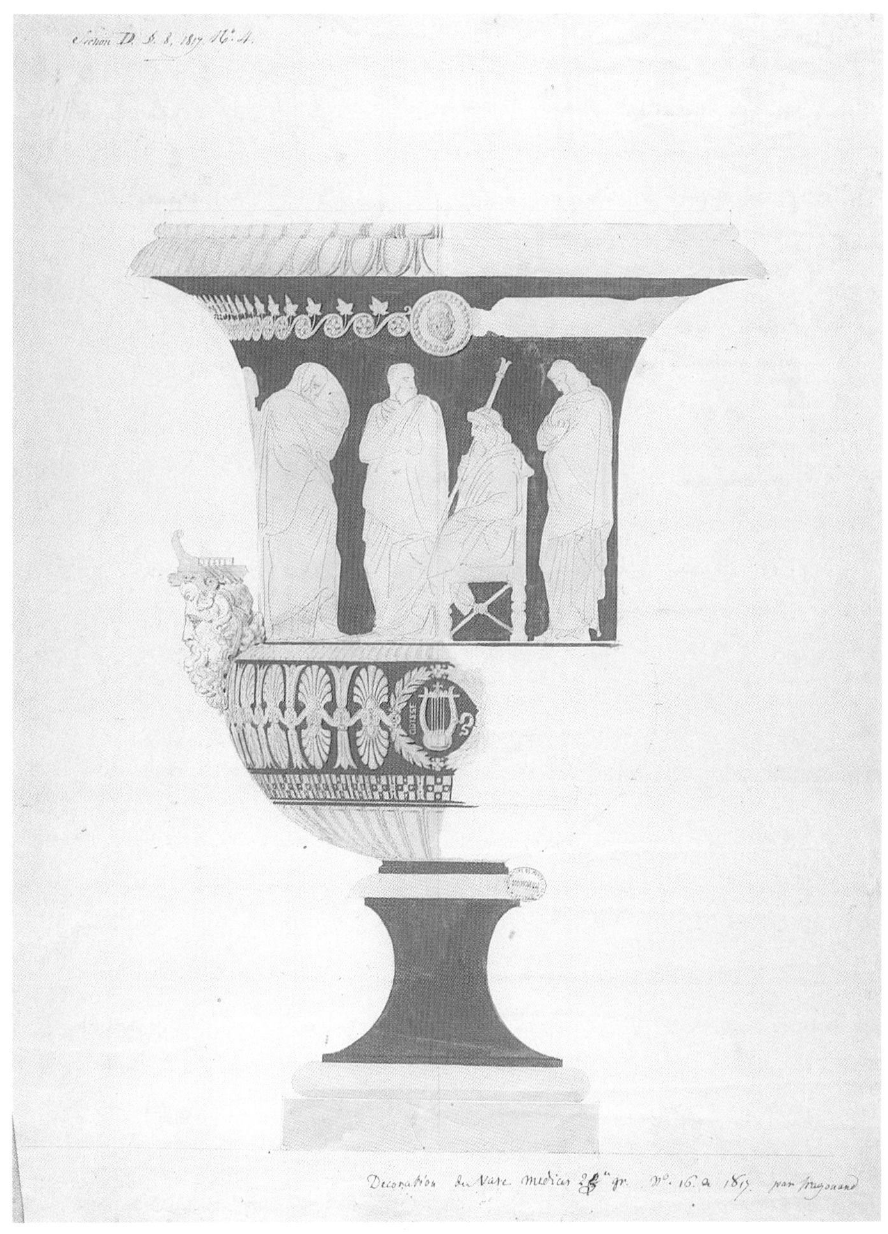

The work allocations for 1816 include a sheet pertaining to Vases No. 16. An entry dated October 10 specifies that it concerned "Two Medici Vases . . . with heads of Jupiter chrome green ground colored subjects scraped on ground copied from figures from the *Odyssey* [illustrated] by Flaxman . . . gold and platinum decorations in the purest and most severe style."

On April 1, 1817, Brongniart noted: "the two vases have been fired with green grounds, but this ground is wretched. We decided to cover it in brown after a successful trial [probably on another piece]. M. Frag[onard] has been charged with the decoration."[1] Alexandre-Evariste Fragonard received 50 francs in the first months of 1817 for "a drawing for the decoration of the green ground Medici Vase," to which was added in July "a drawing of attributes [of] Trojan arms trophies (for the vase [painted] by Béranger)."[2] On March 10, an overall drawing was sent to the chief painter, Claude-Charles Gérard; Antoine Béranger was given the painting-on-porcelain assignment. In January Béranger scraped away the colored grounds to expose the bare porcelain surface, and between April and November he inpainted the figures, receiving 2.250 francs for each vase.

The ornament was assigned to Charles-Christian-Marie Durosey, and the delicate application of a brown ground, in two coats, over the original green ground was completed by Louis Victor Godin. Instructions for the orientation of the drawing are quite vague. The subjects selected correspond to plates 9 and 10 in *The Odyssey*, illustrated by John Flaxman. The catalogue of the exhibition held at the Louvre on January 1, 1818, notes, "these subjects, whose principal dispositions derive from Flaxman's line engravings, were composed in their details and executed by Monsieur Béranger."[3] Béranger probably used the edition of the book that was published in Paris in 1803; it was acquired by the manufactory in 1817.

The two vases entered the sales inventory on December 26, 1817,[4] just before their exhibition at the Louvre, and were delivered to the French ministry of foreign affairs on September 23 of the same year, probably for presentation as gifts.[5]

Although this drawing indicates handles with heads of Neptune surmounted by ships which would be consistent with the overall decorative concept, apparently a variant of one of the more common models with heads of Jupiter was ultimately used instead. Its plaster models may date from 1814. The form of the *vase 'Medici'* itself, which dates from the manufactory's early years, was continually adapted and updated.

1. Carton Pb 4, travaux de 1817.
2. Register Vj' 24, fol. 210 ff.
3. *Notice* . . . (1818), no. 5. The subjects in question are "Ulysses in the palace of Alcinous, beginning to recount his adventures," and "Ulysses in the house of Alcinous, moved by the account of events at the siege of Troy sung by the blind Demodocus." Flaxman's work, in the form of loose plates, had been used as a source at the manufactory before the acquisition of books with his illustrations. On December 31, 1808, a new inventory item is listed as "Two Vase Clodion tortoiseshell ground figure[s] from the Odyssey after Flaxman executed in gold . . . by Béranger . . . Pair 5,470 / 7,500 francs" (Register Vu 1, fol. 69, no. 229 – 18). They were presented to Count Romanzoff on February 11, 1809 (Register Vy 18, fol. 70). Beginning in 1771, John Flaxman, Jr. devised many models for medallions and reliefs in the antique style for Josiah Wedgwood, and the precise contours required by Wedgwood's technique of ceramic molding could well have influenced the development of his characteristic linear style. A.-E. Fragonard adopted this style for his *Recueil de 132 sujets composés et gravés* . . . which is undated, but in 1806 Fragonard used a composition from it to decorate a vase.
4. Register Vv 1, fol. 97, no. 56; the sale price was set at 5,250 francs each.
5. Register Vbb 5, fol. 17v.

43.
Design and Decoration for a Vase, 1817 Called *Vase 'Jasmin Treillis'*

Pierre Huard
Watercolor, gouache, and ink on paper
Inv. no. D § 8 1817 N° 2

A list of new models undertaken at Sèvres between 1817 and 1819 includes a "Jasmine Trellis Vase, model Huard,"[1] dated March 14, 1817. In the June 1817 work allocations, the list of projects assigned to the ornamentalist Pierre Huard included "six model drawings for cup decorations, one ditto for *Jasmin* wicker"; the price of the drawing of the *Jasmin 'Treillis'* had been set at 20 francs the previous April.[2] The drawing of the prototype for the throwers is dated 1818 and bears a manuscript inscription in Alexandre Brongniart's hand indicating that, as with the original *vase 'Jasmin'* of 1801, two versions were initially envisioned, the first consisting of a single piece and the second of two fitted pieces (see cat. no. 1).[3]

Although a list of "pieces to assemble for the exhibition of industrial products" of 1819 includes a reference to "six Jasmin Treillis of various kinds",[4] only two entered the sales inventory on March 19, 1819[5]; in a dessert service described as possessing a "pale blue ground[,] colored ornaments[,] cameo heads" which entered the sales inventory on December 20, 1822,[6] and was delivered on March 25, 1826 to the vicomte de Marcellus, secretary at the French embassy in London,[7] four *vases 'Jasmin Treillis'* priced at 120 francs each were included. It was not until 1841 that two more examples were completed. This is apparently the only form that Pierre Huard designed.

Both the form and the decoration evident in this drawing are typical of the naturalist idiom exemplified by many Restauration productions, some of which have a freshness that sets them apart from the more rigid designs produced under the Empire.

1. Carton Pb 4, travaux de 1819.
2. Register Vj' 24, fol. 51v and Vq', 1ere série, vol. 4, fol. 34v.
3. Tiroir B IV.
4. Carton Pb 4, travaux de 1819.
5. "2 vases Jasmin treillis, fond amaranthe, attributs et ornements en or brunis à l'effet" [two Jasmine trellis vases, amaranth ground attributes and ornaments in gold burnished *à l'effet*] (Register Vv 1, fol. 120v., no. 69); the sale price assigned was 90 francs each.
6. Register Vv 1, fol. 191, nos. 3 and 4.
7. Register Vbb 7, fol. 14.

44 a,b.
Studies for Ornamental Baskets, 1817
Called *Corbeille 'Lion'* and *Corbeille 'Lionne'*

Alexandre-Evariste Fragonard
Pencil, watercolor, and ink on paper
Left: 16 1/2 x 11 3/8 in. (42 x 29 cm)
Right: 16 1/4 x 11 1/4 in. (41.2 x 28.5 cm)
Inscriptions: [recto, both drawings, in the hand of Alexandre Brongniart] *Corbeille Lion (fragonard)* and *Corbeille Lionne (fragonard)*
Inv. no. D § 6 1817 N° 1 and N° 2

A list of new models undertaken between 1817 and 1819 includes an entry dated March 14, 1817, for an "end-of-table basket borne by a lion or a panther"; its design was assigned to Alexandre-Evariste Fragonard. The model was to be made by one of the Brachard brothers, either Jean-Charles-Nicolas Brachard aîné or his younger brother Jean-Nicolas-Alexandre.[1] Apparently the artist's design for a pendant piece, borne by a lioness, was never produced, despite the fact that the original conception called for two "lion" baskets flanking a large central basket called the *corbeille 'canéphore'* which would be supported by four female figures. It was in this configuration that they were exhibited at the Louvre on January 1, 1819.[2] These first examples had entered the sales inventory on December 26, 1818.[3] When they were delivered to "Monsieur le chevallier de La Malle conseiller d'Etat Membre du comité du contentieux" on February 2, 1819, however, they were accompanied by the much simpler *corbeille 'Fragonard'*.[4] The ornament on these baskets was sometimes gilded, but the design exemplifies the new, less formal approach to table decoration that emerged after the Restauration, when pieces like these replaced the rigid centerpieces of the Empire period. This design evidently met with Brongniart's wholehearted approval, for he illustrated it in the catalogue of the Musée Céramique, published nearly a quarter of a century later.[5]

Alexandre-Evariste Fragonard was initially engaged solely to paint gold line decoration, but his many other talents were soon brought to bear on the manufactory's production. Nonetheless, he continued to pursue his career as an independent painter and draftsman.

1. Carton Pb 4, travaux de 1819.
2. *Notice sur . . . au 1er janvier 1819*, no. 20.
3. Carton Pb 4, feuilles d'appréciation de 1818 and Register Vv 1, fol. 278, no. 31.
4. Register Vbb 5, fol. 19.
5. Brongniart and Riocreux, 1845, P., pl. XII, no. 2.

45.
Decoration for a Tabletop, 1817

Charles Percier
Watercolor and ink on paper
11 1/8 x 11 3/8 in. (28.4 x 29 cm)
Inscriptions: [recto, in ink] [in the hexagonal cartels] *Ecole d'Attique / Rhodes / Sicyone / Ecole d'Egine*; [beneath the busts] *Phidias / Agesander / Lisype / Caton*; [verso] [on two strips of paper glued to the sheet] [inventory number] *[pro]jet de la table du Musée Royal par Percier architecte / trav. de 1817 Pièces diverses no 2 – 2 juillet 1817 AlexBrongniart* [in Brongniart's hand]
Inv. no. D § 10 1817 N° 1

The large imperial commission sent to Brongniart on April 26, 1806 (see cat. no. 16) included: "4° make a table with figures from our Museum [Musée Napoleon], namely Apollo, Venus, Minerva, Laocoön, and Hercules." Brongniart initially envisioned a rectangular top that might be used as a console,[1] but insufficient funds and lack of time before the collapse of the Empire prevented him from undertaking all of the pieces ordered and the production of the table was postponed.

The idea was not abandoned, however, and the work allocations for 1817 include, under the heading "various large pieces": "N° 2 – Table illustrating the different rooms of the royal museum after the restoration [of the monarchy]."[2] On the progress sheet concerning this project, Brongniart noted that an overall design had been requested from Charles Percier in March 1817 and was received on July 2 with a note from the architect explaining the program: the four rooms depicted in the large octagonal cartels are the Salle de Diane, the Salle des Colonnes, the Salle de la Melpomène, and the Salle des Caryatides; the four hexagons contain emblematic depictions of the most famous schools of Greek sculpture, each surmounted by a bust of its most famous representative (Cato for Aegina, Phidias for Attica, Lysippus for Sicyon, and Agesander for Rhodes). The central medallion depicts "France to whom Minerva presents these riches with one hand, holding out to her in the other an olive branch, symbol of the peace to which we owe the preservation of these masterpieces."[3] Another sheet in Brongniart's hand provides further instructions regarding the contemporary figures that could be added to the octagons.[4] Percier also designed the entire decorative scheme of the table top, and its "pedestal modeled after a palm tree." The table entered the sales inventory on December 23, 1819, and was exhibited at the Louvre during the New Year's exhibition of 1820. It was presented by Charles X to Prince Leopold of Saxe-Coburg after the New Year's exhibition of 1825.[5]

Inscription: ["design for table of the Royal Museum by Percier the architect / work carried out in 1817 Various pieces no. 2-2 July 1817 AlexBrongniart . . . School of Attica / Rhodes / Sicyon / School of Aegina"]

1. Carton Pb 2, liasse 2.
2. Carton Pb 4, travaux de 1817.
3. Ibid., dossier Tables.
4. Percier was paid 4,000 francs in 1818 for "composition, dessin general 1/3 de l'execution coloré à l'aquarelle developpement des ornements de grandeur d'execution plus 4 dessins de grandeur d'execution de grouppe de monuments et meubles divers du musée pour les cartels hexagones de la table du musée" [composition, general design 1/3 of the execution in color in watercolor ornamental detailing actual size plus four drawings actual size of group of monuments and various furnishings of the museum for the hexagonal cartels of the museum table] (Register Y 21, fol. 65v).
5. For entry in sales inventory, see Register Vv 1, fol. 137, no. 46; the net price was 25,563 francs and the sale price, 35,000 francs; for delivery, see Register Vbb 6, fol. 34v.

46.
Design for a Console, 1818

Alexandre-Evariste Fragonard
Watercolor, gouache and pencil on paper
16 1/2 x 22 1/8 in. (42 x 56.2 cm)
Inscriptions: [recto] [upper left, in ink, in the hand of Denis-Desiré Riocreux] *premier projet d'une console rapelant les trois principales / époques de la vegetation / (travaux en 1818 – 19)*; [upper right, in pencil] *flore . . . . . la nature / flore chimique / flore medicale*; [right edge of drawing] *19 pouces 6 lignes en place de 16 P. / Largeur primitive – bronze doré – bronze – hauteur 3 Pieds 6 pouces 7 Lignes – Bronze*; [top, in ink] *(Console / par M. Fragonard*
Inv. no. D § 10 1818 N° 1

On Brongniart's progress sheet,[1] a note dated April 29, 1818, referring to this drawing, reads: "the overall drawing is done and the program of subjects given price authorized for the overall design and the three drawings by Fragonard 500 [francs]".[2] In another entry under the same date, Brongniart described the subjects that were to be represented on three porcelain plaques designed by Fragonard, depicting the three principal cycles of the growing season (fig. 46a).

His notes for this piece can serve as an example of the specificity of Brongniart's instructions to the artists and the ingenuity needed to devise compositions consistent with these lengthy descriptions. For the first subject, Brongniart wrote: "First cycle: the germination and development of plants (the first spring). Zephyr, or the west wind favorable to vegetation, awakens the slumbering Flora by having rays of the sun fall on her and warm her. He chases away the north wind, which flees with the accompanying clouds, which obscured the sun. The earth near Zephyr and around Flora is already green; some flowers emerge from it: primroses, violets, hazel trees in bloom. Small leaves on the trees and above all buds. Near the north wind the earth is still covered with frost, the trees are bare etc. Seeds of all kinds are contained either within Flora's robe or inside a covered basket to protect them while she sleeps. Near Zephyr these seeds seem already to be opening and we see the sprouts emerge. The decoration can be composed with germinating plants."[3]

Comparison of the overall sketch with the actual object, which survives,[4] reveals that the design's right half was realized as indicated but important changes were introduced in the proportions and decorative details. The production of this table posed a host of problems for the manufactory. On November 3, 1819, Brongniart noted: "the columns are all in the kiln in lapis blue [but] they are of unequal dimensions. The plaques for the upper extremities are in lapis blue [and are both] too high and too short." The problems were eventually solved, however, and the console entered the sales inventory on December 23, 1819[5]; it was delivered to the château de Saint-Cloud between June 30 and July 17, 1821.[6]

Inscriptions: ["first design for a console on the theme of the three principal / stages of vegetation / (work carried out in 1818 – 19)"; "flora . . . of nature / chemical flora / medical flora; 19 inches 6 lines instead of 16 inches / original width-bronze gilt-bronze-height 3 feet 6 inches 7 lines-Bronze"; "Console / by M. Fragonard"]

1. Carton Pb 4, travaux de 1817, chemise: console en porcelaine.

2. Ibid. In fact, the *feuille d'appréciation* indicates that the artist was paid 600 francs.

3. [1ere époque la germination et le dévelopement des plantes (le premier printemps). Le Zephir ou vent d'ouest favorable à la vegetation reveille flore endormie en faisant tomber sur elle les rayons du soleil qui la rechauffent. Il chasse les aquilons qui fuyent vers le nord ainsi que les nuages qui les accompgnoient et qui cachoient le soleil. La terre du cote de zephir et autour de flore est deja verte; quelques fleurs y paroissent: les primeveres, les violettes, les noisetiers en fleurs. De petites feuilles aux arbres et surtout des bourgeons. Du coté des aquilon, la terre est encore couverte de frimats, les arbres sont sans feuilles etc. des graines de toutes especes sont renfermées ou dans la robe de flore endormie ou dans un panier couvert et conservés pendant son sommeil. Du coté de Zephir ces graine semblent deja s'ouvrir et on en voit le germe sortir. Les ornement peuvent être composés avec des plantes en germination] Ibid.

4. Brunet and Préaud, *Sèvres, des origines à nos jours* (1978), ill. 355, p. 391.

5. Register Vv 1, fol. 137v., no. 51 and Carton Pb 4, *Feuilles d'appréciation* de 1819. The net price was set at 12,770 francs; 9,000 francs of this amount was allocated for the production of the bronze mounts by Louis-Honoré Boquet, an enormous sum compared to 2,520 francs for the decoration and 450 francs for the blue-ground porcelains. The sale price was set at 16,000 francs.

6. Register Vbb 6, fol. 26v.

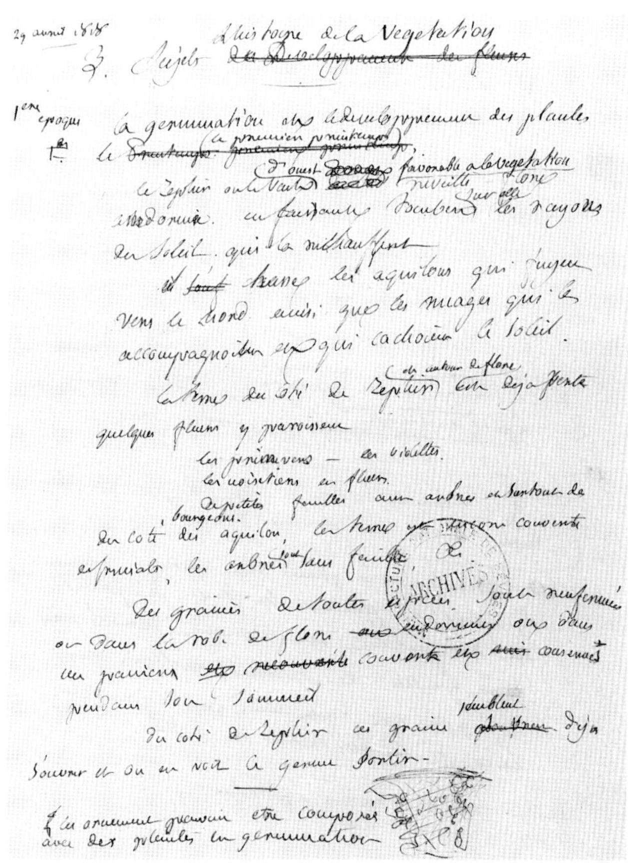

Fig. 46a. Brongniart's instructions to Fragonard for the decoration of porcelain plaques, April 29, 1818. (Archives, Manufacture Nationale de Sèvres, Carton Pb 4, travaux de 1817, chemise: console en porcelaine)

47.
Design and Decoration for a Teapot, 1818
Called *Théière 'Chinoise'*

Alexandre-Evariste Fragonard
Watercolor and pencil on thin paper
6 3/4 x 9 5/8 in. (17.3 x 24.5 cm)
Inscription: [recto] [bottom, in ink, in the hand of Denis-Desiré Riocreux] *Theière chinoise Fragonard*
Inv. no. D § 2 1818 N° 9

This drawing, although not an accurate transcription of authentic Chinese models, borrowed elements of East Asian design in keeping with early nineteenth-century taste. The design was put into immediate production; in April 1818. A.-E. Fragonard was paid 30 francs for a "drawing of a Chinese teapot for the form and the decoration in color,"[1] A list of pieces to be shown at the exhibition on January 1, 1819, includes "four Chinese teapots" under the heading "various small pieces."[2] The first eight examples entered the sales inventory on December 26, 1818;[3] presumably, they were among the inexpensive pieces that Brongniart usually presented on those occasions, without listing them in the catalogue: the documents record that several were sold "at the Louvre exhibition of December 29 to January 8, 1819."[4]

This model, which was always sold separately, never as part of a *déjeuner*, was quite successful. Seventeen examples were produced between 1818 and 1821, probably with similar ornament as all of them were priced at 36 francs.[5] Two others with blue grounds and gold ornament were priced at 55 francs. The form was issued in 1827 with richer decorations.[6] According to the registers, eight of these were decorated between 1827 and 1846. In the meantime, models of several other "Chinese" teapots had been designed, and it is not always easy to distinguish between them in the documents. Here again (see cat. no. 44), Brongniart was sufficiently proud of this design to illustrate it in his catalogue of the Musée Céramique.[7]

1. Register Vj' 25 (1818), fol. 203.
2. Carton Pb 4, travaux de 1819.
3. Register Vv 1, fol. 115v., no. 30 and fol. 117, no. 42.
4. Register Vz 3, fol. 139v.
5. Judging from an example recently on the market (Paris, March 28, 1995, Nicolier Collection, cat. No. 92, ill.), the design of the ornamental band varied but the colors of the drawing were usually, and perhaps consistently, retained.
6. *Nouvelles acquisitions (1979 – 1989)*, exhib. cat. (1989), no. 262, p. 184.
7. Brongniart and Riocreux, *Description méthodique du musée céramique* (1845), P. pl. IV, no. 3.

48.
Decoration for Footed Bowl, 1819 Called *Coupe 'Diatrète'*

Claude-Charles Gérard
Watercolor and pencil on paper
11 5/8 x 17 3/8 in. (29.5 x 44 cm)
Inscription: [recto] [lower right, pencil] *190 fr[ancs]*; [top, center, in ink, in the hand of Denis-Désiré Riocreux] *Coupe Diatrète*; [signature following the inventory number, in ink] *GD*
Inv. no. D § 8 1819 N° 1 (2)

The work registry for 1818 includes a page concerning "three Diatreta footed bowls no. 18 for the 1819 work allocations" by (Claude-Charles) Gérard . They are described in an entry dated June 24, 1818: "frame with twelve colored precious stones along the edge a cameo surrounded by crystal .05 centimeters in the bottom . . . porcelain handle [made] by the Saint-Amand [sic] process, ornament suitable to be made by printing"; three different color schemes were envisioned.[1]

This notation indicates that the objects in question combined the insetting of precious stones, a procedure introduced some years earlier (see cat. no. 40), with two techniques developed by Honoré Boudon de Saint-Amans. In one he devised a special paste and molds that enabled him to attain unusually fine castings. From this process he made cameos that were encased in crystal. These were then secured to porcelain forms.[2] The *coupe 'Diatrète'* required another technique, namely the printing of decorations by means of an etched plate, a technique used at Sèvres since 1806 for monograms but not in general use until about the 1820s.[3]

On March 5, 1819, Brongniart entered the following note: "M. Gérard 1: will produce colored sketches capable of conveying the effect of execution in the three manners [three different color schemes] / 2: will consult with M. Constans regarding the mode of impression and the engraving of the plate / 3: will consult with Messieurs de Saint-Amand, Windinger, and Blaquière regarding the execution of the colored stones and cameos and the way they are to be fitted in."[4]

Only one of these vases was eventually produced. It featured a white ground and shaded gold ornament. After entering the sales inventory on December 22, 1820, it was sold soon afterward in the course of the New Year's Day exhibition of 1820 – 21 at the Louvre. The buyer was identifed as Wilkenson.[5] In the catalogue, it is listed in a special section devoted to vases "with porcelain-paste cameos enveloped in crystal and set into the porcelain, by means of the process of M. de Saint-Amant [sic]," along with two *vases 'Thericléen'* decorated with cameo portraits of past and present members of the royal family. The Latin word *diatreta* refers to ancient glass vessels that were decorated with applied reliefs and skillful undercutting. One contemporary critic observed that this coupe "is a loan from the fifteenth century, but a copy in which richness is allied perfectly with good taste."[6]

1. "Entourage de douze pierres precieuses colorées sur le bord un camée entouré de cristal de 05 centimetres dans le fond. . . Anse en porcelaine par le procédé Saint-Amand, ornements susceptibles d'être faits par impres-

sion" (Carton Pb 4, travaux de 1818).

2. Labit and Lasserre, "Un maître des arts du feu: Le chevalier Boudon de Saint-Amans" (1968). Boudon de Saint-Amans had requested a *brevet de perfectionnement* to refine this process in 1818 and presented pieces at the industrial products exhibition of 1819. The earliest crystal-encased cameos inlaid in porcelain date from 1796 in France. Mme Desarnaud, owner of a Parisian shop called L'Escalier de Cristal, had previously carried out similar experiments with the manufactory's cameos, but these proved unsuccessful, judging from an entry in the archives, dated December 27, 1816, "Losses for biscuit-fired cut medallions namely 415 cut medallions and other biscuit-fired objects delivered in the course of 1816 to Mme Desarnaud, she returned 160 to the manufactory. According to her statement, the rest were destroyed in attempts to set them into crystal. She attributed the failure to the nature of the paste and the extent of firing of the pieces" [Dechets pour médallions découpés en dégourdi savoir sur 415 médallions découpés et autres objets en dégourdi livrés dans le courant de 1816 à Mad[e] Desarnaud, elle en a rendu a la manufacture 160. D'apres sa declaration le reste ayant manqué en les employant dans le cristal et en attribuant la cause à la nature de la pâte ou au degré de cuisson des pièces] (Carton Pb 3, feuilles d'appréciation 1816).

3. Préaud, "Transfer-Printing Processes used at Sèvres" (1997).

4.[M. Gerard 1° etablira des croquis coloriés propres à faire connoître l'effet de l'exécution dans les trois manières 2° s'entendra avec Mr Constans pour le mode d'impression et la gravure de la planche 3° s'entendra avec Mrs de Saint Amand, Windinger et Blaquière pour exécution des pierres coloriées et camées et leur mode d'encastrement] Carton Pb 4, Travaux de 1818. Pierre-Noël Blaquière was a specialist in the inlaying of precious stones (see Ennès, "Un fournisseur de la manufacture de Sèvres" [1995]). Charles-Louis Constans, a gilder and painter, was assigned impressed-ornament projects since 1818 – 19. The Windinger in question is probably Joseph Windinger.

5. For the entry in sales inventory, see Register Vv 1, fol. 154, no. 14 (600 francs) and Carton Pb 4, appréciations de 1820. Curiously, the description here is quite different: "One rich Diatreta Vase with impressed decoration in gold against purple ground painted ornament in brown stone[s] in color . . . mounting and stone and bronze fittings in bronze and vermeil by Monsieur Blaquer [sic]" [1 Vase Coupe Diatrète riche decore par impression en or lesdits sur fond pourpre ornements peints en brun piere de couleurs . . . montage et piere et garniture en bronze et vermeil par Mr Blaquer] (ibid.). For the sale, see Register Vz 4, fol. 27.

6. *Le Courrier français* (December 29, 1820).

49.
Decoration for a Plate from the *Service 'Liliacées', 1819*

Jean-Charles-François Leloy
Pencil, ink and gouache on paper
11 5/8 x 11 3/4 in. (29.5 x 29.7 cm)
Inscription: [recto] [upper right, in ink, in the hand of Alexandre Brongniart] *Leloi 2 fev.no 6 / service Liliacé.1819.no 2.*
Inv. no. D § 5 1819 N° 6

In February 1819 the designer Jean-Charles-François Leloy received 45 francs for this drawing described as "one overall decoration drawing for the *service 'Liliacées'* done entirely in outline, one quarter colored in brown heightened with gold against Nankin ground and the other quarter in gray against a brown ground."[1] A note on the service's progress sheet the same month reads: "make 1° one [engraved] plate with outline of projected ornament 2° try out the execution of this ornament on two plates —in brown heightened with gold against Nankin ground—in white against brown ground . . . some large pieces with ornaments [executed] by hand (coolers)—the others engraved, the flowers by Drouet and Philippine."[2] The fee for painting "groups of two liliaceous plants linked with a convolvulus on the ground of the plate after the work of Redouté in two firings and very carefully done" was set at 25 francs,[3] by comparison with a similar service produced in 1804 – 05.[4]

Work on the service must have been quite advanced January 3, 1820, when it was chosen for the king's table at the Palais des Tuileries. A note in the registry at Sevres reads: "[the first] half promised in three months and the complete service in five by May 15."[5] This schedule was almost met: the service entered the sales inventory on April 17, 1820,[6] and was delivered to the Tuileries on April 18 and May 23. Thereafter, many replacement pieces were provided.[7] As a result of this delivery, the manufactory could present only samples of the service at the

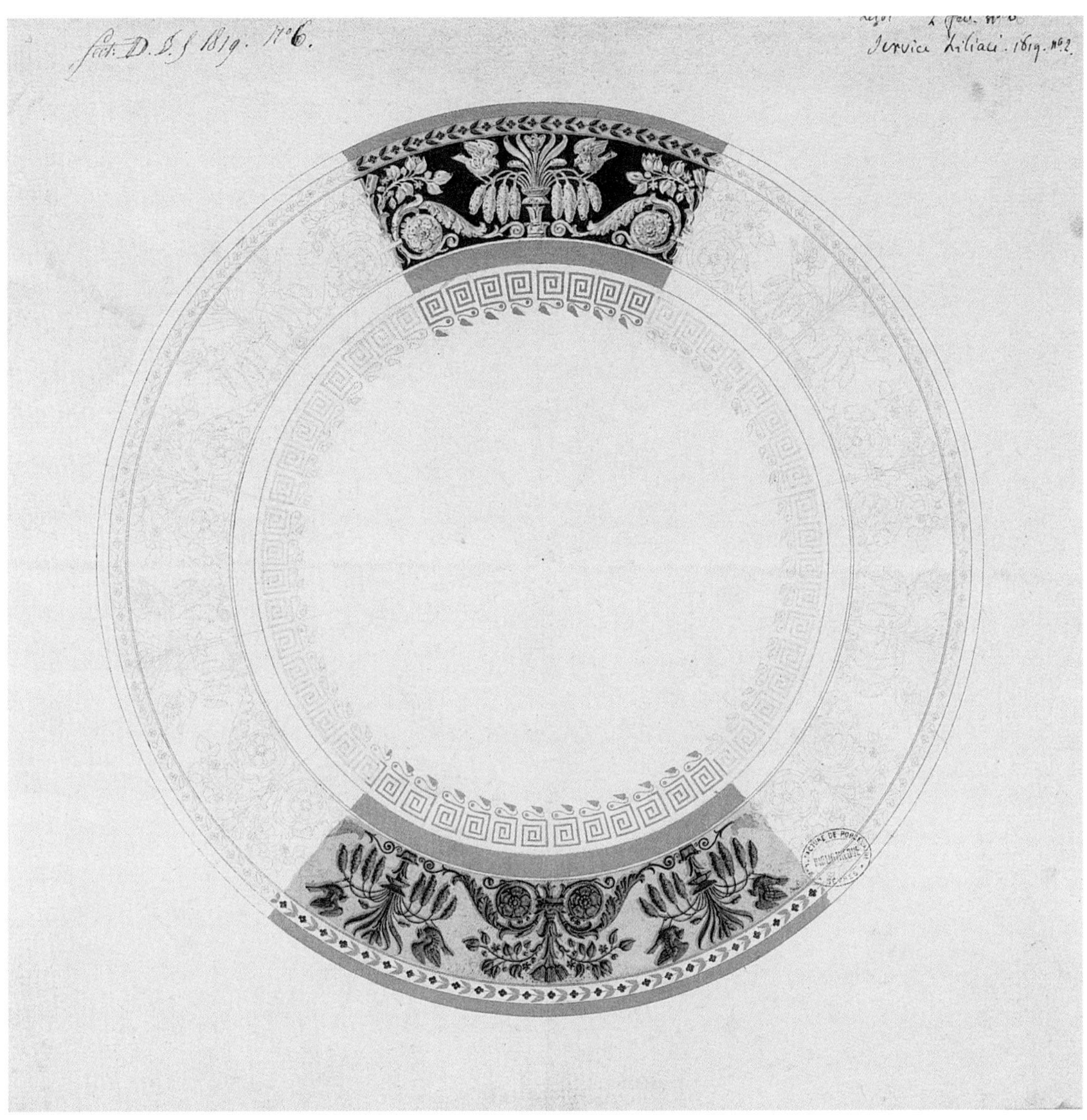

49.

1820–21 New Year's Day exhibition at the Louvre.[8]

It is unlikely that this ensemble was selected by the king's household on the basis of its price. Although it was slightly less expensive than the *service 'Iconographique Italien'*, which was then in use at the Tuileries (plates of the *service 'Liliacée'* cost 75 francs, as opposed to 85 francs for plates from the other service), it seems more likely that it was the brilliantly colored flowers that earned it a place on the king's table. They were more seductive than the severe brown cameo portraits of the other service. In any event, the *service 'Liliacée'* was among the first at Sèvres to feature a ornamental frieze that was transfer-printed on the pieces. This technique, which had been used in England to ornament fine earthenware since the mid-eighteenth century, was only then becoming a regular part of French ceramic production (see cat. no. 67).

1. [1 dessin general du décore du service liliacées fait en totalité au trait, un quart colorié en brun rehaussé d'or sur fond nankin et l'autre quart en gris sur fond brun] Register Vj' 26 (1819), fol. 1.

2. [Faire 1° une planche au trait de l'ornement projeté 2° essayer l'execution de cet ornement sur deux assiettes — en brun rehaussé d'or sur fond nankin — en blanc sur fond brun . . . quelques grandes pièces avec ornements à la main (glacières) — les autres gravées les fleurs par Drouet et Philippine] Carton Pb 4, travaux de 1819, "services de table . . . no. 2. The artists in question are the flower painters Gilbert Drouet and François-Pascal Philippine aîné.

3. [Groupes de deux liliacées liés avec un volubilis sur fond d'assiette d'apres l'ouvrage de Redouté a 2 feux et très soigné.] Register Y 21, fol. 23v., Drouet.

4. Baer and Lack, *Pflanzen auf porzellan* (1979), pp. 53 – 58.

5. [Promis la moitie dans trois mois et le tout dans cinq cad. le 15 mai] Register Vtt 1, fol. 191.

6. Register Vv 1, fol. 143, no. 10.

7. Register Vbb 6, fols. 46, 46v, and 47.

8. Although the documents describe the service's plates as having borders with pale blue grounds with brown decoration, the corresponding entry in the catalogue of the Louvre exhibition reads: "Edge ground of the plates and ornament imitating agates or chalcedonies with cameo engravings. On each piece, one or several flowers of the *liliaceous* plant family, painted after M. Redouté's colored engravings by M. Drouet" [Fond du bord des assiettes et ornemens imitant les agates ou calcédoines gravées en camées. Sur chaque pièce, une ou plusieurs fleurs de la famille des plantes *Liliacées*, peintes d'après les gravures colorées de M. Redouté par M. Drouet].

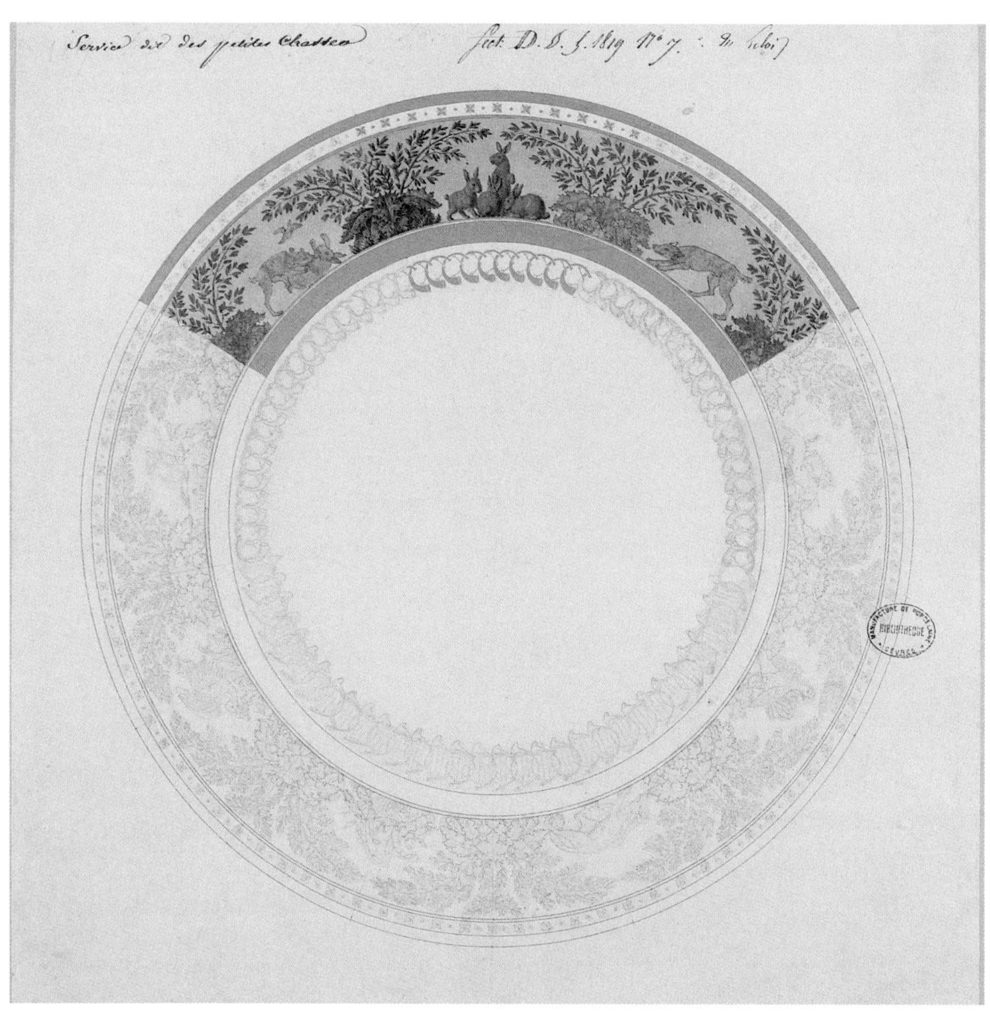

50.

Decoration for a Plate from the *Service 'des Petites Chasses'*, 1819

Jean-Charles-François Leloy
Pencil, ink, and gouache on paper
11 x 11 in. (28 x 28 cm)
Inscription: [recto] [upper left, in ink, in the hand of Denis-Désiré Riocreux] *service des petites chasses*
Inv. no. D § 5 1819 N° 7

In March 1819 Jean-Charles-François Leloy was paid 48 francs for "a design for the *service 'des Petites Chasses'*, complete perimeter [rendering] with variants for the small border and one-third of the drawing colored."[1] Brongniart judged this fee to be too high.[2] Leloy also made illustrations of about fifty small animals, both predators and prey, for this service.[3] The progress sheet for service no. 11 of 1819 describes the decoration: "on the border of the plate a printed frieze of regular undergrowth with animals chasing one another gold ornament on the wall white well."[4] Estimated production costs for the plates included 3 francs each for the transfer printing of the undergrowth, a frieze with hunting horns, and a rosette, all without any painted infilling, as well as 18 francs for the painting of the underbrush and animals. The hand-retouching of the transfer-printed borders resulted in a projected net price of 34 francs and a sale price of 42 francs.

In fact, when the complete service entered the sales inventory on December 22, 1821, the plates were priced at 40 francs each.[5] The ensemble was presented at the Louvre New Year's exhibition of 1821 – 22. Only a few days after its return to Sèvres, most of the service was set aside for one "Milord Herbert," who at the same time commissioned an entrée service described as "white double gold fillet colored coat of arms on the border of the pieces."[6] Both services were delivered on May 16, 1822.[7] Once again, the documents provide contradictory indications regarding the ground color: the sales inventory maintains it was a "bluish gray," while the delivery register describes it as "pale blue" and the Louvre exhibition catalogue as "white"; these discrepancies are evident when examining the actual pieces with their very pale ground color.[8] A low-cost process such as transfer-printing was employed at this time on inexpensive wares. Its use on this service, however, appears to be somewhat contradictory, in view of the undecorated plate wells, a treatment that traditionally indicated a perfect paste and therefore a superlative production.

1. [Un dessin du service des pettites chasses, fait entierement au pourtour avec variantes pour la petite bordure et 1/3 du dessin colorié] Register Vj' 26, fol. 1v.
2. Register Y 21, fol. 66.
3. This drawing depicts rabbits, frogs, and hens with their chicks being pursued or captured by natural predators.
4. [Sur le marly de l'assiette une frise imprimée de broussaille régulière des animaux se chassant dans ces broussailles ornements en or sur le galbe milieu blanc] Carton Pb 4, travaux de 1819, services de table.
5. Carton Pb 5, valuations for 1821, and Register Vv 1, fol. 170v., no. 36 (entry into sales inventory on December 15, 1821).
6. [Blanc double filet d'or armoiries coloriées sur le bord des pièces] Register Vtt 2, fol. 9, January 22, 1822.
7. Register Vbb 6, fol. 103v.
8. Sale Paris, June 13, 1997, O. Coutau-Bégarie, lot no. 111.

51.
Design for a Sugar Bowl, 1819
Called *Sucrier 'Mélissin'*

Alexandre-Evariste Fragonard
Pencil and watercolor on paper
10 3/8 x 14 1/8 in. (26.4 x 36 cm)
Inscriptions: [recto, in pencil, in the hand of Alexandre Brongniart] [within the drawing] *Detail de l'anse adopte-bouton du couvercle-anse adopte-a preferer,* [lower left, in ink] *sucrier de table dit Sucrier Melissin*
Inv. no. D § 6 1819 N° 2

In July 1819 Alexandre-Evariste Fragonard was paid 30 francs each for four new designs for forms. Three were for sugar bowls (called '*Diota*', '*Gaudronné*', and '*Mélissin*'), and one was for a *compotier 'Gaudronné'*.[1] A list of projected new models indicates they were to be produced in 1819.[2] In fact the first examples of these designs entered the sales inventory on December 23 of that year. They featured white grounds decorated with gold-highlighted vegetal friezes, as in this drawing.[3] Thereafter, these pieces were often in dessert services but were also produced individually.

The name of the piece derives from *melitta,* the Greek word for "bee," after the bees that are part of the handle. The form itself has a grace typical of Sèvres productions of the Restauration period.

Inscription: ["Detail of handle adopted-knob on lid-adopted handle-to be preferred"]; ["sugar pot called Sucrier Melissin"]

1. Register Vj' 26 (1819), fol. 242.
2. Carton Pb 4, travaux de 1819.
3. Carton Pb 4, feuilles d'appréciation 1819.

52.
Decoration for a Vase, 1820
Called *Vase 'Cordelier'*

Jean-Charles-François Leloy
Watercolor and pencil on paper
12 1/8 x 7 3/4 in. (30.7 x 19.8)
Inscriptions: [recto, top, in ink, in the hand of Denis-Désiré Riocreux] Dessin d'ensemble du Vase Cordelier 3e les trois graces, d'après Girodet; [bottom, in pencil] Le fond brun pour les sujets coloriés-le fond blanc pr. les sujets en camée; [bottom, in ink] sujet d'après Girodet
Inv. no. D § 8 1820 No 7 (1)

This is probably one of five drawings by Jean-Charles-François Leloy, relating to a "Cordelier Vase third size [to be executed by] Monsieur Le Guay," for which he was paid 110 francs in 1820.[1] The commission is numbered seven in the work allocations for 1820 and described on its progress sheet: "1820 Two Cordelier Vases third size with three-figure colored subjects, sky blue ground, matte gold decoration against gold ground in cameo and in color against gold ground and sky [ground] the whole in conformity with the drawing by Monsieur Leloy. The figures will be painted by Monsieur Leguay. The bronze fittings of the bottom and the handles will be made from models already owned by the manufactory [and made] by Monsieur Boquet."[2]

When the vase was made, the reserve shown in Leloy's design was replaced by figures painted directly on the ground. Perhaps this revision originated with a painter who was paid more when he also provided an original design: for each vase, he received 1,200 francs for the painting and 150 francs "for the composition drawing, retained by the manufactory.[3]" The vases entered the sales inventory on December 20, 1822, and although Brongniart considered them to be "ineffective, even in the view of Monsieur Leguay,"[4] they were shown at the New Year's exhibition of 1822 – 23 held at the Louvre and were presented to the king of Naples on January 14, 1825.[5]

The *vase 'Cordelier'* owes its name to a feature of the first example; the gilt bronze fittings made by Pierre-Philippe Thomire included two infants and thick knotted cords.[6] The vase which had already been produced in several different sizes, was simply reduced to an intermediary size — by Brongniart's father in 1801; several more adaptations were produced before the end of the century.

Inscription: ["Complete design for the Vase Cordelier no. 3 the three graces, after Girodet"]; ["brown ground for colored motifs-white ground for cameos"]; ["subject after Girodet"]

1. [Vase Cordellier 3me gdr. pour Mr. Le Guay] Register Vq', 1ere série, vol. 4, fol. 93 and Register Vj' 27 (1820), fol. 1v.
2. [1820 2 Vases Cordelier 3e gr. sujets de 3 figures coloriées sur chaque, fond bleu de ciel, décoration en or mat sur fond d'or en camée et en coloris sur fond d'or et de ciel le tout conformément au dessin de M.Leloi. les figures seront peintes par M.Leguay la garniture en bronze du culot et les anses seront faites avec les modeles que la manufacture possède deja par M.Boquet.] Carton Pb 5, liasse 2 (1), travaux de 1821). At this date, the artist in question would be Etienne-Charles Le Guay. The use of existing models for the bronze fittings typifies Brongniart's economical approach at the manufactory.
3. Register Vq', 1ere série, vol. 5, fol. 3 (November 1821). The composition drawings are no longer to be found at the manufactory. The Louvre exhibition catalogue attributes these designs solely to Le Guay; this implies that the use of models by Anne-Louis Girodet-Trioson, indicated in the inscription on the present sheet, were subsequently abandoned.
4. [Foibles d'effet, de l'aveu même de M.Leguay.] Carton Pb 5, liasse 2 (1), travaux de 1821.
5. For entry in sales inventory, see Register Vv 1, fol. 190, no. 22. Delivery: Register Vbb 7, fol. 1 and 1v. (sale price 9,000 francs for the pair). See Valeriani, "Porcellane di Sèvres Doni Borbonici" (1990).
6. Register Vf 37 (1787), "December 11, 1787 . . . 3,392 livres paid to Monsieur Thomire to purchase 4 marcs of gold for the gilding of the vase with cords" [11 décembre 1787 . . . 3,392 livres paiée à M. Thomire pour acheter 4 marcs d'or pour la dorure du vase à cordes]

53.
Design for a Mantelpiece, 1820

Charles Percier
Watercolor and ink on paper
16 1/4 x 21 3/4 in. (41.3 x 55.2 cm)
Inscriptions: [recto in pencil] [within the drawing] *coupe-plan-échelles des dessins-profil ou coté de la cheminée*; [below the drawing] [in ink, in the hand of Alexandre Brongniart] *cheminée en marbre et bronze, incrustée en plaques et tableaux sur Porcelaine. mars 1820. / echelle-4 pieds-1 metre*; [bottom center, in red ink] *échelle servant dans le cas où l'on exécuteroit cette cheminée p^r un tres g^d appart^t, elle auroit alors.5^d de haut au lieu de 4 comme dans le dessin cy dessus*; [lower left] [signature] *Charles Percier*; [verso] *Recu le 4 avril 1820*
Inv. no. D § 10 1820 N° 1

Brongniart must have had a previous discussion with Charles Percier about producing mantelpieces decorated with porcelain plaques. In a letter to Percier on February 20, 1818, the director announced that "the moment, Monsieur, that you suggested . . . to occupy yourself with mantelpieces decorated with porcelain . . . has arrived."[1] He asked Percier to submit some drawings for the mantel which was designated number 6, under the heading "*pièces diverses*," on the list of projects anticipated for 1818. According to the progress sheet for the project, however, it was not until March 22, 1820, that the architect finally sent a design for this piece. Work seems to have advanced normally thereafter, for a note of September 7, 1820, records that "all the plaques have been trimmed and brought together."[2]

Although the mantelpiece consistently appeared in the work lists for subsequent years under the same order number, apparently nothing more was done until 1824, when the painting of the figure compositions was assigned to Jean-Baptiste-Ignace Zwinger and the ornamental painting to Charles-Antoine Didier and Pierre Riton.[3] A note dated March 24, on the work allocation list for 1825 indicates that execution of the project had been "postponed." even though another note reads: "assigned before April 1, 1825."[4]

While the mantelpiece continued to be listed from 1826 to 1828, it would seem that work never actually began. When Brongniart eventually made a mantelpiece, it was in a Renaissance revival style quite different from Percier's original neoclassical designs (see cat. no. 87).

Inscription: ["Section-plan-scale drawings-outline or side of the mantel"]; ["mantel in marble or bronze, inlaid with plaques and paintings on porcelain, March 1820. / scale-4 feet-1 meter"]; ["scale to be used when this mantel is installed in a very large room, it would then measure 5 feet in height instead of 4 as in the above drawing"]

1. [Le moment, Monsieur, que vous m'avez indiqué pour vous occuper des cheminées décorés en porcelaine dont je vous ai parlé est arrivé.] Carton Pb 9, liasse 1, dossier Meubles, chemise: "Cheminée pour Fontainebleau."

2. On April 4, 1820, the following note was entered under Percier's name: "A colored drawing section D § 10 1820 N° 1 of a mantelpiece decorated with three compositions representing winter scenes six figures of signs of the zodiac of this season four compositions with figures and allegorical ornament-Overall drawing of the front and both sides the whole very carefully done in color" [Un dessin section D § 10 1820 N° 1 colorié d'une cheminée ornée de trois tableaux representant des scènes d'hiver six figures des signes du zodiaque de cette saison quatre tableaux de figures et ornements alegoriques-Le dessin general de la face et des côtés lateraux le tout très soignés en couleurs], to which Alexandre Brongniart added: "Vu p[ou]r mem[oire]". (Register Vj' 27, fo. 239).

3. Carton Pb 5, "Etat général et sommaire des principaux travaux de 1824."

4. [Donnée en commande avant le Ier avril 1825"; "l'exécution en est ajournée."] Carton Pb 6, liasse 1, dossier 3.

Jeanne d'Arc au Sacre de Charles VII
(par Fragonard 1820)

54.
Design for a Figure of Joan of Arc, 1820

Alexandre-Evariste Fragonard
Pencil on paper
14 7/8 x 10 7/8 in. (37.8 x 27.6 cm)
Inscription: [recto, bottom, in ink] Jeanne d'arc au sacre de Charles VII / (par fragonard 1820)
Inv. no. F § 4M 1820 No 1

Despite the large scale, multiple piece projects for *surtouts* (centerpieces), the sculpture workshop at Sèvres was not the manufactory's most active division in the first half of the nineteenth century (see chap. 8). The number of large *surtouts* of the Empire period consisting of figural groups (see cat. no. 22) were gradually replaced by standing baskets of various sizes (see cat. no. 44) and statuettes increasingly assumed a decorative role. In addition to new busts, medallion portraits, and equestrian figures of members of the royal family, past and present, Sèvres continued to produce models that had originated during the ancien régime. These included divinities and allegorical groups as well as the series of figures known as the Great Men series, which had been begun in the 1780s and was expanded under the Empire. Between 1818 and 1820, Alexandre-Evariste Fragonard designed four new neo-Gothic figures that were probably considered further additions to the same series.[1] They represented French martial heros and heroines of the Medieval and Renaissance periods: Dunois, Duguesclin, Crillon, and Joan of Arc.

Although the manufactory produced two vases commemorating the French medieval figures Jeanne Hachette and Pierre Bayard in 1808,[2] it was only with the return of the Bourbons to power in 1815 that medieval heros of the Catholic, royalist, and nationalist past returned to respectability, above all, Joan of Arc.[3] The beplumed female warrior in Fragonard's design is reminiscent of the one made by the sculptor Etienne Gois in 1804 for the city of Orléans.[4]

Working from two drawings depicting the figure from different angles, Jean-Charles-Nicolas Brachard aîné produced a plaster model between September and December 1820.[5] Two examples were then modeled in porcelain, one by Jean-Nicolas-Alexandre Brachard and the other by Jean-Jacques Oger.[6] The first example to be successfully fired entered the sales inventory on June 8, 1821, and was immediately delivered, with a stand and glass cover, to the Château de Saint-Cloud.[7] Oddly, however, this figure was not exhibited at the Louvre with the three other new ones in the series, at least not according to the catalogues.[8]

1. On June 10, 1823, several porcelain figures from the 1780s Grands Hommes series were delivered to the Garde Meuble de la Couronne, along with others commissioned by Napoleon and the four new figures produced after Fragonard's designs (Register Vbb 6, fol. 29). On the eighteenth-century figures of Grands Hommes, see Samuel Taylor, "Artist and Philosophes as Mirrored by Sèvres and Wedgwood," in Haskell, Levy, and Shackleton, *The Artist and the Writer in France* (1974), pp. 21 – 39.
2. For the entry in sales inventory on March 15, 1808, see Register Vu 1, fol. 57, no 217-3; for delivery to Saint-Cloud on August 14, 1808, see Register Vy 18, fol. 51.
3. *Images de Jeanne d'Arc* (1979), pp. 69 – 70.
4. Ibid., p. 71.
5. Register Va' 23 (1819 – 1820), fol. 147 ff.; in February a payment of 30 francs was authorized for the sketch, and another of 400 francs for the production of the model.
6. Ibid., fol. 151 ff. (Brachard) and fol. 155 ff. (Oger). Each sculptor received 60 francs for their model, but Alexandre Brachard was also allocated two additional sums of 20 francs each for the quality of his work (Register Va' 24, fol. 138 ff.).
7. For entry in sales inventory, see Carton Pb 5, appréciations de 1821; the net price was 180 francs and sale price, 200 francs. For delivery, see Register Vbb 6, fol. 27 (June – July 1821).
8. The figures of Duguesclin and Crillon were shown at the New Year's exhibition of 1818 – 19; that of Dunois was presented two years later, at the exhibition of 1820 – 21.

Fig. 54a. Joan of Arc, Jean-Charles-Nicolas Brachard aîné after designs by Alexandre-Evariste Fragonard; plaster model. (Archives of the Manufature Nationale de Sèvres)

55.
Designs for a *Guéridon*, 1821
Called *Guéridon 'de Henri IV'*

Jean-Charles Develly
Central medallion: gouache on paper; perimeter medallions: ink wash with white gouache highlights
Frame: 21 x 21 in. (53.3 x 53.3)
Inv. no. § 4 M 1818 N° 1

Guéridons, or small tables, were often elaborately constructed and richly embellished. As Sèvres began to produce larger plaques of porcelain in the early nineteenth century, the manufactory produced these pieces of furniture as well. In 1821, Brongniart decided to produce a series of *guéridons*, "primarily to make use of plaques that need to be refired or are too imperfect to receive beautiful paintings. In consequence [of these imperfections] gloss-fired grounds will often have to be used."[1] The project was also meant to make use of surplus balusters and columns, which could serve as the legs of these small tables. Although it was decided to leave the plaque for the present *guéridon* (designated "H" in the documents) with a white ground, it did have a flaw. A note on the progress sheet dated May 25, 1821, indicates that it was to be given "to Monsieur Boquet for sawing after having determined and traced with him the most appropriate place for avoiding the deformation [within the larger plaque] for the circle."[2]

Although the designs by Jean-Charles Develly appear in the 1818 inventory (doubtless having been added after the fact), it was only in June 1821 that this artist was said to be "totally occupied with painting models for the central composition for *guéridon* H, and the twelve small subjects from the life of Henry IV in the style of medals."[3] He was also charged with the actual painting on porcelain, which was sketched in July – August and retouched in September – October. The completed *guéridon* entered the sales inventory on December 15, 1821.[4] It was shown at the 1821 – 22 New Year's exhibition at the Louvre and was delivered immediately thereafter, on the order of Louis

XVIII, to "His Royal Highness Monseigneur le duc de Bordeaux,"[5] the king's great nephew and heir to the French throne.

Although during the Empire the manufactory had produced a *vase 'Cordelier'* decorated with a depiction entitled *Henri IV Returning from the Battle of Joyeuse,*[6] it was only under the Restauration that representations of this most popular of Bourbon monarchs assumed significant proportions.[7] The subject of the central composition of the drawing, the dedication of the equestrian statue of Henri IV on the Pont Neuf in Paris, had previously appeared on two *vases 'Etrusques AB'* with purple grounds, in versions painted by Jean-Charles Develly (1819 and 1820).

The perimeter roundels still resemble medals; imitation Renaissance enamels were used at Sèvres only later. Develly himself executed paintings in the latter style on the *guéridon 'le Paradis Perdu'* of 1830.[8]

1. [Pour objet principal d'employer des plaques qui ont besoin de repasser ou qui sont trop imparfaites pour de belles peintures. Par conséquent les fonds au grand feu doivent être souvent employés.] Carton Pb 5, liasse 2 (2), dossier "*Guéridons* 1821 – 24."

2. [25 mai [1821] Remis la plaque pour le s[c]iage a Mr Boquet après avoir pris et tracé avec lui la place la plus propre pour sauver le gauche dans la grandeur du cercle.] Ibid.

3. [Employé entierement a la peinture du tableau etude du sujet du milieu du gueridon H, et des douze petits sujets de la vie de Henri IV dans le style des médailles.] Register Vj' 28 (1821), fol. 20 ff.

4. Register Vv 1, fol. 169, no. 35 and Carton Pb 5, valuation sheets for 1821; the net price was 4,128 francs (1,000 for mounting and 1,780 for Develly), the sale price, 4,600 francs.

5. Register Vbb 6, fol. 8v. The *guéridon* was among the objects from the Château de Rosny, property of the duchesse de Berry, mother of the duc de Bordeaux, that were auctioned in Paris on February 22, 1836, and the following days (lot 625).

6. For delivery to the Trianon on December 16, 1809, see Register Vy 18, fol. 98v; Ledoux-Lebard, *Inventaire général . . . le grand Trianon* (1975), pp. 92 – 93.

7. Jones, "Henri IV and the Decorative Arts" (1993).

8. Alcouffe, Dion-Tenenbaum, and Ennès, *Un âge d'or,* exhib. cat. (1991), no. 73, pp. 182 – 84.

Fig. 55a. *Guéridon 'de Henri IV',* designed and painted by Jean- Charles Develly, Sèvres, 1821; hard-paste porcelain, gilded bronze, and wood. (Sèvres, Musée National de Céramique)

56.
Design and Decoration for a Vase, 1822

Alexandre-Evariste Fragonard
Gouache, watercolor and pencil on paper
17 7/8 x 21 5/8 in. (45.5 x 55 cm)
Inscription: [recto, lower left, in ink, in the hand of Alexandre Brongniart] *vase etrusque fragonard / fragonard 1822*
Inv. no. D § 8 1822 N° 9

In October 1822, Alexandre-Evariste Fragonard received 60 francs for "a drawing of an Etruscan Fragonard vase with decoration."[1] Neither the projects list for 1822 nor that for 1823 include any items that might correspond to such a vase. On sheets listing "pieces received and credited to the workers's accounts," an entry dated June 30, 1823, notes that Louis Davignon had thrown a *vase 'Etrusque Fragonard de 1822'*.[2] The only pieces modeled by Davignon listed in the firing registers as having been received in the second half of 1822 were several *vases 'Etrusque AB'*, however, which were amended "second size".[3] It is unlikely that a simple name change is in question, for none of the *vases 'Etrusque AB'* decorated in 1822 or later fully corresponds to the present drawing.[4]

Forms and decorative schemes inspired by ancient models never disappeared completely at the manufactory, even during the period that saw the triumph of the "troubadour" or Gothic Revival style, but they seem to have been used almost exclusively for average or small pieces.[5] Antique subjects, however, continued to appear occasionally on important showpieces.[6]

1. [Un dessin de vase et decor étrusque Fragonard.] Register Vj' 29 (1822), fol. 215.
2. [Feuilles des pièces reçues et portées au compte des ouvriers] [Vase Etrusque Fragonard de 1822.] Carton Pb 5, travaux de 1823, "Repareurs et tourneurs."
3. Register Vyy4, fol. 233 and 233v.
4. The original form of the *vase 'Etrusque AB'* is not precisely dated, but decorations for it survive from as early as 1804. The registers almost never specify which of the many variations were used; judging from extant drawings and models, the principal alterations to this model were made between 1823 and 1825.
5. Examples of such objects include: "Two Caraffe Etruscan Vases red and black Etruscan decor" [2 vases étrusque caraffe décor étrusque rouge et noir], which were priced at 360 francs per pair, entered the sales inventory on March 22, 1816 (Register Vv 1, fol. 61, no. 47), and were sold to a "Monsieur Loyd" on December 17, 1824 (Register Vz 4, fol. 167); "One so-called Dripstone Etruscan Vase first [size] green gloss-fired ground Etruscan decor in gold and platinum" [1 vase étrusque dit à larmier Iere fond vert au grand feu decor etrusque en or et platine], which was priced at 1,500 francs and entered the sales inventory on November 12, 1819 (Register Vv 1, fol. 133, no. 28); "Two Etruscan Caraffe Vases third size black ground red ornament" [2 vases Caraffes étrusques 3e grandeur fond noir ornement rouge], which were priced at 65 francs each and entered the sales inventory on April 7, 1821 (Register Vv 1, fol. 159v, no. 37); and "Twelve ordinary flat plates Etruscan ground Etruscan figures and decoration id. the twelve signs of the zodiac and gold fillet" [12 assiettes plattes ordinaires fond étrusque figures étrusques et decor id. les douze signes du odriacre [zodiac] et filet d'or] (Carton Pb 5, valuation of August 22, 1823).
6. At the 1820 – 21 New Year's exhibition at the Louvre, the manufactory presented a green-ground Medici vase of the second size decorated with *Alexander at the Tomb of Achilles*; the 1821 – 22 New Year's exhibition included an Etruscan Cylinder Vase decorated with an episode from the life of Aristotle; the 1822 – 23 exhibition featured the pendant of the preceding vase, commemorating Herodotus.

57.
Decoration for a Vase, 1822
Called *Vase 'Anthophore'*

Joseph Vigné
Watercolor, ink and pencil on paper
16 1/2 x 12 3/8 in. (42 x 31.4 cm)
Inscriptions: [recto, partly obscured by the handle] *nerf bleu / feuille rouge / . . . jaune / fruits vert*; [lower left]-*gothique no 5 vase anthoph.*; [at right] *100 fr[ancs]*
Inv. no. D § 8 1822 N° 12

Joseph Vigné received 15 francs (instead of the 18 francs that he had requested) for Gothic decoration for a *vase 'Anthophore'*. He was paid only 110 francs (instead of 120 francs) for having painted "an Anthophore Vase and its collar, for a Gothic decoration [on] green and purple grounds, large trefoils and ogee arches in gold, Gothic friezes in color ornaments in gold burnished *à l'effet*."[1] The two vases he painted entered the sales inventory on December 20, 1822,[2] but they were judged unsuccessful and were assigned a sale price (250 francs) slightly lower than their net price (255 francs). They were purchased by the duchesse de Berry during the 1822 – 23 New Year's exhibition at the Louvre.[3]

The *vase 'Anthophore'*, which was originally intended to support a high *corbeille 'Calathine'*, was created in 1819. The high neck of the plaster model is detachable. Both the vase and the basket are attributed to Jean-Charles-François Leloy on the form drawings, but a note on the 1819 list of "models to be devised" designates them as "model A.B.,"[4] which could imply that Alexandre Brongniart suggested the concept for this model.

The earliest Gothic friezes to appear at Sèvres were designed by Alexandre-Théodore Brongniart and date from 1806.[5] The first artist to compose and paint decoration of medieval inspiration was Jean-Claude Rumeau who was mentioned in the catalogue of the 1810 salon, where he exhibited for the first time, as a "student of MM. David and Isabey." Most of Vigné's work for Sèvres is in this Gothic Revival idiom, but he occasionally produced neoclassical designs (see cat. no. 61). After leaving the manufactory he seems to have specialized in painting on glass. During the same 1821 – 24 period, the Imperial Porcelain Manufactory in Vienna produced a *surtout* in the Gothic style, ordered by the Emperor Francis I for his castle in Franzensburg.[6] This was an isolated production in this style, only made on special order, whereas at Sèvres similar pieces were regularly produced at the request of Brongniart.

Inscription: ["blue band / red leaf / . . . yellow / green fruits"]; ["gothic no. 5 *vase anthoph*"]

1. Register Vq', first series, vol. 5, fol. 22v, November 1822 and fol. 24v, December 1822.
2. Register Vv1, fol. 190, no. 58.
3. Register Vbb 6, fol. 114, "achats à crédit." They were not included in the catalog of the Louvre exhibition.
4. Carton Pb 4, 1819 work allocations.
5. Gruber, *L'Art décoratif en Europe* (1995), p. 145.
6. Faÿ-Hallé, and Mundt, *La Porcelaine Européenne* (1983), ill. 84, p. 64.

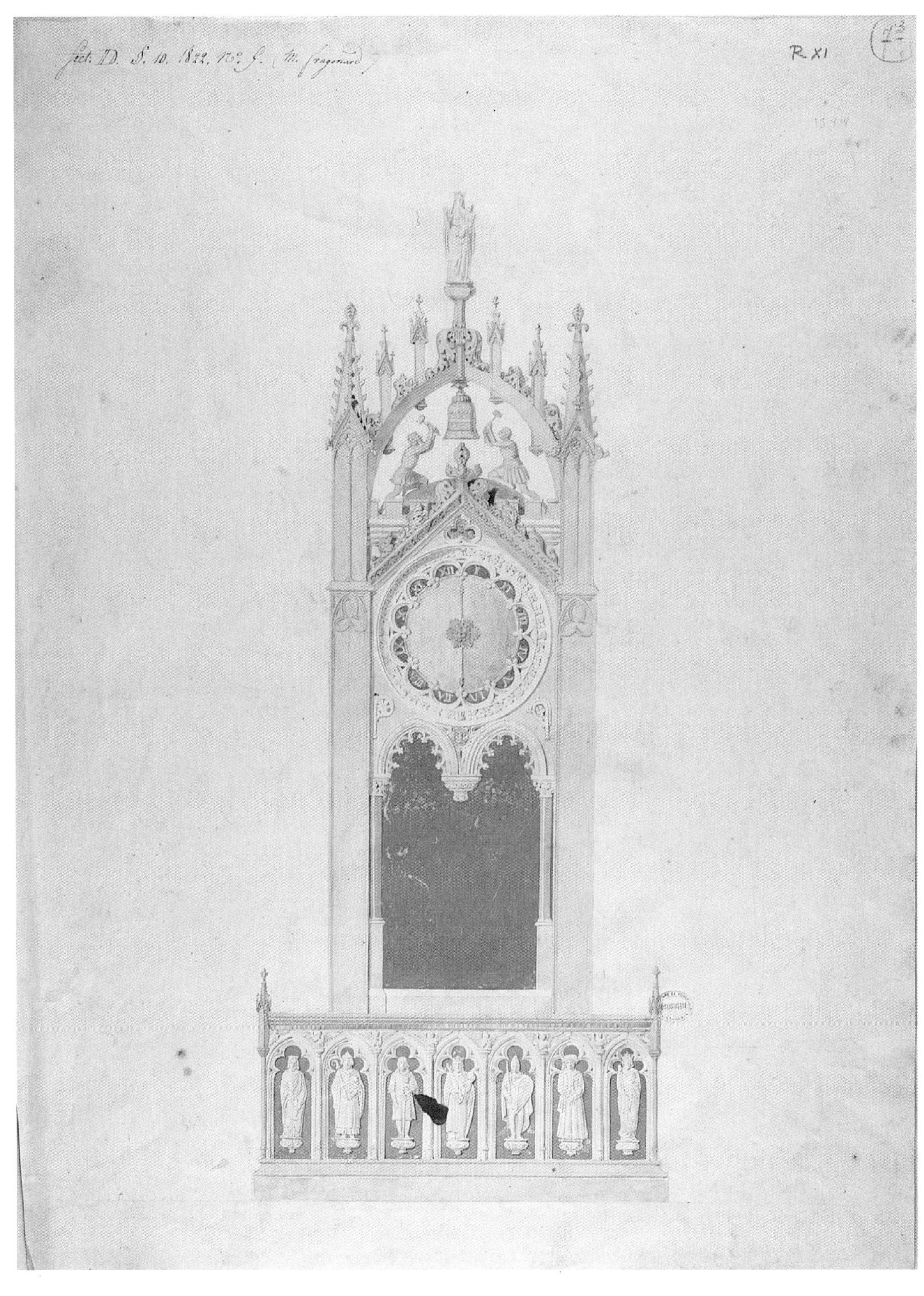

58.
Design for a Clock, 1822

Alexandre-Evariste Fragonard
Gouache, watercolor and pencil on paper
23 5/8 x 17 5/8 in. (60 x 44.7 cm)
Inscription: [recto, lower left, in pencil, barely legible]
Pendule gothique frag.
Inv. no. D § 10 1822 N° 5

In 1820 Brongniart undertook to produce a series of mantel clocks, perhaps as a way to salvage elements of much larger flawed plaques that had originally been made to serve as grounds for paintings. The copying of paintings on porcelain was beginning to proliferate at that time. Large flat plaques were difficult to fire successfully; even when these pieces had defective surfaces, however, portions could be saved and recycled.

A clock, designated "G" in the documents, is described as "in the Gothic style to receive a painting by Monsieur Rumeau [Jean-Claude Rumeau] . . . subject chosen . . . Charlemagne receiving from Caliph Aroun Alraschid a superb clepsydra, or water clock."[1] The choice of this subject demonstrates that the term "Gothic" was very loosely applied in this period, and lexical uncertainty is also evident in the description of this same piece that was given in the catalogue of the 1820 – 21 New Year's exhibition at the Louvre: "No. 14-Mantel clock with form, fittings, mounts, and ornament in the Lombard style against yellowish gray ground." Sèvres produced several other clocks "in the Lombard style," but it is not certain whether these pieces resembled one another.[2]

In November 1822, Alexandre-Evariste Fragonard was paid 150 francs for a Gothic clock design and an additional 100 francs for a Gothic vase design.[3] The first *vases 'Gothiques Fragonard'* were described in the catalogue of the 1823 – 24 New Year's exhibition at the Louvre as having a twelfth-century form and comparable colored decoration. Although listed in this catalogue, they were not completed in time to be presented. Thereafter, the vase form was often produced with varying ornament, not always of medieval inspiration (see cat. no. 97). By contrast, although the *pendule 'Gothique Fragonard'* appears on the list of projects to be undertaken in 1824, a margin note indicates that it was "postponed," and, despite its inclusion in the lists for all the subsequent years, it was never put into production.[4]

Fragonard made relatively few Gothic Revival designs. In addition to those already cited, they included a "piece of furniture intended to serve as a bookshelf for titles concerning the Christian religion . . . [with] Gothic form, fittings, and decoration."[5] This piece was displayed at the 1826 – 27 New Year's exhibition at the Louvre and subsequently delivered to the duchesse de Berry, who was an enthusiastic admirer of this fashionable style.[6]

1. [Dans le style gothique pour recevoir un tableau de M. Rumeau . . . sujet choisi . . . Charlemagne reçoit du calife Aroun Alraschid une superbe clepsydre ou pendule à eau.] Carton Pb 5, liasse 2 (2), "Pendules 1820 – 24." This clock entered the sales inventory on December 22, 1820, when its sale price was set at 3,000 francs (Register Vv 1, fol. 154, no. 17); after the 1820 – 21 New Year's exhibition at the Louvre it was delivered to Madame, the duchesse d'Angoulême (Register Vbb 6, fol. 4v).
2. At least two of these clocks resembled one another. The first was ordered by the principals of the Chambre du Roi and depicted an episode from the life of Bayard. It entered the sales inventory on June 16, 1821 (Register Vv 1, fol. 161, no. 59) and was delivered to the Garde Meuble on the following October 26 (Register Vbb 6, fo. 27v). After its presentation at the 1821 – 22 New Year's exhibition at the Louvre, an exact replica was ordered by a M. Schickler; it was recorded in the inventory on September 14, 1822 (Register Vv 1, folio 185, no 34) but had in fact been delivered the preceding August (Register Vz 4, fol. 87). Both clocks were painted by Rumeau. The same artist designed and painted a third clock — sometimes described as "Gothic" and sometimes as "Lombard" — with decoration evoking the "three times of day in about the eleventh century" [trois époques de la journée vers le XIe siècle]); it entered the inventory on December 18, 1824 (Register Vv 1, fol. 226, no. 76), was shown at the Louvre New Year's exhibition of 1824 – 25, and was purchased by the duc d'Orléans on May 11, 1826 (Register Vbb 7, fol. 106).
3. Register Vj' 29 (1822), fol. 215.
4. Carton Pb 5, liasse 1 and Carton Pb 6, liasse 1, travaux de 1825, 1826, 1827, and 1828.
5. *Notice . . . au 1er janvier 1827*, no. 5.
6. Register Vbb 7, fol. 23v.

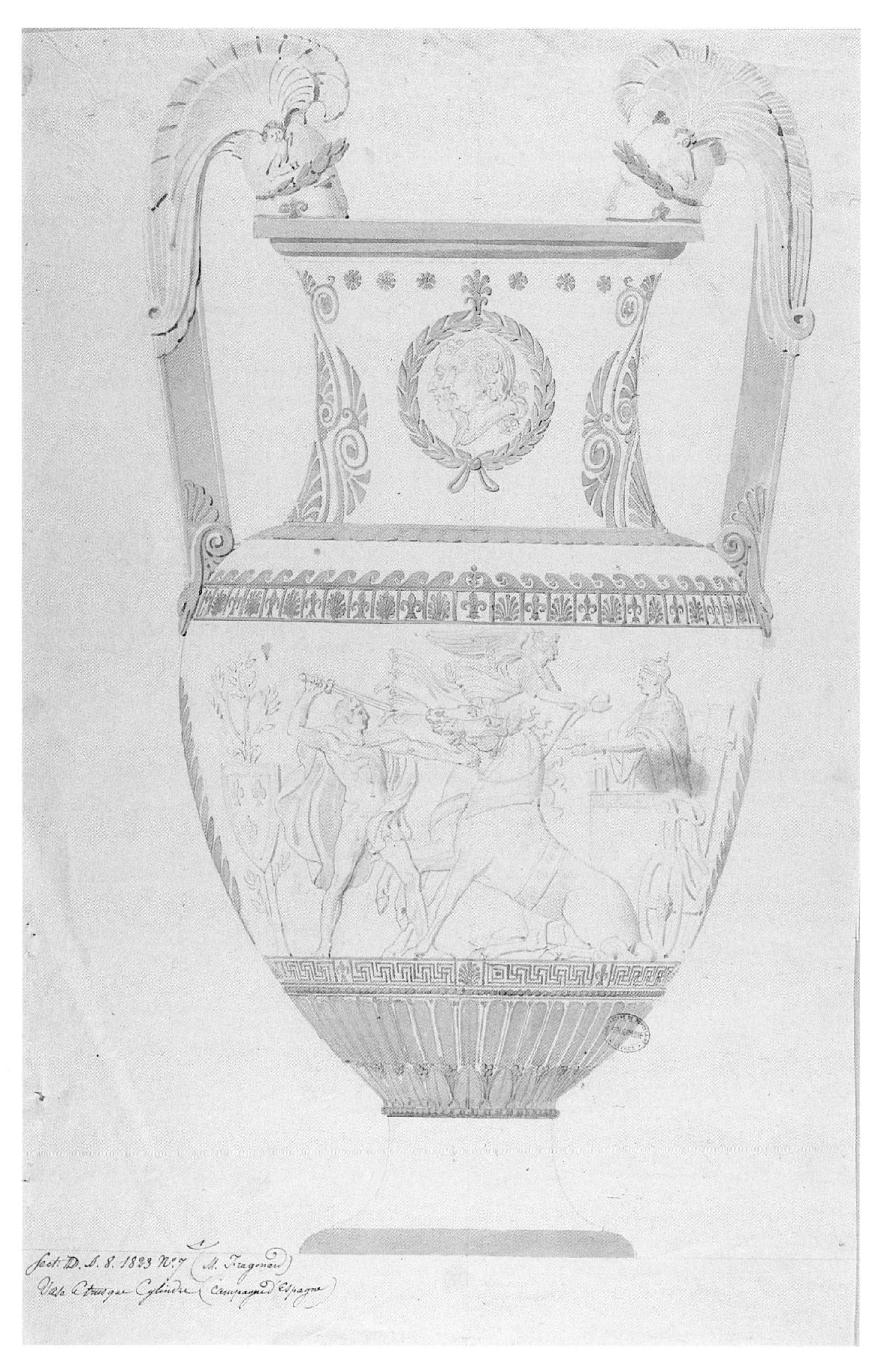

59.

Decoration for a Vase, 1823
Called *Vase 'Etrusque cylindre'*

Alexandre-Evariste Fragonard
Pencil and watercolor on paper
20 5/8 x 13 3/4 in. (52.5 x 35 cm)
Inscription: [recto, lower left, in ink] *Vase Etrusque Cylindre (Campagne d'Espagne)*
Inv. no. D § 8 1823 N° 7

On October 25, 1823, immediately after the military campaign of the duc d'Angoulême, the king's nephew, had helped to restore Ferdinand VII to the Spanish throne, Brongniart wrote to the *ministre de la Maison du Roi*: "I thought it would be appropriate for the king's manufactory to produce without delay a porcelain piece as large and important as time permits, on the occasion of the Spanish expedition and above all in honor of the prince who led and concluded it so gloriously."[1] He added that, to save time, he planned to decorate a green-ground vase with a simple allegorical composition executed in gold and platinum, and that "M. Fragonard is making the drawing of the composition for which I have provided him with a detailed program."[2] On November 13, the vicomte de Senonnes, the minister's deputy, authorized Brongniart to use 5,000 francs from sales revenues to cover unanticipated costs generated by production of the vase.[3] This sum presumably reflects a preliminary estimate of the net price, but it proved overly optimistic. When the piece was entered in the sales inventory on December 23, 1823, the net price was specified as 6,995 francs (including 510 francs for the gilders, 750 francs for the painter Joseph Vigné,[4] 740 francs for the blank porcelain, 3,000 francs for the mount and fittings, and 600 francs for Fragonard's designs).[5] The sale price was set at 8,000 francs.

The vase was delivered for the Crimson Salon of the Château de Saint-Cloud on June 19, 1824,[6] after having been presented at the 1823 – 24 New Year's exhibition. The subject devised by Brongniart, indicated by no more than a vague sketch in the drawing, is described at length in the exhibition catalogue.[7]

The *vase 'Etrusque Cylindre'*, first size, was among the most imposing pieces that the manufactory had in production; for this project Brongniart clearly used a blank (or undecorated piece) that was already in the warehouse, adding specially designed handles.[8]

Other pieces at the 1823 – 24 Louvre exhibition also commemorated the Spanish campaign, namely a pair of *vases 'Medici'*, third size, ornamented and with painted compositions by Jean-Charles Develly, who the following year painted a *vase 'Etrusque AB'* which showed the return of the victorious duc d'Angoulême to Paris on December 3, 1823.

1. [J'ai pensé qu'il étoit convenable que la manufacture du Roi etablit sans delai une pièce de porcelaine aussi grande et aussi importante que le temps le permettoit, à l'occasion de l'expedition d'Espagne et surtout en l'honneur du Prince qui l'a conduite et terminée d'une manière si glorieuse] [Mr. Fragonard fait le dessin du sujet dont je lui ai donné le programme détaillé.] Carton T 10, liasse 1, dossier 2.
2. Ibid.
3. Carton Pb 5, liasse 2 (1), travaux de 1823, "Vases."
4. This figure differs from the one entered in the fee register, where Brongniart noted: "for the whole vase, trials, attributes, large main composition [on the reverse of the vase] 775 francs" [Pour tout le vase, essais, attributs, derriere grand sujet principal 775 frs.] (Register Vq', 1ere série, vol. 5, fol. 44v, December 1823) (for further information on pricing, see chap. 3).
5. Here again the documents are inconsistent, for an entry in the register of work undertaken in the decorations workshops indicates that Fragonard received only 500 francs for "the allegorical design for the victory of the duc d'Angoulême with all the pertinent accessories" [le dessin allégorique pour la victoire du duc d'Angoulême avec tous les accessoires y relatifs] (Vj' 30 [1823], fols. 207 – 208). This design would be one of these "accessory" drawings.
6. Register Vbb 6, fol. 31.
7. The catalogue description reads as follows: "The chariot of the royal government of Spain is pulled by fiery steeds; the reins have been seized away from the hands of the sovereign. The French army, represented by the PRINCE commander-in-chief, subdues the horses, and France returns the reins to the King." [Le char du gouvernement royal d'Espagne est emporté par des chevaux fougueux; les rênes ont été arrachées des mains du souverain. L'armée française, représentée par le PRINCE généralissime, dompte les chevaux, et la France remet les rênes au Roi.]
8. The form of the *vase 'Etrusque à rouleaux'*, modeled after an ancient piece, was developed in 1808 – 9. Normally, its elevated handles and a different shape for the foot made it readily distinguishable from the *vase 'Etrusque Cylindre'*, but the two names are sometimes confused in the documents.

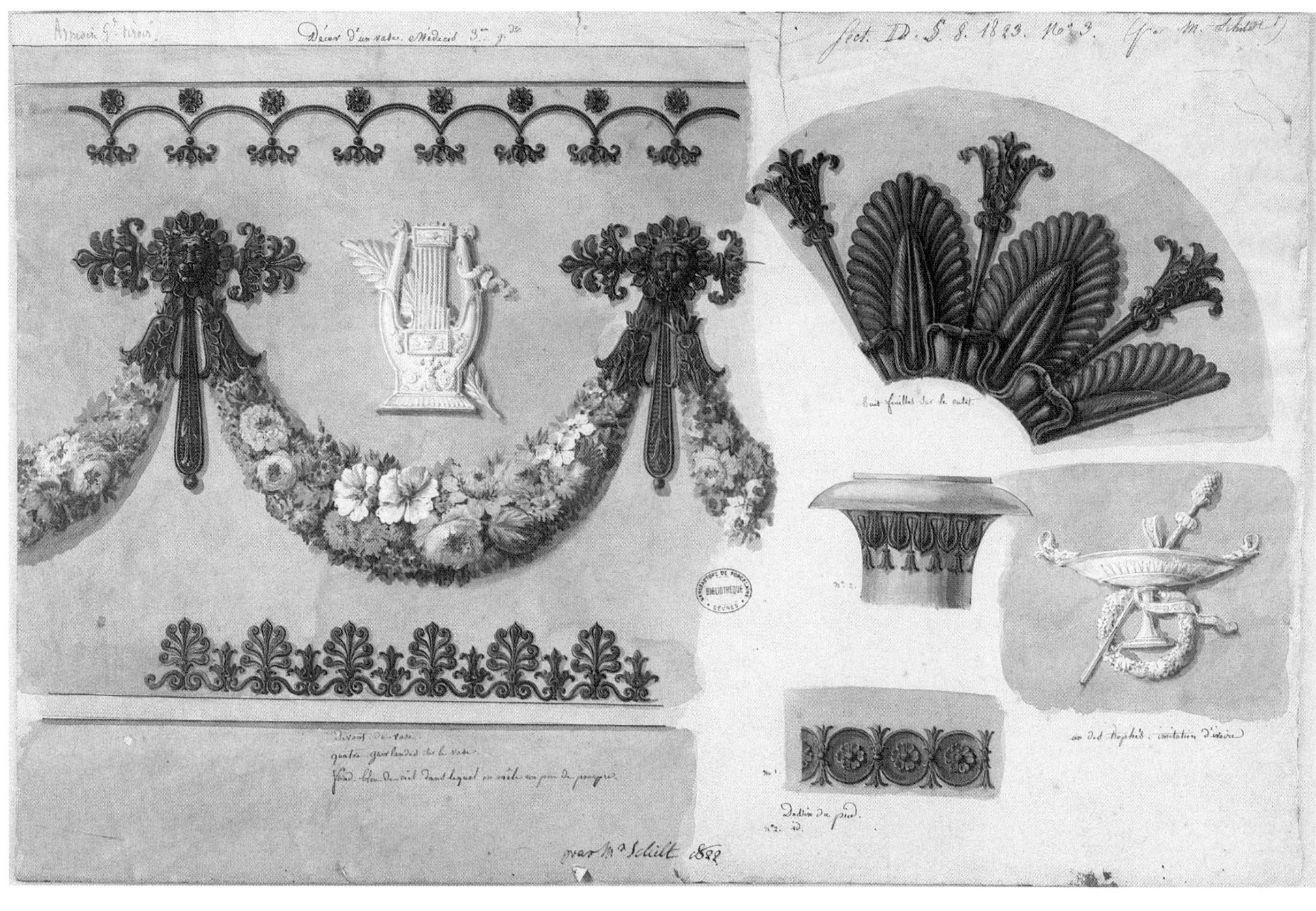

60.
Decoration for a Vase, 1822
Called *Vases 'Medicis'*

Louis-Pierre Schilt
Watercolor, gouache and ink on paper
11 3/4 x 18 in. (30 x 45.7 cm)
Inscriptions: [recto] [within the drawing] *Décor d'un vase Médicis 3em gdr.-devant du vase. / quatre guirlandes sur le vase. / fond.bleu de ciel dans lequel on mêle un peu de pourpre / huit feuilles sur le culot-no. 2-No 1.-Dessin du pied / no 2. id.-un des trophés imitation d'ivoire;* [bottom center, in the hand of Alexandre Brongniart] *par Mr Schilt 1822*
Inv. no. D § 8 1823 N° 3

Louis-Pierre Schilt does not seem to have been paid for these sketches, only for his work on two *vases 'Medicis'*, third size. After applying the overall sky blue coloring to these vases, he was directed to begin: "scraping and painting of a decoration consisting of flower garlands, attributes, and ornaments in brown."[1] He received the vases in May, 1822, returned them for the first firing of the painting in August, and retouched them between September and November. He was paid 225 francs for each vase, according to the valuation sheet established when they entered the sales inventory on December 10, 1822 at a sale price of 450 francs each.[2] Both vases were displayed at the New Year's exhibition of 1822 – 23 at the Louvre without being listed in the catalogue; they were sold to Mme. Ferbach on January 4, 1824.[3] Fresh from this success, Brongniart immediately ordered the production of a second pair; these vases, also painted by Louis-Pierre Schilt, entered the sales inventory on June 25, 1823 at "the known price."[4] They were shown at the next New Year's exhibition and were sold to the duc d'Orléans on December 30, 1823.[5] In 1825 and 1826 Brongniart ordered two additional pairs with similar if not identical decoration, featuring cameos instead of attributes.[6]

Louis-Pierre Schilt worked for the manufactory *en extraordinaire,* or on a freelance basis, beginning in 1818 and became a member of the permanent staff in 1822, the year this drawing was produced. He specialized in painting flowers on porcelain and glass, usually based on his own compositions.

Inscription: ["Design for Vase Medicis, third size-front of vase. / four garlands on the vase. / sky blue ground with a little purple added / eight leaves on the base-no. 2-no. 1.-Design of foot / no. 2 *idem* one of the imitation ivory trophies"]; ["by Mr Schilt 1822"]

1. [Fond bleu de ciel gratage et peinture d'un decor composé de guirlandes de fleurs, d'attributs et d'ornements en brun.] Register Vj' 29 (1822), fol. 248.
2. Register Vv 1, fol. 188v., no. 72 and Carton Pb 5, valuation sheets for 1822.
3. Register Vz 4, fol. 99.
4. [à prix connu.] Register Vv 1, fol. 201, no. 19.
5. Register Vz 4, fol. 133v. The duc d'Orléans became King Louis-Philippe in 1830.
6. Two vases painted by Charles-Antoine Didier entered the sales inventory on November 25, 1825 (Register Vv 1, fol. 243, no. 30), sale price 750 francs each. Two others, again painted by Louis-Pierre Schilt, entered the inventory on April 28, 1826 (Register Vv 1, fol. 251, no. 11), sale price 400 francs each and the artist's fee was 220 francs; they were sold to M. Lormer on July 30, 1826 (Register Vz 4, fol. 230).

61.
Decoration for a Vase, 1824 Called *Vase 'Fuseau'*

Joseph Vigné
Watercolor and pencil on paper
16 3/4 x 10 3/8 in. (42.7 x 26.5 cm)
Inscriptions: [recto, on top, in pencil] *éxécuté sur fond / vert au grand feu / en or et platine.* [right top, in pencil] *vase fuseau 4eme grandr. / avec développement des courbes*; [right side] *Je me suis attaché / a faire ce décors extrê / mement léger, ce /qu'exigeaient les sujets*; [inside detail of collar] *myrthe v.fus.3e. g. / id. / id. / id. / CUPIDON.son époux / id. derriere du collet*; [at center, to right of figure] *figure de platine, / peinte à la/ manière des Etrusques*; [beginning center right, near cornucopia motif] *derrière du vase / platine / peint et / rehaussé- / ce décors est / fait au grattoir, excepté la couronne de souvenirs / PSYCHE. / une petite rosasse sous l'ance de bronze.*; [at level of vessel bottom] *culot de bronze-la figure d'Hébé fait pendentif à celle ci / sur l'autre vase: 7 marguerites composent / l'auréole formée ici par des papillons; / la massue d'hercule et l'aigle de jupiter / sont à ses côtés : hercule nom de son / époux est derrière le collet : / une coupe à têtes d'aigle est dans / la couronne au derrière du vase : / le reste est semblable.*; [beside base] *Perles de platine / feuilles de myrthe en or / feuilles d'eau or, et platine celle de dessous.*; [lower left, in ink] [signature] *Vigné*
Inv. no. D § 8 1824 N° 4

An annnotation in the fee register, dated March 1824, indicates that Vigné was to receive the 75 francs he requested for "a 'Fuseau' vase 4th [size] green ground throughout[,] decoration composed of a platinum figure of Psyche in the manner of the Etruscans[,] the beads of the collar and base the crown of souvenirs painted in the same manner[,] the attributes and ornaments detailed and shaded — drawing included."[1] In fact, a pair of vases was meant; they were in the third size. In any event, work on them must have been well advanced by that time. Vigné returned them after their first painting that same month, and they were finished between May 31 and June 5.[2]

Curiously, the valuation sheet drawn up when the two vases entered the sales inventory on June 24, 1825 indicates that Vigné received only 60 francs; the net price was set at 189.65 francs and the sale price at 225 francs. Both vases were purchased by the king of Prussia on September 29, 1825, along with several busts of members of the French royal family and another vase commemorating the recent accession of Charles X.[3]

This drawing offers a fine example of a neoclassical decoration different in spirit from both the graceful eighteenth-century variant of the style and the more rigid Empire idiom. It also testifies to the varied talents of Joseph Vigné, who is best known for his Gothic Revival designs (see cat. nos. 57 and 62).

Inscription: ["executed in high-fire green ground / in gold and platinum"]; ["*vase fuseau* fourth size / with details of curves"]; ["I have endeavoured / to make this decoration extre / mely light, as / the subject demanded"]; ["myrtle vase fuseau. third size / idem / idem / idem / CUPID her husband idem / back of collar"]; ["platinum figure / painted in the / manner of the Etruscans; ["back of vase / platinum / painted and heightened / this decoration is / executed with a scraper, except for the forget-me-not / PSYCHE. / a small rosette below the bronze handles"]; ["bronze base-the figure of Hebe makes a pair with this one / on the other vase: 7 marguerites compose the halo formed here by butterflies; Hercules' club and Jupiter's eagle / are at her sides: Hercules the name of her husband is behind the collar: / a dish with eagle's heads is in the wreath at the back of the vase: / the rest is similar"]; ["Platinum pearls / myrtle leaves in gold / sheets of water in gold, the lower one platinum"]; ["Vigné"]

1. [Un v. fuseau 4eme fond vert en plin décor composé d'une figure de Psyché en platine a la manière des Etrusques les perles du colet et du pied la couronne de souvenirs peints de même les attributs Et ornements détaillés et ombré au gratoir — le dessin compris." Register Vq', 1ere série, vol. 5, fol. 53v.. Presumably the artist received the same fee for the second vase, decorated with a figure of Cupid.
2. Register Vj' 31, fol. 241 and 241v.
3. Register Vz 4, fol. 197v.

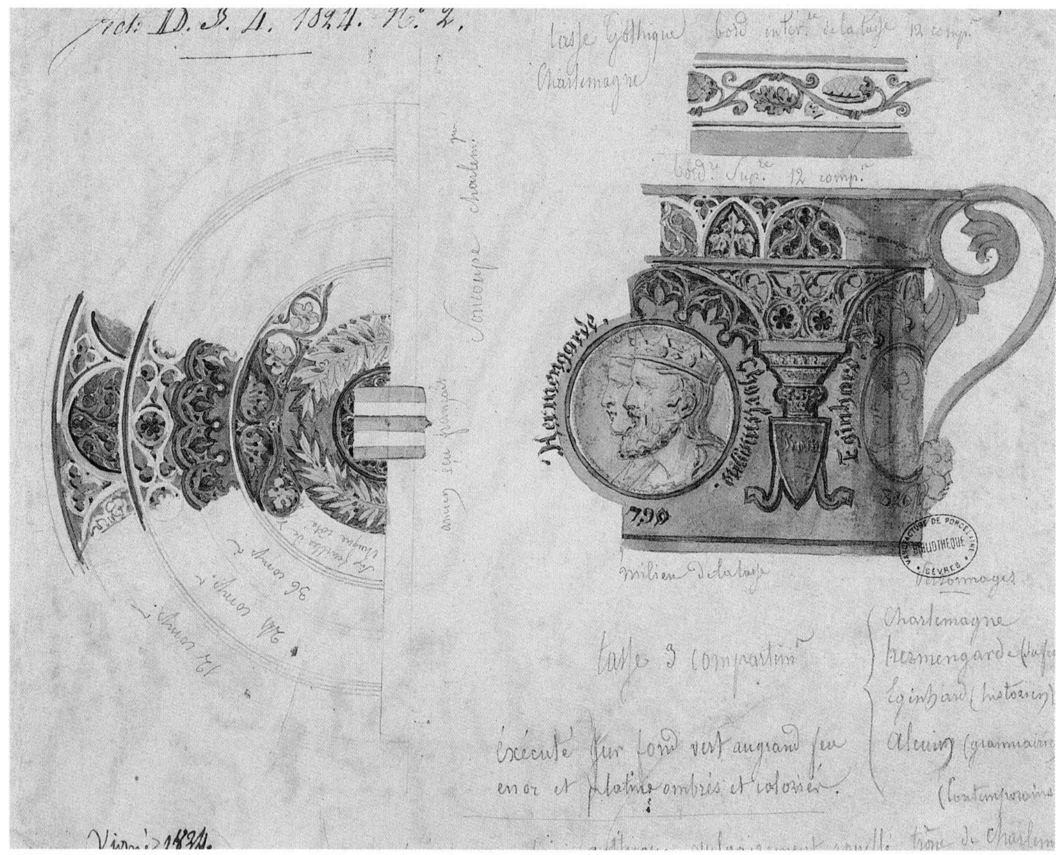

62.
Decoration for a Cup and Saucer, 1824 Called *Tasse 'Gothique' et Soucoupe*

Joseph Vigné
Watercolor and pencil on paper
8 1/4 x 10 3/8 in. (21 x 26.5 cm)
Inscriptions: [on recto, left, in pencil] *12 comps-24 comps-36 comps-six feuilles de / chaque côté-Ancien écu français-Soucoupe Charlem[a]gne*; [right, in pencil] *tasse gothique / Charlemagne-bord intérre de la tasse 12 comp.s-bordre sup.re 12 comp.s* [middle of the cup, in pencil] *tasse 3 compartims-Personnages / Charlemagne / Hermengarde (sa femme / Eginhard (historien) / Alcuin (grammairien) / (contemporains)-éxécuté sur fond vert au grand feu / en or et platine ombrés et coloriés. composé d'après un siège gothique vulgairement appellé trône de Charlemagne*]; [painted within the decor] *Hermengarde. Charlemagne. 790-Eginhard. 820*; [lower left, signature] *Vigné 1824*
Inv. no. D § 4 1824 N° 2

The pricing records for March 1824 suggest that there may have been heated exchanges between Brongniart and Vigné concerning two designs for *tasses 'Gothiques'* and matching saucers. Vigné painted the first cup, described as "green ground from the century of Charlemagne for the decorations on the cup the interior of the saucer executed in gold and platinum without ornament,"[1] and demanded 110 francs, but Brongniart authorized payment for only 100 francs, specifying that the cup was to be completely finished. He also approved a payment of 15 francs for the drawing and 25 francs for the retouching of the cup (instead of the 24 and 40 francs respectively requested by Vigné), specifying again that they were to be "completely finished."

For the second design — "green ground with members of the French monarchy with pertinent [painted] attributes and ornaments for the gilding without ornaments" — Brongniart agreed to a payment of only 85 francs instead of 100 francs, with the same fee being allotted for this drawing as for the preceding one.[2] The two cups were given to the artist to paint in January 1824; the painting on platinum was conducted in March – April, and one of the two cups was painted for the final time in May.[3]

The first completed cup entered the sales inventory on May 14, 1824, where it is described as "one Gothic cup and saucer green ground Gothic figures and ornament in gold and platinum," net price 139.50 francs, sale price 150 francs.[4] The second cup entered the sales inventory on the following July 24, when it was described as "one Gothic cup and saucer green ground rich decoration of Gothic ornament in gold and platinum etc." and was assigned net and sale prices of 192 and 225 francs respectively.[5]

These designs further exemplify the imprecise application of the term "Gothic" in this period; it was used to designate the entire period between antiquity and the Renaissance. The earliest example of a piece for a *déjeuner* decorated in the style seen on this sheet was apparently a *tasse 'Jasmin'* — "yellow and red ground ogee cartel subject from the ninth century Charles the Bald" — painted by Jean-Claude Rumeau that entered the sales inventory on December 27, 1815.[6]

Inscription: ["12 comp(artment)s-24 comps-36 comps-six leaves on / each side-old French shield-Charlemagne saucer"]; ["gothic cup / Charlemagne-inner rim of cup 12 comps"]; ["upper edge 12 comp"];["cup 3 compartms-Characters / Charlemagne / Hermengarde (his wife / Eginhard (historian) / Alcuin (grammarian) / (contemporaries)-executed on green high-fired ground / in gold and platinum shaded and coloured.-designed after a gothic seat commonly known as Charlemagne's throne"; painted within the decoration: "Hermengarde. Charlemagne. 790-Eginhard. 820"]; ["Vigné 1824"]

1. [Fond vert siècle de Charlemagne pour les ornements de la tasse de l'intérieur de la soucoupe exécutés en or et platine sans garniture.] Register Vq', 1ere série, vol. 5, fol. 52.
2. [fond vert personnages de la monarchie française avec attributs et ornements relatifs pour la dorure sans garniture . . . entierement faite] Ibid.
3. Register Vj' 31, fol. 241 and 241v.
4. [1 tasse et S. gothique fond vert figures et ornements gothiques en or et platine] Register Vv 1, fol. 216v, no. 30. It was sold to a private client for cash on September 15, 1825. (Register Vz 4, fol. 196v).
5. [1 t. et S. gothique fond vert riche décor d'ornements gothiques en or et platine etc.] Register Vv 1, fol. 219v, no. 51. It was sold in October 1838 to a George Bagley (Register Vz 5, fol. 221v).
5. [Fond jaune et rouge cartel en ogive sujet du 9eme siècle Charles le Chauve] Carton Pb 3, valuation sheets for 1815.

63.
Decoration for a Plate from the *Service 'des Départements'*, 1824

Jean-Charles-François Leloy
Watercolor, gouache, pencil and ink on paper glued to thin cardboard
9 3/4 x 10 1/8 in. (24.7 x 25.8 cm)
Inscriptions: [recto, beneath the central landscape medallion] [within the design] *Vue du château d'Arques (Seine-Inférieure)*; [within the design, in the border medallions] *Département / de la Seine / Inférieure-Abraham Duquesne-Le Cat / Bernardin de St Pierre / Le Kain-Pierre Corneille-Le Cat-B. Le Bouver de Fontenelle*; [lower right, in pencil, almost invisible and partly cut off] *trav. de 1824 . . . / service des Depar . . . / par Mr. Leloy*
Inv. no. D § 5 1824 N° 1er

The *service 'des Départements'* appears on the projects list for 1824,[1] and a note dated November 25 describes "a single plate completed: Seine Inférieure." This corresponds to the drawing shown here. In March 1824 Jean-Charles-François Leloy was paid for "a colored drawing of the complete decoration of [a plate in] the *service des Départments*" as well as for another drawing for part of the decoration.[2] The plate itself was painted in August and finished in September; Nicolas-Antoine Lebel executed the landscape and Jean-Charles Develly the figures.[3]

In a report concerning "projects undertaken for the coronation of King Charles X, 1825,"[4] which was sent to the vicomte de La Rochefoucauld on December 10, 1824, Brongniart wrote: "No. 1. *service 'des Départements'* 86 plates representing in the center of each a colored view of the most remarkable site in a district with depictions of typical customs when these are noteworthy. On the border of each plate are garlands of fruit or other productions, attributes, instruments, inscriptions concerning the vegetal and agricultural, animal, and industrial productions of [each] . . . district. Cameo medallions contain portraits of famous figures or recall them by their names inscribed within the cartels. Everything, finally, including the gold frieze is linked to the physical, industrial, agricultural, literary, and historical state of the department." [5] In the margin of the report, Brongniart added that for the production: "This very rich service, which only a royal manufactory would dare undertake, has progressed very little despite having been begun last January due to our attempts to find an appropriate mode of decoration, the research it required, and the time demanded by each plate due to its richness. Nonetheless, if His Majesty ordered it we would expend every effort to complete at least two-thirds of it in time for the coronation."[6]

Apparently the new sovereign and his entourage showed no interest this encyclopedic ensemble, for work continued to proceed at a very deliberate pace. Leloy designed friezes, garlands, and emblems to be transfer-printed in gold (in the plate wells) or in brown and subsequently retouched by hand. The first major portion of the service to be completed entered the inventory on December 22, 1827.[7] Despite Brongniart's hopes for the service,[8] Louis-Philippe refused it after he became king in 1830. Following his abdication in 1848, the service was delivered to the residence of the president of the Assemblée Nationale on September 2, 1848.[9] On July 20, 1850 it was returned in exchange for a simpler service. [10] It did not find a permanent home until March 1852, when the service was delivered to the ministry of foreign affairs.[11]

1. For the earliest archival references to the service, see: Carton Pb 5, "Etat général et sommaire des principaux travaux de 1824," progress sheet in table service, no. 1; Carton Pb 5, liasse 2 (2), "services de table, 1824"; and Carton Pb 6, liasse 1, dossier 10 bis.
2. Register Vj' 31, fol. 1 ff.
3. Ibid., fols. 17 and 24.
4. Carton Pb 6, liasse 1, dossier 3.
5. [No 1 service des départements 86 assiettes representant au milieu une vue colorié du site le plus remarquable d'un département avec des scènes caractéristiques des usages quand il y en a de particulier. Sur le bord de chaque assiette sont des guirlandes de fruits ou autres productions, des attributs, des instruments, des inscriptions relatives aux productions vegetales et agricoles, animales, industrielles du département. Des medaillons representent en camés les portraits des personnages celebres ou les rappellent par leurs noms inscrits dans des medallions. Tout, enfin, jusqu'à la frise d'or est en rapport avec l'etat physique, industrielle, agricole, litteraire ou historique du département] Ibid.
6. [Ce service très riche, qu'une manufacture royale peut seule oser entreprendre, est très peu avancé quoique commencé en janvier dernier a cause des tentatives qu'on a faites pour chercher un mode de décoration convenable, des recherches qu'il a exigé et du temps qu'il faut consacrer à chaque assiette en raison de sa richesse. Néanmoins si S. M. l'ordonnoit il n'y a pas d'efforts qui coutat pour qu'il soit terminé au moins aux deux tiers à l'époque du sacre] Ibid.
7. Register Vv 1, fol. 330v., no. 18.
8. In a list of pieces in production as of September 1, 1832, sent on September 26, Brongniart wrote: "It is to be desired that such a service appear on the King's table, and I dare add that this is a possibility, judging from a few words uttered by his Majesty when he saw it" [Il est désirable qu'un pareil service paroisse sur la table du Roi et j'ose ajouter que cela est presumable, d'apres quelques mots dits par S.M. en le voyant] (Carton M 10, dossier 3 [1838]).
9. Register Vbb 11, fol. 26v – 27.
10. Register Vv 5, fol. 39 – 40. In November 1849, Jacques-Joseph Ebelmen, Brongniart's successor, noted: "The main reason the president of the Assemblée Nationale requested this exchange is the elevated price of the plates (300 francs each) in the service currently at his disposition, which he fears to see deteriorate if they remain in use" [Le principal motif qui porte M. Le Président de l'Assemblée nationale à demander cet échange est le haut prix des assiettes (300 francs la pièce) du service actuellement à sa disposition et qu'il craint de voir détériorer par un plus long usage.] (Carton M 14, liasse 3, dossier 2].
11. Register Vbb 11, fol. 267v.

64.
Design and Decoration for a *Déjeuner 'Persan'*, 1825

Watercolor and ink on paper
11 3/4 x 13 1/4 in. (29.8 x 33.6 cm)
Inscriptions: [recto, in red ink]; [Upper left] *Planche no 1 / Fig.1ere / 6 tasses couleur / bleu azur. / 6 d[itt]o carmin vif / 6 do verd clair / 18 . . / N.B. Il sera bon de faire / [e]ntrer dans tous les dessins le / symbole du soleil, même en / les variant*; [within the drawing] *L'intétieur en blanc mat / très pur B intérieur Les caractères en or*; [Upper center] *Observation. / N.B. Il n'est point interdit de varier les dessins / des tasses, lorsqu'on changera la couleur; mais il / faudra conserver les formes autant que possible, / pour ne pas trop s'écarter du goût des persans.*; [upper right, to left of drawing] *figure 3e*; [within the drawing] *L'intérieur en blanc mat / très pur / Ici la même inscription que dans / la soucoupe figure / seconde. / Les caractères en or.*; [to right of drawing] *6 Tasses couleur / bleu azur. / 6 id. Carmin vif / 6 id. Vert clair / 18 tasses*; [lower left] [within the drawing] *Figure 2e A Les caractères en or Le même nombre de soucoupes / que de tasses (fig. 1ere) avec / les couleurs et dessins assortis*; [below the drawing] *A Traduction: Commandé en 1240. Par l'héritier présomptif / Abbas-Mirza; / pour le Chahzadé Sultan Ahmed Mirza (que sa vie soit de / longue durée! (1240.)*; [lower right, to left of drawing] *figure 4e / a / a*; [within the drawing] *(fig.3e) a / a*; [below the drawing] *a a . . . Soucoupe ou zarf de la tasse fig. 3. / N.B. le même nombre de zarfs que de tasses sans anses / avec les couleurs et dessins assortis.*
Inv. no. D § 4 1848 no. 13

On March 26, 1825, the manufactory noted a detailed list of the 108 pieces in a *déjeuner* ordered for Prince Abbas-Mirza of Persia in conformity with instructions delivered to the head of the painters and with the provided drawings.[1] The estimated price was 5,600 francs and the anticipated date of delivery six months later. Both projections proved overly optimistic. Although forms already in production were used for this service wherever possible, some new ones had to be created as well. The *tasse 'Calice'*, for example, which was devised in 1805, was used for the cup and saucer depicted on the left in this drawing. The design on the right, however, a cup without handle accompanied by a matching cup holder known as a zarf, was a form previously unknown at Sèvres. Similarly, it was for this commission that the *tasse 'ovoïde'* was created in 1825 – 26. Many of the decorations were probably also adapted from other schemes. They sometimes incorporate lilac branches and cornflower wreathes which had been used previously. [2]

The complete ensemble, called

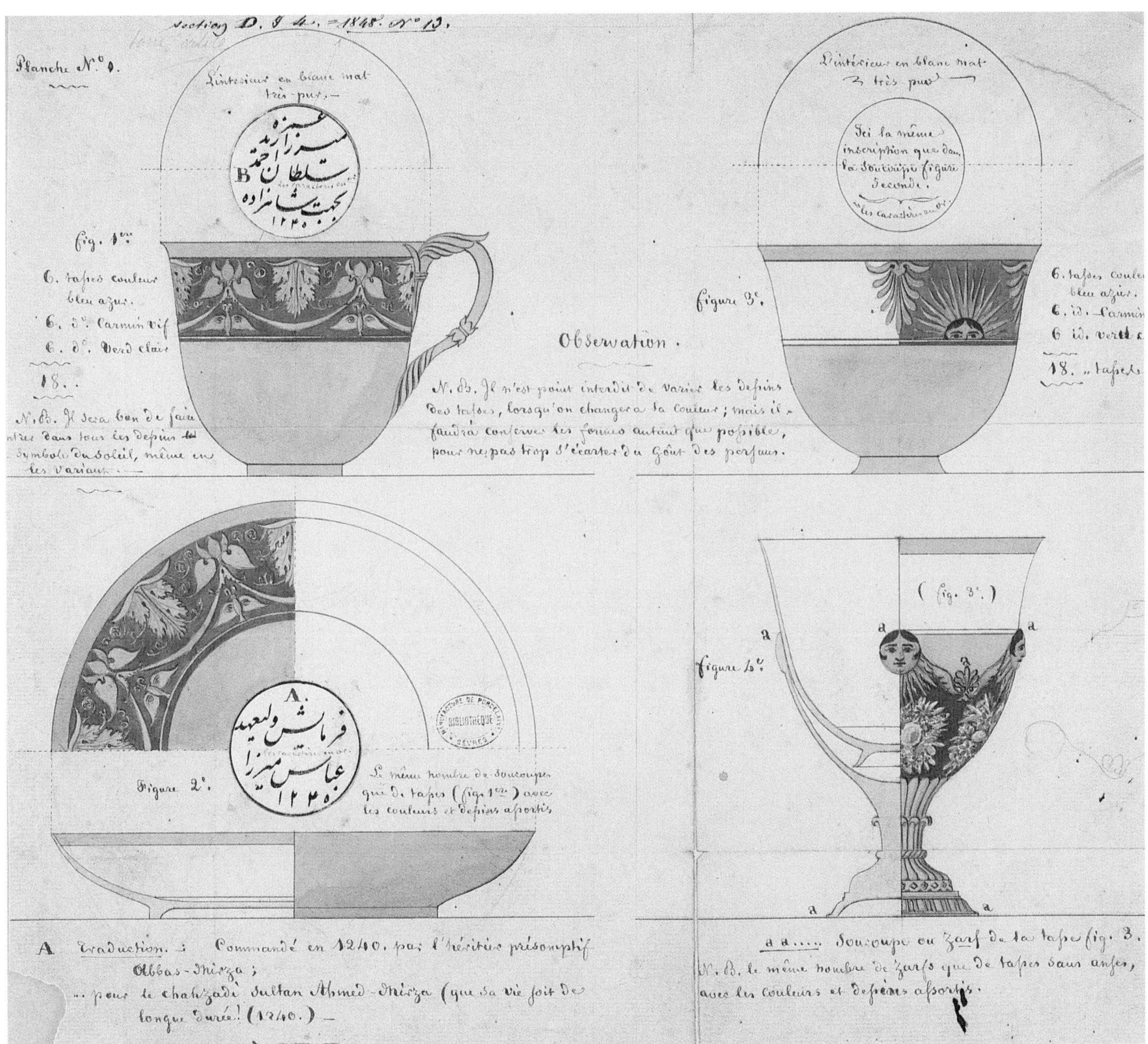

64.

Déjeuner 'Persan', entered the inventory on December 22, 1827 when its total price was set at 9,000 francs.[3] It was shown at the 1827 – 1828 New Year's exhibition at the Louvre, and on April 29, 1829 it was delivered "to His Excellency the Minister of Foreign Affairs for Prince Abbas Mirza of Persia,"[4] which implies that the service was presented to him as a gift.

The manufactory produced more blank examples of each design than were actually needed for the commission, as a precautionary measure against the possibility of pieces being lost, broken or stolen. The list, dated February 28, 1826, of pieces thrown by Louis-Marie Lapierre for the *Cabaret 'Persan'* includes fifty-one zarfs, although only eighteen were actually needed.[5] In 1831 one of the surplus pieces was painted with a "Gothic" decoration very different from those used on the Persian ensemble.[6]

Inscription: ["Plate no. 1 / Figure 1 / 6 coloured cups / azure blue. / 6 ditto bright crimson / 6 ditto light green / 18 . . . N.B. It would be a good idea to / include in all the designs the / sun symbol / varying it as well"]; ["the interior in matte white / very pure B / the characters in gold"]; ["Observation: N.B. There is no harm in varying the designs / the cups, when changing colour; but / the shape should be maintained as far as possible, / in order not to get too far away from Persian taste"]; ["figure 3"]; ["the interior in matte white, very pure. The same inscriptions here as in / the saucer of figure / 2. / The characters in gold"]; ["6 coloured cups / azure blue. / 6 idem bright crimson / 6 idem light green / 18 cups."]; ["Figure 2e The characters in gold The same number of saucers / as of cups (fig. 1) with /colours and designs to match"]; ["A Translation: Order placed in 1240. By the heir-apparent / Abbas-Mirza; / for the Shahzade Sultan Ahmed Mirza (may his life be / long! (1240)"]; ["figure 4/a/a"]; within the drawing:["(fig. 3) a/a"]; ["a a... Saucer or zarf of the cup fig. 3 / N.B. the same number of zarfs as cups without handles / with assorted colors and designs."]

1. [Service de déjeuner commandé pour le prince Abbas-Mirza de Perse conformement aux instructions remises au chef des peintres et aux dessins donnés.] Register Vtt 2, fol. 41v.
2. Carton Pb 6, feuille d'appréciation of December 22, 1827.
3. Register Vv 1, fol. 329v, nos. 59 – 68.
4. Register Vz 5, fol. 9.
5. Carton Pb 6, liasse 1, dossier 9, "travaux des mouleurs-repareurs 1826."
6. Dawson, *A Catalogue of French Porcelain* (1994), no. 182, pp. 221 – 22.

65.
Design for a Four-Footed Fruit Bowl, 1825
Called *Compotier 'à Quatre Pieds'*

Alexandre-Evariste Fragonard
Pencil and watercolor on paper
15 7/8 x 12 3/4 in. (40.4 x 32.5)
Inscription: [recto, lower left] *Compotier 4 Pieds. / fragonard mars 1825.*
Inv. no. D § 6 1825 N° 1

Brongniart's commitment to the production of services with varied shapes and decoration prompted him to develop objects with novel forms to serve very specific functions as well. Under the Restauration, one of the most active designers in this part of production was Alexandre-Evariste Fragonard. He not only developed many new forms for extant table pieces such as butter-dishes, fruit bowls, egg-cups, coolers, cruets, and sugar bowls (see cat. no. 51), but he also designed more picturesque and original objects, including an oyster tray dominated by a seahorse. As a form type, the *compotier 'à Quatre Pieds'* is somewhat similar to a *corbeille,* or footed basket. When a porcelain example of the design was displayed in the 1825 – 26 New Year's exhibition at the Louvre, it was described in the catalogue as "A fruit bowl raised on four feet; the liner can be detached with its contents without disturbing the table setting."[1] Consistent with this description, the valuation entry for the first undecorated example indicates that it consisted of two pieces: a *cuvette,* or shallow bowl, and a liner with two handles.[2] It was rare for these monumental bowls to figure in table services, but two examples with blue grounds were included in the *service 'des Départements'* (see cat. no. 63).

1. [Un compotier élevé sur quatre pieds; la jatte peut s'enlever avec ce qu'elle contient sans que le service soit dérangé].

2. Carton Pb 8, liasse 1, dossier 5, conférence of November 25, 1825 and Carton Pb 16, same date, taking into account the price of this drawing (70 francs).

66.
Design for a Cartouche Called *Porcelain*, 1826

Alexandre-Evariste Fragonard
Gouache and ink wash on paper glued to cardboard
Diameter of drawing: 4 7/8 in. (12.5 cm)
Inscriptions: [recto, below the drawing] *Porcelaine*; [lower right] [in a twentieth-century hand] *(Manufacture de Sèvres)*; [lower left] *fragonard*
Inv. no. F § 5 1827 N° 9

This composition is an allegory of the three basic operations involved in porcelain production at the manufactory, namely the shaping of forms, their firing, and the application of ornament. It is one of a series of twelve compositions designed in 1826 by Fragonard to be used as ornament for two vases — six on each one. The vases were variations he created in 1827 based on the *vase 'Medicis'*. Judging from the progress sheet for these vases, the decoration of one of them was devoted to the literary and lyric arts. The mystifying description of this series in the 1828 – 29 Louvre catalogue accompanying their display, however, indicates the presence not only of the symbols of music and dance but also of the "crown jewelers." The other vase is described as depicting the arts of drawing, with both vases "representing in a figurative manner the various skills of the Département des Beaux-Arts de la Maison du Roi in 1827,"[1] one of which was porcelain making.

Fragonard was paid 300 francs for the set of drawings for these two vases which also indicated the placement and coloring of the ornament. In addition he received 1,200 francs for "developed wash drawing[s] actual size, very precise outlines, showing the shadows of the twelve medallions."[2] This drawing is from the second series. By June 20, 1827 the drawings had already been delivered and "shown to Messieurs Gérard, Turpin, de La Rochefoucauld etc. and generally approved."[3]

Both pieces entered the sales inventory on December 19, 1828; they were shown at the 1828 – 1829, New Year's exhibition at the Louvre, and on January 23, 1829 they were presented to Friedrich Wilhelm III, king of Prussia, the intended recipient from the inception of this project.[4]

The medallions were painted on the vases by Adelaïde Ducluzeau, and the garlands of fruit and flowers were by Louis-Pierre Schilt.

The vases received mixed reviews. According to one critic, "[these vases] deserve praise for the beauty and the perfection of the details but they can be criticized for the choice of subjects which are too much in the manner of the old school. All these attributes are paltry although pretentious . . . we will praise Mr. Fragonard for his manner of executing the program he received, but we will not praise the man responsible for the program."[5]

Some of these elements — including the one exhibited here — appeared again on a second pair of vases made during the reign of Louis-Philippe "representing the arts and industries of the crown budget." The form used then was the *vase 'Medicis'* of 1827, but the grounds were chestnut brown instead of white, and five of the medallion compositions were replaced by new ones. These vases entered the sales inventory on April 25, 1840, and were presented at the Louvre the following May before being returned to the manufactory. They were eventually added to the collections of the Musée Ceramique.[6]

1. [Representant d'une manière figurative les différentes attributions du département des beaux-arts de la maison du Roi en 1827.] Carton Pb 6, liasse 1, dossier 13 bis ("vases terminés en 1828").
2. [Dessin arrêté et au lavis grandeur d'exécution, contours très assurés, effet indiqué, des 12 camées.] Ibid.
3. François Gérard, who was one of Brongniart's most faithful advisors, the vicomte Sosthène de La Rochefoucauld, who was named Directeur des Beaux-Arts in 1824, and Lancelot-Théodore de Turpin de Crissé, who was named Inspecteur des Beaux-Arts in 1824.
4. For entry in sales inventory, see Vv 1, fol. 345, no. 36; for each vase, the net price was set at 5,717.10 francs and the sale price at 7,000 francs. For delivery, see Register Vbb 8, fol. 1v. For placement of the order (November 17, 1826) see Carton M 6, liasse 4, dossier 2, La Rouchefoucauld specified there that he wanted "two vases with forms and dimensions absolutely identical to the one that this monarch deigned to send to me from the workshops of Berlin," adding: "I need not urge you to take every care to assure that these two objects be such as to attest to the superiority of our achievements in this kind of fabrication and to increase abroad the just renown of the establishment that you direct" [Deux vases de forme et de dimensions absolument semblables à celui que ce monarque a daigné m'envoyer et qui est sorti des ateliers de Berlin] [Je n'ai pas besoin de vous recommander d'apporter tous vos soins à ce que ces deux objets soient de nature à constater la supériorité de notre industrie dans ce genre de fabrication et accroître chez l'étranger la juste renommée de l'étalissement que vous dirigez].
5. *La Gazette de France*, January 7, 1829.
6. For entry in sales inventory, see Register Vv 3, fol. 68, no. 14.

67.
Decoration for a Plate from the *Service 'des Arts Industriels'*, 1827

Jean-Charles Develly
Ink and gouache on paper
Back blackened for transfer
7 1/8 x 7 1/8 in. (18.2 x 18.2 cm)
Inscriptions: [recto, in ink, in Develly's hand] [upper left] *accepté le / 13 février / 1827*; [upper center] *impression sur Porcelaine / et fayance*; [upper right (partly cut off)] *1 porte un . . . / 2 tire a . . . / 3 Trempe . . . / 4 découpe / 5 appliqu[e] / sech . . . / mix . . . / usten[ciles]*
Inv. no. 1986 A 3

The earliest mention of the *service 'des Arts industriels'* dates from the work allocations of 1820 (table service no. 5).[1] An entry dated February 24 stipulates that "Monsieur de Vely [sic] will be paid for the drawings according to the time spent on them, at the rate of 10 francs per day with a supplement for carriage expenses."[2] An estimate drawn up on March 20, 1821, anticipated that the fee for painting of each plate would come to 100 francs assuming the use of "blue of the second category," while the fees paid "for composition [and] drawing of the subjects" would amount to 15 francs.[3]

Brongniart also included this service in the list of "Projects Undertaken for the Coronation of King Charles X," describing the plates as follows: "blue plate edge, with a rich gold network. In the middle of the plate, the pictorial and colored representation of a manual art, such as the making of porcelain, forging of iron, glass-making, tapestry weaving, etc.," adding in the margin: "This is a very rich very beautiful and rather interesting service. Fourteen plates are already painted and we began with the royal manufactories. We could hardly finish this service in six months [since] Monsieur Develly is almost the only person who can work on it but if it were wanted as a present we could deliver what's already been made to the person designated by His Majesty along with a promise of the rest."[4] The artist had begun at Sèvres with a series of eight views of the manufactory's own workshops, which were essentially identical to the ones used to decorate the *déjeuner 'L'Art de la Porcelaine'* (see cat. no. 39).[5]

This drawing is a preliminary design for a plate painted in February 1827, whose definitive title was *The Porcelain Printers.* There is no documentary proof that the workshop depicted is the one at Sèvres, but this seems likely: the technique of transfer printing was much used at the manufactory at that time, precisely as shown in Develly's composition.[6]

The work began by etching the design onto a copper plate which was then pounced with a binder containing gold or ceramic powder. A sheet of paper was placed on the plate and both were then passed through the press (seen in the background here). The sheet of transfer paper was then lifted from the plate and put in a tray of water, inked side up.

The three workers in the foreground are transferring the motif onto the porcelain: the one on the left lifts the moist transfer paper while the woman next to him cuts the paper. The worker on the right places the paper face down on a vase and rubs it to transfer the design. In the background, two figures are examining a piece taken out of the drying kiln.

The transfer-printing process created many problems at Sèvres. Decorative schemes were composed of many motifs, each of which required an individual engraving. It was also difficult because these flat sheets had to be adapted to a multitude of different three-dimensional forms. Nevertheless, on occasion it saved a lot of time. Before he decided to use this process regularly, Brongniart had insisted on a series of tests made by his wife over several months on a set of plates decorated with painted and transfer-printed gilding.

The majority of pieces in the *service 'des Arts industriels'* entered the inventory on December 4, 1829. A few pieces had been shown at the New Year's exhibition of 1827 – 1828 in the Louvre, and others figured in the exhibition mounted for the following New Year's. On May 16, 1836, Louis-Philippe presented the service to Clemens Wenzel Nepomuk Lothar Prince von Metternich, the Chancellor of the Austrian Empire.[7]

Inscription: ["accepted on / 13 February / 1827"]; ["impression on Porcelain / and earthenware']; ["1 place a . . . / 2 pull a . . . / 3 soak . . . / 4 cut out . . . / 5 apply / dry . . . / mix . . . / utensils"]

1. Carton Pb 7, liasse 1, dossier 6, "services de tables, 1829" (no. 5).
2. [Les dessins seront payés à Monsieur de Vely suivant la déclaration de son temps à raison de 10 fr. par jour et les frais de voiture en sus.] Ibid.
3. Ibid.
4. [Bord de l'assiette bleue, avec un riche réseau d'or. Dans le milieu de l'assiette, la représentation pittoresque et en coloris d'un art manuel, tels la porcelaine, l'art des forges, la verrerie, la tapisserie etc."; "C'est un service très riche très beau et assez intéressant. 14 assiettes sont déjà peintes et et on a commencé par les manufactures royales. On arriverait avec peine a terminer ce service en six mois M. Develly etant presque le seul qui puisse y travailler mais si on voulait le faire entrer dans un present on livrerait a la personne auquel S.M. le destinera ce qu'il y aurait de fait et on promettrait le reste] (Carton Pb 6, liasse 1, dossier 3, report on "Projets de travaux pour pour le sacre du Roi Charles X . . .," sent on December 10, 1824).
5. A detailed list of the plates is published in Ennes, 1990; a description of all the presently known objects from the service is published in Long, 1996.
6. Préaud, "Transfer-Printing Processes used at Sèvres" (1997).
7. For entry in the sales inventory, see Register Vv 2, fol. 15, no. 9; for delivery, see Register Vbb 9, fol. 8v

68.
***The Paris Stock Exchange*, 1827**

Constant Troyon
Ink wash with white gouache highlights on paper glued to cardboard
6 7/8 x 11 3/4 in. (17.6 x 30 cm)
Inscription: [recto, in ink, in the hand of Denis-Désiré Riocreux] *Le Palais de la Bourse et du Tribunal de Commerce de Paris / 1827*
Inv. no. P § 1er 1827 N° 23

The artist's father, Jean Troyon, was a repairer at the manufactory, and his brother Jean-Marie-Dominique was a painter there. Unlike them, Constant Troyon was never part of the permanent staff. Clearly, his precocious gifts were appreciated, however, for he was given small projects when he was very young. The earliest work by him in the Sèvres archives is a watercolor representing the manufactory building, executed in 1825 when he was fifteen. The following year he was asked to make copies of some engraved portraits at the Bibliothèque du Roi and to draw details of the vestments and uniforms worn at the coronation of Charles X. In 1827 he was paid 8 francs each for nine sepia wash landscapes with white gouache highlights, as well as 20 francs for this view of the Paris Bourse, or Stock Exchange, which had been designed earlier by Alexandre-Théodore Brongniart.[1] Nothing in the documents indicates whether these drawings were executed from their subjects or were copies of existing works. The last payment he received from the manufactory dates from 1837 (for two views of the Château de Villiers la Garenne[2]). Four years earlier, in 1833, he had begun to exhibit paintings at the salon.

The file concerning the *service 'des Départements*[3] (see cat. no. 63) indicates that the plate for the Département de la Seine was to picture the Stock Exchange and Achille Poupart may have used Troyon's view as a model. The drawing may have served the same purpose in 1833, when Louis-Philippe decided to add several new compositions to the *service 'des Vues d'Italie'* to be presented as a gift to Frank Hall Standish, an Englishman who had given his collection of old master paintings to the French king.[4]

1. Carton R 18 (documents comptables, 1827).
2. Carton R 31 (documents comptables, 1837), 50 francs each.
3. Carton Pb 5, liasse 2 (2).
4. Carton Pb 7, liasse 1, dossier 5, "services de table 1830." The service entered the sales inventory on April 8, 1834 (Register Vv 2, fol. 80, no. 9) and was delivered to Frank Hall Standish on December 16, 1841 (Register Vbb 10, fol. 16).

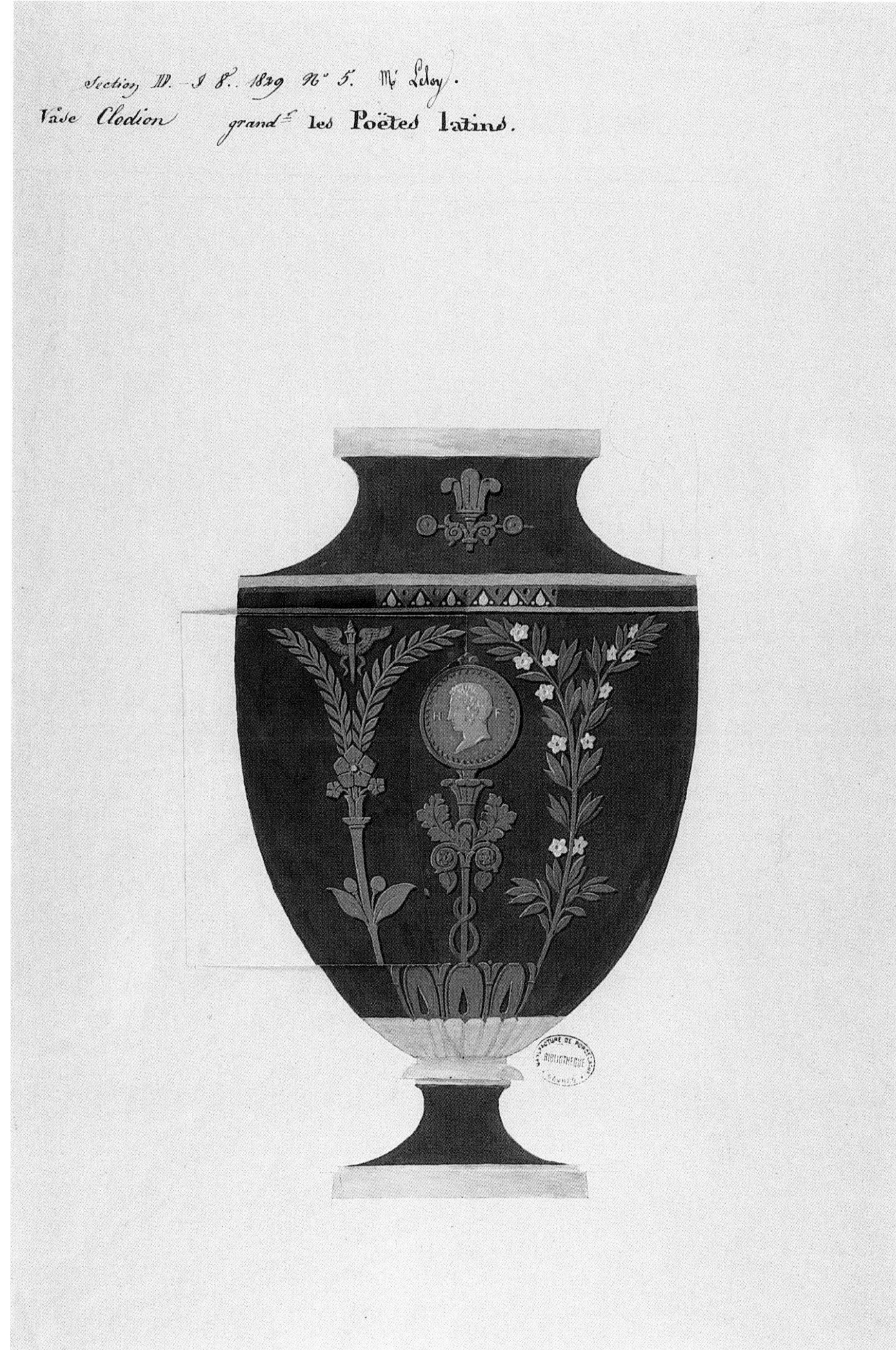

69.
Decoration for a Vase, 1829 Called *Vase 'Clodion'*

Jean-Charles-François Leloy
Gouache and pencil on paper
16 3/8 x 11 1/2 in. (41.5 x 29 cm)
Inscription: [recto, upper left, in ink, in the hand of Denis-Désiré Riocreux] *Section D § 8. 1829 No 5 Mr Leloy. / Vase Clodion [ ] grandr les Poëtes latins.*
Inv. no. D § 8 1829 N° 5

This drawing is probably one of the twenty designs proposed for the decoration of small mantel vases, which were paid for by Brongniart in 1828 and were included in the January 1829 list of work in progress.[1] Some of these decorative motifs may have been made earlier, and this design may have been used by Pierre Huart for two cups and saucers called *tasses et soucoupes 'Régnier uni'*, commemorating ancient poets. These entered the sales inventory on December 19, 1828, and were described as having "gray grounds . . . imitation agate decoration with gilded paint and painted gems."[2] There is no record, however, of a *vase 'Clodion'* with the same decoration produced between 1825 and 1830.

Apparently, Brongniart did not greatly admire the talents of Leloy. He assigned him almost all of the subsidiary ornament on table services and *déjeuners* as well as on vases and furnishings of various kinds. He accepted several new shapes designed by Leloy, but almost never let him design complete decorative schemes. In a note dated February 15, 1844, Brongniart reproached him: "You make too many small sketches of little significance which take you too long, that make the cost of executing your drawings too high, and are too imperfect to be of use. 2° You use too much icy precision in drawings that should not have the dryness and exactitude of mechanical drawings."[3] In addition, Brongniart thought Leloy charged too much for drawings whose inventive fantasy is so appealing today.

A small piece of paper glued over the left side of the central part of the vase shows an alternative decorative scheme.

1. [20 dessins pour décor de petits vases de cheminées, payés en 1828.] Register Vj' 36 (1829), fol. 1 ff., "Leloy"; and Register Vj' 35 (1828), fol. 1 ff., partial payment of 110 francs received in December 1828.
2. [Fond gris . . . imitation d'agate décor en or peint et pierreries peintes.] Carton Pb 6, valuation sheets for 1828.
3. [Vous faites un trop grand nombre de petits croquis peu significatifs, qui vous prennent trop de temps, qui font monter les frais de vos dessins trop haut et qui sont trop imparfaits pour pouvoir servir. 2° vous mettez trop de précision maigre dans des dessins qui ne doivent pas avoir la sécheresse et l'exactitude d'un dessin mécanique.] Carton Ob 7, dossier Leloy.

70.
Design and Decoration for a Jewelry Casket, 1829

Jean-Charles-François Leloy
Watercolor and pencil on paper
15 7/8 x 21 1/2 in. (40.4 x 54.6 cm)
Inv. no. D § 10 1848 No 7 (1er)

In August 1829 Jean-Charles-François Leloy made several designs for a "jewelry box [in the] Gothic style to receive portraits of the duchesse de Berry," placing her likeness alternately on the flat lid or on the sides.[1] The definitive design took the form of a medieval reliquary with the portrait inserted within a brown reserve in the shape of a lancet arch on the front.[2] The completed casket entered the sales inventory on December 21, 1829 and was shown at the 1829 – 30 New Year's exhibition at the Louvre. It was purchased by the duchesse de Berry on April 5, 1830.[3]

By this time Gothic Revival ornament was well established at Sèvres (see cat. nos. 57, 58), and, given the duchesse's predilection for this idiom, its use on this piece is hardly surprising. On January 4, 1823, she had commissioned a *coupe 'Diatrete'* with Gothic motifs very similar to one that had just been presented at the Louvre exhibition and purchased by the duchesse d'Orléans.[4]

The duchesse de Berry, who had a strong interest in porcelain, often commissioned work from freelance porcelain painters. She even tried her own hand at porcelain painting under the tutelage of Dalila Labarchède and Philippe Soiron. In 1821 she had asked the manufactory to send her an assortment of enamel paints for porcelain, as well as some blank plates and another plate decorated with a garland of flowers to serve as a model.[5]

1. [Coffret a bijoux stile gothique pour recevoir les portraits de la duchesse de Berry.] Register Vj' 36 (1829), fol. 1 ff.
2. Alcouffe, Dion-Tenenbaum, and Ennès, *Un âge d'or,* exhib. cat. (1991), no. 82, pp. 197 – 98. A commission for a Gothic casket for the duchesse de Berry was entered on October 1, 1829 (Register Vtt 3, fol. 43v), but the date of the drawing proves that the commission had been initiated previously.
3. For entry in the sales inventory, see Register Vv 2, fol. 16, no. 5 and Carton Pb 7, liasse 2, dossier 5, valuation sheets for 1829. The net price of the casket, composed of eleven porcelain plaques, was set at 3,397 francs "without counting the drawings" [sans compter les dessins], and the sale price was set at 3,600 francs. An "oval portrait plaque of Madame, [la] duchesse de Berry" [plaque ovale Portrait de Madame Duchesse de Berry] also entered the sales inventory on the same date.
4. This coupe, "decorated with sparkling gem decorations with Gothic figures and ornaments etc." [garnie de pierre brillante decor avec figure et ornement gothique etc.], after a design by Joseph Vigné, entered the inventory on December 20, 1822 (Register Vv 1, fol. 190, no. 23), and was sold to Madame between December 26, 1822 and January 7, 1823 (Register Vz 4, fol. 99v). The one commissioned by the duchesse de Berry (Register Vtt 2, fol. 19v) entered the inventory on June 6, 1823 (Register Vv 1, fol. 199, no. 39), and was sold to her on the following June 14 (Register Vbb 6, fol. 118).
5. Carton T 9, liasse 2, dossier 4, letter dated February 18, 1821.

71.
Decoration for an Ice Pail, 1830
Called *Glacière 'à Chimères'* for the *Service 'de la Chevalerie'*

Jean-Charles Develly
Sepia wash with white gouache and watercolor highlights
5 7/8 x 9 in. (14.9 x 23)
Inscriptions: [recto, in the hand of Jean-Charles Develly] [bottom left, in ink] *amour de / dieu et des dames*; [bottom right in pencil] *devise / amour de / Dieu / et des Dames*; [below the drawing in pencil] *1390 a Calais. / Tournois, ou Pas d'armes, Trois chevaliers Français, soutinrent pendant quatre jours / sans vider les arçons, les assauts multipliés de l'elite des chevaliers Anglais et autres. / ou faire / Le Combat des Trente en 1350 entre 30 chevaliers français, et 30 Anglais, pres de Ploërmel en bretagne.*
Inv. no. 1987 D 104

In 1830 Jean-Charles Develly received 200 francs and a 35-franc "research" supplement for four sketches of reserve compositions for the *glacières 'à Chimères'* for the *service 'de la Chevalerie'.* Later the same year Develly executed the actual painting on porcelain, for which he received 750 francs.[1] By that time the service already had a long history, whose origins may date back to the *service 'de l'Histoire de France'*, which Brongniart described as early as 1807: "The plates have borders with chrome green grounds and rich gold friezes borrowed from French monuments from different eras. The plate wells are decorated with polychrome paintings from the history of France and views of French monuments."[2] It was probably for this service that Brongniart's father had designed a series of "Gothic" friezes registered in 1806, but the project does not seem to have proceeded beyond the trial stage.[3]

The service was subsequently put aside. It is not known whether it was at Brongniart's request, or at Joseph Vigné's initiative, that in 1822 the artist drew a plate design featuring several possible "Gothic" ornamental schemes for the border and plate well, which included a figure of Pepin le Bref, an early king of Franconia. In January 1823 it was decided to begin a *service 'de la Chevalerie',* with "white plate edges with printed gold ornament . . . area of glost-fired blue ground in the center reserved for knights of various orders, periods, eras, and families with famous names. On the ice pails, tournaments etc."[4] On March 14 a note was made calling for the preparation of "a list of figures who will be represented . . . they will be taken from the beginning of the monarchy to Francis I included." On May 20 the list was submitted by Vigné, and on November 25 it was recorded that "the seventy-two plates are printed in gold." Then, for reasons unknown, the service was delayed. On July 15, 1830, the ice pails had received their first painting but only twenty-five plates had been completed, six of which had to be replaced because the painting had flaked, possibly from improper handling or firing.

On September 25, 1832, the ice pails had not yet been fitted with their mounts. And on March 22, 1834, it was recorded that "to bring the service to sixty plates there are still four designs to make." The bulk of the service finally entered the sales inventory on December 31, 1834.[5] It was never delivered, but individual plates and small groups of pieces were sold.[6] The ice pails were purchased by M. Charbonné in 1872.[7] (See fig. 71a.)

The *glacière 'à Chimères'*, inspired by an antique vase, was designed in 1808 for the *service 'de l'Empereur'* (see cat. no. 20); it was fitted with two vermeil handles. The form was subsequently incorporated into other services (*service 'à vues diverses'*, and the *service 'à vues Hors d'Europe'*).

Inscription: ["love of / god and the ladies"]; ["emblem / love of God / and the Ladies"]; ["1390 in Calais. / Tournament, or armed engagement, three French knights withstood for four days / without leaving the saddle, repeated attacks by the élite of the English (and other) armies. ' or do / The 'Combat des Trente' (The Battle of the Thirty) in 1350 between 30 French knights and 30 English, near Ploërmel / in Brittany"]

1. Register Vj' 37, fol. 21 ff.
2. [Les assiettes ont une bordure en fond vert de chrôme avec une riche frise en or tirée des monuments français de différents ages. Le milieu de l'assiette represente des sujets coloriés de l'histoire de France ou des vues de monuments français.] Carton Pb 1, liasse 1, dossier 16, travaux 1807.
3. Only two plates for this service appear to have entered the inventory (Carton Pb 1, valuations for 1807). The first one was recorded on June 17, 1807: "One plate [for the] History of France Service with the Continance of Bayard by M. Taunay" [1 assiette service de l'histoire de France La continance de Bayard par M. Taunay]. The second one entered the inventory on July 29, 1807: "One plate [with] border [with] chrome [green] ground [and] Gothic gold frieze painting [by] Swebach [of] the Battle of Austerlitz" ["1 assiette marly fond de chrome frise en or gotique peinture Swebach la bataille d'austerlitz]. The two artists in question are Nicolas-Antoine Taunay and Jacques-François Swebach
4. [Bordure de l'assiette blanche avec ornements en or imprimés . . . zone de fond bleu au grand feu dans le milieu réservé un chevalier de divers ordres, ages, epoque et famille d'un nom connu. Sur les glacières, tournois etc.] Carton Pb 8, liasse 2, dossier 6.
5. Register Vv 2, fol. 91v.
6. The last plates entered the sales inventory in June 1848 (Register Vv 5, fol. 8).
7. Register Vz 12, fol. 240v.

72. Design and Decoration for a Vase, 1830 – 31 Called *Vase 'Egyptien B'*

Attributed to Antoine-Gabriel Willermet
Pencil, ink, watercolor, and gouache on paper
13 x 8 1/8 in. (33 x 20.5 cm)
Inscription: [recto, above the drawing, in ink, in the hand of Denis-Désiré Riocreux] *Vase Egyptien B executé en 1830 – 1832 / sur les dessins et d'après les indications de Mr Champollion jeune*
Inv. no. D § 8 1848 N° 93

It is difficult to determine the date and authorship of this drawing. The file on the vase contains a sketch on tracing paper (Inv. no. D § 8 1830 N° 2 [2]), on which Brongniart wrote "B ou Vase Egyptien Champollion."[1] On this outline drawing of the vase's profile and decoration, each area is numbered to indicate its color, and it is accompanied by two small sheets of details, also keyed to indicate the placement of color. On the design, Denis-Désiré Riocreux wrote: "copy of vase outlines / made in the tombs of Egypt / in 1829 / by M. Champollion."[2] These notations suggest a date of about 1830.

The progress sheet for the vase records that on January 14, 1831, "two of these vases were removed from the kiln," confirming that the form design dates from 1830. This sheet, however, bears the following inscription in Brongniart's hand under the date of April 20, 1831: "Visit to M. Champollion. M. Le Normand in attendance, instructions on the mode of decoration which I send with details and model to M. Willermet to be executed without delay by M. Riton,"[3] meaning Pierre Riton, a Sèvres porcelain painter. A sheet of instructions pertaining to the decoration of the *vase 'Egyptien Champollion'* or *vase 'Egyptien B'*, dated April 22, 1831 by Brongniart, provides the color key to the 1830 drawing and concludes as follows: "make before execution / 1° a drawing approximately the same size as the vase with at least half of it colored and / 2° some samples on glazed pieces of the colors intended to be used."[4] In 1831 Jean-Charles Develly was paid for scraping the platinum ground down to the porcelain and in-painting the gazelle, and Pierre Riton, for the ornament.[5] This drawing therefore probably dates from that year. It may have been made by the head of the painting workshop, Antoine-Gabriel Willermet, whose work is not precisely recorded in the registers.

This vase is one of a series of three undertaken in collaboration with the Egyptologist Jean-François Champollion the younger, whose considerable reputation surely helped to enhance the public's perception of the authenticity of these exotic works. Apparently the archaeologist was especially fond of this model, for it sometimes bears his name in the manufactory register. In a list of important works-in-progress drawn up on September 1, 1831, Brongniart described it: "These vases have a special character that, far from being shocking, is rather agreeable. [They represent] the application of one of the manufactory's principles, that of taking what's best in every style regardless of period or country."[6] Additional evidence of Brongniart's appreciation is provided by his decision to reproduce the three *vases 'Egyptien'* in his *Description du musée céramique . . . .*[7]

The first two *vases 'Egyptien B'* to be completed entered the sales inventory on August 4 and November 9 of 1832, respectively.[8] The first was sold to a Mme Wittingham and the second was delivered

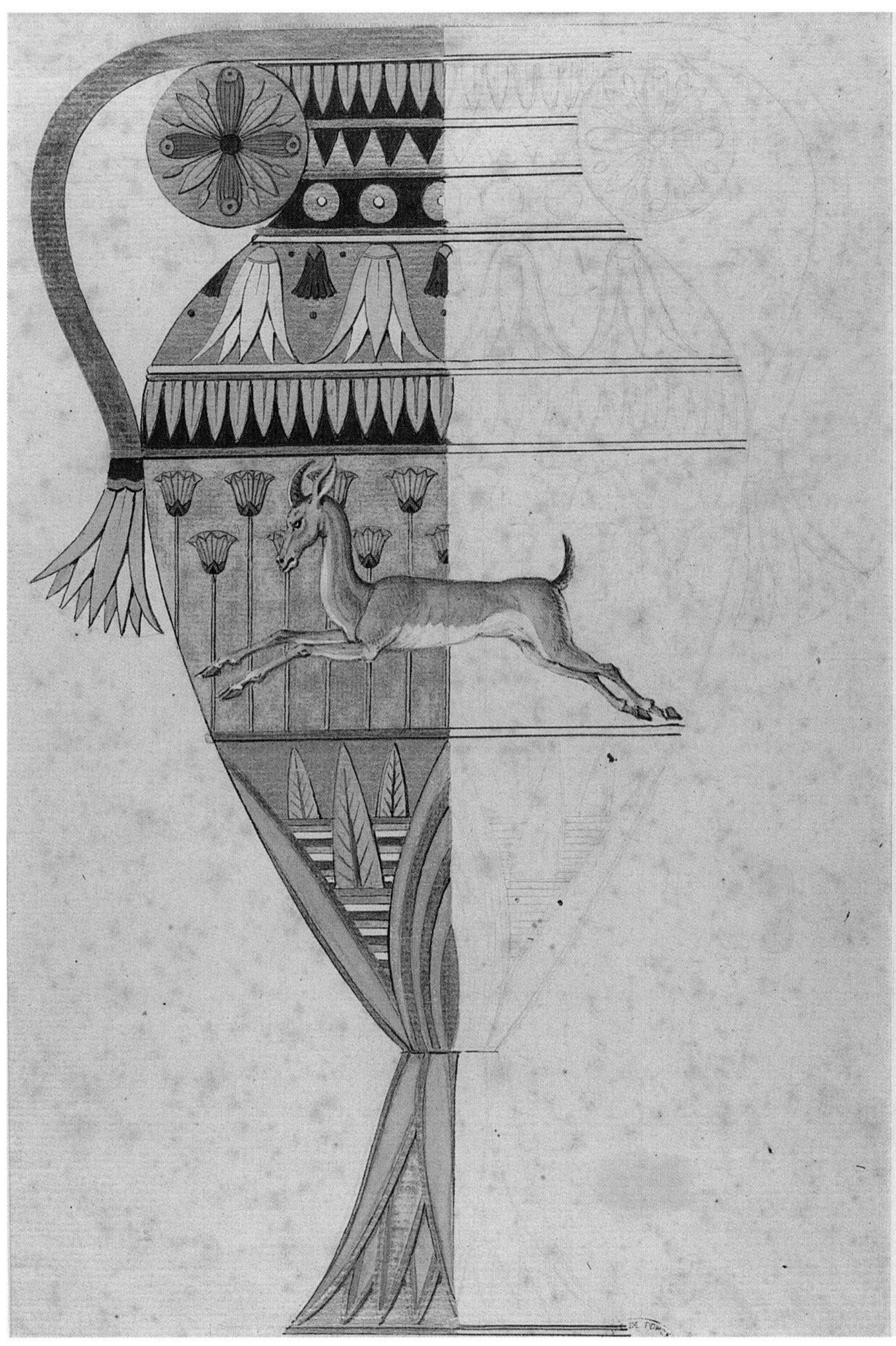

72.

to the Château de Compiègne.[9] Two more vases with the same form but different painted decorations, composed and painted by Pierre Huard, entered the sales inventory on May 28, 1844. They were presented at the Louvre on June 3, 1844, and delivered to the Ministère de l'Interieur on July 21, 1848.[10] Finally, a third pair with simple ornamentation in gold against a blue ground entered the inventory on July 26, 1851, and was delivered to the president of the senate in March 1852.[11] (See fig. 72a.)

1. Carton Pb 7, liasse 1, dossier 1 ("Vases terminés en 1832").
2. [Copie de traits de Vases / pris dans les tombeaux d'Egypte / en 1829 / par Mr. Champollion.] Ibid.
3. [Visite à M. Champollion. M. Le Normand present, instruction sur le mode de decoration que je transmets avec details et modele a M. Willermet pour être mis sans delai a execution par M. Riton.] Ibid.
4. [Instruction sur la décoration du vase Egyptien Champollion ou B"; "Faire avant l'exécution 1° un dessin d'environ la grandeur du vase sur lequel on colorera une moitié ou plus 2° des echantillons sur pièces en couverte des couleurs qu'on se propose d'employer.] Ibid.
5. Register Vj' 38 (1831), fols. 21 ff. and 67 ff.
6. Carton Pb 7, liasse 2, dossier 1.
7. Brongniart and Riocreux, *Description méthodique du musée céramique* (1845), P., pl. 4, no. 4.
8. Carton Pb 9 bis, valuations for 1832 (net price 575 francs, including 160 francs for the blank vase; sale price 700 francs); and Register Vv 3, fol. 53, no. 30 and fol. 57, no. 16.
9. Register Vz 5, fol. 82, August 22, 1832; and Register Vbb 9, fol. 40, August 16, 1834.
10. For entry in the sales inventory, see Register Vv 4, fol. 22, no. 13; and Carton Pb 11 bis, valuations for 1844. These must have been more richly decorated than the first pair: despite the absence of relief elements, each vase was assigned a net price of 1,602.30 francs (including the substantial sum of 1,015 francs for Pierre Huard) and a sale price of 1,800 francs. For delivery, see Register Vbb 11, fol. 22.
11. For entry in sales inventory, see Register Vv 5, fol. 50, no. 28 (net price 574 francs, sale price 750 francs). For delivery, see Register Vbb 11, fol. 268v.

73.
Design and Decoration for a Vase, 1832
Called *Vase 'Carafe Japonais'*

Alexandre-Evariste Fragonard
Watercolor and pencil on thin cardboard
15 3/8 x 11 7/8 in. (39 x 30.3)
Inscription: [recto, below the drawing, in ink, in the hand of Denis-Désiré Riocreux)] *Vase Carafe Japonais, / par Mr Fragonard. (Aout 1832.)*
Inv. no. D § 8 1832 N° 6

Although Denis-Désiré Riocreux described this object as "Japanese," the record of a payment of 70 francs made to Alexandre-Evariste Fragonard in August 1832 speaks of a "drawing for [a] Chinese carafe for decoration and revision of the profile of the form."[1] This is another indication of the pervasive confusion of models from all Far Eastern countries. Auction catalogues of this period almost always listed Asian pieces under the same heading, although the one for the sale of the "Chinese collection" of the dealer F. Sallé, which began on April 11, 1826, testifies to increased historical, technical, and linguistic sophistication in this domain. In that sales catalogue the Chinese inscriptions were translated, the subjects were identified, and the pieces were classified by type.

On January 24, 1808, Brongniart wrote to the Intendant Général de la Maison de l'Empereur, speaking of "our collection of porcelain materials from foreign porcelains. . . . M. Denon was kind enough to think of us as well and brought us a beautiful collection of porcelain from Japan. The manufactory did not have any at all."[2] The catalogue of the Musée Céramique (1845), however, bears witness to the unflagging interest in Far Eastern porcelains, both ancient and modern, that Brongniart and Riocreux had developed in the interim.[3]

Production of the vase-carafe in the drawing seems to have been interrupted. In September 1832, Hyacinthe Régnier was paid 18 francs for "a preliminary model in plaster of the *vase Carafe Japonais* (frag[onard] 1832),"[4] but no corresponding object ever entered the inventory. Perhaps Brongniart came to feel that this strange mixture of relatively authentic elements — elongated women in kimonos and flowers in vases — and distinctly European elements, notably gems and pearls, was insufficiently "pure." If so, this provides evidence of the growing influence on Brongniart of the museum's diverse collection of authentic pieces as it developed.

1. [Dessin de caraffe chinoise pour la décoration et revision du trait pour la forme.] Register Vj' 39 (1832), fol. 162.
2. [Monsieur Denon a eu la bonté de penser aussi à nous et nous a rapporté une belle collection de porcelaine du Japon. La Manufacture n'en avoit aucune.] Register Vc 3, fols. 122 – 122v.
3. Brongniart and Riocreux, *Description méthodique du musée* (1845), vol. I.
4. [Une esquisse en plâtre du vase carafe japonnais (frag. 1832)] Register Va' 29 (1831 – 32), fols. 128 ff.

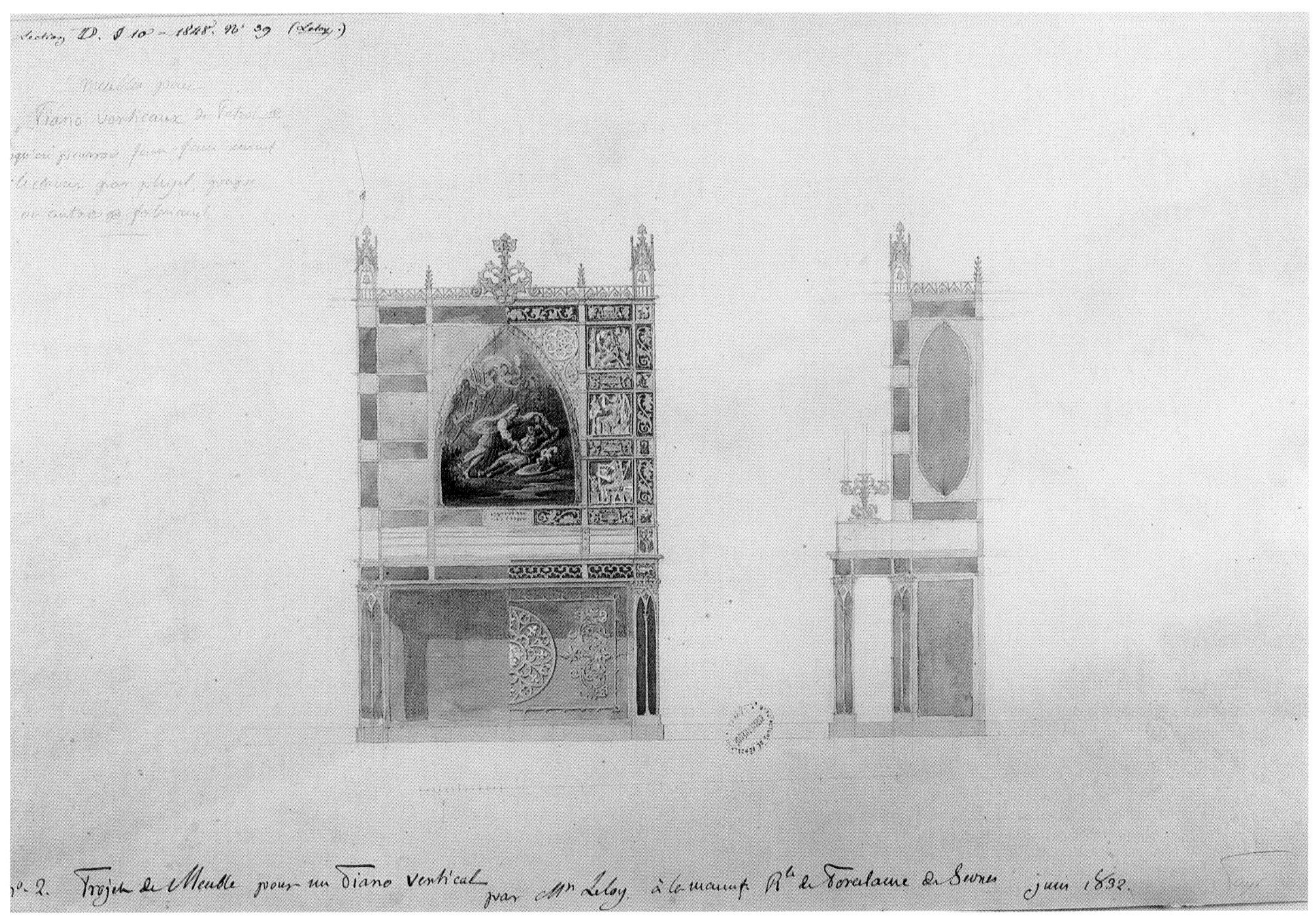

74.
Design for an Upright Piano, 1832

Jean-Charles-François Leloy
Watercolor, gouache and pencil on paper
11 5/8 x 17 3/4 in. (29.5 x 45.2)
Inscriptions: [recto, in the hand of Brongniart] [upper left, in ink] *meubles pour / Piano verticaux de Petrol etc / Lorsqu'on pourroit faire faire ensuit / le clavier par pleyel, pape / ou autre fabricant*; [bottom in ink] *n° 2 Projet de meuble pour un Piano vertical / par Mr Leloy à la manuf. Rle de Porcelaine de Sèvres / juin 1832.*; [bottom right] *Payé*
Inv. no. D § 10 1848 N° 39

This drawing is one of a series of designs for piano cases that are listed among the work for which Jean-Charles-François Leloy was paid in June 1832.[1] They are described in greater detail in an entry made in the price register the following August: "One drawing of grand pianos colored study 70 [francs] One 'ditto' of pediment piano colored study 55 [francs] One 'ditto' of Gothic piano and colored 60 [francs] Three trips to various pianists 15 [francs]."[2] It is impossible to know if the unusual idea of encasing a piano in porcelain sheets is somehow related to a visit made to the manufactory's workshops and collections, on May 11, 1832, by "Jacques Faurin ainé, piano tuner to the king."[3] One can hardly imagine the sound produced by such an instrument, but the consultations with several pianists cannot have been encouraging, for none of these designs was realized.

Inscription: ["case for / Petrol upright Pianos etc / The piano could also be made by Pleyel, Pape / or another manufacturer"]; ["No. 2 Design for case for upright Piano / by Mr Leloy at the Royal Porcelain Factory, Sèvres ' June 1832"]; ["Paid"]

1. Register Vj' 39 (1832), fols. 3 ff.
2. [1 dessin de grand pianos Etude colorée 70 1 ditto de piano a fronton etude colorié 55 1 ditto de piano gothique et colorée 60, 3 voyages chez divers pianistes 15] Register Vq' , 1ere série, vol. 5, fol. 166.
3. [Jacques Faurin aîné, accordeur de pianos du roy] Register Vu 2 (Visitors).

75.
Decoration for a Teapot, 1832
Called *Théière 'Chinoise Ronde'*

Alexandre-Evariste Fragonard
Watercolor and pencil on thin cardboard
10 1/2 x 11 in. (26.6 x 28 cm)
Inscription: [recto, below the drawing, in ink, in the hand of Denis-Désiré Riocreux] *Théyère Chinoise sphérique / par Mr Fragonard (Août 1832.)* [inventory number in lower right corner in ink, inscribed by a later hand]
Inv. no. D § 3 1832 No 12

Long after designing a teapot called *théière 'Chinoise à pans'* in 1818 (see cat. no. 47), A.-E. Fragonard worked on this spherical form, initially introduced on May 10, 1831 in a blank version.[1] Although the manufactory produced warming kettles with bail handles in the eighteenth century, this piece may have been inspired by lot 374 in the Sallé auction of 1826 (see cat. no. 73), described in its catalogue as "une théière anse en dessus."[2] In August 1832 Fragonard was paid 50 francs for this "drawing of a round Chinese Teapot only for the decoration."[3] Neither of the two teapots of this type that were entered in the sales inventory on December 31, 1832, however, correspond to this drawing. The descriptions specify "colored flowers and ornaments" and "colored flowers against a black ground," instead of figures.[4] Both had silver handles with ivory grips.

A recently discovered example has a handle different from the one seen here: it is rounded but made of silver and also features carved ivory motifs at the top and the junction of handle and body.[5] Its form also differs in several respects from this design, but there is no way of knowing whether these discrepancies also characterized the eleven examples that were produced between 1832 and 1846 with varying decorations. The one illustrated in the catalogue of the Musée Céramique features a handle with a floral motif typical of the neo-rococo style, an even richer knob, and floral ornament that no longer reveals any Chinese associations.[6]

1. Carton Pb 7, liasse 1, dossier 4. The artist is not listed here as paid for the drawing of the form.
2. The sale began in Paris on April 11, 1826, and continued for several days.
3. [Dessin de theyere ronde chinoise pour la décoration seulement.] Register Vj' 39 (1832), fol. 162 ff.
4. [Fleurs et ornements en couleurs]; [fleurs coloriées dans un fond noir.] Carton Pb 9, "Appréciations 1832"; sale prices set at 140 and 170 francs.
5. *Faïences françaises,* auction cat. (1991).
6. Brongniart and Riocreux, *Description méthodique du musée* (1845), P, pl. 14, no. 1.

76.
Design and Decoration for a Coffeepot, 1832
Called *Cafetière 'Chinoise Réticulée'*

Hyacinthe Régnier
Watercolor and ink on paper; small paper glued to the upper right
10 5/8 x 8 1/4 in. (27 x 21 cm)
Inscription: [recto, bottom, in ink, in the hand of Denis-Désiré Riocreux] *Cafetière. / du Déjeuner chinois réticulé de 1832. / par Mr h^te Régnier*
Inv. no. D § 3 1832 N° 19

Since the eighteenth century the manufactory had produced several pieces more or less directly inspired by Chinese models[1] (see cat. no. 47). This drawing, however, relates to a deliberate copy based on pieces sold at auction by the Parisian dealer F. Sallé. The catalogue for the 1826 auction of Sallé's "Chinese collection" (see cat. nos. 73 and 75) contains a section devoted to "Openwork White Porcelain," about which the text reported: "The Chinese make a kind of porcelain with openwork designs resembling paper cut-outs. In the center is a vessel for liquid. This vessel forms one unit with the openwork." Lot 462 under this heading is described as: "A teapot, white and blue, and a cup with saucer in openwork, double walled, of great finesse, and very rare due to difficulties of fabrication" (the lot sold for 81 francs).[2] It was certainly not by chance that several years later Sèvres sought to imitate this technical tour-de-force, as Meissen had done so successfully in its early years.[3]

In November 1831 Hyacinthe Régnier was credited with an advance payment for designs for several pieces of a *déjeuner* designated simply as Chinese.[4] The following February he was paid for other drawings and then for definitive drawings and working models; the last to be submitted were for a coffeepot and a tray (August to November). The designation *'Chinois Réticulé'* does not appear in documents until October 1832.

The pattern seen here must not be read as painted decoration applied to a dark ground: carefully rendered shadows indicate the void between the external openwork and the smooth surface of the inner vessel, normally left blank in the porcelain but colored in this rendering to facilitate visual comprehension. The small drawing glued to the sheet's upper right corner offers a schematic plan of the design proposed for the lid.

These pieces were immediately much in demand and became preferred gifts (see fig. 76a),[5] simultaneously functioning as emblems of the technical virtuosity of Sèvres's craftsmen. They remain in production today, for the same reason. Régnier's forms are still used, but the openwork pattern was redesigned around 1900 by Léon Kann. Pieces of this kind are so difficult to produce that Brongniart devoted a plate and a long description to them in his *Traité*.[6]

1. Préaud, "Sèvres, la Chine et les chinoiseries" (1989).
2. [Il se fait à la Chine une espèce de porcelaine qui est toute percée à jour en forme de découpure. Au milieu est une coupe propre à contenir la liqueur. La coupe ne fait qu'un corps avec la découpure"; "une theyere, blanc et bleu, et une tasse avec soucoupe travaillée à jour, à double fond, d'une grande finesse, et très rare par la difficulté de fabrication.] Catalogue of Sallé Sale, Paris, April 11, 1826 and following days. See Slitine, "La Céramique orientale dans les ventes publiques" (1996).
3. *Meissen* (1984), ill. 74, p. 130.
4. Register Va' 29 (1831 – 32), fols. 128 ff.
5. In 1842, a *déjeuner 'Chinois Reticulé'* was delivered to the captain of the ship *Cécilé* with instructions that he exchange it for Chinese porcelains, but it was returned to the manufactory in December 1847, for reasons unknown (Carton Pb 11 bis, valuations for 1847).
6. Brongniart, *Traité des arts céramiques* (1844), vol. 2, pp. 292 – 93.

77.

Decoration for a Cup, 1832
Called *Tasse 'à chocolat AB de 1813'*, for the *Déjeuner 'Fleurs en tableau'*

Jean-Charles-François Leloy
Gouache, watercolor, ink and pencil on paper
6 3/4 x 8 1/2 in. (17 x 21.7 cm)
Inscription: [recto, bottom, in ink, in the hand of Denis-Désiré Riocreux] *Déjeuner Fleurs en Tableau N° 12 de 1832. / Décoration pour Tasse AB. Par Mr Leloy*
Inv. no. D § 4 1833 N° 4a

The manufactory's production was not greatly affected by the accession to the throne of Louis-Philippe in 1830: there were, however, innovations in exotic and historicist modes (see cat. nos. 72, 75, and 76; and 78 and 79), but there were many new designs during this period that were conceived along more conventional lines. Floral decorations, for example, remained quite popular. They were constantly being updated in terms of species, treatment (garlands, bouquets, or bunches), and presentation against various ground colors and patterns such as porphyry. In December 1832 Jean-Charles-François Leloy was paid 200 francs for a series of designs for a *déjeuner des fleurs*, one of which was for "one cup and saucer AB composition on the pieces, one drawing study of the cup overall composition and coloration."[1] The complete *déjeuner* entered the sales inventory on January 31, 1835, when it was described as having a brown ground with groups of flowers against a yellowish ground.[2] The ensemble is not listed in the catalogue of the exhibition held at the Louvre the following May 1; presumably it was not shown there, because the design was considered unoriginal.

1. [1 tasse et soucoupe AB composition sur pièces, 1 dessin etude de la tasse ensemble de composition et coloration.] Register Vj' 39 (1832), fols. 3 ff.
2. Carton Pb 9 bis, valuations for 1835; and Register Vv 2, fol. 94, no. 46. The net price of the cups and saucers with gilded inner surfaces was set at 165 francs, including 60 francs for the ornament painter Joseph Richard and only 30 francs for the floral painter Jean-Joseph Fontaine. The sale price was set at 185 francs.

78.
Design and Decoration for a Cup and Stand for the *Déjeuner 'de François Ier'*, 1832

Alexandre-Evariste Fragonard
Watercolor and pencil on paper
7 3/4 x 5 1/8 in. (19.8 x 13 cm)
Inscription: [recto, bottom, in ink, in the hand of Denis-Désiré Riocreux] *Tasse et Porte-tasse / du déjeuner François Ier*
Inv. no. D § 4 1834 N° 1

Under Louis-Philippe the Château de Fontainebleau was once again an official residence, which must have focused the attention of many artists and designers on its remarkable Renaissance decorative schemes that included sculpture and fresco. In a parallel development, the so-called "Bernard Palissy" earthenware was rediscovered during the same period. Palissy was the only name of a French Renaissance potter known at this time. Contemporary auction catalogues attributed to him most ceramics with colorful relief elements which dated approximately to the time of the Renaissance. Such pieces had been extremely rare in auction sales during the first quarter of the nineteenth century, but soon afterward they became much more common on the Parisian market. The earliest designs at Sèvres in this manner date from 1830 (see cat. no. 79).

In 1832 Alexandre-Evariste Fragonard was paid 370 francs for a *déjeuner 'de François Ier'*. Six watercolor drawings [for the] *déjeuner* design consisting of a coffee cup, coffeepot, sugar bowl, cream jug, tray, and overall view of the *déjeuner* on its tray."[1] Another novelty was that each piece was to be placed on an individual stand instead of resting directly on the tray. The varying heights of the supports added considerable dynamism to the overall effect (see fig. 78a).

Realization of these complex designs was a protracted process, and the first blank examples were priced only in 1835 – 36.[2] The first complete *déjeuner 'de François Ier'* entered the sales inventory on April 29, 1837, and was presented to the king of Naples the following June.[3] A second set entered the sales inventory on July 22, 1837; it was shown at the Louvre exhibition of May 1, 1838, and was eventually delivered to the mayor of Nantes for that city's museum in May 1851.[4]

In 1836, when Brongniart received a commission for a *service d'apparat* for Fontainebleau, he proposed that the *déjeuner 'de François Ier'* be used for presentation, but simpler pieces be employed for the actual drinking of coffee.

1. [Déjeuner de François Ier. 6 dessins coloriés à l'aquarelle projet de Dejeuner se composant d'une tasse a café, caftiere (sic), pot à sucre, pot à crème, plateau et ensemble du déjeuner sur son plateau] Register Vj' 39 (1832), fol. 162.
2. Carton Pb 8, liasse 4, "appréciations en blanc 1833 – 1836," sheet no. 58 (undated; between October 1835 and October 1836).
3. For entry in sales inventory, see Register Vv 3, fol. 20, no. 5. For delivery, see Register Vbb 9, fol. 15, where it is described: "One so-called Francis I Déjeuner in the Renaissance style relief ornament rich gold and colored decoration etc. 6,000 francs" [Un déjeuner dit de François Ier dans le style de la Renaissance ornements en reliefs riche decoration en or et couleur etc. 6,000 francs].
4. For entry in sales inventory, see Register Vv 3, fol. 24, no. 25. For delivery, see Vbb 11, fo. 45v. Same descriptions and prices. This second *déjeuner* is now in the Musée National de Céramique at Sèvres.

79.
Color Scheme for the *Vase 'de la Renaissance'*, 1833

Claude-Aimé Chenavard
Watercolor and ink on paper
17 1/8 x 11 3/8 in. (43.6 x 29 cm)
Inscriptions: [recto, left, in pencil] *filet bronze-bronze-filet en or poli*; right: *poli-pour repondre au filet de la . . .*; [lower left, in ink, in the hand of Alexandre Brongniart] *second vase de la renaissance par M. Chenavard / coloration . remis le 10 decembre 1833 / AlexB*
Inv. no. D § 8 1833 N 4

This design, for which the artist does not seem to have received a specific payment, indicates a new or alternate color scheme for the first *vase 'de la Renaissance'* of 1830. This change was noted in a review of the Louvre exhibition of May 1, 1835: "[the manufactory has been] sensitive to justifiable reproaches that too much color had been used without leaving a single corner of the beautiful material exposed, [the manufactory] has left much of it white, and today the vase is generally found to be more successful than it was."[1]

In January 1830, the ornamentalist Claude-Aimé Chenavard, a new recruit hired by the manufactory and recommended to Brongniart by the painter Jean-Auguste-Dominique Ingres, received 300 francs for a form and color-scheme drawing for the original *vase 'de la Renaissance'*.[2] Documents in the single progress file for the two editions of the vase indicate that the initial production process was protracted.[3] A plaster model without ornament was ready on March 25, 1830, and on April 1 Chenavard suggested that the handles be made by "a young sculptor named Barry [sic]," meaning Antoine-Louis Barye. On July 17 Brongniart noted that Barye, concluding from the fees usually paid him by the bronze casters, had estimated that he would require about 1,200 francs to make the figures and animals on the handles, a sum that the administrator apparently deemed too high.

For the central narrative reliefs, on June 3 Brongniart turned to Félicie de Fauveau, but she formally withdrew from the project on July 15. Eventually, in March 1831, Brongniart reached an agreement with Antonin Moine, who was commissioned to make the handles, profile cameos, and reliefs[4]

The catalogue of the Louvre exhibition of December 27, 1832, where the first example was presented, describes the subjects of these two reliefs: "Jean Goujon in his workshop, showing Henri II and Diane de Poitiers the group of Diana and the Stag, which he has just completed . . . . Leonardo da Vinci painting the portrait known as *Mona Lisa* in the presence of Francis I and amidst musicians."[5]

The first vase to be completed was officially recorded in the sales inventory on December 31, 1832 (shortly after the opening of the Louvre exhibition); it was delivered to the Château de Fontainebleau on September 25, 1838.[6] The second vase, which corresponds to this drawing, entered the sales inventory on April 25, 1835; it was presented at the Louvre on May 1 and was delivered to the official residence of the president of the Assemblée Nationale on August 16, 1848, following the abdication of Louis Philippe several weeks earlier.[7]

In both cases, on the occasion of the exhibition at the Louvre, Brongniart specified in the catalogue: "form, decoration, and coloring in the style of the vases of Bernard Palissy." Sèvres played an early role in the revival of interest both in this ceramist and more generally in Renaissance ceramics which had, until that time, been generally neglected. Palissy's name had probably been kept alive through his many writings and was widely used in this period as a generic identification for most pottery believed to date from the Renaissance period (see cat. no. 78).[8]

Earlier evidence of the emerging interest in this type of pottery is provided by Brongniart's authorization of the glass painter Auguste-Jules-Simon Vatinelle to exhibit a work at the salon of 1831 described in its catalogue (no. 2877): "Subject from the Life of Bernard Palissy; painting on glass in the manner of German stained-glass windows after a design by M. Fragonard." The oil sketch by Alexandre-Evariste Fragonard (today in the archives at Sèvres) depicts an episode that became quite celebrated in which the potter is said to have burned his own furniture to assure completion of an important kiln firing.

Brongniart endorsed the importance of this vase by reproducing it in his *Description méthodique du musée.*[9] Chenavard also illustrated a similar form with different handles, in an album of his designs.[10] He had previously exhibited his first design for the vase at the salon of 1831. Brongniart probably saw relief work of this type as another means of revitalizing porcelain decoration, which had become largely dependent on the use of reserves or cartouches in compositions executed primarily by painters. The novelty of this sculptural decoration enlivened by bright colors was not lost on contemporaries, even if opinions about it differed.[11] In any event, this production technique was cost-effective — it avoided the considerable expense entailed by meticulous miniature painting — and soon became immensely successful throughout Europe, finding favor with both producers and buyers, who were seduced by the vivacity of such pieces.

The first vase (see fig. 79a), made in 1832, remains in the Château de Fontainebleau.

Inscription: ["bronze lattice-bronze-lattice in polished gold"]; ["polished . . . to match the lattice on the lower left"] ["second renaissance vase by M. Chenavard / colouring. Sent 10 December 1833 / AlexB"]

1. [Sensible au juste reproche qui lui avait été fait de l'avoir couvert de couleur sans laisser intact un seul coin de la belle matière . . . [la manufacture] a reservé beaucoup de blanc, et aujourd'hui le vase est généralement trouvé mieux qu'il n'était.] Article in the June 23, 1835 issue of *Le National de 1834*, signed V. S. (Victor Schoelcher?).

2. Carton T 12, liasse 8, dossier 3, letter from Alexandre Brongniart to Abraham Constantin dated March 12, 1831.

3. Carton Pb 7, liasse 1, dossier 1.

4. Moine was paid in two installments: in 1831 he received 1,800 francs for models of the handles, profiles, and one of the reliefs; in 1832 he received 1,600 francs for a model of the second relief and for retouching the whole.

5. [Jean Goujon dans son atelier, faisant voir à Henri II et à Diane de Poitiers le groupe de Diane et du cerf, qu'il vient de terminer]; [Leonard de Vinci, peignant, en présence de François Ier, et au milieu d'un concert, le portrait connu sous le nom de *La Joconde.*] This second subject is surprising, given the preference of some French artists — notably F.-G. Ménageot and J.-A.-D. Ingres — for the alternative subject of Leonardo da Vinci dying in the arms of Francis I (see Haskell, *Past and Present in Art and Taste* [1987], pp. 90 – 115). A similar subject appeared on a monumental biscuit Sèvres vase shown at the same exhibition (December 27, 1832). It is described in the catalogue, "One has imagined that this artist [Phidias], having just completed the full-scale model of his statue of Olympian Jupiter, showed this model to the principal figures of his time" [On a supposé que cet artiste [Phidias] venait de terminer le modèle en grand de sa statue du Jupiter Olympien, et qu'il faisait voir ce modèle aux principaux personages de son temps].

6. For entry in the sales inventory, see Register Vv 2, fol. 58, nos. 27 and 28; Carton Pb 9 bis, valuations for 1832; Carton Pb 7, liasse 1, dossier 1 (net price 8,634 francs, including 5,500 francs for the blank porcelain and 948 francs for the painting; sale price 10,000 francs). For delivery, see Register Vbb 9, fol. 47v. Also see Chevallier, *Musée national du château de Fontainebleau* (1996), no. 58, pp. 88 – 89.

7. A second vase had been planned from the beginning: its components existed in various phases of production (unfired, bisque, glazed) prior to commencement of the decoration process. Unfortunately, the relief had cracked before firing; and the resulting piece was judged defective. Consequently its sale price was set at 8,000 francs, despite the fact that its production costs (8,620.35 francs) were almost identical to those of the first vase. For entry in sales inventory, see Register Vv 2, fol. 96, no. 23 and Carton Pb 9 bis, "appréciations 1835." For delivery, see Register Vbb 11, fol. 25v.

8. Although pieces attributed to Palissy were still quite rare in public sales, Brongniart bought the first to enter the Musée Céramique in 1827 from a sale of Dominique-Vivant Denon's collection. The second was acquired from comte Lancelot-Théodore Turpin de Crissé. (I would like to thank Sylvie Millasseau for this information). The proximity of the dates of these two purchases and that of commencement of the first *vase 'de la Renaissance'* was probably not accidental.

9. Brongniart and Riocreux, *Description méthodique du musée* (1845), P, pl. 2, no. 2.

10. Chenavard, *Nouveau recueil de décorations intérieures* (1833), pl. 31.

11. A review of the Louvre exhibition of productions of the royal manufactories published in the *Journal des Débats* on January 1, 1833 made the following observation about the vase: "Monsieur Chenavard . . . has tried to prove with this effort that colored sculpture can advantageously replace . . . modeled painting. It is said that colored sculpture is more economical and more effective" [Monsieur Chenavard . . . a cherché à prouver par cet essai, que la sculpture coloriée peut remplacer avec avantage . . . la peinture modelée. La sculpture coloriée, dit-on, est plus économique et produit plus d'effet]. On the other hand, the Parisian porcelain producer Nast wrote to Brongniart on January 14, 1833: "Being by taste a zealous partisan of the purest possible classicism, I must acknowledge to you that I am astonished that there are artists at the Sèvres manufactory capable of executing this genre, more bizarre and extraordinary than pure and refined, covered with an overabundance of rich sculpture in a style that, in my opinion, has a more pronounced tendency toward depravation or rather decadence than toward the progress of the arts" [Etant par goût zelé partisan du classique le plus pur qu'il soit possible, je vous avoue que je m'étonne qu'à la manufacture de Sèvres il se soit trouvé des artistes capables d'exécuter ce genre bizarre et plus extraordinaire que pur et recherché, couvert d'une surabondance de richesse de sculpture dans un stile, qui a mon avis, a une tendance plus prononcée vers la depravation ou plutot la décadence que vers le progrès des arts] Carton U 8, dossier "exposition de 1832/1833."

80.
Design and Decoration for a Vase, 1833
Called *Vase 'Flamand C'*

Claude-Aimé Chenavard
Watercolor and ink on paper
16 7/8 x 14 in. (43 x 35.5 cm)
Inscription: [recto, bottom, in ink, in the hand of Denis-Désiré Riocreux] *C. / Vase flamand dans le style du XVIe siècle par Mr Chenavard / Nov.^{bre} 1833.*
Inv. no. D § 8 1833 N° 1

The date inscribed on this sheet tallies with that of a payment made to Claude-Aimé Chenavard for "three wash drawings of Flemish vases in the style of the sixteenth century."[1] In his earlier *vase 'de la Renaissance'*, Chenavard had explored the domain of colored sculptural decoration in ceramics, thereby encouraging a nascent interest in glazed earthenware (see cat. no. 79). In the three *vases 'Flamands'* (A, B, and C) Chenavard again drew inspiration from a type of ceramics that was little known, if not actively despised, by most of his contemporaries: Flemish and German stoneware of the Renaissance, which also features brightly colored relief ornament.[2]

The two first *vases 'Flamands C'* to be completed entered the sales inventory on April 25, 1835; according to the register, one had "gold relief ornament diverse grounds and heightening in various colors" and the other "relief ornament heightened in soft violet and various colors. Some parts of the ornament in burnished gilding."[3] The presence of these bright colors, and especially the gold, can only have served to emphasize the absurdity of imitating stoneware in porcelain. One of the vases was presented at the Louvre on May 1, 1835 (with examples of the two other forms from the series). On May 31, 1837 both completed 'C' vases were presented to Edmond Duponchel, one of the "playwrights whose works have been performed for the royal family."[4] A third example, painted in the Paris workshop that had been set up by Brongniart in the manufactory's salesroom and completed on April 27, 1839, was sold on May 20 to a M. Clodvil.[5] The vase was illustrated in the *Description méthodique du musée* (see fig. 80a).[6]

There is rare documentary proof of the influence of these novel productions. In 1839 Brongniart corresponded with the painter Jules-Claude Ziegler, who was then designing stained-glass window cartoons for the manufactory and at the same time establishing a stoneware workshop with his brother in Voisinlieu. On June 18, 1839, Ziegler wrote to Brongniart: "Chenavard previously designed for Sèvres three vases in the genre of Flemish stoneware that were executed in porcelain; the models exist today as mementos of a kind in the ceramics gallery. I would like to take casts of the pieces of these vases after coating them with thick oil . . . I would not make this request if I did not know . . . that you are interested in my brother's desire to introduce some good taste and some formal beauty in pottery properly speaking; also my brother is full of gratitude for everything you've already done for him."[7]

In 1845 the manufactory began work on a vase of similar inspiration, with "form and decoration in the style of some sixteenth-century German stoneware ceramic vases."[8] It was inspired by a design devised and published in 1842 by the architect Léon Feuchère[9] (see cat. nos. 99, 101, 102, and 110) and was christened the *vase 'Léon'* in his honor. An example was presented at the Louvre exhibition of June 1, 1846.[10]

Inscription: ["C. / Vase flamand in the style of the sixteenth century by M. Chenavard / November 1833"]

1. [3 dessins au lavis de vases flamands dans le style du 16e siècle.] Register Vj', 40 (1833), fol. 282 and Carton Pb 8, liasse 2, dossier 4, "vases." Chenavard received a total of 250 francs for the three drawings.
2. Such pieces were rare on the Parisian market prior to 1833. A few examples include: "pots de Flandre gothique," M[asso]n sale, Paris, May 4 – 8, 1819; "terres de Flandres," Barbier sale, Paris, March 9 – 10, 1829; "grès de Flandres," Paris, November 7 – 9, 1831.
3. "Ornements en relief en or fonds divers et rechampis en couleurs divers" [ornements en relief rechampis en violet tendre et couleurs divers. Quelques parties des ornements en or poli] Carton Pb 9 bis, valuations for 1835. The sale price of the first vase was initially set at 350 francs, that of the second at 275 francs, with the cost of the blank porcelain being set at 120 francs. On June 20, 1835, the prices were changed to 275 francs for the first and 325 for the second (Register Vv 2, fol. 96, no. 25 and fol. 96, no. 50.)
4. Register Vbb 9, fol. 12v.
5. For entry in sales inventory, see Register Vv 3, fol. 52v., no. 2 and Carton Pb 10 bis, valuations for 1839. For sale, see Register Vz 6, fol. 10.
6. Brongniart and Riocreux, *Description méthodique du musée* (1845), P, pl. I, no. 3.
7. [Chenavard a dessiné autrefois pour Sèvres trois vases dans le genre des grès flamands lesquels ont été exécutés en porcelaine; les modèles existent aujourd'huy à l'état de souvenirs dans la galerie céramique. Je désire pouvoir surmouler les pièces de ces vases passés à l'huile grasse . . . Je ne ferais pas cette demande si je ne savais . . . que vous portez quelqu'intérêt au désir qu'a mon frère d'introduire quelque bon gout et quelque beauté de formes dans la poterie proprement dite; aussi mon frère est plein de reconnaissance de ce que vous avez déjà fait pour lui] Carton Ob 11, dossier Ziegler. A replica of this vase was produced in stoneware by Ziegler (Werren, "Jules Claude Ziegler" (1995), figs. 7 and 8).
8. *Notice . . . 1er juin, 1846*, no. 29.
9. Feuchère, *Art industriel* [1842], pt. 1, pl. 3 (left).
10. *Notice . . . 1er juin, 1846*, no. 29.

Fig. 80a. Vases, including *vases 'Flamand A'* and *'B'* by Claude-Aimé Chenavard. (From Brongniart and Riocreux, *Description méthodique du musée de la manufacture royale de porcelaine de Sèvres* [1845], pl. 1)

Guéridon chinois par Mr Chenavard. 1833.
Sèvres

81.
Design and Decoration for the *Guéridon 'Chinois'* and *Déjeuner 'Chinois',* 1833

Claude-Aimé Chenavard
Watercolor, ink, and gouache on paper
15 x 9 1/2 in. (38.2 x 24.1 cm)
Inscription: [recto, bottom, in ink, in the hand of Denis-Désiré Riocreux] *Gueridon chinois par Mr Chenavard. 1833*
Inv. no. D § 10 1833 N° 1 A

The projects assigned Claude-Aimé Chenavard in November 1833 included, in addition to the design of the three *vases 'Flamands'* (see cat. no. 80), "three designs for the Chinese *guéridon,*"[1] a telling indication of this ornamentalist's considerable range. Here again, it might be that the idea originated with the artist or, perhaps more likely, with Brongniart, whose involvement with the museum project had intensified his interest in ceramics of all regions and historical periods. The progress file indicates that Chenavard intervened several times during the creation of this complex ensemble, altering maquettes and models. The white gouache correction of the stand supporting the coffeepot on this sheet may have been made during one of those modifications.

All of the bronze fittings for these pieces were executed by Louis-Honoré Boquet, who was also in charge of executing the ivory decorations which were closely identified with the "Chinese" style during the period (see cat. no. 75). These elements were intended to hide the joinery, as, for example, the small ivory lion heads that masked the seams on the openwork apron of the *guéridon.*

The *guéridon* entered the sales inventory on April 25, 1835, accompanied only by the coffee pot, the individual object most closely linked with composition of this *gueridon.*[2] The ensemble was presented at the Louvre exhibition of May 1, 1835, and delivered, on Louis-Philippe's orders, to the quarters of "His Royal Highness Monseigneur the duc d'Orléans" at the Palais des Tuileries on October 15, 1837.[3]

The rest of the *déjeuner* rendered on this sheet by Chenavard was only realized much later, for the ensemble of the *déjeuner 'Chinois Chenavard'* did not enter the sales inventory until April 29, 1842.[4] When it was exhibited at the Louvre on May 1, 1842, Brongniart noted in the catalogue: "Only the coffeepot was designed by the late Chenavard. M. Hyacinthe Régnier designed the other pieces and tried to make them harmonize with the style of this coffeepot."[5]

It was just at this time that Chinese influence began to have a major impact in the decorative arts, and many Sèvres pieces were inspired by the forms, glazes, and decorations of authentic Chinese models (see cat. nos. 75, 76, and 101). Careful scientific examination of Chinese wares also prompted the development of new immersion techniques for the application of ground colors, which produced results notable for their translucency.

By the second quarter of the nineteenth century, collectors began to emulate their eighteenth-century predecessors, seeking out authentic Chinese monochromatic pieces which they set in elaborate gilt bronze mounts. The richness and subtlety of Chinese glazes, however, primarily interested ceramists, who aspired to develop their own equivalents. In 1845 Alphonse-Louis Salvetat and Jacques-Joseph Ebelmen, then *directeur-adjoint* and subsequently Alexandre Brongniart's successor, were directed by Brongniart to research Chinese glazes and conduct experiments in an attempt to reproduce them.[6]

1. [Trois dessins pour le gueridon chinois.] Carton Pb 8, liasse 2, dossier 3, travaux de 1833 – 34, no. 14 on the list of "grandes pièces diverses"; Register Vj' 40 (1833), fol. 282.
2. This coffeepot resembles a piece illustrated in a work published by William Chambers in London in 1757 (*Designs of Chinese Buildings, Furniture, Dresses, Machines and Utensils*...).
3. For entry in the sales inventory, see Register Vv 2, fol. 96, no. 22 and fol. 97, no. 2, and Carton Pb 8, liasse 2, dossier 3. Production costs for the guéridon were estimated at 7,535 francs, including 1,910 francs for the blank porcelain, 1,120 francs for the mounts, 300 francs for the drawings, and 2,550 francs for the paintings by Pierre Huard. The sale price was set at 8,000 francs.
4. For entry in the sales inventory, see Register Vv 3, fol. 101, no. 17.
5. [La cafetière seule a été composée par feu Chenavard. M. Hyacinthe Regnier a composé les autres pièces et a cherché à les accorder avec le style de cette cafetière] *Notice... 1er Mai 1842*, no. 27.
6. Ebelmen and Salvetat, *Recherches sur la composition des matières* (1852).

82.
Decoration for a Cup, 1833
Called *Tasse 'Litron Fragonard'*, from the *Déjeuner 'Du Guesclin'*

1833
Jean-Charles-François Leloy
Watercolor, gouache and pencil on paper (two drawings originally side-by-side on a single sheet have been cut and the left half glued above the right half, eliminating the left portion of the inscription)
11 3/4 x 5 3/4 in. (29.9 x 14.5 cm)
Inscriptions: [recto, bottom left, in ink, in the hand of Denis-Désiré Riocreux] *dejeuner de Duguesclin* [sic] *de 1833. / Decoration coloriée de la tasse Lit*[on] *fragonard, par Mr Leloy*; [in a roundel on the lower cup (gouache)] *Clisson*; [on a small band of paper glued to the center of the sheet, in ink] *Intérieur de la Tasse*
Inv. no. D § 4 1833 N° 5 A

In August 1833 Jean-Charles-François Leloy was paid 280 francs for six work sessions devoted to the placement of ink guidelines on objects and the execution of color schemes for different pieces of the *déjeuner 'de Clisson'*.[1] This service included parts of an earlier ensemble. The tray decoration was based on an oil study originally made in 1818 by Pierre-Nolasque Bergeret for a *déjeuner* embellished with "subjects taken from the history of Duguesclin (sic) and Clisson."[2]

Apart from the compositions on their trays and the Gothic Revival ornament appropriate to the figures being commemorated, the two ensembles were quite different from one another. The first had a blue ground with gold and platinum decoration, and all of its reserves represented episodes from the lives of these two French heros, whereas the later one was decorated with portraits executed, in the words of the catalogue of the Louvre exhibition of May 1, 1835, "after the most authentic sources that could be found." The lancet arches against a brown ground seen in the drawing correspond with the description inscribed in the inventory register, but this decoration was in fact limited to the upper part of the pieces, the balance having been left white, probably in response to complaints that Sèvres's ornamental schemes tended to obscure the pristine surfaces of the porcelain.[3]

Probably because such minutely detailed Gothic Revival schemes were becoming unfashionable (see cat. no. 97), this *déjeuner* — like the *service 'de la Chevalerie'* completed in 1834 (see cat. no. 71) — never found a buyer, and eventually, in 1875, it was delivered directly to the Musée Céramique.[4] It therefore played no role in fulfilling the mission assigned to the manufactory's commercial products by one critic, who wrote that, if such products were to circulate, "not only would public taste be shaped by the study of good models, but small pieces that are perfectly formed and of the best quality would be sold to the less prosperous, functioning in salons as examples prompting the bizarre objects produced each year by fashionable caprice to be valued no higher than their just worth."[5] (See fig. 82a.)

Inscription: ["déjeuner of Duguesclin (sic) of 1833. / colored decoration for the Litron cup Fragonard, by M. Leloy"]; ["Clisson"]; ["inside of the cup"]
1. Register Vj' 40 (1833), fols. 3 ff.
2. This first *déjeuner*, which included twenty-four plates, was exhibited at the Louvre on January 1, 1819, and was subsequently presented by Louis XVIII to the duc d'Angoulême. For entry in sales inventory, see Register Vv 1, fol. 115, no. 21. For delivery, see Register Vbb 5, fol. 18.
3. For entry in sales inventory, see Carton Pb 9 bis, appréciation of April 10, 1835 and Register Vv 2, fol. 95, no. 10. Also see Alcouffe, Dion-Tenenbaum, and Ennès, *Un âge d'or*, exhib. cat. (1991), no. 140, pp. 271 – 72.
4. Register Vaa 3, fol. 88.
5. [Non seulement le goût public pourrait se former par l'étude de bons modèles, mais encore que de petites pièces parfaites dans leurs formes et du meilleur choix pourraient être vendues à des fortunes mediocres et devenir dans les salons des types qui servaient à apprécier à leur juste valeur les bizarreries que le caprice de la mode produit chaque année]. Nestor Urbain in *Le Temps*, May 14, 1835.

83.
Decoration for a Tray from the *Déjeuner* *'La Récolte du cacao et le chocolat'*, 1833

Jean-Charles Develly
Gouache on paper glued to heavy paper
11 1/4 x 15 1/8 in. (28.5 x 38.3 cm)
Inscription: [recto, bottom in ink, in the hand of Denis-Désiré Riocreux] *La Récolte du Cacao et sa première préparation; composé par / Mr. Develly, d'apres les indications de MM. de Humboldt et Rugendas / et exécuté par le même sur un plateau ovale de Dejené en 1834 – 35*
Inv. no. F § 5 1846 N° 6

This is a rare instance of an ensemble being produced twice. Jean-Charles Develly does not seem to have received separate payment for the composition drawings for this *déjeuner*, but he did receive two fees for painting them on porcelain on two separate occasions. The first ensemble entered the sales inventory on December 28, 1833; it was shown at the Louvre on May 1, 1835, and was presented to Manuel de Miraflorès the following June.[1] The second service, which was very similar, entered the inventory on December 24, 1836 and was delivered to the Queen Marie-Amélie on August 21, 1837.[2]

When the first *déjeuner* was exhibited at the Louvre, Brongniart noted in the catalogue that the tray depicted "a site in Mexico representing, according to MM Humboldt, Rugendas, etc., the harvest and preliminary preparation of cocoa, ... the decoration, consisting of Mexican motifs selected in [the published account] of the voyage of M. Humboldt, was devised by M. Leloy." In fact, the vivid contrast between the genre scenes in sombre colors and the white surfaces of the pieces is considerable, notwithstanding the presence of the brightly hued "Mexican" ornament. Nonetheless, the return of white surfaces met with general approval. *Déjeuners* were among the preferred gifts of Louis-Philippe and Marie-Amélie,[3] and Develly's meticulously rendered genre scenes continued to be appreciated despite changes in taste.

When oval *déjeuner* trays made their first appearance at Sèvres in January 1811, they were sometimes identified in the documents as "Viennese form" (*forme de Vienne*).[4] This designation may have been occasioned by an exchange gift sent by the Austrian manufactory in 1806, which featured a tray of this shape.[5]

Inscription: ["The Cacao harvest and the initial preparation; designed by / M. Develly, according to information supplied by MM de Humboldt and Rugendas / executed by the same on an oval Dejené tray in 1834 – 35"]

1. For entry in the sales inventory, see Carton Pb 8, valuations for 1833, and Register Vv 2, fol. 75, no. 46 (sale price of the ensemble, complete with case, 2,685 francs). For delivery, see Register Vbb 9, fol. 4v.
2. For entry in the sales inventory, see Vv 3, fol. 13v, no. 31. For delivery, see Register Vbb 9, fol. 16v.
3. Barbe, "Déjeuners en porcelaine de Sèvres" (1990).
4. Register Vu 1, fol. 107v., no. 267 – 9, January 31, 1811: "Déjeuner tray oval form gold ground, gold relief etc." [Plateau de dejeuner de forme ovale fond d'or, or relief etc.]. The same object is described as follows on the valuation sheet: "Déjeuner tray Viennese form gold ground gilded relief acanthus leaves in gold and burgos border in gray" [Plateau de déjeuner forme de Vienne fond d'or dorure relief feuilles d'acante en or et burgos bordure en gris] Carton Pb 2, liasse 1.
5. Carton T 2, liasses 1 and 2; and Faÿ-Hallé and Mundt, *La Porcelaine Européenne* (1983), ill. 78, p. 60.

84.
Design for the *Surtout 'des Comestibles'*, 1834

Alexandre-Evariste Fragonard
Pencil and ink wash on paper
11 x 18 5/8 in. (28 x 47.2 cm)
Inscriptions: [recto, top center, in pencil] *vase bon* [word illegible]; [below the drawings, left to right] *liqueurs [lined out]-viande-confiserie-Farine*; [slightly lower] *Echelle de 3 p. . . 3 pieds*; [bottom center, in the hand of Alexandre Brongniart] *Projet d'un surtout des comestibles dans le style grec / par M. fragonard (fevrier 1834)*; [lower left] *remis le 21 fevrier à M. Regnier / pour etre execute en maquette*
Inv. no. 1995 D 11

Brongniart, early in 1834, began to revive the centerpiece format at Sevres by initiating two projects simultaneously, both consisting of five pieces and both based on "dining" themes, but made in different styles. The first commission, in the "Greek" style, was assigned to Alexandre-Evariste Fragonard, while the second, in the "Renaissance style," was assigned to Claude-Aimé Chenavard (see cat. no. 85). The documents leave no doubt, however, that it was Brongniart himself who devised the theme and determined what pieces were to be included.

This drawing, an overall view of the "Greek" centerpiece, corresponds to a set of guidelines sent to Fragonard on February 13, 1834[1]. On March 25, the artist received a payment of 60 francs for this design, described in the register as "composition and general sketch of the dining centerpiece."[2] The initial scheme called for a central element (plinth or tripod supporting a vase) alluding to the meat or game course. It was to be flanked by two bowls, one for fresh fruit (supported by a palm tree) and the other for sweets, such as sugared almonds, and whole cooked fruit (supported by a bundle of sugar cane). The end pieces took the form of rythons, the first for farinaceous plants and the second for liquors.

Although the four side pieces were realized much as they appear in the initial design, the central element was completely reconceived in April 1834, in response to criticism voiced, according to Brongniart, "by myself and at least five other persons."[3] The base had previously been enlarged to accommodate figures of a shepherd and Diana with their attributes, and Brongniart specified further: "take care that this piece [not] have a front and a back, which would be inappropriate for the middle of a table; this requires reflection and experiment; we must discuss it."[4] Apart from designing the pieces to be seen in the round, the principal other change involved replacing the vase originally envisioned in this drawing with a figure of Comus — the ancient god of banquets — accompanied by children. In this unusual assignment, Fragonard was charged not only with producing the drawings but also with personally shaping all of the sculptural elements.

The centerpiece, produced in biscuit porcelain with areas of matte gold, entered the sales inventory on December 24, 1836.[5] It was shown at the Louvre exhibition of May 1, 1838, but remained in the Sèvres warehouse until the Second Republic (1848 – 51).[6] Its individual pieces and a view of the complete ensemble are illustrated in the *Description méthodique du musée* (see fig. 84a).[7]

It is difficult today to understand how this eclectic ensemble could have been thought to be in the "Greek" style. The designation cannot have been prompted by the white and gold color scheme: although this restrained palette was used under the Empire for the *jattes 'Famin'* and the *déjeuner Régnier* (see cat. nos. 19 and 31), both of classical inspiration, it was also used for the *vase 'de la Renaissance Fragonard'*, which was conceived in 1834 but characterized by an ornamental opulence that is anything but Greek.[8] It was probably the use of antique forms — tripods and rythons — that occasioned the description for this centerpiece. Finally, there is a distinct resemblance between the two footed bowls with seated infants on their bases and the large *corbeille 'Palmier'* designed by Fragonard in 1820, an example of which was produced in 1833, also with white and gold decoration.[9]

Inscription: ["vase good"]; ["liqueurs-meat-sweetmeats-Flour"]; ["Scale of 3 ft . . . 3 feet"]; ["design for a surtout in the Grecian style / by M. Fragonard (February 1834)"]; ["sent on 21 February to M. Régnier / for a model to be made"]

1. Carton Pb 9, liasse 1, dossier "Services et déjeuners."
2. [Composition et croquis general du surtout des comestibles] Register Vj' 41 (1834), fols. 250 ff.
3. Carton Pb 9, liasse 1, dossier "Services et déjeuners."
4. Ibid.
5. Carton Pb 9 bis, valuations for 1836 and Register Vv 3, fol. 13, nos. 16 – 18.
6. The bowls were delivered to the official residence of the president of the Assemblée Nationale on August 2, 1848 (Register Vbb 11, fol. 24v.). The central piece and the two rhythons were delivered to the Ministère de l' Agriculture et du Commerce on August 29, 1848 (Register Vbb 11, fol. 26).
7. Brongniart and Riocreux, *Description méthodique du musée* (1845), 1845, P., pl. X.
8. Alcouffe, Dion-Tenenbaum, and Ennès, *Un âge d'or*, exhib. cat. (1991), no. 139, pp. 270 – 71.
9. Casanova, *Le Porcellane francesi* (1974), no. 219, p. 317.

Fig. 84a. A general view and designs for elements in the *surtout 'des Comestibles'* by Alexandre-Evariste Fragonard. (From Brongniart and Riocreux, *Description méthodique du musée* [1845] P., pl. 10)

85.
Confit Dish Design for the *Surtout 'des Comestibles'*, 1834

Claude-Aimé Chenavard
Watercolor, pencil, and ink on paper
23 1/8 x 30 in. (58.6 x 76.2 cm)
Inscriptions: [recto, bottom center in ink, in the hand of Denis-Désiré Riocreux] *La confiserie, pour le Surtout des comestibles / par Mr A. Chenavard, 24 juillet 1834*; [right, level with base] *bronze bronze / un plateau à ajouter*
Inv. no. D § 6 1834 N° 11

On February 13, 1834, Brongniart sent instructions to Claude-Aimé Chenavard asking him to design a centerpiece in "Renaissance style or any other that you like but not antique."[1] The same day he also sent guidelines to A.-E. Fragonard for a "Greek style" centerpiece (see cat. no. 84). Chenavard decided to use a high relief decoration with intensely colored highlights similar to those he had adopted for the *vase 'de la Renaissance'* (see cat. no. 79). The central element of this *surtout* was to represent meat, vegetables, and grains; it was to be flanked by two pieces for fish and game, and end bowls for liquors and sweets. This drawing ("drawing in india-ink wash one half actual size") is for the bowl for sweets, and the artist received 350 francs for it in July 1834.[2]

In this case, little was altered when the ensemble was finally realized. The low-relief elements on the bases were conceived and executed by Alexandre-Evariste Fragonard, but the seated putti were made by the sculptor Jean-Jacques Feuchère. Beginning the same year, Chenavard and Feuchère collaborated on another centerpiece which was very similar in style to this one but executed in bronze, and had been commissioned by the duc d'Orléans.[3]

The complete *surtout* entered the sales inventory at the same time as the Fragonard centerpiece, on December 24, 1836[4]. Like Fragonard's, it was shown at the Louvre on May 1, 1838, and illustrated in the *Description du musée céramique.*[5] In a note of March 25, 1836, concerning the *service 'Historique de Fontainebleau'* then in production, Brongniart proposed to use it in conjunction with this centerpiece, noting that it was in a "style consistent with the dominant decoration of the château."[6] His suggestion was not accepted, and in 1846 Louis-Philippe presented the centerpiece to the sultan of the Ottoman Empire.[7]

The ensemble was criticized by some, particularly for its unusual iconography: "This is certainly not the work of a delicate epicurean; it was conceived at the slaughterhouse and executed in the kitchen . . . The catalogue specifies that this grotesque centerpiece was executed by M. Chenavard in accordance with *a given program.* We can only pity the talent thus subjected to the dictates of bad taste."[8] The designs pointed toward the future, however. Far from emulating past models, like the Fragonard centerpiece, these pieces anticipate productions of the faience workshop that was established at Sèvres under the Second Empire.[9] It was only later, at the Louvre exhibition of June 1, 1846, that the manufactory displayed its first pieces inspired by Italian, rather than French, earthenware.

Inscription: ["The sweetmeat dish, for the *surtout 'des Comestibles'* / by Mr. A. Chenavard, 24 July 1834"]; ["bronze bronze / one dish to be added"]

1. [Style de la renaissance ou comme on voudra mais pas antique.] Carton Pb 9, liasse 1, dossier "Services et déjeuners." The earliest reference to such a centerpiece seems to be a September 1833 note concerning a "Design for a centerpiece composed of the animals and fruit that figure in meals and banquets or contribute to them . . . to be executed by Messieurs Chenavard and Barye in concert" [Projet d'un surtout de table composé d'animaux et de fruits qui entrent dans les repas et banquets ou qui y contribuent . . . à exécuter de concert par Mrs. Chenavard et Barye.] Carton U 15, liasse 3, dossier 3). Antoine-Louis Barye was the principal sculptor of the centerpiece for the duc d'Orléans (see n.3, below).
2. [Dessin lavé à l'encre de la chine de grandeur de moitié de l'exécution.] Register Vj' 41 (1834), fols. 252 ff.
3. Benoist, *La Sculpture romantique* (1995), ill. 13. There is also a noteworthy resemblance between the comfit dish in the present drawing and a "Soup tureen executed by M. F . . . goldsmith in Paris" reproduced in an album of compositions by Chenavard (Chenavard, *Nouveau recueil de décorations intérieures* [1833], pl. 34), notably in the overhanging figures of the handles and the presence of putti on the base.
4. Carton Pb 9 bis, valuations for 1836 and Register Vv 3, fol. 13, nos. 13 – 15. Total sale price 40,000 francs.
5. Brongniart and Riocreux, *Description méthodique du musée céramique* (1845), P, pl. 11.
6. Carton Pb 8, liasse 2, dossiers 1 – 2.
7. Register Vbb 11, fol. 10v.
8. [Certes, ce n'est pas là l'oeuvre d'un délicat épicurien: c'est conçu à l'abattoir et executé à la cuisine . . . Le livret avertit que ce grotesque surtout a été exécuté par M. Chenavard sur un *programme donné.* Plaignons le talent soumis aux écarts du mauvais goût]. From a review of the Louvre exhibition published in the May 25, 1838 issue of *Le Constitutionnel.*
9. The game bowl was later copied in the earthenware workshop of the manufacture by Jean-Denis Larue (see Aslin, *French Exhibition Pieces* [1973], fig. 16).

Fig. 85a. Elements in a *surtout* by Claude-Aimé Chenavard. (From Brongniart and Riocreux, *Description méthodique du musée* [1845], P., pl. 11)

86.
Decoration for a Vase, 1835
Called *Vase 'Jasmin cornet'*

Jean-Charles-François Leloy
Watercolor and pencil on paper
10 7/8 x 8 5/8 in. (27.5 x 22 cm)
Inscription: [recto, bottom, in ink, in the hand of Denis-Désiré Riocreux] *Décoration de Vase Jasmin Ire Les Hommes illustres dans l'Industrie céramique / (par Mr Leloy. Juillet 1835)*
Inv. no. D § 8 1835 N° 2 (1er)

The court of King Louis-Philippe, far more peripatetic than those of Louis XVIII and Charles X, was constantly moving between "private" châteaus and official residences. Refurbishing the many apartments of these royal residences required not only large decorative vases but also many smaller and simpler ones. It was left to Brongniart to anticipate the quantities that would be needed, and above all to determine subjects appropriate for their embellishment. Increasing sophistication about historical ceramics, in part the result of patient research by Riocreux, suggested several new decorative programs. This *vase 'Jasmin Cornet'*, for example, one of a pair, celebrates famous men of "the ceramics industry" and is adorned accordingly with medallion portraits of two celebrated Renaissance ceramists: Lucca della Robbia and Bernard Palissy.

In June 1835 Jean-Charles-François Leloy was paid for two work sessions devoted to these pieces: among others he produced "an overall half-scale color drawing against a white ground."[1] In August of the same year, he received 20 francs for a series of drawings of attributes from French and Italian Renaissance pottery, which were probably for the backs of these vases. Judging from this sheet, the earlier portraits devised by Alexandre-Evariste Fragonard for the vase dedicated to famous potters, which was shown in the New Year's exhibition of 1819 – 20 at the Louvre, were not reused for this project, despite the fact that the two artists in question, della Robbia and Palissy, had also figured in Fragonard's scheme.

Two vases *'Jasmin Cornet'* (first size), with purplish brown grounds, painted cameo portraits, and ornament in gold, platinum, and various colors entered the sales inventory on September 20, 1834. Five days later they were delivered to the Château de Saint-Cloud.[2] Given the absence of any payment records for corresponding new projects, it seems likely that these designs were used again for two *vases 'Gothique Fragonard'* that entered the sales inventory on August 11, 1837, when they were described in identical terms; these vases were delivered to the Château de Compiègne on August 11, 1837.[3]

Although both della Robbia and Palissy are Renaissance figures, Leloy made no accommodating alterations in his customary dry style and used many decorative motifs which do not date to the period. The spareness of the design was probably determined in part by economic considerations.

Inscription: ["Decoration for vase Jasmin 1st famous men in the ceramics industry"]

1. [Un dessin d'ensemble général demi grandeur colorié sur fond blanc] Register Vj' 42 (1835), fols 3 ff.
2. For entry in the sales inventory, see Carton Pb 9 bis, appréciations 1834 and Register Vv 2, fol. 87v., no. 50 (production expenses for each vase, 397.50 francs, including 270 francs for the painter Pierre Riton; sale price, 450 francs). For delivery, see Register Vbb 9, fol. 41v.
3. For entry in the sales inventory, see Carton Pb 9 bis, valuation sheets for 1837 and Register Vv 3, fol. 24v, no. 26 (production expenses for each vase, 442.80 francs; sale price, 500 francs). For delivery, see Register Vbb 9, fol. 46.

87.
Design for a Mantelpiece, 1835

Eugène Dubreuil
Watercolor and ink on paper
8 1/4 x 10 1/2 in. (21 x 26.7 cm)
Inscriptions: [recto, at left, in red ink, in the hand of Dubreuil (?), bottom to top] *12c / 4m515 / 30c*; [within the drawing, at left, in red ink, in the hand of Dubreuil (?)] *A / B / C / D*; [within the drawing, on left pillar] *FP*; [within the drawing, on right pillar] *LP*; [below the drawing in bank ink] *Echelle*; [bottom, in ink, in the hand of Denis-Désiré Riocreux] *cheminée exécutée en biscuit de porcelaine, pour le Salon dit des Tapisseries, au palais de Fontainebleau, Travaux de 1838 / Dessin de Mr Dubreuil architecte du Palais.*
Inv. no. D § 10 1848 N° 15A

On April 26, 1836, Brongniart recounted the history of this mantelpiece in a letter to Agathon Baron Fain, Intendant Général: "On June 2, 1835, M. Dubreuil sent me directly a colored sketch for a mantel ordered by the king for Fontainebleau. On June 28 and 30, I had the honor of discussing it with the king at Sèvres and Versailles. His Majesty confirmed the intentions he had stated to M. Dubreuil, but he also indicated some changes to be made in the composition of this mantelpiece. I communicated these observations to M. Dubreuil."[1] This letter was an answer to another one Brongniart had just received, informing him that King Louis-Philippe desired that the mantelpiece be completed and installed by May 6 or 7; Brongniart protested that this quick delivery was impossible: "Since then I have had no communication from M. Dubreuil. I know only that this architect wanted to have the models made under his own direction . . . . On last March 29th, he asked me for the sketch . . . and on the 18th of this month a skillful modeler, M. Jules Klagmann, who said that M. Dubreuil had asked him to make this model, came to request information about trimming the plaques for mounting. Finally, on the 21st of this month, M. Dubreuil returned the sketch . . . but without an accompanying note of any kind."[2] It is likely that Brongniart did not appreciate the manufactory's being used as a simple fabricant.

Nonetheless, in deference to the royal will, work proceeded rapidly. The models were delivered by Klagmann in early July 1836, and on February 26, 1837, Brongniart made a note listing changes stipulated by the king. Essentially, these amounted to the elimination of ornamental details alluding to his own reign. The completed mantelpiece entered the sales inventory on April 29, 1837,[3] and was delivered to Fontainebleau on May

10 — on the express order of the sovereign and against the wishes of Brongniart, who wanted to display it at the next exhibition at the Louvre. In fact, when this event took place in 1838, the mantelpiece was temporarily returned to the manufactory for the exhibition.[4]

The drawing can offer only a vague approximation of the effect produced by the actual mantelpiece. Its figures and reliefs are in biscuit with matte gilding set against rich, enamel-colored grounds. The illustration in the *Description méthodique du musée* gives a clear representation of it (see fig. 87a), and also accurately reflects the modifications requested by Louis-Philippe.[5] The piece is still at Fontainebleau.

Inscription: ["Mantelpiece made in biscuit porcelain, for the so-called Tapestry Chamber in the Palace of Fontainebleau, work executed in 1838 / Design by Mr. Dubreuil, the palace architect"]

1. [Le 2 Juin 1835 M. Dubreuil me remis directement un croquis coloré pour une cheminée demandé par le Roi poür Fontainebleau. Les 28 et 30 de juin, j'eus l'honneur d'en parler au Roi tant a Sevres qu'a Versailles. S.M. me confirma ses intentions manifestees a M. DuBreuil mais elle indiqua quelques changement à apporter à la composition de cette cheminée; je communiquai ces observations à M. Dubreuil.] Carton M 10, dossier 1, chemise "Pièces commandes par le Roi." The same file also contains documents explaining the various pencil indications on the drawing, and on another sheet Brongniart noted: "Drawing for mounting and decorations for the reduction of the mantelpiece. . . at Fontainebleau delivered on June 2, 1835 by M. Dubreuil, architect of this palace" [dessin pour l'ajustement et la decoration du retrecissement du foyer de cheminée de . . . à Fontainebleau remis le 2 juin 1835 par M. Dubreuil architecte de ce Palais].

2. [Depuis lors, je n'ai plus eu aucune communication de M. Dubreuil. Je sais seulement que cet architecte a desiré faire faire les modèles sous sa direction . . . le 29 mars dernier, il m'a fait demander le croquis . . . et le 18 de ce mois un modeleur habile, M. Jules Klagmann, chargé a-t-il dit par M. Dubreuil de faire ce modèle est venu prendre des renseignements pour les coupes de montage etc. Enfin le 21 de ce mois M. Dubreuil m'a ronvoye le croquis . . . mais sans l'accompagner d'aucune sorte de note.] The *modeleur habile* mentioned by Brongniart is Jean- Baptiste Klagmann. Along with his models he sent a cover letter in which he wrote: "I ardently desire, Monsieur, that this sample of my work might serve to establish professional relations with your beautiful manufactory if I might prove useful to you on some [future] occasion" [Je désire ardemment Monsieur que cet echantillon de mon travail puisse servir à me mettre en relation de travail avec votre belle manufacture si l'occasion se presentait de vous être utile]. Thereafter he was regularly assigned sculptural work, and he also created a few forms.

3. Register Vv 3, fol. 19, no. 97, and Carton Pb 9 bis, appréciations 1837. Total production expenses, 7,789.25 francs (including 4,200 francs for the bronze mounts but not covering payment for the models); sale price, 8,000 francs.

4. Register Vbb 9, fol. 12. See Chevallier, *Musée national du château de Fontainebleau* (1996), no. 201, pp. 207 – 9.

5. Brongniart and Riocreux, *Description méthodique du musée* (1845), P, pl. 7, no. 1.

Fig. 87a. Mantelpiece after Eugène Dubreuil and *déjeuner* (see cat. no. 78), 1837. (From Brongniart and Riocreux, *Description méthodique du musée* [1845], P, pl. 7)

88.
Designs for Plate Borders, 1835
Called *Assiettes 'Ornemanisées'*

Hyacinthe Régnier
Ink wash and pencil on paper
16 7/8 x 11 5/8 in. (43 x 29.5 cm)
Inv. no. D § 5 1835 N° 3.B

The circular plate with flat rim, which had been perfected in the last quarter of the eighteenth century, became the sole format used for plates made at Sèvres in the early nineteenth century. During the reign of Louis-Philippe, however, Brongniart seems to have felt a need for more varied models. The first step in this direction was taken in 1834 with the introduction of embossed ornament, called *bosselage à godrons* and *bosselage à ornements.* In these rim designs the low relief replaced painted or printed ornaments. The overlapping scales of the inner row created a gadrooned border. The plates remained circular in shape, however, and the relief designs only needed to be colored by hand.

In 1835 Hyacinthe Régnier was paid for fifteen designs for decorated plates or *assiettes 'Ornemanisées',* and the following year he was paid for nine more.[1] During the same two years, he made six different plaster models, retouching the impressed wax ornament for three of them.[2] The first blank examples were priced in October 1835,[3] and the first decorated plates entered the sales inventory on June 4, 1836, when they were described as having been highlighted in various colors.[4] Apparently very few of these plates were actually produced, for only one is cited in the form book, and, unlike the more animated designs conceived in the 1840s by Jules Peyre (see cat. no. 103), this design is not illustrated there.

The fact that the models developed by Hyacinthe Régnier are sometimes called *assiette 'Ornemanisé Cuir',* or "plates with leather strapwork ornament,"[5] suggests that he was inspired not by the painted arabesques on Italian Renaissance pottery but by the ornament reminiscent of interlaced leather bands that appeared in many prints of this period and in architectural settings such as the paneling of the Château de Fontainebleau.

Hyacinthe Régnier began his career by devising decorative motifs and then graduated to the design of entire pieces, primarily in the Renaissance and Chinese styles (see cat. no. 91).

1. Carton Pb 9 bis, appréciation February 28, 1835.
2. Register Va' 31, fol. 122 ff. In 1835, six drawings at 6 francs each are mentioned and nine drawings at 3 francs each. There is no fee breakdown for 1836, but fees for establishing the models ranged from 175 to 240 francs.
3. Carton Pb 8, liasse 4, conférence of October 24, 1835, "*assiette ornemanisé cuir* no. 1."
4. Carton Pb 9 bis, appréciations 1836 and Register Vv 3, fol. 5, nos. 12 – 15.
5. Carton Pb 8, liasse 4, conférence of October 24, 1835, "*assiette ornemanisé cuir* no. 1."

89.
Decoration for a Plate, 1835

Charles-Ernest Clerget
Gouache and pencil on paper
7 1/8 x 19 1/4 in. (18 x 26.2 cm)
Inscription: [recto, lower left, in ink, in the hand of Denis-Désiré Riocreux] *pour assiette, par Mr Clerget . . . août 1835*; [below the drawing, pencil, signature] *Clerget inv. et del.*
Inv. no. D § 5 1835 N° 5

In July 1835 the manufactory paid Charles-Ernest Clerget 12 francs for "two drawings of interlace for plate borders, done in watercolor" and 10 francs for "a color drawing of a plate with ornament."[1] One of the border designs was transferred onto a plaster model of a plate by Hyacinthe Régnier, who was then producing several models after his own designs (see cat. no. 88). Perhaps the scheme on this sheet was meant for the "Moresque Service with colored ornament in the moresque genre" initiated in 1826 – 27, abandoned in 1830, but which finally entered the sales inventory in two groups, in December 1836 and August 1838.[2]

Military expeditions and accounts published by travelers to the Middle East explain the new European interest in the decorative arts of this region. Many Sèvres pieces from this period bear witness to this artistic fascination (see cat. nos. 99, 102, 103, 109).

Clerget was a student of the ornamentalist Claude-Aimé Chenavard, but it is not known whether the latter played any role in Clerget's employment at Sèvres. Clerget may well have established contact with Brongniart through the Muséum d'Histoire Naturelle, for which he made many engravings, or he may be the "Clerget" who attended Brongniart's lectures in 1832 (see chap. 2). He also provided models for other Parisian porcelain producers[3] and published several albums of prints of ornament in various styles.[4]

1. [Deux dessins d'entrelas pour bord d'assiettes, fait à laquarelle]; [un dessin colorié d'assiette à ornement] Register Vj' 42 (1835), fol. 251.
2. Carton Pb 9 bis, valuation sheet dated November 26, 1836, dessert service with printed and colored moresque decor; Carton Pb 10 bis, appréciation dated August 24, 1838 for twenty-four similar plates decorated in their centers with portraits of famous Arabs.
3. Plinval de Guillebon, *Faïence et porcelaine de Paris* (1995), p. 305.
4. See, for example, Clerget, *De l'ornementation typographique* (1838); idem, *Mélanges d'ornements divers* (1838); and idem, *Nouveaux ornements* (1840).

90.
Decoration for a Vase, [1836–48]
Called *Vase 'Cratère'*

Antoine-Gabriel Willermet
Pencil and watercolor on paper
8 1/2 x 11 5/8 in. (21.5 x 29.6 cm)
Inscription: [recto, top, in ink, in the hand of Denis-Désiré Riocreux] *Vase Cratère-Vue de Twickenham, etc. travaux de 1840- 42*
Inv. no. D § 8 1848 N° 89 (1)

The head painter at the manufactory did not customarily document his own work in the registers, making it impossible to verify the date inscribed on this sheet. A first "Crater Vase . . . blue ground views of the château des Tuileries and Wickenham [sic]," slightly cracked, entered the sales inventory on April 30, 1836, and was delivered to the Grand Trianon on April 22, 1837.[1] A second example, unflawed but otherwise identical, entered the sales inventory on September 10, 1836 and was "delivered to Her Majesty the Queen as a gift for M. Lelong the owner of Twickenham" on the following October 3.[2] A third example entered the sales inventory on May 18, 1838, and the following July was delivered on Louis-Philippe's orders to his sister, Madame Adélaïde.[3] Yet another example was entered on February 8, 1848; it may well correspond to the present design.[4] Apparently the Orléans family had fond memories of the English country house where they had spent the last months of their long exile during the Napoleonic years.[5] Also in 1836, the painter Justin Ouvrié exhibited a view of the house at the Paris salon. The form of the *vase 'Cratère'*, designed in 1818, was often decorated with landscape compositions.

In 1825 Antoine-Gabriel Willermet was recruited by Brongniart to direct the manufactory's painting workshops. In defending his decision to the vicomte de La Rochefoucauld, Brongniart observed that "he is the most skillful porcelain flower painter who remains in Paris; he was head of M. Dagoty's painting workshops for eight years."[6] Willermet's file, in fact, reveals that he spent a total of seventeen years at Dagoty's establishment, and prior to that had worked for Dihl, another important Paris porcelain maker. This drawing is typical of his dry, meticulous neoclassical style, and it is not surprising to learn that his relations with the artists whose work he oversaw were extremely difficult. Documents reveal that many found his harping over trivial details meddlesome in the extreme. (see cat. nos. 96 and 97).

1. For entry in sales inventory, see Carton Pb 9 bis, appréciations 1836 and Register Vv 3, fol. 4, no. 25 (production expenses 1,043.75 francs; sale price 1,000 francs). For delivery, see Register Vbb 9, fol. 44v.
2. For entry in sales inventory, see Register Vv 3, fol. 9, no. 7. For delivery, see Register Vbb 9, fol. 9v. In fact, the vase was commissioned on August 27, 1835 (Register Vtt 4, fol. 102, "Coupe ou vase avec vue de Twickenham").
3. For entry in sales inventory, see Register Vv 3, fol. 37, no. 1. For delivery, see Register Vbb 9, fol. 21v.
4. For entry in sales inventory, see Register Vv 5, fol. 2, no. 9.
5. A representation of Twickenham, in Middlesex, England, seen from another perspective, appears on a plate in the *service 'Historique de Fontainebleau'* (see Chevallier, *Musée national du château de Fontainebleau* (1996), no. 285, p. 271).
6. Register Vc 7, letter dated February 17, 1825 and Carton Ob 11.4.

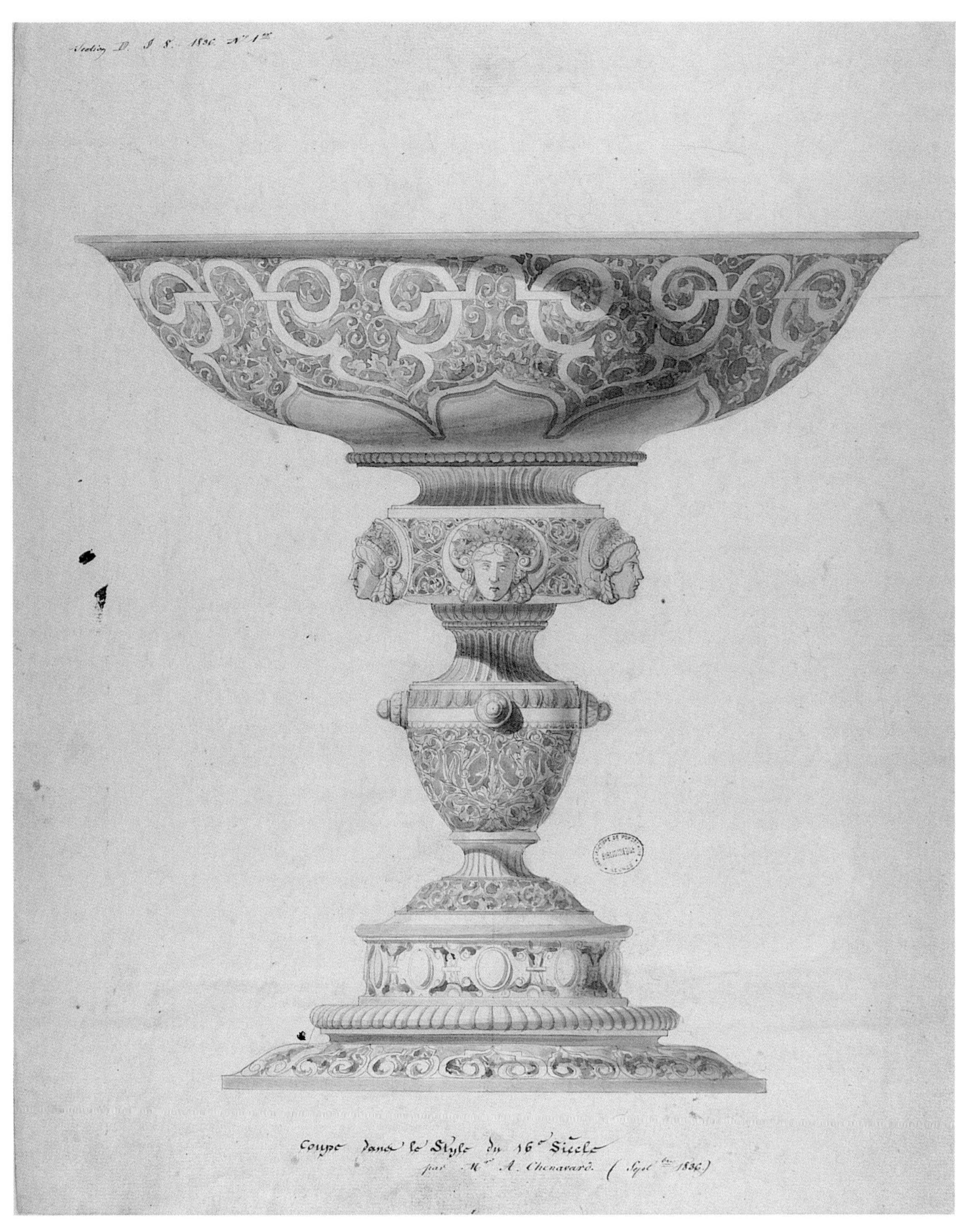

91.
Design and Decoration for a Goblet, 1836
Called *Coupe 'Chenavard'*

Watercolor, ink wash, and ink on paper
17 3/4 x 14 3/8 in. (45 x 36.5 cm)
Inscription: [recto, bottom, in ink, in the hand of Denis-Désiré Riocreux] *Coupe dans le style du 16e siècle / par Mr. A. Chenavard. (Septbre 1836.)*
Inv. no. D § 8 1836 N° 1er

Once again, the date inscribed on the sheet by Riocreux may not be entirely accurate. There is no record of any payment to Claude-Aimé Chenavard in the register that might correspond to this drawing, but between February and April 1836 Hyacinthe Régnier was paid 750 francs "for the complete plaster model of a goblet with relief ornament."[1] The first example of the *coupe 'Chenavard'* was priced as an undecorated blank on December 10, 1836[2]. The first two examples to be decorated entered the sales inventory on February 21 and April 29, 1837, and were exhibited at the Louvre on May 1, 1838.[3]

The first standing bowl was delivered to the queen on April 27, 1837 after one of her visits to the manufactory; the second was sent to her on August 21, 1837.[4] These objects proved to be ideal gifts; they were relatively inexpensive to produce and yet they created a striking decorative effect, largely due to their color-heightened relief elements. They were made in large numbers, with various color schemes and sometimes with painted compositions inside the bowls.

Contemporary documents describe this design as being simply "in the sixteenth-century style" or the "Renaissance" style, without mentioning a specific type of ceramic from that period. Both the relief elements and the interlace pattern, however — despite differences in color scheme — are reminiscent of pieces now thought to have been made in Saint-Porchaire. The first object of this type to be identified as dating to the sixteenth-century was sold at auction in Paris in March 1837 which was after the development of this model. Quite possibly, however, Brongniart, who was always on the lookout for discoveries in ceramics, was aware of such work prior to that time.[5]

Initially, the old technique of using pastes of different colors inset into vessel walls was not used at Sèvres, even for a piece that was shown at the Louvre on May 1, 1842, although it was described in the catalogue as a "covered goblet, known as Henri II . . . blue ground, ornament in white enamel . . . copied from an earthenware goblet of the same size and in the same form from the reign of Henri II."[6] "Henri II Ware" was the name then used to describe those pieces now thought to have been made at Saint-Porchaire. This is all the more surprising since the inset-paste technique had by then been perfected and was indeed used on a Sèvres *vase 'Arabe'* featured in the same exhibition (see cat. no. 99). Furthermore, a drawing now at Sèvres for this *coupe 'Henri II'* bears a long inscription in Riocreux's hand specifying that the model was an object "from the time of Henri II that is in the possession of M. Huteau d'Origny (January 1840)."[7] This notation also lists other French collectors possessing fine earthenware of the same kind. The first *coupe 'Henri II'* decorated with inset paste was only exhibited in 1846.

The *'coupe Chenavard'* was illustrated in the *Description méthodique du musée*.[8]

Inscription: ["Goblet in the style of the 16th century / by Mr. A. Chenavard (September 1836)"]

1. [Pour le modèle en plâtre complet d'une coupe ornemanisée] Register Va' 31 (1835 – 36), fols. 122 ff.
2. Carton Pb 8, liasse 4, appréciations en blanc 1833 – 36. A second size was valued as an undecorated blank on August 22, 1846 (Carton Pb 11 bis).
3. First example: Carton Pb 9 bis, appréciation of February 21, 1837, "a Chenavard Goblet in the Renaissance style, relief ornament heightened in azure blue and rich gold trimming" [une coupe Chenavard dans le style de la Renaissance, ornements relief rechampis en bleu azur et riche garniture en or]. Production expenses were 416.25 francs (including 235 francs for the undecorated blank *de deuxième choix*); sale price 460 francs. Second example: Ibid., valuation of April 29, 1837, "A goblet in the sixteenth-century style relief ornament heightened in orangish red, ground, and various colors, decoration in gold and colors in the interior" [Une coupe dans le style du 16e siècle ornements relief rechampis en rouge orangé, fond, et couleurs diverses, décor en or et couleurs dans l'intérieur]; production expenses were 535.60 francs; sale price 600 francs.
4. Register Vbb 9, fols. 12 and 16v.
5. Monville sale, Paris, March 7 – 10, 1837, lot 55: "Large and magnificent ewer from the time of Henri II . . . decorated with mascarons and relief ornament, as well as with enamel arabesques in various colors" [Grande et magnifique aiguière du temps de Henri II . . . décorée de mascarons et d'ornements en relief, ainsi que d'arabesques émaillées en diverses couleurs]. After being known as Henry II earthenware but before acquiring their current appellation, these productions were thought to come from the area of Oiron.
6. [Coupe couverte, dite de Henri II . . . fond bleu, ornements en email blanc . . . copiés sur une coupe en faïence de même grandeur et de même forme du règne de Henri II].
7. [du temps de Henri II qui est en la possession de M. Huteau d'Origny (janvier 1840)] Petit Casier B IV.
8. Brongniart and Riocreux, *Description méthodique du musée.* (1845), P, pl. 2.

92.
Design for a Table Base, 1836

Claude-Aimé Chenavard
Ink, ink wash, and pencil on paper
11 1/8 x 16 7/8 in. (28.4 x 42.8 cm)
Inscriptions: [recto, top right, in pencil] *elargir la / face de la volute*; [bottom right, in pencil] *augmentation plateau inférieur / plateau supérieur*; [bottom left, in ink, in the hand of Denis-Désiré Riocreux] *pour le pied de la Table de Mr Schilt / (par Mr Chenavard, sept^bre 1836.)*
Inv. no. D § 10 1836 N° 1 B

In the 1836 work register, one of the projects listed under Claude-Aimé Chenavard was the "composition and sketch of a floral table for M. Schilt and of a sculpted base for said table," but there is no record of the sum he was paid for these designs. In February 1837 the same artist provided, among other things, a "half scale colored drawing of the base of said table."[1] Work must have proceeded rapidly, for the completed and decorated piece entered the sales inventory on September 29, 1838.[2] Although this was too late for it to have been shown at the Louvre exhibition on May 1, 1838, it was listed in the catalogue, where it was mentioned that the models had been made by Hyacinthe Régnier. The two children supporting the sphere had been sculpted by Antoine Desboeufs, and the bronze mounts were the work of Louis-Honoré Boquet. On February 7, 1840 the table was presented to Friedrich Wilhelm III, the king of Prussia.[3]

A second table with the same base, its top decorated with a composition of a "group of flowers against a marbled ground" and its "various parts . . . heightened in brown and decorated in matte gold," entered the sales inventory on April 29, 1842, and was presented to Méhemet-Ali, viceroy of Egypt, on December 24, 1845.[4] This example was shown at the Louvre on May 1, 1842; curiously, the catalogue describes it as having a "base consisting of four balusters surrounded by grape vines."[5]

A third example, described for the first time as being "in the Renaissance style" and having a top with a "wreath of flowers and fruit; in the center a group of birds against a sky blue ground; base decorated in matte and polished gold heightened with greenish blue and various [colors?]," entered the sales inventory on May 30, 1846,[6] and was exhibited at the Louvre on the following June 1.

One of these three tables (probably the first) was illustrated in the *Description méthodique du musée.*[7] The illustrations published there (see fig. 92a) seems to correspond most closely with the first example. That table, however, was sent to Prussia in 1840, and it seems unlikely that the engraving would have been completed by that time. It is possible that the engraving could have been made from a drawing and not the actual piece.

Inscription: ["enlarge the / front of the scroll"]; ["enlarge lower table-top / upper table-top"]

1. [Composition et croquis de la table à fleurs de M. Schilt et du pied en sculpture de la dite table]; [dessin au trait et colorié de moitié d'exécution du pied de la dite table] Registers Vj' 43 (1836), fol. 202 and Vj' 44 (1837), fol. 202. According to a receipt dated December 12, 1835, for work already carried out in the course of that month, Chenavard received 300 francs "for the first composition and colored sketches of the flowered table. Top and base included" [pour première composition et croquis colorées de la table de fleurs. Plateau et pied compris] (Carton R. 28). According to another receipt dated March 11, 1837, he received an additional 300 francs "in final payment for the composition and drawings for a large floral table to be painted by M. Schilt" [pour complement et solde de composition et dessins pour une grande table à fleurs à peindre par M. Schilt] and yet another 400 francs for a "tabletop in gouache one meter full-scale sketch of surrounding border design same size, and finished color drawing of the base" [Plateau à la gouache grandeur d'exécution cad. de 1 m., esquisse dessin autour de même grandeur et dessin terminé, et colories pour le pied], all executed in the course of 1836 (Carton R 29).

2. Register Vv 3, fol. 42, no. 37, and Carton Pb 10 bis, appréciation of September 29, 1838: "A porcelain table mounted in bronze consisting of 64 pieces; the top one meter 2 centimeters. Painting of flowers and birds against purplish gray ground, various parts with azure blue ground and matte gold" [Une table en porcelaine montée en bronze composé de 64 pièces; Le dessus d'1m 2cent. Peinture de fleurs et d'oiseaux sur fond gris violatre, divers partie en fond bleu azur et or mat]. Total production expenses were 24,328.30 francs (including 10,000 francs for the painting by Louis-Pierre Schilt, 3,791.80 francs for the blank porcelains, and 5,600 francs for the mounts); sale price was set at 27,000 francs.

3. Register Vbb 10, fol. 8.

4. For entry in sales inventory, see Register Vv 3, fol. 101, no. 10 and Carton Pb 10 bis, appréciations 1842. For delivery, see Register Vbb 11, fol. 7. The decoration of the tabletop was again painted by Louis-Pierre Schilt, who once more received 10,000 francs; sale price again set at 27,000 francs.

5. [Groupe de fleurs sur un fond agatisé]; [les diverses parties . . . rechampis en brun et décoré en or mat].

6. [Dans le style de la Renaissance]; [couronne de fleurs et de fruits; au centre groupe d'oiseaux sur fond bleu de ciel; le pied decore en or mat et poli rechampi en bleu verdâtre et divers.] (Register Vv 4, fol. 67, no. 9 and Carton Pb 11 bis, appréciations 1846). Total production expenses were 15,474 francs, including 7,500 for the painter Moïse Jacobber; sale price was set at 18,000 francs.

7. Brongniart and Riocreux, *Description méthodique du musée* (1845), P, pl. 5.

Fig. 92a. *Table 'Renaissance'* by Claude-Aimé Chenavard. (From Brongniart and Riocreux, *Description méthodique du musée céramique de la manufacture royale de porcelaine de Sèvres* [1845], P, pl. 5)

93.
Two Designs for Glasses, 1836

Claude-Aimé Chenavard

93a.
Champagne Glass called *Verre 'à champagne'*

Watercolor, ink, and pencil on paper glued to cardboard
9 5/8 x 3 7/8 in (24.5 x 9.9 cm)
Inscription: [recto, bottom, in ink, in the hand of Alexandre Brongniart] *verre a champagne / par M. Chenavard*
Inv. no. 1836 nº 8

In 1802, only two years after his appointment to Sèvres, Alexandre Brongniart published a paper entitled "Essai sur les couleurs tirées des oxydes metalliques, et fixées par la fusion sur les différents corps vitreux" (Essay on colors obtained from metallic oxides and fixed by fusion to various vitreous bodies), a text which, among other things, demonstrates that in his view the ceramic and vitreous arts were virtually inseparable.[1] A quarter of a century later, in 1827, he established a workshop at the manufactory for the production of stained glass and paintings on glass (see chap. 7). In addition, the collection he was assembling for the museum at Sèvres included glassware and crystal. On April 5, 1836, writing to Baron Fain[2] about a proposed exhibition at the Louvre, Brongniart recalled that one of the purposes of his trip the previous year to Holland, Rhenish Prussia, and Frankfurt had been to see "the beautiful and numerous results of this application of vitrifiable colors to Bohemian crystal goblets . . . . As you may know, I brought back several samples . . . . The enlightened owner of the glass works in Plaine-de-Walsche in the [Department of] Meurthe, Monsieur the baron of Klinglin, gave M. de Fontenay, director of the glassworks, all the authorizations and clearances he needed to carry out the research and experiments necessary to obtain painted goblets. M. de Fontenay, aided by his practical knowledge of glass goblet production, and M. Louis Robert, in charge of making colors for glass painting at Sèvres, succeeded — the one by hardening the crystal and the other by modifying the color — in decorating French crystal goblets like those of Bohemia. This result was due principally to the king's manufactory."[3] It was probably in the context of this collaboration that Claude-Aimé Chenavard produced a series of forms and decoration for glasses, for which no trace of payment can be found.[4]

Brongniart displayed the fruits of these experiments on the earliest possible occasion, which was the May 1, 1838, exhibition at the Louvre. Brongniart's long preface in the catalogue indicates the importance he attached to the project as a demonstration of the new role he envisioned for the manufactory. Sensitive to criticism that Sèvres had an unfair advantage in competing with private producers, he wanted to show that the manufactory could be useful to them by

93b.
Stem Glass called *Verre 'à pied'*

Watercolor and ink on paper glued to cardboard
7 3/4 x 4 1/8 in. (18.8 x 10.6 cm)
Inscription: [recto, bottom, in ink, in the hand of Alexandre Brongniart] *verre a patte / par M. Chenavard*
Inv. no. 1836 / nº 3

sponsoring costly research that would prove beneficial to all.

The Louvre exhibition catalogue does not provide a breakdown of the objects presented, which makes it difficult to determine whether Chenavard's designs were used. It should be noted, however, that an itemized "invoice for glass goblets cut for the trials with painted glass goblets in the Bohemian manner," submitted by "M. Tissot crystal cutter and engraver" on March 2, 1838, includes entries for "two cut champagne glasses" (30 francs and 25 francs) and "one goblet with engravings against a colored ground" (5 francs).[5]

1. Brongniart, "Essai sur les couleurs tirées des oxydes métalliques" (1801-2).
2. The official in question could be either Agathon-Jean François Fain, who twice occupied the post of Intendant Général de la Liste Civile (Royal Budget) and died the same year this letter was written, or his son Camille, who was the secretary of Louis-Philippe's cabinet.
3. [Les beaux et nombreux résultats de cette application des couleurs vitrifiables sur la gobletterie crystallerie de la bohême]; [J'en ai, comme vous pouvez le savoir, rapporté de nombreux échantillons . . . Le propriétaire éclairé de la verrerie de plaine de Walsche dans la meurthe, M. le Baron de Klinglin, a donné à M. de Fontenay directeur de la verrerie toutes les autorisations et pouvoirs necessaires pour faire les recherches et essais propres à obtenir de la gobletterie peinte. M. de Fontenay aidé de ses connaissances pratiques dans la composition de verres de gobletterie et M. Louis Robert chargé à Sèvres de la Fabrication des couleurs pour la peinture sur verre sont parvenus, l'un en durcissant le crystal et l'autre en modifiant les couleurs A orner de la gobletterie crystalline de France à la manière de celle de Bohême. Ce resultat est dû principalement à la manufacture du Roi] Register Vc 9, fols. 6- 6v. The baron of Klinglin paid a visit to the manufactory on March 10, 1836 (Register Vs 3).
4. After the artist's death, settlement of these outstanding bills was a point of bitter contention between Chenavard's brother Henry and Brongniart, who wrote to the complainant on November 9, 1838: "I will close, Monsieur . . . by telling you that I am ill pleased with the tone that prevails in your letters . . . I would have expected a bit more amenity from the brother of M. Chenavard . . . a person I so loved and *esteemed*" [Je terminerai, Monsieur . . . en vous disant que je suis peu content du ton qui règne dans vos letres . . . J'aurais pu m'attendre à un peu plus d'aménité de la part du frère de M. Chenavard . . . une personne que j'ai autant aimée et *considérée* (Carton Ob 3, dossier Chenavard, emphasis by Brongniart).
5. [Memoire de gobletterie de verre taillée pour les essais de gobletterie de verres peints à la manière de Bohême]; [M. Tissot tailleur et graveur sur cristaux]; [2 verres champagne taillés]; [1 gobelet gravé sur fonds de couleur.] Carton R 31 (1837).

94.
Design for a Goblet, 1837
Called *Coupe 'de François Ier'*

Alexandre-Evariste Fragonard
Watercolor, ink, and ink wash on paper
23 5/8 x 18 1/4 in. (60 x 46.5 cm)
Inscriptions: [recto, bottom left, in ink, in the hand of Alexandre Brongniart] *Coupe de françois Ier. par M.Fragonard / sept. 1837 / AlexB*; [in central cartouche on the rim] *F 1*
Inv. no. D § 8 1837 N° 1

In August 1837 Alexandre-Evariste Fragonard received 200 francs for a drawing of a "rich goblet in the Renaissance style depicting illustrations of the reign of Francis I,"[1] but apparently no such object was put into production. Perhaps it was deemed inferior to Hyacinthe Régnier's design for the *coupe 'de Benvenuto Cellini'*, which also dates from 1837 (see cat. no. 111).[2] Brongniart may also have been concerned about the public's tiring of Fragonard's repeated use of sculptural elements emphasized by contrasts between white biscuit and gilded, matte, and polished surfaces. The *surtout 'des Comestibles'* (see cat. no. 84), then being made, had already been preceded by the *vase 'de la Renaissance'* designed by Fragonard in 1833.[3] When the latter piece was shown at the Louvre on May 1, 1835, one critic had caustically referred to its author as a "Greek artist recently arrived in the fifteenth century."[4] Fragonard's designs for the *déjeuner 'de François Ier'* (see cat. no. 78), then being developed, demonstrate that he was perfectly capable of using the bright polychromy characteristic of the "Renaissance" style.

1. [Coupe riche dans le style de la renaissance consacrée aux illustrations du règne de François Ier] Register Vj' 44 (1837), fol. 200.
2. Alcouffe, Dion-Tenenbaum, and Ennès, *Un âge d'or,* exhib. cat. (1991), no. 230, pp. 408 – 9.
3. For entry in sales inventory on April 25, 1835, see Carton Pb 8, liasse 2, dossier 4, "Vase de la Renaissance Fragonard ou de François Ier"; total production expenses were 3,800 francs; sale price 5,000 francs. The vase was delivered to the Ministère de l'Agriculture et du Commerce on August 31, 1848 (Register Vbb 11, fol. 26) and is now in the Musée National de Céramique at Sèvres.
4. Alcouffe, Dion-Tenenbaum, and Ennès, *Un âge d'or,* exhib. cat. (1991), no. 139, pp. 270 – 71. It is hardly surprising that the eclectic style of this piece dismayed the critics; at least one of them, however, thought it was in "the style of the time of Bernard Palissy," which was exactly what Brongniart had in mind.

95.
Stained-Glass Window Design for the Portal Wall of the Parish Church at Eu, 1837 and 1839 – 40

Achille Mascret
Watercolor and ink on thin paper glued to cardboard. Some of the lower compartments have been covered with new designs with coats-of-arms instead the rinceaus
25 1/2 x 15 5/8 in. (64.8 x 39.8)
Inscriptions: [recto, within the windows, left to right] [top register] *Redemptor-Spiritus Sanctus-Pater*; [penultimate register] *Rollo Dux-Laurent-Michael-Maria-Gabriel-Guillaume-Philippe*; [center right] *Lambel*; [bottom left of drawing] [signature] *Achille Mascret. 1837.*; [immediately below the drawing, in pencil] *Brionne-Artois-Clèves-Lorraine*; [bottom, in ink, in the hand of Denis-Désiré Rioceux] *Dessin d'ensemble de la grande vitre éxécutée en 1837 sur le dessin de Mr A.Chenavard / pour le portail de l'Eglise d'Eu / avec les modifications apportées à la partie inférieure en 1839 – 1840.*
Inv. no. D § 11 1838 N° 6

The painting-on-glass workshop established by Brongniart in 1827 devoted much of its energies to commissions placed by King Louis-Philippe after his accession in 1830. In this case he does not seem to have stipulated the iconographic program or type of decoration to be used, but this was atypical. He often took a personal interest in such matters when they concerned these stained-glass projects, occasioning meetings between the sovereign and Brongniart, who enjoyed his direct contact with the king.

The large stained-glass window for the portal wall of the church at Eu — restored at the same time as the king's private residence there — was commissioned from Sèvres by the architect Pierre-François-Léonard Fontaine on July 4, 1833.[1] This drawing is a reduction of a larger one by Claude-Aimé Chenavard; the original figures and ornament were changed, presumably after Chenavard's death on June 16, 1838. It corresponds to a payment made to Achille Mascret on June 30, 1838, for "thirteen days devoted to making an overall watercolor drawing of the window at Eu".[2]

The stained-glass windows corresponding to this drawing for Eu were exhibited at the May 1 exhibitions of 1838 and 1840 at the Louvre, and installed in the church immediately thereafter.

Inscription: ["Redeemer-Holy Spirit-Father"]; ["Rollo dux-Laurence-Michael-Mary-Gabriel-William-Philip Lambel"]; ["Achille Mascret. 1837"]; ["Brionne Artois-Clève-Lorraine"]; ["General drawing for the assembly of a large window made in 1837 according to the designs of Mr. A. Chenavard / for the portal of the eglise d'Eu / with modifications made to the lower part in 1839 – 1840"]

1. For a complete history of all the stained-glass windows produced for the parish church at Eu, see Morel, "Les Vitraux de l'église d'Eu" (1994); also see chap. 7 in this volume.

2. These efforts were calculated at the rate of 4 francs per day. The payment receipt indicates that the work was carried out in April 1838. (Carton R 32 [1838]}.

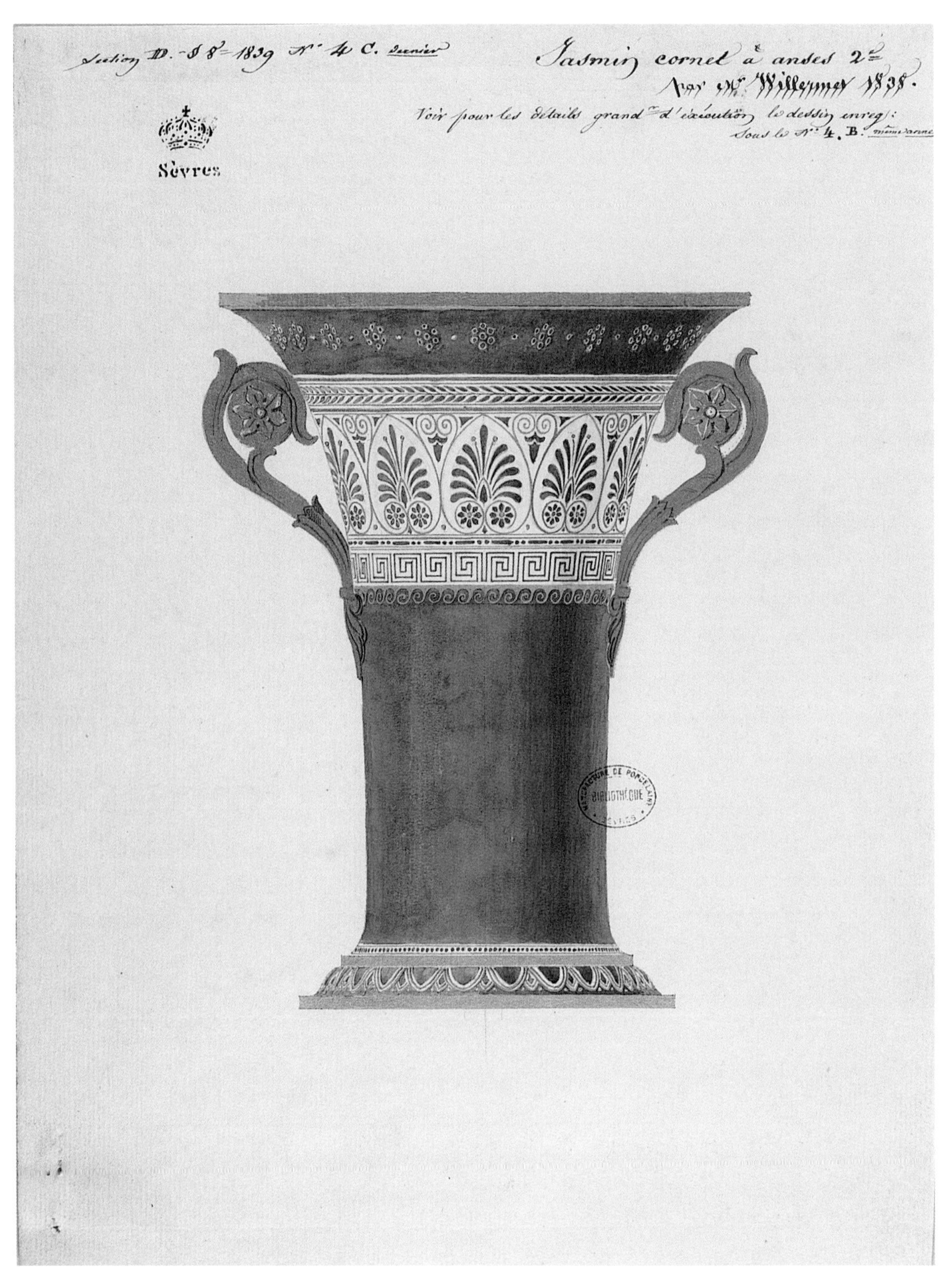

96.
Decoration for a Vase with Handles, 1838
Called *Vase 'Jasmin cornet à anses'*

Antoine-Gabriel Willermet
Watercolor, gouache and pencil on paper
12 1/8 x 9 1/8 in. (30.8 x 23.3 cm)
Inscription: [recto, top right, in ink, in the hand of Denis-Désiré Riocreux] *Jasmin cornet à anses 2e / par Mr Willermet 1838. / voir pour les détails grand^r d'éxécution le dessin enreg: / sous le n° 4.B.même année*
Inv. no. D § 8 1839 N° 4 C. (dernier)

In addition to undertaking ambitious projects intended to demonstrate the manufactory's technical and artistic superiority, Brongniart always kept the warehouse well supplied with more simple objects suitable for purchase by private clients as well as pieces appropriate for furnishing the many royal residences. The classical motifs in the decorative scheme of this vase — rosettes, laurel frieze, Greek palmettes — make it typical of the work of Antoine-Gabriel Willermet, who headed the painting workshops at Sèvres from 1825 to 1848 (see cat. no. 90). One contemporary critic was particularly outspoken in his sarcastic response to Willermet's work: "The ornament . . . of M. Willermet is of an unequaled poverty, paltriness, and nullity. One must deplore the almost unbridled influence that this man exercises at the royal establishment. Considering that he is master of all things there, one wonders whether France is so destitute of artists of merit as to be obliged to turn to an overseer of such miraculous strength. One can only shrug one's shoulders."[1]

It is not even certain that the purplish

ground — the only note of fantasy in this design — was respected, for the only entries in the sales inventory that might correspond to this work describe the ground as blue.[2]

Inscription: ["Jasmin cornet (vase) with handles second size / by Mr Willermet 1838. / for details of size see design recorded / as no. 4.B. of the same year (1838)"]

1. [L'ornementation . . . de M. Willermet est d'une pauvreté, d'une mesquinerie, d'une nullité sans exemple; il faut déplorer l'influence presque sans contrôle que cet homme exerce dans le royal établissement. Quand on songe que c'est lui qui fait la pluie et le beau temps, on se demande si la France est dépourvue à ce point d'artistes de mérite pour qu'on ait été obligé d'avoir recours à un surveillant d'une force si miraculeuse. C'est à faire hausser les épaules] *Journal des Artistes* {1846), vol. 3.

2. Two pairs of vases are in question: Carton Pb 10 bis, appréciation of July 6, 1838: "two flared vases with handles second size blue glost-fired [ground] gold and platinum decor border extending into the interior" [deux vases Cornets à anses 2e gr. Bleu au grand feu décor en or et platine bordure tombante dans l'intérieur]; total production expenses 113.75 francs, sale price 125 francs each; and entry in sales inventory on December 22, 1838 (Register Vv 3, fol. 46v, no 29). The second pair is found in the valuation of December 22, 1838: "two flared vases first size rosette handles blue glost-fired ground rich gold decoration etc." [deux vases Cornets Iere gdr. anses rosaces fond bleu au grand feu riche decoration en or etc.]; total production expenses 179 francs, sale price 200 francs each (Register Vv 3, fol. 46v, nos 30); entered the sales inventory on December 22, 1838. It is not known why the first set of vases, priced in July, did not enter the sales inventory until December. The present design seems to have been used for several years, for it reappeared — still with a blue ground — on two vases produced in 1844 (Chevallier, *Musée national du château de Fontainebleau* (1996), no. 80, p. 117).

Fig. 96a. *Vase 'Jasmin Cornet à anses'*, Sèvres, 1844; hard-paste porcelain. (Fontainebleau, Musée National du Château)

97.
Decoration for a Vase, 1840
Called *Vase 'Gothique Fragonard'*

Alexis-Etienne Julienne, also known as Eugène Julienne
Watercolor, gouache and pencil on paper
16 1/8 x (41 x 27.4 cm)
Inscriptions: [recto: top, in ink, in the hand of Denis-Désiré Riocreux] *Vase gothique Fragonard*; [within the drawing, in pencil, in Julienne's hand] *N° 1-N° 7* [to designate the different parts of the piece on both views]; [lower right, in pencil] *Relevé des / dessins d'ap . . . / le dévelope . . . / de la pièce*; [bottom] *500 f. Compris le sujet et le dessin*; [bottom right, in pencil] [signature] *Julienne / 1840*
Inv. no. D § 8 1848 N° 100

The list of projects for 1839 includes an entry "no. 10 Vases the old royal libraries (sic). Two Fragonard Gothic Vases azure blue ground colored subjects gold and platinum painted decoration, to be executed by M. Julienne."[1] A note added later in the year reads: "design presented and accepted by M. Brongniart." This must have been no more than a simple sketch, for a note dated September 5, 1840, reads: "M. Julienne brought me the completed and colored decoration and requested, for the composition drawing and the execution, 500 [francs] per vase".[2] On September 8, "the drawing was presented and the fee approved. M. Brongniart asked M. Julienne to add some color to the decoration to relieve the monotony."[3] The artist had received the blank vases on the preceding August 21 and received his first payment in September.[4] This must have been for the ornament, since Brongniart did not select the subjects to be depicted — "Alcuin presenting manuscripts to Charlemagne" and "Charles V establishing the library at the Louvre" — until October 2. The vases entered the sales inventory on July 8, 1841,[5] and were delivered by means of "a rush order" to the Château de Saint-

Cloud on April 15, 1843.[6]

Beginning in 1836, Brongniart entrusted Alexis-Etienne Julienne with trial painting and composition projects, maintaining that he executed them "with facility and at a very good price." For his part, the artist submitted "proof-sheets for all kinds of ornament of his own composition that seem of good quality." These had probably been prepared for one of the many print albums that he published under the name Eugène Julienne. In 1839, Brongniart, well satisfied with Julienne's work, offered to add him to the manufactory's permanent staff.[7] As early as the following May, however, an improperly fired ground color occasioned a dispute which prompted the following comments from the disabused Brongniart: "So M. Willermet and M. J[ulienne] are already at odds. Who's at fault, the one thought to have a most accommodating character or the one at war with everyone? . . . We shall see if in the end he doesn't disgust M. J[ulienne], too."[8] To his credit, Julienne did not resign until 1848, after which time he worked for Pichenot-Loebnitz, a ceramist in Paris, and continued to publish albums of prints of ornaments.

The *vase 'Gothique Fragonard'* was designed in 1823. Although the catalogue of the 1823 – 24 New Year's exhibition at the Louvre describes it as a "mantel vase" with a "twelfth-century" form, over the years it was decorated in a number of different ornamental patterns. In Julienne's drawing, the Gothic Revival idiom seems overloaded when compared with earlier examples from the Restauration period (see cat. nos. 57, 58, 62).

Inscription: ["Summary of the / designs after . . . / the develop . . . / of the piece"; "500f. including the subject and the design"]; ["Julienne / 1840"]

1. [N 10 Vases les anciennes bibliothèques royales. 2 V. Gothique Fragonard fond bleu azur sujets coloriés décor en or et platine peint, executer par M. Julienne . . . projet presenter et accepté par M. Brongniart] Carton Pb 10, liasse 1, dossier Vases.
2. [M. Julienne me remet le décor arrêté et colorié et fait la demande pour la composition dessin et execution 500 par vase] Ibid.
3. [le dessin est présenté et le prix accepté M. Brongniart invite M. Julienne a rependre [répandre] dans le decor quelques couleurs pour en ôter la monotonie] Ibid.
4. Register Vj' 47 (1840), fols. 63 ff.
5. Register Vv 3, fol. 88, no. 6, and Carton Pb 10 bis, appréciations 1841. Total production expenses were 796.85 francs (per piece), including a payment of 550 francs to Julienne; sale price 900 francs.
6. Register Vbb 10, fol. 62v.
7. Carton Ob 6, dossier Julienne.
8. "Voila deja M. Willermet et M. J en debats. A qui le tort, a celui qu'on regarde comme d'un caractère très accomodant ou a celui qui est [en] guerre avec tous . . .. Nous verrons s'il viendra a bout de degouter aussi M. J ?" Ibid.

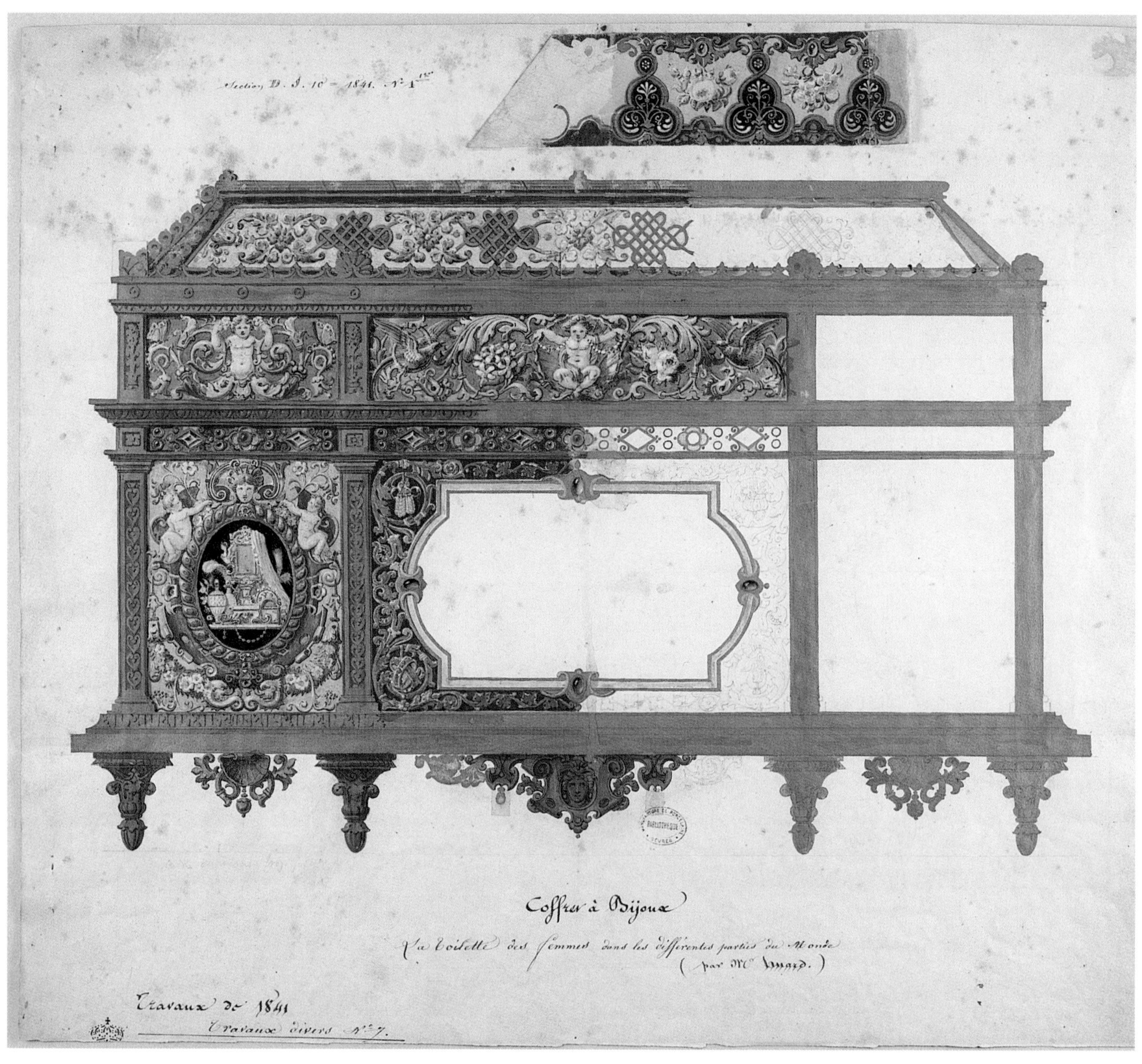

98.
Design and Decorstion for a Jewelry Casket, [1840]
Called *Coffret à Bijoux 'La Toilette des Femmes dans les Différentes Parties du Monde'*

Pierre Huart
Gouache, ink and pencil on paper
16 x 18 1/8 in. (40.5 x 46 cm)
Inscriptions: [recto, bottom center, in ink, in the hand of Denis-Désiré Riocreux] *Coffret à Bijoux / La Toilette des femmes dans les différentes parties du Monde / (par Mr Huart)*; lower left: *Travaux de 1841 / travaux divers N° 7.*; [lower left, in pencil, in the hand of Alexandre Brongniart] *cadre du miroir trop . . .* [the rest is crossed out]
Inv. no. D § 10 1841 N° 1 (1er)

The list of projects for 1840 includes the following terse entry under the heading "Pièces diverses": "No. 7 Jewelry casket [illustrating] the female toilette in the different parts of the world by MM. Huart and Develly."[1] On September 2 of that year, Brongniart noted that there had been a "composition drawing presented by M. Huart and approved aside from some slight changes [to be made]."[2] In January 1841 he was not sure whether "the small cameos will be in relief or painted," but on March 19 he noted: "There will be no cameo reliefs, we will proceed with production. The lid will be pitched."[3]

The task of painting its twelve plaques was divided between two artists: Pierre Huart, who executed the rich "Renaissance" ornament, and Jean-Charles Develly, who painted the five cartouches, one for each of the known continents, as stipulated in a program dated September 1841.[4] The completed casket entered the sales inventory on April 29, 1842[5] and was exhibited at the Louvre on May 1, 1842. On August 18, 1843 it was delivered to Louis-Philippe,[6] who presented it to Queen Victoria during her visit to France the following autumn.[7]

The idea of making a jewelry casket with porcelain plaques was not new. An entry in the work allocations for 1813 reads: "No. 11 An octagonal jewelry box or casket . . . [with] colored and cameo compositions relative to the toilette and tasks of women. This casket was intended to be a New Year's gift but no painter was available and it could not be completed in time."[8] Two more jewelry caskets with related programs were undertaken in 1846 after designs by Jules Peyre. The first one was decorated by Théophile Fragonard with scenes evoking "the industries supporting the female toilette, represented by small genies engaged in making, selling, and buying."[9] The decorative scheme of the second casket, again painted by Develly, incorporated "the presentation of jewelry . . . to queens and other female royalty."[10]

The strip of ornamental design glued to the top of the sheet may represent changes recommended by Brongniart. The extraordinary density of the decoration is altogether characteristic of the period, as is the generous use of Renaissance motifs such as putti and rinceaux, and cameos in a vaguely classical spirit. The inclusion of brightly colored figure compositions can only have further intensified the effect of opulence and preciosity, produced by this relatively small piece. The pitched form of the lid makes the design resemble the medieval reliquaries then beginning to be avidly sought by collectors.

Inscription: ["Jewelry Casket / Lady's toilette in different parts of the world / (by Mr. Huart)"]; ["works of 1841 / miscellaneous work No 7"]; ["frame of the mirror too . . ."] [crossed out]

1. [Coffret à bijoux la toilette des femmes dans les differentes parties du monde par MM. Huart et Develly] Carton Pb 10, liasse 1, dossier Coffrets.

2. [dessin de composition presente par M. Huart et admis sauf quelques leger changements] Ibid.

3. [décider si les petits camees seront en relief ou en peinture]; [il n'y aura pas de camees en relief, on va mettre en execution. Le dessus sera a pentes] Ibid. There is no record of a separate payment for the present drawing; it was included in an aggregate fee paid to Huart for all of his work on the project.

4. The subjects are: "Large plaque (lid): Ball Toilette Europe 160 francs-First [plaque] front: Toilette of a bride in French India, Asia-Second [plaque] back: Indian and half-breed women attired for a procession, Bolivia, America-Third [plaque] for right side: Exchange of toiletry articles [of the] women of Senegal, Africa-Fourth [plaque] for left side: Women being tattooed in Nouka Hiva, Oceania, 135 francs each-Note: These fees include research and execution of the drawings, which are to remain in-house" [Grande plaque (dessus) Toilette de Bal Europe 160 francs-Iere de face Toilette d'une Mariée dans L'inde française-Asie; 2e de derrière indiennes et métis parées pour une procession, Bolivie, Amerique; 3e de côté à droite. Traite d'objets de toilette femmes de la Sénégambie-afrique; 4e du côté gauche femmes parées opération du Tatouage Nouka Hiva Océanie 135 francs chaque-Nota dans ce prix sont compris les recherches et execution des dessins qui doivent rester à la maison].

5. Register Vv 3, fol. 101, no. 18 and Carton Pb 10 bis, appréciation 1842. Production expenses were 5,461.15 francs (including 2,330 francs for Huart and 1,050 francs for Develly); sale price 6,500 francs.

6. Register Vbb 10, fol. 28.

7. Alcouffe, Dion-Tenenbaum, and Ennès, *Un âge d'or,* exhib. cat. (1991), no. 228, p. 406; Bellaigue, "Queen Victoria, A Taste for Sèvres" (1996).

8. [No. 11 une boëte ou coffret a bijoux octogone . . . les tableaux coloriés et en camées representant des sujets relatifs à la toilette et aux travaux des femmes. Ce coffret etoit destiné pour les presents du jour de l'an, mais n'ayant eu aucun peintre disponsible il ne pourra être prêt] Carton Pb 3, liasse 2. It may be that "two colored drawings of a jewelry casket, green ground, actual size § 10 1813 n° 1-2 Brongniart" correspond to this project; the artist (A.-T. Brongniart) received 72 francs for them (Register Y 21, fol. 66).

9. [Les industries qui concourent à la toilette des femmes representees par de petits genies fabricant, vendant, achetant] Carton Pb 10, liasse 1, dossier Travaux 1846, "pièces diverses no. 3." Entered sales inventory on December 30, 1848 (Register Vv 5, fols. 20, nos. 6 and 49, no 23). Delivered to the mayor of Versailles for the Société des Courses in May 1851 (Register Vbb 11, fol. 47).

10. [Hommages de parures d'origines diverses à des femmes reines ou de sang royal] Carton Pb 11, liasse 1, dossier Coffrets. Entered the sales inventory on February 21, 1850 (Register Vv 5, fol. 34, no. 6 and Carton Pb 12, appréciations 1850). Total production expenses were 3,693 francs (including 1,200 for Develly); sale price was set at 4,500 francs. Sold to Gayot, Inspecteur Général des Haras on December 17, 1850, for the reduced price of 3,203 francs (Register Vz 7, fol. 145).

Fig. 98a. Jewelry casket called *coffret à bijoux 'La Toilette des Femmes dans les Différentes Parties du Monde',* Sèvres, 1842; hard-paste porcelain and gilded bronze. This was a gift of King Louis-Philippe to Queen Victoria. (Royal Collection, Her Majesty Queen Elizabeth II)

99.
Design and Decoration for a Vase, 1842
Called *Vase 'Arabe Feuchère'*

Léon Feuchère
Watercolor, gouache, and ink on paper
17 1/4 x 11 1/4 in. (43.7 x 28.5 cm)
Inscriptions: [recto, top, on a sheet of paper glued to the sheet in pencil] [three arabic inscriptions with French translations below] *Monarque dont les mains distribuent des dons aux pauvres / avec autant de profusion et aussi souvent que les vagues se succèdent / Les unes aux autres; Si quel qu'un s'approche de moi se plaignant de la / soif, il recevra pour L'apaiser une eau fraiche et limpide / douce de sa nature; Louange a Dieu / Les doits de L'artiste ont delicatement brodé ma robe apres / avoir monté Les joyaux de ma couronne;* [Bottom, in ink, in the hand of Denis-Désiré Riocreux] *Vase Arabe Feuchère / par Mr Léon Feuchère / (31 Août 1841)* [the same inscription written in pencil by Alexandre Brongniart and then erased is barely legible]
Inv. no. D § 8 1843 N° 1

In 1837 Brongniart had collaborated with Adrien Dauzats on a copy of the immense earthenware vase in the Alhambra in Granada, Spain.[1] As with sixteenth-century Flemish stoneware vases (see cat. no. 80), he had again interpreted another ceramic material in porcelain. He was sufficiently attentive to considerations of authenticity to decorate it with a special inset-paste technique developed for the purpose by Ferdinand Régnier.

The result was a spectacular vase, which was about 54 inches (137 cm) high and entered the sales inventory on April 19, 1842. It was shown in the Louvre exhibition on May 1, 1842, and was delivered to the official residence of the president of the Assemblée Nationale on August 2, 1848.[2]

Perhaps encouraged by growing public interest in the Moresque style, Brongniart decided to undertake more pieces conceived in the same spirit but along simpler lines. For this purpose, he turned to the architect Léon Feuchère who, after the retirement of Alexandre-Evariste Fragonard and the death of Claude-Aimé Chenavard, became the manufactory's most active designer of new forms for a time. On May 8, 1843, Feuchère received payments "for various drawings outlined and colored with details and the necessary follow-up supervision," among them "a colored drawing of an Arab vessel" and another similar drawing of a *vase 'Arabe'* (150 francs for each).[3] Two vases were begun in 1843 and entered the inventory on April 23, 1844; they were exhibited at the Louvre on the following June 3.[4] The catalogue states only that their ornament had been designed and executed by Alexis-Etienne Julienne "after designs of Arab origin," but the progress sheet for the project[5] provides more particulars: "Two arab vases Léon Feuchère second size decorated with a damascened azure blue ground and various *demi-grand-feu*[6] and low-fired colors surrounded with polished gold."[7] Both pieces were delivered to the king on September 12, 1844, for him to use as gifts.[8]

The drawing of an Arab vessel paid for at the same time probably corresponds to the two *glacières 'arabes Léon Feuchère'* that entered the sales inventory on May 28, 1844[9]; they were shown at the same Louvre exhibition as the *vase 'Arabe Feuchère'*.

The identity of the scholar who provided Brongniart with the Arabic inscriptions and translations inscribed on the piece of paper glued to the top of the sheet is unknown.

Inscription: ["Monarch distributing alms to the poor with his own hands / as generously and as frequently as waves succeed each other on the shore / one after the other"]; ["if anyone comes to me complaining of thirst, his thirst will be assuaged by cool, clear water, naturally sweet; Praise be to God / the artist's fingers delicately embroidered my robe after setting the jewels of my crown . . . Arab Feuchère vase / by Mr. Léon Feuchère / 31 / (August 1841)"]

1. This vase was published for the first time by Alexandre de Laborde (*Voyage pittoresque et historique de l'Espagne . . .*, Paris, 1806 – 12). It was probably the vase's unusual size that attracted attention.

2. For entry in the sales inventory, see Register Vv 3, fol. 101, no. 12, and Carton Pb 10, appréciation of April 29, 1842. For delivery, see Register Vbb 11, fol. 24v. Total production expenses were 4,550.50; sale price set at 6,000 francs. A second example, realized in 1848 – 49 with a very different color scheme, was delivered to the museum in Rouen (Alcouffe, Dion-Tenenbaum, and Ennès, *Un âge d'or,* exhib. cat. (1991), no. 234, pp. 413 – 14).

3. [Pour dessins divers arrêtés et coloriés avec les developpemens et les suites de surveillance necessaires]; [1° une Coupe arabe dessin colorié]; [2° un vase arabe id] Carton R 38 (1842).

4. Register Vv 4, fol. 20, no. 38, and Carton Pb 11 bis, appréciations 1844. Production expenses totaled 812 francs (including 550 francs for the painting of the ornament), and the sale price was set at 1,000 francs.

5. Carton Pb 10, liasse 1, dossier "Vases."

6. Ceramic colors are generally derived from metallic oxides, but very few of these are capable of withstanding the 1,410° centigrade temperatures of the *grand feu,* or high-temperature firing, which thus limited the spectrum of available colors at Sèvres and elsewhere. The palette of low-fire grounds is much more varied, but the colors which result are opaque, and must have seemed less seductive as the glazes of Chinese porcelain became known to a wider audience. To address the inadequacy of low-fired glazes, Brongniart sought to develop an intermediary palette of colors which he called *demi-grand feu* grounds.

7. [2 vases arabe Leon feuchere 2eme décorés d'un fond bleu azur damassé et couleurs diverses demi-grand-feu et a feu ordinaire serti d'or poli] {Carton Pb 10, liasse 1, dossier "Vases"}.

8. Register Vbb 10, fol. 38. These vases were probably presented to the landscape painter Paul Huet, for the records indicate that on December 15, 1848 "two handles for the Léon Feuchère Vase turquoise ground gold decoration" [deux anses de Vase Leon Feuchere fond turquoise decor en or] were delivered to this artist (Register Vbb 11, fol. 29).

9. Register Vv 4, fol. 22, no. 15.

100.
Decoration for a Vase, 1842
Called *Vase 'Etrusque AB'*

Jean-Charles-François Leloy
Pencil, watercolor, and gamboge on paper
14 x 10 3/4 in. (35.4 x 27.4 cm)
Inscription: [recto, bottom, in ink, in the hand of Denis-Désiré Riocreux] *Dessin d'ensemble du vase Etrusque AB.2e grand^{r}; les chasses historiques de la cour de france / travaux de 1844 – 46*
Inv. no. D § 8 1848 N° 55[1]

This drawing may correspond to either of two register entries recording payments made in 1842 to Jean-Charles-François Leloy: "drawing one-quarter actual size colored with gamboge and platinum" or "small colored overall drawing."[1] Payment for the first drawing was made in August and for the other in November. It describes a gold and platinum decoration for two *vases 'Etrusque AB'*, second size, first listed in the work allocations of 1841, when Leloy produced his first designs for the project.[2] In addition to ornamental motifs painted against a purplish-brown ground by François-Hubert Barbin, Charles-Antoine Didier, and Pierre Riton, each vase was to feature two large and two small reserves depicting the historic hunts of the French court, composed and painted by Jean-Charles Develly.

Even for large pieces, neoclassicism had not entirely disappeared at Sèvres by the 1840s. The extreme richness of the overall effect, with its invasive plant motifs and detailed reserves, is quite new to the period, while each of the ornaments, however, is in itself quite traditional. Although this manner of dense decoration has come to be closely identified with the reign of King Louis Philippe, it was only in the 1840s that it emerged. Similarly, the subject is not new. Several *déjeuner* and vases (cat. no. 25) based on the same theme had been made since the beginning of the century.

The two vases were begun in 1842 and entered the sales inventory on May 10, 1846.[3] They were outfitted with gilt bronze handles, which means that this feature of the drawing, rendered to be executed in porcelain, was changed. The vases were subsequently separated. One was "delivered to the king for presentation to the Bey of Tunis" on December 9, 1846, while the other was "delivered on the king's orders [to his son], His Royal Highness Monseigneur the duc d'Aumale" on September 2, 1847.[4] (See fig. 100a.)

Both the author and the date of this form are unknown. The initials "AB" could suggest that either the design or the concept for it originated with Alexandre Brongniart. Some decorative schemes for the form survive from 1804, but the form itself does not seem to have been used on a regular basis until after 1817. The vase was produced in three sizes — roughly 5 1/3 feet (165 cm), 3 1/2 feet (100 cm), and 15 2/3 inches (40 cm) in height — and the design was amended twice, in 1823 and 1825.[5]

Inscription: ["Overall drawing for an Etruscan vase AB. 2nd size"]; ["historic hunts of the court of France / works of 1844-45"]

1. [Dessin grandeur d'execution de un quart colores en gomme gutt et platine]; [dessin d'ensemble general de petite dimension colorié] Register Vj' 49 (1842), fols. 2 ff. *Gomme-gutt*, or gamboge, is a gum plant resin used to produce a bright yellow pigment.
2. Carton Pb 11 liasse 1, dossier "Vases."
3. Register Vv 4, fol. 67, no 5 and Carton Pb 11 bis, appréciations 1846. Total production expenses for each vase came to 8,003.75 francs, including 1,265 for the ornamental painters, 3,000 francs for Develly, and 1,500 francs for the gilt-bronze mounts (700 francs also went toward the preliminary drawings, probably those by Leloy); the sale price was set at 9,500 francs.
4. Register Vbb 11, fols. 13 and 17.
5. These amendments must have been limited to changes in the handles and/or slight modification of the moldings to facilitate shaping. On the occasion of the 1825 alterations, the model was said to be "imité de l' antique."

101.
Design for a Cabinet-on-Stand, 1842

Léon Feuchère
Watercolor, gouache, and ink on paper
15 7/8 x 12 5/8 in. (40.2 x 32.2 cm)
Inscription: [recto, bottom, in ink, in the hand of Denis-Désiré Riocreux] *1er projet de Meuble cabinet chinois / par M. Leon Feuchere 1842 – 1843*
Inv. no. D § 10 1843 N° 1 (1er)

In 1841, after producing a limited number of large, rather conventional, *bureaux-secrétaires* at the manufactory,[1] Brongniart decided to undertake a furniture design in a more fantastic vein, a "cabinet Chinese form and decoration subjects taken from studies made in China by M. Borget."[2] The idea may have been suggested to Brongniart by three Chinese landscape paintings by Auguste Borget that were exhibited at the salon of 1841.[3]

According to the progress sheet for the cabinet, Brongniart had already inaugurated the project in July 1841 and discussed it with Borget the following August 19. Subsequently, he asked the architect Léon Feuchère to design the form and ornament of the cabinet itself.[4] In August 1842 Feuchère presented his first colored rendering, which was probably the one mentioned in a payment entry dated May 8, 1843, for 600 francs.[5] In January 1843 he submitted a colored drawing and plan, which took into account the precise dimensions of Borget's paintings. This submission also included a series of detail renderings of the fittings, ornament, and color schemes.

The completed piece entered the sales inventory on May 28, 1844,[6] and was exhibited at the Louvre on June 3, 1844. Its porcelain plaques had been painted by four different artists: Jean-Baptiste-Gabriel Langlacé and Jules André were responsible for the landscape compositions; Jean-Charles Develly executed the figures; and Pierre Huard, the ornament. In the catalog of the Louvre exhibition, Brongniart noted: "Special care has been taken to avoid imitation Chinese ornament,"[7] by which he meant that the decoration was closely modeled after "authentic" Chinese examples, a historically correct approach that was quite new at the time.

The Chinese cabinet-on-stand was illustrated in both the *Description méthodique du musée* (1845), and an album of prints published by Feuchère.[8]

Inscription: ["First furniture project Chinese cabinet / by M. Leon Feuchere 1842 – 1843"]
1. Ledoux-Lebard, "Arredi da Re" (1992).
2. [Dit *Cabinet* forme et decoration chinoises sujet tires des etudes faites en Chine par M. Borget] Carton Pb 10, liasse 1, dossier Meubles et jardinières.
3. Livret of the salon of 1841, nos. 196 – 198.
4. Carton Pb 10, liasse 1, dossier Meubles et jardinieres, July 1841 and August 19, 1841. The architect Léon Feuchère may have been the brother of the bronze-caster Armand Feuchère.
5. "Piece of furniture in the form of an armoire with console support, entirely colored actual size drawing and supervision until execution reaches completion" Carton R 38 (1842). Feuchère was paid for the *glacière 'Arabe'* at the same time (see cat. no. 99).
6. Register Vv 4, fol. 22, no. 18. Total production expenses came to 24,000 francs (including fees for the painted compositions); the sale price was set at 27,000 francs. Napoleon III gave the piece to the king of Sweden in October 1861 (Register Vbb 12, fol. 32). See Alcouffe, Dion-Tenenbaum, and Ennès, *Un âge d'or,* exhib. cat. (1991), no. 229, pp. 404 – 08.
7. [On a mis un très grand scrupule à ne faire aucun ornement d'imitation de style chinois.]
8. Brongniart and Riocreux, *Description méthodique du musée* (1845), P, pl. 15; Feuchère, *Art industriel* (1842), pt. 1, pl. 69.

Pendule turque à musique. (Juillet 1843.)

102.
Design for a Clock, 1843
Called *Pendule 'Turque à Musique'*

Léon Feuchère
Watercolor, gouache, and ink on cardboard
23 x 18 in. (58.4 x 45.6 cm)
Inscription: [recto, bottom center, in ink, in the hand of Denis-Désiré Riocreux] *Pendule turque à musique. (Juillet 1843).*; [bottom right, in ink] [signature] *Léon Feuchère*
Inv. no. D § 10 1843 N° 3 (1)

On June 8, 1843, Brongniart received written confirmation of a verbal commission for a Turkish-style musical clock that King Louis-Philippe intended to present to the viceroy of Egypt, Mehemet-Ali.[1] It was conceived as one of a series of diplomatic gifts for "the Princes of the East," namely the sultan of the Ottoman Empire, the bey of Tunis, and the viceroy of Egypt. The clock was to be presented personally by the duc de Montpensier, Louis-Philippe's son.

On June 8, Brongniart assigned the design project to Léon Feuchère, who on June 22 submitted a quarter-size drawing of this clock. The date of July 1843 inscribed by Riocreux on this watercolor is essentially accurate, for on the following November 30 Brongniart noted: "agreement reached with M. Feuchère regarding the fee for drawings consisting of seven drawings colored in whole or in part supervision of execution etc. etc. in the amount of 800 francs."[2]

In 1844 Brongniart remarked: "it has taken the whole year to make the models, the countless pieces of openwork porcelain, the countless little columns, caryatids, crests . . . etc. that compose this clock."[3] In January and February 1845 Brongniart asked the orientalist Joseph-Toussaint Reinaud, a fellow member of the Institut de France, to select some Arabic sentences and recommend a calligrapher capable of providing flawless models of these inscriptions as well as clockface numbers for the gilders at Sèvres to copy.[4] Beginning in August 1845, production of the musical clock mechanism was entrusted to the highly regarded firm of Breguet, Neveu et Cie. Apart from the complexity of the program, the choice of appropriate music also posed difficulties. Brongniart initially indicated that "two-thirds could consist of some of the prettiest French airs and one-third of the most popular Turkish airs,"[5] but the comte de Montalivet differed and sent a new list of airs — exclusively French ones — that had been expressly approved by Louis-Philippe. As a result, some of the cylinders had to be remade. The completed clock entered the sales inventory on May 30, 1846, the day before the opening of the exhibition at the Louvre.[6] Afterwards, one of Bréguet's employees was charged with accompanying the piece to Egypt to assure the proper operation of the clock mechanism.[7]

It is not known whether Louis-Philippe had seen this piece at any stage during its execution. Nevertheless, on May 18, 1845, he commissioned another clock "in the Turkish style" to give to the sultan, specifying that its clockface was to be "visible from all sides," that it was not to have "the least resemblance" to the one for Mehemet-Ali, and that it was to feature a mechanism with "a carillon, music, etc."[8] This project was apparently never realized, perhaps because it proved extremely difficult to conceive a totally new design for such a similar program.

1. Carton M 13, liasse 3 (1846), dossier "*Présents du Roi aux princes d'Orient*"; Register Vtt 5, fol. 57v.
2. [convenu avec M. Feuchère du prix des dessins portés pour tout se composant de 7 dessins coloriés en tout ou en partie, des soins à donner a l'execution etc. etc. de 800 francs]; an examination of the documents proves that the total fee received by Feuchère for these drawings was, in fact, 1,000 francs (Carton Pb 11, liasse 1, dossier "Pendules").
3. [toute cette année a été employée a faire les modeles, a faire les innombrables pièces de porcelaine decoupées a jour, les innombrables petites colonnes, cariatides, crêtes . . . etc qui composent cette pendule] Ibid.
4. Reinaud recommended the orientalist E. Combarel.
5. [on pourrait y faire entrer deux tiers d'airs français des plus jolis et un tiers d'airs turques des plus populaires] Carton Pb 11, liasse 1, dossier "Pendules."
6. Register Vv 4, fol. 66, no. 85. The flowers were painted by Louis-Pierre Schilt, Joseph Lejour, and Jean-Joseph Fontaine. Total production expenses came to 33,491.90 francs (including 2,600 francs for the flower painting, 5,023 francs for the reticulated plaques and decorative pieces, 1,800 francs for the plaster models, 1,331 francs for the clay and wood maquette, 8,413 francs for the bronze mounts, and 5,500 francs for the musical clock mechanism); the sale price was set at 36,000 francs.
7. Characteristically, Brongniart exploited this circumstance by asking the employee to obtain specimens for both the Muséum d'Histoire Naturelle and the Musée Céramique.
8.Carton M 13, liasse 3 (1846), dossier "Presents du Roi aux Princes d'Orient.

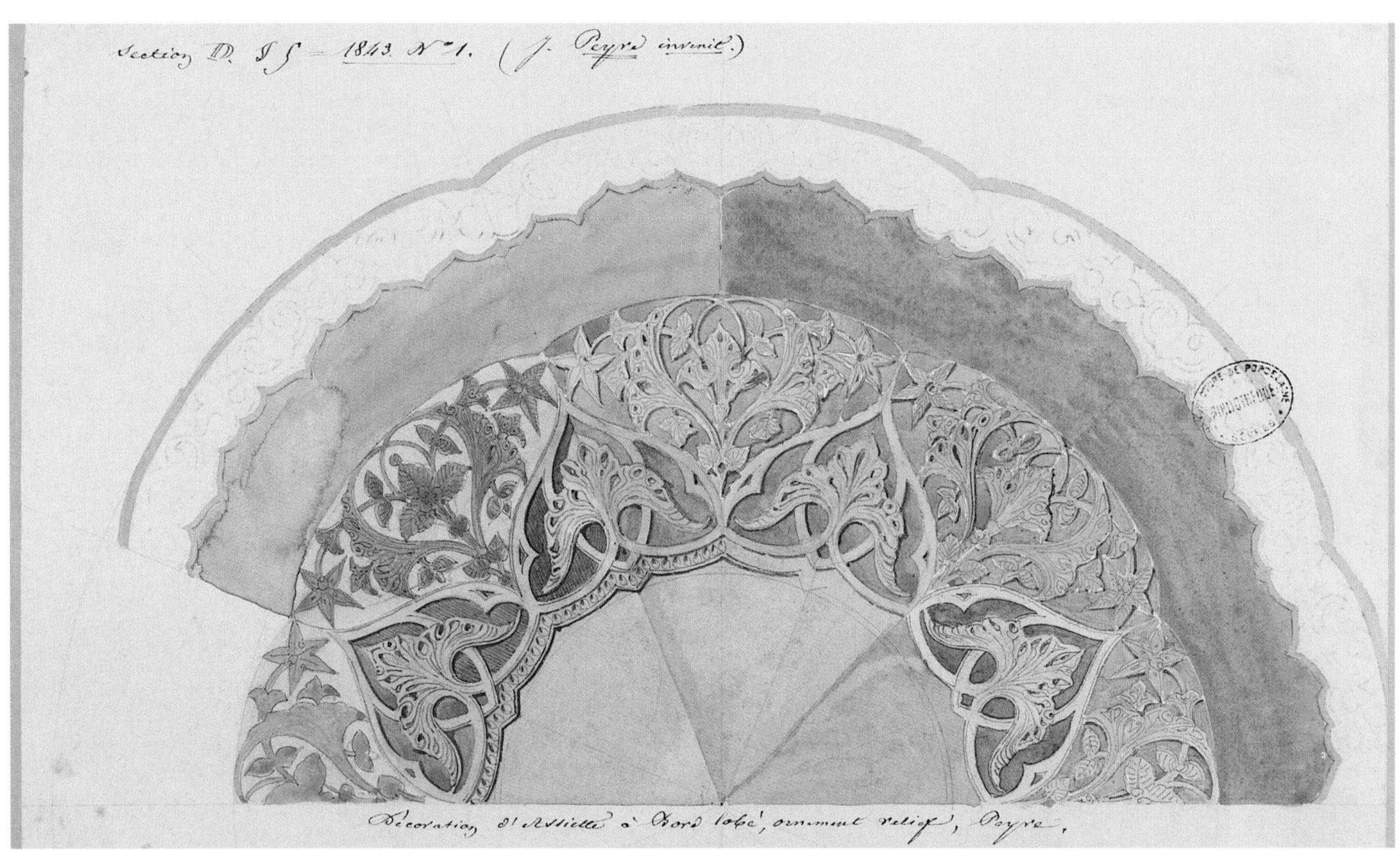

103.
Decoration for a Plate, 1843
Called *Assiette 'A bord festonné N° 1'*, 1843

Watercolor, gouache, and pencil on paper
6 x 10 1/4 in. (15.3 x 26 cm)
Inscription: [recto, bottom, in ink, in the hand of Denis-Désiré Riocreux] *Décoration d'Assiette à Bord lobé, ornement relief, Peyre.*
Inv. no. D § 5 1843 N° 1

While Brongniart began to have Léon Feuchère design furniture and other large pieces to be made at Sèvres, he must have also felt the need to hire a designer capable of reinvigorating the manufactory's more ordinary production — its service pieces, small vases, and ornamental objects. It is not known how he established contact with the sculptor and designer Jules Peyre, but on December 23, 1842, Peyre was paid 80 francs for "two drawings of decorated plates executed in wash on Bristol cardboard."[1] These designs may relate to two more payments, for work done in May 1843: "wax model of border — half with relief ornament — for a plate 40 francs"; and "another wax model of relief ornament covering the border of a plate 70 francs."[2]

The first model could be for the *assiette 'à Bord Festonné No 1'*, which featured a edge with large lobes. This was also produced without relief decoration, in which form it was known simply as the *assiette lobée.* The second model could be for the *assiette 'à Bord Festonné No 2'*, which featured an edge consisting of alternating darts and more pronounced lobes. This was also produced in several versions: one without decoration, one with raised interlace ornament, and another with similar openwork on the border. An August 1843 invoice for "decoration in the moresque style for the plate with relief ornament agreed fee 25 francs," which was paid on October 19, 1843, seems to correspond to this drawing.[3] Apparently, the ornament lightly indicated in pencil along the outer border of the plate was meant to be executed in relief underneath the glaze and left white, while the rest of the surface was to be decorated with one of the colored designs.

Thereafter, Peyre designed a number of vases, ornamental objects, table services, and *déjeuners.* The latter — notably a tea and coffee service that bears his name (see cat. no. 104) — are among the most widely imitated of all Sèvres production. Peyre also designed several models for medallions at the beginning of the Second Empire and published two albums of ornament lithographs, one of which is devoted entirely to the "Moresque" style.[4]

1. [Deux dessins d'asssiettes à ornements composés et exécutés au lavis sur carton bristol] Carton R 38 (1842).
2. [Modèle en cire de bordure a moitie marly d'ornements en relief, pour une assiette 40 francs]; [un autre modele en cire d'ornements en relief remplissant le marly d'une assiette 70 francs] Carton R 39 (1843).
3. [Décoration dans le style mauresque de l'assiette à ornements reliefs Prix convenu 25 francs] Ibid.
4. Peyre, *Orfèvrerie, bijouterie, nielle* (1844); and Peyre, *Ornements mauresques* (n.d.).

104
Decorative Schemes for Pieces with *'Rinceaux bleus'* Ornament, 1844

Jules Peyre

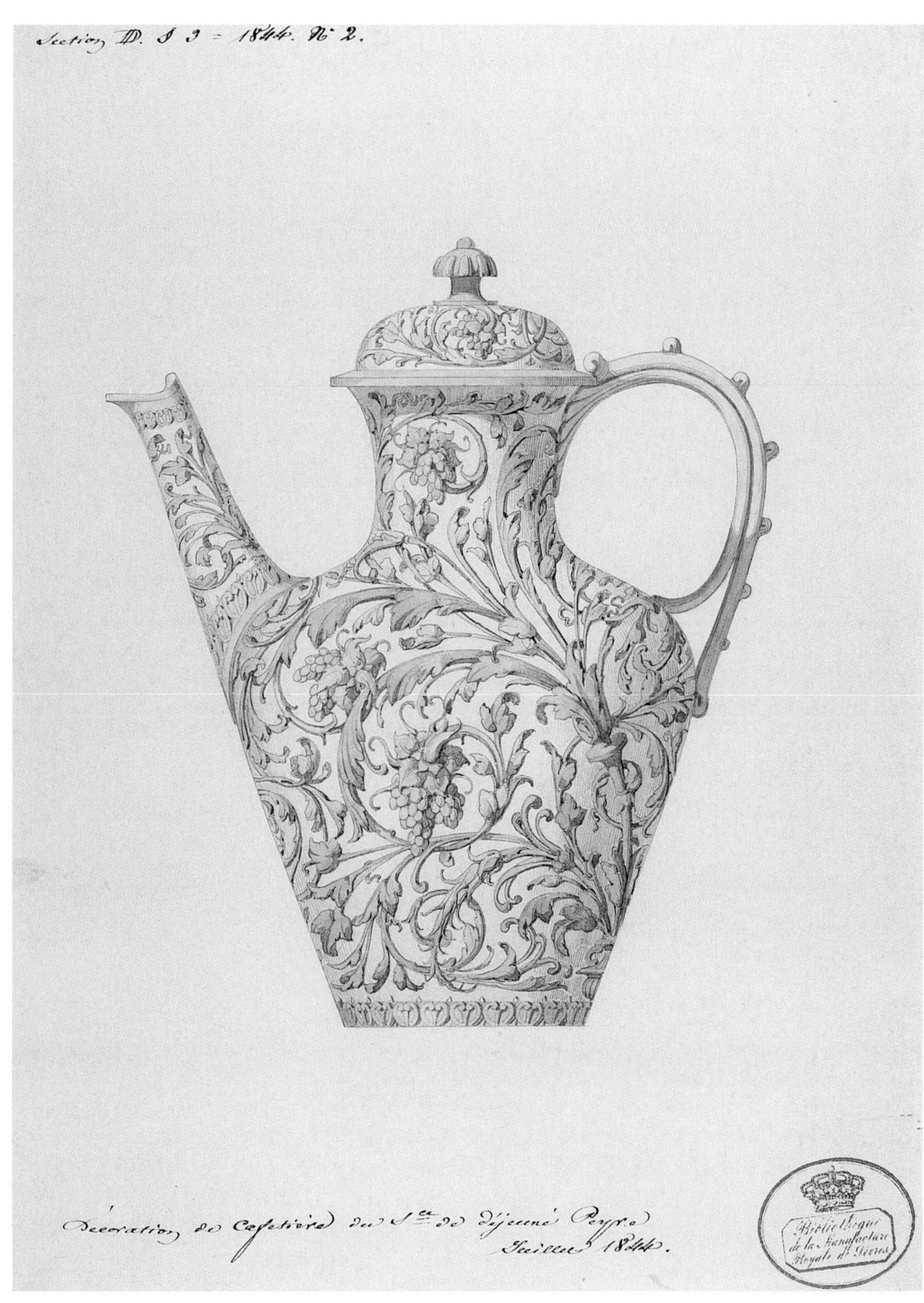

104a. Decoration for a Coffeepot, 1844° Called *Cafetière 'Peyre'*

Watercolor and ink on thin cardboard
11 3/4 x 8 3/4 in. (29.8 x 22.1 cm)
Inscription: [recto, bottom, in ink, in the hand of Denis-Désiré Riocreux] *Décoration de cafetière du S^ce^ de déjeuné Peyre / Juillet 1844.*
Inv. no. D § 3 1844 N° 2

The transfer-printing technique, which uses etched copper plates, was introduced gradually at Sèvres. In was first used in 1806 to imprint crowned "N"s on tableware for the imperial palaces, and in 1813 the manufactory started to use it systematically for its marks. The technique's economy of application eventually led to its being employed for friezes and attributes of various kinds on small vases and tableware, first in gold and then in brown, with colored highlights sometimes added by hand (see cat. nos. 49 and 50). In 1844, when these drawings by Peyre were executed, there had been a further technical advance which enabled the manufactory to transfer-print in color. This technique, used for the decorations in these designs, eliminated a degree of handwork and provided the manufactory with additional savings in labor and time.

Jules Peyre had begun his affiliation with Sèvres in 1842 by designing the so-called *déjeuner 'Peyre'* and several pieces for the *service 'Lobé'* (compote dish, fruit bowl, sugar bowl, and plate; see cat. no. 103). On July 31, 1844, he received several payments,

104b. Decoration for a Plate, 1844
Called *Assiette 'Lobée'*

Watercolor and pencil on cardboard
6 3/4 x 10 in. (17.2 x 25.4 cm)
Inscription: [recto, bottom, in ink, in the hand of Denis-Désiré Riocreux] *Assiette lobée, Peyre, Sce rinceaux bleus, 1844*
Inv. no. D § 5 1844 N° 1a

including one "for the composition of a milk jug, outline drawing and decoration in color" (25 francs) and another "for the composition of a plate decorated with festooned border, and a second rosette" (40 francs).[1] Despite the imprecise language of these entries, there can be little doubt that they correspond to the drawings here, because Peyre included lithographs of the same designs in an album of his original ornamental prints that entered the Sèvres library in 1845. These prints reveal that the same ornament was meant to be used on a complete coffee service.[2] Similarly, the surviving etched plates used in the transfer-printing process indicate that the same rinceaux were adapted for use on all of the pieces from the *service 'Lobé'*.

The first pieces of tableware with this embellishment entered the sales inventory on August 12, 1845.[3] Apparently, an attempt was later made to produce a more elaborate decoration using the same etched copper plate, for the following mention appears in the documents: "Peyre plate no. 2 frieze printed in violet and heightened in blue, medallion and surrounding ornament in gold."[4]

1. [Pour la composition d'un pot à lait, dessin au trait et décoré en couleurs]; [pour la composition d'un décor d'assiette à bord festonné, et d'une seconde rosace] Carton R 41 (1844).
2. Peyre, *Ornements mauresques* (n.d.), pl. 56, 76, and 77.
3. Register Vv 4, fol. 47, no. 14: 75 Peyre plates no. 1 with printed blue ornament (15 francs each); 4 fruit bowls (50 francs each); 6 compote dishes (40 francs each). Eighteen plates, four fruit bowls, six compote dishes, two sugar bowls, and a lobed Peyre tray were sold to a M. Halford in November 1845 (Register Vz 6, fol. 214v.).
4. [Assiette Peyre no. 2 frise imprimée en violet et rechampis en bleu, rosace et entourage en or] Carton Pb 9, liasse 2.

105.
Design and Decoration for a Jewelry Casket, 1845
Called *Coffret 'Roman'*

Ferdinand Régnier
Watercolor and pencil on paper
11 1/2 x 18 1/8 in. (29 x 46 cm)
Inscriptions: [recto, top, in ink, in the hand of Denis-Désiré Riocreux] *Coffret Roman*; [bottom left, in ink, in the hand of Alexandre Brongniart] *travaux de 1844 – 45. Pieces Diverse nº 17*; [bottom center, in ink] *Coffret roman par M. Ferd. Regnier / vu le 6 mars 1845 / L'administrateur.*; [in the hand of the director] *Alex Brongniart*
Inv. no. D § 10 1845 Nº 3 (1)

In December 1845 Joseph-Ferdinand Régnier received 180 francs for a drawing of a coffer composed and colored in the Roman style.[1] The concept of a jewelry casket (see cat. no. 98) combined a form reminiscent of medieval reliquaries with ornament of Renaissance inspiration, but the design shown here was clearly intended to be stylistically unified and historically accurate. It resembles a reliquary, or the porch of a church, while the regular network of ornament recalls medieval inlaid floor and wall patterns. The use of the term *Roman* suggests the imprecision with which terminology was applied in this period.

The inlaid-paste technique used for this design was initially perfected at Sèvres for the first *vase 'Arabe de l' Alhambra'* (see cat. no. 99). The technique was then used in the *pendule 'Turque'* (see cat. no. 102) which was exhibited at the Louvre on June 1, 1846, where the *coupe 'de Henri II'*, also decorated with inset-paste designs, was shown. The form, created in 1841, was initially decorated in a traditional way; the first example to feature inset-paste patterns dates from 1846. The technique proved versatile; it was compatible with a range of stylistic idioms for which Sèvres became known in the mid-nineteenth century.

Another piece in a medieval style resembling this coffer was also shown at the exhibition at the Louvre in 1846: a so-called *pendule 'Romane'* featured a composition depicting Charlemagne receiving a water clock from Caliph Aroun-al-Raschid, flanked by two figures painted in *trompe l'oeil* alabaster. The remainder of the decorative scheme was executed with inset-paste.

The date of the drawing for the *coffret 'Roman'* reveals that it was conceived while the *pendule 'Romane'* was in production. The progress sheet for the project is unusually laconic, but it does specify the three narrative subjects to be represented on it. On the lid is Saint Eloy at the court of King Chlotar II presenting the king with a piece of goldsmith's work, while on the front and back sides Saint Eloy is depicted visiting the Limoges mint, and also ransoming prisoners.[2] An attempt was made to achieve coherence between the object's purpose and its shape, ornament, and iconography.

The actual production process was protracted: the completed piece did not enter the sales inventory until February 28, 1853.[3] In June 1853 it was delivered to serve as a trophy for the winner of the Versailles steeplechase.[4] Among the reasons for the survival of the manufactory during the revolution of 1848 were the need to furnish the "palaces of the nation" and the demand for suitable prizes for the various charitable competitions and good works, which were encouraged by the new republic. Napoleon III had been made emperor in 1852, but by the spring of 1853, this event was still too recent to have affected the use of Sèvres pieces as prizes. Eventually, however, the volume of Sèvres pieces requisitioned by the emperor to serve as diplomatic gifts increased, taking precedent over prizes in the manufactory's production.

1. [Un dessin de coffret composé et colorié dans le style roman] Register Vj' 52 (1845), fols. 15 ff.
2. [Sur le couvercle Saint Eloy à la cour de Clotaire II lui présente une pièce d'orfèvrerie. Face devant et derriere Saint Eloy au monetaire de Limoge et Saint Eloy rachetant des captifs] Carton Pb 11, liasse 1, dossier Coffrets.
3. Register Vv 5, fol. 66, no. 26 and Carton Pb 13, appréciations 1853. Total production expenses 2,923.65 francs (including 910 francs for Ferdinand Régnier's painting of the figures and 650 for the mounts), sale price set at 4,000 francs.
4. Register Vbb 11, fol. 288v.

Section D. 810 – 1848. No 35.
Projet de reliquaire en émail.
AU CINQUIEME DE L'EXECUTION.
Paris. octo. mdcccxlv. E. Viollet Le Duc inv. et del.
DE PORCELAINE
A SÈVRES

106.
Design for an Enamel Coffer, 1845

Eugène-Emmanuel Viollet-le-Duc
Watercolor, gouache, and pencil on paper
13 1/4 x 9 1/8 in. (33.8 x 23.3 cm)
Inscription: [recto, top, in ink, in the hand of Denis-Désiré Riocreux] *Projet de reliquaire en émail*; [bottom center in red ink, in the hand of Viollet-le-Duc] *au cinquième de l'execution*; [bottom right, in red ink] [signature] *Paris.octo.mdcccxlv. E. Viollet Le Duc inv. et del.*
Inv. no. D § 10 1848 N° 35

Alexandre Brongniart probably met the architect Eugène-Emmanuel Viollet-le-Duc in the salon of Etienne-Jean Delécluze,[1] and it was perhaps thanks to ties established there that in 1838 Brongniart asked the young architect to provide some designs for the manufactory's workshop for stained glass and painting on glass (see cat. no. 95). Viollet-le-Duc was to become the most noteworthy proponent of the Gothic Revival in France during the nineteenth century. His teachings and publications brought a scholarly approach to the study of the medieval world. Most of Viollet-le-Duc's projects for Sèvres involved stained glass, but the drawing here — for which no payment record has been found — shows that he was also interested in the enamel-on-metal workshop.

The rediscovery of this vitreous art at Sèvres was incremental. It was most likely encouraged by the historic examples of medieval enamelwork that began to appear with increased frequency on the Parisian market in the first half of the nineteenth century. At the New Year's exhibition of January 1, 1830, at the Louvre, Brongniart presented an octagonal *guéridon* "in the Gothic style" whose principal ornament was a composition inspired by Milton's *Paradise Lost.* This was surrounded by "twelve medallions in grisaille heightened in gold, in the manner of Limoges enamels."[2]

The Louvre exhibition of May 1, 1842, included two *vases 'Adélaïde'* with paintings by Alexis-Etienne Julienne celebrating "famous enamelers of the sixteenth century" as well as two more examples of the same form decorated with "white enamel ornament in the manner of sixteenth-century Limousin enamels" painted by Jacob Meyer-Heine.[3] The Louvre exhibition of June 3, 1844, featured a *jardinière* by Hyacinthe-Jean Régnier decorated with portraits of horticulturists painted in a technique that resembled Limoges enamel. Decorations of this kind may well have been inspired by Parisian production. In a manuscript note dated October 13, 1840, Riocreux remarked: "Currently in Paris, decoration is being applied to porcelains analogous to sixteenth-century enameled coppers from Limoges; this decoration is executed against a glost-fired blue ground in a white enamel so solid that its application seems to have no limits; it becomes extremely rich when combined with gold, making it possible for porcelain to escape the limited possibilities which seem to contain it."[4] Riocreux goes on to attribute work of this kind to a painter named Vion.

In a parallel development, Brongniart soon began trials with real enamel on copper.[5] On the occasion of the Louvre exhibition of June 1, 1846, when the first such pieces produced by the manufactory were presented, Brongniart announced the establishment of a special workshop: "His Majesty has asked us to revive the fabrication of enameled pieces in the manner of the Limousins, perfecting [this technique] in accordance with advances made in the chemical sciences." The workshop was in operation between 1845 and 1872, and it produced both painted Limoges-type enamels — in grisaille heightened with gold — and pieces of Middle-Eastern and Asian inspiration (see cat. no. 109). Unfortunately, nothing in its productions resembled this design, which was probably judged too elaborate.

Viollet-le-Duc's powerful Gothic Revival designs, the antithesis of the more decorative *style 'Cathedrale'* or *style 'Troubadour'* from earlier in the century, had a powerful impact not only on the French-speaking world, but elsewhere as well. This polychrome design for a hanging cabinet predates similar work produced in England in the late 1850s and the succeeding decades.

Inscription: ["Enamel reliquary project / fifth of the execution / Paris.octo.1845. E. Viollet Le Duc"]

1. Leniaud, *Viollet-le-duc* (1994), p. 10.
2. [Douze médaillons en grisaille rehaussée d'or, à la manière des émaux de Limoges]; many French artists depicted episodes from Milton's great poem after the publication of François-René de Chateaubriand's translation.
3. [aux illustres émailleurs du XVIe siècle]; [ornements en émaux blancs à la manière des emaux limousins du XVIe siècle] *Notice . . . 1er Mai 1842.*
4. [On applique actuellement à la décoration de la porcelaine à Paris des ornements analogues à ceux des cuivres émaillées de Limoges du 16e siècle; cette décoration se fait sur bleu de grand feu avec un blanc d'émail si solide que son application paraît n'avoir aucune limite; elle acquiert beaucoup de richesse par l'alliance de l'or et fait sortir la porcelaine des ressources bornées dans lesquelles elle paraissait devoir être limitée] Carton U 15, liasse 2.
5. When he was twenty years old, Brongniart, during a trip to England, wrote an essay entitled "L'Art de l'émailleur sur métaux" (The Art of metal enameling). The first trials at the manufactory were undertaken in late 1838 (Carton U 15, liasse 2)

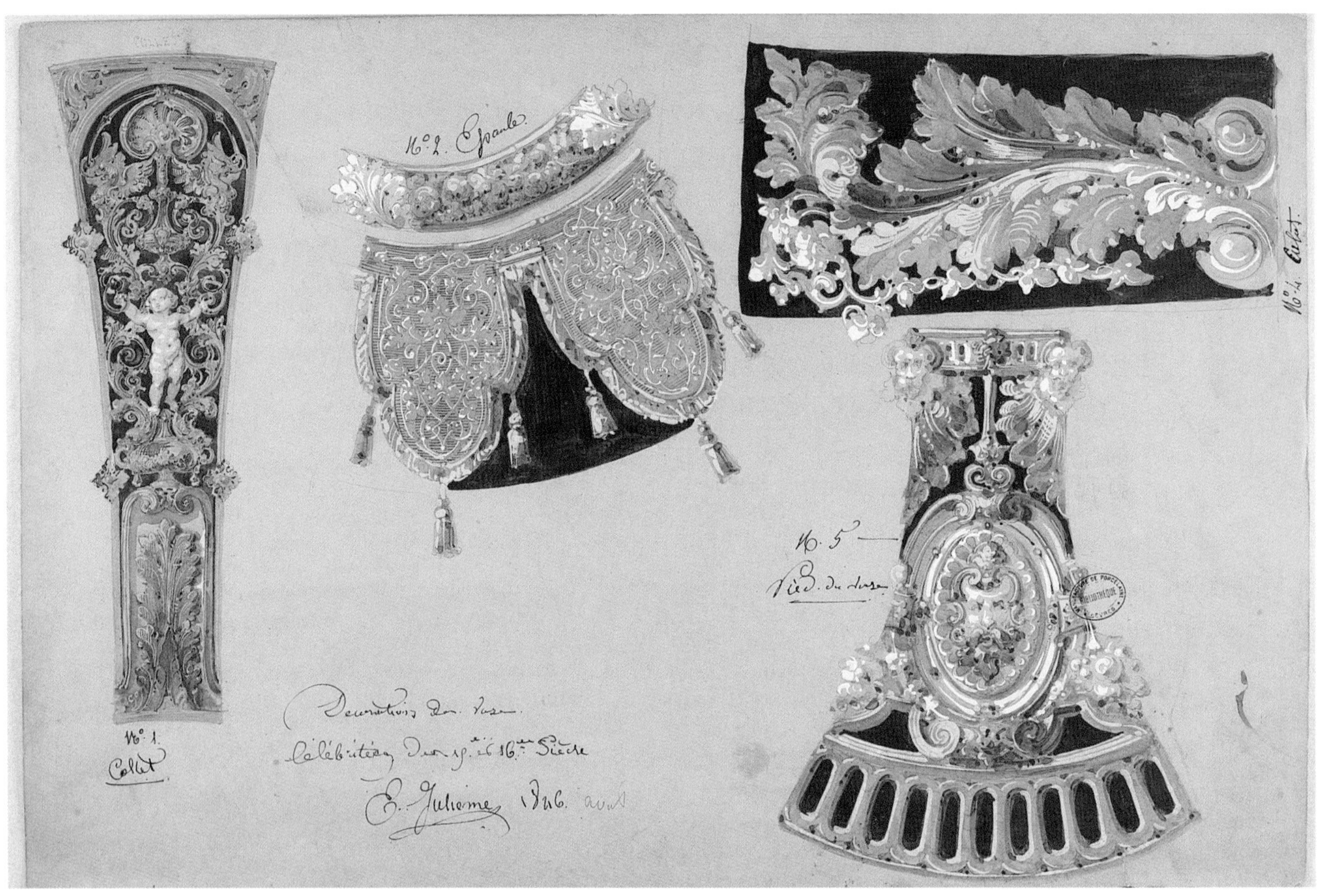

107.
Decoration for a Vase, 1846
Called *Vase 'Oeuf'*

Alexis-Etienne Julienne
Watercolor, gouache, and pencil on heavy paper
11 1/2 x 17 3/8 in. (29.1 x 44.1 cm)
Inscriptions: [recto, variously placed next to corresponding details, in ink, in Julienne's hand] *N° 1 Colet / N° 2 Epaule / N° 4 Culot / N° 5 Pied du vase*; [bottom left, in ink, including signature]: *Decoration du Vase / Célébrités des 15e et 16e siècle / E. Julienne 1846*; [right of signature in pencil] *aout*
Inv. no. 1995 D 12

The composition of this sheet marks a distinct departure from earlier design practices at the manufactory. Instead of rendering the various decorative elements on the form, Julienne detailed each of them separately while the principal composition must have been drawn on a separate sheet. By using this method, and not producing a complete final drawing, it would have been virtually impossible to assess the overall effect produced by a proposed decorative scheme. The practice was nonetheless adopted for most of the projects undertaken in the second half of the nineteenth century.

The artist's inscription makes it possible to link this drawing to *N°2* on the list of work allocations for 1846: "2. Egg vases second size famous sixteenth-century figures from all countries and in all genres. Decoration consistent with this intent and period. Composition and execution of the decoration by M. Julienne figures drawn by M. Gosse."[1] In January 1847 the following note was entered regarding Nicolas-Louis-François Gosse: "announces that the compositions are done. Research for the character of the heads, the costumes, and the poses drawn from nature; and to assure the accuracy of the costumes he had a costumier make them in accordance with his drawings."[2]

A list drawn up by Brongniart includes twelve figures, the only one relating to the arts being Michelangelo. The ornament on this sheet reveals the type of overloaded "Renaissance" style typical of the 1840s in France. The delicate interlace patterns against a gray ground on the lambrequins might correspond to descriptions of "*damassés*," or damascened, ornament that had been associated with the "Renaissance" style for some years in France.[3]

Although Julienne began work on the vases in August 1846,[4] they did not enter the sales inventory until July 12, 1849; Napoleon III presented them to the King of Portugal in 1856.[5]

Inscription: ["No 1 Collar / No 2 Shoulder / No 4 Bottom / No. 5 Foot of the vase"]; ["Decoration of the Vase / celebrities of the 15th and 16th century / E. Julienne 1846 / August"]

1. [2 Vases Oeuf 2me grandeur les personnages illustres du 16e siècle dans tous les pays et dans tous le genre [sic]. Décoration analogues a cette destination et a cette epoque. Composition et execution de la décoration par M. Julienne dessin des figures par M. Gosse] Carton Pb 11, liasse 1, dossier Vases.
2. [Fait savoir que les compositions sont faites. Les recherches pour les caractères de têtes, les costumes et les poses dessinees d'apres nature; et pour que les costumes soient exactes il s'est arrangé avec un costumier qui les a faits d'apres ses dessins.] Ibid.
3. A pair of *vases 'Etrusques de 1810'* decorated by Julienne in 1839 – 40 and now at the chateau of Fontainebleau appear to be among the earliest pieces to feature ornament of this kind (Chevallier, *Musée national du château de Fontainebleau* (1996), no. 76, pp. 111 – 12).
4. Register Vj' 53 (1846), fols. 63 ff.
5. For entry in sales inventory, see Register Vv 5, fol. 26, no. 1 and Carton Pb 12, appréciations 1849. Total production expenses came to 6,289.80 francs, which included 100 francs paid to Julienne for the "*composition et dessin*," another 3,100 francs paid to Julienne for the actual porcelain painting, and 1,080 francs for the "*modèle ou dessin*," probably paid to Gosse; the sale price was set at 7,500 francs each. For delivery, see Register Vbb 12, fol. 13.

108.
Design for a Milk Jug, 1846
Called *Pot à Lait 'Dimère Réticulé'*

Jules Peyre
Watercolor, gouache, and pencil on thick paper
10 3/8 x 13 3/4 in. (26.8 x 34.2 cm)
Inscriptions: [recto, bottom center, in ink, in the hand of Denis-Désiré Riocreux] *Pot à lait / du déjeuné dimère reticulé, Peyre. / (1846.)*; [bottom right, in ink] [signature] *J Peyre*
Inv. no. D § 3 1846 N° 2

Beginning in November 1845, Jules Peyre was paid for a series of designs for a *déjeuner,* eventually christened the *déjeuner 'Dimère'* because it was intended to serve only two persons. From the start, two variants were envisioned — a smooth one and another featuring areas of openwork revealing the actual wall of the vessel within. By analogy with the *déjeuner 'Chinois Réticulé'* with similar openwork ornament (see cat. no. 76), this version was dubbed the *déjeuner 'Dimère Réticulé'*. The first payment relating to this variation dates from December 1845.[1] The drawing here is less successful than the one made for the Chinese-style *déjeuner* by Hyacinthe Régnier, for it offers no hint of the existence of the essential wall of the inner vessel that held the liquid (see cat. no. 76)

The delicate technique of producing openwork patterns in unfired paste, perfected during fabrication of the *déjeuner 'Chinois Réticulé'*, was used subsequently in simpler decorative pieces lacking the inner vessel. At the Louvre exhibition of June 3, 1844 the manufactory presented several "openwork bowls." They were described in the catalogue as being "in the Chinese style," a characterization that links them to the original models for the technique as developed at the manufactory. In contrast, at the Louvre exhibition of June 1, 1846, Sèvres displayed examples of Middle-Eastern and Asian inspiration with openwork elements: the *pendule 'Turque'* (see cat. no. 102), a *vase 'Piriforme réticulé'*, which, judging from a drawing at Sèvres, was "*mauresque*" in form with a decorative scheme that was more European in character; two reticulated coffers (one decorated with reserves painted with flowers and the other with royal châteaus); and some zarfs with delicate openwork.

The 1846 exhibition also featured the simple version of the *déjeuner 'Dimère'*, but the reticulated variant seems to have been abandoned. Perhaps the design was deemed too difficult to produce and too fragile for use. There is a suggestion in the drawing that even the handle of this jug was to include openwork. This hardly seems practical, however, and it would have been all but impossible to permanently secure the handle to an openwork panel, something that is also indicated here. Judging from the shortcomings of this design, Jules Peyre had much to learn about the technical imperatives of porcelain production.

1. Register Vj' 52 (1845), fol. 258 ff., and Register Vj' 43 (1846), fol. 248 ff.

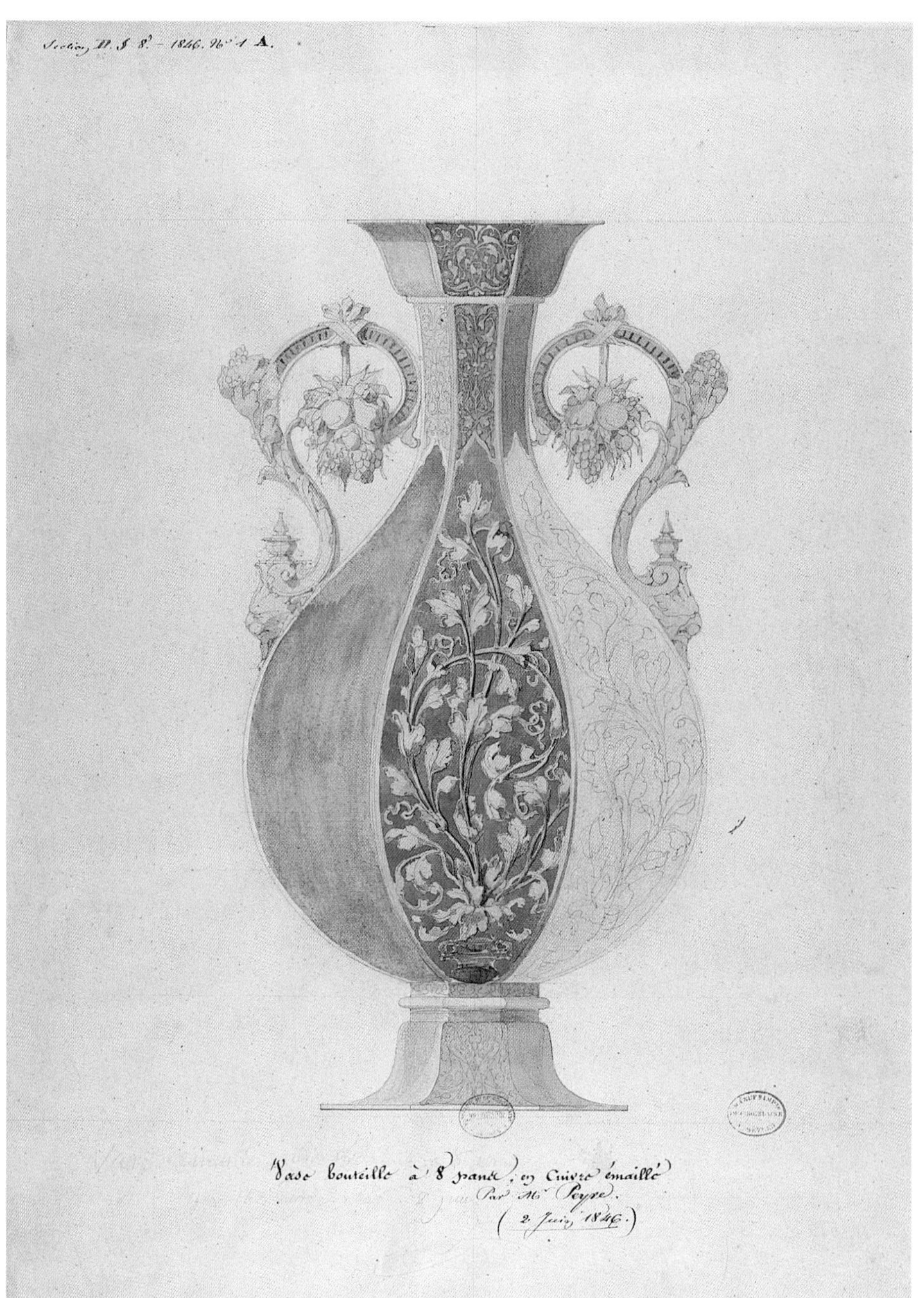

109.
Design for a Bottle-Vase, 1846

Jules Peyre
Watercolor, gouache, and pencil on paper
17 3/8 x 13 1/8 in. (44.1 x 33.4 cm)
Inscriptions: [recto, bottom center, in ink, in the hand of Denis-Désiré Riocreux] *Vase Bouteille à 8 pans, en cuivre émaillé / Par Mr Peyre. / (2 juin 1846.)*; [also legible is an inscription written in pencil by Alexandre Brongniart and then erased] *Vase emaillé dit Bouteille a 8 pans / par M. Peyre 1846 2 juin / Alex B.*
Inv. no. D § 8 1846 N° 1 A.

Although the workshop for enameling on metal that opened in September 1845 had been explicitly charged by King Louis-Philippe with reviving the technique of sixteenth-century Limoges enamels (see cat. no. 106), Brongniart's limitless curiosity prompted him to explore a much broader range of models. Every variety of enamel then known was studied and emulated, including those from the Middle and Far East.

In April 1846 Jules Peyre received his first payment for "three small colored composition designs for vases to be executed on a large scale, in enameled copper."[1] The description that most closely corresponds to this drawing, taken from an inventory valuation sheet dated June 30, 1847, gives some indication of the technical refinement achieved by Jacob Meyer-Heine, director of the new workshop, at a very early date: "Two segmented vases in bottle form with blue grounds on platinum spangles green nielloed collars and feet with silver spangles against green opaque ground the sides separated by opal pearls against gold (cameo painting against the blue)."[2] The spangles referred to on the valuation sheet were actually platinum sequins decorated with colored, translucent enamels that were secured to the vessel wall by a heat-activated adhesive in a low firing. The two vases corresponding to this drawing were delivered to the Ministère de l'Interieur on July 21, 1848.[3]

A very broad historical and geographical range of objects remained characteristic of the enamel workshop's production until its closure in 1872.

Inscription: ["Bottle-vase with 8 sides, in enamelled copper / By Mr Peyre. / (2 June 1846)"]; ["Enamel vase called Bottle with 8 sides / by M. Peyre 1846 2 June / Alex B."]

1. [Trois projets de composition de vases de petites dimensions colories pour être executés en grand, en cuivre émaillé] Register Vj' 53 (1846), fol. 248 ff.
2. [2 vases à pans forme bouteille à fonds bleu sur paillons de platine les collets et les pieds à niellures vertes de paillons d'argent sur fond vert opaque les côtes separées par des perles opales sur or (peinture camaieux sur le bleu)] Carton Pb 11 bis, appréciations 1847 and Register Vv 4, fol. 97, no. 11. Total production expenses for each bottle, 1,244 francs (including 375 francs paid to Jacob Meyer-Heine for the enamel painting); sale price was set at 1,350 francs.
3. Register Vbb 11, fol. 23v.

110.
Design for a Table, [1847]

Léon Feuchère
Watercolor, gouache, and ink on paper
17 1/4 x 22 1/8 in. (43.9 x 56.2 cm)
Inscriptions: [recto, bottom center, in ink, in the hand of Denis-Désiré Riocreux] *Table rectangulaire, les grandes chasses géographiques*; [lower right, below table leg, in ink, signature] *Léon Feuchère*
Inv. no. D § 10 1847 N° 2a

Brongniart's list of projects for 1845, under the heading "*grandes pièces diverses*," includes "No. 20. A table in Louis XV style representing hunts in the five parts of the world."[1] On May 8, 1846 he added: "Conveyed to M. Léon Feuchère the figurative note of M. Develly indicating the dimensions of the top and the general disposition of the nine hunt compositions."[2] As no record of payment for this drawing has been found, it is not known when Feuchère sent it to Sèvres or whether it had already been completed when the compositions began to be painted onto the tabletop in 1846. This element was completed first and it entered the sales inventory separately on December 31, 1849.[3] The valuation sheet also refers to "17 pieces," but whether they correspond to components of this design remains unknown.

It seems clear, however, that the tabletop did not have a base at that time. Perhaps it was the decision, made on December 10, 1851, to present the table to the bey of Tunis that finally prompted the production of this missing element.[4] By that time Léon Feuchère no longer worked for Sèvres, and Jules-Auguste Fossey was paid in January 1853 for "a rectangular table in Louis XIV style, 1 meter 30 centimeters by 90 centimeters in black wood imitating ebony, mounted on four legs with gilded sculpture in gold of various colors. The table to serve as mounting for a porcelain plaque with painted compositions representing hunts in the four parts of the world. 2,000 francs."[5]

It is difficult to reconcile Feuchère's design with the "Louis XV style" called for in the original product description. However misunderstood, this style, with all its vagaries, was returning to favor at Sèvres at this time. It seems likely that Fossey completely ignored the earlier conception, which had already been modified in 1847 by Jules-Pierre-Michel Diéterle.[6] The designation "Louis XIV," which was used to characterize Fossey's design, suggests that he was already working in the opulent "Boulle" style that he would employ for an 1855 jewelry cupboard for the Empress Eugenie, another collaboration with Sèvres.[7]

1. [No. 20 Une table dans le style de Louis XV représentant des chasses dans les cinq [this word written over the original 'quatre'] parties du monde] Carton Pb 11, liasse 1.
2. [Remis à M. Leon Feuchere la note figurative de M. Develly donnant la dimension de la plaque et la disposition générale des neuf sujets de chasse.] Ibid.
3. Register Vv 5, fol. 32, no.2.
4. Carton M 15.
5. [Une table rectangulaire style Louis XIV, d'1m 30c sur 90c en bois noir imitant l'Ebène, monté sur quatre pied avec sculpture dorée en ors de diverses couleurs. La dite table servant de monture à une plaque en Porcelaine avec sujets de peinture représentant des chasses dans les quatre parties du monde 2,000 francs.] Carton R 53 (1853), payment receipt dated January 1853. The table base entered the sales inventory on February 28, 1853 (Register Vv 5, fol. 66, no. 50). The complete table was delivered to the ministry of state on February 4, 1853 (Register Vbb 12, fol. 5).
6. In December 1847, Diéterle was paid 200 francs for "two designs for modifications to the five-parts-of-the-world table." [2 dessins de projets de modifications pour la table des cinq parties du monde] Carton R 49 (1847).
7. Ducrot, *Musée National du château de Compiègne* (1993), no. 241, pp. 301 – 3.

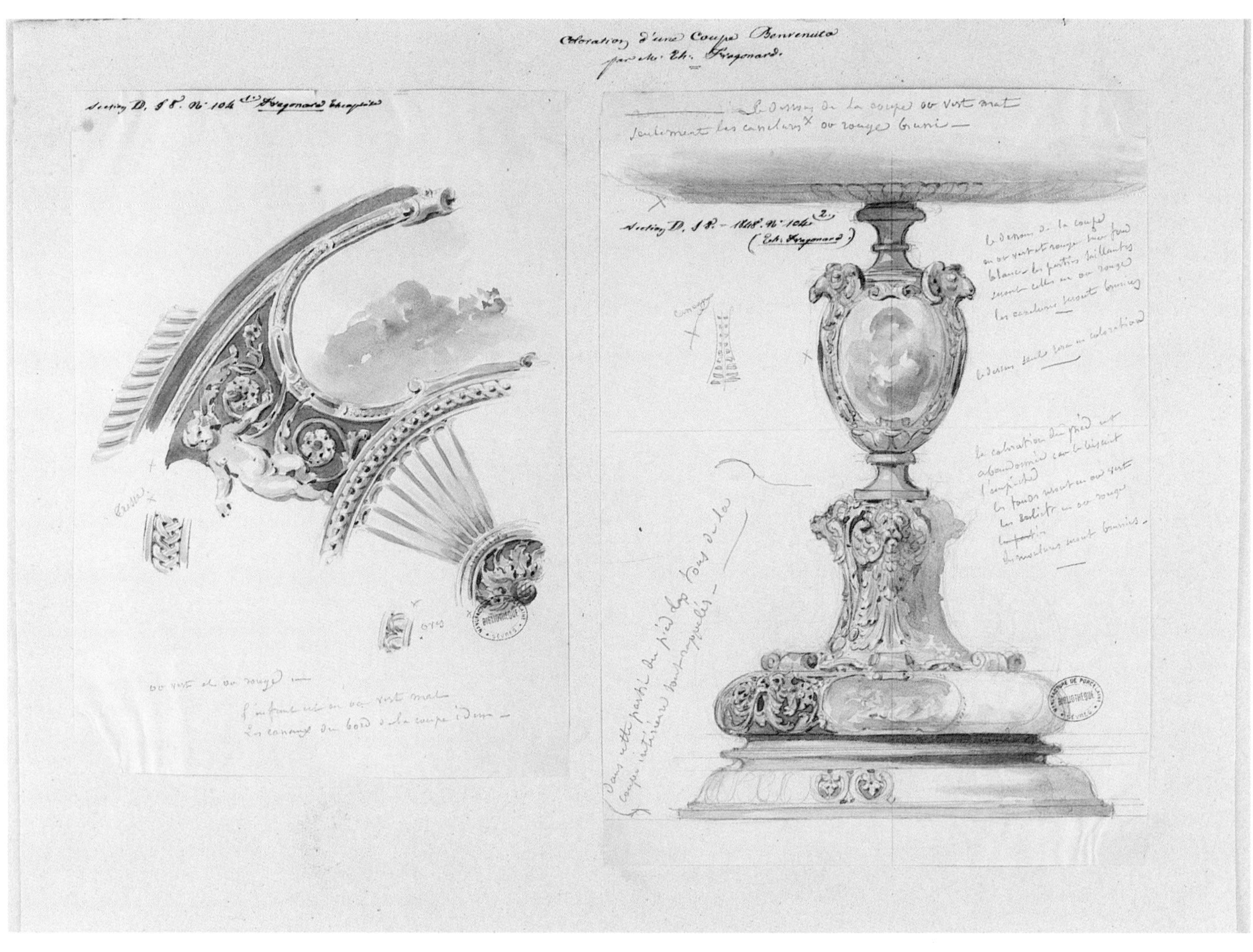

111.
Decoration for a Standing Cup, 1848
Called *Coupe 'de Benvenuto Cellini'*

Théophile-Evariste Fragonard
Watercolor and pencil on paper
9 1/8 x 6 7/8 in. (23.2 x 17.4) and 10 3/8 x 7 1/2 in. (26.2 x 19.1) (two drawings mounted on a single sheet)
Inscriptions: [recto, top center of support sheet, in ink in Riocreux's hand] *Coloration d'une Coupe Benvenuto/par M. Th. Fragonard.* [left drawing: variously distributed, in pencil, in Fragonard's hand): *tresse-or vert et or rouge-oves-l'enfant est en or vert mat / Les canaux du bord de la coupe idem*; [right drawing: from top to bottom, in pencil, in Fragonard's hand] *Le dessous de la coupe or vert mat / seulement les canelures x or rouge bruni-caneaux* [with pencil detail of ornament]- *le dessous de la coupe / en or vert et rouge sur fond / blanc-les parties saillantes / seront celles en or rouge / les canelures seront brunies-le dessus seul sera en coloration-la coloration du pied est / abandonnée car le biscuit / l'empêche / les fonds seront en or vert / les reliefs en or rouge / les moulures seront brunies-dans cette partie du pied les tons de la / coupe intérieure seront rappelés.*
Inv. no. D § 8 1848 N° 104 (1) and (2)

In March 1848 Théophile-Evariste Fragonard received 300 francs for "nine cartel compositions for a Benvenuto Cellini Tazza."[1] Only in February 1849, when he began to work directly on the porcelain, were the subjects specified: "One Benvenuto Cellini Tazza complete blue ground for initial painting of compositions representing architecture, painting, and sculpture."[2] The completed piece entered the sales inventory in February 1850[3]; it was presented to the museum in Bayeux the following December.[4] This is one of the first instances in which the manufactory gave a piece of its production to a museum.

The drawings on this sheet are indicative of a new approach to design draftsmanship then emerging at the manufactory (see also cat. no. 107). The forms are roughly indicated and the decorations only summarily sketched in, producing schematic results that give little indication of the overall effect. While such studies were useful to the designer himself, they would probably have been inadequate as models for other ornament painters. The notation of nine cartels or reserves in the original payment entry, however, suggests that these two were no more than preliminary drawings.

The form of the *coupe 'de Benvenuto Cellini'* was designed in 1838 by Hyacinthe Régnier. Its name may derive from the program used on one of the first decorated examples, whose interior featured "three principal compositions in color from the life of Benvenuto etc."[5] It was delivered to the queen on February 22, 1839. Given the increasing prominence of detailed relief elements in the Renaissance Revival idiom then in favor, the use of thematic ornament commemorating this celebrated sculptor is hardly surprising.[6]

In 1831 Théophile Fragonard, the son of Alexandre-Evariste Fragonard and the grandson of Honoré Fragonard, was admitted to the short-lived Ecole de Peinture en

Couleurs Vitrifiables (School of Painting in Vitreous Pigment) established at the workshop in the Paris salesroom of the manufactory. Brongniart announced his recruitment of this young man in the following terms: "I regard the desire of this young painter [to enroll] as one of the most complete vindications of our intentions in founding this school."[7] Fragonard began to do freelance work for Sèvres in 1839, painting many figure compositions for the manufactory in an eighteenth-century style, but he was also employed simultaneously by other Parisian producers.[8]

Inscription: ["coloration of a *'Coupe Benvenuto'* by M. Th. Fragonard"]; ["Strapwork motif-green gold or red gold-ova-the child is in matte green gold / the grooves round the rim of the dish *idem*"]; ["The underside of the dish matte green gold / only the grooves x burnished red gold-grooves [with pencil detail of ornament]-the underside of the dish / green and red gold on a white / ground-the raised parts will be the ones in red gold / the grooves burnished-the upper side only in color-the color of the foot has been / abandoned because biscuit / prevents it / the backgrounds in green gold / the relief parts in red gold / the moldings burnished-in this part of the foot the colors of the / interior of the dish to be echoed"]

1. [Composition de neuf cartels pour une coupe Benvenuto Cellini] Register Vj' 55 (1848), fol. 9 ff.. In July 1848 he received 100 francs "for new compositions for a second Benvenuto Cellini tazza: 1789, 1830, 1848" [pour nouvelles composition pour 2me coupe Benvenuto Cellini: 1789, 1830, 1848]. Since these dates commemorate the revolutions in France, the project was abandoned, presumably for political reasons, once political stability was reestablished.

2. [1 coupe Benvenuto Cellini complette fond bleu pour 1ere peinture de sujets représentant l'architecture, la peinture et la sculpture] Register Vj' 56 (1849 – 50), fol. 6 ff.

3. Carton Pb 12, appréciation of February 23, 1850. Total production expenses came to 2,513.50 francs, including 50 francs paid to François-Hubert Barbin for the ornamental painting and 750 francs paid to Théophile Fragonard for the figures; the sale price was set at 3,000 francs. See also: Register Vv 5, fol. 34, no. 10.

4. Register Vbb 11, fol. 42, December 27, 1850.

5. [Trois sujets principaux coloriés de la vie de Benvenuto etc.] Register Vbb 10, fol. 3v.

6. In 1843, a *déjeuner 'de Benvenuto Cellini'* was also delivered to Louis-Philippe (Register Vbb 10, fol. 29 v.).

7. [Je regarde le desir de ce jeune peintre comme une des applications la plus complette de l'object qu'on s'est proposé en fondant cette école] Register Vc 8, letter dated June 15, 1831.

8. Plinval de Guillebon, *Faïence et porcelaine de Paris* (1995), p. 360.

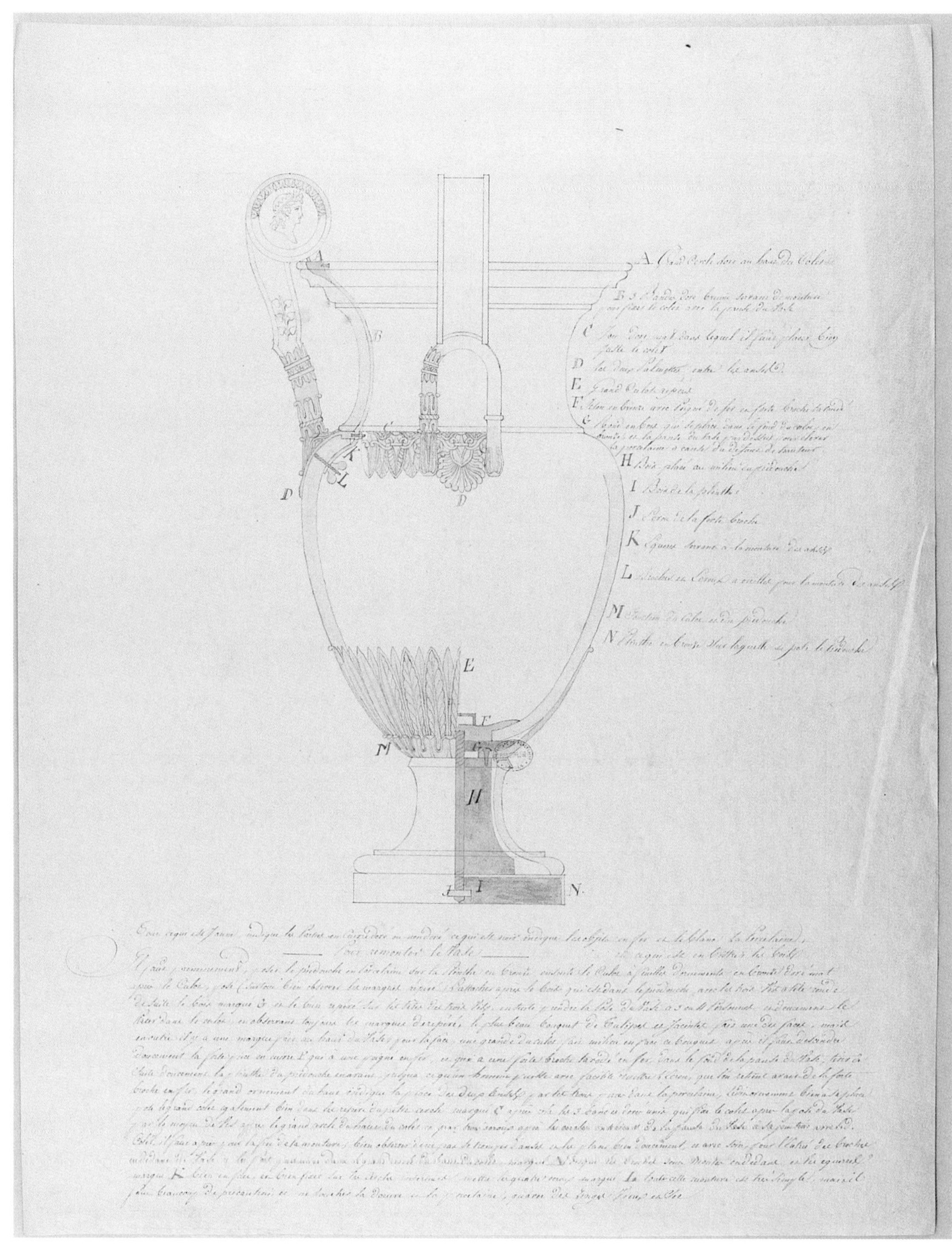

112.
Instructions for Assembling a *Vase 'Etrusque à Rouleaux'*, n.d.

23 x 17 7/8 in. (58.3 x 45.5 cm)
Watercolor and ink on paper
Inscriptions: [on recto, in ink, to right of the drawing, top to bottom: *A grand cercle doré au haut du colet / B 3 Bandes doré brunie servant de monture / pour fixer le colet avec la panse du Vase / C Jon doré mat dans lequel il faut placer bien / juste le colet / D Les deux Palmettes entre les anses. / E Grand culot repérés / F Jeton en bronze avec Poigné de fer et forte broche taraudé / G Rond en bois qui se place dans le fond du culot en / bronze, et la panse du vase par dessus pour élever / la porcelaine a cause du défaut de hauteur / H bois placé au milieu du piedouche / I Bois de la plinthe / J Ecrou de la forte broche / K Equeres servant à la monture des anses / L Broches et Ecroux a oreilles pour la monture des anses / M Jonction du culot et du piédouche / N Plinthe en bronze sur laquelle se pose le Piedouche.* Below the drawing: *Tout ce qui est jaune, indique les Parties en cuivre doré ou non doré, ce qui est noir indique les objets en fer et le blanc la Porcelaine; / et ce qui est en bistre les bois-Pour remonter le vase-/ Il faut premierement, poser le piedouche en Porcelaine sur la Plinthe en bronze, ensuite le culot à feuilles d'ornements en bronze doré mat / après le culot, posé (surtout bien observer les marques repéré) L'attacher après le bois qui est dans le piedouche avec les trois vis a tête ronde / de suite le bois marqué G et le bien repéré sur les têtes des trois vis, ensuite prendre la Pose [sic, for "panse"] du Vase à 3 ou 4 personnes et doucement le / Placer dans le culot, en observant toujours les marques de repéré, le plus beau bouquet de Tulipes et Jacintes fait une des faces, mais / en outre il y a une marque fait au haut du Vase, pour la face, une grande du culot fait milieu en face ce bouquet, après il faut descendre / doucement la forte pièce en cuivre F qui à une poignée en fer, et qui a une forte broche tarodé en fer, dans le fond de la panse du Vase, tirer de / suite doucement la plinthe du piédouche en avant, jusqu'a ce qu'un homme puisse avec facilité mettre l'Ecrou, que l'on retient avant de la forte / broche en fer, le grand ornement du haut indique la place des deux anses par les trous percés dans la porcelaine, le dit ornement*

bien à sa place / posé le grand colet également bien dans les repéré du petit cercle marqué C après cela les 3 bandes dorés unis qui fixe le colet après la pose du Vase / par le moyen de vis après le grand cercle du haut du colet et par trois écroux après les cercles intérieurs de la panse du Vase à sa jonction avec led. / Colet. Il faut après pour la fin de la monture, bien observer de ne pas se tromper d'anses et les placer bien doucement, et avec soin, pour l'Entrée des broches / en dedans du Vase et les fair prisonnier dans le grand cercle du haut du colet, marqué A. Lorsque les broches sont montés en dedans, et les equerres / marqué K bien en place, et bien fixée sur les cercles intérieurs mettre les quatre écroux marqué L. toute cette monture est très simple, mais il / faut beaucoup de précautions et ne toucher la dorure de la porcelaine qu'avec des linges vieux et sec.
Inv. no. 1995 D 13

Large vases with bronze mounts were never transported already mounted. After packing they would have been impracticably large, and their mounts would have broken the porcelain during transit. Accordingly, the component elements were packed separately and sent with detailed instructions for assembly. This drawing is a case in point, and it clearly conveys the fact that such gifts were not always a pleasure to receive. The instructions read:

"A Large gilt ring on upper part of collar
B Three burnished gilt bands serving as mounts / to fix the collar to the body of the vase
C Matte gold ring within which the collar must be carefully placed
D The two palmettes between the handles
E Large bottom with guide-marks
F Bronze disk with iron grip and large threaded pin
G Wooden disk to be placed between bronze bottom / and the body above it, to elevate / the porcelain due to a flaw in the height
H Wood to be placed in the center of the pedestal
I Wood for the plinth
J Thick screw
K Angle-irons for mounting the handles
L Pins and winged screws for mounting the handles
M Junction of the bottom and the pedestal
N Bronze plinth on which the pedestal rests.
Yellow indicates copper [?], both gilded and ungilded; black indicates iron, white indicates porcelain, and sepia indicates wood. To reassemble the vase: First place the porcelain pedestal on the bronze plinth, then [place] the base with matte gilt bronze leaves [to the pedestal], taking care to line up the guide marks. Then secure the base to the wood inside the pedestal with the three round-headed screws, then the piece of wood marked G, lining it up carefully with the three screw heads. Then have three or four men gently lift the vessel of the vase and place it within the base, always lining it up with the guide-marks: the most beautiful bouquet of Tulips and Hyacinths is on one of the faces, but in addition there is a mark partway up the face of the vase that should be lined up with a large one on the base. Then carefully lower the strong copper piece marked F, with the iron grip and thick iron-threaded pin, to the bottom of the vase, then gently slide the plinth of the pedestal forward, until a man can easily place the screw, which is to be kept in front of the thick iron pin. The large ornament on the top shows the place of both handles thanks to the holes in the porcelain. The said ornament having been put in place, insert the large collar in accordance with the guide-marks on the small ring marked C. Then screw the three smooth gilt bands that fix the collar after the positioning of the vase to the large upper ring on the collar, and attach it with three more screws to the interior rings of the body of the vase at its junction with the said collar. Before completing assembly, make certain that the handles have not been reversed. Place them gently and carefully, lining them up with the holes inside the vase so they may be secured to the large ring on the upper part of the collar, marked A. When the pins have been mounted inside, and the angle-irons marked K are in place and securely attached to the interior rings, place the four screws marked L. This assembly procedure is very simple, but many precautions must be taken: above all, do not touch the gilded areas of the porcelain with anything but an old and dry cloth."

Judging from the shape of the vase and the fact that three or four men were required to carry the vessel itself, the piece in question in this drawing must have been a *vase 'Etrusque à rouleaux'* of the first size. According to the registers, the only such example to have been decorated with flowers cited in the assembly instructions was one with "laminated gold [,] relief gold ornament burnished *à l'effet*[,] rich floral torus and colored birds and rich bronze fittings" which entered the sales inventory on December 9, 1813.[1] It was delivered to Charles Maurice de Talleyrand, then *Ministre des Affaires Etranges*, on July 2, 1814;[2] he in turn presented it to Robert viscount Castlereagh, 2nd marquis of Londonderry.[3] The instruction sheet must have been prepared for shipment of the vase to the latter recipient.

The piece is in the collection of the Art Institute of Chicago.

1. [Fond d'or laminé ornements en or relief bruni à l'effet riche torre de fleurs et oiseaux coloriés et riche garniture en bronze] Register Vv 1, fol. 11, no. 4.
2. Register Vbb 5, fol. 2.
3. Springer Roberts, "The Londonderry Vase" (1989).

Undecorated Porcelain Blanks

The undecorated forms, or porcelain blanks, in this section are arranged in chronological order according to the dates of the original models, which are not necessarily those of the exhibited pieces. The marks cited in the entry headings are incisions traced by the workers who shaped the piece: the throwers who fashioned the forms and the workers responsible for molding, adapting and attaching the applied ornament, handle, spouts, and knobs or grips. In principle, such marks should tally with entries in the registers, where the tasks performed by every worker were recorded. In some cases, however, the documents reveal puzzling inconsistencies (see cat. no. 131), and a few of the marks — sometimes the worker's initials — have yet to be reconciled with the documents (see cat. no. 115). Generally speaking, the marks are accompanied by numbers indicating the year and month the work was performed: for example, the "46-6" on the teapot (cat. no. 113) signifies "June 1846."

Chrome-green factory marks were printed under the glaze to discourage forgers. This procedure did not begin, however, until July 1845. In the pieces shown here, the printed marks appear in both their original form (see cat. nos. 113, 122) and in the variation adopted in February 1848 (see cat. nos. 123, 129, 131).

New forms could be produced on the basis of either an artist's drawing (see, for example, cat. nos. 47 and 51) or a model in another material (see cat. no. 119) such as wood or wax. The first step, however, was always the creation of a three-dimensional working model, usually in plaster. If the object was to be thrown, a schematic drawing with clear indications of the prescribed profiles and proportions was prepared first. This could subsequently be modified in response to flaws in the design that emerged in the course of trial firings. Precise models were also prepared for the secondary elements — handles, spouts, grips, and knobs — and molds of these models. It was only after the completion of these preliminary stages that the first pieces could be fired. Hence the considerable delays between the date the design was initiated and the valuation of the first completed blanks (see cat. no. 117) by the manufactory.

The pricing of a model proceeded in two stages. First, an assessment was made of the total production costs to date, which encompassed firing expenses as well as fees paid to the designer, the maker of the model, and the shapers. This aggregate amount was then subdivided into equal portions corresponding to the projected number of examples to be produced. The figure thus obtained remained constant in subsequent valuations of corresponding decorated pieces, as did a sequence of lower figures derived for other categories of the same object. This categorization ranged from perfect pieces (*premier choix*), to pieces with slight blemishes (*les meilleurs rebuts*), to those that were destroyed because of their utter imperfection, and included everything in between. In general, the sale prices assigned to pieces that were only lightly flawed were higher than their estimated production costs.

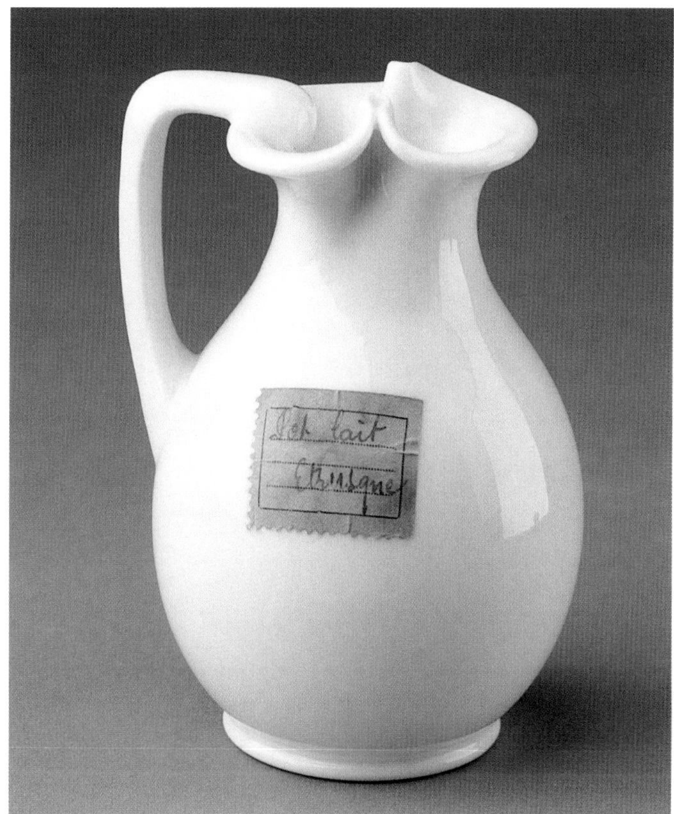

113.

Teapot

Called *Théière 'Pestum anse basse, 2e grandeur'*

Max. height 6 in. (15.3 cm); max. width 6 3/4 in. (17 cm)
Incised marks: *CP* (cursive) *46-6-V* (cursive)
Green mark printed under the glaze *SV LP 46*

For the history of this form, see cat. no. 2. The incised marks present a problem, as there is no entry in the 1846 register for a worker who might correspond to the thrower of this piece. The only thrower cited in connection with a *théière 'Pestum'* — one of the first size, but this could be a simple error — is Michel Tollot. His identifying mark is well documented, however, and cannot be mistaken for the letters incised here (see cat. no. 117).[1] There is no doubt that the piece was finished by Jacques-Marie Vilain, as evidenced by the incised "V" on the bottom.[2]

1. In July 1846 Tollot was paid for throwing 130 teapots of this design of the first size with low handles and lids included (*théières Pestum première grandeur anse basse*), at the rate of 1 franc each. Register Va' 40 (1846), fol. 72, Michel Tollot.
2. In July 1846 Vilain was paid for finishing 130 teapots of the first size with low handles, and lids included (*théières Pestum première grandeur anse basse*), at the rate of 1 franc each (ibid., fol. 100).

114.

Cream Jug

Called *Pot à Créme 'Etrusque Trèfle'*

Max. height 4 in. (10 cm) ; max. width 2 1/2 in. (6.5)
Incised marks: *Lp* (linked cursives)-*Md* (cursives)-*h* (block letter) *24-7*

The earliest valuation of an undecorated blank of this form dates to August 6, 1819, but the working drawing that served as the basis for the original plaster model can be accurately dated to September 1806.[1] The "trefoil" form of the lip itself was inspired by an Etruscan model. The work registers tally with the incised initials: this blank was thrown in 1824 by Louis-Marie Lapierre père[2] and completed by Pierre-Nicolas Marchand.[3]

1. Carton Pb 16. Total estimated production expenses 2.85 francs; sale price of a flawless example (*en premier choix*) set at 4 francs.
2. Lapierre was paid for throwing 82 jugs at the rate of .75 francs each. Register Va' 25 (1823 – 1824), fol. 88v.
3. In May 1824 he was paid for finishing 82 examples at the rate of .80 francs each. Ibid., fol. 129 ff.

115.
Cream Jug
Called *Pot à Crème 'Etrusque à Bourrelet'*

Max. height 3 3/8 in. (8.7 cm) ; max. width 3 1/2 in. (9 cm)
Incised marks: *cn* (block letters)-*27-9*

The model for this cream jug is securely dated to 1807 by the working drawing, but the earliest surviving valuation of a blank example is from August 6, 1829, two years after this example was produced.[1] A gadrooned variant of the form can be dated to 1813 on the basis of the drawing, and other variations are also known.

According to the 1827 working register for shapers, the only cream jugs of this type to be made in the course of that year were thrown by François Michaut[2] and finished by the repairer Victor-François Garnier fils.[3] It is not known whether either of these workers used the letters "cn," incised on this piece, as their identifying mark.

1. Carton Pb 16. Estimated production expenses 1.40 francs; sale price for flawless examples was set at 2.50 francs.
2. On October 31, 1827 Michaut was paid for the throwing of 60 examples at the rate of .50 francs each (Register Va' 27 (1827 – 1828), fol. 139v. ff.).
3. On December 31, 1827 Garnier was paid for the completion of 60 examples at the rate of .20 francs each (Ibid., fol. 172 ff.).

116.
Bowl
Called *Jatte 'Egyptienne'*

Max. height 4 1/8 in. (10.5 cm); diam. 7 5/ in. (19.5 cm)
Incised marks: *DC* (cursives)-*ch* (block letters)-*10*

An approximate date for the model of this form — indiscriminately characterized in the documents as a *déjeuner*, wash, or milk bowl — can be established only by the first known examples, dated 1808. It adheres closely to the profile of an Egyptian piece published by Dominique-Vivant Denon, except for the addition of a base to improve stability.[1]

The present example was thrown in 1810 by Louis-Charles Descoins[2] and finished by Louis-Mathias Chanou.[3]

1. Denon, *Voyage dans la basse et la haute Egypte* (1802), vol. 2, pl. 115, no. 4.
2. In May – June 1810, Descoins was paid for throwing "10 Egyptian wash bowls" [10 jattes à laver Egyptienne] at a rate of 1.25 francs each. (Register Va' 18 (1809 – 10), fol. 53v).
3. In May – June 1810 Chanou was paid for completing "12 Egyptian milk bowls" [12 jattes a lait Egyptienne] at the following rate: .20 francs for each *garniture*, the process of attaching the handles and base, and .40 francs for each *écarissage du socl[e]*, the process of trimming the bases prior to firing to make certain that each was perfectly square (ibid., fol. 120v. ff).

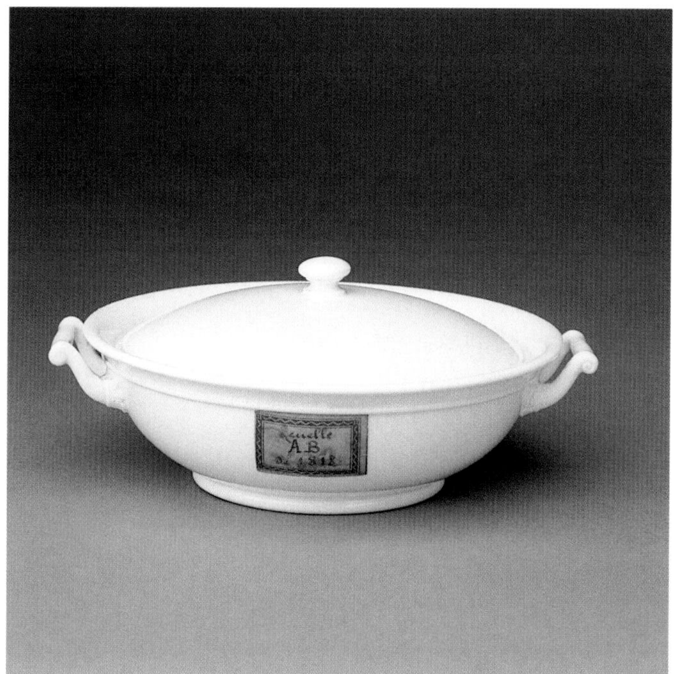

117.
Teapot
Called *Théière 'Litron Fragonard'*

Max. height 6 5/8 in. (16.7 cm); max. width 8 1/8 in. (20.7 cm)
Incised marks: *MT* (cursives)-*42-10-ap* (linked cursives)

This model is a variant of a cylindrical form created in the eighteenth century. Judging from the working drawings, the version shown here was devised in 1817, a date confirmed by Brongniart's summary account of the design's development history: "1817 no. 9. May 10. The drawing is delivered. I give it M. Chanou to make a working diagram. March 1818. The model is sketched; we await M. Fragonard. June 1. The molds are made . . . Fee for the model by M. Brachard 100 [francs]."[1] The earliest pricing of a blank example of this model dates from October 1, 1819.[2] There is also a variation known as the *théière 'Litron Fragonard ornée'*; its earliest valuation record dates from September 16, 1818.[3] It boasts a collar along the upper edge, a scrolled handle incorporating a palmette, and a spout with a more richly decorated base.

This example was thrown in 1842 by Michel Tollot [4] and finished by Alexandre Percheron.[5]

1. [1817 no.9. Mai 10 Le dessin est livré. Je le donne à M. Chanou pour en faire un trait d'exécution. 1818 mars le modèle est ébauché on attend M. Fragonard. juin Ier les moules sont faits . . . Prix du modèle par M. Brachard 100] Carton Pb 18, liasse 1, sculpture.
2. Carton Pb 8, appréciations en blanc. Estimated production expenses 7.25 francs; sale price of a flawless example was set at 9 francs.
3. Ibid. Estimated production expenses 30 francs; sale price set at 45 francs.
4. In October 1842 Tollot was paid for throwing seventeen examples at the rate of 2 francs each (Register Va' 36 (1842), fol. 67 ff.).
5. In October 1842, Percheron was paid for finishing 17 examples at the rate of 1.50 francs each (ibid., fol. 94 ff.).

118.
Covered Bowl
Called *Ecuelle* or *Bol à Bouillon 'AB de 1818'*

Max. height 3 in. (7.5 cm); max. width 7 1/2 in. (19 cm)
Incised marks: *Lg* (linked cursives)-*Lp* (linked cursives)-*23-3*

Despite the presence of "1818" in the name of this object — indiscriminately designated *écuelle* or *bol à bouillon* in the documents — the earliest recorded valuation of a blank example dates from June 16, 1821.[1] Inclusion of the initials "AB" in the name could suggest that Alexandre Brongniart played a role in the genesis of the design.

This example was thrown in 1823 by Louis-Marie Lapierre père[2] and finished by Jules-Pierre-Stanislas Longuet jeune.[3]

1. Carton Pb 16. Estimated production expenses 5.40 francs; sale price of a flawless example set at 7 francs.
2. In March 1823, Lapierre was paid for throwing forty-nine *écuelles AB* at the rate of 1.25 francs (as well as for throwing seventy-four saucers), and the following April he was paid for throwing eighteen more. Register Va' 25 (1823 – 1824), fol. 87.
3. Between January and March 1823, Longuet was paid for finishing 25 porringers at the rate of .50 francs each, and the following April – June for finishing 10 more. Longuet was still an apprentice, however, so these fees were never actually paid but were entered solely to satisfy bookkeeping exigencies (ibid., fol. 193).

119.

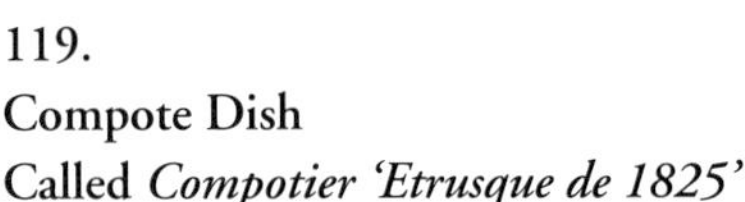

Compote Dish
Called *Compotier 'Etrusque de 1825'*

Max. height 3 3/8 in. (8.6 cm); max. width 10 1/2 in. (26.8 cm)
Partial blue glost-fired ground along upper rim and lower edge of base
Green mark: *D. 22 Jn. 41. d.*
Incised marks: *41-1-DL* (cursives)

This model was among the "forms established in the course of 1825" presented at the Louvre exhibition on January 1, 1826, when the catalogue specified that it was conceived "after an Etruscan bowl lent by M. the comte de Clarac."[1] This piece may be the subject of the comment by the count to Brongniart: "If he [Brongniart] has no further need of my bowl, I would be pleased if he could take advantage of the same occasion to have it returned to me. I would be vexed if he had not profited from it to make, with his usual taste, some pretty porcelain bowl."[2]

This is not the only Sèvres piece modeled after one in this eminent archaeologist's collection. In 1822 the manufactory introduced a *compotier 'Clarac'*. It was the only model to bear the count's name, but he may have provided additional pieces for a similar purpose.[3] In the letter above, he wrote: "I would also say to M. Brongniart that, regarding the small vases in white porcelain with a gold fillet that he modeled after ancient forms and of which I would like to have as simple a set as possible, M. de [illegible] has assured me that if M. Brongniart submitted a request on my behalf at the Ministry, noting that I had provided forms to the Sèvres manufactory from my own collection, it would not be refused."

This example was thrown in 1841 by Antoine-François-Toussaint Delacour.[4] The painted green mark indicates the date on which the blue ground was applied: June 22, 1841.

1. [Formes établies dans le courant de 1825]; [d'après une coupe etrusque remise par Mr. le comte de Clarac]. Charles-Othon-Frédéric-Jean Baptiste, comte de Clarac was not only an archaeologist and scholar but also the curator of antiquities at the Louvre.
2. [S'il n'a plus besoin de ma coupe, il me feroit plaisir de me la faire passer par la même occasion. Je serois faché qu'il n'en eut pas profité pour faire avec son gout ordinaire quelque jolie coupe en porcelaine] Carton T 10, liasse 3, dossier 6, letter dated May 10, 1825.
3. [Je dirai aussi à M. Brongniart que quant à ces petits vases en porcelaine blanc avec un filet d'or qu'il a imités des formes antiques et dont je desirerois avoir la collection aussi simple que possible, M. de . . . m'a assuré que si M. Brongniart la demandoit pour moi au ministère, comme ayant fourni des formes à la Manufacture de Sèvres tirées de ma collection, on ne me les refuserera pas] Ibid. The collection was finally delivered to Clarac in 1829 (Carton M 7).
4. In March 1841, Delacour was paid for finishing sixty examples at the rate of 3 francs each, bases included (Register Va' 35 (1841), fol. 62 ff.).

120.
Butter Dish
Called *Beurrier 'Simple Coquille'*

Max. height 1 5/8 in. (4 cm); max. width 10 in. (25.5 cm)
Incised marks: *S* (cursive)-*49-5*
Green mark printed under the glaze: *S.49*

The earliest valuation of a blank example of this model dates from December 1827.[1] That same year, the manufactory also created a *beurrier 'Double Coquille'*, a composite variant of the same form. The example shown here was molded in 1849 by Théodore Szamowski.[2]

1. Carton Pb 16. Estimated production expenses came to 12.50 francs; the sale price for flawless examples was set at 16 francs.
2. In May 1849, Szamowski was paid for shaping five examples at the rate of 6 francs each. Register Va' 43 (1849), fol. 100.

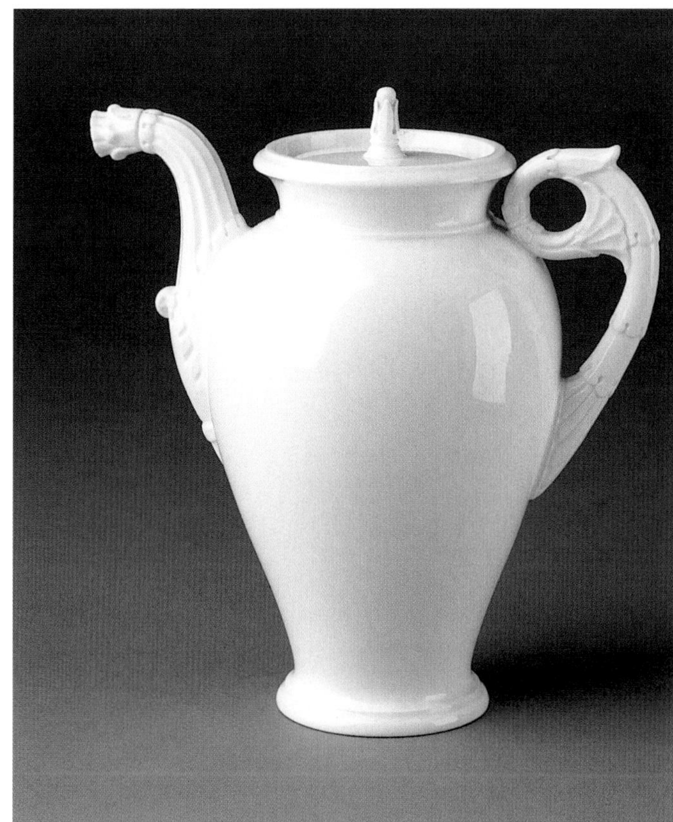

121.
Cream Jug
Called *Pot à Crème 'à Côtes AB de 1830'*

Max. height 3 5/8 in. (9.3 cm); max. width 4 1/4 in. (10.8 cm)
Incised marks: *Lp* (linked cursives)-*40-8-mp* (?)

The date included in the title of this model, used to distinguish it from the p*ot à crème 'à côtes AB de 1840,'* tallies perfectly with the earliest pricing of a blank example, which dates from December 4, 1830.[1] Once again, the presence of Alexandre Brongniart's initials in the title may indicate that he played a role in the design of the *déjeuner 'AB à côtes de 1830'* for which this piece was made.

This example was thrown in 1840 by Louis-Marie Lapierre;[2] it was probably finished by Pierre-Marie Moyez, but some doubt remains because the second set of incised initials on this piece is difficult to decipher.[3]

1. Carton Pb 16. Estimated production expenses came to 7 francs; the sale price for flawless examples was, nonetheless, set at 6.50 francs.
2. In August 1840, Lapierre was paid for throwing thirty-six examples at the rate of 1.25 francs each (Register Va' 34 (1840), fol. 65).
3. In September 1840, Moyez was paid for finishing eighteen pieces at the rate of 3 francs each (Ibid., fol. 84). The other eighteen were completed by Joseph-Germain Boileau, who was paid for this work in December 1840 (ibid., fol. 82).

122.
Coffee Pot
Called *Cafetière 'Campanienne Fragonard'*

Max. height 7 1/8 in. (18 cm); max. width 6 1/2 in. (16.5 cm)
Incised marks: *MT* (linked cursives)-*45-12-g* (cursive)
Green mark printed under glaze: *SV LP 45*

The original model, attributed to Alexandre-Evariste Fragonard on the basis of its name, was conceived in 1830. A series of schematic drawings records a sequence of minor changes introduced between 1831 and 1843. The earliest valuation of a blank is dated May 10, 1831.[1] On November 26, 1830, Brongniart noted: "M. Fragonard's drawing given to M. Régnier so he can have a production model made, such that after the piece has been fired it will have almost exactly the same dimensions as the drawing."[2]

The example shown here was thrown in 1845 by Michel Tollot [3] and was finished by François-Aimé Godin.[4]

1. Carton Pb 16. Estimated production expenses came to 10.50 francs; the sale price of flawless pieces was set at 14 francs.
2. [Donné le dessin de M. Fragonard a M. Regnier pour qu'il en fasse faire le modele pour l'execution de manière que la piece etant cuite, elle ait a peu pres la dimension du dessin] Carton Pb 18, liasse 1, sculpture. It was necessary to make a model larger than the drawing to compensate for shrinkage in the kiln.
3. In December 1845 Tollot was paid for throwing thirty-three examples at the rate of 1.50 francs each (Register Va' 39 (1845), fol. 71 ff.).
4. In December 1845 Godin was paid for finishing thirty-three at the rate of 3.50 francs each (ibid., fol. 95).

123.
Sugar Bowl
Called *Pot à Sucre 'Chinois Réticulé'*

Max. height 4 1/2 in. (11.5 cm); max. width 5 1/2 in. (14 cm)
Incised marks: *M* (cursive)-*79-9-F* (cursive)-*Cg* (cursive)
Green mark printed under glaze: *S.80*

The first valuation of a blank sugar bowl for the *déjeuner 'Chinois Réticulé'* is dated September 15, 1832.[1] The fabrication process was complex and required the skills of three individuals: a thrower to make the interior body; a worker to mold the exterior envelope (on which openwork patterns were outlined by incisions in the mold), attach it to the interior body, and add the handles, which were molded separately; and finally, a cutter to create the openwork patterns in the outer envelope. This was a delicate operation, since unfired paste is extremely fragile. The example here, produced in 1879 – 80, was made by the thrower Michel-Julien Morin the father,[2] the repairer Emile-Augustin Gilbert,[3] and the cutter Catherine Forgeot, née Sire.[4] (Due to the close unit community of workers at Sèvres, women had been added to the workforce at an early stage, though primarily as painters, gilders and burnishers.)

For the history of the *pot à sucre 'Chinois réticulé'*, see cat no 76.

1. Carton Pb 16. Estimated production expenses came to 32 francs; the sale price of flawless examples was set at 42 francs, that of *troisième choix* (third choice) at 34 francs.
2. In September 1879, Morin was paid for throwing forty-six pieces at the rate of 5 francs each (Register Va' 71 (1879), fol. 23).
3. In September 1879, Gilbert was paid for molding and repairing nineteen examples at the rate of 3 francs each (Ibid., fol. 43).
4. Forgeot cut sugar bowls of this type throughout the year, work for which she was paid at the rate of 12 francs each (Ibid., fol. 84).

124.
Teapot
Called *Théière 'Chinoise à Pans Leloy no. 1'*

Max. height 6 3/8 in. (16.2 cm); max. width 7 1/4 in. (18.5 cm)
Incised marks: *D* (cursive)-*38-10-E* (cursive)
Green mark printed under glaze: *S.48*

This form was conceived in 1833 by Jean-Charles-François Leloy. It was designated "no. 1" to distinguish it from a second Chinese teapot designed by the same artist in 1835 and seemingly never produced. The earliest valuation of a blank is dated December 28, 1833.[1]

This example was molded in 1838 by Pierre-Adrien-Jacques Derivière[2]; apparently it was not glost-fired for some time, for it did not receive a printed fabrication mark until 1848.

1. Carton Pb 17. Estimated production cost 21.80 francs; the sale price of flawless examples was set at 25 francs.
2. In October 1838 Derivière was paid for molding fourteen pieces at the rate of 9.50 francs (Register Va' 32 (1837 – 1838), fol. 120 ff.). He also molded the only known decorated example, which recently entered the permanent collection of the musée du Louvre (*Nouvelles acquisitions du département des objets d'arts,* exhib. cat. (1995), no. 119, pp. 272 – 73).

125.
Plate
Called *Assiette 'Ornemanisée'*

Diam. 8 3/4 in. (22.2 cm)
Partial green ground
Incised marks: *ac* (linked cursives)-*36-1*

This may be one of the plates with relief ornament on the border for which Hyacinthe Régnier produced drawings and models in 1835 – 36 (see cat. no. 88). Judging from its dimension, it is a dessert plate.

The example shown here carries the mark of the thrower Hughes-Adolphe Carré, as confirmed by the 1836 work register for shapers.[1] It is surprising, however, that an object featuring low relief elements was thrown and not molded.

1. Carré was paid for "twenty-eight low-relief plates at .75 francs; thirty-nine id[em] at .50 francs," as well as for "two and a half days spent on trials with low-relief plates" at the rate 3.85 francs per day. [28 assiettes à ornements à 0.75 francs; id. à 0.50 francs]; [2 jours _ employés aux essais d'assiettes ornemanisées] (Register Va' 31 [1835 – 36], fol. 88 ff.).

126.
Teapot
Called *Théière 'Wedgwood Godronnée'*

Max. height 5 1/2 in. (13.9 cm); max. width 8 1/8 in. (20.8 cm)
Incised marks: *44-4-DL* (cursives)
Printed marks: *R*

The inspiration for this design was a teapot issued by Josiah Wedgwood about 1785.[1] The Wedgwood piece featured a "seated-figure" knob on the lid, which Sèvres replaced with a simple knob. French nineteenth-century "anglomania" may explain the adoption of this model, but it could also have been produced with English tourists and clients in mind. A blank of the gadrooned version was valued on April 9, 1836, but on that occasion it was noted that there were "modifications to be made: gadrooning throughout / correct the spout / correct the handle / reduce the cost of shaping."[2] A smooth model was valuated on September 17, 1840.[3]

The present example was thrown in 1844 by Antoine-François Toussaint Delacour.[4]

1. Reilly, *Wedgwood* (1989), ill. 622.
2. [Modifications à apporter: guillocher d'une seule pieces / corriger le bec / corriger l'anse / réduire le prix de façon] Carton Pb 18. Estimated production expenses were 11 francs; the sale price of flawless examples was set at 15 francs.
3. Estimated production expenses of first size 6.30 francs; sale price of flawless examples was set at 8 francs; corresponding figures for second size were 5.50 francs and 7 francs respectively (ibid.).
4. In April 1844 Delacour was paid for throwing twenty-three pieces at the rate of 4 francs each, as well as for shaping "six additional replacement lids" [six couvercles en sus pour rassortiment] (Register Va' 38 (1844), fol. 66 ff.).

127.
Teacup
Called *Tasse à Thé 'Semiove, première grandeur'*

Max. height 2 3/4 in (7 cm); max. width 4 in. (10 cm)
Incised marks: *N* (cursive, with the first down-stroke very open and the last one curving at the top)-*37-8-Al* (cursives)

This model was created in 1837 and was first priced on October 28 of that year.[1] The form is one of a set of three for teacups that were designed together (see cat. no. 128); before receiving their definitive name they were designated *tasse à thé 'à godrons A,B,C'*. In the example shown here, the use of the term *ove*, or *ovolo* in the definitive name was probably prompted by the egglike shape, but there is no indication in the name that it was gadrooned. The cup was initially produced in two sizes.

This piece was thrown in 1837 by Nicolas Fischer [2] and finished by Jean-Baptiste Allard.[3] Thus it was among the first examples of this rare form to be produced.

1. Carton Pb 18. Estimated production expenses for examples of first size were 4 francs; sale price for flawless pieces of the same size was set at 5 francs.
2. In August and September 1837 Fischer was paid for throwing "Gadrooned Teacups A 1837, B 1837, and C 1837" [Tasses à thé à godrons A 1837, B 1837 et C 1837] (Register Va' 32 [1837 – 38], fol. 84 ff.).
3. In August and September, 1837 Allard was paid for "finishing 40 gadrooned teacups A,B,C" [40 garnitures de tasses a godrons A,B,C.] (ibid., fol. 117 ff.).

128.
Teacup and Saucer
Called *Tasse à thé 'Angustove' et Soucoupe*

Teacup: max. height 2 1/2 in. (6.5 cm); max. width 4 in. (10 cm)
Incised marks: *N* (see cat no 127)-*38-4*
Printed black mark over glaze, partly worn away: *Sevres LP 18 ...*
Saucer: Diam. 5 1/8 in. (13.1 cm)
Incised marks: *N* (see above)-*38-7*

These pieces are examples of another of the gadrooned teacup and saucer forms designed in 1837 (see cat. no. 127). In this case, it was the narrow configuration of the base as well as the general oval shape that determined the original Latinate name (*angustove* means "narrow egg"). The earliest valuation of a blank dates from October 28, 1837.[1]

Both the cup and the saucer were thrown in 1838 by Nicolas Fischer.[2] There are no repairer's marks on either piece, making it impossible to identify the finisher.

1. Carton Pb 17. Estimated production expenses were 4 francs; the sale price of flawless examples was set at 5 francs.
2. In April 1838 Fischer was paid for throwing seventy-nine "tasses à thé angustove" at the rate of .90 francs each, and in July 1838 for shaping forty "soucoupes angustoves à godrons" at the rate of .75 francs each (Register Va' 32 [1837 – 38], fol. 84 ff.).

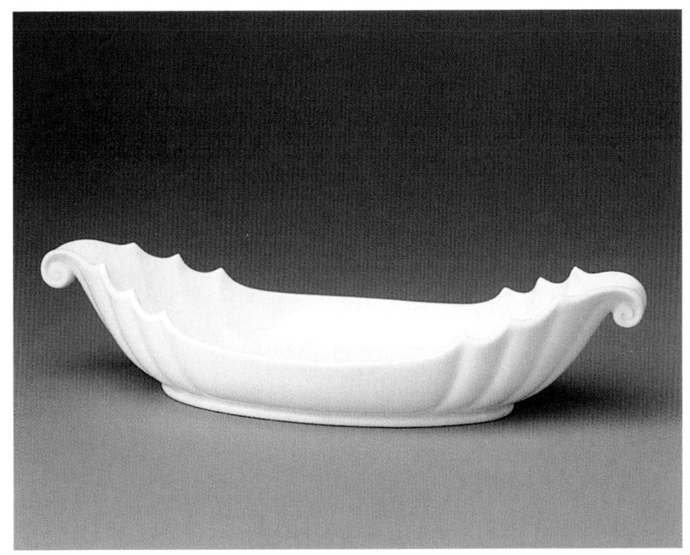

129.
Radish Dish
Called *'Bateau Barquette'*

Length 9 1/4 in. (23.5 cm)
Incised marks: three vertical lines
Green mark printed under glaze: *S.87*

The original French name of this model — *'Bateau Barquette'* — roughly translates as "small boat" and is specified on the working drawing, which bears the date March 6, 1828. This could be an error, however, for the earliest valuation of a blank example is dated March 6, 1838.[1]

Beginning in 1840, this form was often included in table services. Given the absence of both date and identifying mark on the piece shown here, however, it is impossible to specify when it was produced. The mark under the glaze would imply a shaping in 1887.

1. Carton Pb 16.

130.
Soup Tureen and Stand
Called *Soupière 'Karkèse' et Plateau*

Max. height 4 7/8 in. (12.5 cm); max. width 9 in. (23 cm)
Incised marks: *MT* (cursives)-*42-2-Dj* (cursives)

The working drawing for this model, dated October 25, 1842, attributes the design to Hyacinthe Régnier. The earliest pricing of a blank is dated February 28, 1843.[1] In 1836, Régnier had designed a cooler called a *glacière 'Karkèse'*, which featured an elaborate base. The liner designed for the cooler was later produced with a lid and handles to become this soup bowl of the same name.

The piece shown here was thrown in 1842 by Michel Tollot [2] and finished by Jean-Marie-Julien Dieterich.[3]

1. Carton Pb 18. Estimated production expenses 14 francs; the sale price of a flawless piece was set at 18 francs.
2. In January 1843 Tollot was paid for throwing fifteen examples at the rate of 2.25 francs each (Register Va' 37 [1843], fol. 62 ff.).
3. In January 1843 Dieterich was paid for finishing fifteen examples at the rate of 2.75 francs each (ibid., fol. 180).

131.
Plate
Called *Assiette 'Peyre à bord festonné no. 2'*

Diam. 9 1/4 in. (23.5 cm)
Incised marks: *JB* (linked cursives)-*97-4-PN-CV-F* (cursive)
Green mark printed under glaze: *S.98*

Although the basic form of this plate matches a drawing in the Form Book, where it is designated *assiette 'Peyre à bord uni et festonné no. 2'*, the alternating reserves and openwork on the rim of this example differ from the two openwork versions illustrated in the same book.[1] Thus there is some doubt as to the proper name of this model. The designations *assiette 'Hyacinthe Régnier à pointes'* and the *assiette 'Hyacinthe Réticulée'* both appear in the work register for shapers. This could imply that Hyacinthe Régnier created a new openwork border pattern for a form previously designed by Jules Peyre, but the use of these identifying phrases could also have been a simple mistake.

The incised marks are also problematic. It is clear that this is a much later example, as the plate was thrown in 1897 by Julien Bonnafoux[2] and at least some of its openwork was cut by Charles Villion. Villion was relatively new to Sèvres at the turn of the century, however, and the modesty of his fee — 35 centimes per plate — suggests that he performed only a small portion of the cutting.[3] Thus it is not surprising that another cutter's mark also appears on the piece, that of Catherine Forgeot. Unfortunately, there is no record of her having been paid for such a project in 1897; the only corresponding payments entered in the register were made to Irma-Pauline Trager.[4] Perhaps the project was reassigned to lighten the workload of the cutter originally designated to do this work.

The late date of this piece confirms the longevity of some models in the Sèvres line.

1. [Assiette Peyre à bord uni et festonné n° 2]. The "Form Book" is a small volume containing outline drawings of all the forms produced at the manufactory and their official designations. Several copies survive. Some contain only the above-mentioned basic elements; these may have been intended for use by clients to select forms and models of their choice. Other copies, however, are working price books that also indicate the sale price assigned to blanks of each form and size prior to their decoration.
2. In April 1897 Julien Bonnafoux (mark "JB") received "an initial payment for sixty-five *assiettes 'Hyacinthe Régnier à pointes'* made of the new paste" as well as for "one day's work jigging the *assiette 'Hyacinthe'*, and in May 1897 he was paid for throwing "sixty-eight *assiettes 'Hyacinthe Régnier'* new paste" at the rate of .75 francs each [premier acompte sur 65 assiettes Hyacinthe Regnier à pointes P(âte) N(ouvelle)]; [un jour à faire le calibre de l'assiette Hyacinthe]; [68 assiettes Hyacinthe Regnier P.N.] (Register Va' 87 [1897], fol. 16.).
3. In November 1897 Charles Villion (mark "CV") was paid for cutting "seventeen Régnier Plates" [17 assiettes Regnier] at the rate of .35 francs each. Ibid., fol. 213.
4. Between January and December 1897 Irma-Pauline Trager cut nineteen *assiettes 'Hyacinthe Réticulées'*, work for which she was paid 10 francs each (ibid., fol. 220). Her mark is not known.

Finished Works of Art

The lengthy process that culminated in the magnificent finished works of art, made at Sèvres in the first half of the nineteenth century, involved design, fabrication, multiple firings, and the application of decoration—a cycle that often took years to complete. A selection of these pieces, from the simplest to the most ambitious and drawn from American collections, is included in this part of the catalogue. A triumph of art and industry, they reveal how skillfully and meticulously the Sévres artists, throwers, painters, gilders, and other workers interpreted the designers' drawings and plans, transforming them from concepts and works on paper to exquisitely finished objects. When viewed from a variety of perspectives, they also serve to document the complexities of political, economic, and cultural life in France from the decade after the Revolution to the end of the July Monarchy.

In the entries that follow, the objects have been given the names assigned to them in the Sévres archives, which are often vague or incomplete. A precise shape could be known by several names; the most commonly used designation, which is recorded in the manufactory's form books, has been given here. As in other parts of this book, in the translations of material from the archives, nineteenth-century usage and punctuation have been preserved and their idiosyncracies retained, especially with respect to Alexandre Brongniart's unusual syntax.

132 a–e.
Topographical Plates from the *Service 'de l'Archichancelier'*, 1806 – 7

Hard-paste porcelain
Diam. 9 1/4 in. (23.5 cm), each
Private collection

132a. Plate

Inscription: [on the reverse, in black] *no. 51.*; *Restes de quelques Tombeaux antiques / à Syracuse. Le Bucheron et la Mort.*
Marks: [incised] *XI* / [incised, in script] *ch*[1]; [stenciled, in red] *M. Imp.le de Sevres* [with a sign to indicate year 14 and 1806]

132b. Plate

Inscription: [on the reverse, in black] *no. 65* ; *Vue d'une Auberge à Valmontone. / 18. Milles. de Rome.*
Marks: [incised] *II 61*; [incised, in script] *Mon*[2]; [painted in gold] *BT*[3]; [stenciled in red] *M. Imp.le de Sevres* [with a sign to indicate year 14 and 1806]

132c. Plate

Inscription: [on the reverse, in black] *no. 9; Chute d'eau de St. Cosemate. / Le pecheur et le poisson.*
Marks: [incised] *7*; [incised, in script] *T*[4]; [painted] *T*; [stenciled in red] *M. Imp.le de Sevres / 7*

132d. Plate

Inscription: [on the reverse, in black] *Vüe de l'Arc de Trajan à Benevent.*
Marks: [incised] *7*; [incised, in script] *DC*[5]; [stenciled in red] *M. Imp.le de Sevres / 7*

These four plates are part of a service described on the valuation sheet of July 29, 1807, as "purple ground landscapes, fables and views of Imperial Palaces, for the Lord Arch-chancellor."[6] The service was delivered on behalf of the emperor to Jean Jacques Régis de Cambacérès, Lord Arch-chancellor of the Empire.[7] It was one of the innumerable gifts distributed by Napoleon on the occasion of the marriage of Stéphanie de Beauharnais to the prince of Baden.[8] The bride was the emperor's niece by marriage.

In a descriptive table of work in progress on 1 Germinal, year 13 (March 22, 1805) Brongniart writes: "it [the work] has only just been started [on the subject of this] dessert service representing views of Italy after [B]ourgeois and the journey of Mr. St Nom [sic]."[9] Records of the work allocations show that until the end of 1805 only the painter Lebel and the gilder Boitel were engaged on it.[10] In September 1805, however, Brongniart gave assurances that "the views of Italy service . . . will be quickly done,"[11] and on January 1, 1806, he noted

132b. Plate

that "work is being expedited as quickly as possible. Two extra painters have been attached to it. There are 37 plates in progress."[12]

The report of April 1, 1806, makes it clear for the first time that the service is "currently destined for His Serene Highness the Lord Arch-chancellor of the empire," adding that he "has received the modifications and augmentations that his highness has requested. We are adding plates bearing views of France and of imperial palaces."[13] By January 1, 1807, the service was "nearly finished. The final gilding is being added to the plates, and in fact a large proportion of these plates are completely finished."[14] On April 1, he reported that the service "is completely finished as far as the painting is concerned and almost finished for the gilding,"[15] which proves that, in this case at least, the gilding was at least partially laid after the painted decoration. It was not until July, however, that the service was sufficiently complete to be evaluated: twenty-four plates were missing, however, not to be finished until December.[16]

The plate with the view of Syracuse (cat. no. 132a) was painted by Jacques François Joseph Swebach in April 1806.[17] It bears the mark of the gilder Charles Boitel, who was paid on several different occasions in 1806 for working on plates belonging to this service.[18] The plate with the view of Valmontone (cat. no. 132b) must be one of the many to be painted without a precise description and therefore is impossible to identify. The view of the waterfall of Saint Cosemate (cat. no. 132c) was also painted by Swebach, in February 1806.[19] It was copied from an engraving by Bourgeois.[20] Finally, the view of the Arch of Trajan at Benevento was painted by Lebel in June 1807,[21] inspired by an illustration by Abbé de Saint-Non.[22]

The description of the service gives the impression that some of the plates illustrate fables and some are decorated with landscapes. This is true for only a small proportion of the plates. Most of them bear a mixture of illustrations of fables and topographical views taken from engravings.[23] The latter type of decoration was quite new in France and may have seemed a little unusual. Possibly for the same reason, the large pieces laid with the same, rather novel ground color and the same gold ornamentation, are decorated only with a scattering of polychrome insects on a pale blue ground.[24]

132c. Plate

Fig. 132a. *The Waterfalls at Saint Cosemate.* (From Bourgeois, *Vues d'Italie* (1808), pl. 46)

1. *XI* probably indicates year 11 (1802 – 3). There is a mark *ch*, written in slightly different hand, which is attributed to Mathias Chanou; but Chanou, a repairer,

was absent from Sèvres at the time. It may refer here to Claude François Choulet *neveu*: in 1806 it was noted that "his new mark is of two C's" (Register Vc' 6, firing of April 11, 1806); this mark, however, is perhaps the previous one.
2. In year 11 there were two potters at Sèvres by the name of Monginot. Since Pierre Monginot's mark (theoretically) was *MT*, the mark *Mon* could possibly be the mark of Monginot *neveu*.
3. *BT* is the mark of the gilder Charles Boitel.
4. In theory, the mark *7* is considered to belong to the year 1807, but since this plate was decorated in 1806, that is definitely not the case here. It may designate year 7 (1798 – 1799); this would not conflict with the mark (*T*) of the thrower Joseph Thion, who was working at Sèvres between 1783 and 1814.
5. The painting in 1806 suggests that *7* corresponds here with year 7, when the thrower Charles Decoin (*DC*) was certainly at Sèvres.
6. [fond poupre paysages, fables et vues de Palais Imperiaux, pour l'archichancelier] Carton Pb 1, valuations of 1807. Curiously, the service did not appear in the salesroom until August 26, 1807 (Register Vu 1, fol. 45 v, no 205.33); it then comprised seventy-two plates whose net price was estimated at 114 francs (between 30 and 120 francs were paid to the painters) and the selling price fixed at 140 francs. Twenty-four extra plates appeared in the sales inventory on December 28, 1807 (Register Vu 1, fol. 53, no. 213.2).
7. Delivery of August 17, 1807 (Register Vbb 2, fol. 70 v); the twenty-four supplementary plates were delivered on 31 December 1807, along with a vase depicting the wedding and a large bust of the emperor (ibid. fol. 79 v).
8. Stratmann-Dohler, "Zur Hochzeit von Stephanie de Beauharnais" (1995).
9. Carton Pb 1, liasse 1, dossier 13. The books referred to are Bourgeois, *Vues d'Italie* (1808) and Saint-Non, *Voyage pittoresque* (1781 – 86).
10. Ibid.
11. Carton Pb 1, liasse 1, dossier 14 (Aperçu des principaux travaux en train au Ier vendémiaire an 14 [September 23, 1805]).
12. Ibid., Aperçu. . . au Ier Janvier 1806. The names quoted in the work allocations covering this service are the painters Caron and Lebel and gilders Boullemier, Constant, and Boitel (ibid.)
13. Ibid., Aperçu. . . au Ier Avril 1806.
14. Ibid., dossier 16, Aperçu. . . au Ier Janvier 1807.
15. Ibid., Aperçu. . . au Ier Avril 1807.
16. Cf. nn. 6 and 7.
17. Register Vj' 13 (1806), fol. 69 ff. The artist was paid 100 francs for each of the plates. Oddly enough this service is never mentioned under his name in the work allocations.
18. Ibid., fol. 86 ff. The gilders were paid 8 francs for each plate in this service, but the subjects of the individual plates are never itemized in the register.
19. Register Vj' 13 (1806), fol. 69 ff.
20. Bourgeois, *Vues d'Italie*, (1808), pl. 46.
21. Register Vj' 14 (1807), fol. 18.
22. Saint-Non, *Voyage pittoresque* (1781 – 86), vol. 3, no. 1.
23. Sale of May 21, 1997, Christie's, New York, Nos. 101 – 17.
24. Ibid., no. 118.

132d. Plate

Fig. 132b. *View of the Arch of Trajan at Bénévent.* (From Saint- Non, *Voyage pittoresque* (1781 – 86), vol. 3, no. 1)

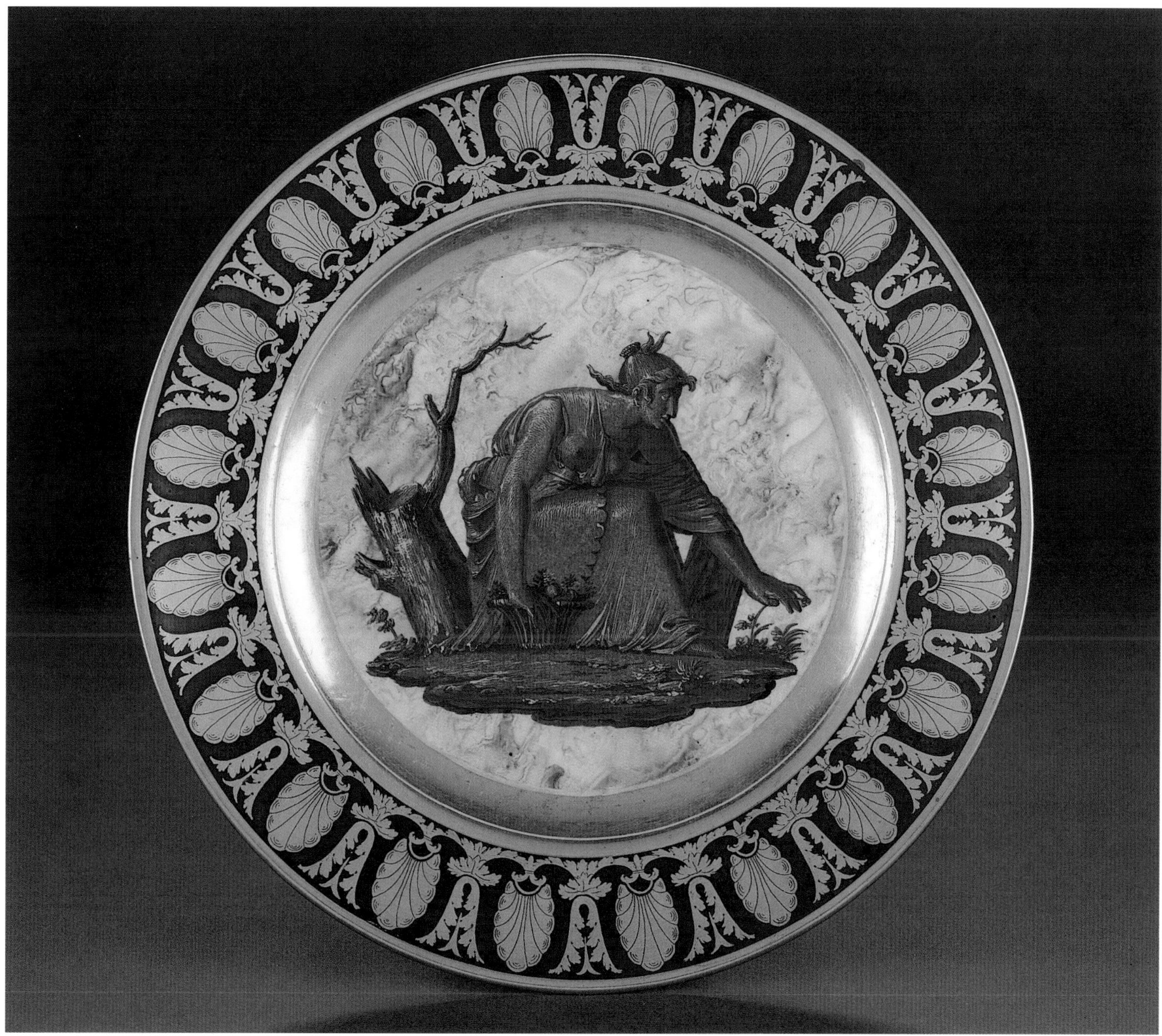

133a.

133 a, b.
Pieces from the *Service 'Fond beau bleu, figures en brun'*, 1808

Hard-paste porcelain
Wadsworth Atheneum
Gift of Reverend Alfred Duane Pell
Inv. nos. 1913.634 (plate); 1913.633 (compote)

133a. Plate

Diam. 9 1/4 in. (23.5 cm)
Marks: [incised] *LD* / *L*[1] [cursive]; [painted in blue, on the foot, very faint, possibly an 18th-century royal monogram]

133b. Compote
Called *Jatte à fruits 'Hémisphérique'*

5 1/2 x 8 1/2 in. (14 x 21.6 cm)
Marks: [incised, year 13, 1804 – 5)-*T* [cursive][2]

These two pieces are part of a service that entered the Sèvres sales inventory on March 9, 1808, where it was described as "Dessert service with dark blue ground figures in brown heightened with gold on pebbled ground etc."[3] It comprised at that time seventy-eight plates and a series of taller pieces including "2 footed bowls" (*jattes à pied*).[4] It is impossible to distinguish between the plates in the work records, but the execution of the bowls can be followed despite the variations in the way they are identified: they received their ground color, called "agate" or *caillouté*, from François Antoine Legros d'Anizy in June 1807.[5] In August they were transferred to the gilder Joseph Léopold Weydinger, who returned them in December.[6] This demonstrates that gilding was sometimes applied before the painting, since the decorative designs were not added by Perrenot the elder until between November/December 1807 and January 1808.[7] Finally the bowls were burnished, one of them by Marie-Josèphe Ganeau and the other by Geneviève Boullemier.[8]

133b.

Probably for the same reason that the plates were on sale at such a low price, or perhaps because after firing, the ground color of the plate well was deemed unattractive, the service did not sell. It was finally included in the auction sale organized between December 1826 and January 1827. By then two sugar bowls and four wine coolers had disappeared, probably having been sold off individually.[9]

1. This double mark may mean that one thrower shaped the plate and a second actually did the turning. As no date for the making of the plate is given it is impossible to suggest any names.

2. In Ventôse of year 13 (February – March 1805) the thrower Joseph Thion père made sixty-three hemispherical bowls (*jattes hémisphériques*), receiving 1.10 francs for each (Register Va' 15, dossier 3)

3. [Service de dessert sur fond beau bleu figures en brun rehaussées en or sur fond caillouté etc.] Register Vu 1, fol. 50, no. 216.3.

4. The set cannot have been considered satisfactory as the selling price of each plate was 40 francs, below the estimated net price of 51.65 francs. On the other hand the price of the footed bowls fixed at 100 francs, exceeds the net price of 82 francs in the normal proportion (Register Vu 1, fol. 50, no. 216-3). Four additional plates at the same price entered the sales inventory on April 7, 1808 (Ibid., fol. 57 v, no. 217-16) For the detailed history of the service, see Dawson, *A Catalogue of French Porcelain* (1994), no. 179, pp. 215 – 217.

5. Register Vj' 14 (1807), fols. 121 ff. He was paid 1.50 for each.

6. Ibid., fols. 63 ff. He received 13 francs "for gold frieze" [pour frize d'or] for each bowl.

7. Ibid., fols. 13 ff. and Register Vj' 15 (1808), fol. 148. He was paid 13 francs for each bowl although Brongniart had in principle offered him 14 instead of the 16 he originally demanded (Register Vq', Series 1, vol. 1, fol. 35, January 1808).

8. Register Vj' 15 (1808), fols. 98 ff. and 81 ff. Each burnisher was paid 3 francs.

9. Carton U 4, liasse 2, dossier 3.

134 a–e.
Tea Service, 1808
Called *Cabaret 'Paysages et Fables'*

Decoration painted by Christophe Ferdinand Caron
Hard-paste porcelain, gilt
Minneapolis Institute of Art
Gift of the Grove Foundation
Inv. nos. 81.101 – .1ab (tea pot with lid), .2ab (sugar bowl with lid), .3 (creamer), .4 (bowl), .5 – .7, .9 – .15, (cups), .17 – .20, .22 – .23, .24 – .28 (saucers)

134a. Teapot called *Théière 'Asselin'*

8 x 8 in. (20.3 x 20.3 cm) with handle
Marks: [on bottom] *Le Lion et le Moucheron / L'Elephant et le Singe de Jupiter*; [incised] *5 DC* [or] *SDC*[1]; [stamped on bottom] *M.Imp.*[te] *de Sèvres, 7*;

134b. Sugar Bowl called *Pot à Sucre 'a pied anse volute'*

6 1/8 x 5 3/4 in. (15.6 x 14.6 cm)
Marks: *Le Rat et la Grenouille / Le Chien qui porte a Son Cou le Diner de Sone Maître*; [stamped] *M.Imp.*[te] *de Sèvres 7*; [incised, sign for the year 12 (1803 – 1804)]

134c. Milk Jug called *Pot à Lait 'Grec'*

8 x 4 5/8 in. (20.3 x 11.8 cm), with handle
Marks: *Les Grenouilles qui demandent un Roi*; [stamped] *M.Imp.*[te] *de Sèvres 7*; [incised] *SD*

134d. Bowl called *Jatte à Fruits 'Hémisphérique'*

H. 5 7/8 in. (14.9 cm), diam. 8 3/8 in. (21.3 cm)
Marks: *La Tortue et les deux Canards / Les deux Coqs / Le Rat et L'Huitre / Les deux Chiens et L'Ane Mort*; [stamped] *M.Imp.*[te] *de Sèvres 8*; [incised, sign for year 14 (1805 – 1806)

134e. Cups called *Tasses 'Jasmin'* and saucers

Cups (10 of 12), H. 4 1/4 in. (10.8 cm), diam. 4 1/4 in. (10.8 cm); saucers, diam. 6 in. (15.2 cm); second size
Inscriptions/marks (cups): [inv. no. .5] *L'Aigle et la Pie*; [stamped] *M.Imp.*[te] *de Sèvres 7*; [inv. no. .6] *Le Lievre et la Tortue*; [stamped] *M.Imp.*[te] *de Sèvres 7*; [inv. no. .7] *Le Loup et L'Agneau*, [stamped] *M.Imp.*[te] *de Sèvres 7*; [inv. no. .9] *Le Milan et le Rossignole*; [inv. no. .10, no inscription]; [stamped] *M.Imp.*[te] *de Sèvres 8*; [inv. no. .11, no inscription]; [stamped] *M.Imp.*[le] *de Sèvres 8*; [inv. no. .12] *Le Renard et le Buste*, [stamped] *M.Imp.*[te] *de Sèvres 7*; [inv. no. .13] *Le Renard et la Cigogne*, [stamped] *M.Imp.*[te] *de Sèvres 7*; [inv. no. .14] *Le Coq et la Perle*, [stamped] *M.Imp.*[te] *de Sèvres*,; [inv. no. 15] *Le Heron*, [stamped] *M.Imp.*[te] *de Sèvres 7*; [incised for year 14 (on two]; [script, on six] *tt*; [rounder script, on two] *tt*; [on three] *SD*[2]
Marks (saucers): [stamped, in red] *M.Imp.*[le] *de Sèvres 8* (inv. nos. .17, .18, .20, .25, .26, .27, .28); *M.Imp.*[le] *de Sèvres 7* (inv. nos. .19, .22, .23); [incised, sign for year 14, on seven]; [on ten] *SD*[3]

In the early years of the nineteenth century, the term *déjeuner* seems to have been used for hot-beverage services that included a tray; if the services did not have a tray it was called a *cabaret*. When this service appeared in the sales inventory it was described as a "Set of Jasmin cups gold ground Landscapes and Fables painted by Caron."[4] The records do not identify the fables as by Jean de La Fontaine, nor do they mention the unusual ground color, called *burgos*, which imitates the pearly glint of a kind of shell ("burgau"). The *burgos* color was first mentioned at Sèvres in the eighteenth century.[5] The use of fables was not new at Sèvres; they appear on the service presented to Cambacérès in

1807. Once the Empire period had ended, however, they seem to have been eliminated altogether as a source. This *cabaret* was presented by the emperor to Friedrich Wilhelm III of Prussia on September 15, 1808.[6]

The production schedule of the cups and saucers is difficult to follow. The first gilding was executed by Godin jeune in April 1807, when he gilded the teapot, the sugar bowl, and the milk jug; between March and August he gilded the cups and saucers; and in August he gilded the bowl.[7] The items were then transferred to the painter Christophe Ferdinand Caron, who painted the landscapes and fables. He returned four finished cups in November 1807, four others in December, and most of the large pieces in January 1808; he finished the bowl in March, and the rest of the cups and saucers between January and April 1808.[8] Most of the inscriptions were added by Legrand in December 1807 and March 1808.[9] The gilding on the sixteen pieces was retouched by Godin, theoretically in April 1808.[10] The pieces were then parceled out to a large group of burnishers[11] before being entered in the sales inventory.

Inscriptions: 134a ["The Lion and the Gnat / The Elephant and Jupiter's Monkey"]; 134b. ["The Rat and the Frog / The Dog who carries his master's dinner around his neck"]; 134c ["The Frogs who ask for a King"]; 134d ["The Tortoise and the two ducks / The Two Cocks / The Rat and the Oyster / The Two Dogs and the Dead Ass"]; 134e ["The Eagle and the Pie / The Hare and the Tortoise / The Wolf and the Lamb / The Kite and the Nightingale / The Fox and the Bust / The Fox and the Stork / The Cock and the Pearl / The Heron"] The two fables not identified by an inscription are "The Monkey and the Dolphin" and "The Swallow and the Little Birds."

1. The mark *DC* identifies Charles Descoins who was paid in Frimaire, year 12 (November – December 1803), for twenty-three teapots in this shape as well as other pieces (Register Va' 15).

2. The *tt* mark identifies Charles Thevenot fils aîné, who was paid in 1806 for trimming and/or making cups in this shape (Register Va' 16 (1806 – 1808), fol. 142 ff.). The mark with the same letters in rounder script has not been identified. *SD* is the mark of the potter Jean Michel Saint Denis aîné, who was paid for making some cups that were initially termed "chocolate cups year 14," then "Jasmin cups" (ibid., fol. 62. ff.)

3. Saint Denis was also paid in installments in 1806 for saucers for *tasses 'Jasmin'* (ibid.).

4. [Cabaret de tasses jasmins fond d'or Paysages et Fables coloriées par Caron] Register Vu 1, fol. 57 v, no. 217 – 27

5. Carton F 22, December 1780, in the work records of the painter Nicolas Schradre: "two Litron goblets third size burgau ground and green ground" [2 gobelets Litron 3eme fond burgaut et fond vert], paid 30 livres each

6. Register Vbb 2, fol. 87. See Brunet, "Le Cabaret" (1965).

7. Register Vj' 14 (1807), fol. 123 ff. He received 10 francs for each cup and saucer, 2.50 francs each for the teapot, the sugar bowl, and the milk jug and 3 francs for the bowl.

8. Ibid., fol. 16 ff. and Vj' 15 (1808), fol. 11 ff. He received 50 francs per cup and saucer, the same for the milk jug, 100 francs for the teapot and the sugar bowl, and 150 francs for the bowl bearing four fables.

9. Registers Vj' 14, fol. 33-33 v and Vj' 15, fol. 87 ff.

10. Register Vj' 15, fol. 49 ff. He received 12 francs for the whole service. As some of the burnishers had been working since the month of March, the date may refer to the completion of this aspect of the work.

11. For the teapot, the burnishing of the plain areas was done by Mme Asselin (Register Vj' 15, fol. 73 ff.; 2 francs) and the burnishing *à l'effet* (with shading) by Mme Baudouin (ibid., fol. 79 ff.; 9 francs). For the sugar bowl, the burnishers were respectively Mesdames Deperais (ibid., fol. 84 ff.; 1.50 francs) and Baudouin (8 francs). For the milk jug, Mesdames Boullemier jeune (ibid., fol. 81 ff.; 1.50 francs) and Baudouin (6 francs). For the bowl, Mademoiselle Frédérique (ibid., fol. 107 ff.; 15 francs) and Mme Baudouin (9 francs; the higher price paid for the burnishing of the plain areas can be explained by the lavish gold lining of each cup). The cups and saucers were portioned out between Mesdames Godin jeune (ibid., fol. 105 ff.), Boullemier (ibid., fol. 86 ff), Ganeau (ibid., fol. 98 ff.) and Mesdemoiselles Baudouin (ibid., fol. 84 ff.), Legrand (ibid., fol. 87 ff.), Laleu (ibid., fol. 91 ff.), Buteux (ibid., fol. 103 ff.), and Parpette (ibid., fol. 138 ff.)

135a, b.
Pair of Vases, 1810
Called *Vases 'Oeuf'*

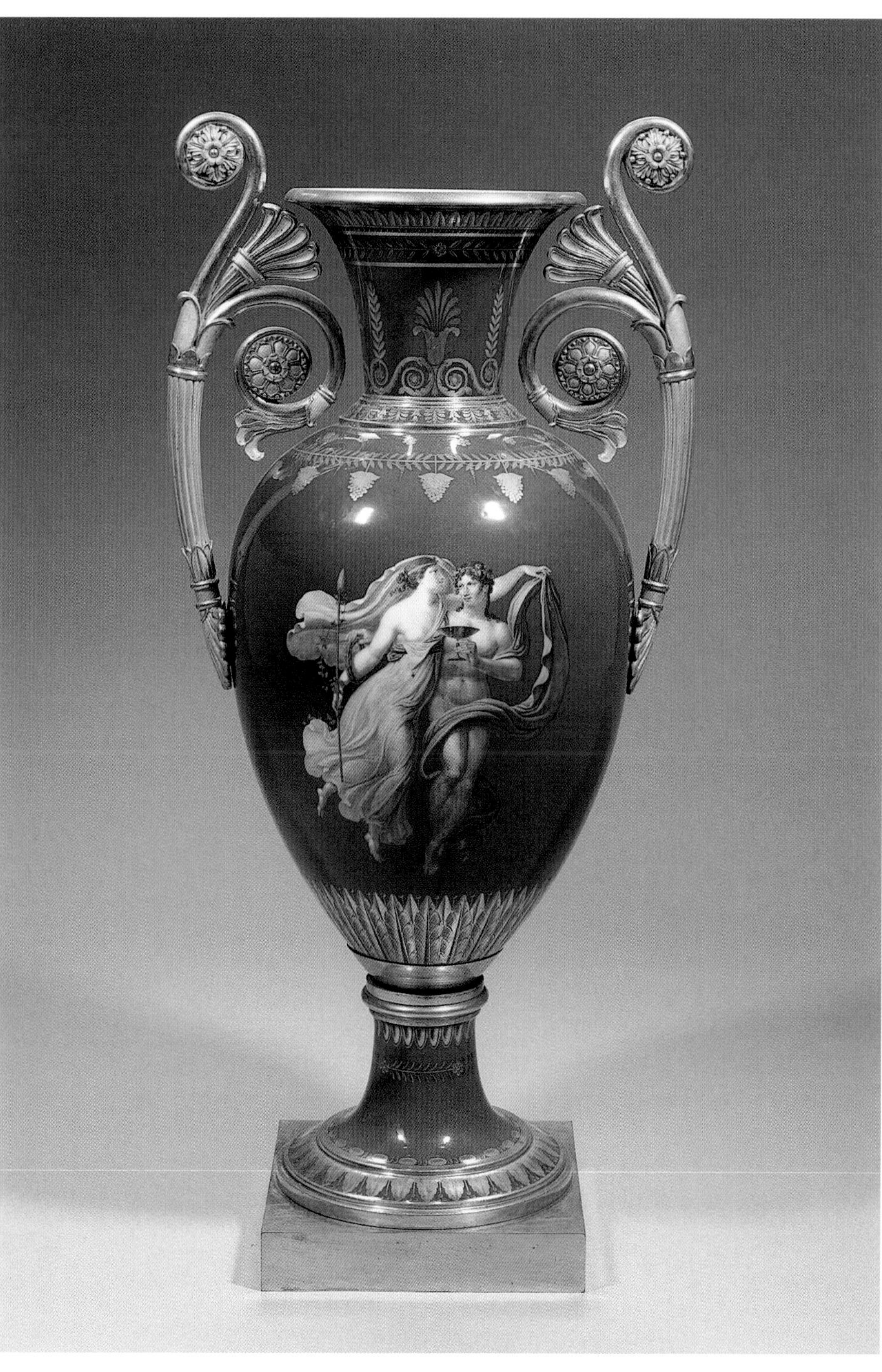

135a
Vase
Called *Vase 'Oeuf'*

Painted decoration called "Bacchus and Ariadne"
Hard-paste porcelain
H. 29 1/2 in. (74.9 cm), third size
Marks: [handwritten] *vasse ouf 3 en T*; [painted in green] *35.36*; [stamped in red, twice] *M.Imple.le de Sevres/1809*
Wadsworth Atheneum
Gift of Mrs. Henry B. Learned
Inv. no. 1948.109

The gilding and painting of these two vases[1] seem to have been executed concurrently: Charles Boitel was paid 75 francs for "gilding and platinum decoration for M. Georget" on each vase in July 1809,[2] and Jean Georget is supposed to have received the two vases in June and to have returned them in January 1810 with "figures of a man and a woman on each, scraped and painted in color on a green ground . . . (price agreed 500 francs)."[3] The vases were then returned to Boitel for adding gold.[4] After having been fired they only needed to be burnished; this was completed between January and March, when Charles Durosey created the shading[5] and Mlle Legrand worked on the flat areas.[6] The two vases entered the sales inventory by May 2, 1810,[7] and were delivered to Prince Louis I of Hesse-Darmstadt on the June 29.[8]

1. As these two vases have been the subject of exhaustive study and have already been published, only a brief historical résumé is given here; see Roth, "Neoclassical Variations at Sèvres" (1995).
2. [decor dorure et platin (sic) pour Mr. Georget] Register Vj' 16 (1809), fols. 39 ff. Boitel had requested 90 francs for each vase (Register Vq', Series 1, vol. 2, fol. 25 v, July 1809).
3. [sujets de deux figures d'homme et de femme sur chaque, gratés et peints en coloris sur le fond vert . . . (prix convenu à 500 francs)] Registers Vj' 16 (1809), fols. 1 ff.and Vj' 17 (1810), fols. 1 ff. Georget had asked for 500 francs for each vase and Brongniart would only pay 450 (Register Vq', Series 1, vol. 2, fol. 22 v, May 1809). The director must have been finally persuaded because the

135b
Vase, 1810
Called *Vase 'Oeuf'*

Painted decoration called "Flora and Zephyr"
Hard-paste porcelain
H. 29 1/2 in. (74.9 cm), third size
Marks: [incised] *A.P.*; [painted in green, under the foot and under the vase] *35.36*;[stamped in red] *M.Imp.1e/de Sevres/1809*
Wadsworth Atheneum
Gift of Mrs. Henry B. Learned
Inv. no. 1948.110

sum of 500 francs appears on the valuation sheet for the vases (Carton Pb 2, liasse 1).

4. Register Vj' 17 (1810), fols. 41 ff, January 1810. Boitel was paid 18 francs for each vase and not the 21 francs he was hoping for (Register Vq', Series 1, vol. 2, fol. 34, January 1810).

5. The information given in the various documents is difficult to reconcile here. Durosey had in principle requested 80 francs "for burnishing the shaded gold and platinum ornamental work" [pour le brunis à l'effet des ornements d'or et platine] and Brongniart only agreed to pay 70 (Register Vq', Series 1, vol. 2, fol. 33 v, January 1810). The valuation sheet (Carton Pb 2, liasse 1) gives the fee of 75 francs for the work, whereas the workshop register (Vj' 17, fols. 69 ff) cites payments to the gilder of 70 francs in January for a complete vase and only 5 francs for "*les effets*" of the second vase.

6. Register Vj' 17 (1810), fols. 94 ff. Here again the information is contradictory: Mlle Legrand is paid 4 francs in January "for the flat areas" [pour les aplats] on one of the vases and its footing, and 2.50 in March for the second vase, probably without its footing. The valuation sheet instances a double burnishing "*à plat*" for 8 francs and it has not been possible (because of the imprecise nature of the documents) to find other references to the burnishing of these vases.

7. Register Vu 1, fol. 93, no. 253-11 and Carton Pb 2, liasse 1. The net price was estimated at 2,150 francs for each vase and the selling price fixed at 3,000.

8. Register Vbb 2, fol. 113.

136
Sugar Bowl, 1810
Called *Sucrier 'Etrusque'* from the *Service 'de l'Empereur'*

Hard-paste porcelain
L. 9 1/2 in. (24 cm)
Marks: [incised] *L*[1]; [painted in green] *35.36*; [stamped in red on sugar bowl] *M. Imp.le de Sevres 1809*; [stamped on stand] idem / *1810*
Collection of Comte and Comtess Alexandre and Elaine de Bothuri Báthory

This object is one of the four "Etruscan" sugar bowls created for "the new service of a highly particular nature" ordered by Napoleon on November 4, 1807 (see cat. no. 20). In spite of the name given to this shape, there does not seem to be any real prototype among the antique vases collected by Dominique-Vivant Denon in Naples and sold by Denon to Louis XVI in 1786. In theory, this collection was to remain at Sèvres only until the Museum des Arts was opened; in fact, it stayed in the manufactory.[2] After the Revolution, Denon became director of the museum (called the Musée Impérial under Napoleon) and one of Alexandre Brongniart's principal advisers. The emperor insisted that Denon be consulted on the design for the new *service 'de l'Empereur'*.

The four sugar bowls were delivered together "for decoration" to the gilder François Antoine Boullemier in 1809, and he returned them in November.[3] In the same month, the ground-painter Louis Victor Godin, painted the four stands in "oriental pink granite."[4] The four sugar bowls were sent to the painter Nicolas Antoine Lebel, who returned them finished in January 1810.[5] The two views of Luxor and of the Elephantine Isle were copied from the *Voyage dans la Basse et la Haute Egypte* published by Denon in 1802.[6] Boullemier aîné received the sugar bowls in February and March 1810 to add "the relief gold and the writing of titles and subjects"[7] and Jean François Philippine burnished the shaded parts in March,[8] allowing the service to appear in the sales inventory on March 31, 1810.[9]

The descriptions of the inventories of the Liste Civile for successive sovereigns is notoriously imprecise, and it would be irresponsible to use these documents to identify the sugar bowls from the emperor's *service*. The Liste Civile itemizes numerous pieces with green ground belonging to a variety of different services, not all of them from Sèvres. Nevertheless, the four sugar bowls were certainly among the stock of porcelain found by Napoleon III when he arrived at Palais des Tuileries in 1852.[10]

Detail of cat. no. 136. Elephantine Island.

Detail of cat. no. 136. View of Luxor.

Fig. 136a. View of Elephantine Island. (From Denon, *Voyage dans la Basse et la haute Egypte* [1802], pl. 64, no. 3)

1. This could be the mark used by Laurent Henry who made various elements of these sugar bowls during 1808 (Register Va' 16 (1806 – 1808), fol. 132ff). he received 4 francs for each of the eight bowls and one franc for each stand and lid.
2. Massoul, *Corpus vasorum antiquorum* (1934).
3. Register Vj' 16 (1809), fol. 35.36; for the "gilding and scraping of the decoration" the artist charged 60 francs but Brongniart only paid him 45 "because of the great difficulty" (Register Vq', first series, vol. 2, fol. 32, December 1809).
4. Register Vj' 16 (1809), fol. 29ff. He was paid 9 francs for each stand.
5. Ibid., fol. 9-9 v and Register Vj' 17 (1810), fol. 9-9 v. He received 100 francs for each landscape.
6. For the view of Luxor see pl. 49, no. 1; for Elephantine Isle, pl. 64, no. 3. The latter image in the book is reversed on the porcelain.
7. Register Vj' 17 (1810), fol. 37 ff. He was paid 20 francs for each sugar bowl, not the 27 he had asked for. (Register Vq', first series, vol. 2, fol. 35).
8. Register Vj' 17 (1810), fol. 21ff. He was paid 21 francs for each sugar bowl although he had requested 24 (Register Vq', first series, vol. 2, fol. 37)
9. Register Vu1, fol. 91 v-92, no. 251-2 and 252-1. The net price of each sugar bowl was estimated at 385 francs and the selling price fixed at 450.
10. The description is as follows: "No 257. Four oval table sugar bowls, fixed to square bases, in Sèvres biscuit in imitation marble, each supported on four small matte-gold turtles; the sugar bowls have green ground decorated with gold, gilded handles with a head of Minerva, and a frieze painted with views of Egypt, each 240 francs." (Archives Nationales, Carton o4 2125, inventory of porcelain belonging to the State, stored in the central depositories, undated [before 1851]).

137
Bust of Napoleon I, 1810

After a model by Antoine-Denis Chaudet (1763 – 1810)
Sèvres Manufactory
Hard-paste biscuit porcelain
20 1/4 x 10 1/2 x 9 1/8 in. (51.4 x 26.7 x 23 cm), without base
Marks: [on back of base, in script] *A.B. 6 dec. 1810 / AL; AB* [front of base, incised] *NAPOLEON /* [impressed] *SÈVRES*
The Detroit Institute of Arts
Founders Society Purchase, European Sculpture and Decorative Arts General Fund with funds from the Visiting Committee for European Sculpture and Decorative Arts and Mr. and Mrs. Stanford C. Stoddard, and Mrs. Jennifer C. Stoddard; gifts from Lauretta R. Boell, Miss Alma l'Hommedieu, Mrs. Orren Scotten, Mr. and Mrs. Edgar B. Whitcomb, City of Detroit, by exchange.

In an agreement signed 16 Fructidor year 12 (September 4, 1804), between Alexandre Brongniart and the sculptor Antoine-Denis Chaudet, Chaudet undertook to deliver to the Sèvres factory "a plaster bust of the Emperor Napoleon larger than life-size . . . selected and prepared by himself."[1] He authorized the factory to "take as many molds and casts in porcelain from this paster model as required," and also authorized the marking of these copies "with his own usual stamp."[2] Rights of reproduction were not to be granted to any other ceramics maker. For this contract Chaudet was to receive the sum of 1,200 francs.[3]

This bust replaced several earlier representations of Bonaparte, some of which depicted him first as a general and later as first consul; these earlier works had been by Louis-Simon Boizot, who had worked at Sèvres since the 1770s. Instead of the earlier figures executed in contemporary clothing, Chaudet made a strongly idealized, "classical" portrait bust. The artist certainly expected to flatter the new sovereign by aligning him with Roman prototypes. The portrait was officially adopted, demonstrating that Chaudet had accurately judged the emperor's desire to be identified with his ancient predecessors. Moreover the large number of copies produced at Sèvres in two sizes[4] and their automatic inclusion in diplomatic and official gifts demonstrate Napoleonic self-promotion.

The full-size bust was a technical challenge: after a first copy was fired in September 1804, a notation was made that it was "to be refired," which suggests that it had faults, but these were judged reparable.[5] The next two copies were fired in October – November and November – December 1804 and were sent to the reject storage.[6] It was not until the firing of 4 Pluviôse year 13 (January 25, 1805)[7] that Brongniart was able to announce to the Intendant Géneral de la Liste Civile that there was "a bust of the Emperor cast from a plaster model by Mr. Chaudet . . . with no apparent defects," at the same time soliciting permission to pay homage to the empress "with one of the most remarkable products of the factory."[8]

There is no documentary evidence to show that Chaudet was consulted over the introduction in 1811 of variations of both sizes; different versions of the portrait head were embellished with a crown and/or rich draperies, or sometimes more of Napoleon's bare shoulder was revealed.

This model must be the one appearing in the accounts of Augustin Liancé (whose mark was *A.L.*) in November 1810, even though it may not have been completely finished by that date.[9] It is almost impossible to link the heads molded with the ones that were fired and that appeared in the sales inventory.[10] It is difficult to reconcile the note on the plinth of this copy, which states that the bust was presented by the emperor to "Joseph Philippe Arrighi de Casanova, Vicar-General of the Island of Elba in 1814" with the fact that all the copies of this model were given away on the orders of the emperor, who seems not to have kept a single one.

1. Carton M 1, dossier 4
2. Ibid
3. The agreement stipulated that he would receive 600 francs in silver and 600 in porcelain, but the accountant's register suggests that he received the entire sum in cash on 14 Ventôse, year 13 (March 5, 1805) (Register Vf 55, fol. 18 v).
4. In a new agreement signed 1 Pluviôse, year 13 (January 21, 1805) the factory obtained Chaudet's authorization under the same conditions to reproduce the plaster bust in a second size; the price of this transaction was 150 francs (Carton M 1, dossier 4).
5. Register Vc' 6, firing of 18 Vendémiaire, year 13 (October 10, 1804)
6. Ibid., firings of 7 Brumaire, year 13 (October 29, 1804) and 28 Frimaire, year 13 (December 19, 1804)
7. Ibid.
8. Carton T 1, liasse 6, dossier 5; the first successful copy was presented to the pope on 2 Prairial, year 13 (May 22, 1805) (Register Vy 16, fol. 26)
9. Register Va' 18 (1809 – 1810), fol. 111 ff. The sculptors received 72 francs for the bust, with a bonus if it was successfully cast. In March 1811 therefore Augustin Liancé received a bonus of 50 francs for the successful casting of the "large bust of the emperor of 6 December 1810" (information kindly provided by M. Bernard Dragesco).
10. It is generally agreed that the mark *A.B.* with a sloping cursive B is the mark of Alexandre Brachard, head of the sculpture workshop, while the one with an upright B is the mark of Alexandre Brongniart (Chevallier, *Musée national du château de Fontainebleau* [1996], p. 411). It is interesting to speculate whether the director actually took the time to come into the workshop to print his mark on the still-soft clay — at this stage a sculpture of this size could not be moved — or whether Brachard had two slightly different marks, one used when he was marking something as a sculptor and one used when he made some kind of intervention as head of the sculpture workshop. At the end of the eighteenth century, biscuit-fired pieces could also receive their identification mark from Josse-François le Riche, head of the sculpture studio, or from Louis-Simon Boizot, artist-in-chief in the sculpture department

138a, b.
Pair of Vases, 1811
Called *Vases 'Étrusque à Rouleaux'*

138a
Vase, 1811
Called *Vase 'Étrusque à Rouleaux'*

Decoration entitled *The Departure for the Army*
Hard-paste porcelain
H. 27 1/2 in. (69.9 cm), second size
Marks: [incised, underlined twice] *9*; [painted in gold] *ii.j.B.T.*; [painted in ochre, handwritten] *as*; [painted in black] *a'o*; [painted in black, under the body] *36a D 10*; [stamped in red] *M. Imp.le de Sevres.10*
Wadsworth Atheneum
Gift of J. Pierpont Morgan
Inv. no. 1919.87

On February 1810 these vases were given to the painter Jean Georget with the chrome-green ground already fired in place.[1] Although Georget was paid an advance in December for scraping away the areas of ground color that he was supposed to paint, he must have passed the vases on to Charles Boitel, since the latter executed the decoration in gold and platinum on one of the vases in June 1810[2] and on the other between December 1810 and January 1811.[3] Georget then took the vases back, and, having received advances in February and March, in April he returned "1 Etruscan vase with 'rouleaux' 2nd green ground . . . for scraping and painting with three figures representing a young man and 2 women (the Departure)" and finished the second vase in May.[4] The pieces were sent to the burnishing workshop,[5] and then to the salesroom on 10 July 1811.[6] They were delivered to Napoleon's brother Jérôme, king of Westphalia, on February 13, 1812.[7]

1. Register Vj' 17 (1810), fols. 1 ff. For a detailed history of these vases, see Roth, "Neoclassical Variations at Sèvres" (1995).
2. Register Vj' 17 (1810), fols. 41 ff. For the first vase, Boitel received 100 francs instead of the 120 he had demanded (Register Vq', Series 1, vol. 2, fol. 44, May 1810).
3. Register Vj' 18 (1811), fol. 45 ff. For the second vase Boitel only received 92 francs. In May 1811, he was paid 8 francs extra for having completed the retouching of the

138b
Vase, 1811
Called *Vase 'Étrusque à Rouleaux,'*

Decoration entitled *The Return from the Army*
Hard-paste porcelain
27 1/4 x 14 x 18 1/2 in. (69.2 x 35.6 x 47 cm), second size
Marks: [obscured by later repairs]
Wadsworth Atheneum
Gift of J. Pierpont Morgan, by exchange
Inv. no. 1994.40.1

four handles. These sums of money do not correspond to the sums mentioned in the valuation sheet (Carton Pb 2, sheet of 10 July 1811), which mentions a payment of 124 francs for gilding. The inaccuracy of some of the information makes it impossible to identify any further payments for the gilding of these vases.

4. [1 vase Etrusq. a rouleaux 2me fond vert . . . pour le gratage et la peinture d'un sujet de trois figures representant un jeune homme et 2 femmes (le Depart)] Register Vj' 18 (1811) fols. 1 ff. Although the system of advances is not very clear, it appears that Georget was paid 650 francs for each of these vases (although he had requested 750) in March 1810 (Register Vq', Series 1, vol. 2, fol. 37 v) and then reduced his demand to 700 in May 1811 (ibid., fol. 71).

5. The muddle in the registers and discrepancies between the different documents are a handicap here. The valuation sheet notes that for each vase 20 francs were paid for burnishing the flat areas and an extra 20 francs for the shaded areas. The register of work done for 1811 (Vj' 18) does not tally at all: Mme Asselin (fols. 92 ff) burnished one vase for 12 francs in March and a second in June; she reburnished one (the flat areas again) in June, for 10 francs; in the same month, Mlle Legrand (ibid., fols. 105 ff) also burnished a vase for 10 francs. This adds up therefore to 22 francs for a double burnishing of the flat areas, instead of the 20 mentioned in the valuation sheet. In addition there is no trace here of the burnishing of the shaded areas. The situation is even more complicated for the handles because five are mentioned here, each burnished for 0.75 franc, two by Mme Asselin in May, two by Mme Ganeau in May (ibid., fols. 117 ff) and one by Mlle Laleu in May (ibid., fols. 113 ff). On the other hand the burnishing of only one foot is mentioned, by Mme Ganeau, in May, for 2.50 francs. There must be some confusion between the foot and the handle, in spite of the marked difference in price.

6. Register Vu 1, fol. 115 v, no. 275 – 32; Carton Pb 2, valuation sheet of July 10, 1811: net price estimated at 2,062 francs, selling price fixed at 3,500.

7. Register Vbb 4, fol. 7 v.

139a–d.
Pieces from the *Service 'Iconographique Grec',* 1812 – 17

139a. Plate from the *Service 'Iconographique Grec'* 1813

Hard-paste porcelain
Diam. 9 1/4 in. diam. (23.5 cm)
Inscription: [obverse] *SOPHOCLE*
Marks: painted [in green] *15.j.11* [painted in gold] *Mo 30;* [painted in color] / *LG*[1]; [engraved and printed in blue, monogram of Louis XVIII with fleur-de-lys and the word *Sèvres* inside it]
Collection of Mr. and Mrs. Richard Baron Cohen

139b. Plate from the *Service 'Icongraphique Grec',*1815

Hard-paste porcelain
Diam. 9 1/4 in. diam. (23.5 cm)
Inscription: [obverse] *SOLON*; *JM de Gault*
Marks: [reverse, incised] *DC-10*[2]; [painted in green] *15.j.11*[3]; [painted in gold] *30 8bre B.T.*; [engraved and printed in blue, monogram of Louis XVIII with fleur-de-lys and the word *Sèvres* inside it]
Museum of Art, Rhode Island School of Design
Georgianna Sayles Aldrich Fund
Inv. no. 1989-010

139c. Plate from the *Service 'Iconographique Grec',* 1817

Hard-paste porcelain
Diam. 9 1/4 in. diam. (23.5 cm)
Inscription: [obverse] *ANNIBAL*
Marks: [painted in gold] *Mo Jo TZ*[4]; [painted in green] 12; [incised] *dZ;* / *DC*[5]; [engraved and printed in blue, monogram of Louis XVIII with fleur-de-lys and the word *Sèvres* inside it]
Collection of Mr. and Mrs. Richard Baron Cohen

139d. Sugar Bowl from the *Service 'Iconographique Grec',* 1812 – 17 Called *Sucrier 'Aigle'*

Hard-paste porcelain
L. 12 1/2 in. (31.6 cm)
Marks: [incised] *116* / *HL*; [painted in green] *13. av. 12*; [painted in gold] *2 juin B.T.*[6]; [stamped, in red] *M.Impˡᵉ de Sèvres*
Collection of Mr. and Mrs. Richard Baron Cohen

These pieces must have formed part of the second *service 'Iconographique'* with blue ground flecked with gold, gold friezes, and cameos of famous men of antiquity. It was made at Sèvres after the first service of this name had been delivered to Napoleon's uncle Cardinal Fesch in 1811 (see cat. no. 23).

The painted elements on the plate bearing the portrait of Sophocles were sketched out in October 1813 by Denise Tard, but there is no record of payment[7] nor of the date of its completion. The medallion is a copy from E. Q. Visconti's *Iconographie*

139a.

grecque, a book that Brongniart had requested from the Intendant Général when the first service was being made:

"You are aware that the factory has on several occasions produced vases, services etc. adorned with the portraits of great men of antiquity, painted in the manner of a cameo. In having these objects decorated in this way I believed that I was fulfilling the wishes expressed several times by His Majesty on the occasion of his various visits to the workshops, and when he requested that we should make a table representing the military heroes of Greece and Rome.

"It has often been very difficult to obtain authentic originals of the said portraits and I have even had to give up the idea when it was a question of painting 150 different heads on a service. The research that would have been necessary to make an informed choice for so many portraits would have been beyond my means, and beyond the capacity of the antiquarians whom I should have had to consult.

"A book has just been published by the most famous antiquarian in the empire, a book commissioned by the emperor and containing most of these portraits. You will understand, I know, M le Comte, that this book is indispensable to the factory; it would be inexcusable for me to allow errors to be made in the execution of any portraits published in this collection; but you also know that the book is not for sale in the shops, and that the emperor has reserved the right to distribute copies of it. For this reason may I humbly beg a copy of the iconography of M Visconti for the use of this factory and may I emphasize the importance of this request by telling you that we are at present engaged in the production of a very beautiful service to be delivered to His Majesty at the Château de Saint-Cloud."[8]

The plate bearing the profile of Solon was painted by Jean Marie Degault, who received it in May 1815 and returned it in September, earning 100 francs for his work.[9] The head of Solon is also inspired by an engraving in Visconti's book.[10] The plate was then gilded by Charles Marie Pierre Boitel in October 1815.[11] Finally, the plate bearing the portrait of "Annibal" was painted by Jean Georget in February – March 1817[12] and gilded by Denis- Joseph Moreau.[13] Again the

139b.

portrait is based on one of Visconti's plates.[14]

The sugar bowl is one of four gilded by Charles Boitel in 1812.[15] Its genesis took several years: it was not until January 1817 that Pierre Huard was paid for "2 sugar bowls Greek iconographic service for four antique attributes painted in cameo."[16] In February Charles Boitel executed "the frames in relief gilding."[17] The sugar bowls were then sent to the burnishers for completion.[18]

As always, the individual pieces of this service were collected as they were completed until the entire service was assembled and entered the sales inventory together on May 9, 1817.[19] The service was delivered on September 17, 1819 "to the court of Rome."[20] This vague reference must be to a member of the pope's entourage, as the pope himself is always clearly identified in the documents of the manufactory when he was the intended recipient.

1. *LG* is the mark of Louis Antoine Legrand, who was paid the sum of 3 francs several times "for the frame of the cameo in gold relief" on plates belonging to this service (see, for example, Register Vj' 20 (1813), fol. 149 ff).
2. The thrower Louis Charles Descoins fils aîné was paid for making ordinary plates throughout the year 1810 (Register Va' 18 (1809 – 1810), fol. 51ff).
3. The marks painted in green refer to the application of the blue ground.
4. *Mo* must be the mark of the gilder Denis-Joseph Moreau. In 1813 he was paid several times for gilding plates belonging to this service; he received 50 centimes "for lapis"; 3 francs for "frame in gold relief" and 6. 25 francs for "frieze on background and lapis in gold" (Register Vj' 20 (1813), fol. 57 ff).
5. *DC* is the mark of the thrower Charles Descoins, who was paid in 1812 for numerous ordinary plates (Register Va' 19 (1811 – 1812), fol. 60 ff).
6. *B.T.* is the mark of the gilder Charles Boitel. In 1812 he was paid in June for three 'eagle sugar bowls complete B(eautiful) lapis blue for the iconographic service for the decoration in gold', receiving 27 francs for each one, he gilded a fourth in July (Register Vj' 19 (1812), fol. 69 ff.).
7. Register Vj' 20 (1813), fol. 198.
8. Carton T5, liasse 2, dossier 3, letter dated 21 January 1811, Visconti, *Planches de l'iconographie grecque* (1811). The service in question is the first iconographic service, finally presented to Cardinal Fesch).
9. Register Vj' 22 (1815), fol. 182 ff. This price is higher than the price paid for plates painted by various artists for the first service, as explained in a note handwritten by Alexandre Brongniart in the register of the sums demanded and the sums paid: "Plates with cameos in the antique manner for the iconographic service; in the future Mr Degault will be paid according to the success of his paintings. . . . if the plates costing 60 francs succeed perfectly the sum will be raised to 100 francs" [Assiettes à camés d'apres l'antique pour le service iconographique Mr Degault devant a l'avenir repondre du succès complet de ses peintures. . . . les assiettes du prix de 60 francs seront portées si elles ont parfaitement réussi a 100 francs] (Register Vq', first series, Vol. 3, fol. 23 v, January 1813). Another register notes that plates that are unsuccessful will not be paid for at all (Register Vy 21, fol. 4).
10. Visconti, *Planches de l'iconographie grecque* (1811). pl. 9.
11. Register Vj' 22 (1815), fol. 88 ff. He received 5.50 for each of the four plates that he gilded. The sum must have paid for only partial gilding: when the first service was made, the gilder Denis Joseph Moreau charged 5 francs for "the gilding of the border around the cameo on the plate of the iconographic service" (Register Vq', 1st series, vol. 2, fol. 70 v, April 1811). Joseph Godin, accepted a payment of 9 francs for the first and 7 francs for subsequent plates, for the "gilding of a decoration consisting of 3 friezes, veined, sanded with gold with bands" (ibid., fol. 44 v, June 1810). The lack of detail in the registers makes it impossible to identify any particular plate in the work records of the gilders and burnishers.
12. Register Vj' 24 (1817), fol. 7 ff. Jean Georget received 80 francs.
13. See n. 6.
14. Visconti, *Planches de l'iconographie grecque* (1811), pl. 55.
15. See n. 7.
16. Register Vj' 24 (1817), fol. 51 ff. He received 8 francs each.
17. Ibid., fol. 86 ff. He received 6 francs each.
18. The bodies of the two sugar bowls were burnished for the flat gold by Mesdames Troyon and Boullemier and on the shaded parts by Mme Noualhier (Register Vj' 24 (1817), fol. 150 ff., 162 ff. and 144 ff. respectively.
19. Register Vv1, fol. 87, no. 26 and Carton Pb 4, valuations of 1817. The net price of the seventy-two flat plates was estimated at 135 francs and the selling price fixed at 150. For the sugar bowls the price was, respectively, 219 and 300 francs.
20. Register Vbb 5, fol. 383.

139c.

139d.

140a–e.
***Déjeuner*, 1812**

Hard-paste porcelain, gilding
Sterling and Francine Clark Art Institute
Inv. no. 1955.1306

140a. Cups called *Tasses 'Jasmin D[enon]'* and saucers

Cups (12), H. 2 3/4 in. (7 cm); saucers, diam. 4 3/4 in. (12.1 cm)
Marks (cups): [incised, joined cursive] *tt*; [cursive] *fd* / *10*[1]; [painted in puce] *B*; [painted in gold on six cups] *18 M*[2]; [stamped in red] *M. Imp. 1e / de Sevres / 1812*
Marks (saucers): [incised on eight saucers] *10 / fd*; [incised on one saucer] *t 8*; [on one] *1 fd*[1]; painted in puce] *B*; [painted in gold] *2 juin*; [stamped] [see above]

140b. Teapot called *Théière 'Étrusque Denon'*

H. 8 3/8 in. (12.3 cm)
Marks: [incised] *10* (?); [cursive] *Ld*; [cursive] *SM*; [painted in puce] *B*; [stamped] [see above]

140c. Milk Jug called *Pot à Lait 'Egyptien'*

H. 7 3/4 (19.7 cm)
Marks: [incised] *tt-9*[3]; [painted in puce] *B*; [painted in gold] *18 M / 2 juin*; [stamped] [see above]

140d. Sugar Bowl called *Pot à Sucre 'Egyptien'*

H. 5 1/8 in. (13 cm)
Marks: [incised] *tte-fd*[4]; [painted in puce] *B*; [painted in gold] *2 / 18 M*; [stamped] [see above]

140e. Bowl called *Jatte à déjeuner 'Egyptienne'*

H. 4 in. (10.2 cm)
Marks: [incised] *Dc-ch-10*[5]; [painted in puce] *B*; [stamped] [see above]

This *déjeuner* must have been painted very quickly, on glazed pieces chosen from the warehouse since the incised marks are all from 1809–10. In June 1812 the painter Charles-Théodore Buteux received fourteen cups and saucers, as well as some tall pieces, "to be decorated with chevrons in purple highlighted in gold"; he returned the cups, finished, in June and the other pieces in July.[6] The entire service was then sent to the gilder Charles Vandé who returned everything within a month.[7] To save time, the pieces were distributed among several burnishers.[8] The service was put on sale on June 29, 1812,[9] but was not actually sold until June 10, 1814, to a M. Charpentier van Moorsel.[10]

The *déjeuner* is typical of the simple, elegant products to which Brongniart gave such importance. The ground color, called "hydrangea," first appeared in 1811 and seems to have been used sporadically until 1816.

There is an interesting variety of stylistic influences in the pieces called "Etruscan" or "Egyptian"; some of the details or shapes are derived from plates to be found in the Denon's book, *Voyage dans la Basse et la Haute Egypte* (1802).[11] There is also a characteristic variety of names given to a single shape. For example in the documents the bowl is called *jatte à lait 'Egyptienne'* (Egyptian milk bowl) and *Bol 'Egyptien à socle'* (Egyptian dish with pedestal), whereas in the form book it is called a *jatte à déjeuner 'Egyptienne'* (Egyptian breakfast bowl).

1. Charles Thevenot fils was paid in February 1810 for fitting handles to 201 *tasses 'Jasmin Denon'* at 0.30 francs each (Register Va' 18, fol. 117 *ff.*) Ferdinand Davignon was paid in January 1810 for having thrown 212 saucers for the *tasses 'Jasmin Denon'* and 201 *tasses 'Jasmin Denon'* at 0.25 and 0.30 francs respectively (ibid., fol. 87 ff.). *10* means 1810.
2. *B* is the mark of Théodore Buteux (see n. 9). *18 M* may refer to the 18th March or the 18th May; the work was not always noted in the registers on the same date as the date marked on the base of the objects, which makes verification difficult. The marks in gold usually refer to the date of gilding.
3. Charles Thévenot fils, *garnisseur*, was paid in March 1809 for attaching handles to 12 Egyptian milk jugs at one franc each (Register Va' 18, fol. 117 ff). *9* means 1809.
4. Charles Thévenot fils was paid in May 1809 for attaching handles to 20 Egyptian sugar bowls at 3 francs each (ibid.). Ferdinand Davignon, thrower, was paid in April 1809 for 20 Egyptian sugar pots at 1 franc each (ibid., fols. 87 ff.).
5. Louis Charles Descoins, thrower, was paid in May – June 1810 for 12 *jattes à laver 'Egyptiennes'* (Egyptian wash basins) at 1.25 each (ibid., fol. 51 ff.); Mathias Chanou was paid in May – June 1810 for 2 *jattes à lait 'Egyptiennes'*: 0.20 for attaching handles and 0.40 for *l'écarissage du socl.* [sic] (squaring the base") on each (ibid., fol. 124 v).
6. Register Vj' 19, fols. 20 ff. Buteux *fleuriste* (the flower painter) received 10 francs for each cup (instead of the 14 he was anticipating; see Register Vq', Series 1, vol. 3, fol. 7 v, June 1812) as well as for the sugar pot and the milk jug, 15 for the tea pot and 20 for the bowl.
7. Ibid., fol. 89 ff. Vandé *doreur* (gilder) was paid for "complete regilding of the ground" [le fond rechargé en plein] 0.20 per cup, 0.30 for sugar bowl and milk jug and 0.40 each for the tea pot and bowl.
8. Mme Boullemier, two cups and saucers at 0.30 francs each (ibid., fol. 112 ff.); Mlle Legrand/Mme Mascret, 2 cups and saucers at 0.40 (ibid., fols. 115 ff.); Mme Troyon, 2 cups and saucers at 0.40 (ibid., fol. 120 ff.); Mme Ganeau, 4 cups and saucers at 0.40 (ibid., fols. 124 ff.); Mlle Parpette the Elder, 4 cups and saucers at 0.35 (ibid., fols. 129 ff.); Mlle Monginot, sugar pot and milk jug at 0.60, bowl at 0.50 and tea pot at 1 franc (ibid., fol. 184).
9. The service was put on sale with only twelve cups; two extra ones entered separately (Register Vu 1, fol. 133, no. 293 – 4 and 293-5). It was a common precaution throughout the nineteenth century to make a few extra cups or plates, in case of accidents. The service is described on arrival as "Hydrangea ground, violet decoration etc." [Fond hortensia, décor violet etc.]. In general the term *cabaret* was reserved for this type of hot beverage service which had no tray; the name *déjeuner* was reserved for similar services that did have a tray.
10. The *cabaret* is described as having a "pink ground, brown decoration" [fond rose décor en brun], but the composition and reference number indicate the same set (Register Vz 2, fol. 97 v).
11. See Denon's book, no. 115 for prototypes of the bowl, the milk jug, and the handle of the sugar pot.

141
Column Clock, 1813
Called *Pendule 'à Colonne'*

Movement by Jean-Joseph Lepaute (1768 – 1846)
Hard-paste porcelain, ormolu, glass, bronze, iron, enamel
51 1/2 x 11 1/2 x 11 1/2 in. (130.8 x 29.3 x 29.3 cm)
Inscriptions: [clock face inscribed] *Lepaute/hr. de l'Emp^{r} & Roy à Paris*; [base engraved] *DONNÉ PAR L'EMPEREUR/ A LA MARÉCHALE NEY/ LE 1er JANVIER 1814*
Marks: [on capital in red] *no 2*; [on column in red] *n° 4*; [in green enamel on bottom on plinth] *24*; [on bottom edge of owl placque] *28-1-V*; [indistinct, in black on bottom of column] *1812*; [gilded, under base of column] *T.Z.*; [printed in red on lower surface of capital] *Manufacture Imperiale/SEVRES*
The Nelson-Atkins Museum of Art, Kansas City, Missouri
(Gift of Mr. and Mrs. Harry J. Renken Sr.)
Inv. no. F66-44

In the factory records, the decorative scheme for this clock is called "The Journey of the Sun" (*la marche du soleil*), an obvious allusion to the measurement and passage of time. Day and night are represented by the cock and the owl, the hours by the twelve winged female figures encircling the base of the column, and years by the twelve signs of the zodiac.[1] It is clear from the manufactory's records that a biscuit figure of Apollo, symbol of the sun, originally stood atop the column. The figure of Napoleon and the sphere on which it stands are later replacements.[2]

Although unsigned, the design (inv. § 10 1807 N° 1) for this clock is attributed to Alexandre-Théodore Brongniart by an inscription on the back: *par Mr. Brongniart père architecte dessinateur.* The design, dated 1807, apparently was not put into production until 1812–13.

It is unclear exactly when production on the column clock began, for it is difficult to trace the work in the manufactory's records. Two similar projects were both under way at the same time: the *colonne 'des Saisons'* by Valois which was part of a *surtout*, an elaborate ensemble of table decorations made to accompany a large dinner service, and a clock based on a design by Percier. It is sometimes impossible to identify the work for each project. Significantly, there is no mention in the factory records of the application of the *beau bleu* ground color to any columns during the period 1812 – 13, leading to speculation that the factory used elements already on hand for the column portion of this clock. Tamara Préaud has suggested that the columns in question were extra ones made for the *surtout* of the *service 'Olympique'*, completed in 1806. The first of the four great *surtouts* made during the First Empire, the *surtout 'Olympique'* featured two large blue-ground columns, one surmounted by a figure of Diana and the other by a figure of Apollo, both executed in biscuit.[3] As the design, ground color, and dimensions of the column on the clock correspond almost exactly to those of the columns in the *surtout 'Olympique'*, it would appear that the factory was indeed using old stock for this part of the clock.

The column and other pieces were delivered to the decorator's workshop in July of 1813 where the gilder Durosey painted the signs of the zodiac and "other ornaments."[4] By August he was finished and in the same month the figure painter Beranger added the winged women representing the twelve hours.[5] In September Pierre-Philippe Thomire, the renowned *fonduer-doreur*, received "seven pieces of porcelain, blue ground, decorated in gold, forming a column clock" for mounting,[6] and at the end of the month, the square porcelain case went to the clockmaker Lepaute for the installation of the clock movement.[7] The biscuit figure of Apollo was the last element to be completed. Brachard aîné made a sketch of it in September and a model the following month. Apollo's lyre presented problems in the molding process, and a new one had to be made in December.[8]

The finished column clock entered the sales inventory on December 24, 1813. Manufactured at a cost of 2,014 francs, the sale price was set at 2,400 francs.[9] On December 29, the clock was delivered to the Palais des Tuileries to be presented by the Emperor Napoleon and Empress Marie-Louise as a New Year's gift on January 1, 1814, to the Princesse de la Moskowa, wife of Marshall Michel Ney, as the inscription on the base indicates.[10]

This entry was contributed by Christina H. Nelson, Curator of Decorative Arts, The Nelson-Atkins Museum of Art, Kansas City, Missouri.

1. The column on the clock was clearly inspired by the column in the Place Vendôme, a monument to one of Napoleon's greatest military triumphs. In the porcelain version, the designer has retained the spiraling arrangement of the decoration seen on the original but has replaced the military scenes with the twelve signs of the Zodiac and their symbols.
2. At an undetermined later date, Apollo was replaced with a figure of Napoleon copied from Antoine Chaudet's bronze that originally surmounted the Vendôme column. The bezel surrounding the clock face is also a later addition.
3. Poulet and Scherf, *Clodion* (1992) pp. 337 – 43.
4. Register Vj' 20, fol. 70 ff.
5. Ibid., fol. 9 ff.
6. Ibid., fol. 177 – 78.
7. Carton Pb3, liasse 2.
8. Register Va'20, fol. 107. ff. The biscuit figure of Apollo cost 40 francs to make and was listed separately on the "Feuille d'Appréciation" dated December 24, 1813.
9. "Feuille d'Appréciation" dated December 24, 1813. Of the total cost of manufacture, roughly one-third was for the clock and the mounts. Lepaute's fee and Thomire's payment are listed together as 700 francs.
10. Aglåe Auguié's marriage to Michel Ney in 1802 was arranged by Empress Josephine. Field Marshall Ney's military career was marked by great successes and equally great failures. He was created prince de la Moskowa in 1812 during Napoleon's Russian campaigns. Early in 1814, Ney turned traitor and supported the royalists only to betray them in turn and rejoin Napoleon. Soon after the Battle of Waterloo, while trying to escape to Switzerland, Ney allowed himself to be captured by royalist forces. He was tried for treason and executed December 7, 1815.

142a
Cup and Saucer, 1816
Called *Tasse 'Gothique' et Soucoupe*

Hard-paste porcelain
Cup, H. 3 1/8 in. (7.9 cm); saucer, diam. 5 7/8 in. (14.9 cm)
Marks (cup): [incised, cursive] *T*[1]; [engraved and printed in blue, cipher of Louis XVIII with fleur-de-lys in the interior] [undated]
Marks (saucer): [cursive] *T*; [painted in gold] *Ier juin BT*; [engraved and printed in blue, cipher of Louis XVIII with fleur-de-lys in the interior] [undated]
Collection of Lee B. Anderson

The two cups and saucers (cat. nos. 142a and 142b) form part of a series of seven "gothic" cups and saucers that were entered in the sales inventory in 1816 and early 1817, all painted by Jean-Claude Rumeau. The list of subjects used by the painter suggests, by process of elimination, that the painted subject of this set is *Sleeping Beauty*.[3] The cup and saucer were given to the painter in March and returned in July with "a rich gothic mosaic a subject with figures".[4] They were sent immediately to the gilder Charles Boitel for "gold ground and decoration," then to the gilder's wife for burnishing.[5] In spite of the June 1 date given with Boitel's signature (*BT*), he gilded *tasses "Gothique"* and saucers only in March, July, and December 1816; his wife burnished this cup and saucer in August, so we can only assume that he made a mistake in the date of the inscription and that the month in which he did the work, July, is when he was paid 2.50 francs for it. They entered the sales inventory on August 21, 1816, priced at 250 francs,[6] and were delivered to King Louis XVIII, with the other six after the Christmas exhibition at the Louvre, to be given to "Monsieur," the king's brother, the future Charles X.[7]

The picture in the reserve seems entirely imaginary, the so-called gothic style of the wall panels appearing with costumes that are closer in style to the Troubadour painting of the period. More effort has been made to be historically accurate in the remaining decoration; the friezes and trellis pattern were directly inspired by one of the plates in *Monuments français* by Willemin.[8]

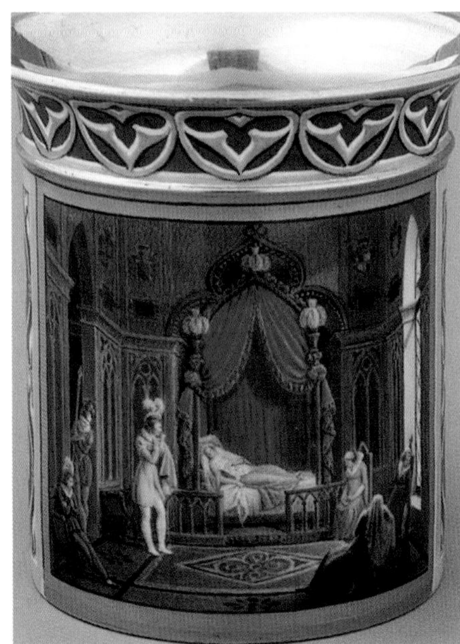

Detail of cat. no. 142a

The shape of this cup, designed in 1815, probably owes its name to the lower part of the handle, which is attached to the cup by the head of a chubby-cheeked angel flanked by two wings. This motif appears quite frequently, with slight variations, and can be found in the plates to Willemin's book.

1. François Joseph Thion fils was paid in October for "8 gothic coffee cups" at 0.35 francs each, and 14 matching saucers at 0.30 (Register Va' 21 (1815 – 1816), fols. 62ff.)
3. According to the records of the work done by Rumeau in 1816, the subjects were entitled: *Lyderic, Philippe d'Alsace*; *Sleeping Beauty*; *Baldwin of Constantinople*; *The Communion of Mary Stuart*; *The Tomb of El Cid*; *Sargine*; and *Bluebeard*. (Register Vj' 23 (1816), fols. 234 and 234 v).
4. [une riche mozaique gautique un sujet de figures] ibid. Rumeau received 150 francs for the work, plus 10 francs bonus.
5. [fond d'or et garniture] ibid., fols. 82ff. Mme Boitel was paid 2 francs (ibid., fols. 125ff).
6. Register Vv 1, fol. 69 v, no. 62 and Carton Pb 3, valuation sheets of 1816; the net price was estimated at 223 francs.
7. Register Vbb 5, fol. 12.
8. "Borders for paintings and chests commonly known as Bahut [a rount-topped chest]" [Bordures de tableaux et coffre vulgairement appellé Bahut] (Willemin, *Monuments français* (1806 – 39), vol. 2, pl. 210). The dates of the cup and of Willemin's publicaton are not contradictory; the illustrations went into circulation as soon as they were printed and were bound into volumes later.

142b
Cup and Saucer, 1816
Called *Tasse 'Gothique' et Soucoupe*

Hard-paste porcelain
Cup: H. 3 1/8 in. (7.9 cm); saucer, 1 1/8 x 5 7/8 (2.9 x 14.9 cm)
Marks: [incised, cursive] *T* [1]; [on the base of the cup, painted in red and brown, some indecipherable letters]; [engraved and printed in blue, cipher of Louis XVIII with fleur-de-lys and Sèvres in the interior] [undated]
Saucer: 1 1/8 x 5 7/8 in. (2.9 x 14.9 cm)
Marks: [incised] see cup; [painted in gold] *9A / Gn / 24.7bre*
Collection of Lee B. Anderson

This cup and saucer belong to the series of seven *tasses 'Gothique'* that were designed and painted by Jean-Claude Rumeau. According to the description on the valuation sheet, the reserve on the cup depicts "The Tomb of El Cid inside a monastery."[2] The painter gave the pieces a preliminary painting and then applied the final touches, all in October, for which he was paid 160 francs.[3] The valuation sheet identifies the gilder as J. B. Pierre-Louis Ganeau fils, who used the mark *Gn.*[4] Both cup and saucer appeared in the sales inventory on December 6, 1816,[5] and were part of the the king's gift to his brother, "Monsieur," after the Christmas exhibition at the Louvre.[6]

Detail of cat. no. 142a.

In this case, Rumeau has faithfully copied an engraving from the *Voyage pittoresque et historique de l'Espagne*,[7] and the back-to-back palmettes of the decoration are taken from one of the plates in Willemin's *Monuments français*.[8]

1. François Joseph Thion fils (see above, cat. no. 142a, n. 1).
2. [Le Tombeau du Cid dans l'intérieur d'un monastère] Carton Pb 3, valuation sheet of 6 December 1816; net price estimated at 226 francs, selling price fixed at 250.
3. Register Vj' 23 (1816), fol. 234-234 v.
4. Ibid., fols. 106ff, and 283ff. Ganeau fils worked on several "Gothic" cups and saucers painted by Rumeau in 1816. Given the *9A* in his mark, this is possibly the cup for which he was paid 5 francs in August "for highlighting of the scraped ornaments, lining and details." It is impossible to be sure which of the burnishers worked on these pieces because no details are provided in the registers.
5. Register Vv 1, fol. 75 v, no. 41 and see note 3.
6. *Notice . . . 1 Janvier 1817.*
7. Laborde, *Voyage pittoresque et historique de l'Espagne* (1806 – 12), P vol. 2, pt. 2, pl. 14.
8. Willemin, *Monuments français* (1806 – 39) vol. 1, pl 38.

143a, b.
Standing Baskets, 1818 – [23?]
Called *Corbeilles 'Lion'*

Hard-paste biscuit porcelain
H. 8 1/4 in. (21 cm); diam. of basket 9 5/8 in. (24.5 cm)
Private collection

143a. Standing Basket

Marks (lion): [incised] *A.B.*; [incised, cursive] *10. oct. 18 / No 2*[1]
Marks (basket): [incised] *18-10*; [painted in gold] *29 juin DG 19*[2]; [engraved and printed in blue, monogram of Louis XVIII enclosing a fleur-de-lys and *Sèvres*]

143b. Standing Basket

Marks (lion): [incised] *3 juillet-19*
Marks (basket): [incised] *ch*[3]; [painted in gold] *24 Al 20*

These *corbeilles 'Lion'* were designed by Alexandre Evariste Fragonard in 1817 and executed soon thereafter (see cat. no. 44). It is extremely difficult to be sure which of the examples mentioned in the documents correspond to the two baskets shown here, which may not have originated as a pair. These two were made very early on in the production of this unusual object.

The two first examples, which entered the sales inventory on December 26, 1818,[4] were exhibited in the Louvre on January 1, 1819,[5] and delivered on February 2, 1820, to the Chevalier de La Malle.[6] A later, isolated example, which theoretically was sent to the salesroom on July 1, 1820, is certainly the one delivered to 'M. Destouches, *préfet*' on June 2, 1820.[7] The next two examples did not enter the sales inventory until May 30, 1823, and were delivered to the Garde-Meuble on the following June 10.[8] The price of the earliest examples was 290 francs, which implies that the gilding on all of them was similar. Subsequently, the baskets were either sold as part of table services or individually.

1. The mark *A.B.* identifies Alexandre Brachard. He was paid in September 1818 for "two basket-bearing lions," 45 francs each (Register Va' 22 (1817 – 1818), fol. 129 ff.) In addition, in June he received a bonus of 10 francs for "one basket-bearing lion no.1 of 10 October 1818," which proves that there may be slight differences between the dates inscribed on the objects and the payments made for them (Register Va' 23 (1819 – 1820), fol. 151 ff.).
2. *DG* is the mark of Catherine Elisabeth Godin; she was paid in July 1819 for "two lion baskets partially gilded," receiving 10 francs for each (Register Vj' 26 (1819), fol. 139 ff.).
3. The mark *ch* identifies Mathias Chanou who, before the date when the basket exhibited here was gilded (April 21, 1820) had previously made only two lion baskets, in July 1819, receiving 20 francs for each (Register Va' 23 (1819 – 1820), fol. 125 ff.)
4. Register Vv 1, fol. 278, no. 31.
5. *Notice . . . 1 January 1819*, no. 20.
6. Register Vbb 5, fol. 19.
7. For entry into the sales inventory, see Register Vv 1, fol. 147, no. 19; for delivery, see delivery; Register Vbb 6, fol. 3.
8. For entry into the sales inventory, see Register Vv 1, fol. 198, no. 11; for delivery, see Register Vbb 6, fol. 29.

144a–e.
Pieces from the *Service 'des Oiseaux d'Amérique du Sud'*, 1819 – 21

Hard-paste porcelain
Hillwood Museum, Washington D.C.
Inv. nos. (plates) 34.136.1, .2, .3, .8; (compote) 24.136.16

144a. Plate

Diam. 9 1/4 in. (23.5 cm)
Inscription: [obverse] *Le Diable enrhumé*
Marks: [painted in gold] *25 January B.T. 20 No. 27*[1]; [engraved and printed in blue, monogram of Louis XVIII, with a fleur-de-lys inside] / *Sèvres. 20*

144b. Plate

Diam. 9 1/4 in. (23.5 cm)
Inscription: [obverse] *Septicolor*
Marks: [painted in gold] *c 12 Aout*; [engraved and printed in blue, monogram of Louis XVIII, with a fleur-de-lys inside] / *Sèvres. 20*

144c. Plate

Diam. 9 1/4 in. (23.5 cm)
Inscriptions: [obverse] *Peruche Toui-été*; [in gold, on either side of the bird's perch] *Pne de Courcelles/Fme Knip*
Marks: [painted on reverse in gold] *MC 5 Juin 19 no10 / DY*; [script, in pale orange] *gmp m*[2]; [engraved and printed in blue, monogram of Louis XVIII, with a fleur-de-lys inside] / *Sèvres. 20*

144d. Plate

Diam. 9 1/4 in. (23.5 cm)
Inscriptions: [obverse] *Euphone teïté*; [in gold on either side of the bird's perch] *Pne. de Courcelles/Fme Knip*
Marks: [incised, in script] *cv*; [painted in gold] *27 Janvier B.T. 20 No. 27*[3]; [engraved and printed in blue, monogram of Louis XVIII, with a fleur-de-lys inside] / *Sèvres. 20*

144e. Compote, 1819
Called *Jatte à Fruits 'Hémisphérique'*

H. 4 3/4, diam. 7 1/2 in. (12.2 x 19.2 cm)
Marks: [incised] *2-81*; [painted in gold] *Mc. 24 Debre 1819-D.Y.*; [painted in black] *no. 7 – no. 8*[4]; [engraved and printed in blue, monogram of Louis XVIII, with a fleur-de-lys inside] / *Sèvres. 20*

144a.

These five pieces belong to a service called the "Birds of South America,"[5] which was numbered three in the list of table services for 1818.[6] The service was begun as a way to display the skills of Mme Knip (Pauline de Courcelles). Brongniart could have first first seen her drawings of birds on vellum in the Salon in 1806. She decorated six plates of the *service 'Marly d'or'* in 1817 and her work greatly impressed the director, who wrote to her: "I have every reason to think that your talent could be of regular use to the factory; you have acquired very sophisticated skills in this short space of time and this makes me think that you will daily give new perfection to your work on porcelain."[7]

She was commissioned to paint all the birds for this service, and on February 2, 1818, she reported to Brongniart: "In the Muséum [d'Histoire Naturelle] galleries among the birds of South America I have found seventy-two birds more brilliant than their brothers . . . none of them needs to be reduced in size for the plates."[8] She explained her preference for working from nature (even if from stuffed specimens) because the illustrated books always exaggerate the colors. Brongniart must have told her of his idea of depicting native plants associated with each of the birds that were to be illustrated as a frieze around the rim of each plate, since Mme Knip points out, "the birds of South America, as you know Monsieur, are seldom seed or fruit eaters; most of them live on insects. The borders will be more uniform as a result, which will in no way detract from the painting."[9] All the friezes and perches were designed by Jean Charles François Leloy.

It took Mme Knip more than three years to paint the entire service, since several pieces were broken and had to be remade or abandoned altogether (see below). The bulk of the service appeared in the salesroom on May 5, 1821.[10] At that time it comprised fifty-one plates whose selling price was fixed at 120 francs, and four compotes at 325 francs, plus twelve *compotiers* decorated with a simple frieze, two ice pails called *glacières 'AB'*, two sugar bowls called *sucriers 'Melissin'* and two swan baskets called *corbeilles 'Cygne'*. Part of the service had already been presented at the annual exhibition of the products of the royal fac-

144b.

144c.

tories at the Louvre on January 1, 1821.[11] Nine more plates appeared in the salesroom on May 10, 1821,[12] and four baskets on December 22, 1822.[13] The service was finally delivered in January 1826, on the orders of King Charles X, to the dauphine.[14] Neither the swan baskets nor the ice pails were included in this delivery.

As is frequently the case, the vagueness of the registers makes it difficult to follow the exact date of execution of each object. A first plate with the *Tangara Diable enrhumé* (No. 3 of the service) was painted between April and November 1818 and then broken. Work on this plate was resumed in March 1820 and completed in June 1821 after a third painting.[15] It may have been gilded by Boitel.[16] The frieze, designed by Leloy, is entitled *Ourouparia guyannensis.*[17]

Plate No. 5, with the [*Tangara*] *Septicolor* has a more obscure history. It was begun in April 1818 and returned in January 1820; the register bears the penciled note "broken" against this date, after which it is not mentioned again in the registry.[18] The design of the frieze bears the inscription *Virola Sebifera* and two notes in the handwriting of Alexandre Brongniart: "taken from Aubert, Flora of Guyana" and "*Myristica sebifera L.*"[19]

Plate No. 10 with the *Perruche Touï-été* was given to Mme Knip to be painted in April 1818 and returned completed in December 1819.[20] The marks identify the gilders Micaud and Durosey.[21] The frieze is the same as on the plate with the *Diable enrhumé.*

Plate No. 27 shows the *Euphone teïté.* The first example was broken in 1818. A second was given to the painter in March 1820 and returned in October of the same year after a second painting.[22] It may have been gilded by Boitel.[23] The frieze is accompanied by the note *Melastoma elegans.*[24]

There seems to have been some confusion over the dishes because the service was originally supposed to include two *Jattes à fruits 'Sirènes',* which were both broken in the course of being decorated. Mme Knip received the four fruit dishes in January 1820 and returned them with the designs sketched in on September 13; they were returned to her for more painting on 11 November. Two were again returned on December 2 and the others received further painting between December 5 and 25.[25] The design for the gold decoration still exists, but no details are given concerning the plants.[26] Here again the marks permit identification of the gilders, Micaud and Durosey.[27]

1. *B.T.* is the mark of the gilder Charles Marie Pierre Boitel. There is no mention of any plates from this service in the summary he made of his work in January 1820. During the year he was only paid in March "for the gilding and decorating" of two plates from the service, receiving 12 francs for each one (Register Vj' 27 (1820), fol. 117ff.)
2. *MC* is the mark of the gilder Pierre Louis Micaud. In June 1819 he was paid for the "gilding" of four plates belonging to the service, 12 francs each (Register Vj' 26 (1819), fol. 124ff.). *DY* is the mark of another gilder, Charles Christian Marie Durosey; this may either be one of the fifteen plates of the service of which "he sanded the decoration" [il a sablonné les décors] for 0.25 francs each, or one of the two for which he received 15 francs for "painting on the gold decoration" [peinture sur or du décor] (ibid., fol. 129ff).
3. See n. 1.
4. The marks pose a problem here. According to the registers, either Micaud nor Durosey seems to have worked on these bowls in December 1819. Micaud gilded them between January and February 1819 and received 35 francs each for "gold decoration and elaborate ornamentation" [decore on or riche garniture] (Register Vj' 26 (1818), fol. 124ff). He took them back to add "2 bunches of leaves on each in gold" at 4 francs per bowl in November 1820 (Vj' 27 (1820), fol. 123ff). On the other hand, they do not appear in Durosey's work records until January 1821, the date when he was paid 38 francs per bowl 'for the painting on gold' (Vj' 28 (1821), fol. 89ff.)
5. Brunet, "The Sèvres service of South American Birds" (1962).
6. Carton Pb 4, 1817 – 1818, summary of work done.
7. Carton Ob 3, dossier Mme Knip.
8. Carton T 8, liasse 2, dossier 4, letter of 16 February 1818.
9. Ibid., same letter.
10. Register Vv 1, fol. 160 v, no. 51.
11. *Notice sur quelques-unes . . . 1 January 1821*, No. 20.
12. Register Vv 1, fol. 191, no. 35.
13. Ibid., fol. 301, no. 18.
14. Register Vbb 7, fol. 12.
15. Register Vj' 27 (1820), fol. 24ff, and Vj' 28 (1821), fol. 33ff.
16. Cf. n. 1.
17. Inventory $ 1 1818 no.22. The drawing in the archives of the design for the perch is different from the one actually on the plate; it may have been changed for the second example.
18. Register Vj' 25 (1818), fol. 24ff, and Vj' 27 (1820), fol. 28ff.
19. [tiré d'Aubert Flore de la Guyanne] Inventory $ 1 1818 no.5.
20. Register Vj' 25 (1818), fol. 24ff. and Vj' 26 (1819), fol. 28ff. The price of 50 francs is mentioned here and appears to have been the same for all the plates.
21. See n. 2.
22. See n. 18.
23. See n. 1.
24. Inventory $ 1 1818 no. 29.
25. Register Vj' 27 (1820), fol. 24ff. She received 60 francs for each of the two birds on each bowl, instead of the 65 she asked for (Register Vq', first series, vol. 4, fol. 91, December 1820).
26. Inventory $ 6 1818 no. 3
27. See n. 4.

144d.

144e.

145
Teapot, 1819 – 20 (not shown)
Called *Théière 'Chinoise'*

Hard-paste porcelain
H. 5 5/16 in. (13.5 cm)
Marks: [incised] *19-10* (October 1819); [painted in gold] *M / 11 / 9* (script) *n 18*; [engraved and printed, monogram of Louis XVIII with fleur-de-lys inside]
Collection of Fred A. Krehbiel

The design for this teapot was paid for in April 1818 and was put into production quickly. The first decorated examples entered the sales inventory the following December 26 (see cat. no. 47). The registers in which biscuit firing and glazed pieces were recorded show that all the copies were made and glazed between 1818 and the end of 1819; they went into the warehouse as blanks and were taken out to be decorated as required.

The incised date on this teapot, October 1819, may indicate that it was one of three pots thrown by François Godin jeune or one of two thrown by Pierre Nicolas Marchand fils aîné in October.[1] The registers lack detail, and it is therefore difficult to follow the decoration of these objects, but it does not seem to have taken place before 1820. Joseph Weydinger put four "in various muffle-kiln colors" in July.[2] These were gilded in August by Jean Moyez[3]; two of them received a "second muffle-kiln ground" by Weydinger in September,[4] but it is not known whether they received a second layer of glaze or a different color fired at lower temperature. Only one came out of the kiln in satisfactory condition.[5] The first two entered the sales inventory on September 29, 1820, and the third on the following October 20.[6] They were not all decorated in the same manner: a teapot in this shape received a ground layer of "'campant' [sic] green marble" from Weydinger in 1820.[7]

1. For Godin, see Register Va' 23 (1819 – 1820), fol. 129ff.; for Marchand see ibid., fol. 137ff. They were both paid 9 francs per pot.

2. Register Vj' 27 (1820), fol. 84ff.; he was paid 2 francs each.

3. Ibid., fol. 283 ff.; he was paid 5.50 francs for each one.

4. Register Vɪ' 8 (firing of painted pieces), fol. 87 v, firing of September 27, 1820, where they were described as "two chinese teapots in muffle-kiln colors ordinary decoration by Mr. Fragonard."

5. Register Vvɪ, fol. 149 v, no. 40 and Carton Pb 4; as for the preceding ones their selling price was fixed at 36 francs (see cat. no. 47). One of the two was sold to the Baron de Cassan at the New Year exhibition of the products of the factory at the Louvre in 1822 (Register Vz 4, fol. 62)

6. Register Vvɪ fol. 150, no. 36 and Carton Pb 4, in which the decoration is described as *ordinaire.* It was sold, also for 36 francs, to an unnamed purchaser who was allowed a 10% discount during the New Year exhibition of the products of the factory at the Louvre in 1821 (Register Vz 4, fol. 26 v).

7. Entered the sales inventory on 2 February 1821 (Register Vv 1, fol. 157, no. 27; although it was described as defective, its selling price was still 36 francs, the same as the price for the perfect ones). It was sold for cash in March 1821 (Register Vz 4, fol. 348).

146a, b.

146a – h
Pieces from the *Service 'Lapis corbilles de fleurs'*, 1820 – 23

Hard-paste porcelain
Private collection

146a. Plate, 1823

9 1/4 in. diam. (23.5 cm)
Marks: [incised] *22-1* / [initials difficult to decipher]; [painted in green] *30 m.22 Rf.*; [painted in red] *SS.*; [painted in gold] *gn / 20 mai 23. / Vd*[1]; [engraved and printed mark in blue, the two *Ls* of Louis XVIII enclosing a fleur-de-lys, *Sèvres*, and two very faint date marks]

146b. Plate, 1823

9 1/4 in. diam. (23.5 cm)
Marks: [incised] *20-1 / CDC*[2]; [painted in green] *15 jer. 20.*[3]; [engraved and printed mark in blue, the two *Ls* of Louis XVIII enclosing a fleur-de-lys, *Sèvres*, and two very faint date marks]

146c. Plate, 1823

9 1/4 in. diam. (23.5 cm)
Marks: [incised] *20-10 / FC* (?); [painted in red] *SS*; [painted in gold] *gn / 20 mai 23*; [in red] *gn*[4]; [engraved and printed mark in blue, the two *Ls* of Louis XVIII enclosing a fleur-de-lys, *Sèvres*, and two very faint date marks]

146d. Plate, 1823

9 1/4 in. diam. (23.5 cm)
Marks: [incised] *20-5 / AC* (very angular)[5]; [painted in green] *30 m. 22 P.*; [painted in gold] *20 mai gn 23*; [in red] *SS*; [in gray-brown] *Vd.*[6] [engraved and printed mark in blue, the two *Ls* of Louis XVIII enclosing a fleur-de-lys, *Sèvres*, and two very faint date marks]

146e. Footed Fruit Bowl, 1820 – 22
Called *Compotier 'Coupe à Pied', rond*

H. 2 1/2 in. (6.5 cm)
Marks: [incised] *dz* / [incised, cursive] *T*[7]; [painted in green] *29 j^n. 15.*; [painted in gold] *M 24 ms 20.*; [engraved and printed mark in blue, the two *Ls* of Louis XVIII, enclosing a fleur-de- lys, *Sèvres*, and two very faint date marks]

146f. Sugar Bowl and Stand, 1820 – 22
Called *Sucrier 'Coupe'*

H. 5 3/4 in. (14.5 cm)
Marks: [incised] *qz-9 / Le*[8]; [painted in green] *29 j^n. 15.*; [engraved and printed mark in blue, the two *Ls* of Louis XVIII enclosing a fleur-de-lys, *Sèvres*, and two very faint date marks]

146g. Fruit Bowl, 1820 – 22
Called *Jatte à Fruits 'Hémisphérique'*

Diam. 5 7/8 in. (15 cm)
Marks: [incised] *Je*; [painted in green] *7 j^et. 20*; [painted in red] *W*[9]; [engraved and printed mark in blue, monogram of Louis XVIII enclosing a fleur-de-lys and *Sèvres*]

146h. Fruit Bowl, 1820 – 22
Called *Jatte à Fruits 'Hémisphèrique'*

Diam. 5 7/8 in. (15 cm)
Marks: [incised] *18 . . .* [figure illegible]; [painted, in green] *7 j^et. 20*; [painted in red] *W*[10]; [engraved and printed mark, in blue, double L of Louis XVIII enclosing a fleur-de-lys, Sèvres, and the last number of an illegible date]

These pieces are part of a service numbered 12 in the record of work for 1819.[11] On the note accompanying the service, written by Brongniart, the heading reads: "service no. 12 Lapis basket of flowers, composed of all the plates in lapis blue, or plain blue with the centers spotted by blue marks. Border lapis blue or with gold continuous frieze. ground an imitation of basketwork in shaded gold, covering almost the whole background for the epergne and other pieces, or leaving a circular space for a bouquet of mixed flowers . . . the basket printed all over and anything surplus to be scraped off by the flower painters."[12]

This seems to have been basically a simple service decorated without great expense, which probably explains Brongniart's decision to present it at the

146c, d.

exhibition of industrial products in 1819, rather than at the exhibition of products from the royal manufactories held at the Louvre. The bulk of the service entered the sales inventory on November 10, 1820; it was described as "service lapis blue ground baskets painted in shaded gold group of flowers in the middle etc." It comprised 99 flat plates whose selling price was 40 francs, ten round bowls at 40 francs, two ice pails at 325 francs, four compotes at 160 francs, two table sugar bowls with stands at 150 francs, and two baskets called *corbeilles 'Jasmin'* at 120 francs.[13] Other pieces were added bit by bit and all were assembled for delivery to "M le Vicomte de Chateaubriand, ambassadeur de France en Angleterre," in several batches.[14] As always with this type of delivery, it is not known whether this was intended for the ambassador personally or for the embassy as part of its official furnishings. The fact that the last delivery, which included these plates, took place in 1823, after Chateaubriand had left London, indicates that they were most likely a personal gift. While he was ambassador in Rome, the Vicomte de Chateaubriand received a second similar service, with a lapis blue ground, a rosette printed in gold in the middle of the plates and a large wreath of flowers (all of the same species) on each plate.[15]

1. The green mark indicates the date when the blue ground was laid (March or May 1822); *SS.* is the mark of the painter Jacques Nicolas Sinsson père, who was paid several times in 1823 for "painting and retouching" plates of this design, seven francs each (Register Vj' 30 (1823), fol. 40 ff.); *gn* is the mark of the gilder J. B. Pierre Louis Ganeau fils, who was paid regularly in 1823 for plates of this design, receiving 60 centimes "for lapis and decoration" and 7 francs "for painting on gold the osiers of the basket" (ibid., fol. 127 ff.); *Vd* is the mark of the gilder Charles Vandé, who painted the gold bands.
2. *CDC* seems to be a variation of the mark of Charles Descoins, plate thrower (Register Va' 23 (1819 – 1820), fol. 81 ff.).
3. The mark in green indicates the date the ground was laid, on 15 July 1820.
4. See n. 1.
5. This mark may belong to Auguste Chanou, who was paid for throwing ordinary plates in 1820 (Register Va' 23, fol. 111 ff.).
6. See n. 1.
7. This is the looped *T* of François Joseph Thion, paid in October 1812 (*dz*) for 120 bowls at 70 centimes each and in December for 25 more (Register Va' 19 (1812), fol. 65 ff.).
8. *Le* is the mark of Jean Charles Leguillier, paid in September 1814 (*qz-9*) for thirty sugar bowls at 1.50 francs each and eight matching trays at 75 centimes (Register Va' 20 (1813 – 1814), fol. 46 v ff.).
9. *W* is the mark of the painter Joseph Weydinger. He received the bowls, two in April and two in May 1820, finished them in July but was not paid until September, 50 francs each (Register Vj' 27 (1820), fol. 84 ff.)
10. Ibid.
11. Carton Pb 4, work records of 1819.
12. [service no. 12 Lapis corbeille de fleurs. composé de toute les assiettes en bleu Lapis ou même bleu uni dont le milieu est gaté par des taches bleues.marly bleu lapis simple ou frise d'or courrante (sic).fond une imitation de corbeille en or ombré, ou couvrant presque tout le fond pour les assiettes montées et autres, ou laissant une place circulaire dans le milieu pour un paquet de toutes fleur... la corbeille imprimée en entier ce qu'il y aura de trop sera gratté par les peintres de fleurs] Ibid.
13. [service fond bleu lapis corbeilles peint en or ombré grouppe (*sic*) de fleurs au milieu etc.] Entry Register Vv 1, fol. 150 v, no. 40.
14. The first delivery on April 15, 1822, corresponded to the entry in the sales inventory, except that the set contained three plates fewer and two bowls more; it was accompanied by an entrée service "blue ground gold decoration" (Register Vbb 6, fol. 11 v). The second delivery, on May 2, 1822, comprised fourteen plates, twelve bowls and eight low baskets, in addition to a tea and coffee set (ibid., fol. 11 v). A third package was sent in December 1822, with ten flat plates and two sugar bowls (Register Vbb 6, fol. 14 v). Finally the last delivery, comprising one hundred plates, took place on 21 August 1823 (Register Vbb 6, fol. 18 v).
15. Entry in the sales inventory was made on December 5, 1828 (Register Vv 1, fol. 345, no. 19); delivery on December 4, 1828 (Register Vbb 7, fol. 53 v).

146e (left) and 146f (right).

146g, h.

147.
Plate, 1822 (not shown)

Hard-paste porcelain
Diam. 9 3/8 in. (23.8 cm)
Marks: [incised] *Lp / 21-10*[1]; [painted in gold] *5 m.rs B.F.*; [painted in orange, handwritten] *a*[2]; [engraved and printed mark in blue, the two Ls of *Louis XVIII* enclosing *Sèvres, 1822*
Cooper-Hewitt, National Design Museum, Smithsonian Institution /Art Resource, New York
Gift of George B. and Georgiana L. McClellan
Inv. no. 1936.13.32

This plate was not part of a service, even though several other plates are known with painted landscapes and the same border with a white ground and friezes of posts and gold stars.[3] The decoration was sketched on the plate by Mlle Delaval in July 1822 and completed by her in August.[4] The plate entered the sales inventory on December 20, 1822, with another by the same artist in the same series, the artist having received 50 francs for each landscape. The total price for making each plate was estimated at 82 francs and the selling price fixed at 75, which implies that there was something unsatisfactory about them.[5]

Although the artist enjoyed the protection of a number of people in the service of the crown,[6] her collaboration with Sèvres was very limited. In 1821 she painted two plates with views of Syria,[7] and in 1822 her second plate bore a "view of the Château de Fontainebleau."[8]

Mlle Delaval probably used an engraving by Duparc after Achille-Etna Michallon (fig. 147a), published by Ostervald, when painting this plate. She included all the details of the engraving, including the peasant in the foreground, but she over-emphasized the bareness of the slope of the Côteau de Bellevue and gave a somewhat curious rendering to the wall extending from the gates in front of the building. Exactly the same engraving was used by Célestin Lamarre on another plate in the same series (now in the Musée National de Céramique in Sèvres, see n. 3). Only the inscription changes from one plate to another: the one now in Sèvres is marked 'Manufacture de porcelaine/de Sèvres', rather than 'Manufacture Royale de/Porcelaine de Sèvres' as here.

1. Among the record of work executed by Louis-Marie Lapierre in October 1821 can be found "75 ordinary plates turned with a template" [75 assiettes ordi(naires) tournassé au calibre] (Register Va' 24 [1821], fol. 84ff.). This probably refers to the first trials of the new technique explored by Ferdinand Régnier after his return to Sèvres (see chap. 4). It may be that because these were experimental pieces the plates were given to students or unproven painters to paint. *21-10* means "October 1821."
2. "Boullemier fils one plate white ground reserve colored landscape for gilding the decoration frieze of posts and 'cossas' in between bands and area of small stars and embellishments" [Boullemier fils 1 assiette fond blanc cartel paysage colorié pour la dorure du décor frieze de postes et cossas entre filets zones de petittes etoiles et garniture] Register Vq', Series 1, vol. 5, fol. 7, February 1822. The gilder demanded 12 francs for this first trial plate, Brongniart agreed, but fixed the remuneration for the following plates at 9 francs each. It is almost impossible to pick out the plates belonging to this series among the work of Boullemier fils, who was paid for a large number of plates at 9 francs during 1822, without any specific details of the design provided (Register Vj' 19, fols. 134 ff.).
3. The same gilded motif was used on a blue ground in 1822, accompanying a bouquet of flowers (see Verlet, Grandjean, and Brunet, *Sèvres* (1954), pl. 120). There is also a second plate with a white ground and the same gilding, painted with a view of the Sèvres porcelain factory by Célestin Lamarre; see Pinot de Villechenon, *Sèvres: Une collection de porcelaines* (1993), ill. 4, p. 12. According to the written sources, about fourteen to sixteen plates of this type should have appeared in the salesroom on December 20, 1822; they were on sale for between 75 and 100 francs; the landscapes were painted by Célestin Lamarre, Binet fils and Mlle Delaval, all students or beginners.
4. Register Vj' 29 (1822), fol. 250.
5. Valuation sheet Carton Pb 5; for entry in the sales inventory, see Register Vv 1, fol. 190, no. 34.
6. Carton Ob 4, dossier Mlle Delaval.
7. *La Montagne du Précipice en Syrie* and *Une vue de Napelouse en Syrie* (Carton R 12).
8. Carton R 13.

148a–f.
Plates from the *Service 'des Arts Industriels'*

Hard-paste porcelain
9 1/4 in. diam. (23.5 cm) each plate

148a. Plate, 1823

Inscription: [obverse, signed] *Develly / 1823*; [in the plate well] *Porcelaine de Sèvres / Couleurs de fond et brunissage de l'or.*
Marks [reverse] [incised, cursive, the "b" is crossed by a horizontal bar) *18-7*; *bd*; [cursive, open capital letter) *D*[1]; [painted in green] *17 J.n 19*; [in gold] *A 17 A* ^{l}; [in red] *D.Y.*[2]; [engraved and printed mark in blue, the monogram of Louis XVIII enclosing a fleur-de-lys, and *Sèvres / 23*]
Bequest of Forsyth Wickes. Forsyth Wickes Collection
Courtesy, Museum of Fine Arts, Boston
Inv. nos. 65.1909

148a.

This is one of the first plates made by Jean-Charles Develly for the *Service 'des Arts Industriels'* (see cat. no. 67).[3] In 1820 he had painted a trial plate, in white ground color, depicting the glass-bottle factory at Sèvres.[4] Brongniart paid the artist the 120 francs that he demanded for the plate and stipulated that the payment was "for the first one only."[5] Another view of the same factory was painted in 1821 – 22, but it was not until 1823 that Develly began to work exclusively on this ambitious project.

For the first eight plates in the series, Develly depicted operations within the Sèvres manufactory, in a manner closely resembling the one he had used for the *déjeuner 'L'Art de la Porcelaine'* (see cat. no. 39). Perhaps the skill he had demonstrated in completing that commission suggested the idea of an entire service illustrating different decorative arts industries.[6] In this plate Develly combined in somewhat arbitary fashion the activities of workers producing the ground colors and, in the room beyond, the burnishers.[7]

As was often the case, the gilding was applied to the entire service before the painted decoration was added; although no related copper-plate has survived from the manufactory's gilding workshop, it is possible that the gold pattern was printed on. The plate was given to Develly for preliminary painting on February 26, 1823 and returned by him on March 19;[8] unlike the remaining plates of the service it apparently needed no final painting.

The date of this plate suggests that it might have been part of the shipment sent in 1836 to Prince Metternich in Vienna. By the time this delivery was made, 113 plates had entered the sales inventory,[9] 108 of which were offered to the prince. The factory must have kept 5, including 3 that showed the manufactory and were delivered directly to the ceramics museum at the factory. Since the registers show that there were in fact 8 plates that had the Sèvres factory as their subject, then 3 of them may have been included in the delivery to Vienna.

1. *18-7* indicates the month of July 1817; the turners marks have not been identified.
2. *17 Jn 1819* is the date the ground color was laid, June 17, 1819. *A 17 A* ^{l} may indicate that one stage of the gilding process took place on 17 April of an unspecified year. The gilder Durosey (whose mark is *D.Y.*) was paid in April 1823 for three "inscriptions on the plates of the service of the industrial arts", 1.50 francs each (Register Vj' 30 (1823), fol.93 ff.).
3. For a detailed history of the service, see Ennès, "Four Plates" (1990).
4. The registers for work done on the *service 'des Arts Industriels'* indicate that this plate appeared alone in the shop on December 20, 1822, with a price tag of 190 francs (Register Vvi, fol. 190, no. 45); it was delivered by the factory to the ceramic museum in September 1849 (Register Vaa 3, fol. 17 v).
5. Register Vq', first series, vol. 4, fol. 88 v, November 1820. The price agreed upon was "without the sketches made." These remained the property of the artist and are as widely dispersed today as are the plates of the service. The Museum of Fine Arts in Boston recently acquired a preparatory sketch for this plate (Ennès, "Four Plates" [1990], fig. 5).
6. In Brongniart's descriptions of pottery-making techniques illustrated in his *Traité des arts céramiques*, he writes: "One of the artists in the factory, M. Ch. Develly, possessing to the highest degree the skill of capturing (with great discernment and precision) the characteristic activities of the different trades carried out by each worker when carrying out the functions to which he is assigned, has made a selection of the procedures carried out in the workshops during the manufacture of porcelain and has portrayed them with his usual skill" (Brongniart, *Traité des arts céramiques* [1844], Atlas, p. 60).
7. This kind of arrangement is explained by Brongniart in the catalogue for the first presentation of part of this service at the Louvre on January 1, 1828: "In the middle of each plate has been depicted in picturesque but accurate manner the principal operations of an industrial process, by grouping together as many operations as possible into one workshop" (*Notice sur quelques- unes . . .*, [1828], no. 13).
8. Register Vj' 30 (1823), fol. 18 ff. Brongniart had first decided that "drawings made by M. Develly will be paid for according to the declaration he makes about time spent . . ." (Carton Pb 7, liasse 1, dossier 6). The first plates depicting the factory were therefore paid at either 110 or 115 francs; the price was apparently fixed thereafter at 100 francs per plate; the days spent making preparatory drawings and transportation costs were added.
9. The bulk of the service entered the sales inventory on December 4, 1829, and comprised seventy-six

148b.

plates whose retail price was fixed at 200 francs (Register Vv 2, fol. 15, no. 9). A group of fourteen plates appeared in the shop on 31 December 1831 (Ibid., fol. 46, no. 15) and twenty-three others on April 10, 1835 (Ibid., fol. 96, no. 11). The last five plates finally appeared in the shop on March 31, 1838 (Register Vv 3, fol. 34 v, no. 68).
10. In March 1836 the factory delivered to the ceramic museum the plate depicting the mill and the preparation of clay (Register Vaa 2, fol. 61); in June 1840 the two plates showing painters and gilders on one and sculptors and trimmers on the other were deposited in the museum (Register Vaa 2, fol. 77 v). Finally, in August 1875, the two plates depicting the utilization of the mill-stone were sent; these were among the five plates that appeared in the shop in March 1838 (Register Vaa 3, fol. 89).

148b. Plate, 1825

Inscription: [obverse, signed] *C.D./1826*(?); *Joaillier./Parures montées*
Marks: [reverse] [incised] two non-parallel vertical lines / *20-7*[1]; [painted in green] *30 nov.20*; [painted in gold] 2 Av. *D.Y.*[2]; [engraved and printed in blue, initials of Charles X enclosing a fleur-de-lys]
Bequest of Forsyth Wickes. Forsyth Wickes Collection
Courtesy, Museum of Fine Arts, Boston
Inv. nos. 65.1908

The *service 'des Arts Industriels'* was produced between 1820 and 1835 (see cat. no. 67) and included a pair of plates depicting the production of jewelry. The overview of the entire service mentions two plates relating to a "jeweler in fine and false gold . . .", as well as a plate depicting a "manufacturing goldsmith"; thc only drawing connected with these objects bears the inscription *Bijoutiers, joailliers*, which gives no clue to their specific subjects.[3]

After a preparatory trip to Paris in April 1825, Develly painted the first plate, "jewelry" in April – May, working on it again in May – June. In early December of the same year (December 1 – 6, 1825), he sketched out the second plate, the one shown here, described as "the jewels mounted," completing it in the same month. In the scene he produced, it has been noted that the artisan's work is neglected in favor of a society woman choosing her finery.[4] He received 100 francs for the plate, plus 10 francs for the day needed to make the drawing and 4 francs for carriage fares when he went to Paris to produce drawings on this plate and two others — one showing the production of artificial flowers and the other depicting dressmakers at work, all activities connected with women's wear.[5]

1. *20-7* means that the plate was produced in July 1820.
2. *20 nov.20* is the date the ground color was laid; in April 1825 the gilder Durosey was paid 1.50 francs "for painting the inscription" on a plate belonging to this service (Register Vj' 32 (1825), fol. 80 ff.).
3. Ennès, "Four Plates" (1990), fig. 7; see Carton Pb 6, liasse 1, dossier 10 bis, "Final progress report on the *service 'des arts industriels'* dated March 1, 1827". The second plate, "Bijoutiers; Joailliers" is much closer in spirit of the rest of the service, showing workers actually performing different functions of their trades (see London, Christie's Sale, June 28, 1993, lot no. 32).
4. Ennès, "Four Plates" (1990).
5. Register Vj' 32 (1825), fol. 15 ff. The date of the signature on the face of the plate is obscured by a gold band but seems more logically to be "1825," the year the artist was paid for the plate.

148c. Plate, 1827

Inscription: [obverse, signed] *Develly /1827*; [in the plate well] *Graveur à l'eau-forte*
Marks: [reverse, incised] *ad* (cursive; *18-12*[1]; [painted in green] *ms.21 E*; [in gold] *a.il Delle B.*[2] [engraved and printed mark, monogram of Louis XVIII with fleur-de-lys and *Sevres 21*[3]
Bequest of Forsyth Wickes. Forsyth Wickes Collection
Courtesy, Museum of Fine Arts, Boston
Inv. nos. 65.1910

This plate was the first of a group illustrating the processes of engraving and printing. It was given to Develly in December 1826 and he returned it with a "first painting" on January 8, 1827, taking it back for finishing from January 10 to 27, 1827.[4] A relatively accurate preliminary sketch exists for the scene.[5] Work on this piece proceeded concurrently with work on a thematically linked plate illustrating the copper-plate printers.[6] Later in the same year, Develly produced another plate depicting lithographers[7] and one more showing transfer-printing on porcelain (see cat. no. 67). These were followed by a second plate portraying lithographers (1828); three plates showing fabric printing (1830 – 31); and two plates on typography (1831), one showing an "ordinary" printing press and the other a steam press.[8]

1. *ad* is the mark of the thrower Alexandre Davignon. He was not paid for making plates in December 1818 (*18-12*), but he may have finished the 200 ordinary plates that figure in his accounts for November 1818, at 30 centimes each (Register Va' 22 [1817 – 1818], fol. 88 ff.).
2. The green mark refers to the laying of the blue background color (March 1821?); the gold mark is the mark of Virginie Boullemier.
3. The presence of this mark seems to suggest that it may have been applied when the ground color was laid, or when the plate was gilded, rather than when it was painted.

4. Registers Vj' 33 (1826), fol. 15 ff. and Vj' 34 (1827), fol. 19 ff.
5. Ennès, "Four Plates" (1990), fig. 10.
6. Registers Vj' 33 (1826), fol. 15 ff., and Vj' 34 (1827), fol. 19 ff.
7. Fairclough, "A Sevres Plate" (1994), no. 4, pp. 410 – 19.
8. Ennès, "Four Plates" (1990), fig. 10.

148d. Plate, 1828

Inscription: [obverse, in the plate well] *Fabrication/Du Blanc de Craie*
Marks: [reverse, incised] *22-6*; *LD* (twisted cursive capitals); *IC* (indistinct)[1]; [painted in green] *13 Xbre 27 G.*[2]
Bequest of Forsyth Wickes. Forsyth Wickes Collection
Courtesy, Museum of Fine Arts, Boston
Inv. nos. 65.1911

The activity depicted on this plate bears more resemblance to industrial production than to that of a workshop. This scene was painted by Develly in October 1828, and the plate received additional painting in November. In addition to the usual 100 francs paid for each of the plates of the service, the artist received 10 francs for the day it took him to make the preparatory drawing.[3] The forty-eight plates of the first batch appeared in the exhibition of products of the royal factories held at the Louvre on January 1, 1828; this one was one of the twenty-one additional plates shown the following year, at the exhibition on January 1, 1829.[4]

1. *22-6* means June 1822; the other marks belong to unidentifiable potters.
2. In December 1827 Godin laid the blue ground color on several plates, receiving 25 centimes for each one (Register Vj' 34 (1827), fol. 75 ff.)
3. Register Vj' 35 (1828), fol. 22 ff.
4. *Notice sur quelques-unes . . . Ier janvier 1828*, no. 13, and *Notice sur . . . Ier janvier 1829*, no. 9.

148e. Plate, 1827

Inscription: [obverse, in the plate well] *Jardinier Fleuriste*
Marks: [painted in green] *30 nov. 20 l*; [in gold] *2.a.il d.elle B*; [in black] *4*; [engraved and printed monogram of Louis XVIII with the two figures indicating the year difficult to read]
The Nelson-Atkins Museum of Art, Kansas City, Missouri
Acquired through the William Rockhill Nelson Trust
European Decorative Arts Deaccessioning Funds
Inv. no. F83-52

Despite the fact that the subject depicted is so bucolic, this plate is part of the *service 'des Arts Industriels'*. It deals with the commercial market garden or nursery in which flowers, flowering shrubs, and trees were grown for sale. The subject must have reminded Develly of another service he worked on in 1821 – 22 relating to "the growing and . . . use of cultivated flowers in

148c.

148d.

148e.

France," in which each plate illustrated a different species of flower.[1] The registers do not show clearly when the plate was sent to the painter; he returned it with the sketch in place on January 16, 1827, and worked on it again from January 19 to 27.[2] Over and above the usual 100 francs fee, he was paid for travel expenses and for the four days required to execute the drawings on a group of four plates: this one, and those depicting bakers, engravers, and copper-plate printers.[3]

1. Carton Pb 5, liasse 2, Followup dossier. The service, which appeared in the shop on December 17, 1822 (Register Vv 1, fol. 189 v, no. 29), was presented to President Boyer of Haiti on December 20, 1825 (Register Vbb 7, fol. 8 v).
2. Register Vj' 34 (1827), fol. 19 ff.
3. Ibid.

148f. Plate, 1827 (not shown)

Inscription: [obverse, in the plate well] *Brasserie / Entonnerie*
Marks: [reverse] *P* [followed by a wavy line ascending and two small vertical liness]; [cursive] *Dc*; [painted in green] *7 ms. 21 E*; [in gold] *D.G. 17 avril*[1]; [engraved and printed mark, monogram of Charles X enclosing a fleur-de-lys] beneath *Sevres 27*
Cooper-Hewitt, National Design Museum, Smithsonian Institution / Art Resource New York
The Decorative Arts Association Acquisitions Fund
Inv. no. 1989.84.1

According to the register of the work of the decorators, this plate belongs to a group of four relating to the brewing industry: the malthouse ("Le Germoire"), the malt kiln (La Touraille"), the fermenting vat ("Le Banc de Cuves") and this one (not shown) which depicts "casking" or putting beer into barrels.[2] The first two, and this plate, were all sketched by Develly in June 1827, taken back for additional painting the same month and delivered on July 13. In addition to the usual 100 francs per plate, the artist was paid for "three days for drawing brewery plates" at 10 francs per day.[3] In the factory archives at Sèvres there is a sketch in ink and wash bearing the inscription "the malt-kiln or drying".[4]

1. The green mark relates to the laying of the blue ground color on March 7, 1821; the gold mark bears no indication of the year.
2. Register Vj' 34 (1827), fol. 19 ff. The progress report on the service drawn up on 1 March 1827 only mentions two plates relating to brewers (Carton Pb 6, liasse 1, dossier 10 bis). The plate depicting the "malthouse" appeared in the saleroom quite recently (London, Christie's, June 28, 1993, no. 51)
3. Register Vj' 34 (1827), fol. 199 ff.
4. Drawer D XII, dossier "service des arts industriels."

149.
Cup and Saucer, 1827
Called *Tasse 'Gothique'* and *soucoupe*

Hard-paste porcelain, gilding
Cup, H. 3 1/4, (8.3 cm), diam. 3 1/8 in. (7.9 cm); saucer, diam. 6 in. (15.2 cm)
Marks (cup): [incised, cursives] MT-ch-23.12 [1]; [engraved and printed monogram of Charles X enclosing a fleur-de-lys]; *Sèvres / 27* beneath the monogram
Marks (saucer): [incised, cursives] MT; 23-11; 6 [2] [painted] M 296 [engraved and printed monogram of Charles X enclosing a fleur-de-lys]; *Sèvres / 27* beneath the monogram
Private collection

Pierre Huard was paid to design the decoration for this cup in March 1826 (fig. 149a).[3] The painting on porcelain was also by Huard; the registers mention two Gothic cups, but it is not clear whether the cups are identical or just very similar. Huard received them for the first painting in January 1827 and returned them in April, taking them back for final painting in October and returning the completed pieces in December.[4] The two cups entered the sales inventory on December 22, 1827.[5] It has only been possible to trace the purchaser of one of them, sold to "Prince Leopold de Saxe-Coburg" on November 10, 1829.[6] Leopold was an uncle of Albert, the prince-consort of Queen Victoria of Great Britain.

The decoration, with its proliferation of Gothic motifs, conforms to the shape of the cup although the kings depicted actually predate the appearance of Gothic architecture. Huard used the same printed source that Rumeau had employed earlier: the depiction of a rose window on the saucer is very similar to the "rose window in the Abbey of Bon-Port in Normandy" which was reproduced by Willemin (see fig. 149b).[7]

1. *MT* is the mark of Michel Tollot who was paid in December 1823 (*23.12*) for forty gothic cups at 35 centimes each (Register Va' 25 {1823-24], fol. 109 ff.); *Ch* is the mark of Mathias Chanou who was paid in the same month for attaching the handles, 1.50 francs for each cup (ibid., fol. 119ff.).
2. Michel Tollot was paid in November 1823 (*23.11*) for 106 saucers for gothic cups at 30 centimes each (ibid., fol. 109ff.).
3. "A design for a gothic cup featuring the three heads of the dynasties 15 francs" [Un dessin de tasse gotique sujet les trois chefs des dynasties 15 francs] (Register Vj' 33 [1826], fol. 42).
4. Register Vj' 34 (1827), fols. 51ff. He received the 200 francs that he requested for each cup (Register Vq', Series 1, vol. 5, fol. 108 v, December 1827).
5. "Two gothic cups and saucers richly decorated with gothic motifs etc." [Deux tasses et soucoupes gothiques riche décor d'ornements gothiques etc.] (Register Vv 2, fol. 330, no. 7). According to the valuation sheet (Carton Pb 6), the manufacturing price was assessed at 280.10 francs and the retail price fixed at 300 francs.
6. Register Vz 5, fol. 28.
7. Willemin (1826), vol. 1, p. 117.

150.
Cup and Saucer, 1828
Called *Tasse 'Litron Godronnée'* and *soucoupe*

Hard-paste porcelain, gilding
Cup, H. 2 1/2 in (6.4 cm); saucer, diam. 5 1/4 in. (13.3 cm)
Marks (cup): [incised] *Lp* (cursive); *27-8* / *Z.9* (the *Z* is reversed)[1]; [painted in gold] *A.28*; [engraved and printed in blue, Charles X with fleur-de-lys inside and date [18]28 below it]
Marks (saucer): [incised] *Lp* (one above the other, cursive) / *26- 3*[2]; [painted in gold] *A.28*; *y*; [engraved and printed mark in blue, monogram of Charles X with *fleur-de-lys* inside and date [18]28 below it]
Wadsworth Atheneum
Gift of Reverend Alfred Duane Pell
Inv. no. 1913.650.A,B.

The term *litron*, taken from a measurement equaling 0.813 liters, applied to this curved shape may seem surprising at first glance. The explanation is contained in a letter sent by Alexandre Brongniart to the steward in charge of expenditures for the king's residence on December 7, 1820, to explain the anticipated delay in the execution of the order placed on December 4: "the fluted cups in the shape of so-called 'Litron' cups; I shall not make them in exactly the same shape as these cups because I think fluting would not suit the square shape, and certainly would not go with the saucer. I have modified it, therefore, giving it a curve that is easier on the eye and better suited to the richness imparted by fluting. This will not change either the capacity or the convenience of the pieces . . ."[3] The new shape was an immediate success with both the royal administration and private individuals; the decoration was always simple but could be embellished with a frieze inside the upper edge of the cup. The rosette on the saucer could be replaced by ciphers or coats-of-arms. Moreover, cup and saucer could be purchased singly or could be added to services with similar fluted tea or coffee pots.

This cup and saucer may have belonged to one of two groups of twelve that were gilded by Auguste Richard and burnished by Rose Angélique Charlot between July and August 1828.[4] One of these groups of a dozen might have appeared on September 26, 1828, in the salesroom[5] and sold at the Christmas exhibition at the Louvre, with tea/coffee pots and other pieces, to the Duc d'Orléans, the future King Louis-Philippe, for 18 francs each.[6]

1. Louis-Marie Lapierre was paid in August 1827 for having thrown sixty-five fluted "Litron" cups, at 0.90 francs each (Register Va' 27 (1827 – 1828), fols. 100ff.) and Louis Victor François Garnier fils for having added handles to fifty in July, fifty in August, fifty in September and seventeen in October at 1.10 francs each (ibid., fols. 172ff.) *27-8* means August 1827.
2. The names of different types of fluted cups must have been confused. Louis Marie Lapierre was paid in March 1826 (*26-3*) for only ninety-one fluted English tea cups and saucers at 0.85 francs each, and eighty-eight saucers for fluted "Etruscan" cups at 0.40 francs each. There is no record of an individual being paid for "fluted 'Litron' cups" in that precise wording (Register Va' 26 (1825 – 1826), fols. 87ff.).
3. Carton T 9, liasse 1, dossier 3.
4. Auguste Richard was paid in June for "foliage decoration" on twelve fluted "litron" cups at 3.75 francs each; and in July for "simple border and border around the centre of the saucers" [bordure s(imple) meme bordure au fond des soucoupes], for twelve others at 5 francs each (Register Vj' 35 [1828], fols. 133ff.); Mlle Charlot was paid for 12 fluted "Litron" cups and saucers in June and 12 more in August, 1 franc each (ibid., fols. 216 v ff.).
5. Register Vv1, fol. 343, no. 1.
6. Register Vz 5, fol. 1 v. The second group of twelve cups and saucers gilded by Richard does not seem to have appeared in the shop before the end of 1829. The pieces here may still have been part of this group as the mark is printed on when the gilding is done.

151.
Plate from the *Service 'des Arts Industriels'*, 1835

Hard-paste porcelain
8 1/2 in. diam. (21.6 cm)
Inscription: [obverse, in the plate well] *Fabrication du Carton./Séchoirs.Etendoirs./Laminoirs*
Marks: [reverse, incised] *ac* (cursive); *32-11*[1]; [painted in green] *D.11 av.33.5*[2]; [engraved and printed in blue: monogram of Louis-Philippe] *Sevres 1835*
Museum of Art, Rhode Island School of Design
Gift of Mrs. Gilman Angier, Mr. Alfred Morris, Jr., and Bequest of The Nickerson Stamp Fund, by exchange
Inv. no. 84.021

This is one of the last plates produced for the *service 'des Arts Industriels'.* According to the archives, it is one of two that depicted cardboard making, although it is not possible to identify which of the two this one is. The second plate was returned from Develly with the illustration sketched out in December 1834, but no mention of when it had been given to the artist can be found; it was worked on again in January 1835.[3] During the same month, Develly sketched out plate number one, taking it back for further painting on February 19 and returning it finished on April 30.[4]

It would be logical to conclude that the last five plates painted for the service, including this one, were the ones that appeared in the shop on March 31, 1838,[5] too late to be part of the shipment sent to Prince Metternich in 1836 (see cat. nos. 67 and 148a). The two last plates, depicting the the mills, were delivered to the museum by the factory in August 1875;[6] the three others may have been sold or delivered individually.

Two preparatory sketches in pencil, representing the two printing presses visible on this plate, survive (see fig. 151a).[7]

1. The thrower Adolphe Carré made 390 "ordinary flat plates," at 30 centimes each, in November 1832 (Register Va' 29 (1831 – 1832), fol. 97 ff.).
2. The green mark refers to the laying of the blue ground color on 11 April 1835.
3. Register Vj' 41 (1834), fol. 19 ff, and Vj' 42 (1835), fol. 15 ff.
4. Ibid.
5. Register Vv 3, fol. 34 v, no. 68.
6. Register Vaa 3, fol. 89.
7. Drawer D XII, dossier "Service des arts industriels."

152a–d.
Pieces from the *Déjeuner 'Culture et Récolte du Cacao'*, 1836

Hard-paste porcelain
Marks: [in additions to individual marks, each piece also bear the monogram of Louis-Philippe stamped on the base, with the date 1836]
The Metropolitan Museum of Art, Purchase
The Charles E. Sampson Memorial Fund and Gift of Irwin Untermyer, by exchange, 1986.
Inv. no. 1986.281.1ab-.4

152a. Tray

L. 17 5/7 in. (44.8 cm), first size
Marks: [incised] *Le* (cursive) / *31-5*[1]

152b. Milk Jug
Called *Pot à Lait 'Ovoïde'*

H. 7 7/16 in. (18.9 cm)
Marks: [incised] *mt* (joined cursive) / *CL* (cursive) / *31-12*[2] [traces of a mark in gold] [illegible]

152c. Coffee Pot
Called *Cafetière 'Campanienne'*

H. 7 1/2 in. (19.1 cm)
Marks: [incised] [a sort of cursive *N* with scrolled first leg linked to a cursive *C*] *j-a* (cursive) *32.12*[3]; [painted in gold] *R* [for Pierre Ritron]

152d. Sugar Bowl
Called *Pot à Sucre 'Ovoïde'*

H. 5 1/2 in. (14 cm)
Marks: [incised] *Al* (cursive) [as under the coffee pot] *36-10*[4]; [painted in gold] *R* [for Pierre Riton]; *M*[5]

This ensemble is the second of two *déjeuners* called '*Culture et Récolte du Cacao*' (The Cultivation and Harvest of Cocoa). The first one, which had already been produced when the second was begun, entered the sales inventory on December 28, 1833, and was shown at the exhibition of the products of the royal factories at the Louvre on May 1, 1835, before being delivered to Louis-Philippe who presented the service to M. de Miraflorès on June 11, 1835 (see cat. no. 83). The painting in the reserves had been designed and painted on the pieces by Jean-Charles Develly. A project description in Riocreux's hand itemizes the subjects illustrated on the different pieces. Because these notations are not dated, however, it is not clear if they describe work to be done or summarize work already completed.[6] All the ornament was done by Jean-Charles-François Leloy.[7]

A drawing in the archives at Sèvres (fig. 152a) shows two designs for the reserves on the sugar bowl, only one of which was used on the first *déjeuner*,[8] the other appearing with minor modifications on the second set. It might be argued that the second set was made just to use the designs that were not used on the first: the same shapes were decorated with the same ornamentation, although identical themes were represented differently.

This second *déjeuner* was begun in December 1835; it was given to Pierre Riton for the entire month of December for the gilding and coloring of the borders of the tray and to Jean-Charles Develly for preliminary painting.[9] The two artists worked simultaneously on the preliminary painting and later detailing of the different pieces. The tray was finished in March 1836,[10] the coffee pot decorated between March and June, the cups painted from June to August, and the milk jug from July to August. The pieces were sent to different burnishers in September, and it was probably then that it was noticed that a sugar bowl was missing; the bowl was produced in great haste and could not be painted and burnished until December.[11]

This second *déjeuner* nevertheless entered the sales inventory on December 24, 1836,[12] and the register carries a curious description of it: "A Cacao tea service; Persian decorations etc."[13] It was delivered to Queen Marie-Amélie on August 21, 1837[14], probably to be used by her as a gift.

1. Charles Leguiller was paid in May 1831 for "30 oval tea-service trays first size" [30 plateaux de déjeuner ovales 1ere], 2 francs each (Register Va' 29 (1831 – 1832), fol. 115); *31-5* indicates May 1831.
2. Michel Tollot was paid in December 1831 for having thrown "39 ovoid milk jugs" [39 pots à lait ovoïde] (ibid., fols. 87 ff.; 0.80 francs each); Charles Delahaye was paid in December 1831 for having added handles to these 39 milk jugs (ibid, fols. 132 ff.; 1.25 francs each); *31-12* indicates December 1831.
3. This mark, which is difficult to describe, identifies the thrower Nicolas Fischer who was paid in December 1832 for 20 "plain *campanienne* coffee pots" [cafetières 'campaniennes' unies] (ibid., fols. 92 ff.; 1.50 francs each). *32-12* indicates December 1832.
4. Jean Baptiste Allard was paid in October 1836 for embellishing 34 ovoid sugar pots (Register Va' 31 (1835 – 1836), fol. 112 ff.; 1 franc each); they had been thrown in the same month by Nicolas Fischer (ibid, fols. 84 ff.; 1 franc each). *36-10* indicates October 1836.
5. The vagueness of the register of painting work (Vj' 43 (1836) makes identification of the gilder impossible.
6. Carton Pb 8, liasse 2, dossier "Déjeuners." The list of subjects, apart from the subject of the tray which is only described briefly as: 'MM. de Humboldt, Rugendas, etc.', is as follows: "Chocolate pot. Early method of preparing chocolate in Mechoacan; Present day method in Spain.-Sugar pot. Travellers stopping to drink chocolate in Mexico, a priest blesses the meal; Creoles and Spaniards selling Cacao.-Milk jug. Creoles drinking chocolate.-Cups. Spain, preparing chocolate in the pantry; Spain, drinking chocolate in the drawing room" [Chocolatière. Manière primitive d'apprêter le chocolat dans le Méchoacan; Fabrication actuelle en Espagne.-Pot à sucre. Halte de voyageurs pour prendre le chocolat au Mexique, un religieux bénit le repas; Des créoles et des Espagnols trafiquent du cacao.-Pot à lait. La prise du chocolat chez les créoles.-Tasses. Espagne, apprêt du chocolat à l'office; Espagne, La prise du chocolat au Salon].
7. Register Vq', Series 1, vol. 5, fol. 183 v, November 1833. Leloi's drawings and plans are listed; in addition allowance is made for his "Research in the [royal] library and at the home of M. Brongniart in Paris" [Reche(rches) a la Bibliothèque [royale] et chez Mr. Brongniart a Paris] for three days, and for the "drawings of Chinese forms originally intended to receive the decoration" [traits des grandes pièces chinoise destinée dans l'origine a recevoir les decor relevé]. He was paid the 260 francs he had demanded. In spite of allusions to Humboldt and Rugendas in the dossier of the service (Carton Pb 8, liasse 2) the only element for which a printed source can be found is the outer border of the tray. See Humboldt, *Vues des cordillères et monumens* (1810), plate "Ruines de Miguitlan ou Mitla dans la province d'Oaxaca."
8. Barbe, "Déjeuners en porcelaine de Sèvres" (1990), ill pp. 62 and 63.
9. Register Vj' 42 (1835), fols. 50 (Riton) and 24 v (Develly).
10. Register Vj' 42 (1836), fols. 68 ff., Riton; Riton was paid only 84 francs for the tray, instead of the 88 that he had been paid for the first one (Register Vq', Series 1, vol. 5, fol. 182, September – October 1833); he received payments identical to those he had received for pieces in the first service: 56 francs for the coffee pot and the sugar bowl; 44 for the milk jug and 48 for each *Tasse 'Litron Fragonard' avec sa Soucoupe 'Gothique'.* Develly received the same pay as for the 1833 *déjeuner.* 700 francs for the tray, 110 for the coffee pot and the sugar bowl, 50 for the milk jug and 45 for each cup (ibid, fols. 22 ff.).
11. Mme Bougon was paid 2 francs in September for the tray and 1.25 for the sugar bowl in December (Register Vj', 43 [1836], fols. 137ff.). Mme Lapierre received 3.50 for a cup and matching saucer "frieze and lining in gold" [frise et doublée d'or] and 2 francs for the milk jug "frieze and groove in full gold" [frise et gorge plein or] in September (ibid., fols. 147 ff.). Mme Chanou was paid 3.50 francs for the second cup in September (ibid., fols. 167 ff.). Mme Troyon received 2.50 for the *frise d'or* on the coffee pot in September (fols. 130 ff.).
12. Carton Pb 6, valuation sheets of 1836; the selling price of the pieces was the same as for the first service: 1.500 francs for the tray, 280 for the coffee pot, 260 for the sugar bowl, 175 for the milk jug, and 175 for each cup and saucer.
13. Register Vv 3, fol. 13 v, no. 31.
14. Register Vbb 9, fol. 16 v.

Fig. 152a. Two sketches for reserves on the sugar bowl in the *déjeuner 'Culture et Récolte du Cacao',* by Jean-Charles Develly. One (left) was for the first *déjeuner,* and the other was for the second service which is shown here. (Manufacture nationale de Sèvres, Archives)

153a.
Vase, 1844
Called *Vase 'Etrusque Caraffe'*

Hard-paste porcelain, gilded with platinum and gold
H. 17 1/2 in. (44.4 cm) [second size]
Inscription: [inside rim, in black] *LP* (in monogram) / *SEVRES* / *1844*; [decoration signed at left] *Moriot*
The Walters Art Gallery, Baltimore
Inv. no. 48.555

Although propaganda for the monarchy appeared very rarely on pieces made during the reign of Louis-Philippe (1830 – 48), straightforward representations of the king and close family members appeared frequently on a large variety of objects, from cups and saucers to ornamental vases. Of this particular shape, called the *vase 'Etrusque Caraffe'*, ten pairs decorated with portraits of Louis-Philippe and Marie-Amélie can be found between the years 1833 and 1847, at least seven of which were painted like this one by Adolphe Moriot.[1]

These vases were sent to Moriot for a preliminary painting in September 1844; he returned them with the design sketched out in October and finished them in October – November, receiving 275 francs for the portrait of the queen and 250 for the king.[2] These vases cannot be identified in the gilders' registers for lack of precise information, and the situation is complicated by the fact that they entered the sales inventory on December 31, 1844, with a notion, "price already known" and therefore without a detailed valuation sheet.[3] Apparently, the two vases were burnished by Mlle Charlot[4] and were "delivered to the Queen by express verbal order of Her Majesty" on January 8, 1845,[5] probably to be given away as gifts.

Despite the similarity of the fees paid the artist for this series of portraits, he did not always use the same models. In the case

153b.
Vase, 1844
Called *Vase 'Etrusque Caraffe'*

Hard-paste porcelain, gilded with platinum and gold
H. 17 1/2 in. (44.4 cm)
Inscription: [inside rim, in black] *LP* (in monogram) / *SEVRES / 1844*; *A AMELIE*; [decoration signed on right] *Moriot* [bottom of each vase, obscured by mount]
The Walters Art Gallery, Baltimore
Inv. no. 48.556

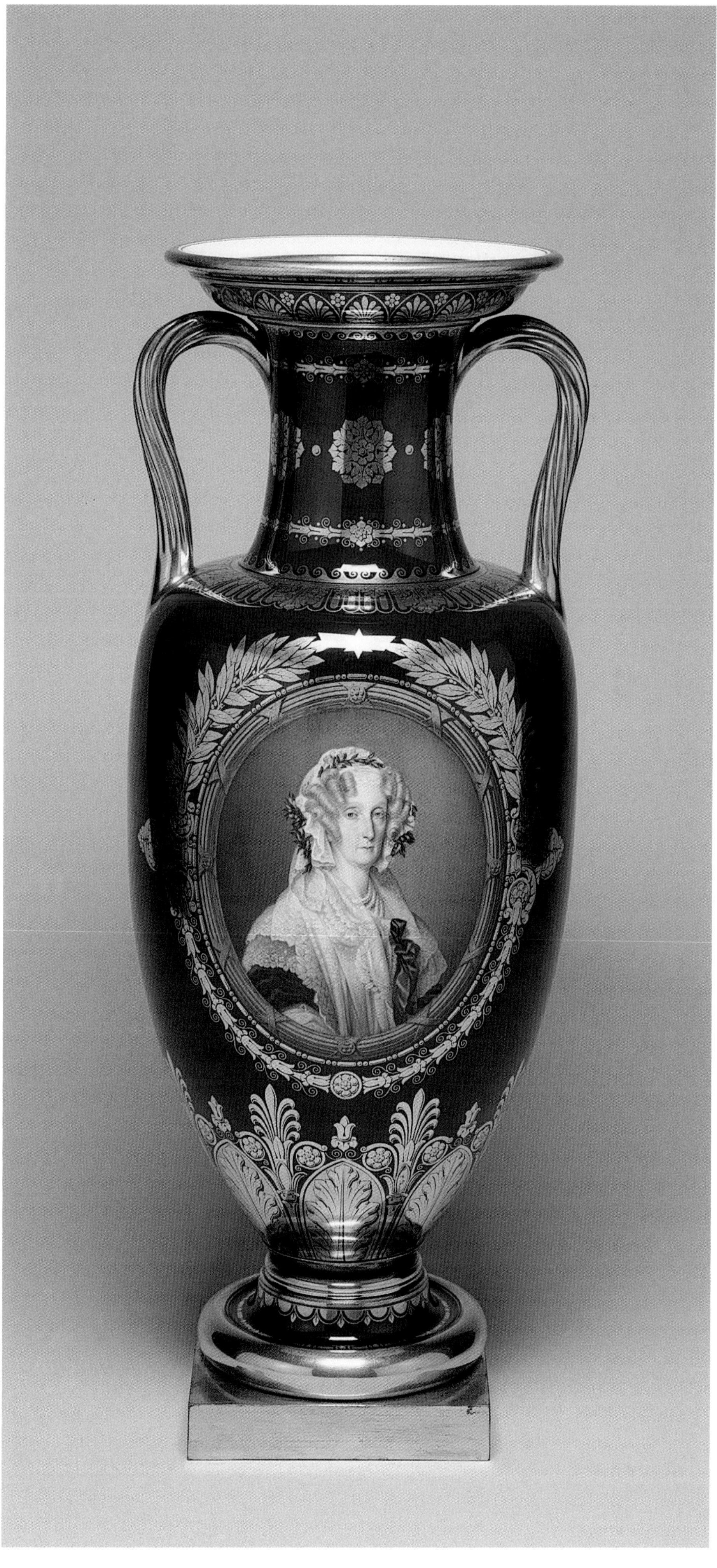

of these two vases Moriot must have used recent lithographs by Léon Noël and H. Grevedon (see figs. 153a and 153b), which were based on two portraits by François-Xavier Winterhalter. The same portraits were used again by Moriot on a pair of *vases 'Floréal'* in 1848, recently purchased by the Musée Louis-Philippe in Eu.

1. The secondary decoration and even the size of the reserves must have varied since the sums paid to Moriot for these portraits vary between 160 and 675 francs. Other artists commissioned to paint royal portraits on this vase form were Adélaïde Ducluzeau in 1837 and Mme Turgan in 1840. All the additional ornament in gold and platinum was designed by Antoine Willermet, as seen from a drawing in the AMNS (Armoire R XVII, dossier 15, inv. $ 8 1848 no. 75(1) and (2). The gilder has made a mistake in the design: the trophy on the back of the vase with a portrait of the queen should bear the legend *M AMELIE* but this has been written as *A AMELIE.*
2. Register Vj' 51 (1844), fols. 19 ff.
3. [à prix connu] Carton Pb 11 bis, valuation sheet 1844 and Register Vv 4, fol. 35, no. 2. The mention of this pair of vases as being *à prix connu* refers to a valuation sheet of July 22, 1837, relating to two vases painted by Adélaïde Ducluzeau. The vases are not identical, however, since the price of the vases painted by Mme Ducluzeau was 800 francs each, whereas the price of this pair was 1,000 francs each.
4. Of the two *vases 'Etrusque Caraffe' 2eme grandeur* for which she was paid 10 francs each in December 1844, one was described as bearing a "portrait of the king, with richly gilded decoration" [Portrait du Roi décor riche en or] (Register Vj' 51 [1844], fols. 167 ff.)
5. Register Vbb 11, fol. 1.

154a–c.
Pieces from the *Service 'Ordinaire de Fontainebleau'*, 1846 – 47

Hard-paste porcelain
Museum of Fine Arts, Boston
Assiette à soupe, Bequest of Miss Susan M. Watson, Inv. no. Res.38.2; *melonnières*, Gift of Dudley Leavitt Pickman, Inv. nos. 34.1364, 24.1363

154a. Melon Dish, 184
Called *Melonnière 'Ovale'*

L: 11 5/8 in. (29.6 cm)
Marks: [incised] *Le* (handwritten)/ *36-8* / [two horizontal parallel lines][1]; [painted in black] *T*; [purple] *Tr*; [gold] *M*[2]; [engraved and printed in gold, cipher of Louis-Philippe with the date 1846]; [engraved and printed in red, mark of the *Château de Fontainebleau*]

154b. Melon Dish, 1846
Called *Melonnière 'Ovale'*

L: 11 5/8 in. (29.5 cm)
Marks: [incised] *Le* (handwritten) / *39-1* / *27*; [painted in black] *T*; [gold] *M*; [red] [sort of cursive open capital *N*]; [engraved and printed in red, mark of the *Château de Fontainebleau*]

154c. Soup Dish, 1847
Called *Assiette 'à Soupe'*

Diam. 9 3/8 in. (23.8 cm)
Marks: [incised] *acbb11* (cursive) / *L* (handwritten); [factory mark engraved and printed under the glaze in chrome green] *SV LP 46*; [engraved and printed in blue, cipher of Louis-Philippe with the date 1847]; [engraved and printed in red, mark of the Château de Fontainebleau]

Returning to a tradition of the ancien régime which began gradually to reestablish itself from the First Empire onward, Louis-Philippe commissioned Sèvres to execute a dinner service for each of his official residences as well as for his private houses.[3] These were in addition to the table services he commissioned for the different divisions of the royal administration.[4]

These three pieces were part of the king's dinner service at the Château de Fontainebleau.[5] The service is often referred to in documents as the *service 'ordinaire de Fontainebleau'*, to distinguish it from an opulent series of plates decorated with historical scenes called the *service 'riche (ou Historique) de Fontainebleau'*, which were immediately mounted in paneling and never used.

When the king ordered the *service ordinaire* in August 1836, he had already decided that it "would bear a bas-relief in the Renaissance style." The Château de Fontainebleau had been built and decorated during the Renaissance and had not since undergone any radical alteration. The items that were delivered from 1839 onward, however, bear no particular relation to the king's request, although they do respect his desire to establish a relationship between the service and the château for which it was designed, a unique circumstance in the royal services of the period. The borders echo the trees in the forest nearby, the animals recall the hunting that was an important feature of the estate, and the shape of the reserves is reminiscent of certain architectural elements of the château.[6] On the other hand, the symbols on the service are

not exclusive to the château and bear only a tenuous relationship with it.

Another important feature of this service is that it has two different ornamental friezes, the overall harmony depending on the Greek frets, rosettes, and ornamental gilding that are repeated on all the pieces. One of the friezes consists of leafy foliage that hides a variety of small animals; between the arabesques of foliage there are transverse reserves containing emblems and a diamond-shaped reserve containing the royal cipher. The other, less common frieze consists of leafy branches that form arbours where birds fly. To complicate matters further, in some cases both friezes exist on different elements of the same piece, on the lid and and container, for example, or even both on the same object; in other examples, the details are switched from one to the other.

A further aspect of this service is that it was frequently copied by counterfeiters. The enormous collection of pieces delivered to Louis-Philippe was sold off after his death; not all, however, had been delivered and a number of the pieces remaining at Sèvres were allocated to the Conseil d'Etat. The stocks were frequently replenished for the Conseil, so that there are quite a few authentic pieces which are too late in date to have been made for Louis-Philippe himself. The fact remains that there are innumerable fakes, however, usually painted by chromolithography and often, but not always, on factory seconds from Sèvres.

The two oval melon dishes illustrate the problems the Sèvres factory experienced with the often anarchic and contradictory demands of the royal administration. Having allowed the household stewards in the different palaces to order what they fancied from Sèvres for years, the royal exchequer suddenly noticed the resultant chaos and abuses. The system was reorganized in 1846 and the quantity of different pieces required for each service in each residence was established. All excess pieces were returned to Sèvres to create a reserve; the factory was told to keep a proportion of the entitlement of each palace on hand so that urgent requests for replacements could be met.

The two melon dishes were probably made with this reserve in mind, since they were not ordered. During the re-organization and inventory that took place in 1846, it was discovered that the twelve melon dishes made for the original order (delivered in 1839 and 1841) were still in reserve.[7] Similar objects are mentioned in the work records of the painter-printer Etienne Joseph Tristan (*T* or *Tr*) and the gilder Jean Moyez (*M*): Tristan received six oval melon dishes from the service in July 1846 and finished decorating them in August.[8] He was also given the job of painting them, sketching out the designs in January – February 1847, and finishing them in March.[9] Between the two painting sessions they were sent to the gilder Moyez.[10] Unfortunately, after that the two pieces disappear without trace; they are not to be found in the records of the burnishers, nor in the lists of porcelain appearing in the

inventory before 1851. In 1851, however, four of them appear in the sales inventory made at the end of the year. These four melon dishes can be found in the inventories every year until 1859; only three were left between 1860 and 1864 and the whole service had disappeared by 1865. In spite of all these gaps and uncertainties the two shown here do not seem to be copies. The foliage frieze, which is certainly the frieze used on the original melon dishes,[11] seems to have been ignored by the counterfeiters.

The soup dish has a much simpler and clearer history. The order placed on September 15, 1846, included, among other things, three soup dishes at 35 francs apiece.[12] Possibly with the reserve in mind, Tristan printed fifty plates in October 1846.[13] Only four of these were sent to the painter Charles Didier in January 1847.[14] The three plates that had been ordered entered the sales inventory on 27 February 1847[15] and were delivered on March 2.[16]

1. Jean-Charles Leguiller was paid two francs each for 48 oval melon dishes in August 1836 (*36-8*) (Register Va' 31 [1835 – 1836], fols. 109ff.). He was also paid the same price for 104 oval melon dishes in January – February 1839 (*39-1*) (Register Va' 33 (1839), fols. 71 v and 72).
2. Marks of the painter-printer Etienne Joseph Tristan (*T* or *Tr*) and the gilder Jean Moyez (*M*).
3. Préaud, "Louis-Philippe et Sèvres" (1993).
4. The services for different ranks of royal administration were the princes' service, with a crowned royal cipher between two branches and a gold ivy-leaf frieze; the officers' service, with the same cipher and gold branches (no frieze); and the kitchen service with a simple cipher printed in blue or red on third grade (or discarded) pieces.
5. Barbe, *Le Service du roi Louis-Philippe* (1989).
6. Chevallier, *Musée national du château de Fontainebleau* (1996), pp. 212 – 316.
7. The selling price of the oval melon dishes delivered in 1839 had risen to 32 francs.
8. Register Vj' 53 (1846), fols. 139ff. He received 3.50 francs for "impression in gold and color" on each.
9. Register Vj' 54 (1847), fols. 134ff. He received a total of 6.50 francs per piece.
10. Ibid., fols. 108ff. He received 0.60 francs per dish.
11. Barbe, *Le Service du roi Louis-Philippe* (1988), ill. p. 35.
12. Register Vbb 12, fol. 118, March 2, 1847, details supplied at time of delivery.
13. Register Vj' 53 (1846), fols. 139ff. He was paid 2.50 francs for "impression in gold and colors" on each plate. Tristan appears to have acted as foreman of a contract workshop: he declared all the work as being his and shared out the wages. This might explain the unidentified red mark under the second melon dish, which may be the mark of one of his assistants.
14. Register Vj' 54 (1847), fols. 63ff. He received 12 francs for coloring and retouching each piece.
15. Register Vv 4, fol. 98, no. 18.
16. Register Vbb 12, fol. 118, March 2, 1847.

155.
Medallion Portrait of Alexandre Brongniart, 1847

David d'Angers (1788 – 1856)
Biscuit porcelain
6 5/8 in. diam. (16.8 cm); frame, 10 x 9 5/8 in. (25.4 x 24.5 cm)
Inscriptions: [obverse, at the base] *David 1842*; [vertically on the left in Brongniart's handwriting] *Alex. Brongniart*; [incised on the back] *Mas*[1]
Label affixed to the reverse: [handwritten] *Souvenir affectueux offert à Monsieur Virlet d'Aoust par la famille de celui auquel il adresse de dernières et touchantes paroles*
Museum of Art, Rhode Island School of Design, Museum Appropriation
Inv. no. 20.015

The link between Alexandre Brongniart and the sculptor Pierre-Jean David, known as David d'Angers is not spelled out in the archives of Sèvres. Both men were members of the Institut de France, however, David having become a member on August 5, 1826, while Brongniart had become a member in 1807. There are also no records of any sittings by Brongniart for this portrait. The plaster model at Sèvres bears the date 1842, probably the date of the original, to judge by the features of the administrator depicted in the medallion.

It appears that the Manufacture de Sèvres started making copies of this medallion in November 1847, very soon after Brongniart's death. The label on the back of this copy suggests that the Brongniart family may have loaned the manufactory the original already in their possession in order to have a memento suitable as a gift for the people who spoke at the funeral.[2] The first mention of the medallion appears in November 1847 in the list of work done by Jean Mascret: "13 cameo medallions blue ground of Mr. Brongniart" for which he was paid 2 francs each and "7 the same white ground" at 1.75 francs.[3] The pieces seem to have caused problems since only three with blue backgrounds appeared in the shop, along with three with white backgrounds (successful) and two others (defective)[4] This first batch of medallions was listed as *pour mémoire* (in memory); in other words they were not priced, and were delivered at once to "Madame Veuve Brongniart."[5] The label on this example suggests that it was part of the first series.

The edition continued in 1848, and a second size was added. The registers mention 7 good copies and 1 defective in the first size, 137 good copies and 9 defective in the second size.[6] The selling price was fixed at 5 francs for the first size and 1.60 francs for the second, but no details are given about background color. One copy of the first size was "delivered to the ceramic museum,"[7] while the rest were sold individually until the end of the 1860s.[8] None appear to have been made after 1848.

One of the explanations for the lack of success of the medallions with blue ground is probably the special technique imposed on the Sèvres factory by the nature of the paste they used. The simplest method would have been to mold a colored paste background in one piece, and to cast the relief in white biscuit clay separately, joining them afterwards as had been done with the Wedgwood jasper ware since the late eighteenth century. The hard-paste porcelain used at Sèvres, however, was not suitable for such a process. One mold had to be used, the white paste was pressed into the hollows to form the relief area, a thin layer of blue paste was laid on top of that, and the mold was filled with white. This process at least had the advantage of producing very fine work with degrees of translucency where the paste was very thin, which may explain why Wedgwood seems sometimes to have adopted the technique, making the identification of certain pieces very difficult.

Many artists who had known Brongniart during his lifetime paid tribute to him after his death in portraits to his memory. There is an oil painting by Emile Wattier and a bronze bust signed by Jean Feuchère, which does not appear ever to have been copied. Oddly enough the busts by Houdon of Alexandre Brongniart and his sister Louise as children were not reproduced by the Sèvres factory until 1905.

Inscription: ["Keepsake affectionately offered to Monsieur Virlet d'Aoust by the family of the man to whom he addressed some affecting last words"]

1. *Mas* identifies Jean Mascret.
2. The Institut published a volume containing the text of the speeches made at the funeral on October 9, 1847, by Elie de Beaumont, Auguste Henri André Duméril (for the Muséum d'Histoire Naturelle), Michel Eugène Chevreul (for the royal factories), Ours Pierre Armand Petit-Dufrénoy (for the Académie des Sciences), Jacques Joseph Ebelmen (in the name of the Sèvres factory) and Virlet d'Aoust (representing Brongniart's students); a speech by Constant Prévost was also included although there had not been time for its delivery (Institut Royal de France, 1847).
3. [13 medaillons camées fond bleu de Mr. Brongniart] [7 idem fond blanc] Register Va' 41 (1847), fols. 109-110.
4. Register Vv 4, fol. 127, nos. 3,4 and 5, entry of 30 December 1847.
5. Register Vaa 3, fol. 10, December 1847.
6. Register Vv 5, fol. 130, nos. 2,8,9,13, to 20 (entries of February 8, March 31, April 22, and May 30, 1848).
7. [livré au musée céramique] Register Vaa 3, fol. 13, July 1848.
8. Register Vz 12, fol. 204 v, 2 August 1870, a second-size copy was sold to a "M. Etienne."

Comparative Illustrations

Fig. 4a. *Vase 'Jasmin'*, Sèvres; hard-paste porcelain. (Musée national du château de Versailles et des Trianons)

Fig. 9a. *Vase 'Fuseau'*, Sèvres, 1806; hard-paste porcelain and gilt bronze. (Compiègne, Musée national du château)

Fig. 6a. *Vase 'Cassolette'*, Sèvres, 1811; hard-paste porcelain. (Musée national du château de Versailles et des Trianons)

Fig. 14a. *Vase 'à bandeau'*, Sèvres, 1806; hard-paste porcelain. (Châteaux de Malmaison et de Bois Préau)

Fig. 15a. Pair of *vase 'Medici's*, Sèvres, 1809; hard-paste porcelain. (Compiègne, Musée national du château)

Fig. 16a. Tabletop, *table 'des Maréchaux'*, Sèvres, 1810; hard-paste porcelain and gilt bronze. (Chateaux de Malmaison et de Bois Préau)

Fig. 16b. *Table 'des Maréchaux'*, Sèvres, 1810; hard-paste porcelain and gilt bronze. (Châteaux de Malmaison et de Bois Préau)

Fig. 18a. Fruit bowl called *jatte à fruits 'sirènes'* from the *service 'des Petites chasses'*, Sèvres, 1821; hard-paste porcelain. (Sèvres, Musée national de céramique)

Fig. 21a. Plate decorated with a view of the Palais des Tuileries and the rue de Rivoli, from the *service 'de l'Empereur'*, Sèvres, 1808 – 10; hard-paste porcelain. (Chateau de Fontainebleau, musée Napoléon)

Fig. 31a. Cup and saucer from the *déjeuner 'Regnier à reliefs'*, Sèvres, 1813; hard-paste porcelain. (Sèvres, musée national de céramique)

Fig. 36a. Cup called *tasse 'Jasmin à pied cannelé'* and saucer, decorated with a view of the Sèvres manufactory, Sèvres, 1815; hard-paste porcelain. (Sèvres, musée national de céramique)

Fig. 71a. A pair of ice-pails called *glacières 'chimères'* from the *service 'de la Chevalerie'*, Sèvres, 1834; hard-paste porcelain and gilt bronze. They are shown in an early photograph taken by Louis Robert, ca. 1850 – 70. (Manufacture Nationale de Sèvres, Archives)

Fig. 76a. *Déjeuner 'Chinois réticulé'*, Sèvres, 1840; hard-paste porcelain and gilt bronze. (Paris, Musée du Louvre)

Fig. 72a. *Vase 'Egyptien B'*, or *Vase 'Champollion'*, Sèvres, 1831- 32; hard-paste porcelain. (Compiègne, Musée national du château)

Fig. 78a. *Déjeuner 'de François Ier'* by Alexandre-Evariste Fragonard, and mantelpiece (see cat. no. 87). (From Brongniart and Riocreux, *Description méthodique du musée* [1845], P, pl. 7)

Fig. 79a. *Vase 'de la Renaissance Chenavard'*, designed by Claude-Aimé Chenavard, Sèvres, 1830 – 32; hard-paste porcelain. (Château de Fontainebleau)

Fig. 82a. *Déjeuner 'Du Guesclin',* Sèvres, 1835; hard-paste porcelain. (Sèvres, Musée National de Céramique)

Fig. 100a. *Vase 'des Chasses Historiques de la Cour de France',* Sèvres, 1844 – 45; hard-paste porcelain and gilded bronze. (Chantilly, Musée Condé)

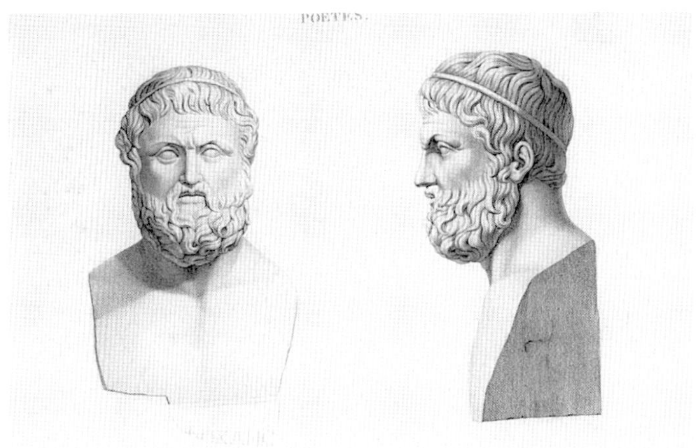

Fig. 139a. *Sophocles.* (From Visconti, *Planches de l'iconographie grecque* [1811], pl. 4)

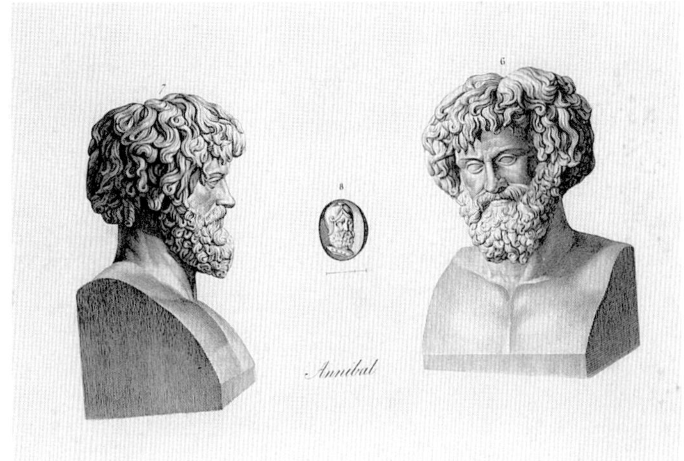

Fig. 139b. *"Annibal."* (From Visconti, *Planches de l'iconographie grecque* [1811], pl. 55)

Fig. 142a. *Tomb of El Cid at S. Pedro de Cardenas* (From Laborde, *Voyage pittoresque et historique de l'Espagne* [1806-12], vol. 2, pt. 2, pl. 14).

Fig. 142b. Designs for pilasters in the cloister of Saint-Sauveur in in Aix-en-Provence, 11th century. (From Willemin, *Monuments français* [1806-39], vol. 1, pl. 38)

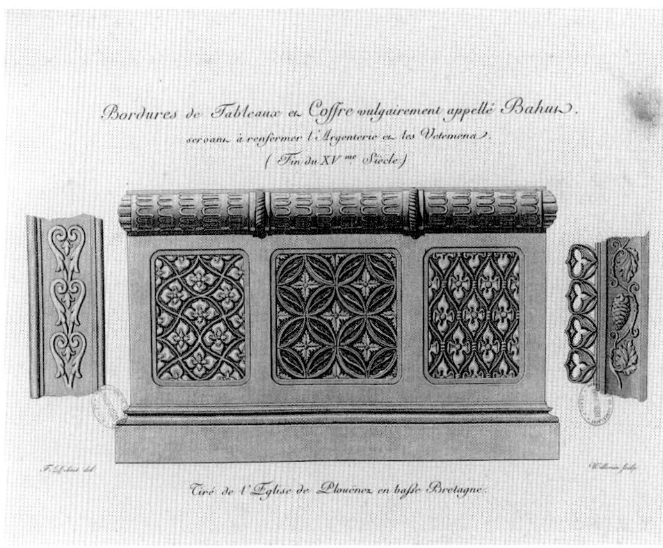

Fig. 142c. Decorative elements in the church of Plouvënez in Bretagne. (From Willemin, *Monuments français* [1806-39], vol. 2, pl. 210.

Fig. 147a. *View of the Manufacture de Sèvres,* engraving by Fortier et Duparc after a drawing by A. E. Michallon. (Manufacture nationale de Sèvres, Archives)

Fig. 149a. Design for a cup called *tasse 'Gothique'*, by Pierre Huard, 1826; watercolor, gouache, pencil, and ink on paper. (Manufacture nationale de Sèvres, Archives)

Fig. 149b. The "rose window" motif (bottom) used for the saucer of the *tasse 'Gothique'*. (From Willemin, *Monuments français* [1826] vol. 1, pl. 117)

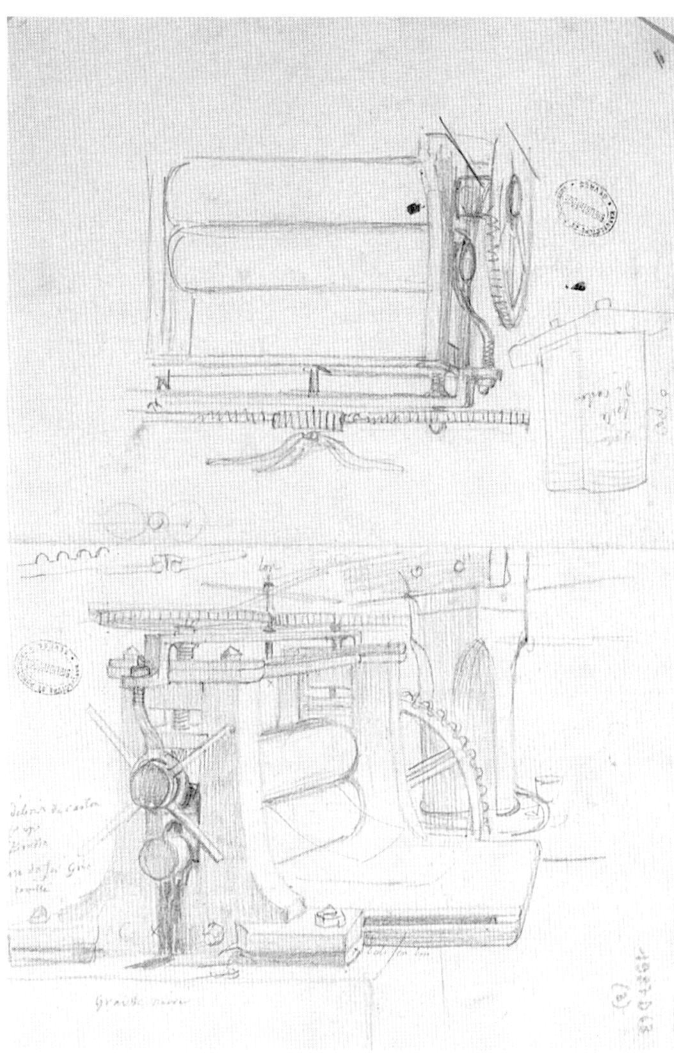

Fig. 151a. Preparatory drawing of two printing presses for a plate from the *service 'des Arts Industriels'*, by Jean-Charles Develly; pencil on paper. (Manufacture nationale de Sèvres, Archives)

Fig. 152b. Sketch for a reserve on a piece in the *déjeuner 'Culture et Récolte du Cacao'*, by Jean-Charles Develly. (Manufacture nationale de Sèvres, Archives)

Fig. 153a. *King Louis-Philippe* by Léon Noël, 1843; lithograph after a painting by François-Xavier Winterhalter. (Manufacture nationale de Sèvres, Archives)

Fig. 153b. *Queen Marie-Amélie* by H.Grevedon, 1843; lithograph after a painting by François-Xavier Winterhalter. (Manufacture nationale de Sèvres, Archives)

Appendix

Marks

During the tenure of Alexandre Brongniart (1800–1847), the Sèvres manufactory used many marks to identify points of fabrication or decoration and to signify special workshops. The list below includes examples of typical marks; some marks varied greatly within a single commission, such as a large table service, and are too numerous to include here.

1. Marks incised into the porcelain body before the first firing. These may identify the artisan or artisans, such as the thrower, molder, or sculptor. They may also give the date of fabrication (day, month, last two digits of the year). The glaze covers such incised marks.

2. Marks painted over the glaze. These may indicate any of the following:
• day and month, usually without the year, painted in green. This mark corresponds to the application of the ground color.
• identity of the gilder, painted in gold. These marks may consist of the gilder's initials.
• identity of the painter or painters who executed the decoration. These included full signatures or initials; they were sometimes applied to the front, appearing with the decoration, and other times to the underside of the piece; and they were applied in various colors.
• Alexandre Brongniart's endorsement. Faint traces of his authorization in red ink can be found on the reverse of some pieces. Often all traces disappeared during the firing, and the presence or absence of this mark may not bear any relation to the quality of the object.

Fabrication Marks

(incised under the glaze)

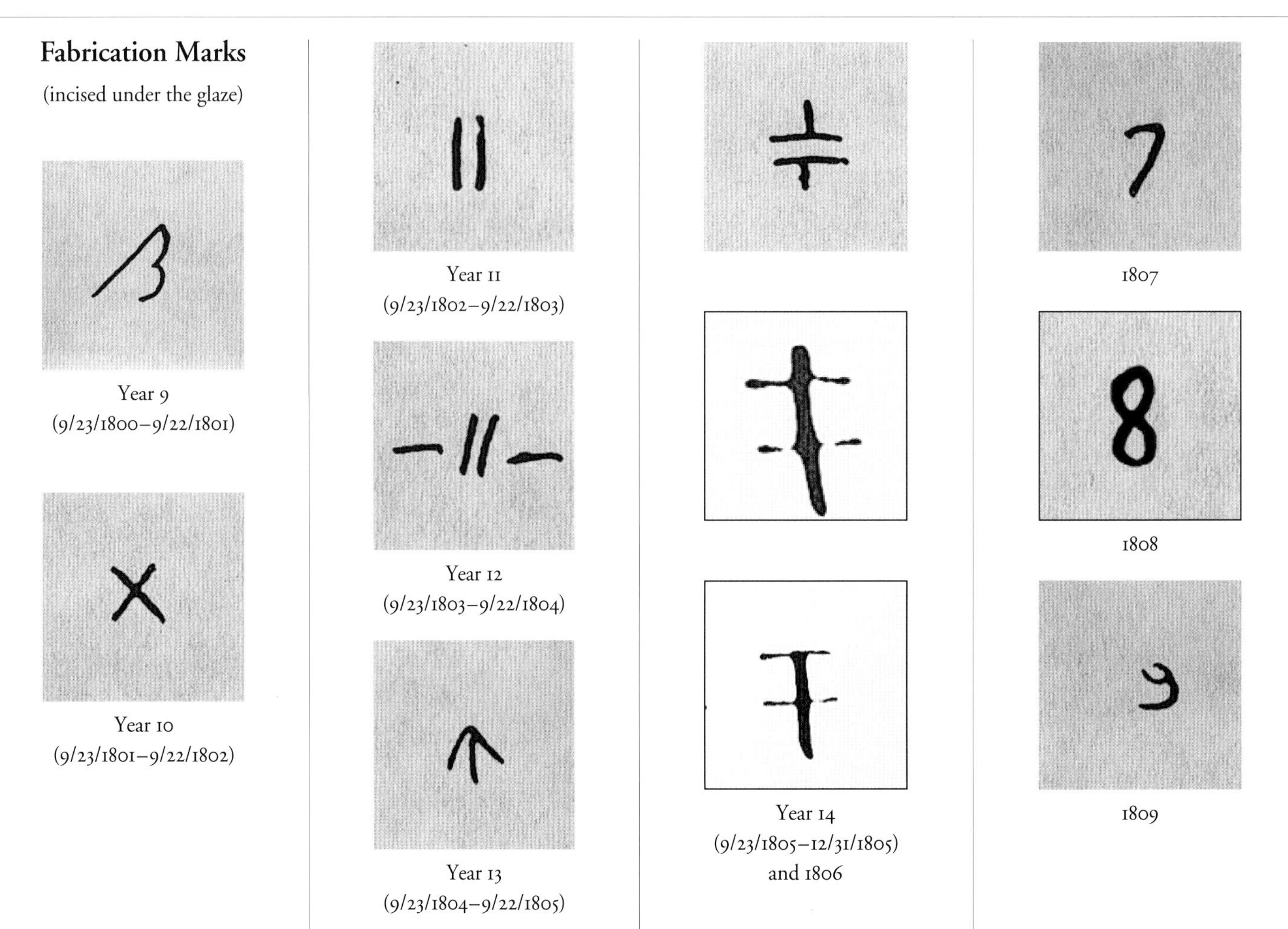

Year 9
(9/23/1800–9/22/1801)

Year 10
(9/23/1801–9/22/1802)

Year 11
(9/23/1802–9/22/1803)

Year 12
(9/23/1803–9/22/1804)

Year 13
(9/23/1804–9/22/1805)

Year 14
(9/23/1805–12/31/1805)
and 1806

1807

1808

1809

1810

1811

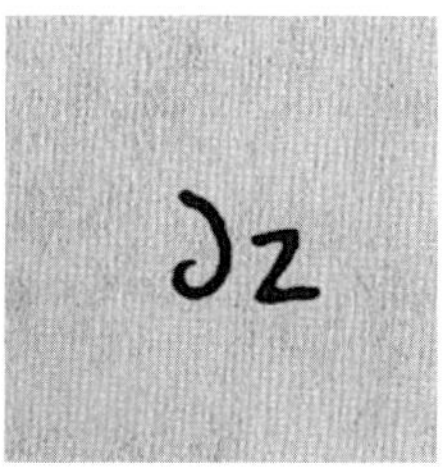

1812

1813

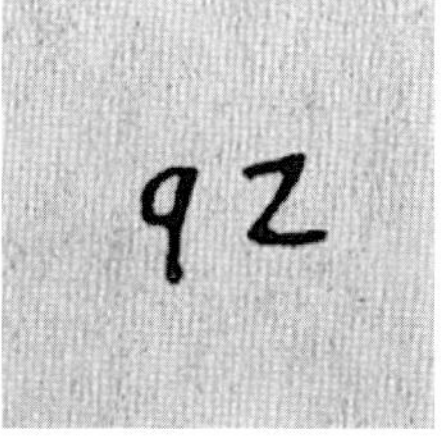

1814

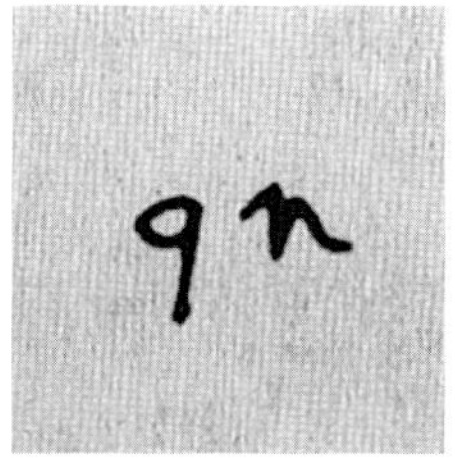

1815

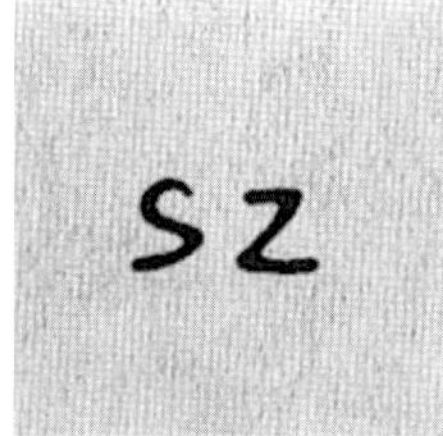

1816

1817

1818–47
Not shown. Numbers were used to indicate the month and the last two digits of the year.

Fabrication Mark

(printed under the glaze)

7/1845–2/1848
in chromium green

Decoration Marks

(printed over the glaze)

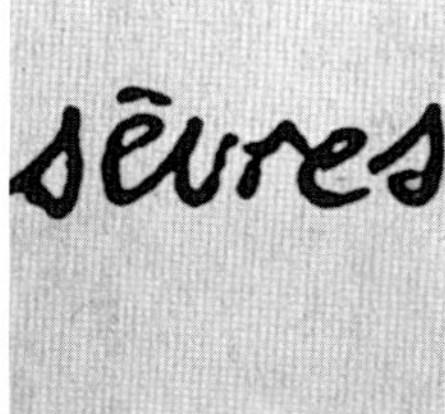

Consulat
(1800–1802) (vignette)

Consulat
(1803–4) (vignette)

Empire
(1804–12) (vignette)

Empire
(1813–15) (engraved)

From 1801 to 1810 the above marks may be accompanied by printed marks, similar to the incised fabrication marks, that indicate the year the piece was decorated.

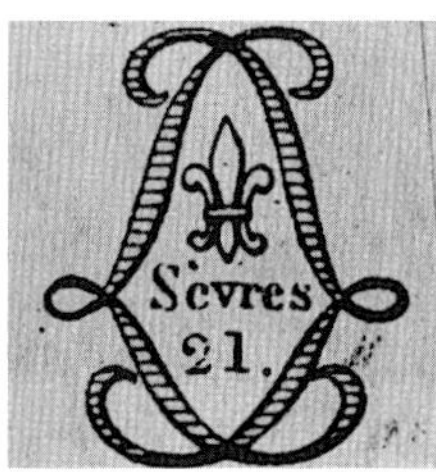

Louis XVIII
(1814–24)
The last two digits of the year could be included either within the mark or below it.

Charles X
(1824–30)
The last two digits of the year could be given below the mark.

Louis-Philippe
(1830–34)

Louis-Philippe
(1834–48)
With the year.

Special Marks

For painted glass and stained glass (printed over the glaze) Louis-Philippe (1830–48)

For sculpture (incised) 1800–1848

For sculpture (incised) 1800–1830

A Note on Fraudulent Marks

Marks on porcelain are easy to counterfeit or imitate and should never be relied upon solely to authenticate a piece. Since the eighteenth century, porcelain blanks decorated only with a thin gold band along the rim, as well as discarded undecorated blanks were widely sold. This encouraged fakes; some of the porcelain painters, in fact, added their own decoration without the permission of Sèvres. The occasional sales by Brongniart of large quantities of undecorated blanks and flawed pieces (see chap. 10), or of pieces to which a ground color had been applied, only exacerbated the problem, a fact frequently pointed out to the director himself. Eventually, a factory mark printed under the glaze was adopted to guarantee that the object had been made and initially fired in Sèvres, but this still gave no guarantee of the authenticity of the decoration. Only in 1880 was an incised slash added to identify an object as a reject.

In addition, skilled forgers were able to produce copies of Sèvres products almost as soon as the manufactury had been established in the mid-eighteenth century. Over time, fakes actually became more numerous than genuine pieces. During the period covered by this catalogue, the most frequent fakes were objects associated with the history of Napoleon (often signed "Bertren" or "Desprez," neither of whom is recorded as having worked in the factory), and pieces made for the everyday table service for the Château de Fontainebleau.

The prevalence of fakes has made the attribution and authentication of individual pieces difficult. They can be made only by a careful examination of the technical characteristics of a piece—the quality of the porcelain body and the glaze, the precision of any sculptured details, and the purity of the colors. There must also be an assessment of the aesthetic qualities, such as the composition of the decoration and the care with which the piece was painted.

Glossary

Compiled by Vincent Plescia

The definitions given below, especially those for technical terms, apply primarily to the use of terminology at Sèvres during the Brongniart years. In many cases, the French terms are also included.

biscuit. Unglazed, fired porcelain or other clay body. At Sèvres, in the second half of the eighteenth century, porcelain figures and sculpted areas of some objects were deliberately left unglazed so that the fine details of the modeling would be preserved. The manufactory became renowned for the quality of its soft-paste biscuit porcelain.

bisque firing or biscuit firing (*dégourdi*). The first firing of the porcelain or other clay body, preparatory to glazing or decoration. Bisque-fired pieces are usually porous.

blank. A fired, usually undecorated piece; porcelain blanks were sometimes given minimal preparatory decoration.

burnishing (*brunissage*). Sometimes called polishing, this decorative technique was used to give luster to a matte gold surface by rubbing the gilded area with a metal tool or a piece of smooth hardstone such as agate. During Brongniart's tenure several degrees of luster could be obtained on the same piece to create highlights and shading (*brunissage à l'effet*) by using different tools or by applying the gilding to the biscuit rather than glazed area of a piece.

cabaret service. A breakfast or tea service that could comprise a teapot (coffeepot or chocolate pot), milk jug, cream jug (or creamer), sugar bowl, and cups and saucers. In the early nineteenth century, the term *cabaret* was used for services that did not include a tray. See also ***déjeuner.***

chrome green. An enamel color introduced at the Sèvres manufactory in the early ninteenth century. The distinctive green color was achieved by adding chromium oxide, a chemical which had been discovered in 1798 by the French chemist Louis-Nicolas Vauquelin. Chrome greens were able to withstand high firing.

compôte. A high-footed bowl, usually for serving cooked fruit.

compôtier. A large bowl or dish, sometimes raised on a pedestal foot.

coupe. A high-footed cup.

crater. A large vase with a wide body and mouth, two side handles, and a small footed base. Several variations on this basic form were introduced by late-eighteenth-century and early- nineteenth-century porcelain manufactories. Of ancient Greek origin, craters were originally used for mixing wine and water.

creamware. A light-bodied earthenware with a transparent lead-based glaze. Creamware was developed in England by Josiah Wedgwood around 1760. Less expensive than porcelain, it was highly successful in the international marketplace. Creamware was decorated by painting under and over the glaze, transfer- printing, molding, and pierced work. In France it was known as *faience fine.*

dégourdi. See **bisque or biscuit firing.**

déjeuner. A French term for a breakfast or tea service consisting of the same elements as in a *cabaret.* In the early nineteenth century if the service also included a tray it was called a *déjeuner.* (See also ***cabaret* service.**)

***demi-grand-feu* colors.** A palette of colors that are fired to temperatures between high-firing colors (*grand-feu* colors) 2012° to 2642° F (1100° to 1450° C) and low-firing colors (*petit feu* colors) 1292° to 1652° F (700° to 900° C). Alexandre Brongniart developed this range to broaden the spectrum of colors available at Sèvres.

edging (*filage*), or banding. A narrow band traced around the rim of an object. At Sèvres edging is applied by a gilder using a slanted brush and pure powdered gold in a liquid matrix while the piece revolves on a banding wheel.

enamel colors. A mixture of flux and pigments derived from metallic oxides. Enamels are applied over the fired glaze and are fused by refiring the piece. This firing takes place in a muffle kiln at a lower temperature, or *petit feu,* which is still high enough to allow the glaze to melt slightly.

faïence fine. A French lead-glazed earthenware produced to compete with English creamware that was flooding the French market in the late eighteenth and early nineteenth centuries.

feldspar (or feldspathic rock). A group of crystalline minerals made up of aluminum silicates with potassium, sodium, calcium, or other elements. Feldspars fuse at a high temperature and vitrify. Many feldspars are used in ceramics production, either in the porcelain body or the glaze or both. Some feldspars are actually complete glazes.

flux (*fondant*). An ingredient, such as borax, potash, soda, or ash, that is added to the glaze or porcelain body to lower the fusion point when fired. It can also be added to enamel colors to assist in their fusion with the glaze.

frit (*fritte*). An ingredient used primarily in glazes and enamels consisting of glass or silica, sometimes derived from sand, which has been fired, cooled, and ground to a powder. In soft-paste porcelain production such a frit was mixed with the clay to produce the working clay body.

glaze (*couverte*). A vitreous coating applied over a porous body to seal it against the penetration of liquids. The glaze is a prepared mixture of powder or a suspension in water which can be sprayed, brushed, or poured on the surface, or the object itself immersed in the glaze.

glost firing or glaze firing. The second firing in the production of porcelain; the glaze is fused to the biscuit body at a temperature of around 2012° F (1100° C) for soft paste and 2552°F (1400° C) for hard paste.

grand feu. See **kiln.**

grand-feu colors. See **high-temperature colors.**

green ware. Potter's term for unfired pottery.

ground. The overglazed or underglazed all-over color, usually monochrome, on an object providing a background for the gilded or painted decoration. At the Sèvres manufactory the overglaze ground colors were spread on the surface with a brush made from the hair of a badger (*blaireautage*) and/or a polecat (*putoisage*).

guéridon. A small table consisting of a pedestal on feet and a tray, usually round.

hard paste, or true porcelain (*pâte dure*). A ceramics body made primarily from kaolin (also known as china clay) and high-fired to vitrification between 2012° to 2552° F (1100° to 1400° C). True porcelain is hard, not porous, white, sonorous, and translucent.

high-temperature colors (*couleurs de grand feu*). Enamels consisting of metallic oxides applied either directly to the bisque-fired body (underglaze colors) or to the glazed piece (over the glaze) and fired in the high-temperature kiln capable of withstanding the intense heat ranging from 2012° to 2552° F (1100° to 1400° C).

hydria. A large urn-shaped jar with horizontal loop handles (for lifting) and one or two vertical handles (for assisting with dipping or pouring). Of ancient Greek origin, hydrias were used to store or carry water.

jigger. A machine designed for the production of large quantities of plates and shallow, hollow forms. A revolving plaster mold forms the inside shape while a die, which is brought down on a pivoted arm, shapes and controls the thickness of the vessel wall and cuts the footring. At Sèvres Ferdinand Régnier experimented with this apparatus in 1820, but the process proved difficult to implement with the porcelain body being used at the manufactory at that time and jiggering did not become part of regular production until 1842.

kaolin. The Chinese word (*Kao-Lin*) for the site where white-firing clay, porcelain, was first discovered in China. Kaolin is composed of a pure aluminum silicate and is also known as white china clay. It is an essential ingredient in true porcelain, responsible for the whiteness, hardness, and translucency of the fired body.

kiln. A furnace used for the firing of ceramic wares. At Sèvres, two types of kilns were used. The *grand feu*, or high-temperature round kiln, was used to high-fire procelain either as biscuit or with high-fire glazes and high-temperature colors. The temperatures reached were as high as 2552° F (1400° C). The *petit feu*, low-temperature, or muffle kiln is used to affix enamel decoration (low-temperature colors), such as gold and platinum, to the glaze; it fires to a temperature of about 1292° to 1652° F (700° to 900° C). The muffle kiln is enclosed in such a way that the firing chamber is relatively clean and the porcelain objects are protected from the flames and smoke.

The first kilns used in France for soft-paste porcelain were rectangular, having only one fire box, in which the fuel was burned, opposite the chimney. The different degrees of heat obtained from one end of the kiln to the other were used to fire different porcelain bodies. These were replaced in about 1770 by round kilns whose interiors were serviced by several fire boxes, allowing a much more even temperature and efficient access to the pieces. Porcelain was fired in the lowest and hottest part, while the upper part (globe) was used for bisque firing. Alexandre Brongniart experimented in about 1842 with the construction of a three-story round kiln.

low-temperature colors (***couleurs de petit feu***). Metallic oxides (enamels) affixed to the glaze at a lower temperature, 1292° to 1652° F (700° to 900° C), than that used for firing the porcelain body.

molds (***moules***). A clay or plaster form used to cast ceramic objects.

muffle kiln. See **kiln.**

oenochoë (oinochoë). An ancient Greek wine jug with a vertical handle and a trefoil or pinched lip and spout.

paste (***pâte***). A white clay body; see **hard paste** and **soft paste.**

petit-feu. See **kiln.**

***petit feu* colors.** See **low-temperature colors.**

pouncing (***poncif***). A technique for applying decoration. Ornamental motifs are copied onto a stencil and the outlines are pricked with tiny holes that allow powdered charcoal to pass through, transferring the outline of the motif to the form for the painter to follow. Pouncing was used to save time.

press-mold (***moulage***). A plaster mold for the fabrication of small decorative elements for applied relief or sprigged decoration. Clay is pressed into the mold by hand. This process is also used for sculpture and other objects that cannot be thrown.

reserve. The areas on the surface of an object left without the ground color. The edges where the ground color and the unpainted area meet were decorated with gilding to hide the uneven boarder, as well as to frame the reserve.

reticulated (***réticulé***). Cut-out or pierced work forming a weblike pattern of interlaced lines in the clay.

saggar (***gazette***). Heat-resistant clay containers created in different shapes and sizes into which pieces were placed before loading them into the kiln. Saggars protected objects from ash fall and fumes during the high-temperature firing. Ferdinand Régnier devised a new type of round bottomed saggar (*gazettes à cul-de-lampe*) that provided a more efficient use of space and a more secure stacking of objects, resulting in an economical use of fuel.

sgraffito. A decorative technique executed by scratching or incising the design through a layer of slip to reveal the colored body beneath.

shrinkage (***retrait de la pâte***). As liquid evaporates from the paste during the drying and firing process a contraction of the clay body occurs. Statistics at Sèvres show that the total amount of shrinkage represents about 7 to 10 percent of the green ware.

skyphos. An ancient Greek pottery form; a large drinking vessel with a flat bottom, tapering sides, and two horizontal handles placed just below the rim.

slip (***barbotine***). A semiliquid mixture of clay and water used to create decorative motifs or change the surface color of an object. Slip is also used in attaching parts such as handles and spouts. This process is called *garnissage* at Sèvres.

slip-casting (***coulage***). A mold process for intricate elements of an object; a slip mixture is poured into a plaster mold. The plaster absorbs water from the slip which then forms a stiff layer. The surplus slip is poured off leaving the form to harden further before the mold is opened and the clay element removed and fired.

soft paste (***pâte tendre***). An artificial porcelain body developed in Europe to imitate hard-paste porcelain. Made with powdered glass, or another ingredient, as a substitute for the kaolin used in hard-paste porcelain. The firing temperature of soft paste was lower (about 2192° F [1200° C]) than that of true porcelain (about 2552° F [1400 C]).

sucrier. A sugar bowl.

surtout-de-table. A large centerpiece consisting of several elements which were often positioned according to a fixed plan down the center of a dining table.

throwing (***tournage***). The making of clay objects by hand on the potter's wheel.

transfer-printing. A decorative technique for applying repeated designs to ceramic wares. For a discussion of this process, see cat. no. 67.

turning (***tournassage***), **or trimming.** A method of finishing a porcelain object after the preliminary shape has been created on the potter's wheel and dried to the leather-hard state. A lathe and various steel tools are used to define the outer and inner profiles giving the form and surface a mechanical precision. Further decoration can also be done by incising concentric circles around an object.

vermiculation (***vermiculé***). A pattern of short, irregular shapes of color surrounded by gold creating channels that produce a marbling effect. This decoration was developed at Sèvres in the 1750s, where it was sometimes executed in blue on a pink ground.

zarf. A footed holder for a handleless cup. This form is thought to have Middle-Eastern origins.

Bibliography

1. Archival Sources

For a list of the principal archives in which documents relating to Alexandre Brongniart and his family are deposited, see the notes to chapter 2 in this volume. Records concerning the administration of the Manufacture Nationale de Sèvres are located in the Archives of the Manufacture Nationale de Sèvres, as well as the Archives Nationales, Cote F21-682, among others.

2. Publications by Alexandre Brongniart

Compiled by Anne Lajoix

In addition to the books, essays, and other publications listed below, Brongniart wrote regularly for the major journals of the period and sent reports to the Académie des Sciences and Conseil des Mines. He also contributed entries to several encyclopedias and dictionaries: anonymously in the *Encyclopédie méthodique* (published by Pancoucke) and *Histoire générale des insectes* (by Olivier, 1792 – 1800); and with credit in the *Dictionnaire des Sciences naturelles* (vols. 1 – 59, 1802 – 29). As president of the ceramics division of the *Exposition des produits de l'industrie française* in 1839 and 1844, Brongniart submitted reports that appeared in the *Rapport du Jury central*, accompanying the exhibitions. Brongniart was not always the primary author of publications written in collaboration; they are listed below according to the title page of the book.

Beudant, F. S., André Jean Marie Brochant de Villiers, and Alexandre Brongniart. "Rapport fait à l'Académie des Sciences sur un mémoire de M. de Beaumont, concernant l'ancienneté relative des différentes chaînes de montagnes d'Europe." *Annales de chimie et de physique*, 1829.

Brochant de Villiers, André, Jean Marie Cordier, and Alexandre Brongniart. *Rapport sur un mémoire de M. de Bonnard intitulé: Notice géologique sur quelques parties de la Bourgogne*, Paris, 1825.

Brongniart, Alexandre. "Art de l'émailleur sur métaux." *Annales de Chimie* 9 (1791), pp. 192 – 214.

—. "Essai sur les couleurs tirées des oxydes métalliques, et fixées par la fusion sur les différents corps vitreux." *Journal des Mines* 12 (1801 – 2), pp. 53 – 80.

—. *Essai d'une classification naturelle des reptiles* . . . Paris, 1805.

—. *Traité élémentaire de minéralogie, avec des applications aux arts, ouvrages destiné à l'enseignement dans les Lycées nationaux* . . . 2 vols. Paris, 1807.

—. *Mémoire sur une nouvelle espèce de minéral de la classe des sels, nommé Glaubérite* . . . Extract from the *Journal des Mines* no. 133 (January 1808). N.p., n.d.

—. *Essai d'une classification minéralogique des roches mélangées.* Paris, 1813. Reprinted in English. *A Selection of geological memoirs*, no. 1. London, 1836.

—. *Notice pour servir à l'histoire géognostique de cette partie du département de la Manche qu'on nomme le Cotentin, suivie de quelques considérations sur la classification géologique des terrains.* Extract from the *Journal des Mines*, no. 206 (February 1814). Paris, n.d.

—. *Sur le gisement ou position relative des ophiolites, euphotides, jaspes etc. dans quelques parties des Apennins.* Paris, 1821. Reprinted in English. *A Selection of geological memoirs*, no. 13. London, 1836.

—. *Notice sur les végétaux fossiles traversant les couches du terrain houillier* . . . Paris, 1821. Reprinted in English. *A Selection of geological memoirs*, no. 14. London, 1836.

—. *Notices sur la magnésie du bassin de Paris et sur le gisement de cette roche dans divers lieux* . . . Paris, 1822. Reprinted in English. *A Selection of geological memoirs*, no. 20. London, 1836.

—. *Sur les caractères zoologiques des formations, avec l'application de ces caractères à la détermination de quelques terrains de craie* . . . Paris, 1822. Reprinted in English. *A Selection of geological memoirs*, no. 17. London, 1836.

—. *Sur les terrains calcaréo-trappéens du pied méridional des Alpes lombardes* . . . Extract from the *Annales des Mines* 7 (1822). N.p., n.d. Reprinted in English. *A Selection of geological memoirs*, no. 19. London, 1836.

—. *Mémoire sur les terrailles de sédiments supérieurs calcaréo- trappéens du Vicentin, et sur quelques terrains* . . . *qui peuvent se rapporter à la même époque* . . . Paris, 1823.

—. *Notice sur Théodore Brongniart.* Paris, 1824.

—. *Introduction à la minéralogie, ou Exposé des principes de cette science* . . . [1824]. 2nd ed. Paris, 1825.

—. *De l'Arkose, caractères minéralogiques et histoire géognostique de cette roche* . . . Extract from the *Annales des sciences naturelle* (June 1826). N.p., n.d.

—. *Classification et caractères minéralogiques des roches homogènes et hétérogènes.* Paris-Strasbourg, 1827.

—. *Tableau de la distribution méthodique des espèces minérales suivie dans le cours de minéralogie fait au Museum royal d'Histoire naturelle par M. Alexandre Brongniart.* [1827] Rev. eds. Paris, 1828, 1833.

—. *Notes sur les coquilles fossiles qui se trouvent dans les terrains décrits par M. Studer; sur les époques géognostiques qu'elles indiquent et sur la montagne des Diablerets au Nord-Est de Bex* . . . Paris, 1827.

—. *Note sur la présence de la Webstérite dans l'argile plastique d'Auteuil près Paris* . . . Paris, 1828.

—. *Notice sur des blocs de roches des terrains de transport en Suède* . . . Paris, 1828.

—. *Observations additionnnelles à la Notice sur les minerais de fer pisiforme de position analogue à celle des brèches osseuses, etc* . . . Extract from *Annales des science naturelles* 26 (1829). N.p., n.d.

—. *Mémoire sur la peinture sur verre (1ere partie: sur les différentes classes de peinture sur verre et sur l'état actuel de cet art, lue à l'Académie royale des Beaux-Arts le 7 Juin 1828).* Paris, 1829.

—. *Tableau des terrailles qui composent l'écorce du globe ou Essai sur la structure de la partie connue de la terre.* Paris/Strasbourg, 1829. Reprint in German. Paris/Strasbourg/Leipzig, 1830.

—. *Du caractère et de l'état actuel de la manufacture royale de porcelaine de Sèvres, et de son influence sur l'art et le commerce de la porcelaine.* Paris, 1830.

—. "Porcelaine." *L'Encyclopédie moderne.* Paris, de Courtin, 1830.

—. *Essai sur les arts céramiques composant l'article "Poteries" du Dictionnaire technologique.* Paris, 1830.

—. *Essai sur les orbicules siliceux et sur les formes à surfaces courbes qu'affectent les agates et autres silex* . . . Paris, 1831.

—. *Institut royal de France. Académie royale des Sciences. Funérailles de M. Lelièvre. Discours de M. Alexandre Brongniart prononcé le 21 octobre 1835*, Paris, n.d.

—. "Sur les délaissements de la mer actuelle et les déplacements du niveau maritime." Unpublished manuscript, 1837.

—. *Extraits et fragments d'un premier mémoire sur les kaolins ou argiles à porcelaine* . . . N.p., [1838].

—. *Premier mémoire sur les kaolins ou argiles à porcelaine, sur la nature, le gisement, l'origine et l'emploi de cette sorte d'argile* . . . Paris, 1839.

—. *Institut royal de France. Académie royale des Sciences. Funérailles de M. Brochant de Villiers. Discours de M. Alexandre Brongniart, prononcé le 19 mai, 1840*, Paris, n.d.

—. *Rapport sur un mémoire de M. Alexandre Leymerie intitulé: "Mémoire sur un terrain crétacé du départment de l'Aube contenant des considérations générales sur le terrain néocomien . . ."* Extract from *Comptes-rendus des séances de l'Académie des Sciences* (June 21, 1841). Paris, n.d.

—. *Traité des arts céramiques ou des poteries, considérées dans leur histoire, leur pratique et leur théorie* . . . 2 vols. and Atlas. Paris: Béchet jeune, 1844.

—. *Coloring and Decoration of Ceramic Ware.* Notes and additions by Alphonse Salvetat. Translated bu George J. M. Ashby. Chicago: Windsor & Kenfield, 1898.

Brongniart, Alexandre, and de Mirbel. *Institut royal de France. Académie royale des Sciences. Funérailles de M. le baron Ramond (discours prononcés le 17 mai 1827 . . .).* Paris, n.d.

Brongniart, Alexandre, and François Malaguti [J. Faustin]. *Second mémoire sur les kaolins ou argiles à porcelaine, sur la nature et l'origine de cette sorte d'argile* . . . Paris, 1841.

Brongniart, Alexandre, and Denis-Désiré Riocreux. *Description méthodique du musée céramique de la manufacture royale de porcelaine de Sèvres.* 2 vols. Paris: A. Leleuse, 1845.

Brongniart, Alexandre, and Anselme Gaëtan Desmarets. *Histoire naturelle des crustacés fossiles sous les rapports zoologiques et géologiques, savoir: les trilobiles par A. Brongniart . . . les Crustacés proprement dits par A. G. Desmarets* . . . Paris, 1822.

Cordier, Pierre Louis Antoine, Adrien Henri Laurent de Jussieu, and Alexandre Brongniart. *Rapport par les professeurs administrateurs du Museum d'histoire naturelle . . . à Son Excellence le ministre secrétaire d'Etat au département de l'Intérieur, sur les travaux de M. Milbert, voyageur naturaliste du gouvernement . . . pendant la mission qu'il a remplie aux Etats-Unis d'Amérique.* Paris, n.d.

Cuvier, Georges, and Alexandre Brongniart. *Essai sur la géographie minéralogique des environs de Paris, avec une carte géognosique et des coupes de terrain.* [1811] Rev. eds. by Alexandre Brongniart. Paris, 1822, 1835.

Hericart de Thury, Louis Etienne François, vicomte, and Alexandre Brongniart. *Rapport fait à l'Académie des Sciences . . . sur un mémoire relatif à la géologie des environs de Fréjus, par M. Ch. Texier.* Paris, 1833.

Lefebre d'Hellencourt, A. M., A. F. baron de Silvestre, and Alexandre Brongniart. *Considérations sur les avantages que le gouvernement pourrait assurer tant au commerce qu'aux diverses parties du service public par l'exploitation de quelques mines dont la République se trouve en possession tant dans les pays conquis et réunis que dans son ancien territoire.* Paris, 1797.

Millin, A., L. Pinal, and Alexandre Brongniart. *Rapport fait à la Société d'histoire naturelle de Paris sur la nécessité d'établir une ménagerie . . . (Paris, 14 décembre 1792).* Paris, 1792.

Pliny the Elder. *Histoire naturelle de Pline.* Translation by M. Ajasson de Grandsagne, with annotations by Beudant, Brongniart, Cuvier, et al. Paris, 1829 – 33.

3. General Bibliography

Actes des journées d'étude du G.R.I.M.C.O. Moulins, 20 et 21 septembre 1991. Moulins: Editions D. Moulinet, 1992.

Albis, Antoine d'. "Le secret de gravent." *Faenza* 1 – 3 (1988).

—. "La Découverte du kaolin de Saint-Yrieix." *Dossiers de l'art.* No. 12 (May – June 1993).

—. "Les 'Faux Sèvres'." *Connaissance des Arts* (October 1994), pp. 70 – 79.

—. "La manufacture de Vincennes-Sèvres à la recherche de la porcelaine dure 1747 – 1768." *Sèvres, revue de la société des Amis du Musée national de Céramique.* No. 4, (1995), pp. 48 – 63.

—. "Les débuts de la porcelaine dure à Sèvres." *The French Porcelain Society* (1996).

Alcouffe, Daniel, Anne Dion-Tenenbaum, and Pierre Ennès, eds. *Un âge d'or des arts décoratifs: 1814 – 1848.* Exhib. cat. Paris: Galeries nationales du Grand Palais/Réunions des musées nationaux, 1991.

Alexandre-Théodore Brongniart (1739 – 1813): Architecture et décor. Exhib. cat. Paris: Musée Carnavalet, 1986.

Anchel, R. "Une famille de pharmaciens au XVIIIe siècle. Les Brongniart." *Revue des Spécialités* (August – September 1933), pp. 563 – 68.

Arizzoli-Clémentel, Pierre. "Les Surtouts impériaux en porcelaine de Sèvres 1804 – 1814." *Bulletin des Amis Suisses de la Céramique* (May 1976), pp. 3 – 63.

—. "Au musée des arts décoratifs de Lyon; note sur une paire de vases en porcelaine de Sèvres à fond laque et décor de chinoiseries." *Bulletin des musées et monuments Lyonnais*, no. 4 (1987), pp. 12 – 14.

—. "Pharaohs et empereur: le surtout égyptien." *Dossier de l'Art*, no. 15 (November – December 1993), pp. 56 – 61.

Arrondeau, Stephane. "La Maison Fialeix. Vitraux d'art religieux." *303. Arts, recherche et créations. La revue des pays de la Loire*, no. 41 (1994), pp. 26 – 33.

Artz, Frederick. *France Under the Bourbon Restauration.* Cambridge: Harvard University Press, 1931.

Aslin, Elizabeth. *French Exhibition Pieces, 1844 – 1878.* London: Victoria & Albert Museum, 1973.

Aubert, Marcel. *Le Vitrail en France.* Paris: Larousse, 1946.

Baca, Albert R. *Napoleon, Russia and the Olympian Gods: The "Olympic Service" of the Armory Museum in the Kremlin.* Los Angeles: CoStar, 1996.

Baca, Albert R. and Irina Gorbatova. "Le 'Service Olympique' du Musée des Armures du Kremlin." *Sèvres*, no. 5 (1996), pp. 32 – 41.

Baer, Winfred, and H. Walter Lack. *Pflanzen auf porzellan.* Exhib. cat. Berlin: Botanischen gartens und botaniches museum Berlin-Dahlem, 1979.

Barbe, Gerard. *Le Service du roi Louis-Philippe au château de Fontainebleau: Introduction à l'étude des services en porcelaine de Sèvres de la table du roi sous la monarchie de Juillet.* [Paris]: G. Barbe, 1989.

—. "Déjeuners en porcelaine de Sèvres de 1830 à 1848." *L'Estampille/L'Objet d'art* (April 1990), pp. 58 – 69.

Barber, Giles, and C. P. Courtney, eds. *Enlightened Essays in Memory of Robert Shackleton.* Oxford, Eng.: Voltaire Foundation at the Taylor Institution, 1988.

Batissier, Louis. "Des procédés de peinture sur verre et des ouvrages relatifs à l'art de la verrerie." *Le Cabinet de l'Amateur et de l'Antiquaire* 2 (1843), pp. 530 – 39.

—. "Histoire du verre et des émaux peints." *Le Cabinet de l'Amateur et de l'Antiquaire* 2 (1843), pp. 49 – 128.

Baudry, Paul. *Eglise paroissiale de Saint-Patrice de Rouen: Description des vitraux*, Rouen: impr. de E. Cagniarol, 1869.

Baulez, Christian. "Le Vase du mariage de l'Empereur, cérémonie civile à Saint-Cloud le 1er avril 1810." *Bulletin de la Société de l'histoire de l'art francais* (1971), pp. 217 – 34.

Bellaigue, Geoffrey de. "Queen Victoria, A Taste for Sèvres." *Cahiers de Mariemont* 24/25 (1996), pp. 29 – 35.

Bellier de la Chauvignerie, Emile, and Louis Auvray. *Dictionnaire général des artistes de l'école française depuis l'origine des arts du dessin jusqu'à nos jours.* 3 vols. Paris, 1882 – 85.

Benoist, Luc. *La Sculpture romantique: Édition d'Isabelle Leroy-Jay Lemaistre.* Paris: Gallimard, 1994.

Benezit, E. *Dictionnaire critique et documentaire des peintres, sculpteurs, dessinateurs et graveurs.* 10 vols. Paris, 1976.

Bensaude-Vincent, Bernadette. "Eaux et mesures. Eclairages sur l'itinéraire intellectuel du jeune Lavoisier." *Revue d'Histoire des Sciences* 48, no. 1 – 2 (January – June 1995), pp. 49 – 68.

Bensaude-Vincent, Bernadette, and Isabelle Stengers. *Histoire de la chimie.* Paris: La Decouverte, 1993.

Bettembourg, Jean-Marie, and Marcel Stefanaggi. "Une exposition: le vitrail. Art et technique (Palais de la Découverte: décembre 1977 – septembre 1978)." *Métiers d'art*, no. 20 (1982), pp. 76 – 83.

Beyer, Victor. *Mille ans d'art du vitrail.* Exhib. cat. Strasbourg: Musée de l'Ancienne Douane, Pont du Corbeau, 1965.

Birembaut, Arthur. "Les Ecoles gratuites de dessin." *Enseignements et diffusions des sciences en France au XVIIIe siècle* (1964), pp. 441 – 70.

Biver, Marie Louise. *Le Paris de Napoléon.* Paris: Plon, 1963.

Biver, Paul. "Vitraux et tableaux des églises parisiennes." *Gazette des Beaux-Arts* (1920), pp. 21 – 42.

Blättel, Harry. *Dictionnaire International, peintres miniaturistes, peintres sur porcelaine, silhouettistes.* Munich, 1992.

Blondel, Nicole. "Les Techniques de vitrail au XIXe siècle." *Vitrea*, no. 3 (1989), pp. 25 – 27.

—. *Le Vitrail: vocabulaire typologique et technique.* Paris: Inventaire général, Imprimerie nationale, 1993.

Blondel, Nicole, and Patrick Bracco. "Le Vitrail religieux au XIXe siècle." *Espace, église, arts, architecture*, no. 9 (1980), pp. 30 – 33.

—. "Un Art retrouvé: le vitrail à Sèvres au XIXe siècle." *L'Estampille/L'Objet d'art*, no. 118 (February 1980), pp. 10 – 19.

Blondel, Nicole, Martine Callias-Bey, and Veronique Chaussée. "Le Vitrail archéologique: fidélité ou trahison du Moyen-Age?" *Annales de Bretagne et des pays de l'ouest* 93, no. 4 (1986), pp. 377 – 81.

Blondel, Nicole, Guy de Goff, and Jean Clèment Marin. "Vitrail et guerre de vendée." *Images du patrimoine des pays de Loire*, no. 31 (1987).

Blouin, Daniel. "La Société d'encouragement: lieux et étapes. I- Les premières implantations, les premières ambitions, les premières manifestations (vendémiaire an X/Octobre 1801 – juillet 1812). *L'industrie nationale* (January – June 1996), pp. 11 – 21.

Blühm, Andreas, et al. *The Colour of Sculpture, 1849 – 1910.* Exhib. cat. Amsterdam: Van Gogh Museum / Leeds: Henry Moore Institute / Zwelle, Waanders, Witgeuers, 1996 – 97.

Blunt, Wilfrid. *Linné, le prince des botanistes.* Paris: Belin, 1986.

Bontemps, Georges. *Peinture sur verre au XIXe siècle: les secrets de cet art sont-ils retrouvés?* Paris: Impr. de Ducessois, 1845.

—. *Guide du verrier.* Paris: Librairie du Dictionnaire des Arts et Manufactures, 1868.

Bouchon, Chantal. *Le Vitrail.* Paris: Editions du Cerf, collection BREF, 1990.

—. "Faits contemporains dans le vitrail au XIXe siècle." *Annales de Bretagne et des pays de l'ouest* 93, no. 4 (1986), pp. 411 – 17.

—. "La Renaissance du vitrail: Eustache-Hyacinthe Langlois." *Etudes normandes*, no. 4 (1989), pp. 35 – 40.

—. "Les Porcelainiers et la peinture sur verre." *Sèvres, Revue de la Société des amis du musée national de céramique*, no. 3 (1994), pp. 15 – 24.

Bouchon, Chantal, and Catherine Brisac. "Le Vitrail au XIXe siècle: état des travaux et bibliographie." *Revue de l'Art*, no. 72 (1986), pp. 35 – 38.

Bouchon, Chantal, et al. *Les Églises du XIXe siècle.* Amiens: Encrage-Picardie, 1993.

Bouquet, Henri. "Petite histoire des membres libres de l'Académie de médecine." *Progrès médical* 1 – 4 (1941).

Bourgeois, Charles Guillaume Alexandre. *Vues d'Italie.* N.p., 1808.

Bouvet, M. "Les apothécaires royaux." *Revue d'histoire de la pharmacie* (1930), pp. 207 – 8.

Breunig, Charles. *The Age of Revolution and Reaction, 1789 – 1850.* New York and London: W.W. Norton & Company, 1977.

Breuille, Jean Philippe, ed. *Dictionnaire de la sculpture.* Paris, 1992.

Brisac, Catherine. "Viollet-le-Duc, cartonnier de vitraux." In *Actes du colloque international Viollet-le-Duc.* Paris: Nouvelles Editions Latines, 1982, p. 205.

—. "La Peinture sur verre au XIXe siècle dans la Sarthe." *303: Recherches et créations — pays de la Loire*, no. 1 (1984), pp. 40 – 45.

—. "Le Vitrail archéologique en France au XIXe siècle: modèles et transpositions." In *Actes du colloque international sur le néo-gothique aux XIXe et XXe siècles.* Paris – Milan, 1985.

—. *Regarder et comprendre un vitrail.* Enghien-les-Bains: Artefact, 1985.

—. "Repères pour l'étude de l'iconographie du vitrail au XIXe siècle." *Annales de Bretagne et des pays de l'ouest* 93, no. 4 (1986), pp. 369 – 76.

—. "Vitriers et peintres sur verre sous la Restauration et le Second Empire." *Etudes normandes* 4 (1989), pp. 41 – 48.

—. *Le Vitrail.* Paris: Editions du Cerf, 1990.

Brisac, Catherine, and Didier Alliou. "La Peinture sur verre au XIXe siècle dans la Sarthe." *Annales de Bretagne et des pays de l'ouest* 93, no. 4 (1986), pp. 389 – 94.

Brisac, Catherine, and Jean-Michel Leniaud. "Adolphe-Napoléon Didron ou les media du service de l'art Chrétien." *Revue de l'Art*, no. 77 (1987), pp. 33 – 42.

Brisac, Catherine, Marie-France Perez, and Daniel Ternois. "Les Vitraux du XIXe siècle dans les églises de Lyon." *Bulletin de la Société de l'histoire de l'art français* (1982), pp. 159 – 79.

Brunet, Marcelle. "A propos de la copie sur porcelaine de la Sainte Therese de Gerard." *Bulletin des Musées de France* (December 1948), p. 299.

—. "Deux vases de Sèvres à portraits de Louis-Philippe et de Marie-Amélie." *Journal of the Walters Art Gallery* 13 – 14 (1950 – 51), pp. 73 – 74.

—. "Contribution à l'iconographie napoléonienne: une figure equestre de Bonaparte en biscuit de Sèvres." *Genootshap voor napoleontische studien* (September 1954), pp. 456 – 67.

—. "Étrange destinée d'un portrait de la duchesse de Berry peint sur porcelaine par Mademoiselle Arsène Trouvé (1821 – 1826)." *Cahiers de la céramique, du verre et des arts du feu*, no. 2 (1956), pp. 33 – 38.

—. "En marge des napoléonides: Une main de femme de biscuit de Sèvres." *Genootshap voor napoleontische studien* (Summer 1957), pp. 281 – 83.

—. "Jean-Charles Develly et la manufacture impériale de Sèvres." *Carnet de la Sabretache*, 5th ser., vol. 6, pt. 4, no. 421 (December 1960), pp. 444 – 53.

—. "The Sèvres Service of South American birds at Hillwood." *The Art Quarterly* (Autumn 1962), 197 – 208.

—. "Les Vitraux de la manufacture de Sèvres d'après Eugène Delacroix." *Cahiers de la céramique, du verre et des arts du feu*, no. 29 (1963), pp. 59 – 66.

—. "Un grand service de Sèvres: le service des "Vues de Suisse" 1802 – 1804." *Versailles*, no. 20 (1964).

—. "Le Cabaret du prince de Prusse." *Connaissance des Arts*, no. 163 (September 1965), pp. 110 – 13.

—. "Le Procédé d'impression de Gonord à la manufacture nationale de Sèvres." *Archives de l'art français*. New series 14. *Les arts à l'époque napoléonienne* (1969), pp. 337 – 40.

—. "Pendule en biscuit de Sèvres d'après Percier." *Weltkunst* (February 1979), pp. 162 – 64.

—. "Le Sacre de Charles X à Reims (1825) vu par un peintre de la manufacture de Sèvres." *Antologia di Belle Arti* 3 (1987), pp. 18 – 28.

Brunet, Marcelle, and Tamara Préaud. *Sèvres, des origines à nos jours*. Fribourg: Office du Livre, 1978.

Burty, Philippe. *Chefs-d'oeuvre des arts industriels*. Paris: Paul Ducrocq, 1866.

—. *Chefs d'oeuvre of the Industrial Arts*. Edited and translated by W. Chaffers. London: Cassell, Petter and Galpin, 1869.

Cabezas, Hervé. *Le Vitrail à Lisieux*. Exhib. cat. Lisieux: Musée de Lisieux, 1987.

—. "Du 'vitrail archéologique'." *Revue d'archéologie moderne et d'archéologie générale*, no 6 (1988), pp. 107 – 26.

—. "La Signature des vitraux français au XIXe siècle." *Revue d'archéologie moderne et d'archéologie générale*, no. 7 (1989), pp. 77 – 97.

—. "Recherches sur la renaissance du vitrail peint à Paris entre 1800 et 1830." *Les arts du verre: histoire, technique et conservation. Actes des journées d'études de la section française de l'Institut international de conservation, Nice, 1991*. Champs- sur-Marne: SFIIC, 1991, pp. 33 – 58.

—. "Rideaux et vitraux, pour le confort des églises de Paris au XIXe siècle." *Revue d'archéologie moderne et d'archéologie générale*, no. 10 (1992), pp. 69 – 85.

—. "Les Vitraux de la basilique de Saint Denis au XIXe siècle." *Vitrea*, no. 9 (October 1996), pp. 31 – 76.

Callias-Bey, Martine, et al. "Les Ateliers [de vitraux au XIXe siècle]." *Revue de l'Art*, no. 72 (1986), pp. 55 – 56.

Calvignac, Marie-Helene. "Claude Aimé Chenavard, décorateur et ornemaniste." *Histoire de l'Art*, no. 16 (1991), pp. 41 – 51.

Casanova, Maria Letizia. *Le Porcellane francesi nei musei di Napoli*. Naples: Di Mauro Editore, 1974.

Caviness, Madeline. "Some Aspects of the Nineteenth-Century Glass. In *Restoration: Membra Disjecta et Collectanea: Some Nineteenth-Century Practices*. Norwich: Crown in Glory, 1982, pp. 68 – 72.

Centenaire de la fondation du Muséum d'Histoire Naturelle, 10 juin 1793 – 10 juin 1893, volume commémoratif publié par les professeurs du museum. Paris: Impr. nationale, 1893.

Chabeuf, Henri. "Les Vitraux de la chapelle royale de Dreux." *Revue de l'art Chrétien* 43 (1900), pp. 512 – 15.

Champfleury [Jules Husson-Fleury]. "Histoire et description des trésors d'art de la manufacture de Sèvres." *Inventaire général des richesses d'art de la France. Province. Monuments civils* 5, no. 1 (1891).

Charleston, Robert J. "A Pair of Vases of the Post-Napoleonic Period and the Working of the Sèvres Factory." *Apollo Annual*, 1950.

Chenavard, Aimé. *Nouveau recueil de décorations intérieures, contenant des dessins de tapisseries, tapis, meubles, bronzes, vases et autres objets d'ameublement, la plupart exécutés dans les manufactures royales, composés et gravés au trait par Aimé Chenavard*. Paris: Emile Leconte, 1833.

Chevallier, Bernard. "Les Emaux de Sèvres." *Estampille/L'Objet d'art* (March 1991), pp. 44 – 57.

—. *Musée national du château de Fontainebleau: Catalogue des collections de mobilier, 2. Les Sèvres de Fontainebleau. Porcelaines, terres vernissées, émaux, vitraux (pièces entrées de 1804 à 1904)*. Paris: Réunion des musées nationaux, 1996.

Chevreul, Michel-Eugène. *De la loi du contraste simultané des couleurs et de l'assortiment des objets colorés d'après cette loi dans ses rapports avec la peinture, les tapisseries des Gobelins, les tapisseries de Beauvais pour meubles, les tapis, la mosaïque, les vitraux colorés, l'impression des étoffes, l'imprimerie, l'enluminure, la décoration des édifices, l'habillement et l'horticulture*. Paris: Pitois-Levrault, 1839.

Clerget, Charles Ernest. *Mélanges d'ornemens divers: recuil destiné aux peintres- decorateurs et aux fabriques dans tous les genres. . . .* Paris: E. Leconte, 1838.

—. *Nouveaux ornements composés, dessinés et gravés . . . .* Paris: Aubert, 1840.

—. *De l'ornementation typographique: essai sur l'art ornemental appliqué à la decoration des livres*. Vienna: L'Imprimerie imperiale, 1859.

Collins, R. D. J. "Porcelain at Sèvres: The New Zealand Connection." *New Zealand Journal of French Studies* 8, no. 1 (1987), pp. 40 – 50.

Comberousse, Charles de. *Histoire de l'École Centrale des Arts et Manufactures depuis sa fondation jusqu'à ce jour*. Paris: Impr. de Gauthior-Villars, 1879.

Cooper, James Fenimore. *Gleanings in Europe*. vol. 1. New York: Oxford University Press, 1928.

Courajod, Louis. *La Collection révoil au musée du Louvre*. Caen: H. Delesques, 1886.

—. *La Collection Durand au musée du Louvre*. Caen: impr. H. Delesques, 1888.

Couvreur, J. "Histoire d'une centenaire. La société de médecine de Paris, 6 Germinal an IV – 22 Mars 1796." *La Presse Médicale* 25, no. 18 (May 25, 1996), pp. 828 – 31.

Cuzin, Jean Pierre, and Dominique Cordellier. *Raphaël et l'art français*. Exhib. cat. Paris: Grand Palais/Réunion des musées nationaux, 1983.

Dahlbäck-Lutteman, Helena, et al. *Porslin från Sèvres*. Stockholm: Nationalmuseum, 1982.

Damien, André. *Le Grand Livre des Ordres de Chevalerie et des décorations*. Paris: Solar, 1991.

Dantec, Dominique. "A chacun son ouvrier ou le dévelopement du culte de Saint Joseph dans le vitrail du XIXe en Trégor et Léon." *Bulletin de la société archéologique du Finistère* (1984), pp. 377 – 89.

Dawson, Aileen. "Two Napoleonic Sèvres Ice-Pails: A Present for an Emperor. A New Acquisition for the British Museum." *Apollo* (October 1986), pp. 328 – 33.

—. *A Catalogue of French Porcelain in the British Museum*. London: British Museum Press, 1994.

Delattre, André. "Jules Ziegler [et son] projet de la réorganisation de la manufacture royale de Sèvres [Hauts-de-Seine, rapport au roi Louis-Philippe sur la peinture sur verre]." *Bulletin de la Société historique et archéologique de Langres* 18, no. 277 (1984), pp. 287 – 90.

—. "Jules Ziegler, chargé de mission du roi [Louis-Philippe: son texte sur le vitrail en Allemagne, 1834]." *Bulletin de la Société historique et archéologique de Langres* 18, no. 282 (1986), pp. 452 – 63.

Denon, Dominique-Vivant. *Voyage dans la basse et la haute Egypte pendant les campagnes du general Bonaparte*. 2 vols. Paris: Didot aîné, 1802.

De Witte, Jean Joseph. *Description des antiquités et objets d'art qui composent le cabinet de feu M. le Chevalier E. Durand*. Paris: Didot frères, 1836.

Dhombres, Nicole, and Jean Dhombres. *Naissance d'un nouveau pouvoir: sciences et savants en France, 1793 – 1824.* Paris: Payot, 1989.

Dictionnaire des sciences naturelles par plusieurs Professeurs du Jardin du Roi et des principales écoles de Paris. Strasbourg- Paris, 1817.

Didron, Edouard. "Le Vitrail depuis cent ans et à l'exposition de 1889." *Revue des Arts Décoratifs* (1889), pp. 39 – 48, 97 – 108, 137 – 54.

Discours . . . prononcés aux funérailles de M. Alexandre Brongniart le 9 octobre 1847. Pamphlet. Paris: Institut royale de France/ Academie royale des Sciences, n.d.

Doyle, William. *The Oxford History of the French Revolution.* Oxford and New York: Oxford University Press, 1990.

Droesbeke, Jean-Jacques, and Philippe Tassi. *Histoire de la statistique.* Paris: n.p., 1990

Du Pasquier, Isabelle, and Luc Georget. *L'Aiglon.* Exhib. cat. Paris: Musée national de la légion d'honneur / H. M. Editions, 1993.

Dubus, Michel. "La Céramique en France à travers l'enquête de Brongniart, 1805 – 1810." Memoire de DEA de l'Ecole des Hautes Etudes en Sciences Socials (October 1988).

Ducrot, Brigitte. "La Collection des porcelaines et terres de Sèvres au musée national du château de Compiègne." *Revue du Louvre,* no. 3 (1993), pp. 61 – 63.

—. *Musée national du château de Compiègne: Porcelaines et terres de Sèvres.* Preface by M. Jean Marie Moulin. Paris: Réunion des musées nationaux, 1993.

Dufief-Moirez, D., and C. Douard. *Le Vitrail en Bretagne.* Exhib. cat. Rennes: Association pour le developpement de l'inventaire en Bretagne, 1980.

Duguet, Claire, and Dorothée Guillemé-Brulon. "Sèvres en gloire: 500 chefs d'oeuvre du XIXe siècle." *L'Estampille / L'Objet d'Art* (August 1975), pp. 44 – 50.

Duhamel, J. "Les Vitraux de la collégiale de la chapelle du Château d'Eu." *L'informateur d'Eu-Tréport-Mers* (July 14, 1961).

Dupont, Patrick. *Porcelaines français aux XVIIIe et XIXe siècles.* Paris: Baschet, 1987.

Ebelmen, Jacques Joseph, and Alphonse Louis Salvetat. *Recherches sur la composition des matières employées dans la fabrication et la décoration de la porcelaine en Chine, executées à la Manufacture Royale de Porcelaine de Sèvres et présentées à l'Académie des Sciences . . .* Paris: Bachelier, 1852.

Ecole Polytechnique: Livre du Centennaire, 1796 – 1896. Paris, 1896.

Ennès, Pierre. "Le Surtout de mariage en porcelaine de Sèvres du Dauphin, 1769 – 1770." *Revue de l'Art,* no. 76 (1987), pp. 63 – 73.

—. "Four Plates from the Sèvres 'Service des Arts Industriels' (1820 – 1835)." *Journal of the Museum of Fine Arts, Boston* 2 (1990), pp. 89 – 106.

—. "Brongniart à Sèvres : Atticisme ou Renaissance?" *Beaux Arts Magazine/Dossier de l'Art* (December 1991 – January 1992), pp. 36 – 42.

—. "Les Vitraux du Pavillon de l'Horloge au Louvre (1838 – 1857)." *Revue du Louvre,* no. 1 (April 1992), pp. 56 – 74.

—. "Un fournisseur de la manufacture de Sèvres, l'orfèvre Pierre-Noël Blaquière, 1811 – 1823." In *L'orfèvrerie au XIXe siècle. Rencontres de l'école du Louvre.* Paris: Réunion des Musées nationaux, 1995, pp. 69 – 76.

Entrecolles, François-Xavier de. *Lettres . . . écrites des missions étrangères: Mémoires de la Chine.* Toulouse, 1811.

Eriksen, Sven. *French Porcelain in Palazzo Pitti.* Florence: Centro di Scala, 1973.

Espagnet, Françoise. "La Céramique commune en France fin XVIIIe – debut XIXe siècles. Mutations et routines." *Revue d'ethnologie française* 11, no. 2 (April – May 1981), pp. 171 – 79.

Explications des ouvrages de peinture, sculpture, architecture et gravure des artistes vivans, exposés au Musée Napoléon, le 14 Octobre 1808, second anniversaire de la Bataille d'Iena." Paris: C.P. Landon, 1808.

Fairclough, Oliver. "Two Pieces from the Sèvres 'Service iconographique grec'." *National Art Collections Fund: Annual Report* (1989), pp. 149 – 52.

Fairclough, Oliver. "A Sèvres Plate and Lithography." *Print Quarterly* 11, no. 4 (December 1994), pp. 410 – 19.

Faïences françaises et étrangères . . . Porcelaine de la Chine et de la Compagnie des Indes. . . . Porcelaines europiennes: Faïences fines. Auction catalogue. Versailles: V. l'Herron, 1991.

Faÿ-Hallé, Antoinette. "De l'esprit dans les formes." *Plaisir de France* (December 1975 – January 1976), pp. 64 – 69.

Faÿ-Hallé, Antoinette, and Barbara Mundt. *La Porcelaine Européenne au 19e siècle.* Fribourg: Office du Livre, 1983.

Faÿ-Hallé, Antoinette, Tamara Préaud, and Henry-Pierre Fourest. *Porcelaines de Sèvres au XIXe siècle.* Exhib. cat. Musée National de céramique. Paris: Editions des musées nationaux, 1975.

Feuchère, Léon. *Art industriel [Recueil de dispositions et de décorations intérieures].* Paris, [1842].

Foster, Kate. "Cameos and Coffee: Two Sèvres Porcelain Déjeuners in the Kestner Museum, Hannover, Germany." *The French Porcelain Society* 11 (1994), pp. 31 – 50.

Foucart, Bruno, ed. *Viollet-le-Duc.* Exhib. cat. Paris: Réunion des musées nationaux, 1980.

Fouilheron, Joël. "Les Vitraux de Viollet-le-Duc à la cathédrale de Saint-Flour." *Revue de Haute-Auvergne* (1980).

Fourmy, Jacques. *Mémoire sur les ouvrages de terres cuites et particulièrement sur les poteries.* Paris: Imprimerie de Gillé fils, 1802.

Fragonard, Alexandre-Evariste. *Recueil de 132 sujets composés et gravé par Fragonard fils . . .* N.p., n.d.

Froidevaux, Yves-Marie. "Vitrail et architecture." *Métiers d'art* 20 (1982), pp. 38 – 39.

Gaillemin, Jean-Louis. "A la table des Pharaohs." *Connaissance des Arts* (January 1994), pp. 84 – 91.

Gallet, Michel. *Les Architectes Parisiens du XVIIIe siècle: Dictionnaire biographique et critique.* Paris: Menges, 1995.

Garnier, Edouard. *La Manufacture de Sèvres en l'an VIII.* Paris: H. Champion, 1888.

Gastineau, Marcel. "La Manufacture de Sèvres et les influences romantiques." *La Revue de l'Art Ancien et Moderne* 58, no. 317 (June 1930), pp. 3 – 24.

—. "Comment A. Brongniart, administrateur de la manufacture de Sèvres, se comportait à l'egard des recommandations." *Revue de l'histoire de Versailles et de Seine-et-Oise* (January – March 1932), pp. 3 – 7.

—. "Rude à la manufacture de Sèvres (1813 – 1814) (d'après des documents inédits)." *La revue de l'art ancien et moderne* 61, no. 335 (April 1932), pp. 181 – 86.

—. "Une menace de suppression de la manufacture de Sèvres en 1807." *Revue des études napoléoniennes* (October 1932), pp. 183 – 88.

—. "Denon et la manufacture de Sèvres sous le Premier Empire (1805 – 1814) (d'après des documents inédits.)" *La revue de l'art ancien et moderne* 63, nos. 341 – 42 (January – February 1933), pp. 21 – 42, 64 – 76.

—. "Les Travaux de la manufacture de Sèvres relatifs au roi de Rome." *Revue des Études Napoléoniennes* (November – December 1934), pp. 270 – 89.

—. "Note sur deux bustes de Napoleon 1er par ou d'après Chaudet édités à la manufacture du Sèvres (1805 – 1811) (d'après des documents inédits.)" *Bulletin de la Société de l'histoire de l'art français* 1 (1934), pp. 159 – 68.

—. "Un projet de tableau de Louis Boilly 'La Famille impériale' (d'après des documents inédits.)" *La Revue de l'art ancien et moderne* (July 1934), pp. 81 – 86.

Gatouillat, Françoise. "Les Vitraux d'Ingres [in the Chapelle Saint-Ferdinand]." *Actes du colloque international. Bulletin spécial des amis du musée Ingres* (Montauban, 1980), pp. 147 – 55.

Gavrilova, L. *Le Service Olympique. Musée des Armures, Kremlin, Moscou.* Moscow, 1979.

Géro, Jules. *Bibliographie du vitrail français.* Paris: La Porte Etroite, 1983.

Gille, Bertrand. *Les Sources statistiques de l'histoire de France.* Genève-Paris: Minard, 1964.

—, ed. *Histoire des techniques.* Paris: Gallimard, 1978.

Gillipsie, Charles Coulstohn. *Dictionary of Scientific Biography.* New York: Scribner, 1981.

Giroux, René. "Technique du vitrail." *Métiers d'art,* no. 20 (1982), pp. 8 – 18.

Grandjean, Serge. "Les Plaques napoléoniennes," *Genootshap voor napoleontische studien* (September 1954), pp. 451 – 55.

—. "L'Influence égyptienne à Sèvres." *Genootshap voor napoleontische studien* (September 1955), pp. 99 – 105.

—. "Une création mi-royale mi-impériale de la Manufacture de Sèvres." *Les cahiers de la céramique, du verre et des arts du feu, no.* 8 (Autumn 1957), pp. 180 – 84.

—. "Napoleonic tables from Sèvres." *Connoisseur* (April 1959), pp. 147 – 53.

—. "Un chef-d'oeuvre de Sèvres: le service de l'Empereur." *Art de France* 2 (1962), pp. 170 – 78

—. "Une messagère de l'Empereur: la porcelaine de Sèvres." *Plaisir de France* (February 1969), pp. 18 – 23.

—. "Deux remarquables souvenirs napoléoniens." *La revue du Louvre,* no. 4 – 5 (1974), pp. 323 – 30.

—. "Le Cabaret égyptien de l'Impératrice Joséphine." *La revue du Louvre et des musées de France* (April 1985), pp. 123 – 28.

—. "Au Louvre: Un biscuit napoléonien de Sèvres." *Antologia di Belle Arti (Melanges Verlet),* no. 31 – 32 (1987), pp. 3 – 15.

—. "Du nouveau sur les collections de Joséphine à Malmaison." In *Hommage à Hubert Landais* (Paris, 1987), pp. 175 – 79.

Gruber, Alain, ed. *L'Art décoratif en Europe: Du Néo-classicisme à l'Art Deco.* Paris: Citadelles & Mazenod, 1995.

Hahn, Roger. *L'Anatomie d'une institution scientifique, l'Académie des Sciences de Paris (1666 – 1803).* Brussels/Paris: Editions des Archives Contemporaines, 1993.

Hardouin-Fugier, Elisabeth. "J-B. Barrelon, P. Campagne: peintres-verriers lyonnais et le vitrail à Lyon au XIXe siècle." *Bulletin de la Société de l'histoire de l'art français* (1981), pp. 239 – 46.

Haskell, Francis. *Past and Present in Art and Taste: Selected Essays.* London/New Haven: Yale University Press, 1987.

Haskell, Francis, A. Levi, and Robert Shackleton. *The Artist and the Writer in France: Essays in Honor of Jean Seznec.* Oxford: Clarendon, 1974.

Haudicquer de Blancourt, François. *L'Art de la verrerie.* Paris: Jean Jombert, 1697.

Herold, Michel. *Le Vitrail en Lorraine du XIIe au XIXe siècle.* Exhib. cat. Metz: Editions Serpenoise, 1983.

Hindré, Jean-Paul. "Aperçus historiques sur le vitrail." *Espace, église, arts, architecture,* no. 13 (1981), pp. 6 – 23.

Holbach, Paul Henri Thiry, baron d', translator. *Art de la verrerie de Néri, Merret et Kunckel. . . ,* by Antonio Neri. Paris: Durand, 1752.

Images de Jeanne d'Arc: Hommage pour le 550e anniversaire de la libèration d'Orlèans et du sa vie. Exhib. cat. Paris: Hôtel de la Monnaie, 1979.

Ingres. Exhib. cat. Paris: Petit Palais, 1967.

Ingres, 2ème série (dessins): Saint-Symphorian, portraits civils et religieux, études de nus, peintures et vitraux de Dreux et de Saint-Ferdinand. Paris, n.d.

Jones, Kimberly A. "Henri IV and the Decorative Arts of the Bourbon Restauration, 1814 – 1830: A Study in Politics and Popular Taste." *Studies in the Decorative Arts* 1, no. 1 (Autumn 1993), pp. 2 – 21.

Jullian, Philippe. "Napoléon sous l'empire des Pharaons." *Connaissance des Arts* (December 1961), pp. 124 – 33.

Julia, Isabelle, and Jean Lacambre. *Les Annés romantiques, 1815 – 1850.* Exhib. cat. Paris: Réunion des musées nationaux, 1996.

Kaempfer, Engelbert. *Histoire naturelle, civile et ecclésiastique de l'empire du Japon.* La Haye: P. Gosse et J. Neaulme, 1732.

Klemm, Gustav. *Die königliche sachsische porzellan-und gefasse- sammlung . . .* Dresden: Walther, 1834.

La Font de Saint Yenne. *Reflections sur quelques causes de l'état présent de la peinture en France.* La Haye: Jean Neaulme, 1747.

La grande encyclopédie: Dictionnaire raisonné des sciences, des lettres et des arts. 2nd ed. Paris: Société Anonyme de la grande Encyclopédie, 1889.

Labit, Anne-Marie, and Charles Lasserre. "Un maître des arts du feu: Le chevalier Boudon de Saint-Amans (1774 – 1858): 1. Les sulfures." *Les cahiers de la céramique, du verre et des arts du feu,* no. 44 (1968), pp. 14 – 31.

—. "Le chevalier Boudon de Saint Amans." *Les cahiers de la céramique, du verre et des arts du feu,* no. 52 (1973).

Laborde, Alexandre de. *Voyage pittoresque et historique de l'Espagne par Alexandre de Laborde et une société de gens de lettres et d'artistes de Madrid. . .* 4 vols. Paris: Didot aîné, 1806 – 12,

Lacambre, Geneviève, and Jean Lacambre. "Les Vitraux de la chapelle de Carheil: Un témoignage de l'art officiel au temps de Louis-Philippe." *Revue de l'Art,* no. 10 (1970), pp. 85 – 93.

Lafond, Jean. "Le Vitrail civil français à l'église et au musée." *Médecine de France,* no. 77 (1956), pp. 16 – 32.

Lafond, Jean. *Le Vitrail: Origines, techniques, destinées.* 3rd ed.. Revised by Françoise Perrot. Lyon: La Manufacture, 1988.

. "Le Vitrail civil en France: un grand passé méconnu." Preface to *Le vitrail dans la demeure.* Exhib. cat. Rennes, 1970.

Lajoix, Anne. "Marie Victoire Jaquotot (1772 – 1855) et ses portraits pour la tabatière de Louis XVIII." *Bulletin de la société de l'histoire de l'art français* (1990), pp. 153 – 71.

—. "Tableaux précieux en porcelaine." *L'Estampille/L'Objet d'art* (May 1991), pp. 109 – 23.

—. "Alexandre Brongniart et la quête des moyens de reproduction en couleurs." *Sèvres,* nos. 1 – 2 (1992 – 93), pp. 64 – 73; 52 – 58.

Lami, Stanislas. *Dictionnaire des sculpteurs de l'école français au XIXème siècle.* 4 vols. Paris, 1921.

Lami de Nozan, Ernest. *De la peinture sur verre, que doit-elle être au XIXe siècle?* Paris, 1860.

Langlois, Eustache-Hyacinthe. *Essai historique et description sur la peinture sur verre ancienne et moderne, et sur les vitraux les plus remarquables de quelques monuments français et étrangers, suivi de la biographie des plus célèbres peintres verriers.* Rouen: Edouard Frere, 1832.

Lasserre, Jean-Claude. "La Commande et les commanditaires [de vitraux au XIXe siècle]." *Revue de l'Art,* no. 72 (1986), pp. 50 – 54.

Lassus, Jean-Baptiste. "Exposition de l'industrie: peinture sur verre." *Annales archéologiques* 1 (1844), pp. 63 – 64, 70.

Lasteyrie du Saillant, Ferdinand de. *Histoire de la peinture sur verre d'après ses monuments en France.* Paris: Didot frères, 1852 – 57.

Launay, Louis de. *Une grande famille de savants: les Brongniart.* Paris: Rapilly et fils, 1940.

Le Bihan, Jean-Pierre. "Notes sur les verriers et les vitraux dans le département du Finistère au XIXe siècle." *Bulletin de la société archéologique du Finistère,* no. 2 (1983), pp. 141 – 64.

Le "Gothique" retrouvé avant Viollet-le-Duc. Exhib. cat. Paris: Hôtel de Sully / Caisse nationale des monuments historiques et de sites, 1979.

Le Mécénat du duc d'Orléans 1830 – 1842. Exhib. cat. Paris: Delegation à l'action artistique de la ville de Paris, 1993.

Le Vieil, Pierre. *L'Art de la peinture sur verre et de la vitrerie.* Paris, 1774;. Reprint, Geneva: Minkoff, 1977.

Le Vitrail. Exhib. cat. Nancy: Musée de l'École de Nancy, 1981.

Lechavallier-Chevignard, Georges. "Le Rachat de la manufacture de porcelaine de Sèvres aux Alliés en 1815." *Archives de l'art français* (1907), pp. 246 – 79.

—. *La Manufacture de porcelaine de Sèvres.* 2 vols. Paris: H. Laurens, 1908.

Lechavallier-Chevignard, Georges, and Maurice Saureux. *Le Biscuit de Sèvres; Directoire, Consulat, Empire.* Paris: A. Morancé, n.d.

Ledoux-Lebard, Denise. *Inventaire général du musée national de Versailles et des Trianons: le grand Trianon, meubles et objets d'art.* Paris: Editions des musées nationaux, 1975.

—. "La Campagne de 1805 vue par la manufacture impériale de Sèvres." *La revue du Louvre et des musées de France,* no. 3 (1978), pp. 178 – 85.

—. *Versailles: Le Petit Trianon, le mobilier des inventaires de 1807, 1810 et 1839.* Pref. by M. Yves Bottineau. Paris: Editions de l'amateur, 1989.

—. "Arredi da Re: Mobili di porcellane" *Antiques* (September 1992), pp. 86 – 91.

Ledoux-Lebard, R. G., and C. Ledoux-Lebard. "Deux effigies peu connues de l'Empereur dues au sculpteur Moutony." *Travaux et documents de l'Institut Napoléon* (1942), pp. 1 – 14.

Lemoine, Paul. "Le Muséum national d'histoire naturelle." *Tricentenaire du museum national d'histoire naturelle,* 6th ser., vol. 12 (1935).

Leniaud, Jean-Michel. "Le Vitrail au XIXe siècle: sources et problèmes iconographiques." *Revue de l'histoire de l'église de France* 67 (1981), pp. 83 – 89.

—. *Viollet-le-duc ou les delires du système.* Paris: Mengès, 1994.

Lenoir, Alexandre. *Histoire de la peinture sur verre et description des vitraux anciens et modernes pour servir à l'histoire de l'art.* Vol. 6 of *Musée des Monuments Français.* Paris: impr. de Guilleminet-Nepreu, 1821.

Lenoir, Alexandre. *Traité historique de la peinture sur verre et description des vitraux anciens et modernes pour servir à l'histoire de l'art.* Paris: J. B. Dumoulin, 1856.

Leproux, Guy-Michel. *Recherches sur les peintres-verriers parisiens de la Renaissance (1540 – 1620).* Geneva: Droz, 1988.

Les Chimistes Français du XIXe siècle. Exhib. cat. Paris: Musée Centennal de la classe 87, arts chimique et pharmacie, 1900.

"Les Vitraux du Louvre et leur déménagement." *Revue des Beaux-Arts* 8 (August 8, 1857), p. 324.

Levy, Edmond. *Histoire de la peinture sur verre.* Brussels: Jircher, 1860.

Loesch, Anette. "Die Napoleonische schenkung, 1809: Französischen porzellan in Dresden." *Dresden Kunstblatter* 36, no. 6 (1992), pp. 174 – 79.

Long, Derek A. "The Sèvres 'Service des Arts Industriels': A Unique Record of Craft Industries in Paris, 1820 – 1836." *Tools and Trades* 9 (1996), pp. 28 – 52.

Lossky, Boris. "Un hommage 'troubadour' à Léonard de Vinci: le vase Chenavard au château de Fontainebleau." *Bulletin de l'Association Léonard de Vinci,* no. 12 (December 1973), pp. 11 – 18.

Magagnini, Vittorio. "Restauration. La table des 'Maréchaux' livre ses secrets." *Société des amis de Malmaison* (1992), pp. 70 – 72.

Maingot, Eliane. *Le Baron Taylor.* Paris: E. de Boccard, 1963.

Manufacture de vitraux de MM. Didron et Thibaud à Paris et à Clermont-Ferrand. Paris: Librairie archéologique de V. Didron, n.d.

Marot, Pierre. "L'Abbé Gregoire et le vandalisme révolutionnaire." *Gazette des Beaux-Arts,* no. 49 (1980), pp. 36 – 39.

Massoul, Madeleine. *Vases antiques du Musée d' Orléans.* Paris: E. Leroux, 1918.

—, ed. *Corpus vasorum antiquorum, France, Musée national de Sèvres.* Paris, 1934.

Meissen: la découverte de la porcelaine européene en Saxe, J. F. Böttger, 1709 – 1736. Paris, 1984.

Micheaux, Robert de. "Un portrait de Louis XVIII sur porcelaine de Sèvres d'après le baron Gérard." *Antologia di Belle Arti* (Mélanges Verlet 3), 1987, pp. 16 – 17.

Middleton, Robin. "Ingres and Viollet-le-Duc: A Roman Encounter." *Gazettte des Beaux-Arts* 95 (April 1980), pp. 147 – 52.

Milet, Ambroise. *Notice sur Désiré Riocreux.* Paris-London: Librairie de l'Art, 1883.

Milly, Nicolas-Christien de Thy, Comte de. *L'Art de la porcelaine dédié au Roi . . .* [Paris], Imprimerie de L. F. Delatour, 1771 – 72.

Montalivet, Comte de. *Le roi Louis-Philippe et sa liste civile.* Paris: Michel Levy freres, 1851.

Montesquiou, Robert de. "Ingres verrier." *L'Art décoratif: Revue de l'art ancien et de la vie artistique moderne,* no. 152 (May 1911), pp. 253 – 68.

Morel, Dominique, ed. *Achille Devéria: témoin du romantisme parisien, 1800 – 1857.* Exhib. cat. Paris: Musée Renan- Scheffer/Musées de la ville de Paris, 1985.

—. "Les Vitraux de l'église d'Eu: Une commande de Louis-Philippe à la manufacture de Sèvres (1833 – 1847)." *Revue de l'Art,* no. 103 (1994), pp. 68 – 76.

Morgan, Sidney Owenson. *Lady Morgan in France.* Edited by Elizabeth Suddaby and P.J. Yarrow. Newcastle upon Tyne: Oriel Press, 1971.

Mosser, Monique, Beatrice de Rocheboüet, and Jean-Marie Bruson, eds. *Alexandre-Théodore Brongniart (1739 – 1813): Architecture et décor.* Exhib. cat. Paris: Musée Carnavalet/Musées de la ville de Paris, 1986.

Mundt, Barbara. "Ein empireservice mit kameenmalerei. Zu einer neuerwerbung des Berliner Kunstmuseum." *Kunst und Antiquitäten* 11 (1990), pp. 20 – 26.

Nicolas Morlaix (1842 – 1912). Exhib. cat. Morlaix: Musée des Jacobins, 1980.

Nora, Pierre, ed. *Les Lieux de mémoire.* Vol. 2 (*La Nation*). [Paris]: Gallimard, 1986.

Nordenfalk, Carl. *Sèvres et les cinq sens.* Stockholm: Nationalmuseet, 1984.

Notice sur quelques-unes des pièces qui entrent dans l'exposition des porcelaines de la manufacture royale de Sèvres, faite au musée royal, le 1er janvier 1818. Exhib. cat. Paris: impr. Hérissant le Doux, 1818.

Notice sur quelques-unes des pièces . . . le 1er janvier 1819. Exhib. cat. Paris: impr. Hérissant le Doux, 1819.

Notice sur quelques-unes des pièces . . . le 1er janvier 1820. Exhib. cat. Paris: impr. de Plassan, 1820.

Notice sur quelques-unes des pièces . . . le 1er janvier 1821. Exhib. cat. Paris: impr. de Plassan, 1821 .

Notice sur quelques-unes des pièces que entrent dans l'exposition des manufactures royales de porcelaine de Sèvres, de tapisseries des Gobelins, de tapisseries de Beauvais, des tapis de la Savonnerie, de mosaïque de Paris faite au musée royal le 1er janvier 1822. Exhib. cat. Paris: impr. de Plassan, 1822.

Notice sur quelques-unes des pièces . . . le 1er janvier 1823. Exhib. cat. Paris: impr. de Plassan, 1823.

Notice sur quelques-unes des pièces . . . le 1er janvier 1824. Exhib. cat. Paris: impr. de Plassan, 1824.

Notice sur quelques-unes des pièces . . . le 1er janvier 1825. Exhib. cat. Paris: impr. de Plassan, 1825.

Notice sur quelques-unes des pièces . . . le 1er janvier 1826. Exhib. cat. Paris: impr. de Plassan, 1826.

Notice sur quelques-unes des pièces qui entrent dans l'exposition des manufactures royales de porcelaine de Sèvres, de tapisseries et de tapis des Gobelins, de tapisseries de Beauvais, faite au musée royal le 1er janvier 1827. Exhib. cat. Paris: impr. de C. Thuau, 1827.

Notice sur quelques-unes des pièces qui entrent dans l'exposition des manufactures royales de porcelaine de Sèvres, de tapisseries et tapis des Gobelins, de tapisseries de Beauvais, de mosaïque de Paris, de laines longues lustrées de la Savonnerie, faite au palais du Louvre le 1er janvier 1828. Exhib. cat. Paris: impr. de Plassan, 1828.

Notice sur quelques-unes des pièces . . . le 1er janvier 1829. Exhib. cat. Paris: Plassan et Cie, 1829.

Notice sur quelques-unes des pièces . . . 1er janvier 1830. Exhib. cat. Paris: Plassan et Cie, 1830.

Notice sur quelques-unes des pièces qui entrent dans l'exposition des manufactures royales de porcelaine de Sèvres, de tapisseries et tapis des Gobelins, de tapisseries de Beauvais, de mosaïque de Paris, faite au palais du Louvre le 27 décembre 1832. Exhib. cat. Paris: Imprimerie Joly, 1832.

Notice sur quelques-unes des pièces qui entrent dans l'exposition des manufactures royales de porcelaine et de vitraux de Sèvres, de tapisseries et tapis des Gobelins, de tapisseries de Beauvais, faite au palais du Louvre le 1er mai 1835. Exhib. cat. Paris: Vinchon, 1835.

Notice sur quelques-unes des pièces qui entrent dans l'exposition des manufactures royales de porcelaine et vitraux de Sèvres, de tapis des Gobelins, de tapisseries de Beauvais, faite au palais du Louvre le 1er mai 1838. Exhib. cat. Sèvres: Adolphe René, 1838.

Notice sur quelques-unes des pièces qui entrent dans l'exposition des manufactures royales de porcelaine et de vitraux de Sèvres, de tapis des Gobelins, de tapisseries de Beauvais, faite au palais du Louvre le 1er mai 1840. Exhib. cat. Paris: Vinchon, 1840.

Notice explicative des six fenêtres en vitraux peints, exécutées à la manufacture royale de porcelaines de Sèvres, et exposées au Louvre le 16 mai 1841. Exhib. cat. Paris: Vinchon, 1841.

Notice sur quelques-unes des pièces qui entrent dans l'exposition des manufactures royales de porcelaines et vitraux de Sèvres, de tapisseries et tapis des Gobelins, de tapisseries de Beauvais, faite au palais du Louvre au 1er mai 1842. Exhib. cat. Paris: Vinchon, 1842.

Notice sur quelques-unes des pièces . . . 3 juin 1844. Exhib. cat. Paris: Vinchon, 1844.

Notice sur quelques-unes des pièces qui entrent dans l'exposition des manufactures royales de porcelaines et émaux de Sèvres . . .faite au palais du Louvre au 1er juin 1846. Exhib. cat. Paris: Vichon, 1846.

Notice explicative des fenêtres peintes en vitraux de couleurs, et des tableaux peints sur glace, exécutés à la manufacture royale de porcelaine de Sèvres, et exposés au Louvre le 18 avril 1847. Exhib. cat. Paris: Vinchon, 1847.

Notice sur les pièces qui composent l'exposition des manufactures nationales de porcelaine, vitraux et émaux de Sèvres, de tapisseries et tapis des Gobelins, de tapisseries de Beauvais, faite au Palais national le 21 avril 1850. Exhib. cat. Paris: Vinchon, 1850.

Nouvelles acquisitions (1979 – 1989). Exhib. cat. Sèvres: Musée national de Céramique. Réunion des Musée Nationaux, 1989.

Nouvelles acquisitions du département des objets d'arts 1990 – 1994. Exhib. cat. Paris: Musée du Louvre/Réunion des Musées nationaux, 1995.

Objectif vitrail Rhône-Alpes. Exhib. cat. Lyon, 1983.

Omalius d'Halloy, Jean-Jacques. "Notice biographique sur la vie d'Alexandre Brongniart." Paper presented at the Société Géologique de France, Paris, March 19, 1860.

"Orientation bibliographique sur le vitrail français au XIXe siècle depuis 1958." *Vitrea,* no. 3 (1989), pp. 40 – 41.

Ottin, Louis. *Le Vitrail: Son histoire, ses manifestations à travers les âges et les peuples.* Paris: H. Laurens, 1896.

—. *L'Art de faire un vitrail.* Paris, 1926.

Ottomeyer, Hans, and Peter Pröschel. *Vergoldete bronzen,* 2 vols. Munich: Klinkhardt and Biermann, 1986.

Oursel, Hervé. "Vitraux du XIXe siècle dans les églises et chapelles de Lille." *Bulletin communal et historique du Nord* 43 (1987), pp. 131 – 62.

Pabois, Marc. "Architecture et vitrail au XIXe siècle." *Revue de l'Art,* no. 72 (1986), pp. 61 – 64.

Pallotino, Massimo, ed. *Les Etrusques et l'Europe.* Exhib. cat. Paris: Grand Palais/Réunion des musées nationaux, 1982.

Passeri, Giambattista. *Istoria delle pitture in majolica fatte in Pesaro e né luoghi circonvicini, descritta da Giambattista Passeri, pesarese.* Pesaro: Delle Stamperia Nobiliana, 1838.

Perot, Jacques. "Le déjeuner de Sèvres de l'apothéose d'Henri IV." *Bulletin de la Société des amis du Château de Pau,* no. 82, pp. 1 – 18, 4 pl. n.

Perrault-Dalbot, A. "La Renaissance du vitrail à la manufacture nationale de Sèvres. Epoque romantique: 1827 – 1854." *Bulletin de la Société de l'histoire de Paris et de l'Ile-de-France* 60 (1933), pp. 4 – 20.

Perrot, Françoise. "La Signature des peintres-verriers." *Revue de l'Art,* no. 26 (1974), pp. 40 – 45.

—. "Les Vitraux et leurs destins." *Monuments Historiques,* no. 107 (1980), pp. 34 – 39.

Perrot, Françoise, and Anne Granboulan. *Vitrail, art de lumière.* 2d ed. Paris: R.E.M.P.A.R.T., 1991.

Peyre, Jules. *Ornements mauresques de l'Alhambra lithographiés par Jules Peyre.* N.p., n.d.

—. *Orfèvrerie, bijouterie, nielle, armoiries et objets d'arts recueillis, composés, dessinés et lithographiés par Jules Peyre.* Paris: Bulla aîné et Jouy, 1844.

Picon, Antoine. *Architectes et ingénieurs au siècle des lumières.* Marseille: Parenthéses, 1988.

Pinault-Sorensen, Madeleine. *Dessiner la Nature: Dessins et manuscrits des bibliothèque de France, XVIIe – XVIIIe – XIXe siècles.* Exhib. cat. Paris: Espace Electra, 1996.

Pinot de Villechenon, Marie-Noëlle. *Sèvres: Une collection de porcelaines, 1740 – 1992, Musée national de céramiques.* Paris: Réunion des musées nationaux, 1993.

Plinval de Guillebon, Regine de. *Porcelain of Paris, 1770 – 1850.* New York: Walker and Company, 1972.

—. *Faïence et porcelaine de Paris, XVIIe – XVIIIe siècles; préface by Jacques Chirac.* Dijon: Editions Faton, 1995.

Plinval-Salgue, Régine de. "La Céramique française aux expositions industrielles de la première moitié du XIXe siécle." *Cahiers de la céramique, du verre et des arts du feu,* no. 22 (1961), pp. 84 – 103.

Pomian, Krysztof, and Annie-France Luarens, eds. *Anticomanie.* Paris: Ecole des hautes études en sciences sociales, 1992.

Pommier, Edouard. "Le Problème du musée à la veille de la révolution." *Les Cahiers du musée Girodet,* no. 1 (1989).

Portet, Mariette. *Sevres en Ile-de-France.* Conde-sur-Noireau: Ch. Corlet, 1975.

Préaud, Tamara. "Alexandre Brongniart et les porcelainiers parisiens (1800 – 1847)." *Cahiers de la céramique, du verre et des arts du feu,* no. 46 – 47 (1970), pp. 13 – 19.

—. "Un fonds méconnu: La série des paysages conservés à la bibliothèque de la manufacture de Sèvres." *Cahiers de la céramique, du verre et des arts du feu*, no. 58 (1976), pp. 36 – 55.

—. "Sèvres, la Chine et les chinoiseries au XVIIIe siècle." *The Journal of the Walters Art Gallery* 47 (1989), pp. 39 – 52.

—. "Sèvres. La Pâte-sur-pâte, un procédé original." *L'Estampille/l'objet d'art* (November 1992), pp. 46 – 57.

—. "La Sculpture à Vincennes ou l'invention du Biscuit." *Sèvres*, no. 1 (1992), pp. 30 – 37.

—. "Louis-Philippe et Sèvres: D'ambitieuses commandes." *Dossier de l'Art*, no. 15 (November – December 1993), pp. 62 – 67.

—. "Sèvres: le vase du bivouac de l'Empereur." *Sèvres*, no. 2 (1993), pp. 48 – 51.

—. "Transfer-Printing Processes used at Sèvres in the late Eighteenth and Early Nineteenth Centuries." *Studies in the Decorative Arts* 4, no. 2 (Spring – Summer 1997), pp. 85 – 96.

Préaud, Tamara, and Antoine d'Albis. *La Porcelaine de Vincennes*. Paris: A. Biro, 1991.

Price, Roger. *A Social History of Nineteenth-Century France*. New York: Holmes and Meier, 1987.

Rabreau, Daniel, and Bruno Tollon, eds. *Le Progrés des arts réunis, 1763 – 1815*. Bordeaux: Université de Bordeaux, 1992.

Raguin, Virginia Chieffo. "Revivals, Revivalists and Architectural Stained Glass [in Medieval Revival Architecture in the Nineteenth Century]." *Journal of the Society of Architectural Historians*, no. 49 (September 1990), pp. 310 – 29.

Ravel d'Esclapon, Alix de. *La Faïence de Rubelles*. Le Mée-sur- Seine: Editions Amatteis, 1988.

Reboulleau, A., and H. Magnier. *Nouveau manuel complet de la peinture sur verre, sur porcelaine et sur émail*. Paris: Librarie encyclopédieque de Roret, 1868.

Regnault, Félix. "La maison des Brongniart." *La Nature* (December 1, 1934), pp. 510 – 12.

Reilly, Robin. *Wedgwood*. 2 vols. New York: Stockton Press, 1989.

Rémusat, Claire Elisabeth de. *A Selection from the Letters of Madame de Rémusat to her Husband and her Son, from 1804 to 1813*. Translated by Mrs. Cashel Hoey and John Lillie. New York: D. Appleton and Company, 1881.

Reneault, Chanoine. *La Paroisse Saint-Patrice de Rouen*. Fécamp, 1942.

Reyniers, François. *Sèvres. Musée national de céramique. Céramiques américaines*. Paris: Éditions des musées nationaux, 1966.

Riou, Yves-Jean. "Iconographie et attitudes religieuses: pour une iconologie du vitrail du XIXe siècle." *Revue de l'Art*, no. 72 (1986), pp. 39 – 49.

Rollet, Jean. *Les maîtres de la lumière*. Paris: Bordas, 1980.

Rosser-Johnson, James. "The Stained-Glass Theories of Viollet-le-Duc." *Bulletin monumental* 122, no. 1 (1964), pp. 108 – 10.

Roth, Linda. "Neoclassical variations at Sèvres: Early Nineteenth-century Vases in the Wadsworth Atheneum." *The French Porcelain Society* 12 (1995).

Rougon, M. "Les Archives de la Société de médecine de Paris de l'an IV (1796) à nos jours." *L'union médicale*, 3d ser., 33 (1882), pp. 80 – 81.

Roussel, Francis. "Le Peintre-verrier au XIXe siècle: un industriel?" *Revue de l'Art*, no. 72 (1986), pp. 57 – 60.

—. "Impressions sur verre." *Vitrea*, no. 3 (1989), pp. 28 – 33.

A Royal Gift: the 1826 Porcelain Jewel Cabinet. Exhib. cat. New York: Cooper-Hewitt Museum, 1994

Rückert, Rainer. "Marie-Victoire Jaquotot, 1772 – 1855." *Weltkunst* 15 (August 1, 1985), pp. 2103 – 9.

—. "Marie-Victoire Jaquotot, 1772 – 1855." *Weltkunst* 17 (September 1, 1985), pp. 2352 – 58.

Rückert, Rainer. "Wiener und Meissener porzellangeschirr des 18. Jahrhunderts alla Turca." *Keramos* 147 (January 1995), pp. 3 – 94.

Salvetat, Alphonse-Louis. "Manufacture nationale de Sèvres. A propos de l'inauguration des nouveaux bâtiments, le 17 novembre 1876." *Bulletin de la Société d'encouragement pour l'industrie nationale*, 3d ser., 4 (January 1877), pp. 3 – 17.

Samoyault, Jean Pierre. "Les Remplois de sculptures et d'objets d'art dans la décoration et 'ameublement du palais de St. Cloud sous le consulat et au début de l'Empire." *Bulletin de la Société de l'histoire de l'art français* (1971), pp. 163 – 91.

—. "Les assiettes de dessert du service particulier de l'Empereur en porcelaine de Sèvres." *Le Souvenir Napoléonien*, no. 369 (February 1990), pp. 2 – 11.

Sandier, Alexandre. *Les Cartons de la manufacture de Sèvres, Epoque Louis XVI et Empire*. Paris, 1910.

Saint-Non, Abbé de. *Voyage pittoresque ou description des royaumes de Naples et de Sicile*. 5 vols. Paris: n.p., 1781 – 86.

Santrot, Marie-Helène. *Ors et splendeurs de Sèvres: Porcelaines 1800 – 1847*. Garenne Lemot: Conseil général de loire-Atlantique, 1996.

S[chlumberger], E[velyne]. "Une belle réussite méconnue: la galerie espagnole de Louis-Philippe." *Connaissance des Arts*, no. 115 (September 1961), pp. 56 – 65.

Schlumberger, Evelyne. "Chef-d'oeuvre ou échec, force est d'admirer le travail de Ingres pour ses vitraux." *Connaissance des Arts*, no. 191 (January 1968), pp. 40 – 47.

Schurr, Gerald. "Les Grands siècles du vitrail: 2. De l'archaïsme d'Ingres à l'abstraction contemporaine." *Gazette de l'hôtel Drouot*, no. 4 (1974), pp. 12 – 13.

—. "Les Grands siècles du vitrail: 2. De l'archaïsme d'Ingres à l'abstraction contemporaine." *Gazette de l'hôtel Drouot*, no. 7 (1974), pp. 12 – 13.

Schwartz, Selma. "The Sèvres Porcelain Service for Marie Antoinette's Dairy at Rambouillet: an Exercise in Archaeological Neo-classicism." *The French Porcelain Society* 9, 1992.

Scott, Barbara. "The Duchess of Berry as a Patron of the Arts." *Apollo* (October 1986), pp. 345 – 53.

"Les Sèvres Restauration." *Connaissance des Arts* (January 15, 1955), pp. 51 – 55.

Shackleton, Robert. "The Enlightenment and the Artisan." *Studies on Voltaire and the Eighteenth Century* (1980), pp. 56 ff.

Shifman, Barry. "Le Déjeuner royal des peines et plaisirs de l'amour en porcelaine de Sèvres, 1816 – 1817." *Revue du Louvre*, no. 5 – 6 (1987), pp. 397 – 409.

—. "'Le Déjeuner royal des chasses' en porcelaine de Sèvres peint par Jean-François Robert, 1817 – 1818." *Revue du Louvre* no. 6 (1990), pp. 470 – 78.

—. "Sèvres Porcelain Given by Charles X in 1825 to the Duke of Northumberland." *Burlington Magazine* (March 1993), pp. 215 – 19.

Un Siècle de vitrail en Picardie. Amiens: Monuments de Picardie, 1987.

Slitine, Florence. "La Céramique orientale dans les ventes publiques au cours de la première moitié du 19e siècle." *Sèvres*, no. 5 (1996), pp. 48 – 64.

Soustiel, Jean. *La Céramique islamique*. Fribourg: Office du Livre, 1985.

Springer Roberts, Lynn. "The Londonderry Vase: A Royal Gift to Curry Favor." *The Art Institute of Chicago Museum Studies* 15, no. 1 (1989), pp. 68 – 81.

Stratmann-Dohler, Rosemarie. "Zür Hochzeit von Stephanie de Beauharnais. Höfische geschenke aus der Kaiserliche Porzellanmanufactur Sèvres." *Weltkunst* (January 1995), pp. 16 – 19.

Suau, Jean-Pierre. "Alfred Gérente et le vitrail archéologique à Carcassonne au milieu du XIXe siècle." *Congrès archéologique de l'Aude* (1973), pp. 629 – 45.

Sudre, Pierre. *La Chapelle Saint-Ferdinand publiée avec l'autorisation de Sa Majesté la reine.* Paris: Imprimerie de Claye, Taillefer et Cie, 1846.

Thélot, P. "Précis historique de la Société de médecine de Paris," *Bulletins et memoires de la Société de médecine de Paris,* 192e année, 17, no. 1, (January – March 1989), pp. 1 – 2.

Théophile. *Diversarum artium schedula.* Rev. ed. by A. Picard and J. Picard. Paris: Picard, 1980.

Thévenot, Etienne. "Essai historique sur le vitrail ou observations historiques et critiques sur l'art de la peinture sur verre, considéré dans ses rapports avec la décoration des monuments religieux, depuis sa naissance au XIIe siècle jusqu'au XIXe inclusivement." *Annales scientifiques, littéraires et industrielles de l'Auvergne* 10 (1837), pp. 385 – 464.

Thibaud, Emile. "De la peinture sur verre ou notice historique sur cet art, dans ses rapports avec la vitrification." *Annales scientifiques, littéraires et industrielles de l'Auvergne* 8 (1835), pp. 667 – 95.

—. *Notions historiques sur les vitraux anciens et modernes et sur l'art de la peinture vitrifiée.* Clermont-Ferrand: Thibaud- Landriot, 1838.

—. *Considérations historiques et critiques sur les vitraux anciens et modernes et sur la peinture sur verre.* Clermont- Ferrand: Thibaud-Landriot, 1842.

Thieme, Ulriche, and Félix Becker. *Allgemeines Lexikon der Bildenden Künstler von der Antike bis zur gegenwart.* 37 vols. Leipzig, 1907.

Thomas, Christine. "Etude du personnel de la manufacture impériale puis royale de porcelaine de Sèvres, 1808 – 1848 (Statuts, salaires, avantages sociaux)." Master's thesis. Université de Paris, 1989.

Toussaint, Helene. *Portraits d'Ingres: peintures des musées nationaux.* Exhib. cat. Paris: Musee du Louvre/Réunion des musées nationaux, 1985.

Truman, Charles. *The Sèvres Egyptian Service, 1810 – 1812.* London: H.M.S.O., 1982.

Tulard, Jean, ed. *Dictionnaire Napoléon.* Rev. ed. Paris: Fayard, 1983.

Valeriani, Roberto. "Porcellane di Sèvres Doni Borbonici." *Casa Vogue Antiques* (September 1990), pp. 112 – 19.

—. "Porcellane di Sèvres a Napoli." *Antologia di belle Arti 2,* Neoclassicismo 3, New Series, nn. 39 – 42 (1992), pp. 47 – 72.

Vaudour, Catherine. "La Céramique normande: l'enquète préfectorale en Seine-Inférieure sous le Premier Empire" *Etudes normandes,* no. 2 (1984), pp. 79 – 106.

Verlet, Pierre, Serge Grandjean, and Marcelle Brunet. *Sèvres.* 2 vols. Paris: G. Le Prat, 1954.

Versailles et les tables royales en Europe, XVIIe – XIXe siècles. Exhib. cat. Versailles: Réunion des Musées nationaux, 1993.

Vigné, Joseph. *Peinture sur verre: Considérations critiques sur cet art.* Paris: Just-Teisseir, 1840.

Vinsot, Jeanne, Catherine Brisac, and Chantal Bouchon. *Les vitraux de la basilique Sainte-Clotilde à Paris.* Paris: Société d'histoire et d'archéologie du VIIe arrondissement de Paris, 1987.

Viollet-le-Duc en Auvergne. Exhib. cat. Clermont-Ferrand: Musée Bargoin, 1979.

Visconti, Ennio Quirino. *Planches de l'iconographie grecque . . .* Paris: Didot ainé, 1811.

Le Vitrail français. Paris: Editions des Deux-Mondes, 1958.

Walton, Whitney. *France at the Crystal Palace: Bourgeois Taste and Artisan Manufacture in the Nineteenth Century.* Berkeley, 1992.

Werren, Jacques. "Jules Claude Ziegler (1804 – 1856) renovateur du grès artistique en France". *Bulletin du groupe de recherche et d'etudes de la ceramique du Beauvaises,* no. 17 (1995), pp. 9 – 224.

Willemin, Nicolas-Xavier. *Monuments français inédits pour servir à l'histoire des arts depuis le VIe siècle jusqu'au commencement du XVIIe, choix de costumes civils et militaires, d'armes, armures, instruments de musique, meubles de toute espèce et de décorations interieurs et exterieures des maisons, dessinés et coloriés d'après les originaux . . . classés chronologiquement et accompangnés d'un texte historique et descriptif par André Pottier . . .* 4 vols. Paris, Willemin, 1806 – 39.

Zafran, Eric M. "Six Drawings by Develly". *Journal of the Museum of Fine Arts, Boston* 3 (1991), pp. 77 – 86.

Index

This index comprises entries for chapters 1 through 11 and includes life dates for the principal figures mentioned in the text. The catalogue of the exhibition is not included.

Photocredits

Unless otherwise noted in the list below, photographs in chapters one through eleven as well as the comparative photographs in the catalogue section are courtesy of the collections, archives, or other sources listed in the captions.

Jean-Loup Charmet: figs. 2-8, 5-3, 7-1 to 7-15
Martine Beck-Coppola: figs. 11-1 to 11-13
Fondation Napoléon — J. Guillot: fig. 6-3; cat. fig. 20a
Giraudon: cat. fig. 100a
Laurent Sully Jaulmes: fig. 4-11; cat. fig. 29a
Jean-Michel Marchand: fig. 2-2
Réunion de Musées Nationales: frontispiece (G. Blot/C. Jean) and figs. 6-2 (Arnaudet), 6-7, 6-8, 9-1, 9-4, 9-8, 9-9, 9-10, 9-12, 9-13, 9-14, (Lagiewski), 6-11 (M. Beck-Coppola), 6-14 (G. Vivien); cat figs. 16a, 21a (Lagiewski), 31a, 36a (M. Beck-Coppola), 55a (M. Beck-Coppola), 76a (Arnaudet), 79a (G. Vivien), 82a (M. Beck-Coppola)
Sèvres, Musée national de céramique: fig. 6-12, 9-2, 9-2, 9-5, 9-6, 9-7, 9-15; cat. figs. 80a, 84a, 85a, 87a, 92a
Bibliothèque Centrale du Muséum National d'Histoire Naturelle: figs. 2-3 to 2-7, 2-10, 2-11
Bruce White: cat. figs. 142a, 142b, 149

Unless listed below, all photographs of the objects in the exhibition were provided by the photography studios of the lending institutions or by the collectors. At the Manufacture Nationale de Sèvres, photographs were taken by Martine Beck-Coppola and Jean-Loup Charmet.
David Stansbury: cat. nos. 135a, 135b, 138a, 138b, 150
Cathy Carver: cat. nos. 132, 136, 139a, 139c, 139d, 142
Dwight Primiano Photography: cat. nos. 139b, 151, 155
Jean-loup Charmet: cat. nos. 143, 146